James Jones

Craig Landes

A+ Exam Cram2 (Exams 220-221 and 220-222)

International Standard Book Number: 0-7897-2867-2

Library of Congress Catalog Card Number: 2002114423

Printed in the United States of America

First Printing: November 2002

05 04 03 4 3

Trademarks

Warning and Disclaimer

Publisher
Paul Boger

Executive Editor
Jeff Riley

Development Editor
Marta Justak

Managing Editor
Thomas F. Hayes

Project Editor
Carol Bowers

Production Editor
Megan Wade

Indexer
Ginny Bess Monroe

Proofreader
Justak Literary Services

Team Coordinator
Rosemary Lewis

Multimedia Developer
Michael Hunter

Page Layout
Michelle Mitchell

Graphics
Stephen Adams
Tammy Graham
Oliver L. Jackson, Jr.
Laura Robbins

Que Certification • 201 West 103rd Street • Indianapolis, Indiana 46290

A Note from Series Editor Ed Tittel

You know better than to trust your certification preparation to just anybody. That's why you, and more than two million others, have purchased an Exam Cram book. As Series Editor for the new and improved Exam Cram2 series, I have worked with the staff at Que Certification to ensure you won't be disappointed. That's why we've taken the world's best-selling certification product—a finalist for "Best Study Guide" in a CertCities reader poll in 2002—and made it even better.

As a "Favorite Study Guide Author" finalist in a 2002 poll of CertCities readers, I know the value of good books. You'll be impressed with Que Certification's stringent review process, which ensures the books are high-quality, relevant, and technically accurate. Rest assured that at least a dozen industry experts—including the panel of certification experts at CramSession—have reviewed this material, helping us deliver an excellent solution to your exam preparation needs.

We've also added a preview edition of PrepLogic's powerful, full-featured test engine, which is trusted by certification students throughout the world.

As a 20-year-plus veteran of the computing industry and the original creator and editor of the Exam Cram series, I've brought my IT experience to bear on these books. During my tenure at Novell from 1989 to 1994, I worked with and around its excellent education and certification department. This experience helped push my writing and teaching activities heavily in the certification direction. Since then, I've worked on more than 70 certification-related books, and I write about certification topics for numerous Web sites and for *Certification* magazine.

In 1996, while studying for various MCP exams, I became frustrated with the huge, unwieldy study guides that were the only preparation tools available. As an experienced IT professional and former instructor, I wanted "nothing but the facts" necessary to prepare for the exams. From this impetus, Exam Cram emerged in 1997. It quickly became the best-selling computer book series since "*...For Dummies*," and the best-selling certification book series ever. By maintaining an intense focus on subject matter, tracking errata and updates quickly, and following the certification market closely, Exam Cram was able to establish the dominant position in cert prep books.

You will not be disappointed in your decision to purchase this book. If you are, please contact me at etittel@jump.net. All suggestions, ideas, input, or constructive criticism are welcome!

Ed Tittel

About the Authors

With over 30 years in the information technology profession and communications industry, **Jim Jones** has held positions from technician, to senior vice president of a Fortune 500 multinational corporation. With a B.S. in education, and an MBA from Michigan State University, Jim is also Microsoft MCSE certified, Novell CNE certified, and Cisco CCNA & CCDA certified. Additionally, Jim holds certificates in A+, network cabling, fiber optics, and microwave transmission, to name a few. Jim Jones is the President of JGJ & Associates, a consulting firm providing executive seminars pertaining to technology, sales, and marketing to some of the world's largest IT corporations, including (among others) IBM, Microsoft, Oracle, Hewlett-Packard, Compaq, and Siemens. Jim has been deeply involved with the A+ program since its inception, and he can be reached by email at **jim@jamesgjones.com**.

Craig Landes has over 18 years experience in information technology, holding numerous positions from database programming to managing information systems in the field of healthcare. Craig has worked with some of today's largest consulting firms, developing technical and educational programs for clients and employees at all levels. Currently, Craig Landes is the president of Triax Corporation, a consulting business providing freelance technical writing, help systems, and educational materials development. Craig can be reached by email at **CLandesAPlus@aol.com**.

Contents at a Glance

Introduction xxvii

Chapter 1 A+ Certification Tests 1

Chapter 2 Motherboards 17

Chapter 3 Memory 49

Chapter 4 Processors 89

Chapter 5 Basic Electronics and Peripherals: Input Devices 117

Chapter 6 Peripherals: Storage Devices 159

Chapter 7 Peripherals: Output Devices 193

Chapter 8 Networking 241

Chapter 9 Cables and Connectors 281

Chapter 10 DOS 307

Chapter 11 Booting, Windows 3.11, and Memory 377

Chapter 12 Windows 95, 98, and Me 449

Chapter 13 Windows NT, Windows 2000, and XP 519

Chapter 14 Troubleshooting 581

Chapter 15 Sample Test 631

Chapter 16 Answer Key 657

Appendix A What's on the CD-ROM 681

Appendix B Using the *PrepLogic Practice Tests, Preview Edition* Software 685

Acronym Glossary 693

Index 711

Table of Contents

Chapter 1
A+ Certification Tests 1

Are You Certifiable? 2
The A+ Certification Exams 3
Where Do I Sign Up? 4
How Do I Schedule the Test? 4
Certification 5
The Exam Site 5
In the Exam Room 5
Testing and Scoring 6
Following the Exam 6
How to Prepare for an Exam 6
Current Exam Requirements 7
Additional Resources 7
The Test Site 8
Adaptive Testing 9
Test Layout and Design 10
Questions and Linguistics 10
Question-Handling Strategies 12
Bogus Choices 12
Duplicate False Responses 12
Mastering the Inner Game 13
Multiple Response Questions 14
Need to Know More? 14

Chapter 2
Motherboards 17

System Boards: A Brief History 18
The Advanced Technology (AT) Form Factor 19
CMOS 21
Clock Speed and Megahertz 22

The ATX Form Factor 23
- Low Profile Extensions (LPX) 25
- NLX 26

Summary—Form Factors 27
Expansion Bus Architecture 28
- Industry Standard Architecture (ISA) 30
- MCA and EISA 31
- VESA Local-Bus—32-Bit 32
- Peripheral Component Interconnect (PCI) 33

Slots and Sockets 33
- Socket 7 34
- Socket A 34
- Slot Technology 35

North Bridge and South Bridge 37
- Chipsets 38
- AMD Chipsets 40
- Supplementary Information 40

Summary—Buses and Slot 42
PC Card (PCMCIA) 43
Practice Questions 45
Need to Know More? 48

Chapter 3
Memory 49

Conceptual Overview 50
Read-Only Memory (ROM) 51
- Basic Input/Output System (BIOS) 53
- CMOS Settings 53
- Flash BIOS 54
- Programmable ROM 55

Memory—an Analogy 55
- Memory Matrix 56
- Wait States 57
- Interrupts (INT) 57
- Timing 58
- DMA Channels 58
- Bus Clocking 59
- Cache Memory 60

Memory Buses 60
- Front Side Bus 61

Cache Memory 62
- The Memory Hierarchy and Caches 63
- L-1 and L-2 Cache Memory 64

Memory Pages 65
Ranges 65
Fast Page Mode (FPM) 66
Extended Data Output (EDO) RAM 66
Supplementary Information 67
Summary—Memory 69
Types of RAM 70
Dynamic RAM (DRAM) 70
Synchronous RAM (SRAM) 70
Synchronous DRAM (SDRAM) 71
Rambus DRAM (RDRAM) 71
Video RAM (VRAM) 72
Packaging Modules 73
Dual Inline Package (DIP) 73
Single Inline Memory Modules (SIMMs) 74
Dual Inline Memory Modules (DIMMs) 74
Rambus Inline Memory Modules (RIMMs) 75
Supplementary Information 76
Summary—Memory Modules 81
Memory Diagnostics—Parity 81
Even and Odd Parity 82
Error Correction Code (ECC) 83
Practice Questions 85
Need to Know More? 88

Chapter 4
Processors 89

Central Processing Unit (CPU) 90
Processor Speed 91
Processor Families 92
A Real Computer—Real Mode 92
The 80286 Processor 93
Real Mode vs. Protected Mode 94
The 80386 Processor 95
The 80486 Processor 97
Pentium Processors 97
First Series 98
Second Series 99
Third Series and MMX 99
Clock Multiplier 100
Over-Clocking 100
The P6 Family: Sixth Generation 101
Intel Celeron 104

AMD Processors 104
Athlon and Duron 105
Supplementary Information 106
Summary—Processors 110
Practice Questions 112
Need to Know More? 115

Chapter 5
Basic Electronics and Peripherals: Input Devices 117

Analog vs. Digital 119
Basic Electricity 120
Negative to Positive 121
Circuits 122
Amps and Volts 122
Cycles and Frequencies 123
Electromagnetic Interference—EMI 124
Electrostatic Discharge (ESD) and ESD Kits 124
Electronic Components 126
Resistors and Ohms 126
Multimeters 126
Dielectrics 127
Capacitors 127
The Power Supply 130
Interrupt Requests (IRQs) 130
IRQ 2 Cascades to IRQ 9 131
Hexadecimal Numbering 132
Direct Memory Access (DMA) 134
IRQs, DMA, and I/O Ports 136
IRQ 14 137
I/O Addresses 138
Ports and IRQs 138
COM Ports 139
LPT Ports 140
Summary—IRQs, DMAs, and Electricity 141
Keyboards 141
Switch Technology: Mechanical 142
Capacitive Technology: Nonmechanical 143
Mice and Trackballs 144
How a Mouse Works 144
Types of Mice 145
Modems 145
UART Chips 146
Basic Modem Commands 147

Scanners 148
Charge-Coupled Devices (CCDs) and Resolution 149
Scanner Connections 150
Supplementary Information 151
Summary—Input Devices 152
Practice Questions 154
Need to Know More? 158

Chapter 6
Peripherals: Storage Devices 159

Floppy Disks 160
Floppy Drive Components 161
Read-Write Heads 162
Head Actuator 163
Spindle Motor 163
Logic Board 163
Floppy Drive Configuration 164
Media Sensor Jumper 164
Write Protect 165
Change Line Jumper 165
Controllers 165
Fixed Disks/Hard Drives 166
Random Access 168
Tracks and Sectors 168
Hard Drive Controllers 169
IDE and SCSI Interface 169
IDE Drives 170
The ATA Specification 171
The ATA-2 Specification 171
Ultra ATA 174
Supplementary Information 175
The PCI Specification 176
Summary—Disk Drives 177
Hard Drive Configuration 178
Removable Media and Drives 180
Tape and Digital Audio Tape (DAT) 180
Optical Storage 181
DVD 184
Flash Memory 186
Practice Questions 189
Need to Know More? 192

Chapter 7

Peripherals: Output Devices 193

Transient vs. Final Output 194
Video Displays 195
Color and Light 196
Pixels, Triads, and Resolution 196
Dot Pitch 199
Screen Size 199
Image Size 200
Contrast Ratio 200
Scan Cycle and Refresh Rate 201
Noninterlaced and Interlaced 202
Standard VGA 204
8514/A and XGA 204
SVGA and UVGA 205
Accelerated Graphics Port (AGP) 205
Frame Buffers 206
Supplementary Information 207
Graphics Accelerator Cards 209
Liquid Crystal Displays (LCDs) 210
Liquid Crystals 211
LCD Panel Construction 212
Color and Light Revisited 213
Passive Matrix 213
Active Matrix 214
Summary—Monitors 214
Printers 215
Dots Per Inch (dpi) 216
Ink Pixels and Resolution 217
Form Feed 218
Dot Matrix 218
Home Position 220
Printer Problems 220
Cleaning 220
Paper Jams 221
Dot Matrix 223
Fonts 224
Raster vs. Bitmap Fonts 224
True Type Fonts (.TTF Files) 225

Laser Printers 226
The Laser Printing Process 227
The Printing Components 227
The Printing Steps 229
Paper Feed Process 234
Summary—Printers 235
Practice Questions 237
Need to Know More? 240

Chapter 8
Networking 241

Chaining Devices 242
SCSI Interface 243
The SCSI Chain—8 ID Numbers 244
SCSI-1 245
SCSI-2 245
SCSI-3 (Ultra SCSI) 247
Universal Serial Bus (USB) 248
USB 1.0 and 1.1 250
Powered USB Hubs 252
USB 2.0 253
Supplementary Information 254
Plug 'n' Play (PnP) 256
IEEE 1394 257
Summary—Bus Transfers 259
Networking Overview 259
Categories and Types 260
Network Interface Card (NIC) 261
The Redirector 261
Media 261
Ethernet (IEEE 802.3) 262
Terminators 263
Throughput and Bandwidth 263
Token Ring (IEEE 802.5) 264
Bus and Star Topology 265
Bridges and Routers 266
The Router 267
The OSI Model 267
Summary—Network Overview 269
The Internet 269
Email Addresses 270
Supplementary Information 271

Practice Questions 276
Need to Know More? 279

Chapter 9
Cables and Connectors 281

Basic I/O Interfaces 282
Floppy and Hard Disk Controllers 284
15-pin VGA 284
Parallel (LPT) Ports: 8 Bits Across 285
DB25 286
RS-232 and DB9 287
36-pin Centronics Connector 288
SCSI Connectors 288
Types of Parallel Ports 289
Serial (COM) Ports: 1 Bit After Another 290
Keyboard or Mouse Connector: PS/2 291
Summary—Standard Cables 293
Network Cables and Connectors 294
Coaxial Cable 294
Twisted Pair 295
Supplementary Information 298
Summary—Network Cables 300
Practice Questions 302
Need to Know More? 305

Chapter 10
DOS 307

Why Read This Chapter? 308
ATTRIB and Windows 309
Operating Systems 310
DOS 312
CP/M 313
Apple 313
86-DOS 314
PC-DOS 315
CP/M into DOS 316
MS-DOS and PC-DOS 317
From DOS to Windows 9x 317
The Command Interpreter 318
The DOS Command Line 318
Parsing 319
Syntax 319
Switches 320

File Mask (Specification) 321
Error Messages 321
Commands and Programs 322
Loading and Running a Program 323
COMMAND.COM 324
Internal and External Commands 325
The Environment 325
SET [variable] 326
PROMPT= 328
SET TEMP= 329
The Path 329
Search Path 331
DOS Commands 332
ATTRIB.EXE 333
Hidden Files 335
The **DIR** Command: File Searches 335
Wild Cards 336
Saving Search Results 338
Vanilla ASCII (Plain Text) 339
Summary—DOS 340
Logical Formatting and Partitions: FDISK 340
Partitions 341
Volumes and Terms 341
Number of Volumes 342
Primary and Extended Partitions 343
LASTDRIVE= 344
SET in AUTOEXEC.BAT 345
FORMAT.COM 345
LABEL.EXE 346
SYS.COM 346
Logical Block Addressing (LBA) 347
File Systems 347
Directories (Folders) 348
Subdirectories (Subfolders) 352
File Management 353
Logical Formatting: Clusters 354
File Allocation Table (FAT) 355
FAT32 Clusters 356
SCANDISK and CHKDSK (Check Disk) 357
DEFRAG.EXE 358
File Names 360
Characters Allowed in DOS File Names 360

Summary—Disk Management 363
Operating Systems vs. Shells 363
File Properties 364
Shells 364
SHELL= 366
Batch Files 367
AUTOEXEC.BAT 367
A Sample Batch File 368
Practice Questions 371
Need to Know More? 375

Chapter 11
Booting, Windows 3.11, and Memory 377

Booting and System Files 378
The Three-Fingered Salute 379
Booting Overview 380
ROM BIOS Looks at the Boot Sector 381
BASIC Bootstrap Loader 381
Partition Loader 382
Bootstrap Loads IO.SYS 383
IO.SYS Checks for CONFIG.SYS 383
SYSINIT 384
The CONFIG.SYS File 384
The DOS F5 Key 385
CONFIG.SYS and MSDOS.SYS 386
IO.SYS Runs Twice 387
IO.SYS and 16-bit Device Drivers 388
MSDOS.SYS 388
MSDOS.SYS Passes to COMMAND.COM 389
Summary—The Boot Process 390
Beep Codes 391
The Bootable Disk 392
DOS Bootable Disk 392
Making a DOS-Bootable Disk from Windows Explorer 393
Bootable Disk Utility Files 394
Bootable Disk Configuration Files 395
Supplemental Information 396
Multitasking 398
Windows 400
Virtual Real Mode 401
The System VM (Virtual Machine) 402
Program Information Files 402

- Windows Resources 403
- Windows 3.1 406

Starting 16-Bit Windows 407
- SETUP.EXE 407

WIN.COM 409
Windows 3.x Core Files 412
Initialization (.INI) Files 412
- SYSEDIT.EXE 413
- SYSTEM.INI 414
- WIN.INI 415
- What Happens if Certain Files Are Missing? 415
- File Associations 416

PROGMAN.INI 417
- Group (.GRP) Files 417

Summary—Windows 3.x 418
Memory 419
- Basic Memory Divisions 419
- Conventional Memory 421
- 80286 and Real Mode 422
- Low Memory (Segment 1) 423
- Upper Memory (Segments 10–16) 425
- Video RAM (B000) 425
- The 640K Barrier 426

Virtual Memory 426
- Swap Files 427
- Controlling Swap Files 428
- The Control Panel (Windows 3.x) 428

HIMEM.SYS and EMM386.EXE 429
- Upper Memory Blocks (UMBs) 430
- Translation Buffers 430
- System Resources 431
- The Windows 3.x Environment: Global Heap 431
- LIM 4 Expanded Memory 433
- EMM386.EXE 434
- Task Switching 435
- Page Frame Memory and Page Swapping 436

Virtual Device Drivers (VxDs) 437
Summary—Windows Memory 438
An Example CONFIG.SYS File 439
- Points of Interest 440
- DEVICE= and DEVICEHIGH= 441

Practice Questions 444
Need to Know More? 448

Chapter 12
Windows 95, 98, and Me 449

A Word of Caution 450
Windows 95 Introduced Changes 451
Wizards 451
The Desktop 452
Right-Click for Properties (Shift-F10) 453
FAT32 453
Windows Versions 455
Finding the Version 455
The Registry 457
.INI Files 458
Editing Registry Files 459
Objects and Shortcuts 460
Pointers 461
Components of the Registry 462
HKeys 462
Automatic Registry Copies 464
Backing Up the Registry 465
REGEDIT.EXE 466
Summary—Windows Registry 468
Installing Windows 95, 98, and Me 468
Installation Phases 470
Startup and Information-Gathering Phase 470
Hardware Detection Phase 472
Copying and Expanding Files Phase 473
Final System Configuration Phase 474
First Restart 474
Installation Log Files 475
Starting Windows 9x 476
POST and Bootstrap 477
DOS 478
MSDOS.SYS 478
WIN.COM 479
Start Sequence 479
Final Steps to Loading Windows 9x 480
Loading Device Drivers 482
AUTOEXEC.BAT 483
Summary—Start Sequence 484
Windows and DOS 485
The MS Explorer 486
Booting to DOS 487

Useful Additional Components 489
  The Control Panel 489
Startup Menu and Safe Mode 490
  Normal and Logged 491
  Safe Mode (F5) 491
  Safe Mode with Network Support (F6) 492
  Step-by-Step Confirmation (Shift+F8) 492
  Command Prompt Only (Shift F5) 493
  Safe Mode Command Prompt Only 494
  Previous Version of DOS (F4) 494
The Installable File System (IFS) Manager 494
  Network Redirectors 496
  VFAT 497
  Saving Long File Names 499
Reports and Utilities 500
  Hardware Diagnostics 501
  Windows 9x vs. Windows 3.x 502
Windows 98 503
Utilities 504
  Microsoft System Information Utility 506
  Registry Checker 507
  Help Desk 508
  MSCONFIG.EXE 509
  Windows Update Manager 509
  Maintenance Wizard 510
Windows Me 511
Summary—Windows 98 513
Practice Questions 514
Need to Know More? 517

Chapter 13
Windows NT, Windows 2000, and XP 519

  Multitasking 520
Windows Versions 521
  NT Versions 3.1 and 4.0 522
  NT Version 5.0, Windows 2000 522
  Windows XP (Version 5.1) 523
NT Architecture 524
  Kernel Mode 525
  User Mode 527
NT Workstation and NT Server 528
The NT Registry 528

NT Networking 529
- Security Account Manager (SAM) 530
- User ID 530
- The Logon Procedure 531
- Local Security Authorization (LSA) 531

The Security Reference Monitor 533
- Access Control List (ACL) 534

Accounts and Profiles 535
- Administrator 536
- User 536
- Guest 537
- Managing User Accounts 537
- Managing Groups 538
- Policies vs. Profiles 539

Starting Windows NT 540
- NT Boot and System Partitions 541
- NT Loader (NTLDR) 541
- Session Manager (SMSS) 542
- Win32 and LSA 543

NT File System (NTFS) 543

NT Disk Administration 545
- The Disk Administrator Tool 546
- Volume Sets 546
- Striped Sets 547
- Disk Mirroring and Duplexing 548
- RAID 549

Troubleshooting Tools 550
- The Event Viewer 550
- Bootable and Emergency Repair Disks 551
- The Task Manager 552
- Performance Monitor 553
- The Network Management Monitoring Agent 554

NT Error Messages 554
- NT Detect 554
- Missing Kernel 555
- Missing BOOT.INI 555
- Missing Files 556

Summary—Windows NT 556

Windows 2000 558
- Starting Windows 2000 559
- Multiple Boot Options 561
- Safe Mode 562

Active Directory 562
Windows 2000 Diagnostics and Troubleshooting 565
System Configuration Utility 565
My Computer and Control Panel 568
The Device Manager 569
Networking (My Network Places) 570
Interactive Partitioning 570
System Agent 571
Windows Update Manager 571
Windows File Protection (WFP) 572
System File Checker 573
The Recovery Console 573
Windows XP 574
Windows Product Activation (WPA) 575
Reduced Startup Time 575
Summary—Windows 2000 575
Practice Questions 576
Need to Know More? 579

Chapter 14
Troubleshooting 581

Startup Function Keys 582
Startup Problems 584
Windows Crashes 585
Troubleshooting Strategies 586
Restoring a System 587
The Device Manager 588
Device Resources (Windows 2000) 589
Windows 9x Safe Mode 589
Windows 95 590
Windows 98 and Windows Me 590
Emergency Repair Disk 591
The Emergency Repair Process 592
Windows 2000 Safe Mode 592
Last Known Good 593
Selective Startup (MSCONFIG.EXE) 594
Windows Me 595
Windows XP Advanced Startup 596
System Information 596
LOGVIEW.EXE 597
BOOTLOG.TXT 597
Event Viewer 599
Task Manager 600

- System File Checker 600
  - Windows Me System File Protection (SFP) 600
  - Windows File Protection (WFP) 601
- Diagnostics Utilities 602
  - Windows 95 Hardware Diagnostics (HwDiag.EXE) 602
  - Administrative Tools 602
  - System Reports and My Computer 603
- Registry Checker (Scanregw.exe) 604
- Windows 2000 Recovery Console 605
  - Available Commands 606
  - Supplemental Information 607
- System Maintenance 609
  - Windows 2000 Disk Cleanup 609
- Boot Problems 610
  - NTLDR Is Missing 611
  - CMOS Problems 611
  - CMOS Error Messages 612
- Hardware Problems 613
  - Master/Slave Jumpers 613
  - Circuitry Failures 614
- Connectivity Problems 615
  - Network Card Configuration Problems 616
  - Services Icon 617
  - Connection Validation 617
  - Access Denied 617
  - PROTOCOL.INI 618
- Viruses 619
  - Types of Viruses 619
  - Scripted Viruses 620
  - Stealth Viruses 621
  - How Viruses Work 622
  - Viruses in Image Files 623
  - Spyware and Adware 624
- Summary—Troubleshooting 625
- Practice Questions 626
- Need to Know More? 629

Chapter 15
Sample Test 631

- The Questions 632
  - Single Choice and Multiple Choice Responses 632
- Picking the Right Answer 633

Confusing Questions 633
The Exam Framework 634
Begin the Exam 636

Chapter 16
Answer Key 657

Appendix A
What's on the CD-ROM 681

PrepLogic Practice Tests, Preview Edition 682
Exclusive Electronic Version of Text 682
Easy Access to Online Pointers and References 683

Appendix B
Using the *PrepLogic Practice Tests, Preview Edition* Software 685

Exam Simulation 686
Question Quality 686
Interface Design 686
Effective Learning Environment 686
Software Requirements 687
Installing *PrepLogic Practice Tests, Preview Edition* 687
Removing *PrepLogic Practice Tests, Preview Edition* from Your Computer 687
Using *PrepLogic Practice Tests, Preview Edition* 688
Starting a Practice Test Mode Session 688
Starting a Flash Review Mode Session 689
Standard *PrepLogic Practice Tests, Preview Edition* Options 689
Time Remaining 690
Your Examination Score Report 690
Review Your Exam 691
Get More Exams 691
Contacting PrepLogic 691
Customer Service 691
Product Suggestions and Comments 691
License Agreement 692

Acronym Glossary 693

Index 711

We Want to Hear from You!

As the reader of this book, *you* are our most important critic and commentator. We value your opinion and want to know what we're doing right, what we could do better, what areas you'd like to see us publish in, and any other words of wisdom you're willing to pass our way.

As an executive editor for Que Certification, I welcome your comments. You can email or write me directly to let me know what you did or didn't like about this book—as well as what we can do to make our books better.

Please note that I cannot help you with technical problems related to the *topic* of this book. We do have a User Services group, however, where I will forward specific technical questions related to the book.

When you write, please be sure to include this book's title and authors as well as your name, email address, and phone number. I will carefully review your comments and share them with the authors and editors who worked on the book.

Email: **feedback@quepublishing.com**

Mail: Jeff Riley
Executive Editor
Que Certification
201 West 103rd Street
Indianapolis, IN 46290 USA

For more information about this book or another Que title, visit our Web site at **www.quepublishing.com**. Type the ISBN (excluding hyphens) or the title of a book in the Search field to find the page you're looking for.

Introduction

Welcome to *A+ Exam Cram!* This introduction is very much like the "Quick Setup" reference section for a software application. Chapter 1 is a description of the testing environment, and where we discuss test-taking strategies. Chapters 2–14 are designed to remind you of everything you'll need to know in order to take—and pass—the **220-221** and **220-222** Computing Technology Industry Association's (CompTIA) A+ certification exam. The sample test at the end of the book should give you a reasonably accurate assessment of your knowledge, and yes, we've provided the answers and their explanations in the final chapter. Read the book, and you'll stand a very good chance of passing the test.

New job listings in the field of corporate information technology (IT) often require applicants to be A+ certified. Additionally, many people who complete the program qualify for increases in pay and/or career-advancement opportunities. Even if the initial job posting doesn't require A+ certification, many companies expect you to complete the certification process within 90 days of being hired.

What This Book Will Not Do

This book will *not* teach you everything you need to know about computers, or even about a given topic. Nor is this book an introduction to computer technology. If you're new to computers and looking for an initial preparation guide, check out **www.quepublishing.com**, there is a whole section on A+ certification. This book will review what you need to know before you take the test. In some cases we refer to the latest-and-greatest trends in coming technology, but our fundamental purpose is dedicated to reviewing the information on the existing CompTIA A+ certification exam.

If you're not already comfortable with command-line operations and getting under the hood of a computer, you'll be much better served by starting off with a comprehensive A+ preparation course or manual. Otherwise, this book uses a variety of teaching and memorization techniques to analyze the exam-related topics, and to provide you with ways to input, index, and retrieve everything you'll need to know in order to pass the test. Once again, it is *not* an introduction to computers.

What This Book Is Designed to Do

This book is designed to be read as a pointer to the areas of knowledge you will be tested on. In other words, you may want to read the book one time, to get an insight into how comprehensive your knowledge of computers is. The book is also designed to be read shortly before you go for the actual test, and to give you a distillation of the entire field of PC hardware, Wintel operating systems, and basic networking, in as few pages as possible. We think you can use this book to get a sense of the underlying context of any topic in the chapters, or to skim-read for Study Alerts, bullet points, summaries, and topic headings.

We've drawn on material from CompTIA's own listing of knowledge requirements, from other preparation guides, and from the exams themselves. We've also drawn from a battery of third-party test preparation tools, technical Web sites, and from our own experience with PCs, going all the way back to the Altair. Our aim is to walk you through your knowledge of PCs and simple networking, looking over your shoulder, so to speak, and pointing out those things that are important for the exam (e.g., study alerts, practice questions, and so on).

The A+ exam makes a basic assumption that you already have a *very* strong background of experience with PC hardware and software. On the other hand, we think that PC technology is changing so quickly that no one can be a total expert. We've tried to demystify the jargon, acronyms, terms, and concepts, and wherever we think you're likely to blur past an important concept, we've defined the assumptions and premises behind that concept.

About This Book

If you're preparing for the A+ certification exam for the first time, we've structured the topics in this book to build upon one another. Therefore, the topics covered in later chapters often refer to previous discussions in earlier chapters. In our opinion, many computer manuals and reference books are essentially a list of facts. Rather than simply listing raw facts about each topic on the exam, we've tried to paint an integrated landscape in your imagination, where each exam fact becomes an obvious conclusion to the problems evolving out of earlier technology.

We suggest you read this book from front to back. You won't be wasting your time, since nothing we've written is a guess about an unknown exam. What may appear to be a detour into rambling discussions is based upon our many years of working with less experienced computer users. We've had to explain certain underlying information on such a regular basis that we've included those explanations here. Time and again, we've found that by understanding the historical, contextual, or conceptual underpinnings of a topic, our audience members were much better able to recall the resulting details.

Once you've read the book, you can brush up on a topic by using the Index or the Table of Contents to go straight to the topics and questions you want to re-examine. We've tried to use the headings and subheadings to provide outline information about each given topic. After you've been certified, we think you'll find this book useful as a tightly focused reference and an essential foundation of PC knowledge.

Chapter Formats

Each *Exam Cram* chapter follows a regular structure, along with graphical cues about especially important or useful material. The structure of a typical chapter includes:

- **Opening Hotlists**—Each chapter begins with lists of the terms you'll need to understand, and the concepts you'll need to master before you can be fully conversant with the chapter's subject matter. We follow the hotlists with a few introductory paragraphs, setting the stage for the rest of the chapter.
- **Topical Coverage**—After the opening hotlists, each chapter covers at least four topics related to the chapter's subject.
- **Study Alerts**—Throughout the topical coverage section, we highlight material most likely to appear on the exam by using a special Study Alert layout that looks like this:

This is what a Study Alert looks like. A Study Alert stresses concepts, terms, software, or activities that will most likely appear in one or more certification exam questions. For that reason, we think any information found offset in Study Alert format is worthy of unusual attentiveness on your part.

Even if material isn't flagged as a Study Alert, *all* the content in this book is associated in some way with test-related material. What appears in the chapter content is critical knowledge.

- **Sidebars**—When we discuss an exam topic that may be based on common knowledge among people in the IT industry, we've tried to explicitly describe the underlying assumptions of the discussion. You may have many years of experience with PCs, or you may be just starting out. Your certification shouldn't depend on "secret knowledge" that you're supposed to "just know" somehow.

Something You May Not Know

A sidebar like this is a way to step outside the flow of the discussion in order to provide you with "insider" information that you may not have heard before. A sidebar is a way to increase the saturation level of your knowledge and apply some "glue" to help keep topical facts from slipping out of your ears.

- **Notes**—This book is an overall examination of computers. As such, we dip into nearly every aspect of working with, and configuring PCs. Where a body of knowledge is deeper than the scope of the book, we use Notes to indicate areas of concern or specialty training.

Cramming for an exam will get you through a test, but it won't make you a competent IT professional. While you can memorize just the facts you need, in order to become certified, your daily work in the field will rapidly put you in water over your head if you don't know the underlying principles of computers.

- **Useful Knowledge Tips**—We provide tips that will help you to build a better foundation of knowledge or to focus your attention on an important concept that will reappear later in the book. Tips are a helpful way to remind you of the context surrounding a particular area of a topic under discussion.

You should read Chapter 1 for helpful strategies used in taking a test. The introduction to the Sample Test at the end of the book contains additional tips on how to figure out the correct response to a question, or what to do if you draw a complete blank.

- **Supplementary Information**—In some cases, the exam-specific material covered in a topic section may be so outdated as to be distracting. Where we think it would be helpful to understand the real-world market technology, we've included supplemental information. This type of information is more than a simple sidebar, but is beyond the scope of the exam.

- **Category Summaries**—In many instances, the topic under discussion is so filled with details, numbers, acronyms, trouble spots, and alerts, that you may become lost in the jumble of words. We've tried to put some breathing space at the end of each generally related category, to provide a sort of reality check as to what ought to be the focus of your memorization efforts.
- **Practice Questions**—This section presents a short list of test questions related to the specific chapter topic. Each question has a following explanation of both correct and incorrect answers. The practice questions highlight the areas we found to be most important on the exam.
- **Need To Know More**—Every chapter ends with a section entitled "Need To Know More?" This section provides pointers to resources that we found to be helpful in offering further details on the chapter's subject matter. If you find a resource you like in this collection, use it, but don't feel compelled to use all these resources. We use this section to recommend resources that we have used on a regular basis, so none of the recommendations will be a waste of your time or money. These resources may go out of print or be taken down (in the case of Web sites), so we've tried to reference widely accepted resources.

The bulk of the book follows this chapter structure, but there are a few other elements that we would like to point out:

- **Sample Test**—A very close approximation of the types of questions you are likely to see on the current A+ exam (Chapter 15).
- **Answer Key**—The answers to the sample test, with a following explanation of both the correct response and the incorrect responses (Chapter 16).
- **Acronym Glossary**—This is an extensive glossary of acronyms. We've tried to include every acronym used in the book.
- **The Cram Sheet**—This appears as a tear-away sheet, inside the front cover of this *Exam Cram* book. It is a valuable tool that represents a collection of the most difficult-to-remember facts and numbers we think you should memorize before taking the test. Remember, you can dump this information out of your head onto a piece of paper as soon as you enter the testing room. These are usually facts that we've found require brute force memorization. You only need to remember this information long enough to write it down when you walk into the test room. Be advised that you will be asked to surrender all personal belongings before you enter the exam room itself.

You might want to look at the Cram Sheet in the car or in the lobby of the testing center just before you walk into the testing center. Keep in mind that if you take both tests together, there is a break between the Core Hardware and the Operating Systems Technologies exam. The Cram Sheet is divided under headings, so you can review the appropriate parts just before each test.

Codes and Commands

In most cases, program commands that are to be issued at a command line prompt are in bold. For example, if you are asked to type **DIR /P** at a command line, the "DIR /P" is an actual command. When you encounter an instruction to type a command, that command will not be bold, and will be surrounded in quotes. The quotes are not part of the command. For example, you may be asked to type "DIR /P" at a command line (without the quotes).

Limitations of printed pages will, many times, introduce false line breaks in programming code, character strings, path names, and other related text. We make every effort to ensure that a line break, or line wrap, generated by the page margins does not change the meaning of the information. In some cases, a hyphen may be inserted into the string by mistake. Where there may be some ambiguity, we try to clarify the intent immediately following the text. If an erroneous hyphen appears in print, we hope you'll understand that these things happen, but do feel free to call it to our attention.

For example, a very long path name might be: C:\WINDOWS\SYSTEM\CatRoot\{127D0A1D-4EF2-11D1-8608-00C04FC295EE}. Note that the first characters in the string are "C:\WI…" and the last characters of the same string, on the same line, are "…5EE}" (without the quotes).

Contacting the Authors

We've tried to create a real-world tool that you can use to prepare for and pass both of the A+ certification exams. We are interested in any feedback you would care to share about the book, especially if you have ideas about how we can improve it for future test-takers. We will consider everything you say carefully and will respond to all reasonable suggestions and comments. You can reach us via email at **aplus@jamesgjones.com**.

Let us know if you found this book to be helpful in your preparation efforts. We'd also like to know how you felt about your chances of passing the exam *before* you read the book and then *after* you read the book. Of course, we'd love to hear that you passed the exam, and even if you just want to share your triumph, we'd be happy to hear from you.

Thanks for choosing us as your personal trainers, and enjoy the book. We would wish you luck on the exam, but we know that if you read through all the chapters, you won't need luck—you'll ace the test on the strength of real knowledge!

Self-Assessment

The reason we included a Self-Assessment in this *Exam Cram* book is to help you evaluate your readiness to tackle A+ certification. But before you tackle this Self-Assessment, let's talk about concerns you may face when pursuing A+ certification and what an ideal candidate might look like.

CompTIA-Certified Computer Technicians in the Real World

Most people will take the two modules of the A+ certification exam in order to serve in the PC hardware and software repair field. Others might see these tests as a great starting point for gaining the basic PC knowledge that can be used in many other fields. You can get all the real-world motivation you need from knowing that many others have gone before, so you'll be able to follow in their footsteps. If you're willing to tackle the process seriously and do what it takes to obtain the necessary experience and knowledge, you can take—and pass—the certification modules involved in obtaining A+ certification. In fact, the entire *Exam Cram* series is designed to make it as easy as possible for you to prepare for certification exams. But prepare you must!

The same, of course, is true for other CompTIA certifications, including the following:

- CompTIA's Certified Document Imaging Architect (CDIA) certification is a nationally recognized credential acknowledging competency and professionalism in the document imaging industry. CDIA candidates possess critical knowledge of all major areas and technologies used to plan, design, and specify an imaging system.

- Network+ certifies the knowledge of networking technicians with 18 to 24 months of experience in the IT industry.

- i-Net+ certification is designed specifically for any individual interested in demonstrating baseline technical knowledge that would allow him or her to pursue a variety of Internet-related careers.

Put Yourself to the Test

The following series of questions and observations is designed to help you figure out how much work you must do to pursue A+ certification and what kinds of resources you might consult on your quest. Be absolutely honest in your answers; otherwise, you'll end up wasting money on exams you're not yet ready to take. There are no right or wrong answers, only steps along the path to certification. Only you can decide where you really belong in the broad spectrum of aspiring candidates.

Two things should be clear from the outset, however:

- Even a modest background in computer science will be helpful.
- Hands-on experience with personal computers is an essential ingredient of certification success.

Educational Background

1. Have you ever taken any computer-related classes? [Yes or No]

   If Yes, proceed to question 2; if No, proceed to question 4.

2. Have you taken any classes on computer operating systems? [Yes or No]

   If Yes, you'll probably be able to handle operating system architecture and system component discussions. If you're rusty, brush up on basic operating system concepts, especially virtual memory, multitasking regimes, user-mode versus kernel-mode operation, and general computer security topics.

   If No, consider some basic reading in this area. A good place to start is *A+ Certification and Training Guide, Fourth Edition* by Charles Brooks (Que Publishing, 2002, ISBN 0-7897-2844-3). This book covers A+ topics in far more detail than the *Exam Cram* series. If this title doesn't appeal to you, check out **www.quepublishing.com**. This site has a whole section dedicated to A+ and offers a wealth of information. CompTIA's Web site (**www.comptia.org**) is also a good location to find all kinds of A+-related material.

3. Have you taken any networking concepts or technologies classes? [Yes or No]

   If Yes, you'll probably be able to handle the A+ certification networking terminology, concepts, and technologies. If you're rusty, Scott Mueller's *Upgrading and Repairing Networks* (Que Publishing, 2002, 0-7897-2557-6) will help you brush up on basic networking concepts and terminology, especially networking media; transmission types; the OSI Reference Model; and networking technologies such as Ethernet, Token Ring, FDDI, and WAN links.

If No, you might want to supplement the material available in this book with other good works. The three best books that we know of are *Computer Networks, Third Edition* by Andrew S. Tanenbaum (Prentice-Hall, 1996, ISBN 0-133-49945-6), *Computer Networks and Internets* by Douglas E. Comer (Prentice-Hall, 1997, ISBN 0-132-39070-1), and *Encyclopedia of Networking* by Tom Sheldon (Osborne/McGraw-Hill, 1998, ISBN 0-07-882333-1). Don't forget Scott Mueller's *Upgrading and Repairing Networks* mentioned in the previous paragraph. This is a great book to have for reference both now and in the future.

Skip to the next section, "Hands-on Experience."

4. Have you done any reading on operating systems or networks? [Yes or No]

   If Yes, review the requirements stated in the first paragraphs after questions 2 and 3. If you meet those requirements, move on to the next section, "Hands-on Experience." If No, you'll find the *A+ Certification and Training, Guide Fourth Edition* by Charles Brooks (Que Publishing, 2002, ISBN 0-7897-2844-3) very helpful.

Hands-on Experience

The most important key to success on all the CompTIA tests is hands-on experience, especially with basic computer hardware, as well as Windows 95, Windows 98, Windows NT Workstation, Windows 2000 Professional, and, to a lesser degree, MS-DOS. If we leave you with only one realization after taking this Self-Assessment, it should be that there's no substitute for time spent installing, configuring, and using PC hardware and software.

Before you even think about taking any exam, make sure you've spent enough time with the related hardware and software to understand how it can be installed and configured, how to maintain such an installation, and how to troubleshoot when things go wrong. This will help you in the exam, and in real life.

Testing Your Exam-Readiness

Whether you attend a formal class on a specific topic to get ready for an exam or use written materials to study on your own, some preparation for the A+ certification exams is essential. At more than $100 a try (pass or fail) you want to do everything you can to pass on your first try. That's where studying comes in.

For any given subject, consider taking a class if you've tackled self-study materials, taken the test, and failed anyway. The opportunity to interact with an instructor and fellow students can make all the difference in the world, if you can *afford* that privilege. For information about CompTIA classes, visit the CompTIA Web site at **www.comptia.org** (follow the Certification link to find training).

If you can't *afford* to take a class, visit the Web page anyway, because it also includes a detailed breakdown of the objectives for both modules of the A+ certification exam. This will serve as a good roadmap for your studies.

Even if you can't afford to spend much, you should use practice exams to their fullest. Practice exams can help you assess your readiness to pass a test better than any other tool. We have included some very good practice exams in the *Exam Cram* book and also on the CD accompanying the book. However, if you feel you need more help in this area, there are numerous practice exams available from commercial vendors. The CompTIA Web site (**www.comptia.org**) is a good place to start looking for additional exams.

5. Have you taken a practice exam on your chosen test subject? [Yes or No]

   If Yes, and you scored 75 percent or better, you're probably ready to tackle the real thing. If your score isn't above that crucial threshold, keep at it until you break that barrier.

   If No, obtain all the free and low-budget practice tests you can find and get to work. Keep at it until you can break the passing threshold comfortably.

When it comes to assessing your test readiness, there's no better way than to take a good-quality practice exam and pass with a score of 75 percent or better. When we're preparing ourselves, we shoot for 80-plus percent, just to leave room for the "weirdness factor" that sometimes shows up on exams.

One last note: We can't stress enough the importance of hands-on experience in the context of both modules of the A+ certification exam. As you review the material, you'll realize that hands-on experience with basic PC hardware, operating system commands, tools, and utilities is invaluable.

Onward!

After you've assessed your readiness, undertaken the right background studies, and obtained some hands-on experience, you're ready to go after the real thing. So pick up the phone and set up a test time at your favorite testing facility. We have even included a coupon with this book to help you with the cost.

1

A+ Certification Tests

As experiences go, taking a test isn't something most people anticipate eagerly, no matter how well they've prepared. In most cases, familiarity helps reduce anxiety. In plain English, this means you probably wouldn't be as nervous taking a second exam, as you will be taking your first one. We've taken lots of exams, and this book is partly about helping you to get rid of some of your anxiety. This chapter is all about what you can expect to see in the exam room itself.

No matter whether it's your first or your tenth try, understanding how much time to spend on questions, the setting you'll be in, and the testing software, will help you concentrate on the material rather than on the environment. Likewise, mastering a few basic test-taking skills should help you recognize—and perhaps outfox—some of the tricks and "gotchas" you're bound to encounter.

Are You Certifiable?

Perhaps a quick way for you to decide where you stand in relation to the current certification process is to leaf through this book and see how well you do with the practice questions at the end of each chapter. We don't recommend that you sneak a peek at the sample test at the end, only because you should consider it to be a final run of the actual exam. If you haven't even looked at the sample test until you're ready to schedule the real exam, you'll have a more accurate sense of your readiness.

Depending on your experience with PCs, we recommend that you begin your studies with a visit to the CompTIA Web site (**http://www.comptia.org**) for a definition of what it means to be A+ certified. As far as we're concerned, the only reason you might not be certifiable would be if you were to suppose that the exam is a simple evaluation of entry-level skills. Don't make that assumption! A+ certification means that you have a comprehensive understanding of first-tier tech support. The CompTIA exam-development team has gone to great lengths to weed out dilettantes and "hot shots."

We *strongly* recommend that you have previously installed, configured, and generally "fooled around" with at least one example of both the Windows 9x environment and the Windows 2000 or XP environment. Sometimes, the only way to effectively do this is through classroom training. In addition, you should be familiar with the underlying DOS operating environment you'll find on most Windows systems. Keep in mind that Windows 9x runs on top of DOS 7.x, and that the Windows 2000/XP Recovery Console is based on many of the original DOS utilities.

The A+ Certification Exams

The A+ Certification Exam actually consists of two separate exams. You will be required to pass both the *Core Hardware* test and the *Operating Systems Technologies* test. These tests are available in Spanish, German, French, and Japanese; however, you should call CompTIA directly, at (630) 268-1818, for more information if you plan to take the test in a language other than English.

The Core Hardware exam tests your knowledge of PC hardware. CompTIA means hardware to include the following:

- Motherboards
- Processors
- Memory
- Peripherals (input, output, and storage)
- IRQs and DMA channels
- Port addresses
- Electronics
- Buses
- Networking
- Cables and connectors

The Operating Systems Technologies exam tests your knowledge of the three most widely used operating systems in the current market. By operating systems, CompTIA means the following:

- DOS and Windows 3.x
- Windows 95, 98, and ME
- Windows 2000

Both the Core Hardware test and the Operating Systems Technologies test are designed to uncover not only your understanding of the technology, but also how to solve problems related to each area. Troubleshooting is an important aspect of the exam, as most certified A+ individuals will be working in the field as tech support personnel. The last chapter in this book is explicitly devoted to areas of troubleshooting.

Where Do I Sign Up?

Many people think that the two components are so closely related that they should be combined into a single exam. Whether or not they're eventually combined, we recommend you treat the two components as one exam. In fact, we have organized this book on that basis, and we urge you to sign up for *both* exams at the same time. You'll be charged $139 for each test you take, whether you pass or fail.

CompTIA is continually evaluating the pricing of these tests, and it may change prior to your enrollment in the exam. We are sure the price will not go down, so the sooner you sign up, the better.

Tests are administered by two organizations: Vue Testing Services and Thomson Prometric. Both services provide the same tests, and you should be able to find a testing location near your home. Additional information can be obtained at the CompTIA Web site (**http://www.comptia.org/certification/test_locations.htm**) or by contacting the testing services directly:

VUE Testing Service
www.vue.com
(877) 551-7587

Thomson Prometric
http://www.prometric.com
(800) 776-4276

How Do I Schedule the Test?

To schedule an exam, you must call at least one day in advance. When calling, have the following information ready for the sales representative who handles your call:

- Your name, your organization, and your mailing address
- The name of the exam(s) you want to take (i.e., A+ Core Hardware exam and/or Operating System Technologies exam)
- Your method of payment

Payment must be received before a test can be scheduled. *To cancel or reschedule an exam without a cost penalty*, you must call at least 12 hours before the scheduled test time. The most convenient payment method is to provide a valid credit card number with sufficient available credit. Otherwise, payments are accepted by check, money order, or purchase order (P.O.).

If you are paying by purchase order, ask the testing service's sales representative for more details.

Keep in mind that if your payment involves the postal service and banking system (i.e., check, purchase order, etc.), you'll have to call to schedule your exam much earlier than one day in advance.

Certification

When you've passed both of the certification exams, you will be A+ certified. Save the test results you are given at the conclusion of the tests, because they are your immediate proof prior to receiving your certification package. Official certification normally takes anywhere from four to six weeks. When the package arrives, it will include a Welcome Kit, a certificate (suitable for framing), and an identification lapel pin. As an official recognition of hard work and broad-based knowledge, A+ certification is a badge of honor.

The Exam Site

On the day of your exam, try to arrive at least 15 minutes before the scheduled time slot. You must bring *two* forms of identification, one of which *must* be a photo ID. Typically, a driver's license and credit card are valid forms of identification. You may also use insurance cards, birth certificates, state ID cards, employee identification cards, or any other legal identification. If you're not sure whether your identification is acceptable, ask the person with whom you schedule your exam.

In the Exam Room

The exams are completely closed-book, and use an interactive computer program to present questions and responses. You will not be permitted to take anything with you into the testing area, other than a blank sheet of paper and a pencil provided by the exam proctors.

We suggest that when you enter the exam room you *immediately write down the most critical information* about the test you're taking on the blank sheet of paper you'll be given. *Exam Cram* books provide a tear-away Cram Sheet, located in the front of the book, listing the most essential, last minute information you'll want to remember before you enter the exam room.

Testing and Scoring

Both A+ tests are multiple choice and adaptive. A computer-based adaptive test means that your second question is based on how well you answered the first question, and so forth. You can expect between 20 and 30 questions, with the actual number of questions depending on the answers to the previous questions. In other words, if you incorrectly respond to a question, the following question will further examine that particular area of knowledge. If you correctly respond to a question, the following questions will increase in difficulty.

The maximum time limit is 30 minutes for each test. However, the test may conclude before the time limit and give you a score. If the software detects that you are either highly competent or unprepared, an evaluation process brings the test to a close rather than spend unnecessary time continuing. The absolute scoring range for each test is 0 through 1300 points. The following are the minimum passing scores for each exam:

- ➤ 596 points in order to pass the Core Hardware test
- ➤ 600 points in order to pass the Operating System Technologies test

Following the Exam

The administrator will give you a report with your overall score, and your score will be broken out into several topical areas when you leave the exam room. Even if you fail, we suggest that you ask for (and keep) a printed copy of the report. If necessary, you can use the printout to help you prepare for another attempt. If you must retake an exam, you must call one of the two testing organizations, schedule a new test date, and pay another $139 per exam.

How to Prepare for an Exam

Preparing for network certification, aerobics certification, or even driving certification (a driver's license) is probably simpler than passing a comprehensive, broad-based examination of your PC skills. In the other cases, the area in which you're being certified is a limited subset of only that field. A+ certification, on the other hand, has no boundary limitations. Anything at all about a PC is a valid subject for testing—even multimeter readings and COM port IRQs!

We've attempted to make no assumptions, whatsoever, about your current knowledge. We've tried to cram as much information as possible about PCs between the covers of this book. However, our main focus is to get you through the exam. Using the self-study method, you might consider us as virtual tutors, coming to your site, at your convenience, and stuffing facts between your ears.

We've "been there, done that" so to speak, and we'll point you in the right direction for your studies. We've also tried to provide a context for the information we're covering, with summaries, sidebars, tips, notes, and supplemental information. Our philosophy is that if you can form a picture of something, you can remember it better.

Current Exam Requirements

The A+ certification exam is constantly being updated, so as to reflect the ever-progressive developments in the PC industry. The best source of current exam information is CompTIA's Web site at **http://www.comptia.org**. If you don't have access to the Internet, you can call or write CompTIA directly at:

Computing Technology Industry Association
450 East 22nd Street, Suite 230
Lombard, IL 60134-6158
Phone: (630) 268-1818

Additional Resources

Self-study candidates may use many individual reference books that, taken together, cover most of the required material on the exam. This is one approach, and a good professional should always have a solid reference library. See the "Need To Know More?" sections at the end of each chapter for lists of some of our recommended references.

If you like a little more structure, there are several good preparation programs available in both a self-paced and classroom format. However, you must be sure the program you select has been developed for the current A+ requirements, released in April 2000. Consider, too, that the cost of a structured class environment is significantly higher than the price of this book.

The Test Site

When you arrive at the testing center, you'll be required to sign in with a test coordinator, or administrator. He or she will ask you to produce two forms of identification, one of which must be a photo ID. When you've completed the sign-in process, you'll most likely have a short wait before you're ushered into the actual exam room. Just prior to entering the room, you'll be asked to surrender any personal belongings for secure storage until you leave the exam room.

When you enter the exam room, you'll be given a pen or pencil and a blank sheet of paper. As we explained in the Introduction, you're allowed to write down any information you want on this, and you can write on both sides of the page. Most likely, the computer you'll be using will be ready to go. The exam begins once you begin using the machine. The timing for the exam is based on the actual question and answer activity, not the amount of time you spend in the room. If you want to spend some amount of time jotting down critical facts on the scratch sheet, do so.

In the Introduction, we suggested that you memorize as much as possible of the critical tips on the Cram Sheet (inside the front cover of this book). Look at that sheet just before you sign in for your test and then write what you remember on your blank sheet as soon as you can, when you've entered the exam room. Timing of the test does not start until you open the first question and from that point on you have 30 minutes. You will be allowed to refer to your notes at any time during the test, but you'll have to surrender the scratch sheet when you leave the room.

Keep in mind that if you've registered for both exams, you can take a break between the Core Hardware and the Operating Systems Technologies exams. If you jam the hardware details into your head just before the first exam, you'll have some time to step out of the testing room, take a break, and jam the software details into your head in a separate process.

After you've signed in and your time slot arrives, you'll be asked to deposit any books, bags, or other items you brought with you. You'll then be escorted into a closed room. Typically, the testing room will be furnished with anywhere from one to six computers. Each workstation will be separated from the others by dividers designed to keep you from seeing what's happening on someone else's computer.

The exam rooms feature a wall with a large pane of glass or a video camera. This is to permit the test coordinator to monitor the room, to prevent test-takers from talking to one another, and to observe anything out of the ordinary that might take place. The exam coordinator will have preloaded the A+

certification test, and you'll be permitted to start as soon as you're seated in front of the machine. The software will take care of the exam times.

You're not required to start as soon as you're seated. You may use a reasonable amount of time to spew (technical term) out those critical facts you memorized, just before you entered the room. Some good examples would be the COM and LPT addresses and IRQs, laser printer print-path components, or any other details you've found it difficult to remember as you've prepared your review.

Adaptive Testing

All A+ certification exams are adaptive, multiple choice, and have an absolute time limit. However, that time limit may not necessarily be reached. Unlike traditional fixed-length tests, where each participant answers a specific number of questions, an adaptive test tailors itself to the person taking the test. Each question is presented based on the response to a previous question. Because of this, each examinee sees a totally different test with potentially a different number of test questions.

Scoring of the test is actually based on the difficulty of the presented questions, *not* the total number of correct responses. You'll have a maximum allowed time of 30 minutes per exam. However, once the software determines that you've answered a sufficient number of questions, or the time runs out, the exam will shut down, and you will immediately be informed as to whether you passed or failed.

Don't panic and have an anxiety attack about what may seem to be a very short time allotment for each exam. The test was developed by many IT professionals, with a widely-accepted agreement as to what ought to be difficult, but typical knowledge. If you know your stuff, you'll have plenty of time. If you don't know your stuff, you'll be found out before the allotted time anyway. Relax, write down the numbers before you start, and take the time to read the questions carefully.

Because of the structure of this type of test, you will not be able to go back and revise an answer. This was possible on earlier versions of the exam, but it is no longer an option. *Read each question carefully before answering!* We can't stress this enough—the exam is designed to confuse you and mess you up with similar-sounding or similarly spelled words.

You may be asked to select the best or most effective solution to a problem from a range of choices, all of which are technically correct. You may be asked to select the best choice from a graphic image. You may also find questions where a series of blanks represent a list of terms used to complete a sentence. All in all, it's quite an adventure, and it involves real thinking. Throughout this book, we will show you what to expect and how to deal with the problems, puzzles, and predicaments you're likely to find on the test.

The Sample Test in Chapter 15 is a very close approximation of the type of questions you will be facing. We've included a sample of every type of question we saw, as well as the phrasing style of the overall exam. We've also provided a few questions with similar uncertainties to what we saw in various questions. Perhaps most importantly, we've tried to show you the underlying psychology of the exam, and the ways the test developers will try to confuse you.

Test Layout and Design

All of the questions on A+ exams are multiple choices. That being said, there are some diabolical ways in which to use multiple choice options. Don't think that every possible way hasn't been thought of! Some questions will provide all of the information in paragraph format, and others will provide an Exhibit (line drawing), asking you to identify specific components. *Paying careful attention* is the key to success! Be prepared to toggle back and forth between a picture and a question, as you work. Often, both the exhibit and the questions are complex to the point that you might not be able to remember either of them from moment to moment.

Each question stands alone in a single, windowed page. The text of the question is near the top of the screen, and each set of response choices is below. Each response has a typical Windows check button, where clicking on the appropriate circle turns it black. You may change your selection at any time, from within the question window.

The time you take to respond, and the number of times you change your response are not factored into the scoring process. Only when you move on to the next question are you finished with the question. There is no going back.

Questions and Linguistics

The most important advice we can give you about taking any test is this: *Read each question carefully*! Are you getting the idea, here? Some questions are deliberately ambiguous, offering several possibilities that could be correct, depending on your reading of the question. We use Exam Alerts and Tips throughout the book, as well as the Practice Questions at the end of each chapter, to point out where you may run into these types of questions.

Some questions use double negatives, such as, "Which of the following files is *not unnecessary* during the boot process?" Observe how easily you could read this as "not necessary" and miss the double negative. This is one of those psychological tricks we've mentioned.

Other questions use terminology in *incredibly* precise ways. We've taken numerous practice and real tests, and in nearly every case we've missed at least one question because *we didn't read it closely or carefully enough*. The use of the word "requires" is a favorite way for questions to mess you up. For example, you might be asked which list of items is required in a CONFIG.SYS file. Each response may offer you a list where all but one of the items is required. Only in one response list, will every item be required.

Another example of a precision question would be, "Windows 95 requires the WIN.INI and SYSTEM.INI files during the startup process in order to load device drivers and user options." The responses are True or False. The correct answer is False, because the WIN.INI file isn't *required*. Windows will create a WIN.INI file if one is not found, but because the file can be created on the fly, that file is, therefore, not required. Neither does 32-bit Windows use the WIN.INI file in the same manner as 16-bit Windows.

Here are some suggestions on how to deal with the tendency to jump to an answer too quickly:

- Make sure you *read every word in the question!* If you find yourself jumping ahead impatiently, go back and start over. Don't schedule your exam on a day when you have lots of other appointments and errands. Take your time!
- As you read, try to rephrase the question in your own terms. If you can do this, it should make it easier to pick the correct answer.
- *Trust your subconscious!* If you've studied the book, and if you feel you're ready to take the exam, then you probably *are* ready to take the exam. The subconscious mind never forgets anything. Every perception, memory, event, fact, or situation you've ever been in, is written to your subconscious database. The problem is getting the data out again. If you just relax and use your imagination, your intuition can come through and often provide you with the answer. Chances are, if the answer you choose feels right, it is right.

Above all, try to deal with each question by thinking through what you know about hardware and software systems. Then, use your imagination and try to picture the page you saw the answer on. By reviewing what you know (and what you've written down on your scratch sheet), you'll often recall or understand things sufficiently to determine the answer to the question.

Question-Handling Strategies

Based on the tests we've taken, a couple of interesting trends in the responses have become apparent. Usually, some responses will be obviously incorrect, and two of the remaining answers will be plausible. Remember that only one response can be correct. If the answer leaps out at you, reread the question to look for a trick—just in case.

Things to look for in the "obviously wrong" category include: weird menu choices or utility names, nonexistent software options, and terminology you've never seen before. If you've done your homework for the exam, *nothing should be completely new* to you. In that case, unfamiliar or bizarre terminology probably indicates a totally bogus answer. As long as you're sure of what's wrong, it's easier to figure out what's right.

Bogus Choices

Our best advice regarding responses that are totally wrong would be to once again rely on your intuition. Nothing on the exam should come as a surprise to you if you've read this book and taken the Sample Test. If you see something in a response that's totally unfamiliar, the chances are high that it's a made-up word.

The following question tries to throw you off this way:

Which is the most useful tool for checking a circuit?

- ❍ a. Differentiometer
- ❍ b. Analytic Resistance Meter
- ❍ c. Multimeter
- ❍ d. Integrity Capacitor

Chances are that you've at least heard of a *multimeter* before. The remaining options sound plausible, but they don't exist.

Duplicate False Responses

Another trend you can use to your advantage, is a tendency to give you two possible responses that say the same thing, but reversed, or in slightly different order. When you see repeating choices, there's a high probability that at least those two choices are wrong. One of the things we've done in our own Sample Test is to play off this and make this trick work against you. If you get through our test, you'll be able to spot duplicate, false responses just fine.

An example of a repeating wrong answer would be in the responses to the following question:

Which of the following files make up the Windows core files?

- ❍ a. user.exe, core.exe, gdi.exe
- ❍ b. core.exe, krnl386.exe, gdi.exe
- ❍ c. user.exe, gdi.exe, core.exe
- ❍ d. gdi.exe, kern386.exe, user.exe."

Examine the preceding question closely, and observe that CORE.EXE repeats in all three responses. The only response in which it does *not* repeat is the last choice. Using this particular strategy, you don't necessarily have to know what the core files are, to begin guessing that response D. is probably the right one.

Mastering the Inner Game

In the final analysis, knowledge breeds confidence, and confidence breeds success. If you study the materials in this book carefully; review the Exam Prep questions at the end of each chapter; and take the Sample Test in Chapter 15, you should be aware of all the areas where you'll need additional studying. Pay attention to all the troubleshooting topics and Chapter 14, "Troubleshooting." If you find yourself scratching your head over any of the problem description terms, then you're not ready to take the final exam.

Follow up by reading some or all of the materials recommended in the "Need To Know More?" section at the end of each chapter. The idea is to become familiar enough with the concepts and situations presented in the sample questions that you should be able to reason your way through similar situations on the real exam. If you know the material, you have every right to be confident that you can pass the test.

Once you've worked your way through the book, take the practice test in Chapter 15. This will provide a very realistic trial run, and will help you identify areas you need to study further. Make sure you follow up and review materials related to the questions you miss before scheduling a real test. Only when you've covered all the ground and *feel comfortable* with the whole scope of the practice test, should you take a real test. It's not an easy test.

Multiple Response Questions

The original A+ exams allowed for questions having more than a single response. As far as we know, the current exam no longer works this way. In the course of revising this book, we made an evaluation as to whether to remove any questions we've listed having multiple correct responses (e.g., "Choose all that apply.") Our decision was to retain these types of questions.

Adaptive tests, as we've said, change according to calculations based on the way the examinee responds to any given question. A printed book cannot match this process. However, by retaining the option of having multiple correct responses, we are able to modify the complexity level of any given question. For that reason, you won't have to worry about picking several correct responses on the actual exam, as you will do in this book.

We continue to believe that one of the best tools we can provide, are the questions we've created. As we've said, these questions are designed partly to test your knowledge; partly to highlight difficult areas on the exam; and partly to demonstrate the kinds of mind games you're almost surely going to encounter on the exam. As we've also said, if you can get through our test and questions, we're confident that you'll be well-prepared for the CompTIA exams.

Need to Know More?

Sooner or later, all the specifics we've shared with you about A+, and the other online resources we mention throughout the rest of this book, will go stale or be replaced by newer information. In some cases, the URLs you find here might lead you to their replacements. In other cases, the URLs will go nowhere, leaving you with the dreaded "404 File not found" error message.

When that happens, please don't give up! There's *always* a way to find what you want online if you're willing to invest some time and energy. As long as you can get to the CompTIA site itself (and we're pretty sure that it will stay at **www.comptia.org** for a long while yet), you can use this tool to help you find what you need.

Examine the topics that CompTIA expects you to know on the test. You can almost always use a copy-and-paste operation to put key words into any search engine. Some of the better technical sites we've found are listed under the additional references, particularly in the operating system section. Several very good sites for technically-oriented information include:

- **www.google.com**—Search engine
- **www.ask.com**—Search engine
- **www.dogpile.com**—Search engine
- **www.zdnet.com** or **www.cnet.com**—Technical publications, magazines, and software
- **www.webopedia.com**—Online technical encyclopedia
- **http://www.techweb.com/encyclopedia/**—Online technical encyclopedia

Often you can use today's search engines to enter a query such as: "understand modem" (without the quotes). In many cases this will lead you to either exactly what you're looking for, or enough information that you can form a better query and try again.

Motherboards

Terms you'll need to understand:

- ✓ Motherboard form factors
- ✓ Megahertz (MHz)
- ✓ Pin grid array (PGA) and staggered pin grid array (SPGA)
- ✓ Cards and integrated circuit (IC) boards
- ✓ Bus types (ISA, EISA, VESA, MCA, PCI, and PC card)
- ✓ Data flow

Concepts you'll need to master:

- ✓ Connectivity
- ✓ System components
- ✓ Slots and sockets
- ✓ Throughput
- ✓ Process and data flow

The motherboard, or main board, is sometimes called the system board or *planar* board. It is the basic foundation of a computer and connects all the components of the system. Nowadays, personal computers (PCs) have consolidated almost all the electronic components onto the motherboard. Aside from the central processing unit (CPU) and its supporting chipset, the motherboard holds the expansion bus, Input/Output (I/O) interfaces, drive controllers, and system memory.

The system board provides connectivity for all system components. Essentially, it's the foundation for all the parts involved in the computer. The motherboard does the following:

- Distributes power from the power supply
- Provides data paths for control signals and data
- Offers various sockets and pads for mounting components
- Provides expansion slots for add-on integrated circuit (IC) cards or printed circuit boards (PCBs).

System Boards: A Brief History

All motherboards are affected by three basic factors: the *form factor*, which determines the actual physical dimensions of the board; the *chipset*, which specifies what supporting chips will be placed on the board to control the flow of information; and lastly, the *bus structure*, which determines the actual design of the circuit traces on the board and the electrical signals that flow across those circuit traces.

In 1981, International Business Machines (IBM) released the original personal computer. This original PC's motherboard had five expansion slots that were configured much like today's Industry Standard Architecture (ISA) slots. The data path for those five expansion slots was 8 bits wide, meaning the bus structure could handle only 8 bits of information at a time. We discuss data paths and data flow under the "Expansion Bus Architecture" heading later in this chapter. Likewise, the main board could support memory between 64KB (KiloBytes) and 256KB. The back of the board had two connectors—the first being a keyboard connector, and the second being a cassette tape connector. At the time, the floppy disk was too expensive to include in most of these machines, and many of them were programmed using a cassette tape.

The eXtended Technology (XT) computer was released in 1983, with three additional expansion slots added to the motherboard. Although the keyboard connector became standard on all later motherboards, the cassette connector quickly gave way to floppy drives and the newly released hard drives. The primary memory capability was increased to 640KB. We will be discussing primary memory, RAM, and other types of memory in Chapter 3.

Finally, in 1984, the PC began to catch on, and one of the most influential changes occurred when IBM released the Advanced Technology (AT) form factor. The AT used a 16-bit data path, allowing information to travel across the motherboard 16 bits at a time. The ISA slots were modified to handle the increase and became predominantly 16-bit slots, although one or two slots were kept to an 8-bit configuration for backward compatibility with XT boards.

The Advanced Technology (AT) Form Factor

The IBM AT form factor, often referred to as an *AT board*, made the motherboard much larger than the XT boards, requiring a larger case to hold all the parts. Additionally, the bus slots were placed flat on the motherboards, with expansion cards inserted perpendicular to the main board, standing straight up. Later motherboards introduced a riser card (discussed later in this chapter), which allowed the expansion cards to be inserted parallel to the board, which made the outer casing smaller.

You will be required to visually recognize various form factors on the exam. You will be shown a series of graphics and asked to assign a correct form factor from a list of question response options.

By this time, other companies were getting into the computer market, producing machines that were exactly compatible with IBM machines. These exact copies were called *clones*, and whenever IBM came up with a new idea, the clone manufacturers produced a copy. The 16-bit expansion cards could still fit on a cloned XT board, but those companies didn't want to market old technology. Instead, they retrofitted the new cards to a motherboard that was smaller than IBM's AT board, and called them *Baby AT* boards. In the process, they accidentally produced a smaller, more streamlined PC that used less desktop space.

Figure 2.1 is a stylized diagram (not a schematic) of a typical AT motherboard. The diagram is for your general reference, showing an outlined representation of a typical motherboard's components. Note that the AT keyboard connector was soon replaced by the PS/2 connector, which is gradually giving way to a USB connector. Although ATX and NLX boards (discussed later in this chapter) can be laid out quite differently, the relative size and shapes of the various components is easier to see on an AT board.

We found it quite difficult to differentiate a power supply from a possible keyboard connector on the exam graphics. Because there are so many motherboards on the market, it is also difficult to present a universal layout. Generally, a power supply is off to the rear of a motherboard representation, but you should look for other examples of motherboard layouts before you take the exam.

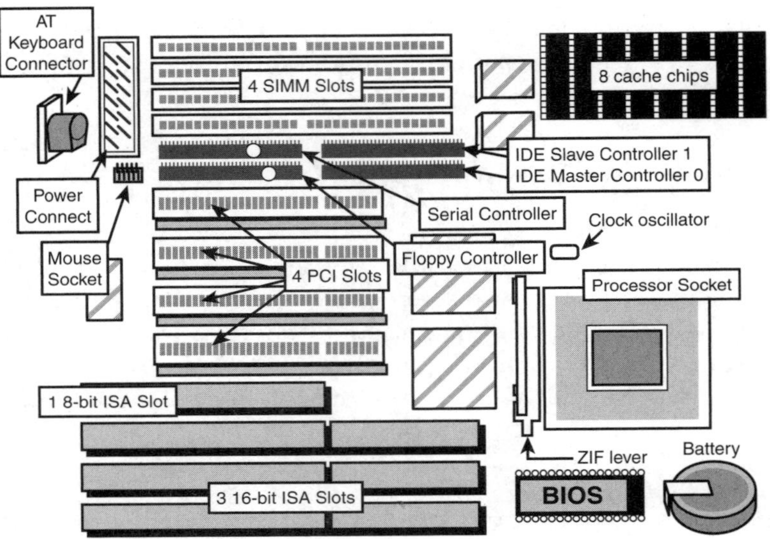

Figure 2.1 A basic AT motherboard.

An extension was added to the original 8-bit slot found on XT boards, which gave the 16-bit ISA technology backwards compatibility. This extension provided for expansion cards having additional edge connectors separated by a small space. The cards themselves acted somewhat like a bridge across the two slots on the motherboard. ISA bus technology eventually gave way to the PCI bus, discussed later in this chapter. Figure 2.2 shows a typical ISA network interface card (NIC)—pronounced "nick"—often found in a modern PC.

Another important change was the introduction of ROM BIOS and CMOS. Essentially, these are two types of memory used for configuring the basic elements of a computer. Although we'll discuss the Basic Input/Output System (BIOS) in further detail in Chapter 3, the use of a memory chip to hold configuration information moved computers away from having to use dual inline package (DIP) switches and jumpers. Additionally, BIOS and CMOS eliminated the need for the special configuration diskette—a boot-up disk or system disk—that earlier PCs used.

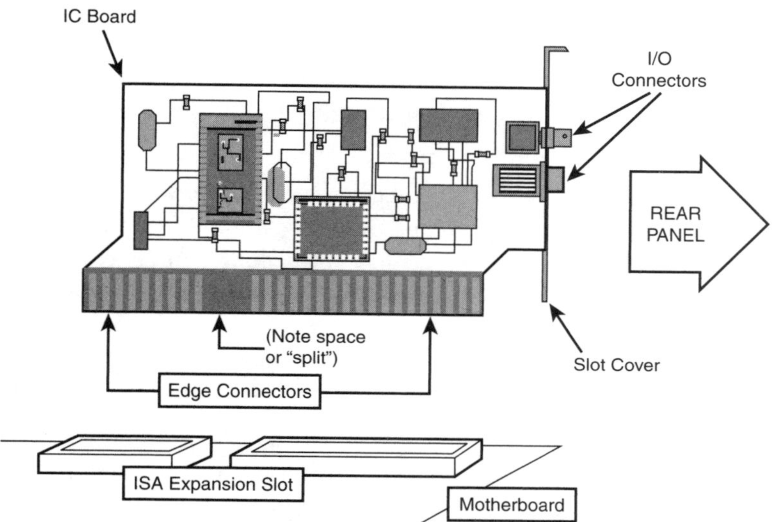

Figure 2.2 A typical 16-bit ISA expansion card.

These system disks should not be confused with emergency startup disks or bootable floppies. These disks were the only way to enter into the basic configuration settings of the machine. Nowadays, you can access these types of settings through the CMOS, usually by pressing a key such as F2, ESC, or DEL, during the initial boot sequence.

CMOS

Complementary Metal Oxide Semiconductor (CMOS) RAM is a small, battery-backed memory bank that stores configuration settings. XT motherboards were relatively simple, so basic configuration changes were done manually through jumpers and DIP switches. The AT form factor had many more configuration options, and CMOS allowed many of those settings to be configured through the keyboard.

CMOS settings are maintained for as long as any electrical current is available. Even when the PC is disconnected from a wall outlet, a small battery on the motherboard provides enough current to maintain the CMOS settings. In the event that those settings become corrupted, or if someone changes the settings, a common way to reset the CMOS is to remove the battery and wait a few minutes.

Another response option for resetting the CMOS is to use a screwdriver tip to short out the CMOS connection. You might see this second way as a option on the exam, but it is neither a good idea nor a safe practice.

Clock Speed and Megahertz

Clock speed is a measurement of frequency, referring to cycles per second. It is usually written in MegaHertz (MHz), where 1MHz refers to 1 million (mega) cycles per second and 1GHz refers to one billion cycles per second. The motherboard has an oscillator—a sort of electronic clock—that is configured through jumpers to yield a specific frequency. This oscillator is the foundation for all the timing cycles used by other components.

The oscillator generates a cyclical wave. That wave has a continuous set of peaks and troughs (highs and lows) passing through a middle point, illustrated in Figure 2.3. A timing wave going up and down along a midline, should be equal in distance from the midline to the top, as it is from the midline to the bottom. A single clock tick, or wave cycle, is measured from the point where a wave begins to move upwards, all the way down and through the midline to the point where the wave moves back up from its lowest point and touches the midline again.

Instructions can be designed to begin from exact points in a wave cycle and this is how processor performance can be improved. When the cycle is going up, we refer to an up tick. When the cycle is going down, we refer to a down tick. To the left of the highlighted clock tick (in the square), we have the leading edge of the tick. To the right, is the trailing edge. We'll discuss the use of clock ticks and CPU speeds in Chapter 3.

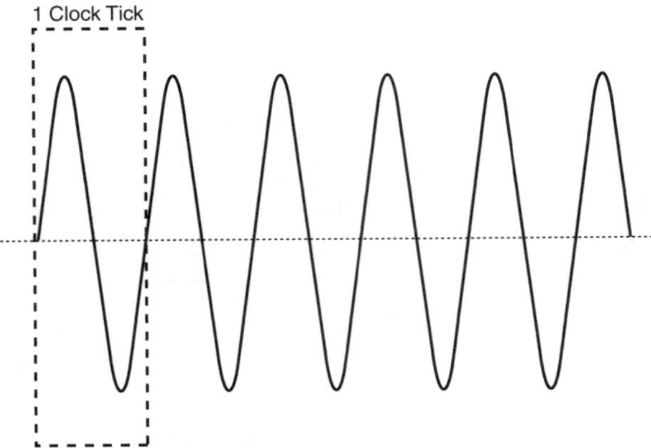

Figure 2.3 An oscillator wave and clock tick.

The motherboard design matches the speed of the oscillator, and the processor chip must be matched to the motherboard clock speed. The frequency of the motherboard determines the processor chip's running speed. Placing a 100MHz processor chip on a 166MHz motherboard can overheat the chip, lead to random lockups and glitches, and destroy the chip. In Chapter 3 we also refer to special cases where *over-clocking* may be allowable.

Newer motherboards are designed to run at multiple clock speeds that can be manually configured. All components on the motherboard should be rated to run at the maximum speed rating for the motherboard.

The ATX Form Factor

The first processor to use an AT motherboard was the Intel 80286, which used a 16-bit internal and a 16-bit external bus. The ISA bus was expanded to 16 bits and CMOS was added so that complex configurations could be set through the keyboard. The primary distinguishing characteristic of a full-size AT motherboard was its size. It was designed around the original XT motherboard, with a large internal space. Tower cases were vertically oriented, usually standing on the floor. Full-size cases were meant for the desktop, and took up a great deal of surface area. Originally, IBM was focused on upgrading the motherboard, and wasn't thinking about the physical size of the components or the space they would take up on a desk.

It wasn't long before IBM lost its dominance in the PC industry. Compaq was one of the first clone manufacturers, leading to the microprocessor revolution that swept across the world in the 1990s. With motherboards directly related to processor chips, the leading chip manufacturer didn't take long to get involved with the design of boards. In 1995, Intel released its specifications for the Advanced Technology eXtention (ATX) form factor, calling for an open standard in the design of future motherboards. An *open standard* means that anyone can use the design freely. Apple Computer chose to use a *proprietary standard*, meaning that anyone who wanted to build an Apple-compatible computer or device had to pay a licensing fee to Apple Computer.

The ATX specification called for several important improvements. One of the changes was a built-in, double-high, external I/O connector panel shown in Figure 2.4. Along with the changes in the connector panel, the locations of the connectors were moved to allow for shorter cables between devices, such as hard drives and floppy drives. Another change was the standardization of single-keyed power connectors. The CPU and memory banks were relocated to allow for easier accessibility and cooling.

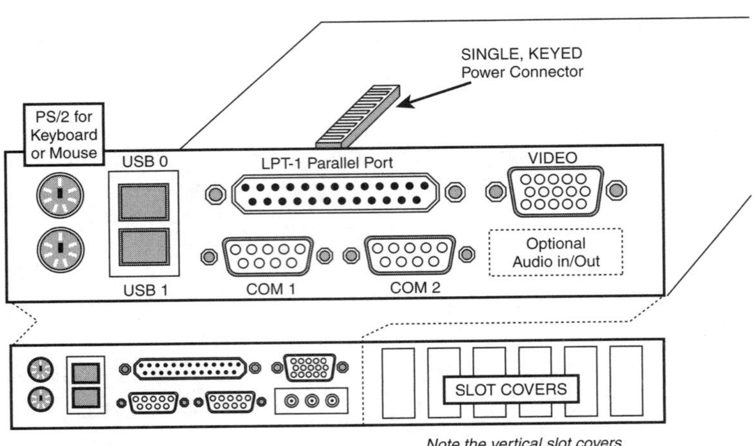

Figure 2.4 The ATX form factor (with double-high I/O panel).

The ATX form factor featured I/O ports built right into the board (as opposed to just their connectors being built-in on AT boards), and there was an integrated PS/2 mouse connector rather than the original DIN connector found on AT boards. The board was rotated 90 degrees, for access to the entire board and better cooling circulation reduces heat. Air blows into, rather than out of the case, and the CPU was placed closer to the power supply with its cooling fan.

The ATX uses a single-keyed, 20-pin power supply connector. A so-called keyed connector means that it can be connected to its opposite connection in only one direction. Usually, this is done by a molded notch or groove in the plastic connector casing or by color coding the ribbon cable attached to the connector. Keying a connector means designing the plug and the socket with matching notches. If the notches don't line up, the plug can't fit into the socket.

These changes in form factor were designed to reduce the cost of manufacturing and provide for faster and easier maintenance. However, competition in the processor manufacturing sector was heating up as Advanced Micro Devices (AMD) and Cyrix began selling their own brands of processor chips. When the original ATX specification was released by Intel, the AMD K-5 and K-6 CPUs were plug compatible. However, AMD later released its own open standard, which was different from Intel's and required a different corresponding chipset.

With the orientation rotated ninety degrees from the Baby AT design, the drive connector cables could be placed closer to the drives themselves. The more efficient use of space allowed for the CPU to be moved back towards the power supply and cooling fan. Figure 2.5 demonstrates this change, which then carried forward to the LPX and NLX form factors.

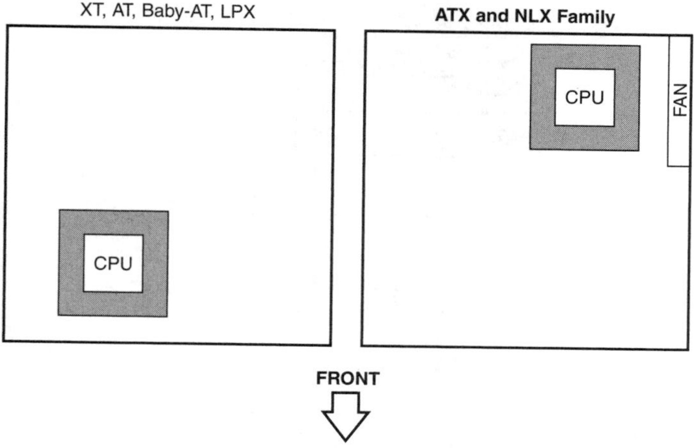

Figure 2.5 CPU moves to the back near the cooling fan on ATX and NLX boards.

The original ATX form factor was smaller than previous designs, but it wasn't long before Intel released a second standard for an even smaller board, which allowed for smaller cases (profiles). This smaller board was called a Mini ATX form factor. Later, even smaller designs were released, including the Micro ATX and Flex ATX. Regardless of the type, all system boards in the ATX family used the same mounting system. ATX boards are installed in most of today's computers

Low Profile Extensions (LPX)

When Lotus released the 1-2-3 spreadsheet, it quickly became a "must-have" application. Corporate America began buying personal computers in very large quantities, and desk space became a problem. Therefore, in 1987, Western Digital Corporation released an even smaller form factor. This was the Low Profile eXtensions (LPX) design, which introduced the *bus riser card*. The riser card was mounted in the center of the motherboard and was narrower than a typical expansion card. By installing the expansion cards parallel to the motherboard, the LPX form factor significantly lowered the overall height of the outer casing. This "low profile" is signified by the LP in LPX. We'll discuss the NLX boards in a moment, but Figure 2.6 shows the movement of the riser card.

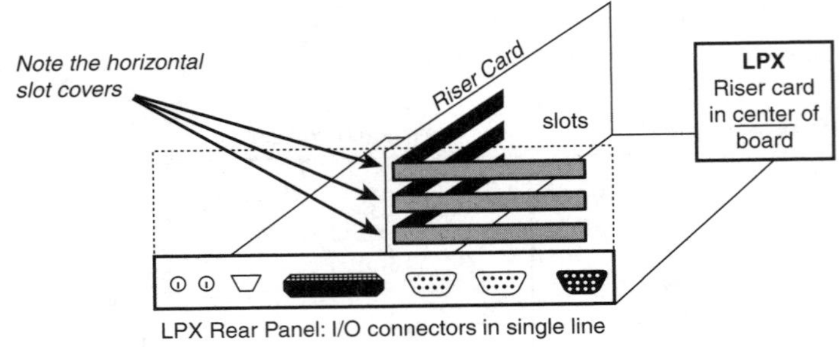

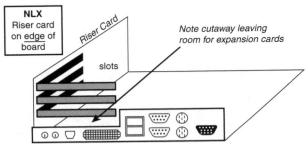

Figure 2.6 Riser card location in LPX and NLX motherboards.

Typically, when you look at the back of an AT or Baby AT computer, you'll see that the slot covers are in an up-and-down, vertical orientation. However, on the back of an LPX machine, the slot covers are in a left-right, horizontal orientation. The AT, Baby AT, and LPX form factors have largely been replaced by the ATX family of motherboards.

The design of a computer's case is engineered to provide an even flow of air around the inside of the machine. Keeping unused expansion slots covered maintains this flow of air. Therefore, an expansion slot should either have an expansion card installed in it, or the slot cover should be in place.

NLX

When the LPX form factor was updated to the NLX form factor (see Figure 2.6), the new design moved the riser card to the outer edge of the motherboard. This provided more room on the board for expansion slots, along with greater accessibility to system components. Both the LPX and NLX retained the parallel (horizontal) slot orientation, with the NLX having a sort of L-shaped profile where the riser card sits on the edge of the motherboard.

An easily recognizable feature of the NLX board, is that it has a sort of step shape to the back panel, as shown in Figure 2.7. Some of the connectors are in a single line, while others are one above the other in a double line. The step shape leaves room for expansion cards.

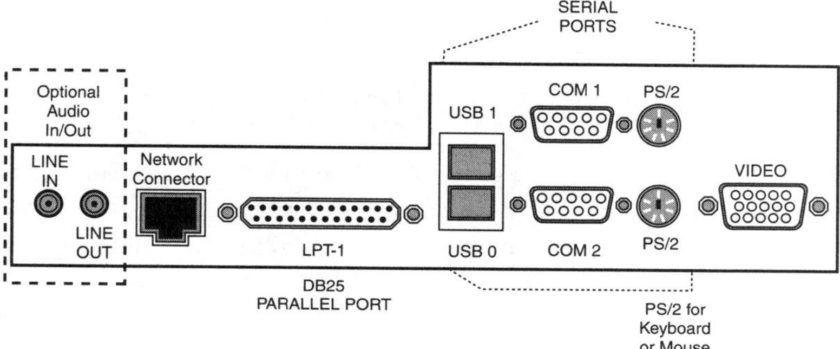

Figure 2.7 NLX step configuration.

Summary—Form Factors

The preceding section covers motherboards, CMOS, clock ticks, and the basic shape and design (form factor) of typical motherboards. Be sure that you understand how the AT form factor evolved into the Baby AT, and eventually became the ATX, LPX, and NLX form factors. Remember the concept of riser cards, and the step design shown in Figure 2.7. The exam doesn't ask you for dates and history, but rather tests you on whether you can recognize various types of motherboards by their shape.

Most importantly, you should examine the diagram of a simple motherboard and learn the relative sizes and shapes of the various components. We've tried to keep the illustration as simple as possible, knowing that motherboards vary greatly. The critical knowledge you must have is how to distinguish an ISA slot from a PCI slot or a DIMM slot. You should be able to see a CPU and distinguish it from a BIOS chip, and separate a CMOS chip from an oscillator. If you're not comfortable with our diagram, be sure that you study physical motherboards, or use additional preparation guides and hardware manuals until you reach a solid comfort level.

Many of today's computers come with a modified tower configuration, or mini-tower designs. Whether they're called mini-desktops, vertical form factors, or anything else, the exam will test you only on the horizontal motherboards we've included in this book. Another term you won't see on the exam is "mobo," short for motherboard. Remember that acquiring knowledge is a life-long event, but passing an exam is a one-time moment. Whether exam terminology is current or not, your A+ certification depends upon your knowing the correct responses to the questions on that specific exam.

Expansion Bus Architecture

New peripheral devices, such as printers, drives, monitors, and so forth, are being developed every day. For a system to take advantage of these new developments, there has to be a common way of connecting them to the motherboard. This common connection point is the *expansion bus*, sometimes called an *I/O bus*.

A *bus* is simply a way to move electrical signals from one place to another on a circuit board. In this case, the circuit board we're talking about is the motherboard. The bus structure provides long, narrow connection slots so that circuit boards—often called *cards*—can be pushed into them edgewise. We often refer to these connections by their architecture, such as an ISA slot or a PCI slot. Expansion cards are designed to work with specific bus structures, and have become known as ISA cards, PCI cards, and so forth, following the convention of including the bus architecture.

Be careful that you don't confuse a PCI card with a PC card designed for a notebook computer. Additionally, you may have to ask for clarification if someone is speaking about a printed circuit card (PC card) or the small expansion card for a notebook computer. The two cards use the same name. Acronyms are not unique in the technology industry, so PC can stand for personal computer or printed circuit, depending on the context.

The expansion bus is a set of standardized connectors (slots), located on the motherboard, which provide connectivity to the data path. You can think of the expansion bus as a toll plaza on a highway. With eight tollbooths on an eight-lane highway, traffic moves fairly smoothly. This is analogous to an 8-bit bus with an 8-bit processor. However, with a 16-lane highway and only 8 tollbooths, traffic jams will occur as the traffic is funneled down from 16 lanes to 8 lanes. This is what happens when a 16-bit processor is connected to an 8-bit bus.

Although the expansion bus provides exceptional flexibility, it can also be a bottleneck as processor speed increases. The design of the expansion bus has changed almost as fast as processors with the need to improve performance. Efforts to constantly improve the performance of the entire system have led to 32-bit and 64-bit buses, as well as changes in how the buses move data signals.

PCs use a processor bus, a memory bus, an address bus, and an expansion bus. The first three relate to moving data in or out of various chips and are discussed further in Chapter 3, but you will need to be able to distinguish the various expansion buses on the basis of their names, shapes, and general location on the board. An expansion bus is usually a visible slot on the motherboard, used to hold add-on cards (e.g., sound card, network card or internal modem).

Remember that a bus is a way to move information around a circuit board. A *signal trace* is the piece of circuitry that allows for the flow of electricity. If we use eight pulses of electricity in a combination, we can call that an 8-bit piece of information. Therefore, if we want to move an 8-bit piece of information, we need eight signal traces—an 8-bit bus.

Bus configurations can be 8-bit, 16-bit, 32-bit, 64-bit, and so on. The more bits of information that can be processed simultaneously, the faster the *throughput* for a given clock speed. Remember that we spoke about the earliest personal computers using an 8-bit signal track, and that a fundamental change in the AT boards was the use of a 16-bit bus. This allowed the AT motherboards to move far more complex information across the system. Throughput is essentially the amount of data that can move through a bus.

Although we say a bus is so many bits, that doesn't mean that there are only 8, or 16, or some other number of connectors on the bus. A bus has additional connectors used for such things as addressing, interrupts, or other functions within the bus itself. However, we always refer to the size of the bus in terms of how many bits of data can move across that bus—the *data path*.

Many of today's motherboards have at least three different buses and several memory buses. These buses include:

- *ISA bus*—This bus is typically a 16-bit bus for compatibility with older machines using legacy cards.
- *PCI bus*—This bus provides a bridge between the processor and slower ISA bus.

- *Accelerated Graphics Port (AGP) bus*—This bus is dedicated to high-speed processing for video.
- *L-2 Cache processor bus*—This Level 2 bus (the backside bus discussed in Chapter 3) uses a high-speed memory management technique.

Industry Standard Architecture (ISA)

The original ISA 8-bit bus was designed to use the edge of an IC card (an edge connector), with 62 contacts. It provided 8 data lines and 20 address lines. This allowed every card installed in the system to be addressed within the first megabyte of memory. Because the original 8086 and 8088 processors could address only 1MB of memory, this was fine.

We can also measure the time it takes for information to move across a bus, much like we measure the speed of a microprocessor. We'll return to clock speed in a moment, having discussed it earlier in this chapter, but for now it's useful to know that, although the CPU in earlier machines ran at various clock speeds, the original ISA buses ran at only 4.77MHz.

As processor speeds increased, new devices and applications were developed that required moving more information through the buses. At 4.77MHz, the original throughput for an ISA bus was 39 megabits (Mb)—not megabytes (MB)—per second.

Bits and Bytes

Everyone throws around terms like bits, bytes, kilobytes, megabytes, and ever-larger numbers referring to larger amounts of storage. You need to know that a 1KB file isn't exactly 1,000 bytes, but 1,024 bytes. A typical page of writing from a word processor generates a file approximately 2KB in size. To avoid any possibility of confusion, Table 2.1 lists the exact number of bits and bytes in single units of each category. Note that a bit uses a lowercase "b," while a byte uses an uppercase "B."

Table 2.1 Standard terminology for bits and bytes.

Term	Number of Bits
bit	Single 0 or 1
kilobit (Kb)	1 bit x 1,024—1,024 bits
megabit (Mb)	1 bit x $1,024^2$ (or 1,024x1,024)—1,048,576 bits (millions)
gigabit (Gb)	1 bit x $1,024^3$—1,073,741,824 bits (billions)
terabit (Tb)	1 bit x $1,024^4$—1,099,511,627,776 bits (trillions)

(continued)

Table 2.1 Standard terminology for bits and bytes *(continued)*

Term	Number of Bits
Byte	8 bits
Kilobyte (KB)	1 byte x 1,024—1,024 bytes (8,192 bits, or 1,024x8) (thousands)
Megabyte (MB)	1 byte x $1{,}024^2$—1,048,576 bytes (millions)
Gigabyte (GB)	1 byte x $1{,}024^3$—1,073,741,824 bytes (billions)
Terabyte (TB)	1 byte x $1{,}024^4$—1,099,511,627,776 bytes (trillions)

Faster throughput means larger buses, so the AT form factor began to use the 16-bit bus. Originally, the 16-bit buses ran at 6MHz. Not long after, they sped up to 8MHz, and the industry soon decided a standard speed should be used. The 16-bit ISA bus speed was eventually set to 8.33MHz, allowing for a theoretical maximum throughput of 8MB per second. The more realistic throughput was approximately 1.25MB per second, but that was still much faster than the previous buses.

The 16-bit bus continued to be the standard far beyond the introduction of 32-bit microprocessors. As is typical of the computer industry, no new standard was set for changing technology, so standards for a new bus didn't exist. To take advantage of the faster processors, many companies began using proprietary (not open) technology in their own buses. At that time, many different types of expansion cards were coming out, but they had to match the particular bus technology on the motherboard. Areas impacted by bus technology were memory cards and video cards.

MCA and EISA

In trying to standardize a 32-bit bus, IBM came out with the Micro Channel Architecture (MCA) bus. MCA took full advantage of 32-bit processing, providing a much faster data path. However, the MCA bus wasn't backward compatible with the ISA bus. If you had a device—for instance, a tape backup unit—that used a 16-bit bus, you couldn't use it in a new IBM machine. Instead, you'd have to buy a whole new card connector, and often you'd have to buy a new backup machine to go along with it. Additionally, IBM required a license fee from any manufacturer that wanted to install the bus on their motherboards, and the clone manufacturers didn't want to do that. Because of the incompatibility, licensing fee, and the rapidly expanding clone machine market, the MCA bus never caught on and died a quiet death.

Meanwhile, the clone manufacturers, spearheaded by Compaq, came up with their own standard, calling it the Extended Industry Standard Architecture (EISA) bus. The EISA bus added 90 new connections and 55 new signal traces, making the slot and card much larger. However, rather than a single row of connectors (like the ISA cards), the EISA cards used two lines of connectors running along both sides of the card's edge. This allowed an ISA card to fit in an EISA connector, and the ISA card would work just fine. However, you couldn't put an EISA card into an older ISA connector. The connector had to have contact points on both sides, and older ISA bus connectors did not.

This idea of using both sides of an edge connector inspired the change in architecture between a SIMM and a DIMM, both memory modules that we'll discuss in Chapter 3.

Although the EISA bus ran at 8.33MHz, the transfer rate was increased to 32 bits of information, making for a theoretical maximum throughput of 33.32MB per second. Both MCA and EISA were superior technologies, but the EISA bus was significantly more expensive and never really caught on for anything other than network servers and high-end PCs. The EISA bus and the VESA bus, discussed next, were eventually replaced by the PCI bus, which is in use today.

VESA Local-Bus—32-Bit

As you can imagine, there was a real gap as processors got faster and faster, but the 16-bit ISA bus continued to limit throughput, causing a bottleneck. To fix the problem, an organization called the Video Electronics Standard Association (VESA) developed a new type of local bus. It was called a *local* bus because it attached directly to the processor itself through what's called the *local processor bus*. This meant that data didn't have to go through the slow ISA bus, but could come right out of the 32-bit processor and move off to whatever device it was targeted for. As we said, these devices usually were memory cards and graphics cards.

VESA continues to be an important player in the standards-setting arena. Although modern flat panel LCD monitors have no particular standard way of connecting with a system, the VESA standard seems to be the front-runner.

Windows was hitting the market in 1992, designed to take advantage of 32-bit processing. The new, graphic user interface (GUI) moved a tremendous amount of information, and the local bus was very useful for speeding up the video monitor and graphics processing. The VESA Local-Bus

(VL-Bus) was actually an extension of the 80486 processor bus. As a result, although it connected with newer chipsets and was inexpensive to produce, the VL-Bus didn't interface well in terms of speed. The VL-Bus had numerous glitches when it connected to other chips, along with timing problems.

The VL-Bus was an important step in the development of graphics accelerator cards, along with inspiring the idea of off-loading graphics processing from the CPU and moving it to the video card. Because of the intermittent problems, the VL-Bus quickly lost favor when the PCI bus was developed. The PCI bus also came out in 1992, promoted initially by Intel. Once again, the power of the world's leading chip manufacturer brought a lot of influence to bear, along with the advantages of better technology and some basic standardization.

Peripheral Component Interconnect (PCI)

Prior to the VESA bus, a video card would have to be inserted into one of the slots on the motherboard's main expansion bus. This led to competition with other cards for the CPU's attention and so the VESA specification created a new bus, separate from the main bus and dedicated exclusively to the CPU. The VESA bus evolved into the PCI specification. As it's used in today's motherboards, PCI places an additional bus between the central processor and the ISA bus. The PCI bus doesn't tie directly to the processor bus, but through the use of bridges, avoids the timing issues of the VESA bus.

The main difference between a PCI bus and a VL-Bus is that the PCI bus is a specifically designed, high-speed main expansion bus to be shared by multiple devices. The VL-Bus was a separate bus dedicated to a single device.

A PCI bus runs at 33MHz, which makes it much faster than the older ISA bus. Many of today's computers have both a PCI and an ISA bus available on the motherboard. However, the ISA bus is gradually falling into disuse.

Slots and Sockets

You may hear about something called "Socket 7," "Slot 1," or "Slot A." Although the following isn't technically correct, it might help to think of this concept as "Socket technology, version 7." Likewise, and again not in proper terminology, you can think of "Slot technology, version 1 or version A." The concept to remember here is that with increasing competition in the motherboard and microprocessor manufacturing market, Intel and AMD have been changing the way a CPU is installed on a motherboard. Most processors today are mounted on the motherboard with either a *socket* or a *slot* arrangement.

Rapid advances in technology, including CPUs running at gigahertz clock speeds, have introduced additional sockets and slots. Although we briefly mention some of these later technologies at the end of this segment, the 2001 CompTIA certification exam is restricted to the socket and slot technologies listed in Table 2.2.

Socket 7

A socket is designed for what's called *Pin Grid Array* (PGA) chip packaging. Typically, this is a rectangular type of chip, with hundreds of tiny pins on the bottom side. The chip plugs directly into the socket itself, which is usually a zero-insertion force (ZIF) socket. A ZIF socket commonly has a lever along one side, making it look much like the handle of a typical paper cutter (see Figure 2.1). Raising or lowering the lever handle moves the chip mechanically in or out of the socket with zero force, eliminating bent or broken pins.

Another common form of the typical pin grid array is the Staggered Pin Grid Array (SPGA). This is where the pins at the bottom of the chip are staggered, decreasing the overall size of the chip and allowing for more pins. Sockets are sometimes referred to as *flat technology*.

The most popular socket was Socket 7, which used a voltage regulator module (VRM) that was either in the circuitry of the motherboard itself, or in a module that could be mounted on the motherboard. This allowed the socket to provide the different voltages required for the many different chips that were designed for that socket. These voltages include 5 volts (V), 3.3V, 3.2V, 2.9V 2.4V, and all the way down to 1.8V.

The design of the Pentium Pro, using a built-in L-2 cache, was much larger than previous Pentiums and led to Socket 8. The complexity of this socket led to its being replaced by Socket 370 (370 pins in PGA), which became popular with the Intel Celeron processor series.

Socket A

AMD created its own socket for the Athlon and Duron chips, using a standard pin-grid array, and calling it *Socket A*. Socket A used 462 pins and 11 plugs, with the same physical layout as a Socket 370, but with different locations for the pins. Each socket is specific to either the Intel or AMD chips designed for it, and neither socket will accept both manufacturers' chips.

Indexing

Socket architecture (sometimes called *flat architecture*) calls for some way to know the correct way to install the chip. This system is called *indexing*, and has changed through the years. Prior to the Pentium family of chips, it was very difficult to find the index. Often, a single (very small) pin was square rather than round. However, modern chips are a bit easier to index, as shown in Figure 2.8, because they use a missing pin on the one side of the chip, with a corresponding indicator (or index marker) on the top of the chip.

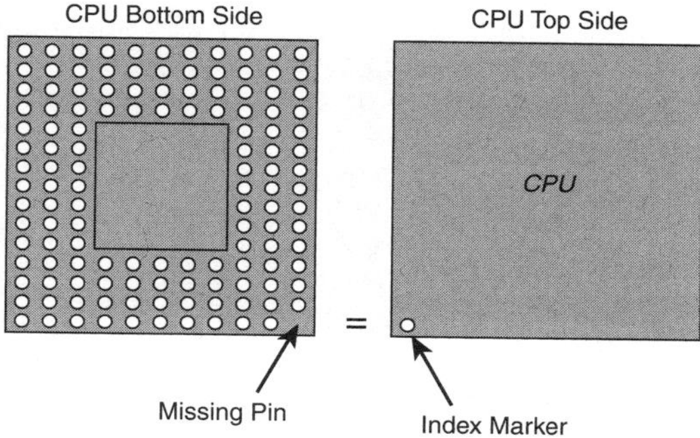

Figure 2.8 Using a missing pin for indexing a chip.

Slot Technology

A second method of mounting a chip is with a slot that uses what's called either *Single Edge Contact* (SEC) or *Single Edge Processor* (SEP) packaging. Pentium II, Pentium III, the Celeron, and AMD's Athlon chip are all provided in SEC or SEP packaging. Rather than needing hundreds of pins, the processor is mounted on its own integrated circuit (IC) board, or "cartridge," using the board's contacts to connect to the motherboard. As you can see from Figure 2.9, these slots look very much like an expansion card.

In Slot 1 or Slot A, the IC board is keyed so that it fits into the slot in only one way. Using a slot (and miniature IC board) is more expensive than a simple horizontal, flat socket. For that reason, and the fact that a Celeron chip is a less expensive version of the Pentium II and III, the Celeron can be purchased in either a socket or a slot configuration.

The slot looks much like a standard Peripheral Component Interconnect (PCI) slot, but it is usually mounted towards the rear of the motherboard, away from the bus (we discuss PCI earlier in this chapter). A common feature of slots is their use of a brace, or bracket, as part of the motherboard, which ensures that once the cartridge is inserted into the slot, it won't move or come free.

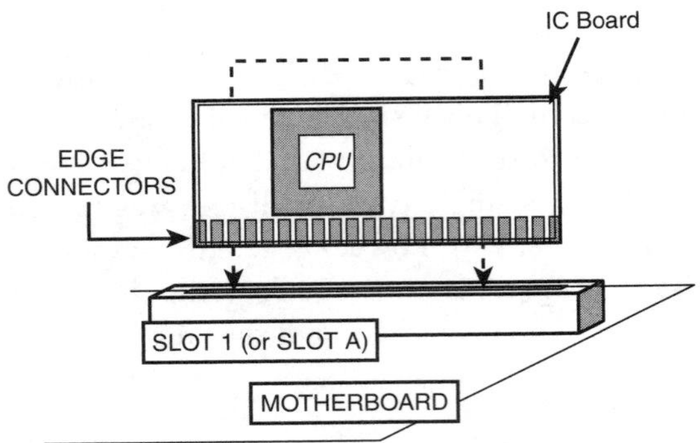

Figure 2.9 Vertical CPU slot technology.

The IC board may sometimes be referred to as a *daughterboard,* or cartridge. Integrated circuit boards may also be referred to as printed circuit boards. Don't confuse a PC board with a motherboard, or a PCB with a PCI card.

Slot 1 is designed for mounting a 242-pin, single-edged chip cartridge. It looks a lot like a very large SIMM (memory modules are discussed in Chapter 3). Slot 2 was designed for the Pentium II and III Xeon processors, using 330 pins with a vertical architecture like Slot 1. Once again, AMD created Slot A to compete with Intel. Slot A was used for the Athlon and Duron processors, and was incompatible with Slot 1 or 2. Table 2.2 shows the differences among the various sockets and slots.

Table 2.2 Sockets and slots.

Name	Pins	Layout	Chips
Socket 7	321	SPGA	Pentium 75-266+, MMX, OD, x86, K-6
Socket 8	387	Dual-pattern SPGA	Pentium Pro
Socket 370 (PGA 370)	370	SPGA	Celeron PGA, Pentium III PGA
Socket A (Socket 462)	462	PGA socket	Duron, Athlon PGA
Slot 1 (SC242)	242	Edge connector	Pentium II, Celeron SEP, Pentium III SEC
Slot A	242	Edge connector	Athlon SEC
Slot 2 (SC330)	330	Edge connector	Pentium II Xeon, Pentium III Xeon

There are a few so-called conversion boards, which use a Socket 370 mounted on a vertical board, where the board will fit into a Slot 1 environment. This allows a processor designed for flat technology to be plugged into the conversion board, which can then be plugged into a Slot 1.

North Bridge and South Bridge

Keeping in mind that the PCI bus is a sort of bridge between the processor and ISA bus, we should point out that there are really two units involved: the *North bridge* and the *South bridge*. The North bridge is generally used for high-speed interface cards, such as video accelerators, Synchronous RAM (SRAM), and memory. The South bridge is generally used for slower cards such as USB ports, IDE drives, and ISA slots. As you can see in Figure 2.10, data flows from the CPU to the North bridge and then out of that to the South bridge in a sort of daisy chain.

We discuss memory and memory controllers in Chapter 3; however, pay attention to the L-1 and L-2 cache locations in Figure 2.10. Note the 100MHz processor bus connecting with the North Bridge. This bus is also referred to as the System Bus, or Front Side Bus (FSB). Also note the connection between the CPU and the L-2 cache. This is a Backside Bus.

The South bridge works in conjunction with what's called a Super I/O chip. Originally, the COMmunications (COM ports), as well as the Line Printer Terminal, or Line PrinTer (LPT ports) were all separate I/O connections on the motherboard. The Super I/O chip brought them all together onto one chip, reducing the space required. Usually, a manufacturer orders the Super I/O chip from a third-party manufacturer, so many people don't consider it part of the chipset.

Pentium machines, in particular, reference the North bridge and South bridge of a PCI bus. Remember that the North bridge is connected to the CPU for high-speed components. Coming out of the North bridge, data passes through to the South bridge, which is used for *slower* components. On a map, North is usually on top while South is usually on the bottom. It may help you if you think of "top" being top speed, or higher speed, with South being lower and slower.

North bridge components are usually accelerated graphics port (AGP), SRAM, and other memory chips. South bridge components are usually the Universal Serial Buses (USB), IDE drives, ISA slots, and the Super I/O chip with COM1, COM2, LPT1, and the floppy drives (A: and B:).

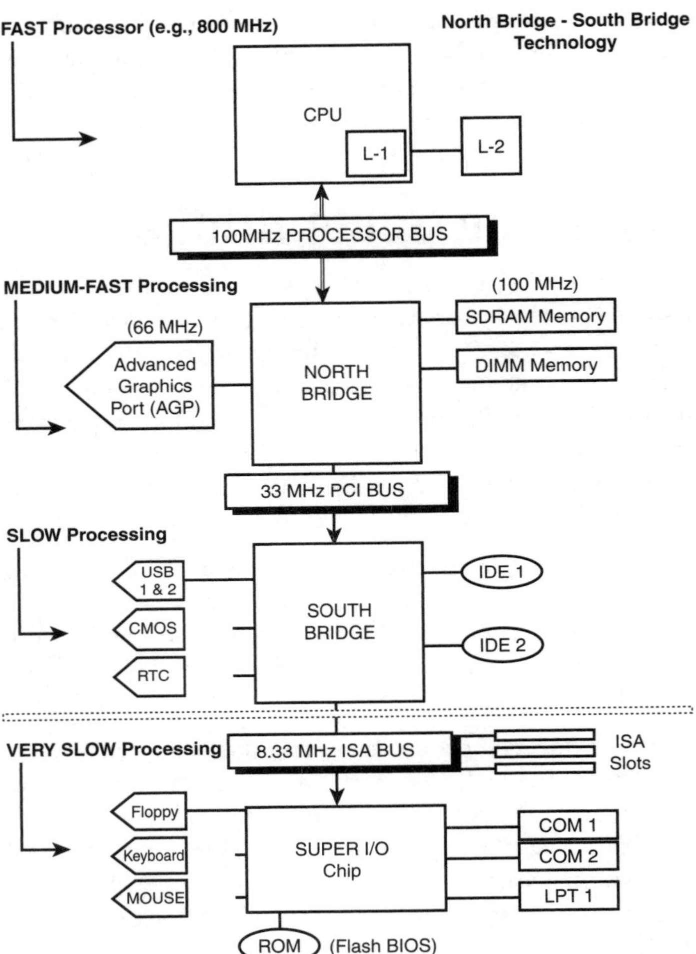

Figure 2.10 North bridge, South bridge, and Super I/O chip.

Chipsets

The chipset is the foundation of the motherboard. It supports every function of the main CPU, including the processor interface, memory controllers, bus controllers, I/O controllers, and more. The chipset determines the way that the main processor connects to everything else. As such, the chipset determines what type of processor you can have; how fast it will run; how fast the buses will run; as well as the speed, type, and amount of memory you can have. Anyone knowledgeable in computers usually refers to both the main processor and the chipset, because the motherboard chipset determines so much about how the CPU will run.

IBM originally designed PCs to use individual microprocessor chips for each individual need. This included the main processor, eventually working with a math coprocessor, or floating-point unit (FPU); clock generators; bus controllers; system timers; interrupt request (IRQ) controllers; direct memory access (DMA) controllers; CMOS; BIOS; RAM; and a number of other chips involved in the motherboard circuit.

The XT boards used six discrete chips, but the AT boards used nine. Then, in 1986, a company called Chips and Technologies released an integrated chip that combined most of the functions of the AT chipset. They used other chips that acted as buffers and minor controllers, making an entire AT motherboard with only five chips. With that, many different companies started combining different chips until, once again, Intel entered the market with its own motherboards and chipsets to go along with its processors.

By 1994, Intel established a dominant market position for integrated chipsets, processors, and motherboards. The Intel design, which is also becoming a standard for non-Intel boards, is built around a three-tier architecture using the North bridge, South bridge, and Super I/O chip. Table 2.3 provides a listing of the various chipsets you're likely to see on the exam.

Table 2.3 Chipsets.

Chipset	Processor Supported
420	80486
430	P5 Pentium
440	P6 (Pentium Pro, Pentium II, Pentium III)
450	P6-Server (Pro, II, III) and Xeon in multiprocessor format

An 800 series chipset was released in 1999. The main difference with this chipset is that it does not use the North bridge and South bridge architecture, but uses a hub architecture composed of three basic components: the Graphics and Memory Controller Hub (GMCH), the I/O Controller Hub (IOCH), and the Firmware Hub (FH). Figure 2.11 shows how a hub sits between the CPU and the various buses in modern, high-speed architecture.

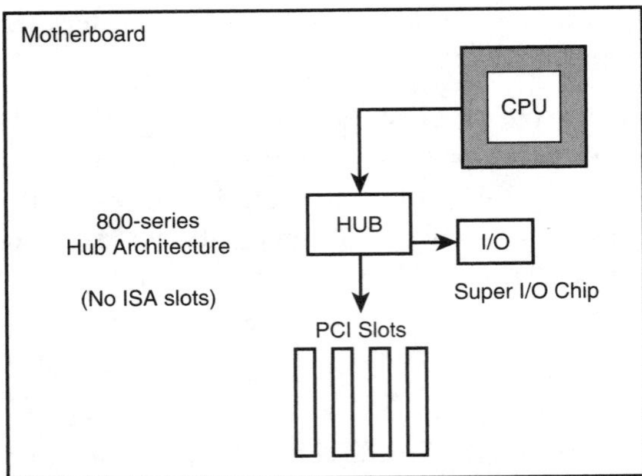

Figure 2.11 The 800-series chipset with hub.

The lowest speed bus in hub architecture is a 33MHz PCI bus. In the bridge architecture, the slowest bus is the 8.33MHz ISA bus. Because processing throughput is often set to the slowest speed bus, hub architecture provides great flexibility in connecting newer, high-speed devices.

AMD Chipsets

Although Intel is still the dominant factor in today's microprocessor manufacturing, AMD has continued to be a significant competitor. The AMD 640 chipset was designed to compete with Intel's Pentium processors, using the AMD K-5 and K-6 series processors. With the release of the Athlon and Duron processors, which are not compatible with Intel's specifications, AMD produced the 750 chipset.

The AMD K-6 series processor could plug into Socket 7 architecture used for Intel Pentium processors. However, the AMD Athlon and Duron are not pin compatible with Intel's Pentium II, Pentium III, and Celeron chip sockets. Therefore, the AMD chips will no longer work with Intel chipsets and motherboards.

Supplementary Information

If you choose, you may jump to the "PC Card (PCMCIA)" section at this time. In 1999, Intel developed Flipped Chip Pin-Grid Array (FC-PGA), where the chip die was mounted upside down. This allowed for a reduction in manufacturing costs that couldn't be achieved with standard slot technology. The Pentium III, Pentium 4, and later chips began using this configuration.

The year 1999 also saw the release of AMD's Athlon processor, competing with the Intel Pentium III. By this time, although Intel and AMD were the leading chip manufacturers, a company called VIA began creeping into the news. Video card manufacturer Nvidia is also entering into the chipset business, competing not only with VIA, but with ALi and SiS, two companies out of Taiwan. VIA, ALi and SiS all offer chipsets supporting the AMD Athlon and Duron CPU, as well as the AMD Palamino.

The increased competition has generated even more diversity in the industry, leading to an increasingly complex array of sockets and slots. The Intel Pentium 4 chip has introduced two additional socket technologies: Socket 423 and Socket 478. The AMD, VIA, ALi and SiS chipets provide a Socket 462 compatibility with the AMD Athlon, Duron, and Palamino processors.

VIA, ALi, and SiS are rising competitors in the chipset business. The VIA KT266 chipset provides three integrated USB controllers, allowing for the simultaneous operation of six USB devices without a hub. Two of the USB ports are located on the board itself, with the third being connected by a cable. We begin to see that additional competition provides for more features and lower prices. The KT266 is by no means the only chipset on the market. As of 2002 some additional chipsets include the Intel 845 and 850 series, the SiS 645 and 648 series, and the VIA P4X266 and P4X33 series, to name only a few. However, once again, this is only for your reference. The A+ exam will test you on only those chipsets listed in Table 2.3.

Accelerated Graphics Port (AGP)

The accelerated graphics port (AGP) is a local bus that was developed at around the same time as the PCI bus. It is similar to a PCI bus, with additional features centering around high-speed video (3D graphics) processing. With the heavy demands of Windows and computer games, moving the video processing into its own channel dramatically speeds up how fast a computer appears to be running. The AGP connects to the North bridge of the three-tier chipset architecture in most of today's computers.

In the past, the video subsystem ran primarily from the main CPU. As soon as the technology was introduced, consumers began buying add-on video cards to boost system performance. The problem with using this extra card was that there were only so many expansion slots on a typical motherboard. Problems with configuration led to headaches and crashes, and increasing graphics software kept pushing the memory limits of available cards. The introduction of the AGP specification provided for a powerful video subsystem as a standard feature on a basically configured PC. Consumers with specialized interests can still purchase add-on video cards, but a basic system almost always comes with an AGP.

According to Intel, AGP X8 is the specification for the next-generation parallel AGP interface. Like AGP X4, it implements a 32-bit wide bus, but the new specification allows for double the previous speed, to 533 MHz, and supports a data rate of two gigabytes per second (2 GB/s). Each AGP s pecification has been developed in order to take advantage of the increasing speeds of Pentium 4 processors. We discuss the AGP at length, in Chapter 7.

Summary—Buses and Slot

Understanding the way add-on cards and interface cards tie in with the underlying motherboard takes a lot of words. If you've had a strong background in hardware, you've seen that it's not all that difficult to tell the difference between an ISA slot and a PCI slot. Bus slots aren't the same thing as the slot and socket technologies used to install a CPU, and you should know the difference.

We've discussed the two types of expansion buses found on the exam, and we mentioned the AGP in the previous supplement, as well as in Chapter 7. Make a note of the VESA bus, because VESA continues to set de facto standards for video interfaces (for example, flat panel LCD connectors). The most important things to remember about buses and slots are as follows:

- The ISA bus is longer than a PCI bus, and the PCI bus is much faster. The ISA bus was a 16-bit bus, clocked at a maximum of 8.33MHz. The PCI bus was originally clocked at 33MHz and connects to the South bridge.
- Sockets almost always refer to Intel chips, and Slots refer to AMD chips. Study Table 2.2 and be sure to remember the associated chips. You won't have to know the layout, but you may get hit with a question on the number of pins.
- Keep track of the few chipsets we've described in Table 2.3. The exam doesn't cover the Pentium 4 or Athlon chipsets, but you'll probably find at least one question on the 400-series boards. That being said, you should know the basic difference between a Pentium and a Celeron chip, and the difference between an Athlon and a Duron chip.

- Learn the overall layout of the North-South bridge architecture. Understand that slow devices (such as USB devices) connect with the South bridge, but that high-speed memory devices connect at the North Bridge. We'll discuss this again in Chapter 3, but that discussion will refer you back to Figure 2.10.

PC Card (PCMCIA)

The Personal Computer Memory Card Industry Association (PCMCIA) card was introduced in 1990 to give laptop and notebook computers an expansion capability similar to that of desktop computers. Originally, the PC card was designed to store memory on a card, but many manufacturers of peripherals came to realize the implications of this for I/O devices. Because no one could remember the acronym PCMCIA, it became known as the PC card (and the way to remember the acronym is now "people can't memorize computer industry acronyms"). These credit card-size expansion boards have the following features:

- Currently exist in four types: Types I, II, III, and IV. Are differentiated into types according to card thickness in millimeters: Type I, 3.3 mm; Type II, 5 mm; Type III, 10.5 mm; and Type IV, thicker than 10.5 mm, but not yet standardized
- Are included in the plug-and-play (PnP) specification
- Introduced the concept of combining the device and its I/O card on the card itself.
- Type I, II, and III form factors share an identical bus connector. Therefore, thinner cards can be installed in computer slots designed for thicker card formats.
- Are hot-swappable, meaning that one card may be removed and another card inserted without turning off the machine.

The PC Card specification eventually was upgraded to include something called *CardBus*. This redefined and enhanced the PCMCIA bus structure, with backwards compatibility to PCMCIA Release 1 and 2. CardBus provided higher speeds than the PCMCIA bus, and support of 32 bit data flow and memory data paths. Note that CardBus cards will not plug into Release 2.x or earlier PCMCIA slots. Windows, for the most part, includes PnP recognition for most PC Cards.

Most new computer systems that have PC Card slots use both Card and Socket Services software, which provide a standardized software interface between the computer and the PC Card itself. Card software, together with Socket Services, is similar to the BIOS and underlying operating system found on desktop machines.

With the standardization of PC Cards, they can now be used not only in laptop and notebook computers, but also in personal digital assistants (PDAs) and other handheld devices. PC Cards are used for many things, including several types of RAM, pre-programmed ROM cards containing software applications, modems, sound cards, floppy disk controllers, portable hard drives, CD ROM and SCSI controllers, Global Positioning System (GPS) cards, large area network (LAN) cards, and pagers, to name a few. A fascinating development in the world of physics indicates that today's nanotechnology has reached a point where an entire device can be added directly to a piece of wire. This is not something found on the exam, but we thought we'd pass the news along.

Practice Questions

Question 1

Motherboards are designed to fit one of two basic form factors.

❍ a. True

❍ b. False

Answer b, false, is correct. Motherboards were originally divided into two, somewhat artificially categorized types: the XT and the AT. Modern specifications now include the LPX, NLX and ATX form factors.

Question 2

Many system boards can support multiple clock speeds, which are set with the DOS **Time** command.

❍ a. True

❍ b. False

Answer b, false, is correct. Motherboards use an oscillator to define the overall timing for components. Although many boards do support multiple clock speeds, those speeds are usually set through jumpers that synchronize the system board speed to the processor speed. The DOS **Time** command is used to set or display the time of day, and that time is also derived from the motherboard clock.

Question 3

What type of expansion bus is included on most current system boards? (Choose all that apply.)

- ❑ a. MCA
- ❑ b. ISA
- ❑ c. PCI
- ❑ d. EISA
- ❑ e. VESA

Answers b and c are correct. Most system boards include both the PCI bus and the ISA bus for compatibility, although this is changing. The MCA bus, developed by IBM, never really caught on. VL-Buses were predominantly used for video controllers prior to the adoption of the PCI bus. The EISA bus became primarily a network file server niche-market bus.

Question 4

Which of the following components are usually connected to the South bridge of a 440-series chipset? (Choose all that apply.)

- ❑ a. L-2 cache
- ❑ b. SDRAM
- ❑ c. USB 0
- ❑ d. Master IDE drive
- ❑ e. AGP

Answers c and d are correct. The North bridge is for high-speed devices such as SDRAM memory chips and an applied graphics port (AGP). The South bridge connects lower speed devices like the USB ports, IDE drive controllers, and CMOS. The Super I/O chip is for very slow COM and LPT ports. The L-2 cache is usually part of the chip die, very close to the CPU.

Question 5

Socket 7 is a technology that ___________?

- ❍ a. Provides a key connector for expansion bus sockets
- ❍ b. Uses a ZIF lever to remove SIMMs
- ❍ c. Installs a CPU using flat technology
- ❍ d. Works with Slot 1 to increase the CPU clock speed

Answer c is correct. Socket 7 is typically a horizontal, flat socket design using a particular type of CPU architecture. Key connectors are mostly found on cables of some kind, while a zero-insertion-force (ZIF) socket is designed for CPUs. Slot 1 technology is designed for vertical architecture CPUs has nothing whatsoever to do with setting clock speeds.

Need to Know More?

Messmer, Hans-Peter: *The Indispensable PC Hardware Book, Third Edition.* Addison-Wesley Publishing Company; May 2000. ISBN 0-201-403-994. This is a comprehensive, up-to-date reference book that covers far more than you will need to know for the exam.

Minasi, Mark: *The Complete PC Upgrade and Maintenance Guide, 11th Edition.* Sybex Network Press, San Francisco, CA August, 2000. ISBN 0-782-128-009. This is considered one of the best reference books available. In fact, Minasi's book was instrumental in the formulation of the first A+ exam.

Rosch, Winn: *Hardware Bible, Fifth Edition.* Sams Publishing, Indianapolis, IN September, 1999. ISBN 0-789-717-433. This is a well-organized reference book that covers software issues as well as hardware.

Mueller, Scott: *Upgrading and Repairing PCs, 12th Edition.* Que, Indianapolis, IN September, 2000. ISBN 0-7897-2303-4. This is one of our favorites! If you are only going to have one reference book, give this one serious consideration.

Freedman, Alan: *Computer Desktop Encyclopedia, Second Edition.* AMACOM, March, 1999. ISBN 0-814-479-855. Great for a fast look-up or refresher course.

Memory

Terms you'll need to understand:

- ✓ Memory controller
- ✓ Read-only memory (ROM) and erasable programmable ROM (EPROM)
- ✓ Capacitor
- ✓ Bus
- ✓ RAM, DRAM, SRAM, SDRAM, VRAM, RDRAM
- ✓ DIP, SIMM, DIMM, RIMM

Concepts you'll need to master:

- ✓ Volatile versus nonvolatile memory
- ✓ Megahertz (MHz) and nanoseconds (ns.)
- ✓ Memory address
- ✓ Synchronization to clock cycle (clock tick)
- ✓ Memory module versus memory chip
- ✓ Odd and even parity checking

Computers use many different microchips and processors, with perhaps the most familiar being the CPU and the main memory—what people commonly refer to as the computer's RAM. Memory is just a temporary place to store information until the CPU can get to it. This information can be program instructions, data, or both. A typical instruction might be a request to store a number or an event somewhere. Another might be to retrieve that information from a particular place—an *address*. *Volatile* memory can only hold information when a normal electrical current is present. *Nonvolatile* memory can hold information without any electrical current.

Volatile, from the Latin "to fly," means that information "flies away" when there's no electricity to keep it in place. Television reporters often refer to an explosive situation as a volatile situation, meaning that it could change at any second. Nonvolatile memory, because it is not volatile, stays the same without any need for electricity.

Conceptual Overview

Memory is fairly easy to understand, once you've grasped the basic concepts. In a nutshell, a CPU moves bits of data into registers (storage places inside a chip). After it's dealt with these data bits to its satisfaction, the CPU works together with a memory controller to move the results out to memory cells (storage places on a memory chip). Both registers and memory cells have memory addresses, and every time a bit of data goes somewhere, it crosses a bus of some kind. That's it! Now go pass the exam.

All right, so it's a bit, so to speak, more complicated than that. Most memory began as dynamic random access memory (DRAM), and the main changes have been to either speed up the memory to match the CPU, or to speed up the CPU to match the memory. For the most part, the history of memory development revolves around synchronizing these two subsystems.

When we refer to speeding up memory, this usually means increasing either the actual speed of the chips or increasing the clock speed of associated buses.

Memory involves several basic concepts, the first of which is a grid or *matrix*. Because of this, we're going to put Table 3.1 to a slightly different use, making it a sort of "mind map." If you can see the way the overall concepts break down on a grid, then perhaps they'll be easier to remember.

A matrix is nothing more than an arrangement of columns and rows, like a spreadsheet or an Etch-a-Sketch. Columns go across the page, and rows go down the side. Cells going left to right (horizontally) have an X coordinate. Cells going up and down (vertically) have a Y coordinate. The direction of rows or columns is called the axis. Combining both the X and Y coordinates gives us an *address* in the grid, like a cell address in a spreadsheet.

Table 3.1 Mind map of basic memory concepts.

Data Storage – Nonvolatile		
Disks Temporary swap files		
ROM – Nonvolatile BIOS		
Programmable ROM CMOS – volatile (trickle charge) Flash BIOS – Nonvolatile		
RAM – Volatile	**Types of RAM**	**Types of Packaging**
Main Memory	DRAM SRAM SDRAM RDRAM VRAM (DDR SDRAM)	DIP SIMM DIMM RIMM
Cache Memory	L-1 and L-2	Card Modules

Read-Only Memory (ROM)

Every computer uses both read-write (RW) memory and read-only (R) memory. Optical disks use a similar designation with CD-RW and CD-R designations. Although the acronym RAM stands for random access memory, for the moment you should think of it as read/write memory. ROM is Read-Only Memory. Information can be temporarily stored in RAM, and then a moment later, it can be taken out and new information can be written to the same place (address). ROM doesn't allow changes. When information is placed in memory, we say that we are "writing to" a memory address. When information is retrieved out of memory, we "read from" that memory.

Picture a bulletin board under glass at the back of a classroom. One way to think of ROM is that it's like the hard-copy notes placed under the glass. At the end of the day, they remain unchanged. The next day, the notes are exactly the way they were the day before. We were able to only read them.

If you think of RAM as a blackboard, it starts out blank. During the day, information is written on it, read from it, and maybe even erased. When something is erased, new information is then written to the same place on the board. If a lot of writing and erasing takes place, a chalk buildup forms on the blackboard. This buildup is similar to *memory fragments*, which can cause computer lockups.

When you go home at the end of the day, you turn off the lights, wash a blackboard clean, and whatever data was on the board goes away forever. This is what happens when you turn off the power to a computer; RAM no longer has the electrical current available to sustain the data in its memory cells.

ROM can have information written into it only one time. From that point on, we can only read the information. No electrical current is required for the information to remain stored—it's nonvolatile. ROM is mostly used for BIOS, although the same concept and acronym apply to commercial compact disks. These are CD-ROM, with the ROM standing for read-only memory.

In some instances, ROM can be changed through the use of certain tools. Flash ROM is nonvolatile memory that occasionally can be changed, such as when a BIOS chip must be updated.

A single letter can really mess you up on the exam if you don't pay close attention. We've seen questions like, "RAM BIOS is used to permanently store instructions for a hardware device: True or False?" (The answer is false.) Keep your eyes peeled, and remember that RAM sounds like RANdom. RAM is never used in BIOS. Since the BIOS instructions are permanent, they almost always use ROM.

RAM is to a computer, like your attention span (i.e., short-term memory) is to your mind. When you cram for this exam, you'll fill your short-term memory with facts and figures just long enough to write them out to a piece of paper in the exam room. Once the data is on the sheet of paper, you can "forget" the information and concentrate on new data, such as the meaning of an exam question. More realistically, your attention span is like a cache (discussed in a moment), and the piece of paper is like RAM. If you were to engrave the information on the surface of the exam-room desk (this is not allowed), it would be more like ROM.

ROM is more like your long-term memory; the things you remember from your past. When you wake up in the morning, you know your name and address. This is like the information stored in BIOS. On the other hand, you may not remember how many glasses of water you had the day before. That information was stored in your short-term memory.

RAM, short-term memory, or attention span, is like a holding tank for data on its way to becoming information. Data becomes information when it takes on context (surrounding circumstances). 76, on its own, means nothing other than the fact that it's a number. Surround that number with context, "Tomorrow, the temperature is expected to reach 76," and it becomes information.

If someone were to ask you to repeat every word on the last page of the previous chapter, you would have to stop what you were doing; turn the pages of this book until you found the requested page, and then read each word. If you were a computer, you would then pause and wait for a new instruction. A human mind continually extracts meaningful information from words, paying little attention to the words themselves. A computer only manipulates bits of data.

Basic Input/Output System (BIOS)

When you turn on a PC, the processor first looks at the basic input/output system (BIOS) to determine the machine's fundamental configuration and environment. This information is stored in a ROM BIOS chip, and largely determines what peripherals the system can support. BIOS instructions are updated regularly by the manufacturer, and if the chip is made to be updated (re-programmed) by the end-user, it is often called *Flash BIOS*. These programmable chips are often referred to as EEPROM (pronounced *ee-prom*) chips, which we discuss later in this chapter.

We examine the boot process in depth in Chapter 11, "Booting, Windows 3.x, and Memory."

CMOS Settings

Although a basic motherboard can be pretty standard, the system can vary in components like hard drives; floppy, CD, or DVD drives; memory; and so forth. The complimentary metal oxide semiconducto*r* (CMOS) is a small memory chip that stores the optional system settings (e.g., hard drive specifications, amount of memory, and so forth). Because these settings are held in CMOS memory with a small electrical charge, CMOS is volatile. However, this trickle charge comes from a battery installed on the motherboard, so even when the main power is turned off, the charge continues. If the battery power fails, all CMOS information vanishes.

Technically, CMOS is different from ROM BIOS in that the CMOS settings require some source of electrical power. Nonvolatile memory doesn't require electricity at all.

Older computers, such as some IBM PS/2 models and the original IBM AT, required a setup program stored on a special floppy disk. When you ran the program, a setup screen allowed you to configure the machine. These configurations were stored in special files on the hard drive. Compaq continued the idea of putting a setup program on a disk. Typically, Compaq's CMOS settings were held in a dedicated 3–4MB, non-DOS partition on the hard drive.

Today, most computers use a keystroke combination, such as ESC, Del, F1, or F2 to access the CMOS. The keys are pressed at startup, before the BIOS transfers control to the operating system. (This is not the same as accessing Windows Safe Mode.)

The CMOS settings are essential to the hardware configuration of any personal computer. A typical symptom of a fading CMOS battery is that the system date begins to fluctuate, sometimes by months at a time. Backing up files and software are a standard part of keeping a current backup, but you should also have a report of the current CMOS settings. On many modern PCs, this can sometimes be done by turning on a local printer, restarting the machine (as opposed to a first-time boot) and going into the CMOS settings. At each screen, press the Print Screen key.

When you exit out of the CMOS setup, the machine will most likely restart. If you boot to DOS, you can send an end-of-form page request to the printer to print the last page being held in printer memory. This can be done by typing "**echo ^L > prn**" (without the quotes). The "^L" is actually created by pressing the Ctrl+L key. From within Windows, open a text editor (for example, Notepad) and print a blank page. The stored page in the printer will come out as part of the print job.

If the Print Screen function doesn't load on a particular machine, the only other way to store the CMOS settings is to manually write them down on a piece of paper. We discuss problems with CMOS in Chapter 14 "Troubleshooting."

Flash BIOS

With advances in technology, most BIOS chips became Flash EEPROM (electrically erasable programmable ROM). These new EEPROM chips made it easier to change the BIOS. Rather than pulling out the ROM chip and replacing it with an updated one, upgrades could be downloaded through the Internet or a bulletin board service (BBS). A small installation program changed the BIOS programming, eliminating the need for pulling apart hardware.

BIOS determines compatibility. Modern BIOS is often stored in the CMOS, whereas older BIOS was stored in nonvolatile ROM, often soldered into the motherboard. Remember that the CMOS is almost always where the computer's configuration is stored. BIOS is where the software instructions for the basic input/output (I/O) operations are stored (for example, COM and LPT ports, expansion bus, and so forth).

Programmable ROM

Compact disks (CD-ROMs) offer another common use for one-time, read-only memory. In the same way that rewriteable CDs (CD-RW) changed the way that we use the disks, programmable ROM chips changed the way BIOS was stored. The formal name for a chip that cannot be modified is *mask ROM* (from the manufacturing mask). ROM chips have a varying capacity for change, named in the following manner:

- Programmable ROM (PROM)—Requires a special type of machine called a *PROM programmer* or *PROM burner* (like a CD burner) and can only be changed one time. The original chip is blank, and the programmer burns in specific instructions. From that point, it can't be changed.
- Erasable programmable ROM (EPROM)—Uses the PROM burner, but can be erased by shining Ultraviolet (UV) light through a window in the top of the chip. Normal room light contains very little UV light.
- Electrically erasable programmable ROM (EEPROM)—Can be erased by an electrical charge and then written to by using slightly higher-than-normal voltage. EEPROM can be erased one byte at a time, rather than erasing the entire chip with UV light. Because these chips can be changed without opening a casing, they are often used to store programmable instructions in devices, such as printers and other peripherals.

Flash ROM

This type of chip is sometimes called *Flash RAM* or *Flash memory* and stores data much like the EEPROM. It uses a super-voltage charge to erase a block of data (rather than a byte). Flash ROM and EEPROM can perform read/write operations, but can only be erased a certain number of times. Flash BIOS relies on this ability to change the program instructions in a ROM chip.

Memory—an Analogy

One of the best illustrations of memory evolution that we've seen, was created by the memory experts over at Crucial Technology, a division of Micron Technology, Inc. (**http://www.crucial.com**). We've modified their original inspiration, expanding it to include many of the related concepts found throughout this book. Imagine a printing business. Back when it started, there was only "the guy in charge" and a few employees. They did their printing in a small building, and things were pretty disorganized.

A motherboard is a lot like this printing business, in that the CPU is in charge of getting things done. The other components on the board have all been developed to lend a helping hand. In the way that a business can make more money by choosing different growth paths, system performance has improved using different evolutionary technologies. One path is by getting things done faster. Speeding things up means shipping out more stuff (technical term) in a given work period. More stuff means more money, and the business grows.

Another way is to provide more time in which to get things done. In the world of computers, events take place according to clock cycles (ticks). If it takes 10 ticks to move one byte, then 5 ticks to move the same byte would mean faster throughput. We can either keep the byte the same size and move it in less time (multipliers and half ticks), or we can increase the size of the byte and move more data bits at the original time (bus widths). The difference in each process underlies Rambus and DDR memory technology (discussed in this chapter).

Memory Matrix

Back in the days of DRAM, when this printing business was just getting started, the boss (CPU) would take in a print job, then go running back to the pressman to have it printed. Think of the press man as the memory controller, and the printing press as a RAM chip. The pressman would examine the document and then grab lead blocks carved with each individual letter (bit). He'd put each block into a form (a grid), letter by letter.

Once the form was typeset, the press man would slop on the ink; put a piece of paper under the press, and crank down a handle, printing a copy of the document. (A bit of trivia: the space above and below a line of printing is called the leading—pronounced as "led-ding." This space was the extra room on a lead block surrounding each carved letter.)

Nowadays, you can buy a toy printing kit from a shop (sort of like buying a 386 machine), where each letter is engraved on a piece of rubber that slides into the rail of a wooden stamp handle. When you've inserted a complete line of letters, you ink them with an ink pad and stamp the line onto a piece of paper. But suppose you could insert an entire line into the rail at once. Wouldn't that be a whole lot faster? That was the idea behind certain memory improvements we'll look at later in this chapter (i.e., FPM and EDO).

Wait States

One of the big problems with DRAM, to follow our story, was that at any given time, the boss wouldn't know what the press man was doing. Neither did the pressman have any idea of what the boss was doing. If the boss ran in with a print job while the pressman was re-inking the press, he'd have to wait until the guy was done before they could talk. This is like the CPU waiting for the memory controller to complete a memory refresh.

Memory cells are made up of capacitors that can either hold a charge (1) or not hold a charge (0). One of the problems with capacitors is that they leak (their charge fades). This is similar to how ink comes off each block on that old printing press. A memory refresh is when the controller checks with the CPU for a correct data bit address and recharges a specific capacitor. When a memory refresh is taking place, the CPU must wait for the controller before it can pass on new data. This is a *wait state*.

You can see that if there were some way to avoid the leakage, the memory controller wouldn't have to constantly waste time recharging memory cells. The CPU could transfer data more often, using fewer wait states, thereby generating faster throughput. SRAM works with transistors, rather than capacitors. Although they don't leak their charge, transistors are more expensive to use on a memory chip.

Interrupts (INT)

Another problem with DRAM was that if the press man had a box of printed documents ready to go, he'd come running out to the front office and interrupt whatever was going on. If the boss was busy with a customer, then the press man would stand there and shout, "Hey boss! Hey boss! Hey boss!" until eventually he was heard (or punched in the face—an IRQ conflict). Once in awhile, just by luck, the press man would run into the office when there were no customers, and the boss would be free to talk.

Interruptions are known as Interrupt Requests (IRQs) and, to mix metaphors, they are like a two-year-old demanding attention. One way to handle them is to repeat "not now…not now…not now" until it's a good time to listen. Another way to handle an interruption is to say, "Come back in a minute, and I'll be ready to respond then." We'll look at IRQs in Chapter 5.

Timing

One day the boss had a great idea. There was a big clock in the front office (the motherboard oscillator), and he proposed putting in a window to the pressroom. That way, both he and the press man could see the clock. The boss would then be able to call out to the press man that he had a job to run, and the press man could holler back, "I'll be ready in a minute."

This could also work the other way around, where the press man could finish a job and call out that he was ready to deliver the goods. The boss could shout back that he needed another minute before he could take them, because he was busy with a customer. Both of them could watch the clock for a minute to go by, doing something else until they were ready to talk.

Data transfers are more efficient when the CPU and memory controller can plan out a specific time to communicate. SDRAM provided a way for the memory controller and CPU to understand the same clock ticks and adjust their actions to match each other. The controller became synchronized with the clock, and memory chips became known as Synchronous DRAM (SDRAM).

DMA Channels

This plan worked very well. Business increased, and the company expanded. The building grew to fill the property, and new problems began cropping up. To begin with, when the press room moved to the other side of the building, the press man couldn't see the clock in the front office anymore. That meant they had to install a separate clock in the press room. When the boss had a print job, he would call down to the press room and schedule a time to meet.

The printing department used one clock to synchronize with the boss, but also had a separate clock used to time print jobs to improve efficiency. CPUs have an internal clock, separate from the motherboard clock. Modern components can synchronize to different clocks, depending upon processing requirements. In other words, a memory subsystem might use the processor's bus to synchronize internal operations. When the resulting information is ready to move out across the motherboard, the system clock becomes the controlling factor.

With business improving, the boss was getting busier and busier. He hired a couple of secretaries to handle walking a print job over to the press room, and the press man hired some assistants to work with some additional printing presses. This is similar to how memory modules came about, where a series of memory chips work together on a single IC card.

Eventually, the boss and the pressman stopped needing to consult about every single piece of paper involved in a particular job. The press man suggested that he be given the authority to make certain decisions as to how to set up the press. You can imagine that by freeing up the boss from having to come down to the press room every few minutes, the boss ended up with more time to work on business matters. This bypass is essentially what Direct Memory Access (DMA) is all about.

When the CPU agrees, certain operations can bypass the ordinary processing channels and access memory directly. We'll examine DMA channels in Chapter 5, but as devices took on more intelligence of their own, the CPU didn't have to waste time on simple routines. The ATA specification and UDMA are an outgrowth of this idea.

Bus Clocking

Another way the boss and the pressman got things done was to widen the hallways and install some conveyor belts. Back when it was a small business, the CPU transferred data over a memory bus at about the same speed as the memory could handle the bits. With increased processor and memory speeds, the transfer process was limited by buses staying at slower speeds.

In our story, the conveyor belts allowed for higher speed movements up and down the hallways. When the boss had a job to send to the press room, he'd hand it to the "bus boy" and tell him to run it over to the printers. The bus boy would jump on a conveyor belt and go sailing off to the other end of the building. Everyone in the building was talking about how fast they could go, and bus boys began timing each other.

A CPU processes some number of instructions per clock tick. We know that synchronous RAM means that memory controllers can also be set to process events according to clock ticks. CPUs used to run faster than memory, but sometimes memory ran faster than the CPU. Either way, both the CPU and memory were faster than the transfer buses.

Eventually, with some new conveyor belts, a bus boy could walk three steps and be carried all the way down the hall to the other side of the building. Surely, you've experienced the thrill of stepping on a conveyor belt and enhancing the speed by walking at the same time as you're being carried? This is somewhat like the concept of clock multipliers.

Modern bus technology brings together the idea of clock ticks and multipliers, using timing cycles to transfer information. Bits can be moved as a clock tick begins and when the clock tick ends, making for two bits per tick. If the clock is ticking at one million ticks per second (1MHz), we can transfer two million bits of data (2Mbps).

Cache Memory

As the company expanded, there was more and more paperwork; with copies of financial statements and records being sent to the accounting department and the government. For a short time, the boss used to send these jobs to the press room—after all, they were a printing company—but that was costing the company money. Finally, he bought some laser printers for his secretary so they could do these quick print jobs on their own.

Whenever the boss was working up a price quote for a customer, he could set up various calculations and have his secretary print them off. Because they didn't have to go all the way to the press room (main memory), these temporary jobs were extremely quick. The CPU uses Level 1 and Level 2 caching in a similar fashion.

Level 1 (primary) cache memory is like the boss' own personal printer, right there by his desk. Level 2 (secondary) cache memory is like the secretary's printers in the next room. It takes a bit longer for the secretary to print a job and carry it back to the boss' office, but it's still much faster than having to run the job through the entire company.

Memory Buses

We measure memory speed in nanoseconds (billionths of a second). On the other hand, we measure CPU speed in megahertz (millions of cycles per second) or gigahertz (billions of cycles per second). Blending the two, we come up with how many million instructions per second (MIPS) a processor can complete. Disk speed is measured in milliseconds (thousandths of a second), and a hard disk typically reads information at around 100 reads per second—not to be confused with Revolutions Per Minute (RPM). A floppy disk generally performs 10 reads per second, while RAM can make a billion reads per second. So moving data in and out of RAM is extremely fast—much faster than moving it to and from a disk.

Modern chipsets use a North-South bridge architecture, as we discussed in Chapter 2. The CPU no longer directly connects with the system memory, but works in combination with the North bridge and the memory controller to move data bits in and out of main memory. In Figure 3.1 we can see how the CPU uses additional buses to connect with the L-1 cache inside the processor housing and the L-2 cache outside the housing. In modern computers, the L-2 cache is usually internal to the housing, and we might find an external Level 3 (L-3) cache. The A+ exam covers only Level 1 and Level 2 caches, and the L-2 cache is considered to be outside the CPU.

A CPU has a number of very small places inside the housing where it stores bits and bytes of data. We've also seen that memory modules store bits of data in capacitors or transistors. Technically speaking, the storage places inside a CPU are called *registers*. The data storage places on a DIMM are called *cells*. Data is constantly moving in and out of registers and being temporarily stored in main memory or cache memory. Figure 3.1 is a highly stylized drawing of the internal registers, the internal L-1 cache, the external L-2 cache, and the two memory buses. Remember that the PCI bus, or expansion bus, is connected to the other end of the North-South bridge—the South bridge. Refer to Figure 2.10 in Chapter 2.

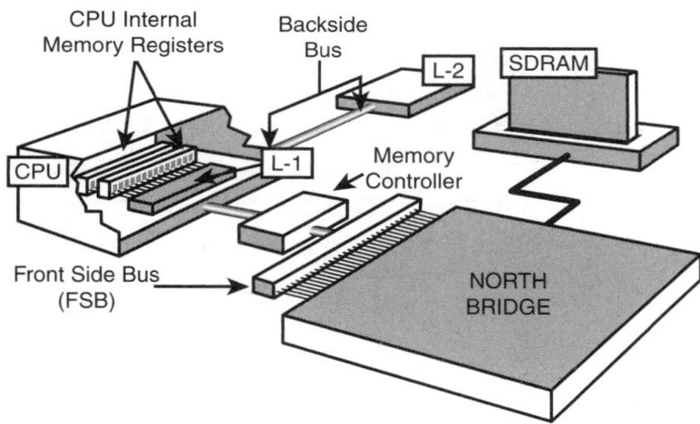

Figure 3.1 Different memory pathways.

Front Side Bus

The North bridge handles fast data transfers into and out of system memory and the AGP, working with the memory controller over a bus. This bus is the subject of a fair amount of controversy, with some people calling it the *system bus* and others calling it the *Front Side Bus* (FSB). You also may find references to a processor bus or a memory bus. For the moment, we'll refer to it as the front side bus. System performance is based on a timing relationship between the CPU and the FSB, with the bus being clocked at a reduced multiple of the processor. In other words, if you have an 800MHz Pentium 4, with an FSB clocked at 133MHz, the FSB is running at one sixth the speed of the chip. Doubling the speed of FSB throughput, making it 266MHz, increases the bus speed to one third of the chip speed. Much of today's performance ratings are based on increasing the clock speed of the front side bus.

Here's another example of FSB speed in relation to CPU speed. Suppose that you have an 800MHz Celeron processor in a machine with a front side bus clocked at 3:1, or a third of the processor speed. Data transfers take place at 266MHz. Now suppose you have a machine with a 1GHz Pentium 4 and an FSB clocked at 4:1, or a quarter of the processor speed. In this instance, data transfers take place at 250MHz (1,000 / 4). Which is the better system, the 800MHz or 1GHz machine? Can we say that a Pentium 4 is always better than a Celeron?

You begin to see that performance is very much tied to the speed of the front side bus. This isn't to say that the entire system is hanging on the FSB, but to point out that performance is becoming a combined measure of many different components.

Backside Bus

The backside bus, shown in Figure 3.1, connects the CPU with an external L-2 cache. Because the data path is extremely short and Level 2 caches are usually comprised of SRAM, data transfers take place at about the same speed as the CPU. We discuss the L-1 and L-2 caches, as well as how a cache operates, in the next sections, but you should have a picture of how the various components of memory are connected. We discuss SRAM in the "Types of RAM" section.

Cache Memory

Cache memory is a type of high-speed memory designed to speed up processing. *Cache* (pronounced "cash") is derived from the French word *cacher*, meaning to hide. A cache attempts to predict which information is about to be used, using an algorithm (logical formula) based on probabilities and proximity. Proximity means how close something is to something else; in this case, instructions or data bytes.

Typically, a memory cache is a separate SRAM chip, running much faster than DRAM. Whichever instruction or data is most likely to be used next, is stored in the cache. When the CPU looks for the next instruction, the chances are good that it will find it faster in small cache memory than in large main memory.

The Memory Hierarchy and Caches

A cache is like an expectation. If you expect to see a piece of information and it's right beside you, you can access that information much faster than if you had to go look for it. When you open a book and look at page 22, logic dictates that you'll look at the top of the page, then at the middle of the page, then at the bottom of the page, and then at the top of page 23. That's how computer caching operates.

Think of the example at the beginning of this chapter—the one where you're asked to repeat the words on the last page of the previous chapter. If you were expecting to be asked this question, you could cache the page by putting your finger in the book at that location. This would create a pointer to the page you were going to be asked to read, and you would be waiting for the probable next request—the instruction to read the page.

Because memory size is always increasing, more time is needed to decode increasingly wider addresses and to find stored information. Larger numbers mean we can have more addresses, but a memory register can store only one digit of an address. The larger the numbers, the wider the registers must be, and the wider the corresponding data bus used to move a complete address.

One solution is a memory hierarchy. "Hierarchy" is a fancy way of saying "the order of things; from top to bottom, fast to slow, or most important to least important." Memory hierarchy works because of the way that memory is stored in addresses. Going from fastest to slowest, the memory hierarchy is made up of registers, caches, main memory, and disks. When a memory reference is made, the processor looks in the memory at the top of the hierarchy (the fastest). If the data is there, it wins. Otherwise, a so-called *miss* occurs, at which time the requested information must be brought up from a lower level of hierarchy.

A miss in the cache (that is, the desired data isn't in the cache memory) is called a *cache miss*. A miss in the main memory is called a *page fault*. When a miss occurs, the whole block of memory containing the requested missing information is brought in from a lower, slower hierarchical level. Eventually, the information is looked for on the hard disk—the slowest storage media. If the current memory hierarchy level is full when a miss occurs, some existing blocks or pages must be removed for a new one to be brought in.

A hierarchical memory structure contains many levels of memory, usually defined by access speed. A small amount of very fast SRAM is usually installed right next to the CPU, matching up with the speed and memory bus of the CPU. As the distance from the CPU increases, the performance and size requirements for the memory are reduced.

SMARTDRV.SYS and SMARTDRV.EXE are DOS program utilities that provide disk caching. The efficiency of a cache is reported as its hit ratio. To send an efficiency report to the screen, issue the command **SMARTDRV /S** from a DOS command prompt.

L-1 and L-2 Cache Memory

The Intel 486 and early Pentium chips had a small, built-in, 16KB cache on the CPU called a *Level 1* (L-1), or *primary cache*. Another cache is the Level 2 (L-2), or *secondary cache*. The L-2 cache was generally (not all the time, nowadays) a separate memory chip, one step slower than the L-1 cache in the memory hierarchy. L-2 cache almost always uses a dedicated memory bus, also known as a *backside bus*.

For the purposes of the exam, you should remember that the primary (L-1) cache is internal to the processor chip itself, and the secondary (L-2) cache is almost always external. Modern systems may have the L-1 and L-2 cache combined in an integrated package, but the exam differentiates an L-2 cache as being external. Up until the 486 family of chips, the CPU had no internal cache, so any external cache was designated as the "primary" memory cache. The 80486 introduced a 16KB internal L-1 cache. The Pentium family added a 256KB or 512KB external, secondary L-2 cache.

Technology tends to move toward consolidating components, for speed and cost efficiencies. The Super I/O chips combined many of the original XT adapters (for example, keyboard, COM and LPT ports) into a single package, and central processors soon moved in the same direction. Although caches were originally placed outside the chip die, new developments paved the way to move them inside the chip. A die, sometimes called the *chip package*, is essentially the foundation for the multitude of circuit traces making up a microprocessor. Today, we have internal caches (inside the CPU housing) and external caches (outside the die).

Internal and External Memory

When we speak of a chip's internal bus, we mean that the bus is cast right on the manufacturing die, along with the chip. These chip packages are sort of like an extremely small motherboard, in that they're the foundation for the many transistors, diodes, buses, caches, and a host of other electrical components we call a central processor. Don't confuse a chip package with a chipset—the entire set of chips used on a motherboard to support a CPU. The CPU is a chip package.

A manufacturing mask is the photographic blueprint for the given chip. It is used to etch the complex circuitry into a piece (chip) of silicon.

An external bus is the place where information moves out of the chip die to another destination (for example, an L-2 cache). Because bus width is typically measured by the number of bits that the bus can process at one time, we can have an 8-, 16-, 32-, and 64-bit bus. The number of data lines, each carrying a stream of bits, indicates the width of the bus. The bus width generally depends upon where the processor is directing information.

Memory Pages

Typically, memory is divided into chunks (or blocks). At the main memory level, a chunk is referred to as a *memory page*. At the cache level, a chunk is called a *cache block* or a *cache line*. Keep in mind that if a register is 8 bits wide, a cell contains one of the bits in that register. Technically, only a CPU has registers. Memory chips have capacitors and transistors.

The memory controller keeps track of the state and location of the charges held in the capacitors and transistors of a memory chip, as we indicated earlier, in our printing business story. This combination of states and locations is called an *address*. The charges in the memory chips are created by the original byte transmissions, coming from the CPU's registers. The CPU sends data to memory in order to empty its registers for more calculations.

In other words, the CPU has some information it wants to get rid of. It sends that information to the memory controller. The memory controller shoves it into whichever capacitors are available and keeps track of where it put the data. It keeps track of the bits by assigning memory addresses to each bit of information.

Ranges

Changes in memory chips and controllers are similar to how flat, one-page spreadsheets developed the concept of named ranges. DRAM is usually accessed through paging. A page is a related group of bytes (with their bits), similar to a range on a spreadsheet. It can be from 512 bits to several kilobytes, depending on the way the operating system is set up.

Without ranges, a spreadsheet formula must include every necessary cell in the spreadsheet. For example, we might have a formula something like =SUM(A1+B1+C1+D1+E1). Now suppose that we assign cells C1, D1, and E1 to a range, and call that range "LastWeek." We can now change the formula to include the range name: =SUM(A1+B1+"LastWeek").

When a spreadsheet formula uses a named range, this is analogous to the memory controller giving a unique name to a range of charges. This range of charges is called a *page address*, and with a page address, the controller doesn't have to go looking for data in every single capacitor or transistor.

Fast Page Mode (FPM)

Dynamic RAM (DRAM) originally began with Fast Page Mode (FPM) back in the late 1980s. In fast page mode, the memory controller makes an assumption that the data read/write following a CPU request will be in the next three pages (ranges), very much like a cache. This is somewhat like having a line of letters all ready to go in the toy stamp we spoke about in our printing business story.

Using FPM, the controller doesn't have to waste time looking for a range address for at least three more times: it can read-assume-assume-assume. Note the three pauses, as we'll mention burst cycles in a moment.

When the controller passes through the memory chip, it turns off something called a *data output buffer* when it reads the page it just read or wrote to. This process takes approximately 10 nanoseconds.

Fast Page Mode is capable of processing commands at up to 50 ns. Fifty nanoseconds is fifty billionths of a second, which used to be considered very fast. Remember that the controller first moves to a row; then to a column; then retrieves the information at an X-Y coordinate—a matrix address.

Once the information is validated, the controller hands it back to the CPU. The column is then deactivated, and the data output buffer is turned off. Finally, the column is prepared for the next transmission from the CPU. The memory enters a 10 ns wait state while the capacitors and transistors are precharged for the next cycle.

Extended Data Output (EDO) RAM

FPM evolved into Extended Data Out (EDO) memory. The big improvement in EDO was that once the column of data was deactivated, the data remained valid until the next cycle began. In other words, FPM removed the data bits in the column address and deactivated the column (data output buffer). EDO, on the other hand, kept the data output buffer active until the beginning of the next cycle, leaving the data bits alone.

EDO memory is sometimes referred to as hyper-page mode, and is a specially manufactured chip that allows a timing overlap between successive read/writes. The data output buffers are not turned off when the memory controller finishes reading a page. Instead, the CPU determines the start of the deactivation process when it sends a new request to the memory controller. The result of this overlap in the process is that EDO eliminated the 10 ns. per cycle delay of fast page mode, generating faster throughput.

Both FPM and EDO memory are asynchronous. (In the English language, the "a" in front of synchronous is called a prefix. The "a" prefix generally mean "not," or "the opposite.") In asynchronous memory, the memory controller and the system clock are not synchronized. DRAM is asynchronous memory. In asynchronous mode, the CPU and memory controller have to wait for each other to be ready before they can transfer data. Remember that everything on an asynchronous motherboard listens to the clock ticks coming from the motherboard oscillator.

Originally, motherboard clocks ran between 5–66MHz. The early x86 processors ran at 5–200MHz. When Pentium Pro motherboards stabilized at 66MHz, CPU speeds went up to between 200MHz and 660MHz. Suppose a motherboard has a 66MHz clock with a clock multiplier of 2. In this situation, the CPU runs at 133MHz (66 * 2). Remember, the CPU runs at the speed of the motherboard clock.

Now suppose a memory chip is synchronized to that same motherboard's 66MHz clock. The memory controller will have to wait 2 clock ticks before it can interrupt the CPU, unless it accidentally happens to catch the CPU at exactly the right time. Think about it: the CPU is hearing two ticks for every one tick the memory controller is hearing. If the CPU processes one instruction for every clock tick, then it will do two things before it's ready to be interrupted by the memory controller. This makes the controller seem a bit slow in the head.

Supplementary Information

If you choose, you may jump to the "Types of RAM" section at this time. This section is a more technical discussion of wait states and the memory standards used in rating memory performance.

A 60 ns. DRAM module, using fast page mode, might run in *5-3-3-3* burst mode timing. The first access takes 5 cycles (on a 66MHz system), or about 75 ns. The next three accesses take only 3 cycles, because they "assume" the range addresses. It happens that this works out to about 45 ns, with a ninety nanosecond savings in time (about 40 percent). Regular old page mode would be 5-5-5-5 burst mode.

EDO RAM became popular for a time, with a typical burst cycle of 5-2-2-2, yielding about a 22 percent savings in time over FPM memory. 50-nanosecond FPM isn't used anymore. Both FPM and EDO memory eventually gave way to Synchronous DRAM (SDRAM), then to Rambus memory, then to DDR-SDRAM (discussed later in this chapter). SDRAM developed a burst cycle of 5-1-1-1, which is even faster than EDO RAM, so SDRAM became the most popular type of memory toward the end of the 1990s.

The PC100 Standard

The speed of the actual memory chips in a module is only part of how we evaluate memory speed. The other factor is the underlying printed circuit board. Due to the physics of electricity and electronic parts, a module designed with parts that can run at 100MHz may never reach that speed. It takes time for the signals to move through the wire, and the wire itself can slow the signal speed. This led to the same old ratings problems that processors were causing.

Motherboard speeds eventually increased to 100MHz, and CPU speeds went beyond 500MHz. The industry decided that the original SDRAM chips should be synchronized at 100MHz. Someone had to set the standards for the way memory modules were clocked, so Intel developed the PC100 standard. This initial version of the standard made sure that a 100MHz module was really capable of, and really did run at 100MHz. Naturally, this created headaches for memory manufacturing companies, but the standard really helped in determining system performance.

The PC100 SDRAM modules required 8 ns DRAM chips, capable of operating at 125MHz. This provided a margin of error, making sure that the overall module would be able to run at 100MHz, according to the standard. The standard also called for a correctly programmed EEPROM, on a properly designed circuit board.

At 100MHz and higher, timing is absolutely critical, and everything from the length of the signal traces to the construction of the memory chips themselves is a factor. The shorter the distance the signal needs to travel, the faster it runs. Noncompliant modules, those that didn't meet the PC100 specification, could significantly reduce the performance and reliability of the system. The standard caught on. Note that unscrupulous vendors would sometimes use 100MHz SDRAM chips and label the modules as PC100 compliant, a similar situation occurred with processor chips (mentioned in the next chapter). This didn't necessarily do any harm, but consumers weren't getting what they were told they were getting.

As memory speeds increased, the PC100 standard was upgraded to keep pace with the new modules. Intel released a PC133 specification, synchronized to 133MHz, and so it went. PC800 RDRAM was released to coincide with the 800 series chipset, running at 800MHz, and these days, we see a PC1066 specification, designed for high-speed RDRAM memory. As bus speeds and module designs change, so too does the specification.

Summary—Memory

We've seen that memory can be broadly divided into two categories: memory that the system can change, and that which the system cannot change. RAM and ROM are the beginning concepts for understanding memory. The BIOS is where the motherboard remembers the most basic instructions about hardware, but the CMOS is where basic system settings are stored. BIOS and CMOS are different, in that CMOS requires a small amount of electricity to maintain its settings.

BIOS and CMOS can be changed, but not without some effort. Make sure you know the acronyms associated with these chips and the ways in which they can be updated. Additionally, you should have a comfortable sense of understanding about the following points, having to do with memory:

- The central processing unit, the memory controller, cache memory, and the system clock
- How timing affects performance, and the difference between asynchronous and synchronous data transfers
- The North bridge and South bridge architecture, and how the front side bus stands between the CPU and the North bridge (see Chapter 2).

Be sure that you have a good understanding of how data can be stored in memory cells, using ranges and range addresses. You should be able to differentiate between FPM and EDO memory, and dynamic (asynchronous) versus synchronous RAM. You won't be asked to calculate or remember burst cycles, but you should understand the concept of moving data as opposed to waiting cycles. A critical concept is the relationship between clocks (oscillators) and data transfers. If you can't remember how the motherboard uses timing cycles, go back and skim Chapter 2.

Types of RAM

As you've probably noticed, RAM is a sort of universal name for memory. Beyond that, each new name refers more to the mode of operation than an actual type of memory. The "D" in DRAM refers to the dynamic access. The "S" in SRAM and SDRAM refers to synchronizing the chip to the motherboard. EDO RAM refers to the extended data output whereby the column address isn't turned off after a read.

Dynamic RAM (DRAM)

First, *dynamic* means moving or always changing. In dynamic RAM, electricity always has to be moving through the chip to keep refreshing the memory. DRAM is the basic type of memory chip, and everything that came later was mainly a way to get address information faster. Dynamic also means that data can be moved into or out of memory, over and over again, for as long as power is available.

Data in a DRAM chip is stored in very compact form, with each bit using only its own capacitor and accompanying transistor. Once again, if the capacitor has a charge, the computer reads that as a 1. If it does not have a charge, it's a 0. Capacitors have a tendency to leak their charge fairly quickly. For that reason, they often have to be refreshed. The controller refreshes the DRAM sequentially during any given operation.

Synchronous RAM (SRAM)

SRAM introduced a clock that was actually built onto the memory module. This allows the module to be synchronized to the motherboard clock, introducing the term synchronous, or synchronized memory. Another feature of SRAM chips was that they weren't as dense as DRAM. The chips used a matrix of 6-transistors and no capacitors. Transistors don't require power to prevent leakage, so SRAM didn't have to be refreshed on a regular basis. By staying charged, the data changed only when a register changed, making the chips a lot faster than DRAM.

Because of the extra space in the matrix, SRAM uses more chips than DRAM for the same amount of storage space. Manufacturing costs are higher, so although DRAM was slower, the higher density and lower cost still made them popular in many machines. However, combining the best of both technologies quickly led to the development of SDRAM chips.

L-2 memory caches are usually on SRAM, which is extremely fast (as fast as 7–9 ns and 2–5 ns for ultra fast SRAM). Level 2 cache is usually installed in sizes of 256KB or 512KB.

SRAM is also used for CMOS configuration setups and requires a small amount of electricity, provided by a backup battery on the system board, to keep its data. It comes on credit-card-sized memory cards, is available in 128KB, 256KB, 512KB, 1MB, 2MB, and 4MB sizes, and has a battery life of 10 or more years.

Synchronous DRAM (SDRAM)

When the concept of synchronizing a memory chip to the motherboard proved successful, the idea was retrofitted to DRAM chips. Synchronous DRAM synchronizes the interrupt requests to the motherboard and works just like SRAM, only with the higher density (and lower cost) of the DRAM chip. Most SDRAM controllers are built into the North bridge of the motherboard chip set.

SDRAM uses the synchronization feature to eliminate the waiting problems between the CPU and the memory controller. When the CPU is ready to access data from memory, it goes to a specified clock point. The CPU knows when operations are going to be completed and when data is going to be available. No wait states means better performance (approximately 20 percent better than EDO memory, in most cases).

As we've seen, DRAM, fast page mode, and extended data output mode all measured memory speeds in nanoseconds (billionths of a second). A 70 ns part would be a "7," a 60 ns part a "6," and so on. The lower the number, the faster the memory. With the introduction of SDRAM, this measurement became less accurate. At such short intervals, per-second time began to lose any real value. Instead, the transfer speed of the front side bus began to make more sense as a measure of speed. For this reason, SDRAM modules began to be rated as 66MHz, 100MHz, 133MHz, 800MHz, and so on.

Rambus DRAM (RDRAM)

RDRAM comes out of technology developed originally by Rambus, Inc., for the Nintendo 64 gaming system. It's not that new, but it seems new because Intel started to use it with its Pentium 4 processors and 800-series chipset. Rambus memory is integrated onto Rambus Inline Memory Modules (RIMMs). The modules use Rambus DRAM (RDRAM) chips. We discuss the Rambus modules later in this chapter.

RDRAM chips are synchronized to the processor's memory bus (not the motherboard clock). Therefore, the processor won't request something at mid tick (the reverse of an interrupt). In DRAM, the CPU is synchronized to the motherboard (which is fairly slow), but the memory chip is not. In SRAM and SDRAM, both the CPU and the memory are synched to the motherboard. In RDRAM, the synchronization is no longer tied to a slow motherboard, but is synchronized to the memory bus. The memory bus clock is derived from the processor, but it still uses a multiplier of the motherboard clock.

Video RAM (VRAM)

VRAM and WRAM have been supplanted by DDR memory chips, but you may find a question about VRAM (pronounced "vee-ram") on the exam. Video RAM was designed to provide two access paths to the same memory address. It's as if VRAM were a café that has two doors, one in the front and one in the back. Information came in one "entrance" at the same time that other information flowed out the other "exit." When the video controller read the memory for information, it accessed an address with one of the paths. When the CPU wrote data to that memory, it accessed the address via the other path. Because of these two access paths, we say that VRAM was dual-ported.

Manipulating graphics is processing-intensive, and so this ability to push data in and out of the chip at the same time helps a moving image appear continuous. VRAM chips were about 20 percent larger than DRAM chips, due to extra circuitry requirements. Modern computers usually have modest graphics processing integrated right onto the motherboard, with the AGP as a convenient way to add an extra video card.

VRAM, WRAM, and AGP

The AGP acronym stands for Accelerated Graphics Port. Most computers include this accelerated port, which is an integrated part of the I/O system. An AGP is not the same thing as VRAM or a video accelerator card, nor is it the same thing as today's integrated graphics. Although some video cards still use the expansion bus, most connect with the port.

To say that a computer has "AGP memory," or "comes with AGP," can be confusing at best. At worst, it can demonstrate a faulty knowledge of the distinction between video memory and I/O subsystems. AGP is discussed in Chapter 7.

WRAM is short for Windows RAM, and has no connection with Microsoft, even though the acronym includes the word "Windows." WRAM, like VRAM, was dual-ported, but used large block addressing to achieve higher bandwidth. Additional features provided better performance than video RAM at lower manufacturing costs. With the advent of AGP and DDR RAM, both video and Windows RAM have faded from the marketplace. That's not to say that add-on graphics accelerator cards have vanished.

Packaging Modules

We've discussed how memory chips work on the inside, but you'll need to know how these chips are installed on a motherboard. Once again, most of the changes came about either to make maintenance easier, or to avoid bad connections. Keep in mind that installing a combined "unit" or module of some kind is less expensive than having many individual units to install.

Dual Inline Package (DIP)

Originally, DRAM came in individual chips called *dual inline packages (DIPs)*. XT and AT systems had 36 sockets on the motherboard, each with one DIP per socket. Later, a number of DIPs were mounted on a memory board that plugged into an expansion slot. It was very time-consuming to change memory, and there were problems with chip creep (thermal cycling), where the chips would work their way out of the sockets as the PC turned on and off. Heat expanded and contracted the sockets, and you'd have to push the chips back in with your fingers.

To solve this problem, manufacturers finally soldered the first 640 kilobytes of memory onto the board. Then the problem was trying to replace a bad chip. Finally, chips went onto their own card, called a *single inline memory module* or SIMM. On a SIMM, each individual chip is soldered onto a small circuit board with an edge connector (Holy Pentium II architecture, Batman!).

Connectors: Gold Vs. Tin

SIMMs and DIMMs come with either tin (silver-colored) or gold edge connectors. Although you may assume that gold is always better, that's not true. You want to match the metal of the edge connectors to the metal in the board's socket. If the motherboard uses gold sockets, use a gold SIMM. Tin sockets (or slots) should use tin edge connectors. The cost difference is minimal, but matching the metal type is critical.

Although it's true that gold won't corrode, a gold SIMM in a tin connector will produce much faster corrosion in the tin connectors. This quickly leads to random glitches and problems, so look at the board and match the color of the metal.

It's important to note, too, that each module is rated for the number of installations, or insertions. Each insertion causes scratches, and the more metal that is scratched off, the worse the connection becomes. In flea market exchanges and corporate environments, modules are subjected to constant wear and tear, and nobody is looking at the rated number of insertions.

Single Inline Memory Modules (SIMMs)

When DRAM chips were placed in a line on their own circuit board, it gave rise to the term inline memory. Once the chips were formed into a *module*, the entire module would fit into a socket on the board. These modules and sockets are referred to as *memory banks*. Depending on how the chips are connected on their own little circuit board, the module is called either a single, or dual inline memory module (SIMM or DIMM).

SIMMs come in both 30-pin and 72-pin versions. The 30-pin module is an 8-bit chip, with 1 optional *parity* bit. The 72-pin SIMM is a 32-bit chip, with 4 optional parity bits.

The memory bus grew from 8 bits to 16 bits and then from 32 bits to 64 bits wide. The 32-bit bus coincided with the development of a SIMM, which meant that the 32-bit-wide data bus could connect directly to 1 SIMM (4 sets of 8 bits). However, when the bus widened to 64 bits, rather than making a gigantic SIMM, we started using two SIMMs in a paired memory bank. The development of the 64-bit-wide DIMM superseded the SIMMs, and only used one module per socket again.

SIMMs and DIMMs are sometimes referred to as chips, but they are really a series of chips (modules). DRAM itself is a chip, and DRAM chips are grouped together to form SIMMs and DIMMs. SIMMs can come with a varying number of pins, including 30-pin and 72-pin. (Even though the 72-pin module could have chips on both sides, it was still a SIMM.)

Be careful when you read a question on the exam that you don't accidentally agree that a SIMM is a memory chip. A good way to keep alert is that chips have RAM in their name.

Dual Inline Memory Modules (DIMMs)

Dual inline memory modules are very similar to SIMMs, in that they install vertically into sockets on the system board. DIMMs are also a line of DRAM chips, combined on a circuit board. The main difference is that a DIMM has two different signal pins, one on each side of the module. This is why they are dual inline modules.

The differences between SIMMs and DIMMs are as follows:

- DIMMs have opposing pins on either side of their board. The pins remain electrically isolated to form two separate contacts—a dual set of electrical contacts.

- SIMMs also have opposing pins on either side of the board. However, the pins are connected, tying them together. The connection forms a single electrical contact.

DIMMs began to be used in computers that supported a 64-bit or wider memory bus. Pentium MMX, Pentium Pro, and Pentium II boards use 168-pin modules. They are 1 inch longer than 72-pin SIMMs, with a secondary keying notch so they'll only fit into their slots one way.

Don't Mix Different Types of Memory

Mixing different types of SIMMs or DIMMs within the same memory bank prevents the CPU from accurately detecting how much memory it has. In this case, the system will either fail to boot, or will boot and fail to recognize or use some of the memory.

You can, however, substitute a SIMM with a different speed within the same memory bank, but only if the replacement is equal to or faster than the replaced module.

All memory taken together (from all memory banks) will be set to the speed of the slowest SIMM.

Rambus Inline Memory Modules (RIMMs)

Rambus inline memory modules (RIMMs)—as opposed to dual inline—use Rambus Dyamic RAM (RDRAM) chips. Previously, on a standard bi-directional bus, data traveled down the bus in one direction, then returning data reversed back up the same bus in the opposite direction. It did this for each bank of memory, with each module being addressed separately. A wait occurred until the bus was ready for either the send or reverse.

RIMMs use a looped system, where everything is going in one direction (unidirectional). In a looped system, data moves forward from chip to chip and module to module. Data goes down the line, then the results data continues forward on the wire in the same direction. The results data doesn't have to wait for downstream data to finish being sent.

These chips are set on their modules contiguously (next to each other in a chain) and are connected to each other in a series. This means that, if an empty memory bank socket is in between two RIMM chips, you must install a continuity module, which is a low-cost circuit board that looks like a RIMM, but that doesn't have any chips. All it does is allows the current to move through the chain of RDRAM chips. It's like Christmas tree lights wired in series, where one bulb is missing.

Latency is a combination of two things: You don't have to wait for the bus to turn around, and the cycle time is running at a fast 800MHz, so you don't have to wait very long for the next cycle. Using RDRAM chips, signals go from one module to the next to the next, and the throughput is triple that of 100MHz SDRAM. You can also use two to four RDRAM channels (narrow channel memory) at the same time. This can increase throughput to either 3.2GB or 6.4GB.

Why Memory Becomes Corrupted

Most DRAM chips in SIMMs or DIMMs require a parity bit because memory can be corrupted in the following two ways: Alpha particles can disturb memory cells with ionizing radiation, resulting in lost data, or electromagnetic interference (EMI) can change the stored information.

A DRAM cell (transistor) shares its storage charge with the bit line. This creates a small voltage differential, which can be sensed during read access. The differential can be influenced by other nearby bit line voltages. This, along with other electrical noise, can corrupt the electrical charge in the memory cell.

Supplementary Information

Throughout this book we've taken the time to explore technical details outside the scope of the A+ exam. In some instances, these supplementary segments serve as real-world examples of how the concepts you'll be tested on are used out in the field. In other instances, you should be aware that low level physics, electronics, engineering, and design schemes have produced long-term consequences. You'll be faced with questions that result from how modern computers have come to terms with these consequences, and you can either remember "just the facts," or have a sense of history as to how the facts came into being. If you choose, you may skip to the "Memory Diagnostics—Parity" section at this point.

The following section is a more technical examination of how Rambus memory went in one direction, and DDR memory went in another. Each type of memory develops problems based on RIMMs using serial transfers and DDR using parallel transfers. By seeing the problems, you should end up with a much better understanding of some of the other concepts covered in this book, and the underlying reasoning behind many of the exam questions. If you can figure out the reason for the question, many times you can also figure out the answer—even if you can't remember the specific details.

Serial Transfers and Latency

Aside from some other technical features we'll explore in a moment, RDRAM has a latency factor. In order to understand latency, let's take a look at the difference between serial and parallel transfers. We'll refer to these concepts again in Chapter 9, as they are fundamental concepts to computer technology. Think of a train, like the ones you often see in movies. When the hero has to chase the bad guy through the train, he starts at one end and goes from car to car. This is a serial process, where he moves through a series of cars. He begins at one end of a car, then walks all the way through it, usually looking for someone, and leaves by a door connecting to the next car in the series. Then the process starts all over again, until he either reaches the end of the train or someone gets killed.

Now suppose we take that same train, but this time we don't have a hero chasing a bad guy. Instead, let's imagine a train full of people on their way to work. If there was only one door at the back of the train, it would take forever when the train pulled into a station and everyone wanted to get off. To fix that problem, each car has its own door. When the train comes to a stop, everyone turns to the side facing the platform: The doors in each car open up, and a stream of people leaves each car simultaneously. This is a parallel transfer, with eight passengers leaving their own car in parallel (side by side) with each other.

One of the problems with Rambus memory is that the RIMMs are connected to the bus in a series. A data item has to pass through all the other modules before it reaches the memory bus. The signal has to travel a lot farther than it does on a DIMM, where the bus uses parallel transfers. The longer distance introduces a time lag, called *latency*. The longer the delay before the signal reaches the bus, the higher the latency. In a game, data generally moves in long streams, so serial transfers aren't a problem. But in a typical PC, data routinely moves in short bursts, and latency becomes a problem.

In a DDR or SDRAM system, each DIMM is connected, individually and in parallel, to the data bus. Regardless of whether the system uses a single DIMM or multiple DIMMs, transfer times are essentially the same. We'll discuss DDR memory at the end of this chapter.

Narrow Channel Bus

Earlier Pentiums had a data bus up to 64 bits wide and transferred data using a parallel process. The DIMM was also 64 bits wide, which meant that data could be moved across the memory bus in 64-bit chunks, or 8 bytes, per second. Remember that a byte is equal to 8 bits. Another way of looking at it is that a bit is one-eighth of a byte. Therefore, 64 bits divided by 8 equals 8 bytes.

All the memory systems that we've talked about are known as *wide channel* systems because the memory channel is equal to the width of the processor data bus. RDRAM is known as a *narrow channel* system because data is transferred only 2 bytes (16 bits) at a time. This might seem small, but those 2 bytes move extremely fast. The Rambus data bus is 18 bits wide, as opposed to the standard 32 or 64 bits, but the system sends data more frequently. It reads data on both the rising and falling edges of the clock signal, a process also used in Dynamic Data Rate (DDR) memory (discussed at the end of this segment).

Up until RDRAM, the fastest chips had a throughput of 100MHz. Remember that 8 megabytes moving in parallel means that 8MB is transferred every 1 second. At 100 clock ticks (cycles) per second, that means 100 times 8, or 800 megabytes per second. RDRAM chips move 2 megabytes per cycle (one on the up tick, one on the down tick). At 800MHz, that means RIMMs move 1,600MB per second (800 times 2 bytes), which translates to 1.66 gigabytes (GB) or a billion bytes—about twice as fast as SDRAM.

Another way to think of it is an example we heard, involving driving to the store. If you go out of your way, you can take 10 minutes to drive 10 miles on a highway at 60 mph. If you go directly to the store, you can take 4 minutes to drive only 2 miles at 30 mph. You might drive a whole lot faster on the highway, but you'll get to the store faster on the straight-line route. In this example, the store is the memory controller and bus.

Continuity Modules

Because Rambus memory works with serial transfers, all memory slots in the motherboard must have an installed module. Even if all the memory is contained in a single module, the unused sockets must have a PCB, known as a continuity module, to complete the circuit. This is similar to old strings of Christmas tree lights, wired in series, where every socket required a bulb. Since the current moved through each bulb in order to get to the next, a missing or burnt-out bulb would stop the flow of current to the entire string.

One of the interesting things about very high-speed memory is that as signals move across the circuits in different ways, the modules begin to look more like microscopic networks. When we speak about network architectures in Chapter 8, we'll refer to signal interference as packets collide. This is similar to what's taking place in modern memory modules. At such high speeds, the physics of impedance and capacitance have more of an impact on the way data signals arrive at their destinations. Configuring a serial pathway has one set of problems, while parallel pathways have different problems. We won't go into all the low-level details, but you may find it interesting to do some research on the technical specifications of Rambus and DDR memory.

Double Data Rate SDRAM (DDR SDRAM)

DDR SDRAM probably won't be on the exam, but we'll mention it because technology is rapidly abandoning the previous types of SDRAM, along with RDRAM. Intel has stopped developing chipsets for RDRAM technology, and has shifted its resources to DDR SDRAM and DDR-II, using a newer version of the i845E chipset. Double Data Rate (DDR) came about as a response to RDRAM specifications put together by Intel and Rambus. Intel eventually bought Rambus and began licensing the technology for a fee. In much the way that IBM created Micro Channel Architecture (MCA) and charged a fee, both situations led to the development of separate consortiums for a different standard. DDR is an open architecture, and comes from a consortium of non-Intel manufacturers.

DDR and Rambus memory are not backward compatible with SDRAM.

In our discussion of motherboards in Chapter 2, we mentioned that AMD developed faster processing by using a double-speed bus. Instead of using a full clock tick to run an event, they use a "half-tick" cycle, which is the voltage change during a clock cycle. In other words, as the clock begins a tick, the voltage goes up (an up tick) and an event takes place. When the clock ends the tick, the voltage goes down (a down tick) and a second event takes place. Therefore, every single clock cycle can have two memory cycle events. The AMD Athlon and Duron use the DDR specification with the double-speed bus.

DDR (double data rate) memory is the next generation SDRAM. Like SDRAM, DDR is synchronous with the system clock. The big difference between DDR and SDRAM memory is that DDR reads data on both the rising and falling edges of the clock tick. SDRAM only carries information on the rising edge of a signal. Basically, this allows the DDR module to transfer data twice as fast as SDRAM. For example, instead of a data rate of 133MHz, DDR memory transfers data at 266MHz.

DDR modules, like their SDRAM predecessors, are called *DIMMs*. They use motherboard system designs similar to those used by SDRAM; however, DDR is not backward compatible with SDRAM-designed motherboards. DDR memory supports both ECC (error correction code, typically used in servers) and nonparity (used on desktops/laptops.)

Aside from the royalty fee to Intel, Rambus memory is more expensive to produce than DDR SDRAM. DDR is designed around an open architecture, meaning no royalties. Rambus die (chips) are much larger than SDRAM or DDR die, which means that fewer parts can be produced on a wafer. Even so, Silicon Integrated Systems (SiS), the manufacturer of the first DDR400 chipset for the P4, has launched a PC1066 RDRAM system. Intel is still validating PC1066 support for the i850E chipset. DDR is the most popular DRAM at the moment, but RDRAM is still being used in a few high-end desktops and workstations.

RDRAM uses a 16-bit bus for the data signals, and this narrow 16-bit path is the main reason why RDRAM is able to run at speeds up to 533 MHz (with double data rate, an effective 1066 MHz). However, one of the problems with parallel transfers at high speeds is something called *skew*. The longer and faster the bus gets, the more likely it is that some data signals will arrive too soon or too late, based on the clock signal. This is where the very high speeds in today's systems are rekindling interest in serial transfers. The parallel port used to be the fastest port, but fast serial USB ports and serial ATA transfers (IDE drives, discussed in Chapter 6) are making parallel transfers seem out-of-date.

RDRAM also developed a different type of chip packaging, called *Fine Pitch Ball Grid Array* (FPBGA). Most DDR SDRAM uses a Thin Small Outline Package (TSOP). TSOP chips have fairly long contact pins on each side, as opposed to FPBGA chips, which have tiny ball contacts on the underside. The very small soldered balls have a much lower capacitive load than the TSOP pins. DDR SDRAM using the FPBGA packaging is able to run at 200-266MHz, whereas the same chips in a TSOP package are limited to 150-180MHz.

DDR-II and "Yellowstone"

DDR-II may be the end of Rambus memory, although people have speculated that RDRAM wouldn't last for quite some time. DDR-II extends the original DDR concept, taking on some of the advantages developed by Rambus. DDR-II uses FPBGA packaging for faster connection to the system, and reduces some of the signal reflection problems (stubs) of the original DDR. However, as bus speeds continue to increase, so too does latency. DDR-II is expected to enter the consumer market sometime in 2003. RDRAM is expected to continue to exist in 2003, but with very little chipset support. This makes it likely that DDR-II will take over from both DDR SDRAM and RDRAM.

The current PC1066 RDRAM can reach 667 MHz speeds (PC1333), so Samsung and Elpida have announced that they are studying 1333MHz RDRAM and even 800MHz memory (PC1600). These systems would most likely be used in high-end network systems, but that doesn't mean that

RDRAM would be completely removed from the home consumer market. Rambus has already developed a new technology, codenamed "Yellowstone," which should reach 400MHz, using octal data rates. This may lead to 3.2GHz memory, with a 12.4GB/s throughput. With a 128 bit interface Rambus promises to achieve 100GB/s throughput. Yellowstone technology is expected to arrive in game boxes first, with PC memory scheduled for sometime around 2005.

Summary—Memory Modules

Everything about the packaging of memory chips rests on the concept of modules. These modules are vaguely like tiny motherboards within a motherboard, in that they, too, are integrated circuit boards. The big difference between DRAM and SDRAM is the synchronization feature. Be sure you understand how SDRAM uses timing cycles to more efficiently interrupt the CPU. Remember, SRAM is extremely fast and is used in secondary caches; SDRAM is a type of main memory.

It's all well and good to know how SDRAM differs from Rambus RAM, but you're also going to have to be able to differentiate between SIMMs and DIMMs. Inline memory modules are the small IC cards you install in your machine when you upgrade your memory. You won't have to remember clock speeds and the exact number of pins, but you'll definitely be tested on the different types of modules.

Memory Diagnostics—Parity

Parity is the state of either oddness or evenness assigned to a given byte (not bit) of data. Parity checking is the way that the computer uses a special set of logical rules and chips to make decisions based on the parity (state) of a particular byte. When a PC runs through the POST (Power On Self-Test), commonly called a *cold boot*, memory integrity is one of the first things tested. On many machines you can see this taking place as a rapidly-increasing number displays on the screen before the operating system begins to load. This checking is designed to verify the accuracy (integrity) of the bits contained in memory, and it happens after every read/write operation.

Remember that computers think in binary bits and bytes. The binary computer language uses "words" composed of 1s and 0s.

Originally, parity checking was a major development in data protection. At the time, memory chips were nowhere near as reliable as they are today, and the process went a long way towards keeping data accurate. The parity circuit allowed the CPU to compare what it sent to main memory with what it read from main memory. Parity checking is still the most common (and least expensive) way to check whether or not a memory cell can accurately hold data. A more sophisticated (and expensive) method uses Error Correcting Code (ECC).

Even and Odd Parity

Parity checking puts a byte into memory along with its parity bit and then reads the byte from memory. If the byte plus the parity bit matches what was sent, the memory is okay. Otherwise, we have a parity error. Parity can be set to odd, even, or off. The parity circuit works by adding one bit to every byte of data, resulting in nine bits. (Remember that a byte is already eight bits.) The value of any given bit (1 or 0) is determined at the time that data is written to memory. Then, a 1 or 0 is assigned to the parity bit, depending on whether the overall byte is made up of an odd or even number of 1s. Figure 3.2 shows various bytes of data with their additional parity bit.

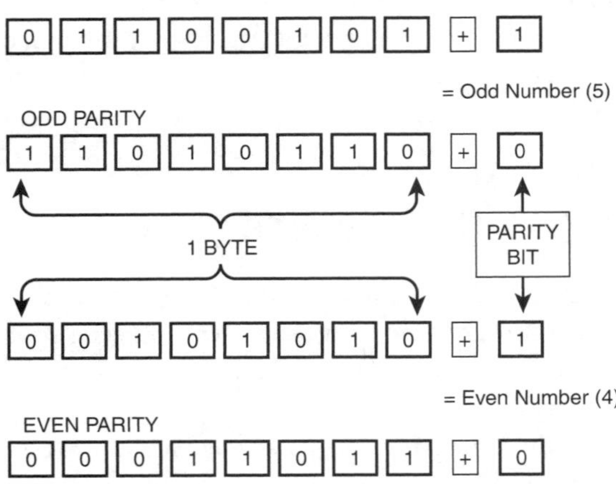

Figure 3.2 Odd and even parity.

In plain odd and even parity, every byte gets 1 parity bit attached, making a combined 9-bit byte. Therefore, a 16-bit byte has 2 parity bits, a 32-bit byte has 4 parity bits, and so forth. This produces extra pins on the memory module, and this is one of the reasons why various DIMMs and SIMMs have a different number of pins.

Even parity checking, is where the total of all the 1 bits in a byte must equal an even number. If five of the bits are set to 1, the parity bit will also be set to 1 to total six (an even number). If 6 bits were set to 1, the parity bit would be set to 0 to maintain the even number six. If the parity is set to "even" and a returning byte contains an odd number of "ones," the system knows the data is corrupted. This is called a *parity error*.

In even parity, the overall number of 1s must come out to an even number.

Odd parity works in the reverse of even parity, but the concept is the same. The total number of 1s in any given byte must come out to an odd number. Once again, this is done by using either a 1 or a 0 for the parity bit, as you can see in Figure 3.2.

You'll receive a parity error if the parity is odd and the parity circuit gets an even number, or if the parity is even and the parity circuit gets an odd number. The circuit can't correct the error, but it can detect that the data is wrong.

Fake or Disabled Parity

Some computer manufacturers install a less expensive "fake" parity chip that simply sends a 1 or a 0 to the parity circuit to supply parity on the basis of which parity state is expected. Regardless of whether the parity is valid, the computer is fooled into thinking that everything is valid. This method means no connection whatsoever exists between the parity bit being sent and the associated byte of data.

A more common way for manufacturers to reduce the cost of SIMMs is to simply disable the parity completely, or to build a computer without any parity checking capability installed. Some of today's PCs are being shipped this way, and they make no reference to the disabled or missing parity. The purchaser must ensure that the SIMMs have parity capabilities, and must configure the motherboard to turn parity on.

Error Correction Code (ECC)

Parity checking is limited in the sense that it can only detect an error—it can't repair or correct the error. This is because the circuit can't tell which one of the eight bits is invalid. Additionally, if multiple bits are wrong but the result according to the parity is correct, the circuit will pass the invalid data as okay.

Error correction code (ECC) uses a special algorithm to work with the memory controller, and it adds an error correction code bit to each data bit when it's sent to memory. When the CPU calls for data, the memory controller decodes each error correction bit and determines the validity of its attached data bit.

The system requires twice the number of bits, but the benefit is that ECC can correct a single-bit error. Because approximately 90 percent of data errors are single-bit errors, ECC does a very good job. On the other hand, ECC costs a lot more, due to the additional number of bits.

Remember that ECC can correct only single-bit errors, but it can also detect multi-bit errors. Parity checking understands only that the overall byte coming out of memory doesn't match what was sent into memory. Parity checking cannot correct anything.

Usually, whoever is buying the computer will decide which type of data integrity checking they want, depending mainly on cost benefits. They can choose ECC, parity checking, or nothing. High-end computers (e.g., file servers) typically use an ECC-capable memory controller. Midrange desktop business computers typically are configured with parity checking. Low-cost home computers often have nonparity memory (no parity checking or "fake" parity).

Practice Questions

Question 1

Part of a computer's RAM chip is dedicated to storing key system settings required for boot-up.

- ❍ a. True
- ❍ b. False

Answer b, false, is correct. Random access memory (RAM) is volatile and loses all of its data without a source of power. RAM comes in modules, and is almost never referred to as a chip. System boards commonly use non-volatile CMOS to store system settings. CMOS memory uses very little current (a trickle charge) and continues to be powered for extended periods of inactivity by a small battery on the system board.

Question 2

Over-clocking allows a microprocessor to run considerably faster than motherboard components. What type of memory structure was developed to minimize the delay of accessing RAM on the motherboard?

- ❍ a. Processor resident pipeline
- ❍ b. L-2 cache
- ❍ c. CMOS memory
- ❍ d. Duplex memory

Answer b is correct. Intel 486 and Pentium processors have a small amount of memory integrated in the chip called an L-1 cache. However, as processor speeds increased, additional high-speed memory was needed. This second block of memory was called an L-2 cache and was located on a special high-speed bus. Later, some designs included an L-2 cache on the processor cartridge or the die itself. Duplex memory and a processor resident pipeline do not exist.

Question 3

DIMMs and SIMMs are interchangeable, provided speed and capacity requirements are observed.

❍ a. True

❍ b. False

Answer b, false, is correct. SIMMs and DIMMs look similar, and both use edge connectors. However, DIMMs use both sides of the connector to support a 64-bit or wider memory bus, and they have two separate connector pins, one on each side of the module board.

Question 4

Parity chips on SIMMs no longer provide a useful purpose and have been largely removed.

❍ a. True

❍ b. False

Answer b, false, is correct. Parity chips allow memory to be tested during the POST, and they also monitor memory during computer operations. Some manufacturers have eliminated them or bypassed their function to cut costs. This allows less expensive SIMMs to be used, but at the expense of reliability.

Question 5

Which of the following choices best describes what is meant by cache memory?

❍ a. A place where instructions are stored about the operations of a device or application

❍ b. Extended memory that can be made accessible with the **SMARTDRV /ON** command

❍ c. Memory that holds applications and data that the CPU isn't running

❍ d. Memory that holds data that the CPU will search first

Answer d is correct. The CPU will look in cache memory first. If it fails to find the necessary data, it will look in main memory. If it fails to find what it needs in main memory, the CPU will look on the disk.

Question 6

A 64-bit EEPROM is an inline memory module with 32 connecting pins located on either side of the memory bank.

❍ a. True

❍ b. False

Answer B, false, is correct. EEPROM refers to programmable read-only memory chip that is used to store the BIOS. This chip is not a part of the main memory, and it is not a "module."

Need to Know More?

Freedman, Alan. *Computer Desktop Encyclopedia, Second Edition.* AMACOM, 1999. ISBN 0-814-479-855. This is great for a fast look-up or refresher.

Messmer, Hans-Peter. *The Indispensable PC Hardware Book, Third Edition.* Reading, MA: Addison-Wesley Publishing Company, 2000. ISBN 0-201-403-994. This is a comprehensive, up-to-date reference book that covers far more than you will need to know for the exam.

Minasi, Mark. *The Complete PC Upgrade and Maintenance Guide, 11th Edition.* San Francisco, CA: Sybex Network Press, 2000. ISBN 0-782-128-009. This is considered one of the best reference books available. In fact, Minasi's book was instrumental in the formulation of the first A+ exam.

Mueller, Scott. *Upgrading and Repairing PCs, 12th Edition.* Indianapolis, IN: Que, 2000. ISBN 0-7897-2303-4. This is one of our favorites. If you are only going to have one reference book, give this one serious consideration.

Rosch, Winn. *Hardware Bible, Fifth Edition.* Indianapolis, IN: Sams Publishing, 1999. ISBN 0-789-717-433. This is a well-organized reference book that covers software issues as well as hardware.

http://www.aceshardware.com
Ace's Hardware—Technical Information for the Masters and the Novices
A comprehensive site covering everything you would ever want to know about memory.
Brian Neal - Publisher, Webmaster
All Content is Copyright (c) 1998-2002 Ace's Hardware. All Rights Reserved.

Processors

Terms you'll need to understand:

✓ Microprocessor, processor, chip
✓ Megahertz (MHz)
✓ Chip die, chip package
✓ Throughput

Concepts you'll need to master:

✓ On-die versus external central processing unit (CPU) functions (internal and external bus)
✓ Bus speed
✓ Clock speed, clock cycle, or clock tick
✓ Clock multiplier and over-clocking

At the heart of every personal computer is the central processing unit, often referred to as a *chip* or *processor*. Traditionally, processors are referred to by their clock speed in megahertz. IBM and Intel originally worked together to develop a PC that would take advantage of microprocessors. Today, other manufacturing companies have taken an important share of the chip-manufacturing market. Two of the better-known chip makers are Advanced Micro Devices (AMD) and Cyrix. An interesting lawsuit came about when Intel tried to trademark the numbers 80386, 80486, and so on, only to discover that it wasn't legal to do so. That's why Intel created the Pentium name; a name can be trademarked.

In this chapter we'll get into the details of the various processors you'll encounter on the A+ exam. Many of the performance improvements that came about with each new generation of processors did so as a result of problems with throughput bottlenecks. In Chapter 3 we discussed how memory works, differentiating some of the ways memory chips and bus speeds are interrelated. You should be comfortable in your knowledge of data transfers and memory utilization as you begin this review of microprocessors.

Central Processing Unit (CPU)

The CPU is where most of the software instructions, math, and logic calculations are performed. Early CPUs added a math coprocessor, or floating-point unit (FPU), where some of the more complex mathematical calculations were offloaded to improve performance. Beginning with the 80486 family of processors, the math coprocessor began to become an integral part of the CPU.

When you open up a PC and look at the motherboard, the CPU is usually the largest chip on the board. On many motherboards, the CPU is inserted into a plastic holder, or socket, making it easy to spot. Modern motherboards tend to have the CPU in a slot, standing vertical, and making them more difficult to spot. Slots and sockets were covered in Chapter 2, "Motherboards."

If the CPU is in a large, square socket, it will often have its own cooling fan and heat sink directly above it, hiding the actual chip from view. In a vertical configuration, you'll often see what looks like a very deep comb, or a vertical piece of metal with many small ledges coming out at right angles. This is also a heat sink, and will typically have an integrated cooling fan.

Most of today's sockets have what's called a zero-insertion force (ZIF) design. ZIF design means that you don't need a chip extractor to remove the chip, which reduces the chance of breaking the connector pins. It takes about 100 pounds of insertion force to install a chip into a standard machine socket. ZIF goes a long way toward reducing damaged sockets, chips, and pins.

Processor Speed

Starting with the original 8088 processor, CPUs were referred to by their clock speed. This continued through the 80486 family of chips (486 machines) and even into the early Pentium chips (e.g., P-133, P-166). Today, companies try to use a name that can be trademarked, so most CPUs are referred to by a name instead of a number.

Internally, a processor always operates on instructions at its rated speed (133MHz, 700MHz, 1.2GHz, and so forth). At various points in the processing, the CPU stores results in its own memory registers. The internal registers become filled very quickly, and the CPU begins moving data to various types of additional memory. In some cases, this additional memory is extremely short-term.

As the need for immediate processing reduces, the CPU moves data results farther away from its internal registers. Eventually, when all the instructions in a given routine have been completed, the resulting data is moved out to main (system) memory. The rate at which the CPU transfers information to memory is controlled by various clock speeds, depending on the type of memory involved. In Chapter 2 we discussed oscillators and clock ticks. In Chapter 3 we discussed memory buses and short-term cache memory (i.e., L-1 and L-2).

The 486 DX2/Overdrive chip ran internally at twice the clock speed of the motherboard. A DX4 could be configured to run at two or three times the motherboard clock speed. However, even though the internal processing took place at double, triple, or quadruple the speed of the original chip, the transfer rate of the results of all that processing was still tied to the original motherboard clock speed.

Bus Speed

System performance is directly related to the width of several closely related buses. The chip speed is fairly straightforward, but bus "width" includes several variables, such as the processor bus, data input/output (I/O) buses, and various memory address buses. For instance, an internal address bus may be one size, but an external bus may be a different size. Generally speaking, the faster the bus speed, the faster data can move across that bus. When data in a wide bus (for example, 32-bit channel) arrives at a 16-bit-wide bus, the narrowing of the stream produces a bottleneck. Ideally, all the buses in a system should be the same width.

AT boards run at either 33MHz or 66MHz, and we call this speed the motherboard bus speed. The 80486 DX2, followed by the Pentium family of processors, introduced running speeds that went far beyond the motherboard's bus speeds. To that end, we now have differing bus speeds in different locations on the motherboard. Keep in mind that memory modules, network connections, and anything else related to system speeds, all depend on the physics of circuits and wiring.

Processor Families

When IBM introduced the first PC, it contained an Intel 8088 processor chip. Although the 8086 was the first CPU in existence, the 8088 was actually the first chip to be released on the market. IBM used the 8088 in its XT computers. Features of the 8088 included the following:

- A clock speed of 4.77MHz, or 4,770,000 cycles (ticks) per second. Each cycle represents the execution of one instruction or part of one instruction. Later, it was designed to run at 8MHz, which is close to double the speed of the original.
- An 8-bit external bus that could move 8 bits of information into memory at one time.
- A 16-bit internal bus.

A Real Computer—Real Mode

The 8088 chip was designed with a 20-bit address bus that enabled it to access 1 megabyte (MB) of Random Access Memory (RAM). This was considered far more than adequate for any expected application. However, the introduction of GUIs and Windows quickly demonstrated the need for a chip that could address far more memory.

An MS DOS session in Windows and the Virtual Machine discussed in Chapters 12 and 13 are based on the history of the original 8086 processors used in XT machines. These processors worked only with their registers and the memory cells on installed memory chips. Because of this direct, physical relationship between the chip and the memory addresses, we refer to it as a "real" machine.

The 8086 chip, produced prior to the 8088, was a somewhat faster chip. The 8086 was a true 16-bit chip that used 16 bits for both the internal and the external bus. However, at the time IBM felt that people would be unwilling to pay a premium price for this capability, and it adopted the less expensive 8088 for the first PCs. The 8086 had approximately 20 percent faster throughput than the 8088 because of its ability to communicate at 16 bits with the other system components. For the moment, understand that throughput is basically how much data can travel across a bus in a given time segment. Both the bus speed and bus width impact on the throughput. We'll discuss throughput more thoroughly in Chapter 8.

IBM could say that the 8MHz 8086 PS/2-30 was two and a half times faster than the 4.77MHz 8088 PC/XT because of the change in the external bus from 8 bits to 16 bits. This was one of the first indications that performance could be increased by making the data path larger.

The 80286 Processor

Although the 8088/86 CPU could address 1MB of memory, software applications and the operating system rapidly took over the entire megabyte and demanded more. Unfortunately, a number of engineering decisions had been made that would affect the PC industry for the next 10 years. As a result, Intel developed the 80286 CPU, which was a fundamental turning point in how chips accessed memory. The release of the 286 coincided with the new AT motherboard design.

The 80286 was used in the new IBM AT, along with the original PS/2 models. Later PS/2 models began using the 80386 chip. Windows 2.0 was starting to catch on, and in an effort to reduce the boxy size of computers, IBM also moved away from the standard five-pin DIN connector. A smaller connector—known as a *PS/2 connector*, or Mini-DIN—lives on today as one of the standard keyboard and mouse connectors.

The increasing market for PCs led to the emergence of many new companies that manufactured computers. These computers came to be known as IBM *clones*, which were referred to as *AT-compatible* or *AT-class* computers, leading to the standardization of the AT-type motherboard.

Beginning with the 80286 chip, references to Real Mode meant that the newer chips could imitate the original 8088 chip when they were running in a particular way. Put another way, the chip addressed the first 1,024 bytes of conventional memory (discussed in Chapter 11) by assigning real addresses to real locations in memory. Even in today's Windows machines, DOS application imitate a virtual 8086 PC called a *Virtual Machine* (VM).

The 8088 could directly assign memory addresses to 1MB of memory with its 20-bit address bus. A CPU operating in Real Mode addresses memory in the original 1MB range that the 8088 used. The 286 could address a total of

16MB of memory, but it had to maintain backward compatibility with the many PCs and applications already on the market. Many of the applications had to be rewritten to take advantage of any memory beyond the first 1MB of conventional memory.

Virtual Real Mode (or Virtual 86 Mode) allows several Real Mode sessions to run concurrently in what's called a *virtual machine*.

Real Mode vs. Protected Mode

The 286 chip introduced the concept of real mode, along with protected mode. In Real Mode, the 286 acted essentially the same as the 8088/86 chips and could run older software with no modifications. Once again, Real Mode means that the chip addresses the first 1,024 bytes of conventional memory by assigning "real" addresses to "real" locations in memory.

As software began requiring more memory, the 286 introduced a way for software to access 1 gigabyte (GB) of memory. This was called *virtual memory*, and it was done by "swapping" code held in RAM to a disk. This enabled the software to use the freed-up actual memory, and to think that it could use up to 1GB of RAM while remaining unaware of the swapping.

With an appropriate operating system and software, the chip could run multiple programs at once, using the 286 Protected Mode feature. This sparked the development of OS/2, and later, the Windows 3.0 Standard Mode. As we've said, we will discuss operating systems later in this book, but consider that even today, DOS applications running in Windows and the way that Windows manages virtual memory can be traced all the way back to the 80286 microprocessor.

Switching from Protected Mode to Real Mode

Both the operating system and the CPU control virtual memory, or information being swapped out of RAM to a disk. 286 Protected Mode introduced this capability, but software development was slow to catch up. The 286 was unable to switch from Protected Mode to Real Mode without resetting (warm rebooting) the computer. However, it could go the other way and switch from Real Mode to Protected Mode without resetting.

The next generation of chips, the 386, allowed switching to either mode without a system reset. This inability to come back from protected mode without a warm reboot changed history when IBM continued to develop OS/2 for the 80286 and began to fall behind in relation to Microsoft's desire for a multitasking operating system. Microsoft built the Windows GUI into New Technology (NT), and OS/2 became an also-ran.

The 80386 Processor

The introduction of the 80386 represented another fundamental change in the world of PCs. At that time, the PC was catching on and bringing major changes to the business world. The graphic interface of Windows was demanding lots of processing power, and Intel was beginning to dominate the chip market. The constant demand for more speed and more power was pushing development efforts, and new chips were coming out every year.

Applications were becoming larger, requiring more memory to hold their code and data, and customers were prepared to spend more money for RAM if it would make their machines faster. The PC had hit a critical acceptance point, and the expanding market was bringing software that could work with as much memory as a chip could address. The 80386 opened the door to that memory, and finally provided enough speed for the new multitasking operating systems and programs.

The 386 chips had a full 32-bit processor (32-bit internal registers, 32-bit internal data bus, and 32-bit external bus); a 32-bit memory address bus; and clock speeds from 16–33MHz. Manufacturers other than Intel offered chips up to 40MHz, but all 386s had the ability to address 4GB (4 billion bytes) of physical memory. The main difference from the 286 was that the 80386 had the ability to switch between Protected Mode and Real Mode through software control, and didn't have to reset the system. This made multitasking (more properly, "task-switching") more practical.

With built-in memory management, the 386-DX enabled software to access 64 terabytes (TB) of memory, or about 1 trillion bytes, so software written for the 386 chip could access 64 trillion bytes of memory. (Current estimates of the space requirements of the human mind suggest that a complete lifetime of memories can be stored in about 15TB.)

SX Versions

Market forces and the dramatic increase in consumer interest led Intel to develop a chip for people who wanted 386 capability at a price closer to that of the older 286 chips. This budget-conscious buying is essentially what led to an entire line of derivative chips—the SX chips—being developed. Later, with the same market forces at work, but with the names of CPUs moving away from clock speeds, Intel and AMD continued the practice of releasing less expensive chips with reduced capabilities (for example, Celeron and Duron).

The 386SX ended the reign of the 286 because of its better memory management unit (MMU) and the new Virtual Real Mode feature. The 386DX and the 386SX could both run Windows 3.x in Enhanced Mode (formally called *386 Enhanced Mode*). Enhanced Mode allowed Windows software to take advantage of the 80386 chip's ability to continually switch between Real Mode and Protected Mode.

Along with the increased market for PCs, both in business and at home, people wanted portability and a general reduction in the space that their computers were taking up. Portable computers were introduced, but didn't really excite the market the way that laptop computers did.

Laptop computers came about with the development of liquid crystal display (LCD) panel technology, and they began driving the research into size reduction and lower power consumption. To meet those needs, yet another line of chips—the SL line—introduced lower power consumption and something called *System Management Interrupts* (SMI), with power management features for battery conservation, including several sleep modes.

Coprocessors

Starting with the Intel 80386, another major marketing push began stressing the performance advantages of adding a math coprocessor, or floating-point unit (FPU). Models were differentiated by changing the last digit of the main CPU's number to a seven, but the "87" chips were always the same speed as the primary "86" chip. For example, the 33MHz 80386 was paired with an optional 33MHz 80387. These math coprocessors had been available as far back as the 8086, but at that time they affected only arithmetic calculations (add, subtract, multiply, and divide). Therefore, they greatly speeded up spreadsheet applications, but did not necessarily speed up all applications.

This marketing campaign was so effective that when the 486 chips internalized the floating point unit, it was simply disabled in the SX line and a separate—so-called 487—math coprocessor was offered (for an additional fee). This coprocessor was actually a fully functional 486 CPU, and when inserted in its special socket, it disabled the preexisting 486.

Remember that a math coprocessor is a floating point unit (FPU) and affects only applications that do a lot of arithmetic. Such a processor greatly speeds up spreadsheet applications, but not necessarily other applications.

The 80486 Processor

With the introduction of the 386 AT-class machines and Windows 3.0, more and more businesses began to move to computers, and a PC on every desktop became typical. This led to bigger, more feature-packed software that demanded faster computers, more memory, and increasing storage capacity. The GUIs of Windows and OS/2—along with huge spreadsheets, databases, and computer-aided design (CAD)—increased the demand for intense mathematical calculations and higher clock speeds.

The 486 processor, about twice as fast as the 386 chip, had 32-bit internal, external, and memory address buses. It could execute one instruction at two cycles (clock ticks) rather than the 4.5 cycles of the 386, and it introduced an internal Level 1 cache (with a typical hit ratio of 90–95 percent). The 486 also used burst mode (see Chapter 3), and used a built-in synchronous math coprocessor (also known as a *Floating Point Unit*, or *FPU*) in some versions.

With the advent of the 486, and because it was nearly twice as fast as the 386, the graphic user interface finally came into its own. Market acceptance of the Windows GUI prompted the sale of more expensive hardware, larger hard drives, and faster video cards. This ultimately began the price competition that has brought the prices of PCs down and driven their capability continually upward.

The 486 primarily differed from the 386 and 286 in its integration and *upgradability*. *Integration* refers to the number of components that have been moved onto the chip. *Upgradability* means that the CPU can be taken off of the motherboard and replaced with a better (faster or feature-enhanced) chip. *Scalability* means that the entire system can be made larger in order to handle more capacity.

80386 and 80486 processors typically ran at 100MHz, with a front side bus of 33MHz or 66MHz. Although processor speeds continued to increase, bus speeds stayed the same, for the most part. It wasn't until 1998, when Intel released the Pentium II and BX chipset that bus speeds increased to 100MHz.

Pentium Processors

The Pentium, introduced in 1992, was entirely compatible with previous processors from Intel, but it added a fundamental difference: superscalar technology. Superscalar technology is based on a twin data pipeline, meaning that the Pentium can execute two instructions at the same time. All previous chips executed one instruction at a time.

Superscaler technology allows the Pentium to execute two instructions per cycle (1 hertz [Hz] clock tick), which moved the chip's execution factor beyond the single clock-tick barrier for the first time. Another way of looking at this is to say that the Pentium performs one instruction in 0.5Hz (half of one cycle).

After improving processor speed, Intel turned its attention to increasing the bus width. Like the 80386 DX and 80486 processors, Pentiums have a 32-bit-wide address bus, allowing them to address up to 4GB of memory.

Although the memory address bus was 32 bits wide, the Pentium's data bus was expanded to 64 bits, meaning that data could be moved around the system almost twice as fast as previous chips. For this reason, first-series Pentiums also required two 32-bit-wide single inline memory modules (SIMMs) for each data bank on the motherboard. Initially, these memory chips had to be mounted in pairs, as opposed to later Pentiums, which could use a single 64-bit-wide SIMM.

First Series

When Intel discovered it couldn't trademark a number, the company began releasing each new CPU with its own registered name. Most people were used to calling a CPU a 286, a 386, or a 486 and understood that a bigger number meant a faster CPU. As we'll see in a moment, this led to a marketing problem with later generation processors. Even though the Pentium name was owned by Intel, other manufacturers (and many consumers) carried on the tradition of using a number. Fifth generation chips refer to the 586 line of CPUs, just as fourth generation refers to the variations of a 486 processor.

The original Pentium came in three basic series, and had variations within each series. The first series (of fifth generation) Pentiums began to phase out the tradition of differentiating a chip primarily by speed. They were available in both 60MHz and 66MHz, used a 273 pin grid array (PGA) form factor, and ran on approximately 5 volts (V). Because the processor ran at about the same speed as the motherboard, the chips were said to have a "1X clock speed," referring to the 1:1 relationship between the processor speed and the motherboard's clock speed.

The 66MHz Pentium required 16 watts (W) of power and drew 3.2 amps, making it a very "hot" processor. For the first time, designers had to come up with ways to cool the chip. This led to chip-cooling fans and heat sinks, and eventually helped change the overall design of motherboards.

Second Series

In 1994, Intel released the second series of Pentiums, with variations running at 75MHz, 90MHz, or 100MHz. Soon after, the speed was increased to 120MHz, 133MHz, 150MHz, 166MHz, and 200MHz. This second series of processors used a different manufacturing technique, allowing for a significantly smaller die and a current requirement of 3.3V (running somewhat cooler than the 5V series). The chips used a 296 staggered pin grid array (SPGA) form factor and were physically incompatible with the first series chips. One of the improvements to the second series Pentiums included a programmable interrupt controller (PIC) and a dual-processor interface that allowed two processors to be installed on a single motherboard.

The smaller, or thinner the piece of silicon that a chip uses, the more wafers can be sliced from a silicon bar (or ingot). Smaller dies mean smaller wafers, which in turn mean more chips and fewer manufacturing costs. Larger chips mean a reduced "yield" (fewer chips per bar), thereby increasing manufacturing costs.

Third Series and MMX

In late 1996, in an effort to capitalize on the expanding market for multimedia applications, Intel introduced the third series Pentium processors, or Series 3 Pentiums (not to be confused with a Pentium III), with MultiMedia eXtensions (MMX) capabilities. MMX technology is a set of basic, general-purpose, integer instructions that can be applied to a wide variety of multimedia and communications applications. MMX introduced 57 new instructions for accelerating calculations typical of audio, two-dimensional (2D) and three-dimensional (3D) graphics, video, speech synthesis, and voice recognition. Acceleration can be as much as eight times faster than without MMX. This should have provided an apparent 50–100 percent performance improvement in multimedia programs—particularly in PC games.

MMX is a hardware technology in which the instructions are built into the system. To take advantage of MMX, software must be written specifically for these enhancements.

Many of these newer chips ran on 2.8V, lower than the previous generation of chips, and were designed for installation on 66MHz motherboards. The speed for these third series Pentiums climbed from 166MHz to 200MHz or 233MHz.

A Pentium mobile chip, running at 266MHz, was used in laptops.

Clock Multiplier

The original Pentium motherboards came with three basic, or "core" speed settings: 50MHz, 60MHz, or 66MHz. Even at their introductory speed of 120MHz, the second series Pentiums ran much faster than the motherboards on which they were installed. When we compare the speed of the motherboard to the speed of the CPU's bus width, we refer to that comparison as the "core-to-bus frequency ratio," or the "clock multiplier."

Originally, pins BF1 or BF2 on the chip were used to synchronize the processor to the motherboard. Even today, there are still either jumpers or switches on many motherboards, which allow you to control the BF pins, and subsequently, the clock multiplier ratio.

Over-Clocking

Pentium chips can be set to run faster than their design specification, which is called *over-clocking*. For example, a 75MHz Pentium can be set on the motherboard (using jumpers) to run at 133MHz. Due to conservative estimates on the part of the manufacturers, this over-clocked chip may continue to function quite well in the short term. However, as time passes, the chip may begin to perform unreliably.

It is important to check that the speed setting on the motherboard is at the design specification for the installed Pentium chip. In some cases, unscrupulous third-party distributors will re-mark the speed setting on the chip, making it very difficult to correctly identify the optimum performance configuration.

Advances in manufacturing and technology began making it difficult to produce RAM and other components that could keep up with the processor. Over-clocking was used more and more, to get around this problem. The first indication that this might become a standard practice was the 486/50 DX2. Here, the processor ran at 50MHz while the rest of the system ran at 25MHz. This is a 2:1 multiplier, and became known as 2X. Over-clocking has increased over the years, making it difficult to clearly define processor speeds.

An example of formal over-clocking is the 1.33GHz Athlon. The chip itself runs on a 133MHz system bus with a 10:1 multiplier (10 times 133MHz =

1330MHz or 1.33GHz). This means that the processor can only access other components of the system on every tenth clock cycle. Therefore, if the CPU has to store or retrieve data from, say, main memory, it may waste several clock cycles waiting for a clock cycle to arrive where it can again connect with the system.

To improve bus speeds, certain designs are capable of transferring data on both the up-tick (rising edges of the clock) and the down-tick (falling edge). In this case, a bus with a 133MHz clock speed becomes a 266MHz bus. This is the same principle used in DDR memory, discussed in Chapter 3. The Pentium 4 goes a step further, transmitting data four times per clock cycle.

This trend towards increasing the clock multiplier in order to produce faster-sounding chips is probably a result of the original marketing strategy used for computers. As we've said, consumers have come to identify faster MHz numbers with better computers. At the end of this path we see chips such as the Athlon XP, where the bus is so slow in comparison to the over-clocked processor that benchmark tests begin to show performance degradation.

The P6 Family: Sixth Generation

In November 1995, Intel released the Pentium Pro, the first of the sixth generation chips. With the P6 family, Intel finally broke away from using chip speeds in marketing the CPU. Even so, the "6" in P6 refers to the traditional x86 number, with 686 following 586. Members of the P6 family include Pentium Pro, Pentium II, Pentium III, and the bargain priced Celeron. The Pentium Pro was designed to run at different speeds, depending on its underlying motherboard:

- On a 60MHz motherboard, the Pentium Pro ran at 150MHz or 180MHz.
- On a 66MHz motherboard, the Pentium Pro ran at 166MHz or 200MHz.

Up until the introduction of the P6, motherboards used a single motherboard *host processor bus*, which sometimes created bottlenecks in the data path. The way around this was to create a *backside processor bus* (as opposed to the front side bus) that would run at the processor speed. This bus went around the back door of the motherboard processor bus and connected the processor directly to an L-2 cache.

The main feature change in the Pentium Pro was moving the previously external L-2 cache onto the chip die itself and giving it a dedicated bus.

Some of the earlier Pentium Pros had an L-2 cache built directly into the chip. However, the cost of manufacturing was so high that most Pentium Pros were later released with a separate L-2 cache that was accessed through the backside processor bus running at full, core speed.

Pentium II and VID Pins

Pentium Pro chips could not be installed in a Socket 7 (see Chapter 2), which brought about the development of Socket 8 technology, with 387 pins. These very large sockets cost a lot to manufacture, and they brought about the relatively quick replacement of the Pentium Pro by the Pentium II.

Pentium II processors moved away from the socket and chip design, and introduced Slot 1 and Slot 2 architecture. Once again, the L-2 cache was moved onto the integrated circuit (IC) board (often called a *cartridge*), maintaining its close proximity to the central processing unit. These sixth generation Pentiums all ran at different voltages. However, instead of having the motherboard set that voltage with jumpers, DIP switches, or a voltage regulator module (VRM), the voltage could now be set automatically by something called the *voltage identification (VID)* pins. These four special voltage identification pins are located directly on the processor cartridge itself. Table 4.1 shows the wide variety of processor speeds, depending on the variation in motherboard bus speed and clock multiplier.

Table 4.1 Pentium II speeds in relation to clock multipliers.

Motherboard	Clock Multiplier	Speed
66MHz	3.5	233MHz
66MHz	4	266MHz
66MHz	4.5	300MHz
66MHz	5	333MHz
100MHz	3.5	350MHz
100MHz	4	400MHz
100MHz	4.5	450MHz

Pentium III

The Pentium III was released in 1999, using either flipped-chip pin grid array (FC-PGA) Socket 370, or Single Edge Contact (SEC) Slot 1 packaging. The primary difference between the Pentium III and the earlier Pentium II was the addition of 70 new instructions working in something called *Streaming SIMD Extensions* (SSE) mode. Single Instruction Multiple

Data (SIMD) is a way to process many different instructions at once—simultaneously. These instructions dramatically improved the chip's performance in advanced imaging, 3D graphics, streaming audio, video conferencing, and speech recognition.

Another important (and somewhat controversial) feature of the Pentium III was a self-reportable processor serial number. Although this was introduced originally for security, it was possible to use the serial number for managing corporate inventories of computers (asset tracking). However, some people felt the feature might be used as an invasion of privacy if the serial number could be reported out (stolen by the site developers) during a visit to an Internet site.

The Pentium III had a locked clock multiplier, which was designed in such a way that it could not be reset. However, unscrupulous dealers were able to actually disassemble the chip itself, making the necessary modifications to overclock the chip. They would then reassemble the chip with different markings. Be careful at flea markets and other places where the price seems "too good to be true," and remember Robert Heinlein's TANSTAAFL (*There ain't no such thing as a free lunch!*).

The Pentium III had many different speeds, depending on its underlying motherboard and the clock multiplier being used. As we saw in Table 4.1, both the motherboard and clock multiplier work together to generate an advertised processor speed, so perhaps the best way to think of the Pentium III is as follows:

- Pentium III chips were installed on motherboards with an original clock speed of either 100MHz or 133MHz.
- The clock multipliers could be 4 (133MHz only), 4.5, 5, 5.5, 6, 6.5, 7, 7.5, 8, or 8.5.
- On a 100MHz motherboard, chip speeds became 450MHz, 500MHz, 550MHz, 600MHz, 650MHz, 700MHz, 750MHz, 800MHz, and 850MHz.
- On a 133MHz motherboard, chip speeds became 533MHz (multiplier 4), 600MHz, 667MHz, 733MHz, 800MHz, 866MHz, 933MHz, and finally breaking the 1 gigahertz (GHz) ceiling.

3DNow!™ Technology

AMD developed a technology to compete with the Intel SSE instruction set. 3DNow! added an additional twenty-one instructions, designed to improve K-6 integer and floating point calculations. Like MMX, the additional instructions were designed to enhance the rendering of 3D graphics found in computer games, as well as other multimedia applications. 3DNow! is particularly helpful in processing single instruction multiple data (SIMD) instructions.

Intel's multimedia extensions were originally developed to improve graphics and heavy mathematical processing. However, there wasn't an immediately noticeable performance improvement in computer games—a primary consumer market multimedia application. As a result, not many games were written to take advantage of the technology.

Intel Celeron

With the need for faster computers at lower costs, Intel developed the Celeron processor in much the same way that the old 386 and 486 chips came out in both the full DX version and the bargain SX versions. Although the older chips lowered prices by adding or removing the floating point unit (FPU)--the math coprocessor--the Celeron's core processor is actually either a Pentium II or a Pentium III, depending on its version.

Celeron processor packaging is generally found in one of two formats: a PGA 370 socket (Socket 370) or FC-PGA. Both packaging formats are less expensive to manufacture than a PII or PIII, with the Socket 370 being similar to the typical flat installation of an older 486 or Pentium. The FC-PGA package looks similar to the vertical architecture of the Pentium II and III, but the Celeron uses a less expensive cartridge that can be placed in a Slot 1. In terms of speed, the Celeron was configured as follows:

- Celeron chips were only installed on 66MHz motherboards.
- The multipliers ranged from 4 through 9, generating chip speeds of 266MHz, 300MHz, 333MHz, 366MHz, 400MHz, 433MHz, 466MHz, 500MHz, 533MHz, 566MHz, and 600MHz.

AMD Processors

Although you may get a few questions on the different AMD chips, most of the questions will be about Intel-designed processors up through the Pentium III series. Intel is the largest chip manufacturer in the world, with AMD being the second largest. AMD chips are in direct competition with the Intel Pentium line, with the first of these being called the K-6. The company soon found that they too, would have to match the market demand for variations based on either price or performance. Taking a lesson from Intel, AMD created the Athlon and Duron processors.

The K-6 performed somewhere between a Series 1 Pentium and a Pentium II, and was designed to fit into a Socket 7. It had a higher performing L-1 cache, helping the K-6 to get around limitations in the Socket 7 architecture. Remember that an L-1 cache is internal to the processor. Competitive Pentium chips generally used 32KB of L-1 cache, but AMD increased K-6 cache to 64KB. Because of this, the K-6 could sometimes perform on a par with the Pentium II, and even sometimes match a Pentium III.

K-6 processors were found on motherboards that ran at 66MHz, 95MHz, and 100MHz, generating chip speeds from 166MHz to 450MHz.

Athlon and Duron

When the K-6 was replaced by the Athlon chip, the manufacturing process led to a completely different design process. The Athlon, similar to the Pentium II, mounted vertically on a cartridge using a single edge connector. It had a large (512KB) external L-2 cache mounted on the cartridge, which used a separate bus for direct access by the CPU (like the Pentium II and III). With the introduction of the Athlon processor (and its subsequent Slot A architecture), AMD chips could no longer be installed on Pentium motherboards.

Although the overall vertical form was similar in shape to the Pentium chips, the Athlon used a different pinout from the Pentiums, thereby requiring AMD's Slot A design, as opposed to Intel's Slot 1 design. This pin incompatibility means that AMD uses Slot A ("A" like in AMD), while Pentium uses Slot 1.

A good way to remember this is that both Socket A and Slot A have the AMD "A" in their name, and the "A" from Athlon. Everything else is the Intel specification.

Sockets (Celeron, Duron) are cheap, while Slots (Pentium, Athlon) are expensive. "*Socks*" are cheap, but a *slot* for your boat at the marina is expensive!

Motherboards designed for the Athlon and Duron originally ran at 100MHz, using an unusual method of increasing throughput. This method was called an EV6 bus, and worked by doubling the data transfer rate per clock cycle. However, the chips were clocked at the original motherboard speed (100MHz) using varying clock multipliers, depending on which chip was installed.

Using Slot A, the initial Athlon series ranged in speeds from 500MHz to 1GHz. On the other hand, using Socket A, the chips ran at 650MHz to

1GHz. If you noticed the higher speeds in what was supposedly older technology (Socket A), you can understand why today's chips are tending to go back to flat technology. Regardless of whether it was installed in a Slot A or a Socket A, the Duron ran in speeds ranging from 550MHz to 700MHz.

The Intel Celeron used a less expensive Socket 370 packaging, and AMD reduced packaging costs by developing Socket A. Both the AMD Athlon and Duron were designed to use either Slot A or Socket A technology. The more expensive Athlon used a 512KB L-2 cache, as opposed to the Duron's 64KB cache, and the Athlon's cache was external. The Duron's L-2 cache was moved from outside the chip, becoming an internal L-2 cache.

The AMD Duron has a 128KB L-1 cache, whereas the Celeron has a 32KB L-1 cash, split evenly as a 16KB data and 16KB instruction cache. The Celeron, however, has a 128KB L-2 cache, compared to the Duron's 64KB Level 2 cache. The Celeron has moved from a 66MHz to a 100MHz front-side bus. However, the Duron still has the edge here, because while its front-side bus is 100MHz, it transfers data on both the rising and falling edges of the clock. This means that the Duron effectively has a 200MHz bus. Finally, the memory interface of the Celeron is 100MHz, while the Duron typically has an interface allowing for memory running at 133MHz.

Supplementary Information

Although none of the following discussion is part of the A+ exam, we thought you might be interested to see where the industry seems to be heading. If you choose, you may jump to the end of the chapter and test yourself on the Practice Questions at this point.

The Pentium 4 was initially released with clock speeds in excess of 1GHz, using a 400MHz system bus and a new 850-series chipset. The chipset was optimized for the P4 and Rambus dynamic RAM. This combination provided a throughput of 3.2GB/s, meaning that the combination can transfer 3,200,000,000 bytes every second.

AMD and Intel were both trying to be the first to release an x86 processor capable of a 1000MHz (1GHz) clock speed. AMD ended up releasing the Athlon just days before Intel released the 1GHz Pentium III. The battle for bigger numbers escalated almost out of control, as AMD pushed the Athlon up to 1.4GHz, and Intel responded with a Pentium 4 running at 1.8GHz. At some point, we would hope that marketing hype gives way to real performance measures.

32-bit Processing

Certain applications, often referred to as high-end applications, require extremely sophisticated processing. An example of this kind of throughput demand would be a file server in a network (networking is discussed further in Chapter 8) running an immense database. The Pentium Xeon package was much larger than a Pentium II, Pentium III, or Celeron. The L-2 cache typically began at 512KB, but could hold up to 2MB of memory. All the cache chips in a Xeon run at the same, core speed of the processor itself, making the cache very expensive (often more expensive than the processor itself). The Xeon was designed to run 32-bit programming code, with far better performance than 16-bit code. We discuss 16-bit Windows and 32-bit Windows at length in Chapters 10–13.

Xeon systems were very expensive, and would run only 32-bit code. The Xeon didn't do very well in the corporate market, as customers were looking for less expensive ways to increase capacity. It wasn't long before Intel announced the release of 64-bit Itanium processors, but by this time, customers were using inactive mainframe cycles to create virtual file servers. When a mainframe isn't using processing power for some other task, it can be configured to act as a PC server, using certain network management software tools. Virtual servers reside on a single mainframe, as opposed to requiring many separate computer boxes.

64-bit Processing

IBM (Power4) and Hewlett-Packard (Superdome) are already shipping 64-bit processors, with the capability of running anywhere from 1 to 64 processors simultaneously. Some of these new systems are capable of providing 1TB (terabyte) throughput. Sun Microsystems (UltraSPARC) and AMD also have 64-bit processors that will be backward compatible with 32-bit code. The Intel Xeon has, for the most part, been bypassed, and it remains to be seen whether the Itanium, now the Itanium 2, will be able to hold a strong market position. Intel, along with the Hewlett-Packard-Compaq conglomerate, seems to be pushing customers toward 64-bit applications alone, running on the Itanium series. AMD, IBM, and Sun Microsystems are hoping to capitalize on the fact that their processors will run the thousands of pre-existing 32-bit applications, as well as 64-bit applications.

Reduced Instruction Set Computers (RISC [pronounced "risk"]) use an architecture where microprocessors are designed to work with a limited number of individual instructions PCs using chips designed to work with a full list of instructions are referred to as *Complex Instruction Set Computers* (CISC). Reduced instruction set computers are generally faster because they function with a smaller list of potential instructions.

Athlon XP

To improve speeds for what many consumers came to understand was a "cheap" version of their Pentium line, Intel started running the Celeron on a 100MHz front-side bus. For a long time, the Celeron stayed on a 66MHz bus while the Duron originally shipped on a 100MHz bus. Both the Intel Celeron and the AMD Duron have been taking part in a clock speed war, and the 1GHz Duron was the first move to a new programming core (Morgan). The result of the change was a processor that ran significantly cooler, consumed less power, and offered better clock-for-clock performance than its predecessor.

The Athlon ran at 1.4GHz, and when Intel hit the 2GHz point in their Pentium 4 series, AMD released the Athlon XP. This chip ran at only 1.53GHz, but performed better than the P4. With advanced chips, such as the XP, AMD has released chipsets capable of supporting memory running at 166MHz or 333MHz. However, benchmark tests show the front-side bus is running at approximately 266MHz. To that extent, the Athlon XP can't take advantage of faster memory, which is actually running faster than the processor can get to it. Development is underway to create a system where the system bus runs at the same speed as the RAM, leading to a complete 333MHz bus integration.

The P4 has hit the 2.53GHz range and is moving upwards, with rumors of 3GHz before the year end of 2002. The Athlon is holding on, based on their lower system prices and often better benchmark performance. However, the Pentium 4 is definitely the emerging leader, and the Athlon series is fading. AMD is hoping that its upcoming Hammer chips will turn things around, but until this new series is released, AMD hopes to retain market share with its next revision of the Athlon. The revised Athlon will have 512KB of L-2 cache, and the possibility of putting the Athlon XP onto a 333MHz bus. Rumor has it that the next series will be called the *Palamino*.

The Athlon XP uses an Organic Pin Grid Array (OPGA) package. This package has a fiberglass foundation, like a printed circuit board, and is similar to the packaging on Intel chips. AMD claims the new organic packaging is cheaper to produce and offers lower impedance than the ceramic packaging they've used in the past. This new design may prevent cracked or chipped cores that Athlon chips have been prone to in the past.

Names and Performance

We've seen how, since the first IBM XT with its 8086 chip, performance has been mostly measured by the processor speed. The Pentium 4 and Athlon XP were designed to be scaled to much higher clock speeds, but performance on an instructions-per-clock tick basis has begun to degrade. For example, comparing a 2GHz Pentium 4 with an Athlon XP 1900+, there's an apparent performance edge of 400MHz in the Pentium. However, in nearly every industry benchmark test, the Athlon XP outperformed the Pentium. One of the problems coming out of this discrepancy is that the consumer market will have to be re-educated as to how different chips are rated.

AMD tried a new naming convention, starting with a 1533MHz clock speed and calling it "1800+." Every time a new processor's speed increased 66MHz, AMD added 100 to the name. So a 1599MHz processor became a 1900+. This worked for as long as the system performance was tied only to the CPU. When bus speeds went from 166MHz to 333MHz, AMD needed a new way to market its systems.

The Pentium 4 eventually crossed the 2.53GHz mark, and processors are still on target to reach 10GHz by around the year 2007. Apple and some PC vendors have tried to recapture the buying frenzy of yesteryear with different colors and shapes, but with so many consumers having amply sufficient systems, faster and better-looking machines are really only luxuries. Whether processor names will continue to reflect system performance is anyone's guess, but for now, the buying public continues to assume that larger numbers mean better performance, regardless of reality. Technically educated people understand that system performance is better understood by reading the results of industry-standard benchmark tests.

Given the choice between a 1.7GHz Intel and a 1.2GHz AMD at about the same price, uneducated consumers will most likely choose the Intel. AMD is promising "an industry-wide initiative (for sometime in 2002) to develop a new and more complete measure of performance that end-users can trust." There has been no word yet on whether an organization will be formed to sanction the new metric, nor does anyone know much about how the ratings will work. For example, there is no information on whether the rating would take into account performance across multiple operating systems, or whether it could be used to compare Pentiums and Athlons with non-x86 chips.

Then there's QuantiSpeed, the name AMD has given the new Palomino chip. The name implies that the chip will process even faster on each clock tick. Although this may make AMD seem vulnerable to their marketing department, Intel tried the same thing with NetBurst. That name was chosen to go along with Intel's "makes the Internet go faster" marketing strategy. Other marketing names we've seen that mean nothing in the real world include advanced transfer cache, hyper-pipelined technology, rapid execution engine, and advanced dynamic execution. Although these might make excellent exam questions, they aren't valid technologies.

Manufacturing Technology

AMD's Athlon chip was the fastest x86 processor available at the time that Intel was having trouble scaling the Pentium III past 1GHz. The Pentium 4 was designed on a new 0.18 micron process, with its longer pipeline and lower instructions per clock. Even so, the Athlon hung in there for a lot longer than Intel would have liked. Eventually, Intel's Northwood Pentium 4 with its 0.13-micron process technology, 512KB L-2 cache, and 533MHz bus, took back the lead.

The Athlon still uses a 0.18-micron manufacturing process, and it will take a while for AMD to make the conversion to 0.13 microns. However, AMD points to the fact that even a 0.13-micron Pentium 4 has a larger die size than a 0.18-micron Athlon XP. At the same time, the Athlon XP 3DNow! instructions just happen to correspond to the instructions the original Athlon needed in order to be compatible with Intel's SSE. These extra instructions do not provide compatibility with the Pentium 4's new SSE2 instructions, but they should yield improved performance in applications optimized for SSE.

Meanwhile, Intel has announced a new 90 nanometer (nm) process. To show the conversion, 0.13 microns is the same as 130 nanometers, and 0.09 microns is the same as 90 nm. A nanometer is one billionth of a meter, and the average human hair is 150 microns wide.

Intel says the new process combines higher-performance, lower-power transistors, strained silicon, high-speed copper interconnects, and a new low-k dielectric material. This is the first time all of these technologies will be integrated into a single manufacturing process. This should allow Intel to make better products and reduce manufacturing costs. "Prescott" is pegged as one of the first 0.09-micron parts, scheduled to enter the market sometime in 2003. All things considered, Intel is clearly well ahead in the manufacturing technology race. Aside from allowing for faster chips that consume less power, it will also let them cram more processor dies onto each silicon wafer.

Summary—Processors

Anyone who wants to buy a computer knows that the type of installed CPU is an important part of the decision process. Prior to the advent of modern bus technologies, we could use the speed of the processor to gauge system performance. The current exam doesn't cover the subtleties of front side buses, processor buses, and such things as bus clock multipliers. All of these concepts are necessary to understanding how computers work, and a solid grasp of each concept should help you remember much of the information on which you'll be tested. As for processor-related questions, be sure that you know the following:

- The 80286 was the first chip to access more than 1MB of real memory. It provided a Protected Mode, as well as Real Mode. Know the difference between these two modes and how they operate.
- Be aware of how the 80386 introduced an SX version as a budget chip, and that an FPU is the same as a floating point unit and a math coprocessor.
- The 80486 series was where clock multipliers began having an important impact on the computer market. Understand what an SX and a DX version means, and how a chip package could use an internal or external feature.
- Pentium series names (1, 2, and 3) are different from the processor names within each series. You should know the Pentium II and its rated speeds, and you should know what MMX technology refers to.

Try not to get too caught up in the details of individual chip speeds right before the exam. It's important to understand how the various processors evolved, because the underlying technology was directly associated with other components. Different people remember things in different ways, and we've tried to provide several memory paths in this book. If you find yourself getting bleary-eyed with numbers and details of speed ratings, relax and move on to a different chapter. You can always return to this chapter at a different time.

Practice Questions

Question 1

The floating point unit or coprocessor was internally integrated into which Intel microprocessor?

- ❍ a. Intel 8088
- ❍ b. Intel 8086
- ❍ c. Intel 80286
- ❍ d. Intel 80386
- ❍ e. Intel 80486

Answer e is correct. The floating point unit (FPU) or coprocessor was first integrated into the Intel 80486. The unit was disabled in the Intel 80486-SX for marketing reasons, but still present.

Question 2

Which was the first Intel microprocessor to be able to address more than one 1megabyte MB of memory?

- ❍ a. Intel 8086
- ❍ b. Intel 80286
- ❍ c. Intel 80486
- ❍ d. Intel 80386

Answer b is correct. The Intel 80286 could address 16MB of memory and was the first Intel microprocessor to break the one 1MBmegabyte limit.

Question 3

Flat CPUs use ______________, while vertical CPUs work with ______________ technology. (Choose all that apply.)

- ❑ a. ZIF, Slot
- ❑ b. Socket 7, Slot A
- ❑ c. Socket 8, Slot 1
- ❑ d. Slot B, Socket 7

Answers a, b, and c are correct. Socket 7 and Socket 8 are both referred to as flat technologies, and the sockets mostly are zero-insertion force (ZIF) sockets. Vertical processors can use Slot 1 or Slot A, depending on whether they are Intel or AMD chips. Answer d is backwards in the use of "slot" and "socket," and there's no such thing as Slot B.

Question 4

MMX enhancements refer to ______________.

- ❍ a. Video accelerator cards
- ❍ b. L-1 and L-2 cache improvements
- ❍ c. Memory management extensions
- ❍ d. Multimedia extensions

Answer d is correct. multimedia extensions (MMX) are a set of instructions on a CPU that help speed up such things as video, audio, and speech recognition. Modern PCs have an accelerated graphics port (AGP). There's no such thing as "memory management extensions," and neither the Level 1 or Level 2 cache have any sort of multimedia enhancements.

Question 5

Level-1 L-1 and Level-2 L-2 caches were provided to speed CPU operation by reducing the need of the processor to access system RAM. The difference between the two types is that the L-1 cache is internal to the processor and the L-2 cache is external to the processor.

❍ a. True

❍ b. False

Answer a is correct. The internal L-1 cache provided 8KB to 16KB of fast memory to the processor, but the external L-2 cache provided 256KB or more of memory.

Need to Know More?

Karney, James. *Upgrade and Maintain Your PC.* New York, NY: Hungry Minds, Inc. 1998. ISBN 1-55828-460-5.

Messmer, Hans-Peter. *The Indispensable PC Hardware Book.* Reading, MA: Addison-Wesley, 2001. ISBN 0-201-87697-3. This is the resource to consult if you are unclear on any aspect of memory or CPUs.

Rosch, Winn. *Hardware Bible.* Indianapolis, IN: Sams Publishing, 1996. ISBN 0-672-30954-8.

http://www.amd.com
The Advanced Micro Design (AMD) home site

http://www.cyrix.com
The Cyrix home site

http://www.intel.com
The Intel Corporation home site

Basic Electronics and Peripherals: Input Devices

Terms you'll need to understand:

- ✓ Resistor, capacitor, ohms, potentiometer (POT)
- ✓ Electrostatic discharge (ESD), electromagnetic interference (EMI)
- ✓ Alternating and direct current, cycle and frequency
- ✓ Pixels, charge-coupled device (CCD), and dots per inch (dpi)

Concepts you'll need to master:

- ✓ Interrupt request (IRQ) lines and direct memory access (DMA) channels
- ✓ Binary and hexadecimal numbering
- ✓ Electricity and circuits
- ✓ Image resolution versus optical resolution

Human beings understand information through written and spoken language, but computers communicate and process in binary machine language (ones and zeros). The results of machine processing—*digital* information—must be turned into something that people can understand—*analog* information. Standing between the human mind and the mechanical PC is some kind of interface, and the three hardware aspects of that interface are input devices, output devices, and storage media devices (i.e., a hard drive).

Whenever we connect something to a motherboard for the purpose of input, storage, or output, we refer to that thing as a *device*. When a device is outside the computer's main case, we generally call it a *peripheral* device. "Peripheral" means on the edge or outside of an area. Standard devices include keyboards, internal disk drives, monitors, and mice. Peripheral devices include scanners, printers, modems, external CD-ROM or DVD drives, and sound cards, to name a few.

The operating system, programs, and applications constitute the software aspects of the interface. The motherboard and associated chips make up the foundation of a basic computer—the core system. Anything else is a peripheral device of some kind. We need a way to talk with a machine, and the various tools we use to accomplish this are called *input devices*. On the other hand, the machine has to talk back to us and this requires *output devices*. We discuss the main output devices (monitors and printers) in Chapter 7.

Typical input devices include such things as keyboards, mice, scanners, and modems. People mostly define peripherals as devices that aren't critical to the operations of a computer. However, even though the devices we just mentioned are considered critical elements, for the sake of this discussion, we'll address them as peripheral devices.

Finally, because RAM doesn't keep information intact when the power is turned off, there must be some way to keep the applications (ways of getting work done) and the work that the applications produce, from disappearing at the end of a session. This requires the storage devices, discussed in Chapter 6.

This chapter and the next two chapters focus on hardware devices. We've mentioned interrupt requests and direct memory access channels in Chapters 2 and 3, but the concepts are more closely related to the devices themselves, rather than to the underlying core system. For this reason, we've decided to examine IRQs and DMAs, as well as computer numbering systems and the basic elements of electronics in this chapter.

Although we could have listed the following segments as concepts you'll need to master, we believe that some of the obscurity associated with computer technology is due to the prevalence of undefined assumptions. By now, you should be familiar with clock ticks as not only a word with a definition, but as a conceptual image. Computers are an interface between the analog world we see around us and the digital world of numbers and steps. The following discussion highlights the difference.

Analog vs. Digital

In the fields of electronics and electrical engineering, analog and digital refer to whether a curve has an infinite number of steps, or whether it has a set of numbered (incremental) steps. Analog information has a potentially limitless number of settings (values) for varying states and conditions. Digital values are either on or off—one or zero, yes or no, exist or not exist. Remember that a "state" is basically the way something is at a specific time. In the analog world, everything changes all the time. In the digital world, there are only encoded "snapshots" of a thing.

Relative to the human mind, analog refers to the perceptions of the world around us. Our minds store mental images, and we interpret those images as information. Computers operate in a digital environment, and are not (yet) capable of interpreting anything. To "interpret" something means to make sense of that thing—to understand it, grasp it, conceptualize it, or provide an explanation. For example, you interpret the words of this book and form a visual concept of the meaning of the word "computers." A machine works only with the encoded characters and their positions in a grid. You might say, "Ah-hah, I see…I get it!" A computer can only be programmed to output a series of characters following a specified condition.

Analog information is abstract (not associated with any specific thing); digital information is concrete (factual). A computer can assign a value of two when it's told to, but it can't hold the infinite values of all possible sets of two. The human mind understands the abstract concept of two, or "two-ness," and can apply it to any set of two specific apples, people, fingers, and so forth. The digital computer understands only a specific two, in a specific situation, at a specific time, in a specific context, and in a specific state.

The digital process can approximate an analog event and assign digital values to represent changing moments of the event over time. For example, the analog concept of "up" can mean many things, with infinite increments of direction and distance relative to gravity. Human beings perceive gravity directly as a feeling of weight, and we know that "up" is "up there." A computer doesn't feel gravity and would ask, "What is up? Starting when, and from where? Which direction, and for how long? What's the definition of direction?"

Because analog information essentially has no boundaries, it includes the presence of noise (random information from random sources). Digital information never varies, has no noise, and always has an exact initial and ending state. An analog brain interprets a pattern of dots on a page of newspaper and sees a picture that means something. The analog mind sees shapes, patterns, and shades of gray.

Magnifying the image shows the underlying digital format of the image, composed of black dots on a white field. The separation values of the dots, along with their sizes and even the yes/no value of a dot's existence, are exact values. There are no shades of gray. Each dot is only black or white. The interpretation of the dots into a shaded picture, then linking the picture with stored memories to form meaningful information, is part of the analog process.

Basic Electricity

Before we move into keyboards, this is a good place to review some of the essential elements of electricity. The exam has some questions relating to concepts like AC, DC, voltage, multimeters, ohms, and basic electricity, so you should know something about the terms. You won't need to be overly concerned with the definition of electrical measurements, but you do need to be familiar with the terms.

If you're already familiar with ohms, resistors, capacitors, and computer electronics, you may choose to skim ahead.

Electricity is actually a flow of electrons. The electrons can be flowing in one direction (Direct Current, DC), or they can change direction, going back and forth (Alternating Current, AC). Both types of flow have unique benefits. Alternating current goes first in one direction, then reverses to the other direction, and then reverses back again in a regular *cyclical* process. In the United States, common AC runs at 60 cycles per second.

We're going to use a common analogy for electricity, where water moves through various hoses, plumbing equipment, and objects. The analogy begins to break down with the idea of AC, given that water usually flows only in one direction. That being said, we'll propose some amount of electricity coming from a power source, and go on from there.

Negative to Positive

Atoms contain an equal number of negatively charged electrons and positively charged protons. Protons are inside the nucleus of an atom and don't move around very much. Electrons travel around the outside of the nucleus, moving all the time—it's in their nature. An atom has a neutral charge because it normally contains an equal number of electrons and protons.

Electrons are actually waves, and protons aren't fully responsible for positive charges, but we'll leave it up to you to research the particle physics.

Electricity flows from a negative charge to a positive charge, not the other way around. Back in the 1700s, when Benjamin Franklin was out there flying his kite in that famous thunderstorm—where he had the metal key attached to the string—he was developing two things. The thing he became famous for was his original theory of electricity. The second—a footnote in history—was that he was trying to think up some kind of a clever comeback for his wife who had told him to go fly a kite.

Franklin theorized that electricity was composed of two charges—positive and negative—and he assigned active movement to the positive charges. For the next 250 years, children would be taught that electricity flows from the positive to the negative. This isn't how electricity works, and neither are electrons little planet-like balls orbiting around a sun-like nucleus. We knew that electrons were waves all the way back in 1910; it's just that nobody told our teachers.

Think of it this way: electrons are used to moving around—it's in their nature. When a bunch (technical term) of electrons take a hike, they leave behind their positive counterparts. A surplus of protons is a positive charge. Something doesn't actually *build* a positive charge, so much as it *loses* negative electrons.

Now suppose that something else comes wandering by with a surplus of electrons. In the first place, electrons are all charged the same way (negative), and so they repel each other. In the second place, opposite charges attract each other, just like in love. Finally, it's a natural law that charges will tend to equalize, moving towards a neutral balance of the same number of electrons and protons.

The thing containing the extra electrons is trying to get rid of the freeloaders, in an attempt to get back to a neutral state. Meanwhile, the thing with the surplus of protons is looking to fall in love with some electrons and hook up for awhile. When the two things reach a critical distance, the extra electrons on the first thing jump to the waiting space on the second thing. The process is called a *discharge*, and if the jump takes place over a gap, we might see a spark. In a moment, we'll refine the story and call the two "things," *plates* in a capacitor.

Circuits

Most of us learned that in order for electricity to flow, we had to build a complete circuit. In other words, electricity had to come out of one terminal; cross through a number of wires and stuff (another technical term); then flow back into a second terminal, using a closed circuit. When you plug a wire into a wall socket, electricity will actually flow out into the wire, giving the wire a potential (possibility) of some kind. The wire carries the same potential (voltage) as the socket.

Electricity will not flow out of a bare-ended wire, all over the floor, creating a mess. Electricity will flow into the wire, but most of it will stay within the wire. However, if you are exceptionally allergic to electrons, you may notice one or two of them in the surrounding carpet.

A capacitor has two plates, separated by a gap. Electricity flows into one plate, somewhat like the way it flows into a wire plugged into a wall socket. The gap prevents the continued flow of current, and so the plate begins to build a potential charge. Remember that electrical properties vary according to length, size, thickness, atomic structure, and various other factors. A wire is a thin piece of metal, but a capacitor plate is much larger and wider than the wire. The plate is capable of holding many more electrons than the wire itself, and you can imagine a sort of funnel, or bottleneck effect, where the wire joins the capacitor plate.

Amps and Volts

Current is the actual number of electrons moving through wire, and we measure it in amps. Voltage, on the other hand, is a measure of the pressure pushing electrons through a medium such as a wire, and is often called "potential." In the United States, most PCs connect to wall sockets providing 110 volts (V). Watts (W) are what you get when you multiply volts by amps, and are often called a "measure of work."

You can think of the current as the amount of water flowing through a hose. The water pressure in the hose is like the voltage. A stream of water hitting you from a garden hose may make you wet, but it won't do much more than that. On the other hand, a stream of water coming from a water cannon can knock you halfway down the block. Even if the water pressure in the water cannon is fairly low, the volume of water coming from it may knock you down. This is similar to the way low voltage with high amperage can do significant injury.

If you multiply the amount of water (amps) by the water pressure (volts), you can figure out if you have enough power (watts) to turn a particular water wheel or light a light bulb. Too little wattage, and a bulb won't work well; too much, and the filament will burn out.

Cycles and Frequencies

Although the power supply converts AC to DC, that doesn't mean that from the point where current enters the PC, we never see alternating current again. Consider the oscillator, vibrating back and forth very quickly. How would that be possible, unless the associated electrical charges were moving back and forth? In fact, some components in a computer re-convert the incoming direct current to very low amperage alternating current. This isn't the AC we've been talking about, but means that small amounts of cyclical current are used for timing and signaling purposes.

If you go back and look at Figure 2.3 in Chapter 2, "Motherboards," you'll see that cycles are represented as waves moving up and down through a midpoint. The height between the top (peak) and bottom (trough) of a single wave cycle is called the *amplitude*. The number of waves being generated in a single second is called the *frequency*.

We can assign a positive association to the half wave moving from the midline up through a peak and returning to the midline. We can assign a negative association to the bottom half of a wave cycle.

Signal information moving through a network cable does so at some frequency number. In Chapter 9 we reference various types of wire specifications, but as an example, Category 4 low-grade cable specifies a transmission rate of 20MHz. This means data signal cycles are passing through the wire at a rate of twenty million per second. Understand that to produce both the timing of the cycles and the characteristic up-reverse-down pattern of a wave, the direct current must be changed back to an alternating, cyclical flow pattern.

Electromagnetic Interference—EMI

When something holds an electrical charge, it also produces a field. A field has a direction of flow, and you've probably seen magnetic fields when you held a magnet under a piece of paper holding some iron filings. All electrical circuits produce fields and have an influence, to some degree or another, on the atomic structure of their surrounding environment. When electricity modifies a surrounding area, we call it (simplistically) an *electromagnetic field*. When an electromagnetic field modifies the surrounding environment, we call that a *field effect*. The modification generated by strong electrical currents and their fields is called *electromagnetic interference* (EMI).

By way of example, a device called a *ballast* generates a powerful spark in order to fire the gases contained in a fluorescent lighting tube. The power required by the ballast is sufficient to radiate a field quite a distance from the unit itself. Fluorescent lights produce a large amount of EMI.

Electricity flowing through a conductor generates a field moving roughly similar to the flow of current. Small currents, such as those in a parallel or video cable, have a lesser impact than large currents. Even so, when you bundle many cables next to each other, where the current is moving in similar directions, each cable enhances the field effect and can increase their combined EMI.

ESD means Electro-Static Discharge. EMI means Electro-Magnetic Interference. When many electrical wires are placed near or next to each other, you can have EMI. Fluorescent lights (with their ballast) can also cause EMI. However, rubbing a cat's fur the wrong way or walking on a carpet when you work on a computer, can generate ESD.

Electrostatic Discharge (ESD) and ESD Kits

Your body routinely builds up static electricity that discharges to the ground when you touch something conductive. When this takes place, we call it an *ElectroStatic Discharge* (ESD). Before we get into our discussion of microprocessors, you should understand how static electricity could easily destroy the tiny components and circuits inside a computer. Computers are excellent conductors and because of this, you'll be required to understand exam questions related to ESD.

Microprocessors are manufactured on extremely small bits of silicon, with well over 1,000 components packed into wafers much thinner than a human hair. In this kind of crowd, an amazingly small electrical discharge can wreak havoc. Keep in mind that most processors run on less than 5 volts of current. Many people think that an ESD incident either will totally destroy an IC board or cause no damage at all. In other words, if you've worked on a computer and it functions when you've finished, then apparently there was no problem with static electricity. This isn't the case.

Human beings have an "awareness threshold" of approximately 3,000 volts, meaning that we probably won't feel a spark discharge below this level. On the other hand, walking across a carpet can produce anywhere between 1,500 to 35,000 volts of static electricity, depending upon the humidity of the surrounding air. Picking up a plastic bag can charge your body with between 1,200 and 20,000 volts. As long as the charge is contained within your body, you probably won't even notice it (until your hair begins standing on end).

ESD problems fall into three categories, with catastrophic failure—the component is killed—being only one of them. Latent failures are where a component has been damaged, but it continues to function. Over time, these weakened components begin to fail, losing data integrity or capabilities, until they eventually fail completely. An upset failure is where the discharge current is just enough to produce intermittent failures (gateway leaks). In many instances, an IC board with an upset failure will pass every quality control test and enter the field. However, like a damaged memory cell, the machine may develop a history of software losses, data corruption, and other hard-to-find problems.

ESD Kits

Before you touch anything inside a computer, you should at least ground yourself by touching a metal part of the chassis (e.g., the power supply casing or the metal frame of the chassis). The problem with this solution is that although the computer and your body have equalized, the charge is still contained within the combined system. It hasn't been removed (discharged). A better way to ground yourself is to use an ESD kit.

An ESD kit consists of a wrist strap with a built-in resistor (discussed in Chapter 5), connected to a ground wire. The kit also includes a special floor mat that discharges a current into the ground, bypassing the computer. An ESD kit with a floor mat is the only way to move the charge to the ground, thereby fully removing the charge.

Remember that an ESD kit uses a wrist strap (with a resistor), and the strap is connected to a ground wire. The kit should also include a grounded floor mat, but the exam may not include the mat in a choice of responses.

By the way: perhaps you've heard someone suggest that you should place circuit boards, system boards, and loose chips on a piece of aluminum foil. This is not a good idea. Placing these pieces on aluminum foil can result in a small explosion, due to the fact that many motherboards, expansion cards, and other boards have built-in lithium or nickel cadmium (Nicad) batteries. If these batteries become short-circuited, they can overheat and react violently; exploding and throwing off pieces of their metal casings.

Never place a circuit board of any kind onto conductive surfaces, such as metal foil. Remember the ESD is electro*static* *d*ischarge. On the other hand, EMI is *e*lectro*m*agnetic *i*nterference (when several wires are placed in close proximity).

Electronic Components

There are hundreds of basic electrical components, but two important ones to know (for the exam) are resistors and capacitors. Keep in mind that when you connect a number of electrical components together and move electrical current through them, you have a circuit. Transistors are foundational to computer technology, but you won't be expected to answer any questions about transistors or diodes on the exam.

Resistors and Ohms

Resistors "resist" (hold back) the flow of electricity. You may have encountered a sentence such as, "The pilgrim's progress was impeded by the thick vegetation and many rivers he encountered along the way." Impedance means that forward movement is blocked, resisted, or slowed down. Resistors and the structure of wire slow down current. The more the resistance, the more the flow is impeded, and we measure that impedance in ohms.

Some resistors, called *potentiometers* (or "pots"), can change the amount of resistance. A good example of a potentiometer is the volume control on a radio. When you turn the volume control, you vary the resistance. This directly affects the current flowing to the speakers, and as such, controls the volume.

Multimeters

At one time, individual meters were used to measure different electrical values; voltmeters measured electrical potential, ohmmeters measured resistance, and so on. Often, one instrument was used for direct current and a different one for alternating current. Today, most of these instruments have been combined into one instrument called a *multimeter*. Most multimeters are small and portable, and they can measure ohms, volts, and amps for both DC and AC. They are simply the most versatile test instruments you can have.

When you use a multimeter to check a circuit, remember that a complete circuit has no resistance. A complete circuit has a reading of 0 ohms.

Dielectrics

The amount of resistance in a circuit usually depends on three things: the length of a wire, the thickness of a wire, and the type of metal. However, not all circuits require wire. A dielectric is a material that does a poor job of conducting (directing movement) electricity to one degree or another. When a material is a poor conductor, we call it an *insulator*, or *insulation*, and it has a high *dielectric constant*. The material may still pass electrons (conduct) to some degree, but not very efficiently.

You will not be tested on dielectrics, but you should know that air has a dielectric constant of 1.0. The higher the constant, the less conductivity, and the more the material is an insulator. Rubber, with a high dielectric constant, is a good insulator. Water and gold, with low dielectric constants, are good conductors.

Capacitors

Technically, a capacitor (once known as a *condenser*) is formed by separating (a gap) two conductive plates (things) with a dielectric—the insulating material we just mentioned. You might imagine a tiny battlefield with small hills on either side. The hills are the plates, and the battlefield is the dielectric. Electrons really don't like each other very much—it's in their nature. In a capacitor, they constantly stare across the dielectric at each other, waiting for the chance to go grab some positive proton babes and have a party.

If we push electrons into one plate of a capacitor, the electrons would like to move across the dielectric to the other plate; grab all the positive charges; and kick butt on any electrons they find over on the other plate. Instead, because of the insulating qualities of the dielectric, they just keep piling up on the plate, staring across the gap until the flow of electrons (current) eventually stops.

When increased direct current is applied to a capacitor plate, electrons continue to build up until they reach a high enough potential to jump across the dielectric (or charge across the battlefield). If the current is powerful enough, that jump (discharge) will destroy the dielectric, killing the capacitor. But let's examine what happens when alternating current is sent to one plate. Remember that in half a cycle, the flow goes in one direction; in the next half-cycle, the flow reverses.

Imagine a current flowing into one plate of the capacitor. Electrons begin to build, forming a negative charge. At the same time, the force of repulsion in those electrons is pushing away any electrons on the other side of the dielectric—the gap in the circuit. If enough electrons on the opposite side of the dielectric are pushed away, that other plate takes on a positive charge. When the flow reverses, electrons go with the flow, so to speak, reducing the negative charge in the first plate, which leads to a positive charge. This attracts the electrons back to the other plate, making it negatively charged.

Let's summarize all this, setting aside the analogies. Capacitors contain two plates with a dielectric between them. They create a small gap in a circuit. Electricity flows into one plate, forming a negative charge. The negative charge "influences" the other plate, repelling its electrons. As those electrons "run away" from the first plate, the second plate takes on a positive charge. When the current cycle reverses, the two plates change roles, and the first plate takes on a positive charge.

In this way, a capacitor is able to pass alternating current across a small gap in a circuit. Capacitors are sometimes used in a circuit, to prevent or slow—filter—the passage of direct current, allowing for the passage of alternating current.

Storage Capacity

Suppose your friend holds a small barrel, where the top "plate" and the bottom "plate" are separated by the air in the barrel. You've connected a small hose (wire, or lead) to the bottom of the barrel, and the other end of the hose is connected to a faucet (power supply). When you turn on the faucet, water (electrons) flows through the thin hose (current) and up into the barrel. When you turn the faucet off, gravity pushes the water in the barrel back down into the hose until the pressure is equalized.

There isn't much time for water to flow out of the barrel, because very quickly, you turn the faucet back on again. In a small barrel (capacitor), most of the water leaks out fairly quickly. In a large barrel, it takes time for the water to leak out across the bottleneck of the connection to the thin hose. In this way, capacitors can be made to build a stored charge. Alternating current is like turning the faucet on, then turning it off, then turning it on, then turning it off; over and over again in cycles.

Now suppose you decide to play a trick on your friend, and you connect the hose to a fire hydrant. The next time you turn on the water, the pressure drives so much water into the barrel that it blows off the top. Imagine the shock on your friend's face! This is what happens when direct current is applied to a capacitor beyond its design rating.

Capacitors store a charge for a short period of time. Small capacitors quickly leak away their charge (as we mentioned in Chapter 3, "Memory"). Large capacitors, such as those used in power supplies, can store a huge charge, and are capable of delivering a nasty shock even when the power cord has been disconnected. We've seen the tip of a screwdriver vaporized by accidentally shorting the terminals of a capacitor! Replace the word "screwdriver" with "finger," and you can see why power supplies are given a great deal of respect.

Power supplies contain capacitors that can store very high charges. Batteries and power supplies must be disposed of according to local government ordinances. Improper handling of a power supply can result in electrocution and other depressing problems.

HAZMAT and MSD Sheets

Keep in mind that power supplies and integrated circuit (IC) boards can be classified as *Hazardous Material (HAZMAT)*, which may require special disposal considerations. Whenever hazardous materials are present in the workplace, U.S. law requires that a readily accessible Material Support Data (MSD) sheet be on-site and in a known location. These sheets, usually in a looseleaf binder, provide the details of that material and how to handle it properly. MSD sheets can almost always be downloaded or printed from the Internet.

Disposing of power supplies, a battery backup Uninterruptible Power Supply (UPS), integrated circuit boards, and printed circuit boards may be subject to federal laws and/or local ordinances.

Lastly, capacitors may be used in situations using a powerful jolt of electricity to produce work. No, you can't call a cup of coffee in the morning a capacitor! Imagine a thin wire connected to a big, heavy motor. The wire can only carry a limited amount of current, partly because of its size. If we were to connect that wire to a capacitor with very large plates, then we could build up a very high charge inside that capacitor. If we were then able to discharge the capacitor, the resulting current would flood into the motor at many times the level possible with only the wire. This is somewhat how an automobile ignition system functions.

Capacitance—literally a capacitor's capacity—is the number of electrons a plate in a capacitor can hold under a given electrical pressure (voltage). We measure capacitance in farads (not on the exam), and the more charge a device can hold, the greater its capacitance.

The Power Supply

The power supply converts alternating current to direct current at the voltages required by the system components, usually 24V, 12V, 5V, and 3V. In the United States, typical wall outlets provide 110VAC (Volts in AC form). Although the power supply is technically not a component of the motherboard, it is physically attached to the computer case, and connects to the motherboard through either a single, keyed connector, or a set of two connectors. The single-key connector was developed to eliminate the possibility of destroying a motherboard by reversing the connectors.

Keying a connector means designing the plug and the socket with matching notches. If the notches don't line up, the plug can't fit into the socket. Note that connectors are keyed, but chips are indexed.

The motherboard distributes power to all its system components, except for high-current components, such as the main cooling fan, or disk drives that connect directly to the power supply. Today's power supplies may be rated at anywhere from 300 to 400 watts or more, and are capable of powering almost any configuration of system components. Older computers, such as the early XTs, had power supplies rated at less than 100W and often failed to meet the demand of additional components.

The power supply is a swap-out, or exchange component, rather than a repair item. Voltage and current levels within a power supply can be lethal. Furthermore, computer-grade capacitors can hold a charge even after the supply is unplugged. Always treat a power supply with respect and replace it if defective. Do not repair it!

Interrupt Requests (IRQs)

We saw in Chapter 3 that, when the CPU is busy with a process, any request by the memory controller must interrupt what the CPU is doing. The specific instructions for these interruptions are provided by the ROM BIOS on both the motherboard and on many devices. The operating system also understands interrupts, and uses part of low memory to store something called the *interrupt vector table*. Low memory is discussed in Chapter 11.

We'll explore the Windows Device Manager in Chapter 14 "Troubleshooting," but even in Plug-and-Play systems, resolving IRQ conflicts can be a real chore. The Device Manager reports out the IRQ and DMA channel being used by various devices attached to the core system.

If you think of the CPU as the Wizard of Oz, then an IRQ line is like an 8- or a 16-lane yellow brick road. An IRQ is a signal from a piece of hardware (for example., a mouse) indicating that it needs the CPU to do something. To take pressure off the CPU, IBM created a chip called an *interrupt controller*, which is analogous to that weird gatekeeper to the Emerald City.

When a piece of hardware sends a demand to the busy CPU, it tries to interrupt the processing by sending an IRQ down its own, assigned IRQ line. The IRQ signals (Dorothy and pals) run along the IRQ lines (yellow brick road) to an interrupt controller (that bizarre gatekeeper), which assigns priorities to incoming IRQs (puts them in the waiting room) and then delivers them to the CPU (the Wizard).

Because the interrupt controller (different from the memory controller) expects signals from only one hardware device per IRQ line, an IRQ conflict occurs when two devices try to use the same IRQ line, much like two cars using the same lane at the same time. When that happens, computers (like the cars) usually crash. The gatekeeper loses his mind, and you're left in the poppy fields! This is why assigning IRQs to new hardware as you install it is so important—and why it can be such a pain when it goes wrong. A technical term for this pain is *major aggravation*. This is also why so much effort went into developing "Plug and Play," which helps the computer and new devices figure out all the IRQs on their own.

Plug and Play was commonly contracted to plug 'n' play when spoken out loud. In the typical way that computer terminology is often a result of irreverent language usage, reference manuals contracted the term even further and abbreviated it as PnP. Computers were invented by people who wanted to get things done faster, and so most of the language, programming words, execution steps, and mechanics are founded on the shortest way possible of accomplishing a task. Additionally, severe memory restrictions in the original computers required the bare minimum of characters in any set of instructions.

IRQ 2 Cascades to IRQ 9

The original XT interrupt controller chip could handle only eight IRQs at once. Starting with the AT and continuing through the ATX to modern PCs, motherboards began using two interrupt line controllers. Each controller is able to handle eight lines (0–7 and 8–15). To get the two controllers working together, IRQ 2 on the first controller is set aside to pass certain requests to IRQ 9 on the second controller. This is known as *cascading*.

By daisy-chaining the two chips—running them in series—the AT motherboard could handle 16 IRQs at the same time. ATX motherboards continue the precedent set by the AT boards, so all in all, there are 16 IRQ lines—IRQ 0 through IRQ 15. The concept of daisy-chaining spread throughout the hardware industry, beginning with IRQ and SCSI controllers, and continuing with USB and FireWire devices. These devices, along with chaining are discussed in Chapter 8.

The AT controllers began using interrupts 8–15 and left the original XT lines 0–7. Because of this, the old IRQ 2 is often borrowed by the new IRQ 9 using something called *cascading*. Be sure to know the term *cascading* for the exam.

Make a note that if IRQ 2 is being used by BIOS instructions, IRQ 9 is also being used. IRQ 9 is cascading, vectoring, or redirecting to IRQ 2. All three words refer to the same process of pointing to somewhere else. This is a typical question on the exam. When source information is redirected to a destination, the destination receives cascaded information from that source.

Hexadecimal Numbering

We just presented a concept that you may not have encountered before. We said that AT boards had 16 IRQs, and we then made the highest number 15. The decimal, hexadecimal, and binary numbering systems all start with zero. Our habit is to think of the "first" of something as being number 1, but in the world of computers and technology, you need to become accustomed to the first thing being numbered 0.

Never forget that in computer technology, the "first" of something is numbered with a 0 (zero). For instance, the primary (master) hard drive is Drive 0.

If you remember your high school math, the number of digits that can fit into the units (ones) column, is called the *base*. The word "decimal," from the Latin "ten," allows 10 digits in the ones column (0–9). Decimal numbering is also called *base-10*. In base-10 numbering, when you have more than 10 digits, you cross over and put a 1 to the tens column.

In regular counting, we start with a one and go to a nine. When we add one more number, we put a 0 in the ones column, a 1 in the tens column, and make a "10." In computer math, we start with zero! When we get to the end of the allowed numbers in the ones column, we go back to the beginning, put down a zero, and move a one to the tens column.

Binary Numbers—Base-2

Someone once said that there are only 10 kinds of people in the world: those who understand binary, and those who don't. Binary refers to base-2 numbers, in that only two units are used before you begin using the tens column. In base-2 numbering, you can have only a 0 and a 1 in the ones column. There is no "two," and you have to go to the tens column instead. You put a 1 to the left of the zero after two digits (binary), just as you do after ten digits in base-10 numbers (decimal).

There's actually no "10" symbol in decimal numbering. The word "ten" actually describes only a one in the tens column and a zero in the ones column. Ten is the same word in any base of numbering, but we get to that 10 by a different number of units in the ones column. In base-3 numbers we would count zero, one, two...ten.

Binary (base-2) counting would be: zero, one, ten, eleven, one hundred, one hundred and one, one hundred and ten, one hundred and eleven, one thousand. The same sequence in symbols would be 0, 1, 10, 11, 100, 101, 110, 111, and 1000. Because binary has only ones and zeros, there's no such thing as a "two." The two is replaced by what we think of as a 10. Confusing? Of course! That's what computers are all about. The exam probably won't have any binary or hexadecimal math, but you need to know the concept.

The largest eight-bit binary number is 11111111, which is made up of eight "ones," and converts to 255 in decimal. By an amazing coincidence, the last character in the American Standard Code for Information Interchange (ASCII) keyboard character translation table is 255, which is a blank space. On the other hand, decimal/binary zero is also a space, so maybe it's not that incredible.

Hexadecimal Numbers—Base-16

Hexadecimal is base-16 numbering, where numbers in the ones column must go beyond 10 digits, all the way to 16 digits. For that, we need to use letters, because decimal numbering (base-10) has only ten available digits—0, 1, 2, 3, 4, 5, 6, 7, 8, 9—before we make a 10. Hexadecimal (often abbreviated as Hex, H, or h) adds A, B, C, D, E, and F. Fortunately, computers were invented long after we stopped using Roman numerals!

Counting a full, hexadecimal sequence would be: 0, 1, 2, 3, 4, 5, 6, 7, 8, 9, A (no ten), B (11), C (12), D (13), E (14), and F (15). Note how the A replaces the 10. The "F" represents the "tens" column crossover point, just like the nine does in decimal numbers. In this case, 15 (the F) is the sixteenth digit and the last that can fit in the ones column. Don't forget that zero was the first digit.

Following F (in base-16) would come a "tens unit," so the next number is 10. The sequence continues as 11, 12, 13, 14, 15, 16, 17, 18, 19, 1A, 1B, 1C, 1D, 1E, 1F, and then another tens unit, making 20.

Hexadecimal numbering allows for cramming more information into a smaller space. For example, the decimal 255 is three bits—two, five, five. However, it becomes FFh (two bits) in Hex. Observe the small "h" following the number. This references the number as being a hexadecimal number, and is *not* a third symbol in the number itself.

Be sure to remember that computer memory addresses are usually written in hexadecimal notation. Hex notation can appear as 10h, 10H, &H10, or &h10, but the first two formats are the most common. Therefore, decimal 255 is typically written as FFh in hexadecimal format. The actual hex address is "FF" with the "h" letting the reader know that this is a hexadecimal number.

Direct Memory Access (DMA)

A number of semi-intelligent chips work together with the CPU. The interrupt controller, which handles IRQs, is one of these chips. We've mentioned the memory controller, and another peripheral chip is the Direct Memory Access (DMA) controller. Following the IRQ technology, the first DMA controller had four channels. A second one was soon added and chained to the first. Like IRQ lines, DMA channels are limited in number, and you can allocate only one channel to one device. There are 8 DMA channels.

No matter how fast the CPU runs, it can easily be loaded down if it wants to send data to something like a very slow (relative to the CPU) hard drive. If this is the case, the CPU then has to wait around for the drive to report back. This movement of data from slow disk to fast memory used to have to pass through some very small memory registers in the CPU. The DMA controller was developed to offload this sort of drudge work and to avoid bottlenecks in processing.

Offloading work from the CPU has been a driving force behind the development of such things as synchronous RAM, video cards, and the AGP, to mention only a few.

The DMA controller is like a highway bypass. It bypasses the CPU registers and moves information directly into and out of RAM. In another astounding coincidence, this is why it's called "direct memory" access! The DMA controller chip is capable of taking over control of the system, but must first request control from the microprocessor. When this happens, the CPU makes itself appear as though it has been removed from the circuit.

When the hard drive needs to access RAM for addresses or instructions, those interrupt requests don't have to interrupt the CPU. Fewer interruptions means more work gets done (just like in real life) and better system performance.

Originally, a motherboard had only one DMA controller. The system worked so well, that a second DMA controller was added. Each controller allows four channels, so today we have 8 DMA channels (0–7) available on most systems.

DMA Channels

Modern (AT-class) PCs have two DMA controllers. Each controller provides four channels for fast DMA. Again, a device can use a DMA channel to bypass the CPU and send information directly into main memory. DMA is used to increase performance. IRQs are used to connect hardware devices.

The original 8088/86 (8-bit/16-bit) processors provided 4 DMA channels that were capable of supporting both 8- and 16-bit cards. The 80286 added 4 more 16-bit-only channels. Table 5.1 lists the DMA channels and the most common devices configured to use them.

Table 5.1 Direct memory accessing channels.

DMA Channel	Bus Width	Default Device
0	NA	DRAM refresh
1	8- or 16-bit	Sound cards (low)
2	8- or 16-bit	Floppy disks
3	8- or 16-bit	Not assigned
4	NA	Cascade to DMA 5-7
5	16-bit	Sound cards (high)
6	16-bit	Not assigned
7	16	Not assigned

It's very good policy to follow the instructions for setting IRQs, DMA channels, and I/O ports according to the manufacturer's recommendation, especially with sound cards and scanners. Install the sound card first and then let it find the IRQ and DMA channel it needs. Install everything else next. Install the sound card before CD-ROM drives as well; then let the CD take whatever DMA channel is open.

32-bit Windows provides a listing of the in-use DMA channels by selecting the My Computer properties and then the Device Manager's "View Resources" tab.

IRQs, DMA, and I/O Ports

The certification exam has a number of questions about IRQs, COM and LPT port addresses, and direct memory addressing (DMA) channels. Remember that IRQs interrupt the CPU. A DMA channel is a shortcut around the main expansion bus that allows a device to access memory directly.

DMA channels and IRQ lines interconnect devices, the CPU, and memory. You should document the current devices and their IRQs and DMA settings before you install and configure a new device. Table 5.2 lists IRQ lines and their default device services. In Chapter 14 "Troubleshooting," we discuss several utility tools used to find IRQs. One of the original diagnostic tools provided with DOS was the MicroSoft Diagnostics executable, MSD.EXE. This can still be found on Windows 9x installation CDs.

Table 5.2 A typical MSD.EXE report of IRQ usage.

Device	IRQ	Handler
Timer output	0	WIN386.EXE
Keyboard	1	Block device
Cascade from IRQ 9	2	BIOS
COM2, COM4 (serial ports)	3	BIOS
COM1, COM3 (serial ports)	4	BIOS
LPT2 (parallel port, XT drive)	5	BIOS
Floppy disk controller	6	Default handler
LPT1 (parallel port)	7	System
Real-time clock	8	Default handler
Redirected IRQ2 (video, network)	9	BIOS
(Reserved)	10	BIOS
(Reserved)	11	BIOS
(Reserved), built-in mouse	12	Default handler
Math coprocessor	13	BIOS
Primary fixed disk controller (IDE)	14	BIOS
Secondary fixed disk controller	15	Default handler

IRQ 5 and IRQ 7 are usually taken by a printer. Typically, IRQ 7 is always taken (LPT1), but IRQ 5 might be available in a configuration situation (e.g., for a sound card).

Remember that 16 IRQs are available to devices. Because the IRQs are numbered in the hexadecimal numbering system, the first IRQ is 0. The upper limit is IRQ 15. There are 16 IRQs to conform with hex memory addressing (base 16) and the 16 segments of conventional memory.

IRQ 14

IRQ 14 is set-aside for the primary IDE (AT) drive controller. The primary controller is often referred to as a master controller, the master drive, Drive 0, the primary hard drive, or the first hard disk. Note that the device is Device 0, but the IRQ is 14. Most motherboards have two drive controllers, and each controller can have two devices. In most cases, we speak of the master controller and the secondary controller. The second controller uses IRQ 15.

Each IDE or EIDE controller can have two devices chained to it. The first device is usually the *master*, with the second device being the *slave*. A slave might be a second hard drive or a CD-ROM drive. IRQ 15 (the last IRQ) is typically set-aside for the secondary IDE drive controller, *not a second drive*.

Ordinarily, a second disk is chained to the IDE controller. Remember that IDE controllers allow for a daisy chain of two devices, so the master and slave usually connect to a single controller.

Remember that the default IRQ 14 is used for the primary hard disk IDE controller. IRQ 15 most likely is used for either a *third* physical disk, or a slower drive of some kind. More typically, two physical disks use the primary controller on IRQ 14. Adding a third disk requires using a second IDE controller, which then uses IRQ 15.

Be sure you don't get confused by a response on the exam that refers to IRQ 16. There isn't any number 16. If you can remember that hex (Latin for *6*, e.g., *hex*agon) numbering uses 16 numbers starting at 0, at least the numbers assigned to the last IRQs make sense; 14 is primary and 15 is secondary for the disk controllers.

Pay close attention to questions that ask about a master controller and a secondary drive. IRQ 14 and 15 are the two important IRQs, but there can be four IDE drives.

I/O Addresses

We know that a PC has a number of Input/Output devices connected to the motherboard. Each device requires a unique I/O hardware address. Programs and the operating system send instructions to, and read instructions from, the hardware by placing calls to an I/O address. The first megabyte of conventional memory has room for one million real addresses used by data (Real Mode). Extended memory allows for many millions more data addresses. Usually, only about 800 addresses can be used as hardware addresses.

Some memory addresses are reserved for system use, and a typical device uses 4, 8, or 32 bytes of address information. Some of the hardware addresses have been predefined as available for use by the most common devices (although they might not always be used for that purpose).

We did see questions having to do with the origin of a hardware address. During the POST, the BIOS checks the CMOS tables for the existence of an I/O port interface. If this port exists, the CPU assigns a hardware memory address and stores the address in memory for the length of the running session. The main I/O ports (for example, LPT and COM ports) have common default settings.

After the device has a hardware memory address (from the CPU), the operating system uses the low-memory IRQ vector table (see Chapter 11) to point to their addresses. These addresses are used when moving instructions back and forth between the device and the software.

User-configurable devices store configuration settings that tell the device to use a particular port and an I/O address. Often, the I/O address is described in either the CONFIG.SYS or the AUTOEXEC.BAT file.

Ports and IRQs

"Port" is derived from "portal," which is an entranceway to something. A door is a physical portal, but a computer interface is a logical port. Because we carry things through a doorway, another use of the word carry is "portage," which also reduces to "port." When an application can be carried (ported) over to another platform, we say it is portable. Finally, port interfaces like the COM and LPT ports are divided into logical ports with separate memory addresses. The Internet (TCP/IP) often uses virtual ports as the final entryway into a destination computer. If this all sounds impossible, implausible, or immaterial, remember that it's imPORTant!

Physical or Logical

When you can pick something up and hold it in your hands, it is a physical something. Physical things are also called concrete, actual, real, or tangible. Ideas cannot be picked up and handled, but they have consequences in the physical, real world. To differentiate between concrete components (ware) and the written instructions contained in a program, we use "hard" and "soft." Hardware can fall on your foot and break your toe. Software is physical, in that it has actual symbols and characters, but it won't fall on your foot and break your toe.

But what differentiates the characters in a program from the ideas and logic behind those characters? Ideas and logic are abstractions, in that they exist in a mental, or abstract realm. Abstractions are concepts that aren't limited to a specific instance. When abstract ideas are used to construct devices that aren't physical but act in the same way as a physical device, we call the device a *logical* or *virtual* device. This is the idea behind partitions (FDISK) and logical drives (FORMAT).

A physical disk is round and has many cylinders. A logical drive is an idea held in the "mind" of the operating system. Physical RAM is made up of modules, capacitors, and transistors. Virtual memory, such as a RAM disk, is a nonphysical area of memory that acts in the same way as a disk. Virtual memory can be made to act as a virtual drive, which acts like a logical drive on a physical disk. You have the right to remain silent, and the right to be totally confused!

Real memory is made up of things you can put in a shopping bag and install onto a motherboard. Windows uses Real Mode to address this real memory. Hardware has real instructions in a real software program called a *software driver.* Windows can also control disk space and extended memory, and create virtual storage, or virtual memory. Windows can create an abstraction of a specific device driver and load it into memory. This is a virtual device driver, otherwise known as a *VxD.*

COM Ports

Each logical port has its own default memory address. Most modern computers have several, physical, serial interfaces built into the motherboard. Two of those physical interfaces are broken up into four logical COM ports. COM1 and COM3 go together with the first serial interface. COM2 and COM4 go together with a second serial interface. USB ports, discussed in Chapter 8, are also serial ports, designed for fast serial transfers.

In the real world, you'll be able to research memory addresses such as those of the COM and LPT ports on a given PC. However, the exam contains questions about ports and memory addresses. Even on an old DOS machine, MSD.EXE prints out whether a device is attached to either of the serial ports and which address the device is using. For the purposes of the exam, Table 5.3 lists the default memory addresses assigned to each COM port.

Table 5.3 Default COM port addresses and IRQs.

I/O Serial Interface	Port	Address (Hexadecimal)	IRQ
Controller 1	COM 1	03F8	4
Controller 1	COM 3	03E8	4
Controller 2	COM 2	02F8	3
Controller 2	COM 4	02E8	3

Here's a mnemonic that might help you build COM addresses during the exam. Observe that the only changing address values are "2-3" and "F-E." All four default addresses begin with 0 and end with 8. The only IRQ choices are 4 and 3.

It might help to think of COM3 and COM4 as "Extra," with an "E" hex address. COM1 and COM2 are "First," with an "F" hex address. The exam is multiple choice, so you won't really need to remember the 0 or the 8.

Using an odd/even trick, COM1 and 3 use the "3" (odd address) and COM2 and 4 the "2" (even address). In other words:

- Port 1 (odd), COM1 and 3, use odd "03" (03xx).
- Port 2 (even), COM2 and 4, use even "02" (02xx).
- First (Ph)ysical interfaces 1 and 2 use "F" for First (xxF8).
- Extra logical interfaces 3 and 4 use an "E" for Extra (xxE8).
- The even ports (2 and 4) use odd IRQ 3. The odd ports (1 and 3) use even IRQ 4.

LPT Ports

Aside from the COM ports, the default printer (LPT) ports and their IRQs are also considered testable knowledge. The good news is that although the default COM port memory addresses are considered common knowledge, the LPT addresses aren't. LPT ports have a range of addresses, though they commonly try for a default address. Table 5.4 lists the two LPT ports and their default IRQs.

Table 5.4 LPT2 and LPT1 and their default IRQ lines.

Parallel Interface	IRQ
LPT2 (parallel port)	5
LPT1 (parallel port)	7

LPT2 is rarely used these days, except on network print servers (PCs under the control of a network operating system and dedicated to managing a shared printer). IRQ 5 is much more often assigned to a sound card on stand-alone systems. In fact, IRQ 5 is the default for SoundBlaster cards, with LPT1 going to IRQ 7. If LPT2 is being used, it is usually assigned to IRQ 5 and 278h.

LPT2 comes first because IRQ 5 was originally the XT hard drive controller's IRQ. Later PCs had a normal configuration of two parallel ports, so LPT2 took over from the obsolete XT controller. Nowadays, most likely you'll never see a workstation with more than one parallel port.

We've tried to come up with some ways to help you remember the proper order of the LPT ports and their default IRQs. Here are some suggestions, although you might have your own method:

- "There's only 1 God and only 1 heaven, and LPT1 uses IRQ 7."
- P-R-I-N-T-E-R has 7 letters.
- You have two hands with five fingers (each). LPT2 uses IRQ 5
- 1 (LPT1) and 2 (LPT2) make "12." In the same way, 7 + 5 = 12

Summary—IRQs, DMAs, and Electricity

It may seem, at this point, that the discussion so far has had little to do with input devices. In one sense that may be true, but all of the devices we're about to explore connect with the motherboard in the real world. You can't really isolate a keyboard, and analyze it without understanding how the motherboard and operating system views the keyboard. You're going to have to know the following main points on the exam, and we felt that by putting them into this first chapter on peripherals, it would help form a surrounding context:

- EMI and ESD—related to field effects and electrical discharges.
- Resistors, capacitors, ohms, and multimeters—basic electronic components used in all computer environments
- Hexadecimal numbering—knowing how to recognize a hex address.
- IRQ lines—the commonly referenced interrupts for hard drives, and how to differentiate a master from a slave. You'll also have to know the IRQs for printer and COM ports.
- DMA channels—how many channels, and how many controllers.

Keyboards

Arguably, the most important peripheral component is the keyboard. A keyboard has a set of keys with language symbols for a human operator. When you press a key, it generates an electrical signal, and a microprocessor in the keyboard changes the signal to a digital code—a scan code. It then sends the scan code to the computer. Most PCs check to see whether a keyboard is attached during the Power-On, Self-Test (POST) process, and generate a keyboard error message if a keyboard can't be found. We discuss the POST at length in Chapter 11.

Switch Technology: Mechanical

Depending on how an electronic signal is generated by the key, there are two basic types of keyboards: switches and capacitive. Switch technology tries to solve two problems: how to produce an electrical contact, and how to get the keycap back up after it's been pressed. The four basic switches are:

- *Pure mechanical*—Metal contacts and a spring, providing audible feedback with a "click," along with resistance feedback for touch typists. They are durable and usually self-cleaning, and they last around 20 million keystrokes.
- *Foam element*—Like a plunger, but using foam, metal foil, and a spring. Compressible foam attaches to a stem, with a foil contact attached under the foam. Circuit board contacts are closed when the foil bridges them. The spring pushes the key back up after it's pressed. Foil gets dirty with corrosion, leading to intermittent key strikes. The foam reduces bounce, but at the same time, it gives the keyboard a "mushy" feel. Because the lack of audible feedback tends to hinder touch typists, they sometimes resort to sending a clicking sound to the PC speaker to provide audible feedback.
- *Rubber dome*—A rubber dome, similar to half of a handball with a carbon button contact on the underside of the dome, which resists corrosion better than the foil of the foam switch. On a key press, the dome begins to collapse and then "snaps through" like the handball, which is good tactile feedback. Key release allows the rubber to re-form, pushing the key back up. This type of keyboard is sealed, protecting the contacts from dust and dirt, and has few moving parts, making it reliable and inexpensive. However, it doesn't provide enough tactile feedback for the touch typist.
- *Membrane sheet*—A simplified version of the rubber dome, placing all keys together on what looks like a single-sheet rubber dome. This limits key travel, making membrane switches impractical for touch typists. Because the keys and membrane are sealed together, the keyboard is practically spill- and dustproof. This type is often used in commercial and industrial environments for simple data entry (for example, cash registers).

Debouncing

In mechanical and dome-type switches, most keys bounce somewhat when you press them, leading to several high-speed contacts. Keyboards also generate some amount of electrical noise whenever you press a key, which the CPU could interpret as something you meant to do. To clean up the noise, and to help the keyboard processor determine real key presses from noise, the processor constantly scans the keyboard, looking at the state (condition and status) of every key. This constant scanning is why you should never plug in or unplug a keyboard while the power is on.

Typically, *debouncing* waits for two scans before deciding that a key is legitimately depressed. Usually, key bounce is far faster than a human being can press a key twice.

Capacitive Technology: Nonmechanical

Capacitive switches are the most expensive keyboards. They last longer, resist dust and dirt even better than rubber dome keyboards, and are the only nonmechanical keyboards currently in use. Additionally, they offer the highest level of tactile feedback of any switch.

A capacitive switch puts the two conductive plates of a capacitor inside a switch housing. The upper plate connects to the key plunger (stem), and the bottom plate connects to a voltage sensor on the integrated circuit board inside the keyboard housing. Every key on the keyboard has its own voltage sensor.

A tiny amount of voltage continually charges the bottom plate under the key. When a key is up (normal state), the voltage and charge remain constant, and the flow is static (not changing). Electrons gather on the bottom plate until it can hold no more and the system reaches a balance point. However, when the key is pressed downward, the positive plate on the plunger begins to approach the bottom plate, narrowing the gap between the two plates.

As the plates move closer together, the electrons on the bottom plate are drawn towards the positive plate on the plunger, causing a small current to flow as electrons are drawn into the bottom plate. With moving current, the voltage in the wire slightly drops, and the voltage sensor wakes up. The sensor is responsible for one character, say the $ symbol. As soon as it detects a change (drop) in its line voltage, it signals the microprocessor on the circuit board. That signal generates a scan code, the digital number the system uses to output a $ sign.

If two voltage sensors make a notification to the microprocessor that their keys have been activated, the microprocessor makes a value calculation, and outputs a key-combination character scan code. This is what happens when you press Shift+j and see a resulting capital "J."

Usually, a mechanism provides tactile feedback, and a strong click when the upper plate crosses a center point (discharge point) makes these keyboards exceptionally well suited for touch typists. Because of the enclosed housing and the lack of metal contacting metal, the capacitive switch is essentially corrosion free and immune to dust and dirt. The switch is highly resistant to bounce because the strike is not produced by closing a contact. Therefore, there is no physical structure capable of accidental, multiple contact connections. These keyboards are expensive, but they are the most durable type, rated at around 25 million or more keystrokes.

Mice and Trackballs

Although people might think that Apple Computer invented the mouse, it was actually invented in 1964 by scientists at Stanford University. Then, Xerox applied it to an experimental computer system called the Alto. The story of how Xerox pretty much gave away most of its modern computer industry technology, including the original laser-printer technology, is legendary: Xerox didn't think much money could be made from a so-called X-Y position indicator, but Apple Computer did, so in 1979, Apple Computer bought the mouse technology and lured away most of the innovative scientists from the now-famous Palo Alto Research Center.

How a Mouse Works

Two thin rollers are set at a right angle to each other inside a mouse or trackball. The rollers are attached to a notched wheel mechanism called an *encoder*. The rollers touch the rubberized ball as the ball moves, and the friction turns the rollers, which moves the encoder.

The encoder wheels have very small notches on their edges, with fine contact points where they touch the wall of the mouse. By calculating the number of times a contact is made from both encoders, the system can calculate where to put the pointer (or cursor) on the screen. This is the X-Y matrix again.

Mice come in many shapes and sizes, but a mouse is essentially a case with a rolling rubber ball underneath it. Turning the mouse upside down and putting a plastic ball on top makes it into a trackball. For convenience we use the term *mouse*, but the following discussion applies to trackballs as well. With the mouse, the case moves the ball against a mouse pad. With the trackball, the case stays in one place and your fingers move the ball.

Generally, a mouse requires some sort of software program (a device driver) to tell either the operating system or an application how to relate the physical movement to an on-screen pointer. Either the device driver is loaded (installed) with special software, or it is built into an operating system such as OS/2, Windows 9.x, Windows NT, and so forth.

Types of Mice

The different ways that a mouse tracks the movement of the ball distinguish the types of mice. A basic mouse is mechanical because the encoder wheel and contacts are metal and make physical movements.

Optical Mouse

An optical mouse has no moving parts, and works in conjunction with a reflective mouse pad. As the mouse moves, a beam of light bounces from the inside of the casing to the reflective surface (e.g., a desk top or special pad), and then back onto a sensor inside the mouse. The sensor calculates the changes in the light beam to define the X-Y coordinates of the screen cursor.

Some mice are called *optomechanical* devices. These are hybrids of mechanical and optical mice, using a rubber ball, but they replace the encoder contacts with a photo-interrupter disk. The X-Y calculations are performed by counting the interruptions to a beam of light, rather than by making contacts with a mechanical wire.

Wireless Infrared

Although the way a mouse develops X-Y information is almost always the same, the way that it sends (outputs) the information to the computer can vary. A newer and sometimes more convenient way is through the use of wireless infrared technology. This technology uses a specific frequency of infrared light, much like the remote control of a television or VCR.

Modems

It isn't easy to decide whether a modem is an input device, used for downloading information to the local machine, or an output device, used for uploading information to another computer. For that reason, we'll include the basics of dial-up modems here, before we go any further, as the exam may ask you about a few of the basic modem commands. In Chapter 8, we examine other types of online connectivity.

Modems come in many types and varieties, including dial-up modems, cable modems, digital subscriber line (DSL) modems, and wireless modems, to name just a few. On the A+ exam, the word "modem" usually refers to those used with analog telephone lines—dial-up modems.

The word "modem" is really an acronym for MODulator DEModulator, which is the way analog signals are converted to digital signals and then back again. Computers work with digital information, whereas phone lines work mainly in analog mode. However, telephone systems are gradually being converted to all-digital signaling technology.

UART Chips

Modems can either be internal or external. An internal modem is usually installed as an expansion card, using an IRQ to configure it through the operating system and/or a setup program. An external modem is easier to install because it connects to one of the COM (serial) ports, which the computer already understands.

Computers work with bytes, but the serial port transfers information in bits. Serial transfers take place 1 bit at a time in series, so we needed a device to break apart each byte into its component bits. That device must then remember how to fit the bits back together again, into their original bytes. The device is the Universal Asynchronous Receiver Transmitter (UART) chip.

Three Types of UARTs

Most of today's PCs have a 16550A UART chip installed. The difference among the three types of UARTs is primarily how fast they can transfer information. The UARTs are as follows:

- *8250*—The original chip in XTs and PC-AT, with a 1-byte buffer.
- *16450*—Introduced with the AT, with a 2-byte buffer.
- *16550A*—Popular in 486 and Pentium computers; adds 16-byte *first in, first out* (FIFO) buffering to eliminate data overrun when a port receives data faster than it can process that data (needed for speeds faster than 15.5 kilobytes per second [KB/s]). Comes in two types: 16550AN and 16550AFN.

16550AN vs. 16550AFN

The original 16550AN had some problems limiting the buffer. This was fixed by the 16550AFN replacement chip.

The 8250 and 16450 UARTs send one interrupt to the CPU after each character is received. Adding the 16-byte buffer to the 16550A accumulates more characters without losing some of them (*buffering*). Another feature of the 16550A is that it uses only one interrupt to handle all the characters in the buffer. The buffer stores characters, waits for the CPU to be available, and interrupts only once at that time. This is a significant improvement in reliability with high-speed communication rates.

Windows 3.x couldn't take advantage of the 16550A's buffering, but Windows 9.x can.

Basic Modem Commands

You'll almost never have to remember simple modem commands; however, you may find some questions on the exam relating to them. Some simple terminal emulators are still buried in among the many accessories that come with most operating systems. One of the original companies to develop low-cost modems for PCs was Hayes. As a result, many of today's commands originate from those first modems, leading to what is often referred to as a "Hayes-compatible" modem.

Table 5.5 lists the typical commands for manually controlling a modem, using their generic syntax (typed structure). Usually, the operating system or online service's installation routine performs this drudgework. These commands may not work on all modems, so consult the particular modem's reference manual for the exact commands. Most commands begin with an **AT** statement, with the exception of a few that begin with a **+++** statement.

Table 5.5 Basic modem commands.

Command	Translation
+++	Escape (for configuration or hang-up)
A/	Repeat
ATA	Answer incoming call
ATD [string]	Dial, or attention. [string] might be a phone number.
P	Pulse dialing, as in ATDP
T	Tone dialing, as in ATDT
, (comma)	Pause 2 seconds, as in ATDT 9, 123-4567 for an outside line
!	Flash (depress the hook and then release)
W	Wait for dial tone, as in ATDT 9 W 123-4567

Table 5.5 Basic modem commands *(continued)*

Command	Translation
H	Hang up, as in AT H
O	Online (often used after working in +++ mode), as in ATO
Zn	Reset the modem to defaults, where *n* is usually 0 or 1, as in AT Z0
ATE	Echo to host (show command information on screen)
ATFn	Select transmission mode or speed, where *n* is a number
ATZ	Reset the modem (e.g., AOL uses **ATZHO^M** for fast disconnect)
AT&Fn	Return to factory defaults (if any)
ATI	Show product identification (e.g., diagnostics and who made the modem)
ATLn	Speaker volume, where *n* is number 0, 1, 2, or 3
ATMn	Turn off the modem sound, as in AT M0 (n = 0, 1, 2, or 3)
AT&C	Carrier detect
XON or XOF	Software flow control

Scanners

By now, you should be thinking of input as anything that sends or helps you send information to the CPU. Output, in our breakdown, is anything that receives information from the CPU. We sometimes think of input devices as being only mice or keyboards, but suppose you want to send a picture to the hard drive? To do this, information must be sent to the CPU through an adapter interface. The DMA controller will probably perform some of the details of transferring data to the disk because it's good at that sort of thing.

Simply stated, a scanner is a device that converts an analog image—a pattern—into digital information. On the other hand, a photocopier or a camera transfers an analog image to paper or to film, keeping it in analog form. An image can be a graphic, an alpha character, a bar code, a fingerprint, a retina, or any other pattern stored on a solid material. Naturally, a digital camera is like a scanner, only it converts real-life analog patterns to digital information.

Scanners capture an image optically by using a light source and capturing the reflection. Some scanners, such as Magnetic Ink Character Recognition (MICR), capture a magnetic pattern. Other specialized scanners capture transparencies using a light source, but they don't capture reflections. A slide-transparency scanner works this way.

A scanner is a peripheral input device, primarily because it is not directly connected to the motherboard, but uses an interface. Scanners require either some sort of expansion card, often a SCSI interface, or they work with an existing parallel or USB port. Using a port often means a reduction in the speed of scanning. We discuss interface ports, connectors, and cables in Chapters 8 and 9.

Charge-Coupled Devices (CCDs) and Resolution

A typical scanner or digital camera uses a series of photosensitive cells called *Charge-Coupled Devices* (CCDs), which are mounted in a fixed row. Each CCD registers whether or not light is present. The point (or spot) of light being registered by one CCD is a roughly equivalent to a dot on a piece of paper. The smaller the physical size of the CCD, the more dots per inch (dpi) of image it can acquire. For more information on dots and resolution, see Chapter 7.

Scanners are usually measured in terms of resolution in optical dpi. This means the actual number of dots the scanner can discern, based on how many CCDs are built into it. Any image or pattern can be broken down into a number of discrete areas, or pixels (picture units). The smaller the area, the more pixels that area contains, and the finer the resolution. A CCD is often said to roughly correspond to one picture unit (pixel); however, this isn't technically accurate.

A CCD is composed of many small diodes, and a decision process defines how many diodes will generate a pixel. Today's digital cameras use fewer diodes on a CCD to capture a "unit of picture." This allows other diodes to capture other pieces of the picture, generating many more pixels—the so-called *megapixel* resolutions.

The optical resolution of a scanner is the one-to-one ratio of a physical CCD with a single dot. Software enhancement (*interpolation*) is a way to add pixels beyond a scanner's capability to scan a picture area. When software is used to change the image clarity, we refer to that difference as software resolution, interpolated resolution, or enhanced resolution. Resolution is usually divided into the two following categories:

- Horizontal resolution depends on how close together the CCDs are placed in a single row. The smaller the CCDs and the closer they can fit together, the higher the number of pixels in a row.

- Vertical resolution depends on how slowly the light source and mirror mechanism move from the top to the bottom of the image. A slower speed means smaller incremental steps. Again, the smaller the increments, the finer the resolution.

In the rating of 300x600 optical dpi, the first number applies to horizontal placement—in this case, 300 CCDs in a row. The second number (600) refers to vertical movement. Today, most scanners have an optical resolution of 300x600, 600x600, or 1200x1200 dpi. However, the amount of memory and storage space a 1200 dpi image requires is more than a typical person is willing to work with. In addition, no matter how high a resolution an image has, the resolution of the output device limits the resolution that can be displayed. Monitors generally have a 96 dpi resolution, with many printers being easily capable of 750 dpi resolutions or more.

A megapixel image will produce a high-resolution printed photograph, but will also result in a very large file. If you intend to use a digital camera to capture images for display on a monitor (for example, a Web site), remember that monitors are low-resolution devices. Large files also use a lot of bandwidth during transfers, leading to viewing delays when accessing a Web site.

As an example of scan resolutions in the real world, consider that the typical photographs you see in a magazine are scanned at about 200 dpi. Once again, there is an important relationship between the resolution possible from a scanner (for example, 1200 dpi) or digital camera, and the final output of the scanned image. A good rule of thumb is to scan an image at approximately one third of the final print resolution. Following that rule, a 720 dpi photo-inkjet printer would do very well with an image scanned at 240 dpi, using photo-quality paper. For plain old regular paper, a better scan resolution would be 120 dpi, so as to print at 360 dpi.

Scanner Connections

The primary difference between the parallel port and a SCSI adapter card is the data transfer rate. A parallel port moves eight bits of information at a time, whereas an internal interface card transfers at bus speeds. Therefore, parallel ports are slower than internal card adapters. We'll discuss transfer rates more in Chapter 8.

Some sheet-fed scanners are built into a keyboard, interfacing with an internal keyboard processor in the casing. The scanner borrows the keyboard cable to transfer data. On the other hand, handheld scanners are very small and portable, often connecting through their own interface cable, which also provides power to the scanner.

This concept of borrowing a cable for power became a problem when many devices began using a single cable. USB technology (discussed in Chapter 8) had to deal with the problem, and introduces powered hubs.

Installing an internal SCSI adapter is another exercise in IRQ/DMA conflicts. Also, some inexpensive scanners don't provide Advanced SCSI Programming Interface (ASPI) support, which is necessary if you want to run the scanner on the same SCSI bus as other peripherals (see the "SCSI" section in Chapter 8). Scanners and sound cards are legendary for their installation and configuration difficulties, creating a strong market for the Plug-and-Play specifications.

Nowadays, many (if not most) scanners connect to the core system with a USB connection. USB and FireWire provide fast serial transfers and avoid the expense and configuration issues of SCSI controller. USB and FireWire are discussed in Chapter 8.

Supplementary Information

We discussed binary and hexadecimal numbering earlier in this chapter, but this is a good place to mention bit rates in relation to scanners. 255 is an 8-bit number. We've referenced how bus widths are directly associated with the number of bits and bytes being transferred. We've also said that 8 bits equal 1 byte, so 255 is also a one-byte number.

When we speak about monitors in Chapter 7, we'll get into pixel units and color triads, but for the moment, we'll say that a 24-bit scanner is capable of recognizing 256 levels of colors (8 bits time 3 colors—Red, Green, Blue—is a 24-bit number). Remember that 0–255 is two hundred and fifty-six numbers. Taken together, these 256 levels are capable of generating the 16 million colors we see in monitor resolutions (also discussed in Chapter 7). Working the math, 24 bits provides for 16.77 million addresses at 256 levels of intensity, or depth. Working the numbers a bit more, we find out that

16-bit color addressing allows for 65,000 levels of intensity. These numbers should be familiar to you, if you've ever played with your monitor resolutions. Video resolution and color depth is dependent upon the amount of RAM available to the video subsystem.

Think about 8-bit addressing and 24-bit resolution. In this instance, using the three RGB colors, each color takes 8 bits of information in storage. When we speak of a 24-bit scanner, this means that the scanner is capturing the three colors in this fashion. If we move up to a 30-bit scanner, we have an extra 2 bits available per color (30 - 24 = 6, and 6 / 3 colors = 2). A 36-bit scanner provides an extra 4 bits per color.

Essentially, video technology and the ability of the human eye to perceive variations in color mean that we probably won't be seeing any increase in the overall number of color levels. Going back to our discussion of Analog versus Digital at the beginning of this chapter, we can begin to see that the more incremental steps that a digital process can capture, the closer the result will come to the analog world.

Put another way, you've probably seen older digital images of a rainbow. In the images, you could easily see division points between color variations. These bands of color are a result of the incremental steps. If light red is 1 and plain red is 2, our eye can perceive many colors in-between but the computer only knows 1 and 2. If we can make the incremental steps smaller, we could have 1, 1.25, 1.5, 1.75, and 2.0. Using those extra steps, we could have light red, medium light, not too light, darker regular, pretty-close-to-regular, and regular red.

Each increase in the number of incremental steps requires additional addressing space. This is why a line drawing can be captured in 2 bits, but a black-and-white photo with shades of gray might use 8 or even 16 bits of information. Since the resolutions levels are basically capped at 24 bits, any further information we can capture is assigned to the extra bits we find in 30-bit, 36-bit, or 48-bit scanning addresses. The bottom line is that although scanning an image with a 48-bit scanner set at 1200 dpi optical resolution will allow you to have a great deal of control over shadows and shading, the resulting file may easily be larger than 64MB. That's megabytes!

Summary—Input Devices

All things considered, the preceding discussion wasn't all that complicated. Be sure you remember the IRQs and port addresses, but as far as keyboards, scanners, and mice are concerned, here are the main ideas to remember:

- The various switch technologies used in keyboards: mechanical, foam element, rubber dome, sheet membrane, and capacitive nonmechanical.
- Mice use a pair of rollers and X-Y coordinates. Know how to clean a mouse ball and rollers, just in case you see a related question, and understand how an optical mouse uses reflected light.
- External modems use COM ports (know the addresses) and you may find a question or two on the most basic modem commands, particularly answer, attention, and disconnect. Know how to explain a UART chip.
- We'll cover dpi and pixels in Chapter 7, but you should understand a CCD and the concept of optical resolution, and the difference between horizontal and vertical resolutions.

Practice Questions

Question 1

Modems that interface with analog telephone lines require parallel transmission paths, and because of this, are almost always connected to the parallel port of the computer.

❍ a. True

❍ b. False

Answer b, false, is correct. Modems transmit data 1 bit at a time and, as such, are serial devices. The parallel port transfers 8 bits at a time.

Question 2

What kind of keyboard is considered mechanical? (Choose all that apply)

❑ a. Foam element

❑ b. Capacitive

❑ c. Membrane

❑ d. Rubber dome

Answers a, c, and d are correct. Foam element, membrane, and rubber dome keyboards are considered mechanical. Answer b is incorrect because the capacitive switch doesn't rely on metal contacts, but instead puts two plastic plates inside a switch housing designed to sense changes in capacitance of a circuit.

Question 3

Why is an optical mouse different from other types of mice?

❍ a. Optical mice do not require a cable connecting them to the PC.

❍ b. Optical mice have no moving parts.

❍ c. Optical mice do not require the use of a mouse pad.

❍ d. The friction ball in an optical mouse rarely requires cleaning.

Answer b is correct. An optical mouse has no moving parts and works in conjunction with a reflective mouse pad. As the mouse moves, a beam of light from the inside of the casing hits the reflective pad and then bounces back onto a sensor inside the mouse. The sensor calculates the changes in the light beam and defines the X-Y coordinates of the screen cursor.

Question 4

Most optical scanners use photosensitive devices called _______ to convert the scanned image into a machine-readable format.

- ❍ a. Quartz tube emitters
- ❍ b. Light-emitting diodes
- ❍ c. Electro-optical couplers
- ❍ d. Charge-coupled devices

Answer d is correct. Charge-coupled devices (CCDs) are photosensitive cells mounted in a fixed row. Each CCD registers whether there is light or no light—on or off. The point or spot of light being registered by one CCD is equivalent of a dot on a piece of paper. A light-emitting diode (LED) is used as a light transmitter, not a light sensor. There's no such thing as a "quartz tube emitter," nor is there an "electro-optical coupler."

Question 5

What basic electrical component can store a charge for a short period of time?

- ❍ a. Resistor
- ❍ b. Transistor
- ❍ c. Capacitor
- ❍ d. Diode

Answer c is correct. Capacitors store a quantity of electrons for a short period of time. Large capacitors can store a huge charge and are capable of delivering a shock even after the power cord has been disconnected. Resistors impede the movement of electrical current, and are measured in ohms. A diode does not store current, and a transistor is a small switching device.

Question 6

How many IRQ lines are on a typical, modern-day motherboard, and which line is used for cascading various requests?

- ❍ a. 15, 2
- ❍ b. 16, 9
- ❍ c. 15, 9
- ❍ d. 16, 2

Answer d is correct. IRQs 0–7 were the original interrupt lines, and the AT boards added IRQs 8–15, making a total of 16. IRQ 2 is often used to pass requests to IRQ 9, which is called *cascading*.

Question 7

A dial-up modem uses the following command to connect to the Internet:

- ❍ a. **ATD**
- ❍ b. **ATA**
- ❍ c. **ATX**
- ❍ d. **AOL**

Answer a is correct. A dial-up modem uses the ATD (AT(tention) Dial) command to connect to the Internet. Answer b is incorrect because the **ATA** command answers an incoming call. Answer c, refers to the ATX form factor for a motherboard. Answer d is the acronym for America OnLine.

Question 8

What is the default address of COM 2?

- ❍ a. 02E8
- ❍ b. 03E8
- ❍ c. 03F8
- ❍ d. 02F8

Answer d is correct. The default address of COM 2 is 02F8.

Question 9

What is the default IRQ for LPT1?

- ❍ a. 5
- ❍ b. 7
- ❍ c. 3
- ❍ d. 2

The correct answer is b. The default IRQ for LPT1 is 7.

Question 10

The power supply (usually mounted to the case) performs what function?

- ❍ a. Provides consistent 110V AC to the system board.
- ❍ b. Converts AC to DC at the voltage required by the system board and system components.
- ❍ c. Protects the system components from power outages.
- ❍ d. Boosts power coming from the power utility to acceptable AC voltages for system components.

Answer b is correct. Computers require direct current (DC) at several voltages, including 5V+, 5V-, 12V+, and 12V-. Standard wall outlets in the United States provide 110V alternating current (AC). The power supply's main purpose is to convert that AC to DC at the voltages required by the computer.

Question 11

Two common causes of electrical trouble in a PC are ______ and ______.

- ❍ a. ESD, EMM
- ❍ b. EMI, DMA
- ❍ c. EMI, ESD
- ❍ d. EDS, AMD

Answer c is correct. EMI, or electromagnetic interference, is caused by multiple cables running too closely together. ESD, or electrostatic discharge, occurs when static electricity build-up in a technician's body is accidentally passed to the computer system, possibly destroying the circuitry. EMM is an expanded memory manager, while AMD is a chip-manufacturing company.

Need to Know More?

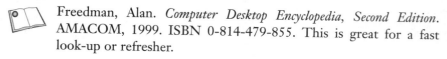

Freedman, Alan. *Computer Desktop Encyclopedia, Second Edition*. AMACOM, 1999. ISBN 0-814-479-855. This is great for a fast look-up or refresher.

Messmer, Hans-Peter. *The Indispensable PC Hardware Book, Third Edition*. Reading, MA: Addison-Wesley Publishing Company, 2000. ISBN 0-201-403-994. This is a comprehensive, up-to-date reference book that covers far more than you will need to know for the exam.

Minasi, Mark. *The Complete PC Upgrade and Maintenance Guide, 11th Edition*. San Francisco, CA: Sybex Network Press, 2000. ISBN 0-782-128-009. This is considered one of the best reference books available. In fact, Minasi's book was instrumental in the formulation of the first A+ exam.

Mueller, Scott. *Upgrading and Repairing PCs, 12th Edition*. Indianapolis, IN: Que, 2000. ISBN 0-7897-2303-4. This is one of our favorites. If you are only going to have one reference book, give this one serious consideration.

Rosch, Winn. *Hardware Bible, Fifth Edition*. Indianapolis, IN: Sam's Publishing, 1999. ISBN 0-789-717-433. This is a well-organized reference book that covers software issues as well as hardware.

Peripherals: Storage Devices

Terms you'll need to understand:

- ✓ Disk, storage
- ✓ Floppy drive, hard drive, revolutions per minute (rpm)
- ✓ Sectors and clusters
- ✓ Integrated Drive Electronics (IDE) and Enhanced Integrated Drive Electronics (EIDE)
- ✓ Advanced technology attachment (ATA) and Peripheral Component Interconnect (PCI)
- ✓ Removable disk

Concepts you'll need to master:

- ✓ Data transfer rates
- ✓ Master/slave configurations for physical drives
- ✓ Controller and bus specification
- ✓ Small Computer System Interface (SCSI) chains

If we want to keep the results of our input, we need a place to put everything after the power is shut down. Remember that without a steady power supply, RAM loses whatever it was holding. Software applications, work, and new information we've created, all have to be stored somewhere for continuity, sharing, and output. The most common way to store information and data is on a disk of some type (although this is changing). The original floppy disks were inexpensive, easy to use, and could be shared among computers. Today, we have hard disks, CDs, DVDs, floppy disks, tape drives, removable hard disks, flash memory cards, and network file servers.

A hard drive is far more complex than a floppy drive, obviously, but we've chosen the original floppy disk and drive system as our entry point into the various components making up storage technology. They use the same concepts and basic technology, for the most part. We believe that focusing on these essential concepts will help you better retain the many details involved in the exam.

Floppy Disks

The floppy disk drive was developed by Alan Shugart of Shugart Associates, who also developed the Shugart Associates Systems Interface (SASI). Later, SASI was renamed Small Computer System Interface (SCSI) when the American National Standards Institute (ANSI) committee approved the interface in 1986. *Floppy disk* refers to a round, flimsy, bendable piece of Mylar coated with magnetic material and in a protective jacket. The first minifloppy disk, which we know as the 5 ¼-inch disk, followed the original 8-inch disks used prior to 1974. The protective jacket was changed from somewhat floppy on 5 ¼-inch disks, to rigid on 3 ½-inch disks.

Shugart created the floppy disk, hard disk, SCSI drive, and controller interfaces that are still used in most PCs today. The Shugart Technology, Inc. (ST)-506/412 interface was the accepted standard for all PC hard disks and stood as the basis for the Enhanced Small Device Interface (ESDI) and Integrated Drive Electronics (IDE) interfaces. Because Shugart left his company (for some reason) right before the market release of the 5 ¼-inch floppy drive, he never profited fully from his inventions. In 1979, he resurfaced and formed a partnership with Finis Conner. They created Seagate Technology, Inc. and developed the now-obsolete 5 ¼-inch hard drive. However, Windows 98 introduced a much better backup utility than had been available previously in Windows 95, and this utility was licensed from Seagate.

Floppy disks are available in different densities, using one (single) or two (dual) sides of the disk. *Density*, in this case, means that floppy disks originally used eight tracks and then changed to nine tracks. The original disks used only one side for data storage and were referred to as *single-sided, single density*. Almost any floppy disks you find today use both sides for data storage and therefore are called *double-sided, double density*. This same concept carried over into DVDs.

Density

We spoke about the concept of density in Chapter 3 when we described the capacitors and transistors used on memory chips. Magnetic disks use tracks and sectors, also measured in density. Keep in mind that the amount of space a given number of bits takes up, regardless of what the space is made of or how the bits are formed, is called *density.*

The density of a newspaper graphic could be defined in terms of how many dots can fit into a given square inch on a matrix. We generally think of the matrix as having X-Y coordinates and being in two dimensions. The more dots in a square inch, the higher the resolution, hence "dpi." DVDs use a third dimension—depth. This requires a so-called Z coordinate, generating X-Y-Z addresses. This isn't any different than measuring a box or a cube. Using all three coordinates, we can find a single point anywhere within the volume of the cube.

The number of sides used on a floppy disk, along with its density, are still referred to as: double-sided (DS), low density (LD) and high density (HD). The four typical floppy disk sizes and densities are named as follows:

- *DS, DD*—360KB 5 ¼-inch double sided, dual density
- *DS, HD*—1.2MB 5 ¼-inch double sided, high density
- *DS, DD*—720KB 3 ½-inch double sided, double density
- *DS, HD*—1.44MB 3 ½-inch double sided, high density

The IBM 2.9MB floppy disk developed for OS/2 distribution was referred to as "extra" density. Microsoft also had a proprietary disk-formatting process for storing 1.7MB on a typical floppy. Microsoft disks were referred to as *Distributed Media Format* (DMF). Windows 9x and above can read all normal sizes, along with the extra sizes, but neither the 2.8MB nor 1.7MB formats are supported by DOS.

Floppy Drive Components

The inside of a floppy drive uses many of the same general components as a hard drive. Remember your hexadecimal numbering, and the fact that the first cylinder and track on a disk are numbered *cylinder 0, track 0*. The exam sometimes uses the informal term *head* in place of the technical term *cylinder*. The boot sector could also be said to be on head 0, track 0.

For the remainder of this book, we will relate the boot sector to head 0 and track 0. That being said, due to the low-level nature of cylinders, heads, and actuator arms, this isn't an absolute fact in all instances. However, the level of detail for a total explanation of head 0 goes far beyond the scope of this discussion, as well as being relative only to an engineering perspective. This book is intended to help you pass the exam by understanding the normal use of the concepts.

Read-Write Heads

Most floppy drives have two read-write heads, which is why disks can be made dual sided. The first head (head 0) is actually the bottom one, and the second head (head 1) is the top one. Read-write heads are the hardware pieces that actually change the magnetic state of the disk surface. When the magnetic state is changed by the head, it writes to the disk. When the existing state is sent back to the CPU, the head reads from the disk.

The two heads are spring-loaded and physically touch the surface of the disk to read or write data. A 3 ¼-inch floppy disk spins at 300 revolutions per minute (rpm). The original 5 ¼-inch high-density drives spun at 360 rpm. (By comparison, a typical hard drive spins at 7,200 rpm.)

Each head is actually a combination read-write head. The separate heads are each centered within a pair of tunnel erase heads. In other words, each tunnel erase head contains both a read and a write head, and they move together. The heads are made of soft iron materials with electromagnetic coils.

When a track of information is produced, the trailing tunnel erase heads erase the outer edge of the track, making the data stand out cleanly on the disk. This forces the data to be confined in a narrow "tunnel" in the middle of the track, and prevents peripheral magnetic interference from nearby tracks of data. The process also removes fading magnetic changes trailing off to the sides of the written data, which could lead to some confusion during reading.

Either/Or State

We first brought up the concept of "state" when we talked about how AMD uses the changing state of voltage on a motherboard clock oscillator. Anything that is "either/or" can be translated into a 1 or 0—a binary bit. If voltage always is either 4V or 2V, we can assign a one or zero to either voltage.

Voltage can be either "steady" or "not steady," and so we can also assign a bit-status condition to either of those two states. Think of a voice-activated answering machine. If someone talks, the machine records. If the person pauses too long, the machine stops. If noise is present, the machine is on, but when noise ceases, the machine turns off. Continuous/Broken, Regular/Irregular, Quiet/Loud, Yes/No, and On/Off are all binary conditions that can be assigned a 1 or 0.

Head Actuator

Moving the read-write heads is done by a stepper motor called a *head actuator*. This motor moves the heads back and forth over the disk (or platters on a hard disk). The heads go from edge to center and back again, moving over tracks that were created by low-level formatting (usually performed by the manufacturer).

Computer disks are not like the old vinyl music records (disks). On an old record player, a rotating platter would spin the disk while a needle picked up analog information from one, very long groove on each side of the disk. You had to physically turn the disk over in order to use the second side.

The head actuator motor is also controlled by a disk controller. The disk controller works with the operating system and ROM BIOS so that the PC can move the read-write heads to specific locations on a disk, in order to find data (files).

Spindle Motor

To get a disk spinning at 300 rpm, the spindle motor works very much like the old record players. Older floppy drives used a belt-driven system with inconsistent speeds, making them unreliable. The belts would wear and slip over time, making them even more unreliable. Just as record players evolved from belt driven to direct drive, so did computer floppy drives. The direct-drive motor doesn't have any belts, so the spindle doesn't slip, making for very consistent speed.

Newer disk drives use automatic torque compensation to provide greater spin force, and have very little slippage. Therefore, these drives rarely need adjustment, unlike older drives. However, with a typical 3 ¼-inch drive costing around $30, it's often simpler and cheaper to replace the drive.

Observe how the operating system takes control of the head actuator through the drive controller. CD-ROMs and DVDs use the way information is stored to take control of the spindle motor and further guarantee a consistent speed. (We discuss optical disks in the "Optical Storage" section later in this chapter.)

Logic Board

The drive mechanism is attached to one or more logic boards (printed circuit boards), located underneath the main housing. This board contains the controls for the head actuator, spindle motor, disk sensors, and any other drive components. A CMOS setting may need to be changed, depending on the installation context (for example, switching the A: and B: drives).

Floppy Drive Configuration

Installing a floppy drive or a hard drive may require configuring some jumper settings. One difference between the drives is that floppies are designated A: or B:. Hard drives are either a *master* or *slave*. The drive select jumper defines the unique drive number, and in the overall scheme of drives and controllers, every drive must have its own drive number! The drive select jumper defines a floppy drive as either drive 0 or drive 1.

Drive 0 does not necessarily correspond to Drive A: drive, just as drive 1 does not necessarily correspond to Drive B:. This is because IBM wired its system to make installing preconfigured drives as easy as possible. Assigning a letter to a disk drive is part of the operating system's logical formatting, and we cover this in the "FDISK" section of Chapter 10.

One of the fundamental things you must remember for the exam is that IBM (and all clone makers) designed Drive A: and Drive B: into every system. This will affect your understanding of partitioning, because all PCs continue to set aside two drives (A: and B:) for the basic floppy drives. The C: drive is always the third drive. Any additional drives take on the next consecutive letters of the alphabet.

Media Sensor Jumper

Have you ever noticed the small hole in the upper right corner of a 3 ¼-inch disk? That hole is for the media sensor. If a beam of light (media sensor light) can pass through the hole and make contact with a photo sensor, the system knows that a high-capacity 1.44MB disk is in the drive. Extended-capacity 2.8MB disks have a different hole on the disk jacket, so a multicapacity floppy drive actually has two media sensors: one for 1.44MB and one for 2.8MB disks. (A 1.7MB disk uses 21 sectors per track, rather than 18, and doesn't require a special media sensor.)

Low-density 720KB disks have no hole in the media sensor position, so the media sensor light fails to make contact with the photo sensor. This led to an interesting scheme in which a special hole-punch tool was marketed for converting cheaper 720KB disks to 1.44MB disks. The reformatted disk eventually becomes unstable because of the density of the magnetic structure of low-density disks. This led to a rapid degradation of the format, with a catastrophic loss of data. (On the other hand, placing a piece of tape over the media sensor hole on a 1.44MB disk will fool the drive into thinking that it has a 720KB disk that can be formatted with no data loss.)

Write Protect

Looking at the back (or bottom) of a high-density disk, notice that there's a hole in the upper left corner with a sliding piece of plastic. When this hole is covered, it locks the disk and prevents any writing to it, making it write protected.

Write protection makes it physically impossible to write data to the disk. This is a way to guarantee that a virus program can't be placed on the disk. There's no way to write-protect RAM, but a virus in memory won't be able to transfer to a write-protected disk.

Change Line Jumper

AT boards use pin 34 to carry a signal called the *diskette change line*. This signal is used to tell the system whether a disk in the drive is still the same disk since the last time a disk access was requested. This control signal is a pulse sent to the controller (to a status register) that changes one time on insertion and one time on ejection.

When the drive responds with information that the heads have moved, the system knows whether or not a disk has been inserted. If a change signal isn't received between accesses, the controller assumes that the same disk is in the drive. This allows information that is stored in RAM (having been read from the floppy) to be used without rereading the disk.

Controllers

Most PCs have some amount of peripheral control right on the motherboard. To distinguish this rudimentary control from the more sophisticated I/O control of later PCs, we refer to various *controllers*. A controller is a component containing additional microprocessors and logic, and works through a connection with the motherboard BIOS. Depending on the age of the computer, controllers take on more or less of the actual management of their specific device. A SCSI drive controller, for instance, can work directly with a multitasking operating system, bypassing the CPU and allowing for faster access to the disk.

Controllers don't usually have a ROM BIOS chip. The motherboard BIOS contains instructions for working with different types of controllers. The devices that the controller manages may have their own BIOS chips. Although peripherals can be Plug and Play, controllers are part of the motherboard system platform and aren't referred to as PnP controllers.

Different peripherals have different controllers. A typical PC can have a keyboard controller, floppy drive controller, and hard disk controllers. There are also memory, IRQ, DMA, and video controllers. With all these controllers working around the CPU, you can imagine the number of instructions flying around the motherboard circuitry. The places where those instructions cross over to other devices are the buses.

You might think of a controller as a traffic cop working at a busy intersection. Traffic laws (software instructions) define the way that the traffic flows through the intersection. At certain times, traffic (processing) is so heavy that it speeds things up to have a human being in the intersection, who can override the standard laws with individual decisions. Peripheral controllers take on "localized" processing management, and help speed up overall performance.

Modern systems have a floppy disk controller and two hard disk controllers built into the motherboard. AT computers often had an adapter card with both controllers attached to it. Drive controllers use interrupts, the same way that serial and parallel ports do. Because almost every PC has a hard disk, the ROM BIOS includes a default IRQ (14) for the master (primary) hard disk, along with default IRQs for the floppy drives and other basic ports.

Remember that IRQ 14 is usually assigned to the primary disk controller. IRQ 15 is assigned by default to any secondary disk controller. The obsolete XT used IRQ 5 for its disk controller. Later PCs used IRQ 5 for a secondary printer port (LPT2). Modern PCs tend to assign a sound card to IRQ 5.

Fixed Disks/Hard Drives

Because hard disks cost so little these days, the preferred storage device is an internal, nonremovable storage media, or *hard disk*. Tape storage may be cheaper, but its use of sequential access makes it much slower. The hard disk is actually called a *fixed disk drive* because you don't remove it except to permanently replace it. (Presumably, once it's replaced, it's fixed.) Many people call it a *hard drive* because the platters aren't flexible and floppy, and in fact you can replace it like any other drive. However, you should note that a drive usually refers to the logical formatting of a disk. The technical name given by the IBM PC Institute is a Direct Access Storage Device (DASD).

When we speak of high-capacity removable storage media, we refer to them as *removable* drives. These include the Iomega Zip and Jaz drives, which are designed to be quickly disconnected. Removable drives offer the advantage of a removable disk with storage capacity similar to a fixed disk, where the entire drive bay can be unplugged and carried to another machine.

Although the disk, drive mechanisms, drive controller, and cable/interface subsystem are separate components, familiar language joins them together as the hard drive or simply "the drive." In the following discussion, we often refer to fixed disks as either the hard drive or the drive. Many disks are partitioned with a single, Primary, Active Partition making them Drive C:. Drive C: and the fixed disk are often referred to as the same thing, even though this leads to a great deal of confusion when it comes to understanding logical drives as opposed to physical disks. FDISK.EXE, FORMAT.COM and logical drives are covered explicitly in Chapter 10.

Be very careful that you don't confuse a physical disk and a logical drive. Although many people call the fixed disk a hard drive, the physical disk can contain anywhere from 1 to 24 logical drives. Additionally, a system can have more than one physical disk, where each disk can have many logical drives. Tricky exam questions can trip you up by asking whether a fixed disk can contain 23 or 24 drives. (The answer is 24. See Chapter 10 for more information on FDISK and partitions.)

A hard drive has many internal components, consisting mainly of several plates of highly electroconductive metal spaced extremely close together. These plates are called *platters*. A spindle motor, connected to the plates at their centers, spins the platters. Each side of each platter has a read-write head. The heads are attached to an actuator arm under each platter to move the heads back and forth over the disk.

The boot sector explicitly points to head 0, cylinder 0, track 0, sector 0 of the first platter. In common usage, either the head 0 or cylinder 0 may be dropped.

Hard disks spin at thousands of revolutions per minute (for example, 5,400 rpm, 7,200 rpm, 10,000 rpm [SCSI]), making them dramatically faster than floppy disks. The disk drive also has a circuit board and connectors to transfer data and to supply power to the drive. Although we speak of a single disk, you can see in Figure 6.1 that, technically, a hard drive has a number of physical disks.

Figure 6.1 A typical hard drive, showing the platters and spindle.

Random Access

When the CPU requests data from the disk, the platters rotate, and the heads move back and forth over them. The back-and-forth movement allows for random access of the data, rather than the sequential data reads of a tape cassette. Sequential reading means that if you have a file stored somewhere on a tape, the tape machine must spin through an entire length of tape before it gets to the beginning of that file. A hard drive, on the other hand, skips over whole platters and tracks, going directly to the first cluster of a file. (We discuss sectors and clusters in a moment, and again in Chapter 10.)

Random access means that if an area (cluster) of a platter is near a read-write head and available for storage, the head can begin storing a file immediately. A tape must have enough room to store the complete file from beginning to end. If a tape doesn't have space for a complete file, we either have to wait for it to spin all the way through to the end of used space, or we must use a new tape. A hard drive can also store pieces of a file in many different sections.

Tracks and Sectors

All disks, including floppy disks, are divided into tracks and sectors by the manufacturer. The same track on each platter is part of a cylinder. A formatting process, defined by the operating system, then further subdivides the disks into clusters. Initially, a fixed disk is magnetized (physical, or low-level formatting) by creating magnetic tracks and cylinders on the plates of the disk.

If you were to take an apple corer and smash it down on a hard drive (not recommended), it would cut through one cylinder. The edge of the corer would be like the width of one track. Tracks and cylinders are characterized by the following:

- *Tracks*—Concentric, circular paths placed on both sides of the platter. They are identified by number, starting in the center with track 0.
- *Cylinders*—A set of all the tracks on all sides of all the platters located the same distance from the center of the stack of platters.

Each track is subdivided into sectors that store a fixed amount of data. Sectors are usually formatted to store 512 bytes of data. Binary data is stored in the sectors using various combinations of zeros and ones. The ones are magnetized areas, and the zeros are not.

A way to remember the difference between sectors and clusters is that the formatting process adjusts the size of file clusters. Perhaps files, like chickens, can cluster around a disk, changing from larger to smaller clusters (depending on the amount of food). Sectors never change size. Perhaps all those chickens like to cluck and cluster in a particular sector of the yard? The sector dimensions of the yard never change, only the cluster-size of the chickens. The exam always uses 512 bytes for a sector size.

Over time, the magnetic coating of the platters begins to deteriorate, preventing them from holding a magnetic pattern. When this happens, the heads can't read or write data from a sector. Reformatting the disk or using certain software programs such as SCANDISK or Norton Disk Doctor, will label the sector as a *bad sector*. Even with modern engineering, most brand new disks have some number of bad sectors that are marked as unusable by the manufacturer during physical formatting.

After physical formatting, the operating system performs logical formatting, which we cover in the discussion of FDISK.EXE in Chapter 10. The formatting process also marks unusable sectors as bad.

Hard Drive Controllers

Hard drives have such a huge responsibility in a PC, that a lot of attention has been focused on how to make the drive controllers more intelligent. We've seen that controllers can take over a lot of the management for a particular type of device, and hard drive controllers are in constant development. Hard drive controllers include:

- IDE (Integrated Drive Electronics), EIDE (Extended IDE), and XT IDE (eXtended Technology IDE)
- SCSI (Small Computer Systems Interface)
- ESDI (Enhanced Small Device Interface)
- ST-506/412 (Shugart Technologies 506/412. Remember the story of Alan Shugart of floppy fame? Don't worry; the story isn't an exam topic.)

IDE and SCSI Interface

Part of what makes understanding drive controllers difficult is that each controller interface has even more acronyms and descriptive words used for different features. Some of these acronyms include:

- ATA IDE (AT Attachment IDE)
- MCA IDE (Micro Channel Architecture IDE)
- Fast, Wide, Ultra, and Ultra-wide SCSI

The exam covers the IDE, EIDE, and SCSI interfaces for the most part. The ATA IDE bus and the PCI bus show up as well. Remember that ATA is a specification, but IDE is an interface architecture. The IDE controller is built into the drive.

IDE Drives

You'll find an IDE controller in most of today's computers. Strictly speaking, IDE refers to *any* drive that has a built-in controller. The actual interface bus uses the AT Attachment (ATA) specification, which refers back to AT-class motherboards. The specification was "attached" to the AT form factor. Until recently, an IDE controller was typically a 16-bit ISA motherboard interface. Keep this in mind, because newer computers dropped the ISA bus completely in favor of the PCI bus (discussed later in this chapter) and the hub architecture of the North-South bridge technology.

The ATA IDE combination was first developed by Compaq, Control Data Corporation (CDC), and Western Digital Corporation, who decided to use a 40-pin keyed connector with a 5 ¼-inch form factor. As we've said, the keyed connector is designed to be plugged in only one way (plugging in a drive backward can damage both the drive and its related circuits). These original drives were physically large, and could hold only 40MB of data. (That's megabytes, not gigabytes! Everyone thought 40MB was far more than sufficient—in those days.)

IDE and EIDE controllers work with a 40-pin keyed connector.

The drive and built-in controller plugs into a bus connector on either the motherboard or an expansion card. Because the controller is on the drive unit, these drives are easy to install and require a minimum amount of cabling. Fewer parts are involved, so signal paths are shorter, which improves the reliability of the drive.

Because of the physical properties of wire, especially cheap ribbon cable wires, signals traveling along a piece of wire are subject to various types of degradation. Electromagnetic interference and structural resistance (not to mention signals bouncing back from improperly terminated cables) make a trip from the CPU to the drive heads a risky business for any given byte of data. The shorter the path, the more likely the data byte will arrive safely. We discussed this problem earlier, in relation to modern memory chips and signal traces (see Chapter 3).

Another advantage of the integrated controller is that the manufacturer doesn't need to worry about compatibility issues with the drive. This makes the overall hard drive unit easier and cheaper to build, and cheaper to sell, which is partly why IDE drives are so common.

Make a note that an ATA IDE cable should be a maximum of 18 inches long. The drives use a 40-pin keyed connector, with a cable 40 wires wide that carries all signals to and from the controller. Some connectors don't use a physical notch for keying, in which case the ribbon cables have matching colored stripes to indicate the correct orientation. SCSI connectors are generally 50-pin connectors.

The ATA Specification

A controller works with the ROM BIOS on a motherboard. In 1989, ATA IDE was accepted as the ANSI standard, ending many compatibility issues. ATA is an ongoing set of specifications, with each development aimed at increasing the access speed between the software, the operating system, the CPU, and the drive.

Because ATA is a specification, it defines, for example, a standard for the signals on the 40-pin connector, the functions and timing of signals, and cable specifications. The ATA specification does the following:

- Provides a way for two separate drives (each with its own controller) to interface with the same bus
- Creates the master drive (drive 0) and secondary (slave) drive (drive 1) hierarchy

Remember that auto-configuration in a CMOS file is different than Plug and Play. PnP uses a combination of system BIOS, operating system, and device BIOS. Auto-configuration applies only to CMOS.

The ATA-2 Specification

The ATA-2 specification, released in 1994, is the same thing as EIDE, or an Extended IDE controller. ATA was "extended" to add Programmed

Input/Output (PIO) modes, along with DMA transfer support. PIO is available in five modes. The first three, 0, 1, and 2, are the ATA-1 specification. The ATA-2 specification added modes 3 and 4, bringing the total to five. Let's pause for a sanity check, and take another look at this alphabet soup:

- The underlying device that we're talking about is the IDE drive controller. IDE is a type of hard drive with a built-in controller. Ordinarily, a controller is separate from the disk and tells the drive system how to operate. IDE puts the controller right in the housing, along with the read-write heads and the platters.
- Instructions get from the controller to the drive by crossing over a bus—an interface. Data transfers from the drive back to RAM across a bus. The amount of data that can move from the disk to memory is measured in MB/s, or how many megabytes can move in one second.
- Different drives require different ways of communicating with the motherboard's BIOS. ATA specifies a standard for that communication. Part of the specification means that IDE drives and their controllers have to be made a certain way.
- The first ATA specification defined most of the manufacturing process and included a way to hook two drives to a single controller.
- ATA and ATA-1 changed as the sophistication for controlling the hard drive increased. ATA was one set of rules, and ATA-1 was the next set of rules. ATA-2 is the third set of rules, and each set builds on the previous set of rules.
- Original ATA started with 4MB/s, eventually hitting 8MB/s
- ATA-2 allows even more complicated instructions to go between the controller and the hard drive. Along with the new instructions, the controller can take charge of other ways that the system moves data into memory, such as PIO modes. PIO stands for *programmable I/O*. The five PIO modes helped speed things up to 16MB/s.
- Another way the controller speeds things up is by using direct memory access (DMA).

PIO Modes 3 and 4

ATA-2 added PIO modes 3 (11.1MB/s) and 4 (16.6MB/s). However, to run in these modes, the IDE port on the motherboard must be on either a VESA local bus (a VL bus), or a PCI bus. Many motherboards have two IDE controllers, but on older systems, only the first controller is connected to the

PCI bus. The second controller is connected to a legacy ISA bus and is limited to PIO mode 2. (Legacy means carried over from back in the old days.) The manufacturers claim that the ISA connection is required because slower devices, such as CD-ROM drives, don't need the higher speed of the PCI bus. As we've said, many new systems don't even come with any ISA slots.

Mixing fast and slow devices (such as hard disk and CD-ROM drives) on the primary controller can cause slower data transfer for the hard disk. Typically, all transfers travel at the speed of the slower device. Connect only hard disks to the primary controller, and make the faster of two disks the master.

Fast ATA

By 1994, ATA-2 had done a number of things to speed up data transfer. It provided support for drives larger than 504MB, and included PIO 3 and 4 modes, which allowed for faster data transfers. The updated PIO modes were referred to as ATA-3, or *Fast ATA*, and required upgraded device drivers, along with an enhanced BIOS.

EIDE used the ATA-2 specification, with its PIO 3 and 4, along with the DMA channels on the motherboard. ATA-2 and Fast ATA used a burst transfer rate of 16.7MB/s. Fast ATA also introduced a Secure Mode.

Burst Transfer Rate

Hard drive controllers have a small, built-in memory buffer. This is due to the difference between how fast the drive heads can move information, relative to how fast the timing strobe, cables, and DMA channels can transfer information to the CPU. At the drive itself, reading or writing small files and portions of a file is done in small bursts of data. These small packets are then transferred in bursts—the burst transfer rate.

For more sustained file operations, such as during the boot process, when a very large application begins to load, or gaming, data is transferred in a long, continuous, sequential mode. The sequential transfer rate for earlier ATA controllers would often fall to just above 10MB/s as the buffer filled up. One reason the buffer fills up is that the time it takes for a host machine to send 4KB commands to the controller is longer than the time it takes for the hard drive to act on that command.

Another reason a drive controller buffer fills up is that a command has to wait for a timing signal from the controller. The signal is somewhat like a motherboard clock tick, using a timing strobe with an "up" (positive) and a "down" (negative) transition cycle. Fast ATA used only the positive cycle to send data, but Ultra ATA uses both the positive and negative transition of the timing signal. Using both transitions doubles the frequency of data transfers, so data can be sent twice as fast without doubling the speed of the timing strobe.

Ultra ATA

In 1997, Quantum introduced a way to double the data transfers from IDE hard disks, calling it *Ultra ATA* (also known as ATA/ATAPI 4). Intel backed the technology and included support for the process in their new chipsets. The rest of the industry and disk manufacturers followed suit, and Ultra ATA became the standard. EIDE drives became a direct competitor to SCSI drives, in terms of speed. Ultra ATA (using DMA channels) doubled the existing performance, with burst transfer rates of 33MB/s, and was fully backward compatible with Fast ATA. A new ATA Packet Interface (ATAPI) was added, which allowed extra drives (for example, tape drives or CD-ROM drives) to connect to the ATA connector.

Fast ATA specified that the drive had to wait for the strobe from the host (propagation delay) before responding by putting data into the buffer (data turnaround delay). The timing signal was a two-way (bi-directional) event between the host (computer) and the drive. Ultra ATA, much like double data rate (DDR) DRAM, doubles the data transfer rate by making the drive the single source for both the timing strobe and the data transfer—a unidirectional process. Both the strobe signal and data signal travel simultaneously down the cable in the same direction, eliminating the propagation delay where the drive is waiting for signals coming from the opposite direction.

Ultra ATA also uses something called a *Cyclical Redundancy Check* (CRC) as a way of verifying data (somewhat like parity checking). The CRC is calculated for each burst of data by both the host and the drive, and stored in CRC registers on both the host and the drive. After each burst, the host sends the contents of its CRC register back to the drive, which compares it against its own register's contents. Matching CRCs indicate the data sent was the same as the data received. This provides better data integrity, making an Ultra ATA drive more accurate, as well as faster.

Ultra DMA (UDMA 2, or UDMA/33)

We won't go any deeper into the details of transfer rates, buffers, and command overhead. Ultra ATA essentially brings the process of transferring data from the controller to the CPU more into conformity with the internal transfer rates of fast disks. In order to keep the process synchronized from the read/write heads of the drive all the way through to the CPU, the DMA channels had to be upgraded. Quantum improved the way DMA works by doubling the transfer rate to 33MB/s, and then applied those improvements to the ATA specification. PIO modes 0-4 continue on, but became secondary to UDMA 2 and UDMA 3.UDMA 2 is also known as UDMA/33, where the "33" refers to the 33MB/s transfer rate through the UDMA channels. In order to use an Ultra ATA drive, the motherboard chipset must also have UDMA 2.

Ultra ATA is sometimes known as Advanced ATA.

Supplementary Information

This is not on the exam, but since we're discussing the ATA and Ultra ATA specifications, ATA/ATAPI-5, also known as *Ultra ATA/66*, was released in 1999 and increased throughput to 66MB/s. Ultra ATA/66 kept the PIO modes 0–4, and added support for UDMA 3 (44.4MB/s) and UDMA 4 (66.6MB/s). As we've seen before, faster speeds began to create bottlenecks when very slow components began to catch up with fast components. We saw this when memory bus speeds caught up with processor speeds. The same thing happened with ATA drives. Another problem with Ultra ATA/66 was that the signal strobe began flashing so quickly it introduced EMI problems. To solve this, the specification introduced a 40-pin, 80-conductor cable, with forty secondary ground lines to go along with the original forty signal lines.

ATA/ATAPI-6 is scheduled to be released in 2002, and should include Ultra DMA mode 5. This new specification may take a year before it shows up in consumer workstations, but UDMA 5 should provide for transfer rates up to 100MB/s. Most modern IDE hard drives are already capable of this transfer rate, so the new ATA should better consolidate data transfers. The current 28-bit Logical Block Addressing (LBA) system (512-byte sectors) provides for a maximum hard drive size of 137GB. UDMA 5 is expected to support 48-bit or 64-bit addressing, which would allow for drives millions of times larger than today's drives.

Although it's way beyond the scope of this book, DOS BIOS uses Int13h (Interrupt 13) to understand the cylinders, tracks, and heads of a hard disk. Due to limitations of a 24-bit addressing scheme, hard drives were limited to a size of slightly over 8GB. To get around this, Int13h extensions were developed, which work in combination with the BIOS and Windows operating system, and provide a 64-bit disk-addressing scheme. This allows for a maximum hard drive size of 9.4 trillion gigabytes.

Meanwhile, a company called *Nexsan Technologies* has created an ATAboy2 specification as part of its trademarked InfiniSAN RAID storage systems. We'll discuss the redundant array of inexpensive disks (RAID) in Chapter 13, but ATAboy2 provides options for connecting 2Gb Fibre Channel systems to Storage Area Network (SAN) servers running ATA drives. This allows for multiterabyte storage and up to 400MB/s throughput (peak). These kinds of storage needs are used in the broadcasting industry and graphics industry (for example, movie special effects). 1.68TB is enough storage for over 100 hours of digital video.

Like a regular SCSI interface, ATAboy2 supports 8 logical unit numbers (LUNs) per host controller. The ATAboy2 can also use the Ultra ATA 160/230 SCSI specification, with transfer rates of 160MB/s. The ATAboy2 is designed to use ATA disks in heavy network storage situations, and brings the ATA specification into competition with SCSI drives. However, ATA disks tend to run at 7,200 rpm, as opposed to high-end SCSI drives capable of running at 15,000 rpm.

The PCI Specification

Think back for a moment to the intersection with the traffic cop. Recall too, that a bus is like a toll plaza where traffic moves through the tollbooths and back onto the highway. If you think of different types of roads being developed for cars, trucks, pedestrians, or bikes, then the PCI specification isn't really a specific road, so much as the rules for how to build all roads. The PCI specification is really a way to connect various types of processor chips together. After a device takes on the PCI specification, it can work with roads designed for it. In other words, a PCI bus can work with an old ISA card and slow down, or work with an Ultra ATA controller and go very fast.

We're still talking about a hard drive with integrated drive electronics, but the description and capabilities keep changing. The actual performance of the disk gets better, and the disk can store more data. However, the connection between the IDE disk and the rest of the system has to improve as well. That improvement is described with the letters A-T-A.

- ATA is a specification—a set of rules for doing things.
- A different type of bus had to be developed in order for PIO and DMA to work correctly. This meant that a different kind of connection had to be made for the controller—the PCI bus.

- ATA-2 changed the original IDE controller so much, that the industry began calling the new version an enhanced version—the *enhanced* IDE (EIDE)—with transfer rates from up to 8.3MB/s.
- The PCI bus could be improved so as to handle increasing speeds (i.e., Ultra ATA): the ISA bus had reached its peak.

Like the IDE and ATA specifications, the PCI specification allows developers and manufacturers to follow a set of rules for connecting their devices. Rather than having to rebuild a device, hoping it will be compatible with everything in the market, PCI takes care of the compatibility as long as the new device follows the PCI rules.

PCI cards come in two lengths: full-sized and short. The full-size card is about 12.2 inches long, and the short card is about 6.8 inches long. The cards can have varying numbers of pins, but the physical bus connector is a 32-bit 124-pin slot.

Summary—Disk Drives

We've covered a lot of information in the preceding sections, and it can be confusing at times. Unfortunately, you're going to have to know a lot about hard drives, controller specifications, cylinders and tracks, and the differences between logical and physical drives. You should have a solid grasp of the following concepts at this point:

- The component parts of a disk drive, including read-write heads, tunnel erase heads, spindle motor and head actuator. You should also know what an IDE controller is. Pay particular attention to IDE and SCSI, but remember the ESDI controllers.
- The media sensor and write-protect locks, and the different types of densities on floppy disks (for example, 720KB and 1.44MB).
- Tracks and sectors, and their relationship with cylinders and heads
- The difference between a drive controller (e.g., IDE) and an interface specification, particularly the ATA specification and PIO modes
- The PCI bus and Ultra DMA (UDMA).

The following sections on removable storage, optical drives, and flash memory are not so easy to summarize, so we'll use this segment to let you know that you should be prepared for a question or two relating to CDs or DVDs.

If you're in a rush, we highly recommend that you spend your time getting clear and focused on the hard drive controllers, the ATA specification, and the PCI bus.

Hard Drive Configuration

After you've installed an IDE, EIDE, or SCSI drive (SCSI is discussed in Chapter 8), the drive still won't be ready to run without going back to the motherboard. The BIOS must properly recognize the drive. IDE drives are usually auto-configured (in CMOS), and today, almost any BIOS can query an IDE drive for its settings.

As we've stated, SCSI manufacturers have opted for their own closed architectures, so almost every adapter is different. The immediate problem that this presents is the lack of auto-configuration. Be sure to keep the reference manual for any SCSI device, because this is the only place to find which BIOS settings are required by the device.

Although people say that SCSI drives are faster than IDE drives, that's not always true. SCSI—like PCI and USB—is a bus, not a controller. Hard drive speed is partly related to the interface, but is mostly related to average seek time. Other parts of the drive also contribute to overall speed.

Hard drives typically move data into a command buffer at about 10MB/s on a sustained basis. With a transfer rate of 16.7MB/s, you would think that Fast ATA would be capable of keeping the buffer from becoming full. The reason it can't, has to do with the turnaround time that the PC takes between the commands it issues to the drive. This command turnaround time is what causes most of the slowdown in overall performance.

Command turnaround time delays come from the number of commands a PC makes to a drive, depending upon the size of the command requests. The requests are typically 4KB in size and are equivalent to the page size supported by a virtual memory operating system like Windows. It takes approximately 4 milliseconds for a drive to read a 4KB instruction command.

Command Turnaround Time and Overhead

When a 4KB command comes from the host machine to save a file, it takes approximately 400 microseconds for the drive controller to read the command data into its buffer. Fast ATA, with a burst transfer rate of 16.7 MB/s, had a sustained sequential data rate of 10.2 MB/s. The buffer emptied 4KB in about 250 microseconds, leaving 150 microseconds of overhead between commands, to keep the filling and the emptying of the buffer in balance. A typical desktop PC has a command turnaround time of around 275 microseconds, and takes approximately 525 microseconds to empty the buffer. This reduces the effective transfer rate of Fast ATA to approximately 7.8MB/s (4096 bytes divided by 525). Keep in mind that the drive has a burst transfer rate of 16.7MB/s.

7.8MB/s is 75 percent of the drive's 10.2 MB/s sequential data rate. What this means, is that for every 3 bytes being sent to the host, 1 byte accumulates in the buffer. A typical buffer holds 64KB worth of data, and 1 buffer's worth of data is accumulated for every 3 buffers of data being sent to the host. At that point, the drive "slips a rev" (a rev, or revolution), meaning that before the host can drain the buffer, the system has to wait until a requested sector rotates past the head a second time. The buffer typically holds 64KB, which means 1 slipped rev occurs for every 256KB of data being transferred.

The effective data transfer rate of the bus equals the burst transfer rate minus the command turnaround time. By doubling the rate at which the buffer is emptied, Ultra ATA compensates for command turnaround overhead. Ultra ATA's 33MB/s burst transfer rate allows a 4KB data block to transfer in 125 microseconds (half the time of Fast ATA), leaving 275 microseconds for overhead. 125 plus 275 equals 400 microseconds (the buffer fill rate), and as a result, the buffer doesn't accumulate data and can avoid slipped revs.

Most PCs use the IDE interface because it's inexpensive and performs reliably. Many manufacturers sell the same drive in both IDE and SCSI models, and put an extra chip on the SCSI circuit board. In that case, the extra chip is a SCSI *adapter*. Because this extra chip requires data to go through an extra step, the IDE model performs slightly better.

One of those extra steps is the command buffering, whereby up to 256 commands can be sent by the system and rearranged by the SCSI adapter. On a system using multitasking, where several programs are running at once, the extra intelligence of the SCSI adapter boosts system performance. A couple of hundred microseconds here and there, and pretty soon you're talking about real time!

Another advantage of the SCSI interface is that if bad sectors develop on the disk, a SCSI system can mark the sector as bad and avoid crashing on a disk read. IDE systems require either reformatting the disk or running a disk repair utility.

SCSI devices can communicate independently of the CPU and can operate at the same time. IDE devices have individual controllers that can operate only one at a time. Similar to DMA transfer, this allows SCSI devices to run a bypass around the CPU for simple device-related tasks. This bypass keeps the CPU from bogging down.

Removable Media and Drives

Many years ago, a very inexpensive notebook appeared on the market that used a stylus-based operating system. It was available in various sizes, stored data in character recognition and graphic format, offered many color styles, and cost about $1 at the local stationery supply store. The stylus cost about $.29. The main thing about these spiral bound notebooks (SBNs), as they were called, was that the stored data could be easily transported. You ripped a sheet of paper out of the notebook and jammed it into your pocket.

Portability and extra storage have always been issues for computer customers, which is why 3 ¼-inch floppies lasted so long. If you needed to mail a file to someone, drop a copy of a file off at a service bureau, or even make backups of your hard drive, you had to use either floppy disks or a tape drive. Email changed all that, of course, but who wants to email a 100MB attachment?

Tape and Digital Audio Tape (DAT)

Dating back to the IBM mainframes, which used magnetic tape for data storage, auxiliary tape machines have stored data as backups. Prior to removable hard drives and write-enabled CD-RW drives, backups often involved 10MB to 50MB of a PC's hard disk. Tape drives usually interface with a SCSI connection and an internal expansion card.

The basic tape cartridge used in most home-market tape machines was the quarter-inch cartridge (QIC) analog tape format. QIC was replaced by digital audio tape (DAT) storage, which is a competitive technology to the CD-ROM and DVD optical storage (see below). Tape transfer on a high-end tape system ranges from 1MB/s to 3MB/s.

Tape storage has both high capacity and low cost. Modern cartridges can store more than 7GB of information, and both the tape and the backup software use a high degree of error correction. The error checking results in very reliable data backup, and many networks continue to use either analog QIC or DAT systems for archiving data.

The introduction of DVDs, CD carousels (multiple CDs available in a single drive), and optical read-write technology is having a strong effect on the consumer market for tape. Redundant Arrays of Inexpensive Disks (RAID), the multigigabyte capacity of removable drive cartridges, Iomega's Zip and Jaz drives, along with the downward trend in costs may make the last remaining advantage of tape systems their complex error checking. However, that checking comes at a cost in terms of time, and consumers may be willing to sacrifice error-free backups for convenience and speed.

Optical Storage

Since the introduction of the compact disk (CD), both the music industry and the computer industry have been coming together in the way they use optical storage technology. At the moment, standards are still sketchy, and we can only generalize about the main concepts relative to CDs and digital versatile disks (DVDs). That being said, we can break the optical storage disk into four, broad categories:

- *CD-ROM*—Information is written by a manufacturer and becomes Read-Only Memory.
- *CD-R*—Information can be written only once by a consumer, making these disks Recordable. CD-R disks are technically called *Write Once, Read Many (WORM)*.
- *CD-RW*—Information can be written to and erased from 1 to approximately 25 times, making these disks ReWritable. These are significantly more expensive than other CDs, and do have a limit as to the number of rewrites.
- *DVD*—These disks have a much higher storage capacity than a CD and a different storing process.

CDs

CDs started out as a layer of highly reflective aluminum foil sandwiched between layers of transparent plastic. These original disks used a writing laser beam to etch microscopic marks, or pits, in the foil. A reading laser beam then bounced the reflections from nonpitted (flat) areas of the foil back to a photo sensor. The combination of the pits and the flat areas (lands) results in the binary 1s and 0s of digital information. A standard CD can hold up to 640MB of information (approximately 74 minutes of music).

Optical disks, unlike hard disks, return to the old, vinyl record method of writing in a long, single track. The track spirals from the outer edge of the disk to the center. Tracking is where the laser maintains a specified optical path to read correct information. The reading laser tracks the spiral, reading a 1 for reflective surfaces, or a 0 for nonreflective surfaces.

A track on a magnetic disk is one of many independent and concentric circles. The track on an optical disk is a single spiral that begins at the outer edge and terminates at the center. "Laying down tracks" in a recording studio means recording a song. For a time, there were magneto-optical drives that worked like typical floppies and hard drives. They used a track and sector system in concentric rings around the center of the disk.

A problem with audio CDs is that the surface at the outer edge is moving faster than the surface near the center, making music sound slower and slower as the laser reads data closer and closer to the spindle motor. To overcome this, audio CDs use a process called *Constant Linear Velocity* (CLV). As the reading laser moves inward, the revolutions per minute of the spindle motor increase. A mechanical feedback system works to sustain an exact velocity (speed) as the reading laser moves closer or farther from the center. Unfortunately, this is an expensive manufacturing process.

Data disks, originally distinguished as CD-ROMs, developed a different method of handling velocity. Constant Angular Velocity (CAV) uses a small buffer to vary the data stream through a microprocessor. In other words, it doesn't matter how slow or fast data enters the buffer (from variable surface velocity) because the data coming out of the buffer is adjusted for speed.

A feature of the CAV process is that information regarding the mechanical environment is included with the data being stored. This means that the CD-ROM is constantly correcting itself for speed and signal strength, resulting in extremely reliable data reads. With the CLV CD, the spindle motor uses a mechanical process to adjust the head mechanism as it moves closer or farther from the center, keeping speed constant.

The two methods used with CDs for handling variable surface velocity are CLV, where the speed of the spindle motor is controlled, and CAV, where processing adjusts the data stream.

The distinguishing feature of a data CD is that it reads information in segments that can be located anywhere on the disk, much like random access to a hard drive. Audio CDs are more like the sequential reads of a tape backup unit. The seek, or access time, is how fast the reading laser can be repositioned at the start of a requested segment of data. Repositioning doesn't matter on an audio CD, but on a typical data CD, the average access time is approximately 95ms (milliseconds) on a 24X drive. A typical hard drive has an average seek time of 4–10ms.

Increasing the spin velocity and size of the buffer in a CAV CD drive multiplies the throughput from the original (1X) buffer speed of 150KB per second (KB/s). Various multiples led to the designation of 2X, 4X, 16X, and so on. Audio CDs slow down the buffer for music, but data CDs favor faster throughput. A so-called 100X CD actually copies data to the hard drive before reading it.

CD-R

The original CD-ROM worked with actual pits that were "burned" into the surface of a piece of foil by the manufacturer. To give consumers the ability to write their own CDs without putting someone's eye out, CD-Rs use a type of organic dye (not to be confused with a chip die, or engraved stamp). The dye is layered into the plastic of the disk, and heat from the laser as it passes by, changes the reflective properties of the dye.

After the dye particle changes, it stays that way. Once again, reflection equates to 0 and less reflection equates to 1. Different colors of dye have different properties. Gold-green has a rated life of 10 years. Silver-blue has a rated life of 100 years. Reading a disk is one simple sweep over a disk, but in order to write a disk, the laser has to generate a certain temperature to change the dye, which takes time. Original 1X CD-Rs could take up to 90 minutes to write an entire disk. Current disks are much faster.

Transfer Ratios

Original specifications are usually referred to as a 1:1 ratio, written as 1X. In other words, the first AGP specification was 1X (sometimes X1), and the first CD players operated at 1X speeds (i.e., one-to-one). Each stage of the technology has evolved to increase performance ratios with a multiplier. When we say a CD "burner" is rated at 24X, we mean that the writing process takes place 24 times faster than the original technology. Generally speaking, 1X is roughly equal to a transfer rate of 150KB/s, or about 9MB per minute.

If the stream of data to be written to a CD-R isn't uniform, any interruption in the data flow destroys the CD. Writing or "burning" software uses either a series of buffers to ensure data continuity, or creates an image of the data as it will appear on the disk. It then reads out the image in a steady, continuous stream.

Referring to the types of CDs we listed just a moment ago, you can see that today's performance specifications are commonly listed as a speed ratio of: CD-R (write once), CD-RW (write many times), and CD-ROM (play only). Using the "X" numbers as multipliers of the original technology speeds, a 16X10X40X CD drive has three different speeds, according to the feature being used. This example uses a 16:1 multiplier when writing to a CD-R disk, a 10:1 when writing to an RW disk, and can play a CD-ROM at 40:1, or forty times the speed of the original CD drives. A few of these ratios applied to actual files provide the following approximate transfer rates:

- 1X records 650 MB in 74 minutes
- 2X records 650 MB in 37 minutes
- 4X records 650 MB in 19 minutes
- 8X records 650 MB in 9 minutes
- 12X records 650 MB in 6 minutes

DVD

CD-ROMs, CD-Rs, and CD-RWs are gradually being replaced by digital versatile disks. Because these DVDs were initially developed for the movie industry, the "V" is sometimes thought to stand for "video," but be sure to call them digital versatile disks. A DVD uses the same diameter as a CD-ROM, but varies somewhat in thickness.

Once again, the technology quickly migrated to PCs, and we ended up with DVD and DVD-ROM. Both types of disks are read-only, and a video disk is differentiated from a data disk in much the same way that the "ROM" in CD-ROM distinguishes a computer disk from a music disk. An audio CD player can't use the data tracks from a CD-ROM, but a computer can read the data tracks and also play music. The same principle applies to DVDs and DVD-ROMs; a video DVD player is designed to work only with a video or audio installation.

For the moment, there aren't any real standards in DVD technology. DVD Recordable (DVD-R) disks are entering the market, but they're still somewhat expensive. Typical DVDs can either use one or both sides, and can have single or dual layers, not unlike the division of floppy disks. The four current types of DVDs at the moment are:

- Single-sided, single-layer (SS/SL)—Holds 4.7GB
- Single-sided, dual-layer (SS/DL)—Holds 8.5GB
- Dual-sided, single-layer (DS/SL)—Holds 9.4GB
- Dual-sided, dual-layer (DS/DL)—Holds 17GB

The reason storage is higher on a DVD than a CD is that the data markings on a DVD are much smaller and closer together. Therefore, the pit length is shorter, and the optical path is much narrower, requiring a reading laser with a shorter wavelength to read the pits and lands. Some combination units actually have two reading lasers: one for DVDs and one for standard CDs.

A dual-layer DVD uses two layers of media. One layer is set deep in the plastic, and one layer is shallow. The focal length of the laser is set up so that it can read both layers even though one is behind the other.

The photo sensor connects to a digital-to-analog converter for music and video. For computer data, as in the case of CD-ROM data disks, the information continues straight through in digital format. DVDs use an IDE/ATAPI (see "Fast ATA and Ultra DMA [UDMA]") interface, with a dual-connector 40-pin cable, and they require configuration as either a master or slave (primary or secondary) drive.

All DVDs require bus mastering, which means that they connect to a PCI bus, not an ISA bus. If the drive is used to play video, it also requires an MPEG decoder. The decoder, usually a hardware device, also requires a slot in the bus. To conserve slots, many decoders are now integrated onto a video expansion card.

Beginning with Windows 95, the software drivers (instructions) for all DVDs are part of the PnP specification. Older systems require manual installation of the drive, using the generic MicroSoft CD EXtensions (MSCDEX.EXE) program and the specific ATAPI driver for the DVD device.

Although dust is the main problem in optical drives, a can of compressed air can usually keep them clean. However, because optical disks use transparent plastic around a data layer, a smudge, scratch, or anything that impairs the optical transparency generates read errors. A good nonabrasive plastic polish, such as those found in automotive stores, can sometimes buff out minor scratches. There are also small machines (e.g., Disk Doctor) that work well for minor repairs.

MPEG Formats

The Motion Picture Experts Group (MPEG) is another bunch of people who set standards. MPEG files, .MOV files, and .AVI files are all specifications for storage and/or compression. MPEG-1 was designed mostly for small images (352x240) transferring at 1.5MB/s. MPEG-1 works well with animated .GIF images on Web sites.

MPEG-2 (the second version) incorporated support for High-Definition TV (HDTV), and resolutions up to 1920x1152. This release allowed for 135 minutes of video, with 3 channels of digital audio and 4 channels of subtitles. By only using 1 audio channel, a DVD can store more than 160 minutes of video. MPEG-2 is the current standard format for digital video and DVDs.

MPEG-3 is not the same as an .MP3 audio file. MPEG-3 is specifically for HDTV and is incorporated into MPEG-2

MPEG-4 is the next version of MPEG-2. With video-conferencing and 3D graphics taking up more bandwidth on the Internet, two things are happening: The first is that streaming applications are pushing for higher compression rates; the second is the development of Internet2 (mentioned in Chapter 8). MPEG-4 will use a higher compression factor, and include intelligent audio-video controls for conferencing. At the moment, the two leading streaming media companies are RealNetworks and Microsoft. Following closely behind them is Apple Computer, using its QuickTime format. Version 6 may increase the market share for QuickTime, given that it supports the MPEG-4 format.

Flash Memory

We saw how the CCD brought about the development of scanners, and how these charge-coupled devices could be used to capture analog images. Naturally, the chips were almost immediately put to work in photographic equipment. The CCDs could be used to convert an image to digital information, but cameras still required film in order to store the image. Disk storage was physically still too large to help in that department.

The laptop and notebook computer market have been driving development efforts toward smaller-sized components. Smaller size means less weight, easier transportation, and perhaps most important, less power consumption. Flash memory comes out of the desire for small storage devices, and has migrated first to the digital camera market and now to the general storage market. Ongoing sophistication in CCDs has joined with memory "cards" to produce a new demand for digital still cameras and video cameras, and the recent MPEG Audio Layer 3 (MP3) compression format has carried flash memory into the music industry.

Flash memory is divided into *blocks*, as opposed to the bytes of conventional memory. Because it is nonvolatile memory, it requires a way to both write and erase information. The cards use a very small amount of voltage to change the blocks, and they operate very quickly. This makes flash memory fast, with very low voltage requirements, and very compact in size. Four types of flash memory are succeeding in the market at the moment: CompactFlash, SmartMedia, ATA Data Flash, and Sony's MemoryStick. Table 6.1 shows the way that these memory cards interface with a device, as well as their varying amounts of storage memory.

Table 6.1 Flash memory types and storage.

Card Name	Interface	Storage
CompactFlash	Proprietary	8–128MB
Smart Media	Proprietary	2–64MB
ATA DataFlash	PC card, type II	8–512MB
Sony Memory Stick	Proprietary	4–32MB

Memory capacities continue to increase, and the numbers given are as of 2001.

CompactFlash emulates (imitates) a disk drive to the degree that once the card has been formatted, it can be plugged into a PC and will act like any other disk drive. The cards are about an inch-and-a-half long, and include an interface adapter on the card. They can be plugged directly into a camera, or into an adapter that plugs into a PC card. The adapter can then be inserted into a laptop. The other three types of cards require a proprietary adapter to install in a device.

SmartMedia was originally called a *Solid State Floppy Disk Card* (SSFDC), and it is actually a NAND-type EEPROM "chip," about the size of a postage stamp. What makes these cards so interesting is that unlike an integrated circuit board, a SmartMedia card is made up of only logic gates. As technology shrinks the size of the gates, more of them can be put on a standard-size card. Toshiba has already announced a 512MB die, with a proposed 1GB card coming next.

Logic Gates

Have you ever wondered how a microprocessor actually thinks? How does it know if something is true or false? How does it distinguish between AND and OR, TRUE and FALSE? Microprocessors have an area on their die that's taken up by *logic gates*. These gates are extremely small electronic components somewhat like transistors. The fundamental unit of a digital circuit, most logic gates have 2 input terminals and 1 output terminal, along with a single evaluation instruction for the comparative voltage levels at the input terminals. If the voltage is the same, the output sends a signal. If the voltage is different, the output sends a different signal. The output signals can represent a 1 or a 0.

There are seven basic logic gates: AND, OR, XOR, NOT, NAND, NOR, and XNOR. SmartMedia cards use NAND gates, but other EEPROM chips can be NOR-type chips. NAND technology has a speed advantage in storage processes, making them ideal for nonvolatile storage. NOR-type chips have an advantage in terms of random byte access but are slower when storing information.

The simplicity of a SmartMedia card makes it compatible with a wide variety of devices. Although the cards were initially used in the digital camera market, so-called *card readers* are becoming widely available for anything that requires storage. These readers attach to a system with a USB cable and make the flash memory look like another disk drive. Advances in this technology have produced hard drive flash cards with built-in USB connections. We can now carry a 1GB extra drive (or main drive) in a shirt pocket and connect it with any USB-compliant machine. (USB is covered in Chapter 8.)

The ATA-compliant PC card, which was used for everything from game adapters to modems to SCSI interface cards, was originally designed as ATA-compliant memory. These memory cards also act like a disk, and they use the ATA specification much like an IDE and EIDE drive.

The main difference with a Sony MemoryStick is an erase-protection switch and the rectangular shape. Like the CompactFlash and SmartMedia, the Sony cards use a proprietary interface, but a memory stick is about .5 in. wide and 4 in. long.

Practice Questions

Question 1

Which 3 ½-inch floppy disk format is the most common?

- ❍ a. DS,SD 1.44MB
- ❍ b. DS,SD 720KB
- ❍ c. DS,DD 1.44MB
- ❍ d. DS,DD 1.7MB

Answer c is correct. 3 ½-inch floppy disks are usually double-sided, double-density (DS,DD) and hold 1.44MB of information. Double-sided, single-density (DS,SD) 720KB disks are almost obsolete. Certain 3 ½-inch floppy disks can be formatted in 1.7MB (Microsoft distribution format) and 2.8MB (super disk) densities are rare.

Question 2

The read-write heads for a platter are all that are necessary to read and write data to the disk.

- ❍ a. True
- ❍ b. False

Answer b, false, is correct. Unless data is erased, a disk will run out of room. Each read-write head is contained within a tunnel erase head.

Question 3

On a typical IDE or EIDE controller, Drive 0 is called the ________ drive, with a default IRQ of ______.

- ❍ a. Slave, 15
- ❍ b. Slave, 14
- ❍ c. Master, 15
- ❍ d. Master, 14

Answer d is correct. When two drives are connected, one must be configured as the primary, or master (drive 0). The second must be configured as the secondary or slave (drive 1). IRQ 14 is set aside as the default for a primary, or master hard drive controller.

Question 4

The organization of a platter in a hard drive is described using the following pairs of terms? [Choose all that apply]

- ❑ a. Cylinders and tracks
- ❑ b. Sections and FAT
- ❑ c. Segments and clusters
- ❑ d. Sectors and clusters

Answers a and d are correct. Tracks are concentric, circular paths placed on both sides of the platter. They are identified by numbers, starting with track 0. Tracks in the same position on multiple platters are called *cylinders*. Tracks are divided into sectors during formatting, and the operating system stores data in clusters. A hard drive does not use sections or segments. The File Allocation Table (FAT) is used by the operating system to locate files.

Question 5

An IDE hard drive controller connection on a motherboard can operate up to how many disk drives?

- ❍ a. One
- ❍ b. Two
- ❍ c. Four
- ❍ d. Seven

Answer b is correct. Many motherboards have two IDE controllers, each of which can run two drives. The drives are not limited to only IDE hard drives. The system can run a total of four drives, using both controllers; however, the question asks about a single controller.

Question 6

Which of the following statements is true?

- ❍ a. An ATA drive uses an IDE controller.
- ❍ b. An IDE controller uses an ATA bus.
- ❍ c. An IDE drive uses an ATA controller.
- ❍ d. An ATA bus uses an IDE controller.

Answer b is correct. An IDE controller uses an ATA bus. Any drive with a built-in controller is technically called an *IDE drive*. However, the question makes a distinction between a drive, a controller, and a bus. ATA is a specification for an interface bus. ATA is never a controller or a drive. Answers b and c have the correct use of IDE, but answer c includes an ATA controller.

Need to Know More?

Bigelow, Stephen. *Troubleshooting, Maintaining, and Repairing Personal Computers.* New York, NY: TAB Books, 1995. ISBN 0-07-912099-7. Detailed information from a break-fix standpoint can be found on the following pages: hard drives (pages 341-358), CD-ROM drives (pages 207-220), floppy drives (pages 310-325), and tape drives (pages 792-803).

Karney, James. *Upgrade and Maintain Your PC.* Indianapolis, IN: MIS Press, date. ISBN 1-55828-460-5. Hard drives are covered on pages 303 through 340.

Messmer, Hans-Peter. *The Indispensable PC Hardware Book.* Reading, MA: Addison-Wesley, 1995. ISBN 0-201-87697-3. More information is provided than you need for the exam, but this reference goes into great detail. Storage devices are discussed on pages 651 through 835.

Minasi, Mark. *The Complete PC Upgrade and Maintenance Guide.* San Francisco, CA: Sybex Network Press, 1996. ISBN 0-7821-1956-5. Here is your source for information on peripherals from a repair standpoint: hard drives (pages 427-479), CD-ROM drives (pages 1017-1047), and floppy drives (pages 753-789).

Rosch, Winn. *Hardware Bible.* Indianapolis, IN: Sams Publishing, 1994. ISBN 0-672-30954-8. Again, far more information is provided than you need for the exam: storage technology and interfaces (pages 367-482), floppy drives (pages 541-563), hard drives (pages 483-530), CD-ROM drives (pages 563-601), and tape drives (pages 603-632).

Peripherals: Output Devices

Terms you'll need to understand:

- ✓ Video display terminal (VDT), cathode ray tube (CRT), liquid crystal display (LCD)
- ✓ Red, green, and blue (RGB); cyan, magenta, and yellow (CMY)
- ✓ Pixel, dots per inch (dpi)
- ✓ Triad (triangular color units)
- ✓ Dot matrix, ink jet, and laser printers

Concepts you'll need to master:

- ✓ Display resolutions
- ✓ Interlaced versus noninterlaced screen refresh
- ✓ Resolution versus dpi
- ✓ Electrophotographic (EP) drum and relative negative electrostatic charge
- ✓ Laser printing process steps

Chapters 5 and 6 looked at getting data into the system and then storing that data when the power is turned off. The last part of the process is getting data back out of the system—the *output.* If everything goes well, the information coming out of the computer makes sense to a human being. On the other hand, output can just as easily be meaningless garbage or noise. An *output device* is the thing that produces the output. If a keyboard is a standard input device, with a hard drive being a standard storage device, the display screen (monitor) is usually the standard output device.

Transient vs. Final Output

Output relates to time, in the sense that you can have transient output and final output. Transient output is the stream of data being sent somewhere for fleeting observation or temporary storage. Final output is data that moves away from the system completely and stays fixed in time. "Transient" is a fancy way of saying "just passing through."

An example of transient output is pressing a key on the keyboard and inputting a scan code to the system. The code exists only long enough to be picked up by the CPU. Additionally, you have no way to verify which code you sent because you have no way directly to see a translation of that code. The CPU accepts the code and then sends it on to the video subsystem. The video subsystem is in charge of outputting a representation of the scan code to the screen, where it becomes a letter or a number. The screen displays the output only long enough for you to act on it.

Another example of transient output is when an application is holding too much information for the installed RAM and sends part of that information to the hard disk for temporary storage. This is called a *swap file* and is part of virtual memory. After the data in the swap file has been used, it's erased by new temporary (transient) data. A swap file is somewhat similar to a buffer. We'll discuss Windows swap files in Chapter 11.

Buffers

Imagine a faucet, a sink, and a drain at the bottom of the sink. The water is like a data stream coming to a modem (the drain). If the water from the faucet is coming out slowly, then it goes right down the drain. If the water starts pouring out of the faucet faster than it can drain, the sink begins to fill up. The sink is a buffer, and can only hold so much water (data). When the sink becomes full, water pours over the edge onto the floor. In a buffer, data is thrown away. If the data source and the buffer are intelligent, meaning that some sort of software logic is being used by the devices, the speed of the data stream can be adjusted so that no data will be lost.

This would be like having a drain that could control the faucet. On the other hand, making a bigger drain would be like widening a bus or increasing the processing speed of the device.

Final output is just that: final. After you've completed inputting and the system has finished its calculating, the result (you hope) is something useful (e.g., a report, spreadsheet, or database) and that result must stay put—in a storage device. When you save a file and copy it to a disk, you're creating output from both an application (the file) and from the overall system (the copy on the disk).

When a sound card produces sounds from a speaker, we have two forms of output. The sound you're hearing with your ears is final output, and you store the results in your brain. The .WAV file being modified in the system is output being held in RAM or stored to disk.

The video monitor is the standard output device for working with a computer. The printer is the most common peripheral for creating final output. Characters on a screen are transient and change from moment to moment. A screen capture of a particular set of characters at a particular moment in time can be sent to the printer. The paper with the image of what was on the screen is final output. Final output can be stored and retrieved for use at a later time.

Video Displays

Monitors have been called *cathode ray tubes* (CRTs), *Video Display Terminals* (VDTs), *CONsole* (CON), which is the DOS device name, or simply the *screen*. In this section, we refer to display monitors generically as *monitors*. The two main categories of monitors are cathode tube and liquid crystal display (LCD). A CRT is a vacuum tube. There is an electron gun at one end (usually narrow) of the tube and a large piece of glass (wider) at the other end.

The inside surface of the viewing pane is coated with a layer of dots made up of three different kinds of phosphor (a chemical). The electron gun is made up of three different electron beams. Each beam shoots a stream of electrons at the phosphors, with each beam making one of the phosphor types glow. When we look at the glass face of the monitor, we're actually seeing through the glass to the backside of the phosphor layer. In monochrome monitors, there is only one layer of phosphors, either green or amber, and a single electron beam.

Color and Light

Color CRT monitors have a separate electron beam for each of the three primary colors. We can create every color of *light* by using three primary colors: red (R), green (G), and blue (B), making the so-called RGB colors. RGB colors are used when we're working with direct light. If we're working with reflected light (e.g., light bouncing off of paper to our eyes), we use three different colors. Reflected color is composed of cyan (bluish [C]), magenta (pinkish red [M]), and yellow (Y). Commercial color-separation printing works with solid colors (ink) and reflected light (paper). RGB monitors create their own light, but color printing uses a CMY process.

CMY is also used in LCD panels. Solid materials reflect light and react differently than glowing light does when they're are blended together.

When three different phosphors are arranged in a triangle of dots, they become a triad (discussed in a moment). The video card can manipulate the electrons so as to change how each dot glows. By combining red, blue, and green glowing light, we can fool the eye into thinking that it sees all sorts of colors in-between. One triad in an RGB monitor makes up one pixel.

Pixels, Triads, and Resolution

A pixel is a fancy name for a dot. Each phosphor dot on the inside of a monitor is a pixel (a picture unit). We use three pixel dots to create all the colors of the rainbow, and the combination making up an RGB "dot" is called a *pixel triad*. A pixel is loosely defined as a "picture unit," which is a term invented by Microsoft. Depending on how closely pixels can be bunched together per inch, we can say that a monitor has a resolution measurement.

The word "resolution," in the context of computer video, should technically be replaced with "pixel addressability." We're really discussing how many pixels can be addressed in something called the video frame buffer, but you won't need to worry about a frame buffer for the exam.

Triads are very small, so the inside of the CRT has a lot of them next to each other in horizontal and vertical lines. The combined lines of triads running across and down the inside face of the tube forms a large matrix of triads. Take a look at the lower right corner of Figure 7.1, where you can see how a pixel is made up of three-dot triads.

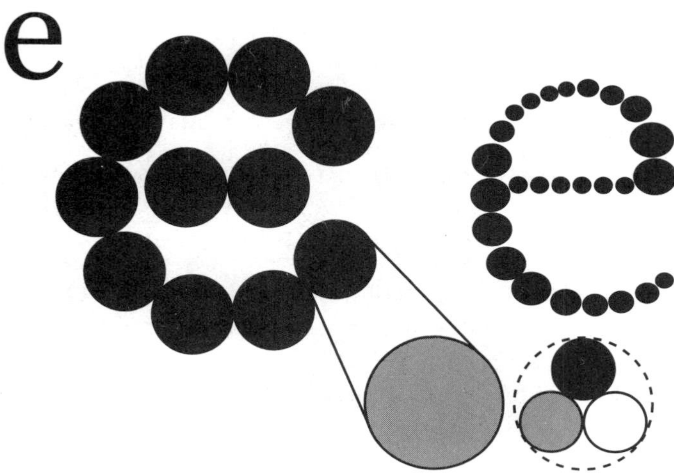

Figure 7.1 Smaller pixels mean sharper resolution.

True resolution should refer to the smallest object capable of being displayed on the screen, and therefore would be more related to dot pitch. A neurotically correct definition of resolution is "the degree of detail visible on a monitor, and therefore is related to the size of the electron beams, the degree of focus in their alignment, the arrangement of the pixel triads, and video bandwidth." But who's neurotic?

Scanners and monitors both define optical resolution by the number of pixels per inch. The only difference is that a scanner pixel is equal to one charge-coupled device (CCD). The optical resolution is limited by the physical size of the CCD. A CCD is a small piece of electronic equipment (diode) that registers whether light (photons) is or is not present—on or off. Electronic circuitry is joined to the light-sensing area, designed to convert the photon data into electrical impulses. The combined unit is one charge-coupled device. The point, or spot of light being registered by one CCD, then, is the "pixel" equivalent of a dot of ink on a piece of paper.

CCDs are arranged in a matrix and the information from each device is read in a serial process. CMOS imaging takes advantage of a different structure, and allows data to be read from the entire grid (matrix) at once. CCD imaging has a much greater market share than CMOS imaging.

The smaller the physical size of the CCDs in the scanner, the more dots per inch (dpi) of image can be acquired. An important measurement of a scanner's quality is its resolution in optical dpi. Printers use dots of ink, and the smallest dot of ink that can be produced is equal to a printer "dot." The more dots per inch, the higher the image resolution.

A scanner acquires an image and during the process limits each dot of the image to the size of the CCD. A printer outputs an image already in memory. Regardless of the resolution of the already-acquired image, the printer limits the dots of the image to the size of ink dots.

An RGB monitor uses lighted dots, each of which is one pixel. LCD panels use a molecular crystal as a pixel device, and gas-plasma screens use a pinpoint flash of heated gas to describe a pixel. A typical 640×480 pixel screen contains 640 dots on each of the 480 lines. This equals approximately 300,000 pixels.

Both printers and scanners measure resolution in dots per inch (dpi). Monitors measure resolution in pixels. Scanners measure *optical* resolution in pixels.

Regardless of how resolution is defined, if we follow common terminology, the smallest piece of light or darkness that a screen can physically display is the resolution of that screen. A standard VGA monitor has 640 pixels in a horizontal axis (line) and 480 pixels vertically. We use the × to mean the word "by," so the measurement is commonly written as 640×480. (To remember that the horizontal measurement comes first, just remember that "H" is before "V" in the alphabet).

HHH *x* VVV *x* CCC

You've probably heard carpenters and builders talk about two-by-fours. They're referring to a length of wood two inches in width by four inches in height. That means measuring one pair of sides produces two inches, and measuring the other pair (at right angles) produces four inches. In a computer matrix, the horizontal (left to right) measurement and the vertical (top to bottom) measurement become dots, pixels, addresses, and so on.

Different graphics modes can also have varying numbers of colors. We use a third number to refer to the number of colors associated with pixel resolution. A monitor resolution of 640×480×256 means that the monitor uses 640 pixels horizontally by 480 pixels vertically, and has 256 colors to display information. The Super Video Graphics Array (SVGA) standard of today's monitors is typically 1,280 by 1,024 pixels or 1,600 by 1,200 pixels. Typically, this is written on a specification sheet (spec sheet) as 1028×1024 or 1600×1200.

CRT monitors are capable of displaying a range of resolutions and scaling them to fit the screen. Most LCD panels have a fixed number of crystals, leading to a typical resolution of 1024×768. Generally, LCD monitors can display only one resolution at full-screen size, using one cell per pixel. Although they can be set to display at lower resolutions, and in some cases higher resolutions, the resulting image quality often becomes unstable. Lower resolutions are usually accomplished by using only a portion of the screen and then using software to rescale the images to fill the screen. However, this can lead to jagged edges (aliasing) in text, lines, or fine details, making the process more suited to photographs. Removing the jagged edges is called anti-aliasing.

We saw an interesting question that had to do with a change to the image size on the screen. Ordinarily, if a true black border appears around the image, then either the monitor is failing, or the image controls need to be adjusted. However, if the resolution of a monitor is changed from lower to higher, it can shrink all the images on the screen. Normally, this would not produce a black band around the entire image.

On an LCD panel, an image resolution change could potentially cause a black band to appear around the edge of the panel. Because the display is designed to match the number of pixels in an image, the LCD process turns crystals on and off, based on usage. If the resolution were set too high for the panel, the images would be too small to go all the way to the edges of the panel.

Dot Pitch

Dots-per-inch is not the same thing as dot pitch. Technically, dot pitch is the diagonal measurement between the centers of two neighboring triads. Because the triangles are all arranged in the same way, this works out to be the same measurement as from the center of any two dots of the same color.

Dot pitch is the space between each pixel triad, measured in millimeters. Generally, the smaller the dot pitch, the sharper the images, though a very small dot pitch can result in a loss of brightness and contrast. Typically, a good dot pitch ranges from .28 mm to .25 mm.

Screen Size

After resolution, the next most popular way of differentiating monitors is by screen size. Monitors have borrowed from the television industry by measuring screen size diagonally. The box that holds the cathode ray or the LCD panel has a physical diagonal dimension. The actual tube or panel has another size. The actual size of a displayed image is somewhat smaller than the physical edges of the tube or panel against the casing. Monitors often provide both a physical measurement and the dimensions of the actual viewing area.

Any monitor larger than 16 inches is called a *full-page monitor* because it can display a full page in a one-to-one (1:1) ratio. A monitor that is wider than it is tall is called a *landscape monitor* and can usually display two pages side by side. A monitor that is taller than it is wide is called a *portrait monitor*.

Portrait vs. Landscape

Silly as it may seem (and computer jargon is often downright goofy), the orientation of a page or monitor is called *portrait* or *landscape* because of the way painters turn their canvases one way or the other. A painter who was painting a person usually did the head, shoulders, and upper torso, which created a taller, narrow painting—a portrait of that person.

On the other hand, to capture the expanse of an outdoor scene, a painter would turn the canvas sideways to achieve a wide view—a landscape view of the scene.

To this day, when the paper is tall and narrow (e.g., a letter), it is said to have a portrait orientation. When the paper is wide and short (e.g., a spreadsheet), it is called landscape orientation.

Image Size

The actual area used to display the image is called the *raster*. The raster varies according to the resolution of the monitor and the internal physics of the screen. VGA at 640×480 on a 15-inch screen displays differently than SVGA at 1024×768. Television monitors usually *over scan* the image, putting the actual edge out beyond the physical edge of the screen. However, because a computer image contains information up to the edge and often beyond the raster edge, PC monitor images are designed to be smaller than the physical edges.

Many video cards have logic to automatically resize the raster, depending on the brand name and model of the monitor. On the outside of the monitor are a number of physical controls that can manually adjust the raster, along with the brightness, contrast, centering position, and so on.

Contrast Ratio

Contrast is essentially the difference between the black text of letters on a page and the white background of the piece of paper. Measuring this difference is often done by using a contrast ratio. Contrast ratio is, for the most part, what we tend to use when we judge the quality of a picture. If a picture has a high contrast ratio, we think of it as being sharper than a picture with a lower contrast ratio—even if the lower contrast picture has a much higher screen resolution.

Higher contrast provides both a sharper image and a more pure-looking white. Older passive matrix LCD panels had a typical contrast ratio of 15:1, showing washed-out colors and lack of detail. Normal room lighting could easily make the image impossible to see. Active matrix LCD panels, used in today's flat panel displays (FPDs), offer contrast ratios of more than 400:1. The lower-quality FPDs may provide a contrast ratio of 200:1, whereas slide film has a typical contrast ratio of over 500:1. Some flat panel displays (costing over $4,000) offer contrast ratios as high as 850:1.

Scan Cycle and Refresh Rate

Phosphors only glow for a short time when struck by an electron beam. The glow quickly fades away (kind of like a capacitor) and the image must be redrawn. A *redraw* is simply a technical term for blasting those phosphor triads with electrons a second time to make them glow again. In other words, the electron beam must strike the chemicals again and again, in order to refresh the level of light (like a memory refresh).

Because the electron gun is a kind of mechanical device, it can only blast electrons into one triad at a time. When you view a document on a monitor, it stays on the monitor; it doesn't appear for an instant and then fade away. When an electron gun redraws a screen of information, it typically begins at the upper left corner (as we face the monitor) and progresses back and forth across the monitor, moving down one line at a time like a typewriter. Eventually, it reaches the bottom right corner. The scan cycle is the time it takes for the beam to sweep from the top left to the bottom right of the screen.

When the beam of electrons reaches the lowest-right set of dots, it starts over again at the top left. If the image hasn't changed at all, it does the whole thing over again, refreshing the image. If the image has changed, the new information is processed and the image is drawn to the screen. Whether there is a new or old image, the electron beam is constantly moving back and forth across the inside layer of phosphors.

The video card tells the monitor how to time the scan cycle by sending a scan frequency to the monitor. Recall from our discussion of motherboards that frequency is measured in cycles per second, hertz (Hz) and megahertz (MHz). The electron beam must synchronize with the scan frequency to redraw the screen. The entire cycle from top to bottom then back to top is called the *refresh rate*.

Noninterlaced and Interlaced

When the electron beam sweeps across the pixels from top to bottom and left to right, all in one pass, we call it the *noninterlaced* mode. This involves sweeping past every pixel triad, one after the other, covering the entire screen once and then beginning over again.

Interlaced mode, on the other hand, means that the beam sweeps from top to bottom in *two* passes. First, it refreshes the odd lines and then the even lines—like weaving, or lacing a shoe half a side at a time. Figure 7.2 shows an interlaced monitor in the process of redrawing a screen. Every other row of pixels is glowing, and each row in-between is black (the phosphor has lost its glow).

Be sure to understand that noninterlaced means a big wad (technical term) of glowing chemicals, but that interlacing is weaving two things together. You can count on this being on the exam! Noninterlaced is a one-time pass by the electron gun. Interlaced is a two-time pass. You might even remember that "non" is very close to "one," which could stand for 1 pass over the screen. Intermixed uses the prefix "inter," meaning between, among, or in the midst of.

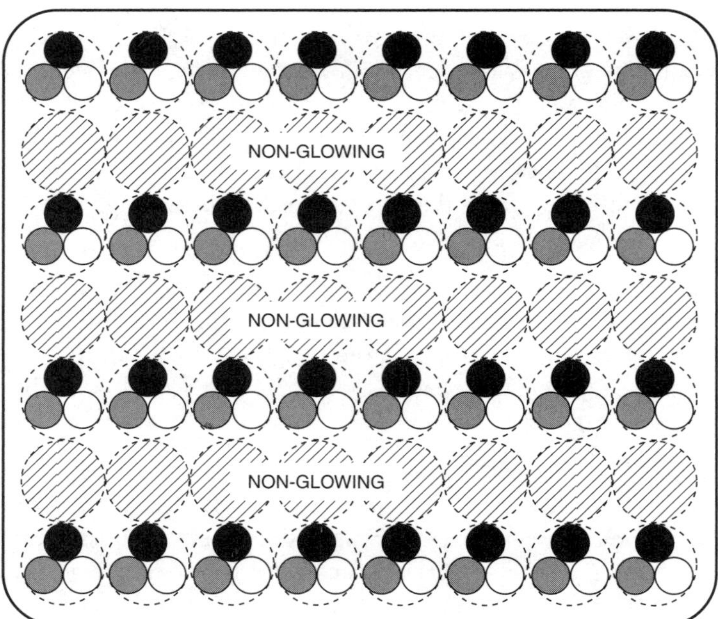

Figure 7.2 An interlaced monitor during a screen redraw.

Both modes take the same amount of time. However, given the same refresh rate, interlaced mode provides a more stable image and less flicker to the human eye. The problem is that manufacturers slow the refresh rate in interlaced monitors, and this slower rate allows for cheaper manufacturing and therefore cheaper monitors. The ideal would be to have an interlaced monitor with the *same* refresh rate as a noninterlaced monitor.

If you've ever watched a movie shown on an old projector, you know that the flicker comes from the spaces between each frame as it passes the projector's beam of light. The refresh rate includes a momentary pause during which the upper lines of triads are starting to fade and the electron gun is swinging into action to light them up again. We see this as a flicker (technically called a flicker).

You can see the actual interlacing process if you stand in front of, and a bit off to the side of a video monitor in a typical office environment. Florescent light flickers as the ballast triggers the explosive gases in the lighting tubes. The rate of flicker in the light is different than the refresh rate of the monitor, causing a so-called *beat wave* every half second or so. Another way to see interlacing, is by videotaping a television set.

Let's say a single-pass noninterlaced process means the gun has to sweep across the whole screen two times per minute, taking 30 seconds to go from top to bottom. The gun hits the starting point at the top two times in that minute, but in the 30 seconds it takes to travel down the back of the screen, the upper phosphors begin to fade. By the time the ray hits the bottom of the screen, the top phosphors have faded, and the ones in the middle of the screen are on their way out. At the 30-second point, we notice the upper half of the screen has gone black.

In a two-pass, interlaced example, the ray gun hits the top of the monitor four times every minute. Granted, it actually hits the very top odd row (row 1) twice and the even row (row 2) twice, but our eyes can't distinguish that small a distance (the width of 1 row). In 15 seconds all the odd rows light up as the gun skips the even rows and goes to the bottom of the screen. The physics of the delay time for the phosphors to start fading means that we can't tell they're fading in that short a time.

The faster the electrons can refresh the phosphors, the faster the refresh rate is and the less flicker the human eye perceives. Flickering can become a distraction with 16" and larger monitors. Higher resolutions require different refresh rates. Larger monitors can easily have resolutions of 1280×1024, and the spec sheet should include the refresh rates for different screen resolutions. For minimum flicker, the refresh rate should be at least 70 times per second (70Hz).

Be sure to take your time on a question involving interlacing. Stop, think, and remember that interlacing is like weaving your shoelaces together. Remember that just as you wear two shoes, it takes two passes to interlace a monitor.

Standard VGA

Following the Color Graphics Adapter (CGA) and Enhanced Graphics Adapter (EGA) monitors, a new technology was developed called *Video Graphics Array* (VGA). Actually a superset of EGA, VGA was developed by IBM to provide higher pixel resolution and graphics capabilities.

The VGA system didn't really support any processing, so the CPU still had to manage all the new calculations and logic. This made VGA very dependent on processor speed and linked it directly to the computer's processor in terms of speed comparisons. Installing the same model VGA monitor on either a 386 system or a 486 system, gave the appearance of making the monitor on the 486 faster, cleaner, and sharper. This was one of the first examples of apparent speed, as opposed to actual speed generated by technical specifications.

Safe Mode, in Windows, is when the monitor resolution goes to 640×480×16 (colors) as the original and default VGA standard. Windows will set the monitor to standard VGA mode, regardless of what higher resolution was last set during normal operation.

8514/A and XGA

IBM was on a quest for ever-increasing video resolution, the higher transfer rates necessary for graphic interfaces. The 8514/A adapter was developed to work with the proprietary MCA bus, and required a VGA controller that provided three new graphics modes. Using the rudimentary graphic commands that began with VGA, the 8514/A could perform a few video memory transfers, draw a few lines, and calculate rectangular areas in a display image.

The eXtended Graphics Adapter (XGA) followed on the heels of the 8514/A, and it was the first IBM video adapter to use video RAM (VRAM). The XGA specification could include an additional 500KB or 1MB of video memory, and it supported resolutions from 640×480 to 1024×768 for graphics, and 1056×400 for text, with a color palette of up to 65,535 colors (640×480 mode with additional memory installed).

SVGA and UVGA

Super VGA (SVGA) and Ultimate VGA (UVGA) aren't standards, and they mean different things to different manufacturers. "Ultimate," in particular, seems a bit optimistic, given statements from IBM like "10MB of hard disk is all anyone will ever need." IBM, like so many corporations involved with PCs, has a history of making failed assumptions about the market. Many of those assumptions led to the complex series of patches and bug fixes we deal with every day in modern computers. However, the common ground for standardization seems to be the (Video Electronics Standards Association) VESA VGA BIOS extensions, sometimes (improperly) called VESA SVGA. These VESA (discussed in Chapter 2) extensions at least allow programmers to try and provide a common software interface. Most monitors come with software drivers designed specifically to optimize their performance. Windows usually includes virtual drivers for common monitors as part of the Plug-and-Play feature.

Advantages of SVGA include the following:

- SVGA can produce millions of colors at a number of different resolutions, depending on the card and the manufacturer.
- The VESA resolution standards range from 640×400 to 1280×1024, with 256 colors.

Remember 15-pin Video and 9-pin COM. Modern monitors use a 15-pin connector, where the back panel of the PC has a *female* connector and the cable has a male connector (also 15-pin). Serial (COM) connectors are usually nine-pin connectors. (See Chapter 9.)

Accelerated Graphics Port (AGP)

Displaying data involves a number of subsystems, all of which work together to bring a visual pattern to the human eye. The basic display subsystems are a monitor, a video adapter (controller), and a graphics card. A typical motherboard has a video interface connector as part of the system board. Earlier motherboards typically used a specialized ISA or PCI slot for a graphics accelerator card. In the real world, so many people were adding processing power to their video system that by 1997, motherboards evolved to include an Accelerated Graphics Port (AGP).

The accelerated graphics port differs from previous motherboard expansion slots, in that it is a specialized bus dedicated to fast graphics processing. The AGP slot is usually located near the memory slots, but is shorter than DIMM slots and closer to the CPU. (Due to timing requirements, the maximum AGP bus length is 9 inches.) The data bus may be 8-, 16-, 24-, 32-, or 64 bits wide. AGP slots are almost always brown. The specification allows certain graphical processing (texture maps) to be done in system memory, bypassing the local memory found on add-on graphics accelerator cards.

Although a motherboard may come equipped with an AGP, this doesn't mean that an add-on video accelerator card isn't required. The AGP is only a bus, and, on its own, doesn't add additional video capability. Modern systems often advertise "onboard graphics" as a feature. This doesn't necessarily mean they come with an AGP.

Frame Buffers

Any image being sent to a monitor begins as a series of instructions programmed into an application. The application may be a drawing program, or it may be a mouse driver asking the computer to display a pointer picture (cursor) on the screen. The image on the monitor takes up the whole screen, and every part of it is placed on the screen in a specific location. All this is done by software working with the CPU.

You probably know that a strip of movie film contains a number of still pictures. As the film moves across the light source, the eye perceives movement. Each still picture on the strip is called a *frame*. The same term applies to the single picture being shown on a monitor at any given time. The difference is that some parts of the picture stay still while other parts of the picture change. For example, a menu and toolbar stay constant while a new cursor position and new characters are formed during typing.

The CPU keeps an area of memory—a buffer—where it stores the information being displayed on-screen at any given time. When it's ready, the CPU lets data out of the buffer. The keyboard has a small buffer that allows you to press keys faster than the system can process the presses. If you hold down a key, you'll eventually fill the buffer, in which case the CPU sends an alert tone to the PC's speaker. Likewise, the video system uses a buffer for image data, and the whole amount of data that goes to the screen is called the *frame buffer*.

SVGA and high-resolution monitors that take advantage of video RAM (VRAM) include a more complex set of graphics instructions than VGA does. These instructions, working together outside of main memory, allow for faster data transfers between the CPU and the screen. The older VGA instructions were not sophisticated enough for independent intelligence between the monitor and CPU.

Early VGA circuitry was integrated onto the motherboard in a very large-scale integration (VLSI) chip, and IBM developed the PS/2 display adapter to use the chip's functions. This adapter, part of the IBM PS/2 line of computers, was just like the early VGA card. It used an 8-bit expansion slot, and clone makers jumped on the bandwagon to produce many third-party VGA cards.

VLSI is the process of placing thousands (or hundreds of thousands) of electronic components on a single chip. Modern chips are almost always VLSI or ultra large-scale integration (ULSI) chips. There is no specific dividing point between VLSI and ULSI.

Supplementary Information

The information in this segment is not on the exam, and you may skip to "Liquid Crystal Displays (LCDs)" if you want. The AGP was designed to deliver increased bandwidth and graphics processing speed. Based on the PCI 2.1 standard, the port used clock doubling to double the 33MHz PCI bus (133MB/s transfer rate) found on Pentium II motherboards. Even though the PCI bus was capable of a 33MHz transfer rate, the AGP used a 66MHz timing signal, allowing for a 266MB/s transfer rate. AGP uses an "X1" mode and an "X2" mode. In X2 mode, the port uses—what ought to be familiar to you by now—both the rising and the falling edge of the clock. This doubles the transfer rate yet again, producing 532MB/s throughput. If X2 mode is supported on the video card, the AGP can provide graphics processing at four times the speed of the PCI bus.

The accelerated graphics port uses additional signal wires, providing for something called *pipelining and queuing*. It isn't just the timing that allows for enhanced graphics processing, but the overall combination of several features. AGP is able to actually reach the hypothetically defined peak transfer rates, bringing it into the realm of system memory. Pentium chips use a wider bus (64 bits), clocked at 66MHz. The AGP uses a smaller bus with a faster clock.

Textures (often used in computer games) are large data transfers, often larger than 128KBs. With transfer rates close to main memory speeds, the port is able to bypass the local memory on a video card, moving the textures directly in an out of main memory. In a way, the AGP is capable of acting like direct memory access channels for the specialized processor on a video card. Intel happened to notice this, one afternoon, and invented the term DIrect Memory Execute (DIME) to distinguish ordinary DMA from the ability of the AGP to directly "execute" texture instructions in main memory.

AGP provides an overall system performance increase for several reasons. Aside from high transfer rates, video cards no longer have to share the PCI bus controller with other devices. With large texture information executing directly in system memory, AGP is able to bypass the previous method of signal routing (unified memory architecture, or UMA) and video buffers.

Finally, AGP uses its own chip with AGP RAM. This isn't so different from the way add-on accelerator cards include specialized processors, but AGP is designed to be built into the motherboard and integrated with the CPU. Instead of using main memory, the CPU can send graphics data directly to the integrated AGP memory. This is much faster than trying to transfer data through the PCI bus controller. Better integration provides for a sort of teamwork between the AGP and CPU, with the central processor being able to access main memory at the same time (concurrently) as the AGP chip.

AGP X4 provides for 1GB/s throughput. Understand that these high speeds are designed to move information in and out of main memory to the graphics accelerator. In order to reach the gigabyte transfer rates, the other bus speeds have to be increased. The introduction of a 100MHz bus and an 800MB/s transfer rate, along with the movement to SDRAM and DDR SDRAM, was just what AGP needed. To that extent, AGP X8 mode is now being prepared for release.

Each change to the AGP specification is designed to be backwards-compatible with the previous modes. The following is a listing of the various AGP modes, their clock speeds and their transfer rates:

- AGP X1—66MHz clock, 266Mb/s throughput
- AGP X2—66MHz clock, 533MB/s throughput
- AGP X4—66MHz clock, 1.07GB/s throughput
- AGP X8—66MHz clock, approximately 2.1GB/s throughput

Intel Released the AGP 8X specification in November of 2000, as part of its planned migration to the 64-bit Itanium chips and other systems. AGP 8X is currently entering the market, and there is also a 32-bit version of the specification. The 32-bit version of AGP 8X should allow motherboard makers to use the same connector, although it defines a "universal" motherboard that will allow any previous version of AGP to coexist with X8 mode signals.

AGP has some competition from high-speed video accelerator cards. Modern VRAM and WRAM cards, not to mention Rambus RAM cards, are offering video memory with transfer rates of up to 1.6 GB/s. This is more than AGP X4 mode, and will use their own local memory for texture. AGP

RAM isn't as fast as these new memory chips, and although these cards use a PCI slot, they take advantage of the higher data transfer speed of AGP. Dropping prices and inexpensive RAM may make these cards a preferred installation over AGP. However, the likelihood is that AGP will be installed on all motherboards anyway.

Graphics Accelerator Cards

Most of today's computers come with integrated graphics and an AG port. Increased PC gaming, slide presentations, multimedia, video, and the overall demands of the GUI environment are all driving the development of higher speeds and better quality images (for example, 3D and movement). When a computer is sold with so-called onboard graphics memory, the motherboard has some amount of built-in dedicated memory and processing. For basic, everyday use, this integrated graphics capacity is fine. It's only when the PC is used for more complex graphics that an accelerator card begins to make sense.

Not long ago, video cards boasted 8MB of VRAM and anyone who had such a card considered their machine to be very powerful. Of course, not too long before that, anyone with a 10-megabyte hard drive was considered to be a power user. Time passes and everything changes. For the moment, graphics accelerator cards commonly have anywhere from 32–128MB of DDR SDRAM. The card uses its own graphics processing unit (GPU), designed to convert digital information into pixels, and new releases of video card chipsets appear on the market every six months to a year.

Microsoft has released the specifications for Pixel Shader 1.4, part of the DirectX 8.1 multimedia standard. Leading manufacturers of video cards (e.g., ATI, 3dfx, NVidia) can use these specifications to render textures. Textures (shaded polygons) are used in games for such things as walls, hair, water, wood, or other object surfaces. The 1.4 specification provides for single-pass rendering of up to six textures, as opposed to four in the previous version (1.3). The AGP is designed to help with texture processing, but the bulk of the work is done on the graphics card. Integrated graphics processing is not designed to handle textures or 3D graphics…yet. (Rumor has it that Microsoft would like to incorporate 3D graphics into the Windows interface.)

To give you an idea of how much processing power goes into graphics processing, a screen resolution of 1024×768 requires a system to calculate and produce the exact color and data for 786,432 pixels for every screen refresh. The screen is then redrawn anywhere from 30 to 90 times per second.

Before the screen can display the pixels, they must be converted from digital information back to analog, in a RAMDAC. This is a RAM digital-to-analog converter, and works with most of today's monitors to break down the pixel information into RGB colors (for each electron beam). The refresh rate is directly dependent upon how quickly the RAMDAC can process data. Upcoming monitors are designed to directly accept digital information, reducing the need for the middleman, so to speak.

An important aspect of add-on graphics cards is that they typically include specialized connectors for evolving display technologies, such as S-Video (S-VHS), DVD, and the new Digital Visual Interface (DVI) used by digital monitors. Popular trends, today, include using multiple monitors or watching movies via the PC. Integrated graphics and AGP don't always provide the connectivity that an add-on card has to offer.

Modern graphics cards support resolutions of up to 2048×1536 pixels, in True Color. The number of colors a monitor can display depends upon whether the colors are using 16- or 32-bit addressing. A graphics card must fill each line of the screen with some number of pixels, and the speed by which this is done is called a *fill rate*. High-end cards have a fill rate of nearly one billion pixels (gigapixels) per second, and a faster fill rate also affects the refresh rate. For the human eye to see fluid motion, the refresh rate must be at least 30 times per second. Video cards also handle the special 3D processing need for lighting changes (direction, reflections, etc.) and anti-aliasing.

Less expensive video cards continue to use VRAM, but the trend is moving towards DDR SDRAM. In some cases, both the CPU and video card may share the additional 4–8MB of video RAM, reducing the overall cost of the PC (for example, less than $400 for commodity machines).

Liquid Crystal Displays (LCDs)

Whereas a CRT produces a beam of light, liquid crystals rely on another source of light to pass through each crystal. If light can pass through the crystal, our eye can see it. When the crystal is turned off, it won't let light pass, and we see an area of black. Each crystal can be either on or off, much like binary computer numbers can be either 0 (off) or 1 (on).

LCD technology allows for a much thinner screen than the bulky CRT, which gives rise to a group of monitors called *flat-panel displays*. Because a CRT monitor uses a vacuum tube to contain the beam of electrons, physics mandates that the tube be a certain depth. Flat-panel technology is most often thought of as an LCD monitor, but other displays can be categorized as flat panel (e.g., LCD panels, gas plasma panels (or Plasma Display Panels [PDPs]), and electro-luminescent display (ELD) monitors.

A flat technology monitor (FTM) is not the same as a flat-panel display. Flat technology monitors technically describe a CRT that uses a flat screen to reduce glare. Flat panel displays are the typical screens used in laptops and notebooks. FTMs are still tubes, featured in today's monitors as having "Very Flat Screen" features.

Until recently, LCD panels were almost always found on laptop or notebook computers. As color technology and the use of active matrix advanced, full-size LCD monitors reached the consumer market. Flat panel technology also brought new television screens and high definition television (HDTV) to the home market. The ability to control the size of the crystals (and therefore the size of the pixels) allows for ways to produce very high resolutions. Potentially, LCD technology will replace cathode ray technology and bring film-quality video capability to the market.

Flat panel displays work with the computer using either an analog or a digital connection. Although analog LCD monitors are fairly standardized, requiring no additional hardware, digital LCD monitors usually require a digital video card. At the moment, there isn't a strong industry standard for these digital video cards. The two market leaders are the Digital Display Working Group's Digital Video Interface (DVI), and Digital Flat Panel (DVP) from the Video Electronics Standards Association (VESA).

Plasma Display Panels (PDPs)

Plasma Display Panel (PDP) is a type of flat panel display. Instead of sandwiching liquid crystals, an ionized gas is placed between the panels. One panel has wires going across in rows, and the other panel has wires going up and down in columns. By combining a specific horizontal and a specific vertical wire on the two panels, a charge can be sent through the gas, making it glow as a dot of light. The type of gas determines the color of the glow.

Plasma displays are monochrome only, and most use neon gas and glow orange. Although advances are being made in colorizing gases, current technology makes these panels very expensive and provides no gray scale capability. However, the panels can be scaled to very large sizes and provide excellent brightness and contrast, making them an attractive technology for signs and public information displays.

Liquid Crystals

A fascinating property of liquid crystals is that they exist in either a solid or a near-liquid state, depending on electrical conditions. In their near-liquid state, the crystals can pass light. Another interesting feature is that the crystals have a tendency to be straight (like rods) in their natural state, but they twist into a right angle under electrical stimulation. This ability to pass light when they're straight or to turn at right angles and block light gave rise to the LCD panel.

Polarization

Have you ever used polarized sunglasses? The science used in making these glasses works on the principle that most light tends to be polarized (lined up) according to its wavelength. It's somewhat like iron molecules facing the same direction around a magnet. The molecules in lenses of polarized glasses are constructed so they line up in rows leaning over at an angle. The molecules of regular glass don't line up this way. Because polarized sunglasses have this alignment property, the lenses allow only light waves traveling at the correct angle to pass, which is only a fraction of the entire spectrum of sunlight.

If you hold a polarized lens in front of another polarized lens and rotate the first lens, all the light will gradually be blocked, and the background will turn black. When the polar alignment of one lens is 90 degrees (at right angles) against the other, no light passes.

LCD Panel Construction

An LCD panel is made of two polarized planes of glass placed at right angles to each other. Sandwiched between the panes of glass is a layer of liquid crystals (with that weird bending quality). Behind the back panel is a fluorescent light source that tries to get through the two misaligned panels of glass. In the default state, the light is blocked, and the panels appear black.

Each liquid crystal is in a matrix, with very thin wires leading to a set of switches along the top and side edges of the glass panels. When electrical current is sent to a specific X-Y location on the grid, the crystal at that point goes into its act, bending 90 degrees and turning almost transparent.

What's so cool about this process is this: Let's say the light coming in from the back is vertically aligned (straight up and down). The crystal is also up and down, but the front pane of glass is horizontally aligned (left and right). When the liquid crystal becomes transparent and twists over on its side, it carries the light over sideways and passes it through the front pane. Let there be light! We can envision all these little liquid crystals doing the Macarena dance, and when they bend down, they form images.

In any event, forming an image pattern always involves making a series of dots. If you can create a dot of light against a background of black, you've met the basic criterion for making an image. Depending on how often a crystal is turned on in relation to the crystals next to it, the human eye can be fooled into thinking that it sees about 16 shades of gray.

Color and Light Revisited

Eventually, liquid crystals were developed that could cut out all colors of light except one. Using the cyan, magenta, yellow process (discussed earlier in this chapter), the number of crystals in the matrix was tripled. Once again, triads of three crystals (each able to pass only one primary color) were put together in the matrix, and the switches were tripled to access each subcrystal. By turning one of the three crystals in each triad on or off, the same effect was produced as with an electron beam and phosphor triads.

Because the crystals are only acting like a very tiny camera shutter, they can't produce light on their own. On the other hand, a fluorescent light doesn't need the space of an electron gun and beam. LCD panels can have very thin light sources behind them, making the entire panel far thinner than a CRT, which is perfect for notebook and laptop computers.

Twisted Nematic

LCD panels have a limited angle of viewing because of the physics of polarization and light transmission. Therefore, the types of crystals have been modified to allow light to branch off to the sides. Without getting into scientific jargon, we can see three modifications to the crystals:

- Super-twisted nematic (also known as super-twisted nematic display [STND])
- Double super-twisted nematic
- Triple super-twisted nematic

The first two modifications allow a wider viewing angle and a brighter contrast in the panels. The third kind, triple super-twisted nematic, allows for the color subtraction method of CMY along with added brightness and side viewing.

Passive Matrix

As we just mentioned, LCD panels have a matrix of wires. VGA resolution is 640×480 pixels in a matrix. Therefore, a VGA liquid crystal display panel requires 640 transistor switches along the sides and 480 along the top and bottom to produce 640×480 dots of light. As in a CRT, the rows are activated sequentially, moving from top to bottom, resulting in a refresh rate and limited contrast.

Dual Scan

Some LCD panels divide the screen into a top half and a bottom half, allowing a simultaneous refresh of two rows, one in each half, which is similar to interlacing (but not the same thing). On the one hand, this dual scanning process decreases the contrast, making the screen less bright. On the other hand, it consumes less power than panels that use a single refresh rate.

Either way, the response time of LCD panels is slow. It takes from 40–200ms to move the crystal through its twist-and-relax cycle. This explains why earlier LCD panels showed a shadowy trail when the cursor moved, and why the expected position of the cursor seemed to take a moment to catch up with an actual picture of a cursor. This is now an optional feature in Windows, known as "*mouse trails*."

Active Matrix

The fundamental difference between passive and active matrix, is the number of switches. Passive matrix has only one switch per column. In Chapter 5, we discussed how a capacitance field allows a charge to be sent to a specific part of a wire, somewhere between two transistors. Using capacitance, an active matrix gives every liquid crystal its own switch address.

Oddly enough, in reverse of burst mode memory (see Chapter 3), giving every crystal in the matrix a separate address increases the speed of pinpointing a specific X-Y coordinate. In an LCD matrix, this allows each crystal to be turned on and off more quickly and provides better control over how long a crystal stays on in relation to its neighboring crystals. Individual addressing also provides better control over each crystal in a triad at a grid point. Active matrix LCD panels are basically huge integrated circuits, much like microprocessors.

The number of components in an active matrix LCD is at least three times the number in a passive matrix panel. Although active matrix panels are much more expensive to manufacture, they have far better contrast and response time than the passive matrix models.

Summary—Monitors

Think of the preceding discussion on monitors as if you were in the process of buying a new monitor for your own system. What would you want to know, and how would you go about analyzing the various types of monitors on the market. We've tried to use each heading as a reflection of the categories you would see on a spec sheet for a monitor. The exam is going to test your knowledge of monitors in terms of how they develop problems. If you understand the specifications, you'll have no problem understanding exam questions. Focus your attention on the following points:

- Monitors fall into two basic categories: CRT and LCD. CRTs use the RGB colors and LCD panels use reflected CMY colors.
- All monitors use pixels and work at some level of resolution. You should understand dot pitch and how monitor resolutions are defined. The VGA standard is part of the most basic video configuration used in Windows Safe Mode.
- Resolution relates to screen size, in that if you have a large screen and a low resolution, you'll see a lot of jagged edges (aliasing) on diagonal lines. Monitors work with video drivers in order to produce varying screen resolutions. The size of the screen is not the same as the image resolution, and you should understand the two concepts.
- Be sure you understand scan cycles and refresh rates. You'll definitely run into a question on interlacing versus noninterlaced monitors. If you're not clear on the definitions, skim the chapter again.

We've included a substantial amount of information on the accelerated graphics port and frame buffers. Although you most likely won't encounter specific questions on the AGP, there's no doubt that you'll have to understand the concepts and principles. AGP is closely related to the PCI bus, primarily because they both use bus technology that you'll have to understand in relation to the universal serial bus. If you want to skip ahead to the next chapter and review the USB, then come back and re-read this section, feel free to do so. The PCI bus evolved in an effort to overcome the 16-bit limitations of the ISA bus. The AGP evolved in a similar fashion, to offload high-speed graphics processing from the PCI bus.

Printers

Printer output is by far the most common way to share information among people. The driving forces in printer technology have been speed and resolution. Printer resolution is measured in dots per inch (dpi). Think of a newspaper picture composed of black-and-white dots. The more dots in a given area, the darker the area. The smaller the dots, the sharper the edges of the area.

When they hear the term "output," most people think of a printer. A printer is a way to capture information on paper, film, transparencies, or anything else (sometimes, even thin cloth) that can be handled by the roller mechanism and that won't get stuck in the printer. In a moment, we'll examine some of the problems with printers, but for now, we'll focus on the basic differences between the types of printers and how they work:

- *Impact printers*—Includes the daisy wheel and dot matrix.
- *Direct thermal printers*—Includes some fax machines and inexpensive and high-portability printers.
- *Thermal ink/color printers*—Includes ink jet and bubble jet.
- Laser printers

For the exam, remember that the most common printer cable is a 25-pin male DB25 connector on one end and a 36-pin male Centronics connector on the other. Serial interfaces (ports) use a male 9-pin connector on the back panel of the PC's chassis.

Typically, printers connect to the CPU by either a serial interface or a parallel interface. You must remember the difference between a 9-pin serial cable and a 25-pin parallel cable. The confusing part is the 25-pin *serial* printer cable.

Dots Per Inch (dpi)

If you've ever used a graphics program that allows you to zoom in on an image (making an area incrementally larger or smaller), imagine zooming in on the pupil of a person's eye in a photograph. At low resolution, zooming in to a certain pixel level shows that all the pixels are square. You'll discover that only seven or eight squares were used to form the pupil, making the pupil look like a mix between a rectangle and a cross.

If you scan that same photograph again with, say, a 1200 dpi optical scanner, then zoom in to the same pixel level, you'll discover a difference. First, you'll need to click the zoom button a few more times to get down to the pixel squares. Second, the pupil is now made up of perhaps 25 or more pixels. The pixel squares are much smaller than those in the first image.

We've seen that the smaller a series of dots used on a monitor, the sharper the resolution is. This principle applies exactly the same way with printing dots. Under a microscope, the dots in printer resolution are actually round. The phosphorus spots on the back face of a CRT are generally also round. Pixels in a graphic image are square.

Remember that printed images resolve with dots per inch (dpi), but displayed images resolve with picture units (pixels).

Ink Pixels and Resolution

Advances in ink jet technology allow for the controlled breakup of a single dot into even smaller parts, guaranteeing the size and spread of pieces. These pieces of an ink drop are how ink jet printers can improve on the resolution of a laser printer. However, the slight amount of drying time it takes for the ink to be absorbed into the paper, allows a microscopic amount of capillary bleeding (spreading out into paper threads) into the paper. This reduces the original resolution. With newer, glossy papers and appropriate drying time, a modern ink jet printer can reproduce photographic-quality resolution.

Ink Bubbles

Print heads in an ink jet printer have extremely tiny nozzles (orifices) for spewing out the dots of ink. A hole can be engineered to be much smaller than the rods used by a dot matrix printer, because the hole doesn't require the structural strength to withstand being smashed into a ribbon hundreds of times per minute.

Not only can the dot of ink be much finer than the diameter of a pin, but multiple cartridges can contain the four typical colors of ink (CMY plus black). Depending on the color required, any or all of the cartridges can be told to put a drop of ink on a specific spot on the paper.

Ink is held in a containing well in the print head until the CPU sends a control signal for that color of ink. The control signal generates a rapid heat increase in a thermal resistor, heating the ink and causing it to expand to form a bubble under the ink in the well. The bubble expands just enough to force a tiny drop of ink from the orifice and onto the paper.

Ink/Bubble Jet vs. Piezoelectric

The problem with ink bubbles is that the resulting dot is a single size when it leaves the orifice, and it has a tiny amount of splatter when it hits the paper—much like a raindrop hitting the ground. Another problem is that we can only guess at the size of the original bubble. Incremental differences from one bubble to the next are extremely small, but they do exist.

To solve these problems, the bubble-forming process changed from a thermal resistor to a piezoelectric crystal. These crystals have the unusual attribute of changing size when an electrical charge is sent through them. This change is exactly related to the amount of charge and the size of the crystal. By sending an exactly increasing charge across a crystal, the crystal contracts and pulls an exact amount of ink down from the well above it. When the charge ends, the crystal returns to its original size, forcing the drop of ink out of the orifice.

We can use electronic frequencies to "bend" a drop across a cutting edge as it emerges from the orifice. With a specific frequency and a drop of a specific size, we can cut exact subdrops with a controlled "splatter pattern." This allows for resolutions of greater than 1440 dpi (some printers currently have a resolution of 2880×720 dpi).

Ink jet technology is faster than impact-pin printing because the jet of ink has only a single mechanical step: the movement of bubbling. Also, blowing liquid ink drops is a lot quieter than ramming a metal pin against a piece of paper and a roll bar (platen).

Form Feed

Printers almost always require a piece of paper—a *form*—that must be moved at the front end of the printing process, then out of the printer. The old printing press used human labor as a paper-feed mechanism. A human being inserted paper into the press and used a letterpress to lay down a series of aligned letters on the paper. The letterpress was then raised, and the human laborer reached in and lifted off the sheet of paper. Very few people use human labor for printing anymore, and this printing process has become nearly obsolete. However, we still see it in the $1.95 laptop notebook systems being sold on the market these days, where the printer is integrated into the system. In these instances, the integrated printer is called your hand.

Feeding a form—a *form feed*—involves pulling a piece of paper into a printer, aligning it in front of a printing mechanism, and moving it back out of the printer. If only one piece of paper (a single form) is moved through the printer at a time, the printer is commonly called a *sheet feed printer.* If the pieces of paper are connected into one long sheet and move through the printer continuously, the printer is called a *continuous feed printer.*

Dot Matrix

Impact printers will have a place in society as long as there are multipart forms. A typical environment for a dot matrix printer is in medical offices, where Medicare reimbursement forms use carbon copies attached to a front sheet. Laser printers might print faster and sharper, but because they use a heat-transfer process, printing works on only one sheet of paper at a time. Thermal color printers can also work only on single sheets of paper, which leaves impact printers alone in the field of multisheet forms.

Thermal Paper and Thermal Printers

Thermal paper is a type of paper used mainly in small calculators, inexpensive fax machines, and some very small thermal printers designed for cash registers and laptop computers. This paper is chemically treated so that a print head can heat it in the typical dotted patterns. The print head is essentially the same as a dot matrix print head, but it uses heated pins to form a mark on the thermal paper rather than pressure on an ink ribbon.

Thermal paper is somewhat expensive, and it is very sensitive to ultraviolet (UV) light (i.e., sunlight), which can fade the images on the paper to the point of being illegible.

The term *impact* applies to dot matrix printers because a mechanical device is driven forward in space and rams into the surface of the ink ribbon with great impact. Think about the process of impact printing with a pin-based dot matrix printer. A rod of metal—the pin—must be held in a ready position within the print head. This is done with an electromagnet that pulls the base of the pin back against a coiled spring. A control signal from the CPU turns off the power to the magnet, and the spring gathers momentum to push the pin forward. Gradually, the pin gathers speed until it slams into the ribbon, driving the ribbon backward into the paper and stopping.

Ink is forcibly thrown from the back of the ribbon, splattering all over the paper, with the paper crushed between the pin, the ribbon, and the roller platen behind the paper. The ribbon and the pin exchange phone numbers and insurance information; then the CPU calls the electromagnet to turn on the magnetism again. The pin is hauled away by the magnetic tow truck and returned to its housing in the print head. The paper is left to recover in the hospital. The piece of ribbon moves away from the scene with only a few scratches.

All this happens very quickly from a human perspective, but at a microcosmic level, it takes a lot of time. No matter how strong the spring is, it must be very small. It has to overcome inertia in the pin, and then the electromagnet has to overcome the resistance when it pulls the pin back into the head. In addition, the pins themselves must be able to withstand the carnage and "pinslaughter" of being smashed into the paper again and again, at least a few million times. Let's take a moment of silence to remember those heroic pins that have paved the way to the modern day ink jet and laser printer.

A dot matrix printer uses a print head housing a number of very small pins. The print head moves back and forth along a guide rail. As each line is printed, the paper moves up one line. The pins in the print head are pushed toward the ribbon and paper in various combinations to form letters. The number of pins defines the quality of the letter, just as the number of dots defines printer resolution.

With only nine pins, there's a limit to how many pins can form the curve at the top of, for example, the number 9. However, with twenty-four pins, the pins are much smaller, so more of them can be used to form the curve at the top of the number 9, resulting in a sharper-looking character.

Make a note that dot matrix printers are distinguished by how many pins the print head uses. Common varieties are 9-pin, 18-pin, and 24-pin print heads.

Home Position

Dot matrix and many inkjet printers require the print head to start in an exact location—the *home* position. Some printers use a system of counting a series of pulses sent by the printer's motor. When the correct number of pulses has been counted, the print head is in the home position. Other printers use an optical sensing device to locate the print head in the home position.

Typically, when power is supplied to a printer at startup, part of the initialization procedure is to set the print head to its home location. When the print head is aligned, many printers will sound two beeps to let you know the printer is ready to accept print jobs.

Printer Problems

Problems with printers are so common and, in many cases, so complicated that many corporations have a dedicated information systems person assigned to working with printers. The only questions we saw on the certification exam dealing with printer problems related to cleaning, paper jams, and the printing process.

Cleaning

Electronic components made of plastic usually come with a reference manual of some kind. Somewhere in the beginning of these manuals is a short statement about cleaning the components with a damp cloth and mild detergent. This instruction applies to computer parts and external printer parts as well.

Paint and lacquer thinners are designed to take paint and grease off metal or wood that you're about to paint. Electronic components are *delicate*, so use some common sense when answering questions dealing with how to clean devices such as printers. If the component is delicate, you don't use hydrochloric acid to clean it!

Paper Jams

A likely cause of paper jams in printers is either the wrong type of paper (inkjet) or too many sheets of paper trying to get into the printer (laser). A laser printer uses a paper pickup roller and registration rollers to grab a piece of paper from the paper bin. A rubber separation pad prevents more than one sheet of paper from entering the printer at a time.

Remember that laser printers tend to develop paper jams if the separation pad fails to prevent more than one sheet of paper at a time from being pulled into the printer.

Continuous/Tractor Fed

Continuous-form paper is a very long, single sheet of paper with a perforated divider line every 11 (US letter) or 14 (legal) inches and with a series of holes along both sides. The perforations allow individual sheets to be separated after the print job; the holes along the sides fit over a pair of form tractors or a sprocket that rotates and then pulls the paper forward (or backward) into the printer. Today, most continuous-form paper is several sheets thick and can be preprinted and multipart, containing blanks to be filled in with variable data.

The difference between a form tractor and a sprocket is that a form tractor is a belt that has knobs protruding from the outer surface. A sprocket-feed (also called a *pin-feed*) printer uses a less expensive plastic wheel with molded pins protruding around the edge of the wheel. Again, the pins align with the holes on the edge of the paper. Because a tractor belt has more knobs per inch than a sprocket, tractor-feed printers can work with smaller increments of movement, so line spacing can be smaller. However, the tractor belt has a tendency to slip with usage, whereas the sprocket wheel is usually glued onto a kind of axle.

Friction Feed

One of the original single-sheet, friction-feed printers was a typewriter. This device used a biochemical software application, called the *human typist*, to produce output, and it pulled a single sheet of paper through the printer with friction and rollers. Friction-feed devices rely on the friction of a pinch roller to catch the leading edge of a piece of paper and then draw it forward into the printer. The leading edge is the first edge (although not always the top edge) that goes into the printer. A roller mechanism then presses down on the surface of the paper, rolling it along a paper path. These rollers continue to turn, moving the paper along the paper path until there's no more paper to work against—usually when the paper has reached the output tray and the print job is complete.

While oil is beneficial in places where constant mechanical movement can wear down a part, it becomes a detriment where friction is required. Common areas of a printer that depend on friction are: pinch rollers, platens, tractor belts and sprockets, and paper separation wheels.

Consumer products have followed a trend over the years of reducing the amount of maintenance as much as possible. Other than general cleaning, many of today's printers use replaceable components instead of providing for the owner's mechanical know-how. When a part is used up (consumed) and then thrown away, we call it a *consumable*. The cost of a printer is a one-time expense. However, the overall cost of operating a printer depends on how expensive the various consumables are. Typical consumables are paper, ink cartridges, and toner cartridges.

We saw some questions on the exam that had to do with lubricating parts of a printer. Aside from possibly using some light oil on a bi-directional print-head rail, most printers don't provide for this type of general maintenance.

Print rollers are designed to rub against a piece of paper and pull it through a printer. Print rollers need friction to work, so they're often made of rubber. Rubber against paper tends to produce a lot of friction. Grease on rubber is like wax on a ski. The more grease buildup, the less friction the rubber has.

When oil or grease begins to build up on surfaces that require a lot of friction, the most common way to clean them is with rubbing alcohol. Alcohol is a liquid solvent that evaporates, leaving almost no residue of any kind. Rubber wheels used in various rollers, areas under tractor belts, and sometimes the platen roller behind the paper on a dot matrix printer can benefit from cleaning with alcohol.

The solvent properties of alcohol break down oils, grease from fingers, and ink residues for removal, and then evaporates cleanly, leaving a clean surface. Electrical circuits should be as clean as possible in order to minimize an accidental connection between two lines (short circuit) in the wrong place.

Rubbing alcohol is a grease solvent that evaporates into the air, leaving no residue. Use alcohol on parts that need to retain their friction. Use alcohol on any parts that can't have any liquid residue on them (electronic or electrical conducting parts).

Special cleaning kits are available that include a cleaning solvent that leaves no residue, rubber restorers for cleaning roller wheels, and pressure dusters. A blast of compressed air can blow dust out of keyboards and printers without allowing pieces of a physical duster to fall into a delicate mechanism. In addition, you should always check the instructions on rubber-cleaning chemicals. Some chemicals are destructive to various types of rubber. Check the printer's reference manual as well before using solvents.

Always be sure that you've disconnected components from all electrical power sources before cleaning them with liquids. Liquids tend to conduct electricity and can lead to electrocution.

Dot Matrix

Remember that dot matrix printers use either a tractor-feed or pressure roller (friction) method of pulling paper through the printer. The pressure rollers press down on a piece of paper and hold it tight against the platen (the big roller behind the paper that backs the paper and ribbon). When the print head pushes the pins into the ribbon and paper, the platen takes the pounding. After the line of characters has been printed, the platen turns, as do the tractor gears on the sides of the platen. As the gears turn, they pull the paper forward one line.

The platen has no real effect on moving the paper, so it doesn't need to be cleaned. However, the tractor gears don't always turn at the same speed, so if the paper isn't lined up exactly and the tractor wheels don't turn at the same speed, the paper begins to develop a slant as it moves through the printer and eventually will jam.

Cleaning a dot-matrix printer is usually a preventative maintenance measure. Naturally, vacuuming out dust and debris periodically, or using a can of compressed air to blow out dust, is a simple process. The internal tractor belts and the rubber parts of the pressure rollers can often be cleaned with a proper chemical rubber-cleaning compound. Keeping torn pieces of paper out of the internal drive mechanism is another periodic cleaning task.

Fonts

The words *font* and *typeface* are used to describe two ways of looking at a letter. A font is the overall way a set of characters looks. A typeface refers to whether the font characters are bolded, italicized, or plain (regular). In the days of hot-metal type, three different character sets had to be created to produce the three changes in the typeface of a single font.

Without going deeply into the process of mathematically creating lines, points, and curves on a computer screen, we can say that software can produce graphics in two different ways: by vector calculations and by pixel points. Remember that a pixel (picture element) is the smallest dot that can be represented on a graphic display.

DOS uses a grid and BASIC to fill in sets of squares created by intersections of columns and rows (a matrix). Windows converts information being sent to the screen to a graphic—the GUI. Rather than working with the fixed character spacing of the DOS rows and columns, Windows uses pixels to draw everything, including letters.

Raster vs. Bitmap Fonts

Imagine a blue square with black lines making up the outline of the square. You can draw that square in two different ways. One way is called a *vector drawing*. You send a mathematical point coordinate to the computer, which puts the point on the screen and virtually extends a line for a specified length in a specified direction. From the end of that line, the computer can extend the line in a different direction. Each time you click the mouse one time and move in a new direction, you tell the computer to remember the new length and direction.

When it comes time to print, the printer prints the line(s). Because the computer knows where every intersection for each part of the line is located, it can fill in any area enclosed by that line with some color. This fill color is a single color (in this example, blue) that is surrounded by the connecting line points, and it exists virtually until the printer converts it to ink.

In other words, you're telling the computer to keep track of when you click in an area, and how far you moved the mouse pointer before you clicked. The computer only remembers numbers and doesn't care what kind of shape you're drawing. When you use a coloring book to connect numbered dots and make a picture to color, the dots and their numbers are similar to the data the computer stores about a vector graphic.

Another way to draw the square is with dots (pixels). Starting at a certain point, the computer draws small dots to the left or to the right as you move the mouse along. The next line in the drawing begins at a new point, and does the same thing all over again with some number of dots. The dots are pixels when they're created on a monitor, and dots per inch (dpi) when they're created by a printer. These types of images are called *bitmaps*, because every single bit (dot) of the image just created is stored by the computer. If you draw lines and then color them in, every dot used for every line and every part of the coloring is a separate piece of data to be stored.

In summary, raster images are mathematically created by a vector-drawing process. Microsoft calls vector-based fonts *vector fonts*. You might also hear them called *raster fonts*. Bitmap images are grids of pixels; a grid position either has a dot of some color or is blank (containing the background color).

To change the size of a vector image, you simply tell the computer to change the image's stored numbers and recalculate the lengths of the virtual lines. To change the size of a bitmap image, the computer has to change the size of every one of the image's dots and recalculate the overall image.

True Type Fonts (.TTF Files)

We've seen that dot matrix and thermal ink technology printers place dots of ink on paper. Because of this ability to reduce anything to a series of dots, an application can create a font in memory, break down each letter to a dot, and send it to the printer as a bitmap graphic image. It takes a lot of time to create a grid for every letter and to determine which squares in the grid will be dots.

Another problem with bitmaps involves the size of the dots. If you create a square using 16 dots, where each dot is one inch in diameter, you would have a nice four-inch square. But suppose that you wanted to enlarge that square to 16 inches? The original dots are only one inch wide, so the bigger square would look fuzzy because of the spaces between the one-inch dots.

Adobe's Postscript font description language provides a way to tell a computer how to draw a letter from a mathematical description (vector drawing). The advantage of this is that regardless of how large or small the letter is, the computer sees it only as a series of mathematical line segments. The virtual lines and the places where they change directions can be as long or as short as you choose, making for very little degradation at the edges and therefore a sharper-looking font. The color of the font can be changed on-the-fly by telling the computer which fill color to use.

Microsoft and Adobe had an argument over how much it would cost Microsoft to license the Adobe process. Eventually, Microsoft figured out a way to make its own raster fonts and named the process TrueType. The original invention wasn't perfect, so Microsoft worked on it and released a second version that fixed the problems in the first version.

TrueType and TrueType II fonts are vector-based raster fonts. TrueType fonts can be scaled (enlarged or shrunk), in increments of 1 point, by the computer from the minimum display capabilities of a printer or monitor, to as large as 999 points. A point is $^{1}/_{72}$ of an inch, making a 72-point letter 1 inch tall.

Modern laser printers can often allow a font to be scaled in increments of less than 1 point.

Windows 3.x includes three vector-based fonts stored in files that use a .FON extension, as well as a number of TrueType fonts in a TTF file and a companion FOT file for each typeface. When a laser printer contains the stored calculations for a vector font, those fonts are called internal fonts. Windows added a feature whereby it could work with printers to convert its TrueType fonts to graphics, and the printer would print what Windows was showing on the screen even if there were no matching internal fonts.

Laser Printers

Around 1980, a new technology was being moved forward from the famous Xerox Palo Alto Research Center (PARC) labs. It was called *ElectroPhotographic* (EP) printing, better known as the laser printer. Dot matrix and ink jet printers put dots on paper in blocks, from 7 to 64 dots at a time, depending on the number of pins or ink nozzles being used.

A laser printer still puts dots on a piece of paper, but these dots are made up of tiny pieces of plastic toner, heated until it bonds with the paper. Regardless of how small those pieces of plastic are, they're still solid matter and probably can't be made smaller than a liquid dot of ink. For this reason, current ink jet printers can attain resolutions of 1400 dpi or higher, but current laser printers are limited to around 600 dpi.

Laser printer toner is a near-microscopic combination of plastic resin and some organic compounds bonded to iron particles. Remember that toner powder is a combination of plastic, metal (iron), and organic compounds.

The Laser Printing Process

The A+ exam devotes a number of questions to the specific mechanics of printing with a laser printer. We suggest that you take the time to understand the step-by-step movement of paper through the printer. Although the technical science behind the electrostatic and electrophotographic (EP) process may seem obscure, we found that by knowing the process, we could usually puzzle out a correct response to these questions.

Remember that EP is short for "electrophotographic." The EP drum in a toner cartridge is where images are created and developed.

In a laser printer, a page of information is formed in RAM first and then transferred as a whole unit to the paper (similar to how a photocopier works). This speeds up the process of printing. On the other hand, the process requires a heating time to fuse (set) the image on the paper permanently.

Ink: How Long Will It Last?

Remember that an ink jet printer puts ink on paper. The ink soaks into the fibers of the paper itself. A high-quality ink is designed to be resistant to ultraviolet light and won't fade or otherwise degrade. Because the ink is literally a part of the paper, it usually will last as long as the paper lasts.

Laser printing uses bits of plastic that effectively are melted onto the surface of the paper. Although the plastic is also impervious to UV light and its fading effects, the bond between the paper and the plastic is degradable. At the moment, laser-printed information hasn't been around long enough to really test its longevity against embedded ink. However, for historical and archival documents, it's worth keeping in mind that the fused bond between the paper and the plastic is an area of weakness.

The Printing Components

A laser printer is a complex grouping of subsystems, all of which interact exactly to move a blank piece of paper from the input side to the output side. In-between, information is stored to the paper. The components of a laser printer are as follows:

- *AC/DC power supply*—The main power supply takes in AC from the wall. The DC power supply converts the AC to the DC voltages typically used in a computer system.
- *High-voltage power supply*—Electrophotography (EP) requires around 1,000 volts or more to create a static electricity charge that moves the toner particles into position.
- *Fusing assembly*—Heat and pressure are required to fuse the plastic toner particles to the paper.
- *Erase lamp assembly*—The laser beam writes a preliminary, or *latent*, image to the photosensitive drum before transferring the image to paper. To clear the latent image, an erase lamp resets the drum to clear.
- *Writing mechanism*—The image in RAM must be initially written as the latent image on the drum. A laser beam is moved across the photosensitive material by the writing mechanism.
- *Main motor*—A number of small motors drive various rollers, the drum, and mechanical processes. The main motor provides the mechanical energy needed by the submotors.
- *Scanner motor assembly*—To move the laser beam across the photosensitive drum, a mirror and motor direct the reflected light beam.
- *Paper control assembly*—This includes the entire process and all the mechanics of grabbing the leading edge of a piece of paper and moving it through the paper path to the output tray.
- *Main logic assembly*—Sometimes called the *electronic control package* (ECP), this includes all the circuitry for communicating with the CPU, the control panel, and the internal memory of the printer.
- *Toner cartridge*—Technically, this is the EP cartridge. The cartridge includes a number of subassemblies for cleaning, developing, and moving toner particles.
- *Control panel assembly*—This is the user interface where the printer control codes can be entered for configuration or manual paper operations. The control panel is also where the printer communicates various internal problems to the user.

A camera uses reflected light from an object to influence the molecular structure of a piece of film and to capture an image. A scanner also uses reflected light, but it's bounced onto a CCD and transferred to a file for storage. A laser printer is called a *laser* printer because it uses a laser beam to draw a sort of photograph of an image onto a photosensitive drum.

The Printing Steps

Nonlaser printers mainly use a single system to put a tiny part of a pattern onto paper, one part at a time. Laser printers depend on a whole group of systems and processes to get an image from memory onto paper. The heart of the Image Formation System (IFS) is the photosensitive EP drum.

This drum is an extruded aluminum cylinder coated with a nontoxic organic compound that reacts to light in an unusual way: It turns light into electricity, a process called *photoconductivity*. When light touches the compound, it generates a bit of electricity that is conducted (moved) through the compound.

Figure 7.3 is a stylized representation of the various parts involved in the printing process. We didn't see any questions on the exam asking you to identify parts by letters, but we feel it may help you to keep the steps in their right order if you can visualize them. A good starting point is with the EP drum covered in toner. It has a neutral charge in its photoconductive surface. Creating an image creates an electrical charge.

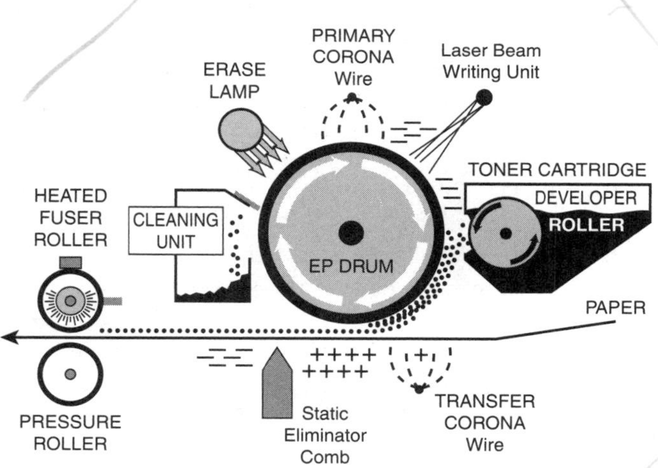

Figure 7.3 The main parts of a laser printing cycle.

Cleaning

Latent images are like a memory of a picture. If a drum simply accumulated images and printed them, it wouldn't take very long before we'd have a piece of paper covered in black. All the remembered images would build up, one on top of the other. (Take 5 or 10 photographic slides, put them on top of each other, and then try to look through them.)

To get the drum ready to accept a new image, it has to be cleaned and erased. No matter how high the quality of the drum and toner, one way or another, a microscopic amount of residue will stay on the drum from the previous image transfer.

The printer uses a rubber cleaning blade to gently scrape the drum clean of any residual toner. This residue drops into a debris cavity on the side of the cartridge, down below the cleaning blade. Some cartridges allow the residual toner to be returned to the main toner supply.

The EP drum must be clean in order to take on a new image. (This is one of the cases where, if you think about it logically, you can almost work out the details in your mind when you're facing a question.)

Erasing

As soon as the laser beam touches a point on the drum, it changes that point to a "less negatively" charged spot. This creates a relatively positive point that stands out from the overall negatively charged surface. An image is written on the drum this way, line by line, in a series of positive dots against a negative surface, until the entire image is stored. In its default state, the drum surface has no electrical charge. The stored image is the latent image mentioned earlier.

To remove the previously charged dots from the drum, a series of erase lights are set up near the drum's surface. The erase lights are filtered to provide a specific wavelength that bleeds away any electrical charge from the drum. After the drum has been erased, it has a neutral charge—that is, no electrical charge at all.

An area that can be confusing during the exam is the difference between "cleaning" old toner particles from the EP drum, and "erasing" an image from the drum. Think of it this way: You erase a picture. You don't clean a picture.

Conditioning

The neutral surface of the drum has no sensitivity to light at this point and can't store any kind of image. The drum must be given a negative charge that's completely and evenly distributed across the entire surface of the drum. That electrical charging is called conditioning.

To condition the surface of the drum, an extremely powerful negative charge of electricity is swept across the surface of the drum. This voltage is in about

–6,000 volts (negative charge) and is distributed by a very thin wire called the *corona wire*, which is located close to the drum. The drum and the corona wire share a "ground" with the high-voltage power supply, and their proximity generates the electrical field. After the conditioning and a negative charge have been applied to the drum, it again becomes photoconductive.

Corona Ionization

Essentially, the high voltage being sent through the corona wire causes a short circuit between the wire and the image drum. The air around the wire breaks down, causing a corona to form. The corona ionizes the molecules in the air surrounding the drum, and negative charges migrate to the drum surface.

Because a short circuit isn't healthy for high-voltage power supplies, a primary grid is put between the wire and the drum, allowing for a regulating process of controlled voltages—the regulating grid voltage, or typically -600 to -1,000 volts. The charge on the drum is set to this regulating voltage.

Writing

When a beam of light touches the surface of the drum, it discharges a small amount of electricity, usually about -100 volts. Because the surrounding area of the drum is between -600 and -1,000 volts, this spot (or dot) is "more positively charged" than the surrounding area. In other words, the dot is less negatively charged, and we say that it has a *relative positive charge*. In other words, the spot charge is somewhat positive, relative to its surroundings.

Because we've started with negative charges (that is, -600 to -1,000 volts) and the light from the laser beam siphons off about 100V, there is a more negative charge where the light missed, and a higher (less negative) charge where the light touched. The background charge is the -600 volts, and the lower charge (-600 volts with 100 volts siphoned off) is -500V.

The image held in memory, which was sent there by the software program, is transferred to the writing mechanism. This is a sophisticated device that controls the way in which the laser beam moves over the surface of the drum. It also controls when the beam is lit or turned off. The beam produces a dot on the drum each time that the beam is on.

Developing

At this point, an invisible pattern of electrostatic charge differentials is sitting on the surface of the drum. Overall, the charge is negative, but at each data point, there's a relatively positive dot standing out from the surrounding area.

Somehow, we're going to have to move toner from the cartridge onto the drum, in such a way that an image is made visible. ("Visible" is a debatable term because it's pitch black inside a laser printer after the laser beam has finished writing the latent image.) To do this, we use a long metal sleeve with a permanent magnet inside. This sleeve is called a *toner cylinder*, or sometimes called the *developer roller*.

The toner cylinder is constantly turning in the middle of all the toner powder. Toner powder is held in the toner trough. As the cylinder turns, it attracts particles of toner to its metal sleeve. Now the high-voltage power supply sends current, but this time through the toner cylinder, which charges the toner particles with a negative charge. The charge is somewhere between the charges on the drum, averaged for the places where the light touched and where no light touched.

The toner on the toner cylinder is kept at one microscopic layer by a restricting blade. The rotation of the cylinder is moving charged toner on the cylinder ever closer to the drum. Where there was no light, the higher negative charge repels the less negatively charged toner particles. Where light touched the cylinder, there's less of a charge than the charge of the toner particles, so the toner particles are attracted to the surface of the drum. (A fluctuation mechanism helps ensure that toner particles are more attracted to the drum than the cylinder.)

Stop for a second. Think of the drum surface as a flat surface. It's clear colored. Wherever the laser beam touches, the surface sinks downward. This leaves a sort of hole, or "dip" in the surface. The dips are also clear, without any toner in them.

Toner particles are attracted only to the dips, and they're pushed away from the main surface area. Therefore, the developing process is sort of like shoveling toner particles into the holes until the surface of the holes reaches a level with the original surface of the flat surface. An image develops wherever the black toner particles fill in the electrostatic holes on the drum.

Remember that you can't develop an image unless you first write it to the EP drum. The process is very much like taking a photograph, and you can't develop an image unless you first "snap the picture" (write the image).

Transferring

The surface of the drum now has a layer of toner powder in an image pattern. The powder has to be laid down on a piece of paper in that precise pattern—that is, it has to be transferred to the paper. The problem is that although the toner was originally attracted to the drum by feelings of electromagnetic love, it now has to be pried away from the drum, kicking and screaming.

A different corona wire, this time called the *transfer corona wire*, charges the paper at this point, similar to the way the drum was charged. This time, the paper takes on a very high positive charge. If you've ever rubbed a comb against cloth and then held the comb over a piece of tissue paper, you saw how the comb attracted the tissue. This is a problem with laser printers: The paper must be charged enough to pull the toner particles off the drum, but not so much that the paper wraps itself around the drum.

The size and stiffness of the paper, along with the relatively small size of the drum, work to prevent the wrapping problem. Additionally, a static charge eliminator called an *eliminator comb* works to counteract the attraction between the paper and the drum. Just like in rock music, everything is attracted to the drum(mer).

Fusing

After the toner particles get onto the paper, they're held there only by a combination of gravity and a residual electrostatic charge in both the paper and the toner. If you've ever had a printer jam and pulled a piece of paper out of a laser printer before it was fused, you've seen how easily the toner rubs off onto anything it comes in contact with. Toner must be "bonded" to the paper, before the print process is complete. This bonding process is called *fusing*.

The fusing assembly is a quartz heating lamp inside a roller tube, positioned above a rubber pressure roller. This heating roller is made of a high-quality, nonstick material. As the paper with the toner on it is drawn between the heated upper roller and the rubber lower roller, the toner is subjected to enough heat to melt it (180 degrees Celsius), and it is then pressed into the paper by the bottom roller. The combination of the fusing roller and pressure roller, is called the *fusing rollers*, but only the upper roller produces the heat.

The temperature of the heating lamp must be highly controlled to prevent fires and internal damage to the printer. Remember that the temperature sensor on the heated fuser roller is designed to shut down the system in the event that the temperatures get high enough inside the printer to cause a fire.

End of Cycle

Finally, a fabric cleaning pad, located on the opposite side of the heated upper roller, rubs off any residual melted toner. The paper with its fused image is rolled out of the printer and deposited in the output tray. During the final stages, the drum is in the process of being cleaned and erased, as we saw at the beginning of the cycle.

An even distribution of light is passed over the entire surface of the drum, causing the entire drum to bleed away all electrostatic charges. The drum is then ready to be conditioned and the next page printed. This happens for every sheet passing through the laser printer.

Be sure to remember the difference between the primary corona and the secondary corona wires. The primary wire charges the EP drum, so it can attract toner. The secondary wire charges the paper, so it can pull toner away from the EP drum. First comes the drum; then comes the paper. There's no logical sense in running the paper under a blank drum.

Paper Feed Process

When you send a **PRINT** command to the laser printer, the main motor begins to turn. This starts the EP drum, the fusing rollers, and the feed rollers that move the paper along. However, there are three mechanical rollers that aren't part of this process: the paper pick-up roller, and the pair of registration rollers. They are controlled by a separate clutch mechanism, and stay stationary.

Figure 7.4 shows the outside of a typical laser printer. We've made the larger pick-up roller and the two registration rollers a darker shade. Once the printing cycle is under way, a clutch engages the pick-up roller, dropping the roller down onto the surface of the top piece of paper in the paper tray. The pick-up roller is "notched," and only makes one turn—just enough to pull the edge of the paper in-between the registration rollers.

Just as the paper leaves the paper tray, a small rubber separation pad, right below the pickup roller, tries to make sure that only one piece of paper is pulled into the printer. One of the most common causes of paper jams in laser printers is when more than one piece of paper moves between the registration rollers, and tries to go through the printer. The registration rollers continue to turn until the entire sheet of paper has passed between them.

When a paper jam occurs and no paper is in the paper tray, the most common cause of the jam is either more than one page entering the system, or the paper separation pad. Typically, if the wrong type of paper is being used, the pick-up roller can't move the first page. If the pick-up roller can move the paper, then the other most likely problem is that the separator pad can't separate two sheets.

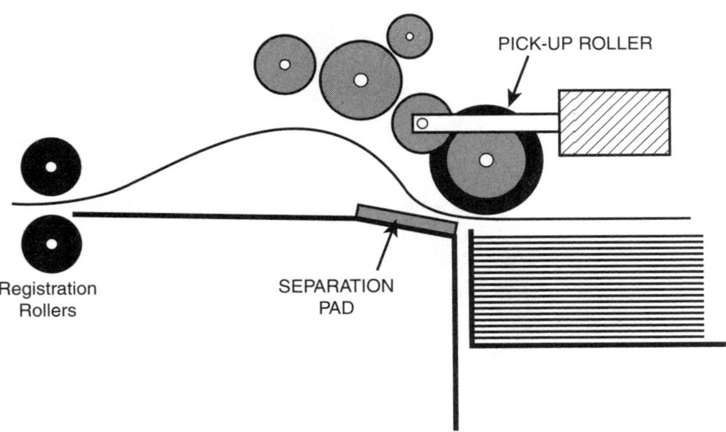

Figure 7.4 The laser printer's paper feed process.

Summary—Printers

Unfortunately, the exam is going to test you on the raw memorization of how a laser printer runs a print job. In our opinion, there are only a few areas on the test that require brute-force memory, with the rest of the topics being context related. In other words, if you understand computers and you've worked with Windows, then you can generally figure out the answers to a question based on experience, and visual images of how each area works. The exceptions to this are the port IRQs and addresses, the order in which certain files load at startup, and the steps involved in laser printing.

Examine the details in Figure 7.3, and commit them to memory in whatever fashion suits you. If you have the basic sense of how the EP drum works, and you understand the cleaning, erasing, and conditioning steps, you can generally make an educated guess at a correct response to a question by comparing the responses themselves. Please read the test-taking strategies we've discussed in Chapter1, if you haven't already done so. You should know that at the back end of the process, after developing, the printer must somehow put an image on a piece of paper. Transferring comes before fusing, and if you can remember the first few steps and the last few steps, you should be able to figure out the middle steps.

As for troubleshooting printer problems, we've chosen the topics in the section to point you to the specific areas you'll encounter on the exam. Obviously, there can be many other problems with printers, but you won't be tested on the entire realm of every printer problem in the world. Know how a dot matrix printer works, and how the print head goes back and forth over a rail. Be sure you understand paper feeding, and how both dot matrix and laser printers can develop problems with paper jams.

Practice Questions

Question 1

A black band around the screen image of an LCD panel can indicate what type of problem?

- ❍ a. Resolution has been set higher than the panel maximum.
- ❍ b. There is a device driver mismatch.
- ❍ c. More colors have been selected than the panel can display.
- ❍ d. The scan rate is too slow for the resolution.

Answer a is correct. On an LCD panel, changing the image resolution can potentially cause a black band to appear around the edge of the panel. Because the display is designed to match the number of pixels in an image, the LCD process turns on crystals based on usage, and if the resolution is set too high for the panel, the images would be too small to go all the way to the edges of the panel.

Question 2

What is the standard resolution for a VGA monitor?

- ❍ a. 480 horizontal × 640 vertical
- ❍ b. 800 horizontal × 600 vertical
- ❍ c. 640 horizontal × 480 vertical
- ❍ d. 600 horizontal × 400 vertical

Answer c is correct. A standard VGA monitor has a resolution of 640 pixels horizontally and 480 pixels vertically. We use the X to mean the word "by," so the measurement is commonly written as 640×480. The other answers are invalid screen resolutions.

Question 3

What is a pixel?

- ❍ a. A dot of ink on a page
- ❍ b. A 1-micron unit of image
- ❍ c. A fairy-like creature
- ❍ d. A single picture unit

Answer d is correct. Microsoft invented the term "pixel" to mean a single picture unit. Pixels are used mostly in image resolutions where some kind of light is involved. Dots per inch (dpi) are used where some kind of ink is involved.

Question 4

How many times does the electron beam sweep from top to bottom to fully refresh an interlaced monitor's screen?

- ❍ a. Two
- ❍ b. One
- ❍ c. Four
- ❍ d. None of the above

Answer a is correct. Interlaced mode means the electron beam sweeps from top to bottom, taking two passes to do so. First, it refreshes the odd lines and then the even lines. Noninterlaced mode is where the beam moves across the tube only one time.

Question 5

What is the purpose of the erase lamp in a laser printer?

- ❍ a. The erase lamp places spaces between dots.
- ❍ b. The erase lamp removes toner from the drum.
- ❍ c. The erase lamp allows printing of special fonts.
- ❍ d. The erase lamp resets the photosensitive drum to clear.

Answer d is correct. The laser beam writes a preliminary, or latent, image to the drum before transferring the image to paper. To clear the latent image, an erase lamp resets the drum to clear. Remember that toner is removed by the cleaning blade.

Question 6

The main motor in a laser printer turns which of the following subsystems? [Choose all that apply]

- ❑ a. EP drum
- ❑ b. Fusing rollers
- ❑ c. Paper pick-up roller
- ❑ d. Feed rollers
- ❑ e. Registration rollers

Answers a, b, and d are correct. The paper pick-up roller is used to move the top sheet of paper in a paper tray far enough that the registration rollers can grab it and pull it into the printer. The EP drum, fusing rollers, and feed rollers are all part of the main assembly being moved by the main motor.

Question 7

Print rollers should be cleaned with what type of solvent?

- ❍ a. Alcohol
- ❍ b. Mild soap and water
- ❍ c. Thinner
- ❍ d. Print rollers are brushed clean, solvents are not recommended

Answer a is correct. Print rollers need friction to work properly. Therefore, they must be cleaned with a solvent that will dissolve grease and leave no residue. Alcohol has these properties and is an excellent solvent for cleaning print rollers. Answer b is incorrect as soap will leave a sticky residue. Answer c is incorrect because thinner is a corrosive solvent. Answer d is incorrect because a brush will not remove the grease that causes a loss of friction.

Need to Know More?

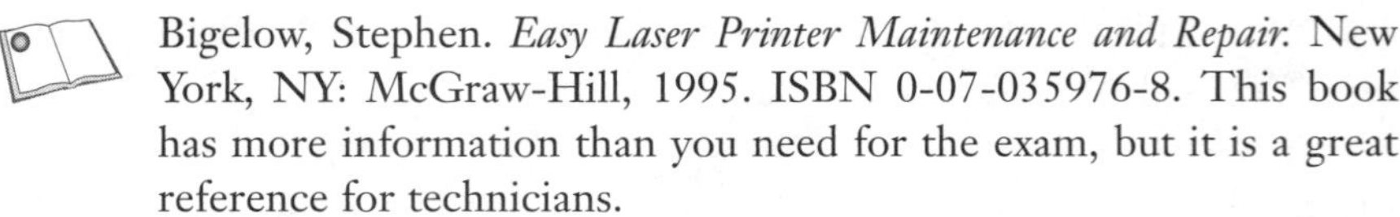

Bigelow, Stephen. *Easy Laser Printer Maintenance and Repair.* New York, NY: McGraw-Hill, 1995. ISBN 0-07-035976-8. This book has more information than you need for the exam, but it is a great reference for technicians.

Bigelow, Stephen. *Troubleshooting, Maintaining, and Repairing Personal Computers: A Technical Guide.* New York, NY: TAB Books, 1995. ISBN 0-07-912099-7. This book contains detailed information from a break-fix standpoint for displays; LCD panels; and dot matrix, ink jet, and laser printers.

Messmer, Hans-Peter. *The Indispensable PC Hardware Book.* Reading, MA: Addison-Wesley, 1995. ISBN 0-201-87697-3. This book contains much greatly detailed information about monitors and displays.

Minasi, Mark. *The Complete PC Upgrade and Maintenance Guide.* San Francisco, CA: Sybex Network Press, 1996. ISBN 0-7821-1956-5. This book is a great source of information on peripherals from a repair standpoint.

Rosch, Winn. *Hardware Bible.* Indianapolis, IN: Sams Publishing, 1994. ISBN 0-672-30954-8. This book covers everything you'd want to know about computer hardware.

Networking

Terms you'll need to understand:

- ✓ Small Computer System Interface (SCSI), Universal Serial Bus (USB), FireWire
- ✓ Megabits per second (Mbps) and megabytes per second (MB/s)
- ✓ Network interface card (NIC)
- ✓ Ethernet and token ring architectures
- ✓ Collisions and collision domains
- ✓ Backbone and backplanes
- ✓ Hub, bridge, router

Concepts you'll need to master:

- ✓ Serial connectivity
- ✓ Client/server and peer-to-peer network
- ✓ Baseband vs. Broadband
- ✓ Star, ring, and bus topologies

Before you start stressing about the complexities of networking, remember that a computer is only a bunch of parts put together by human beings just like you. Someone wanted to do something with information, and was inspired to invent a particular way to do it. When it worked, lots of people started using it, and they soon started complaining that it was too slow and too expensive, or that it had some problems. Then, someone came along and figured out a better way. Part by part, each area of computer technology grew out of previous problems.

Let's start our network section by reviewing three technologies that are not networks. Strange, right? Well, the reason is that these three are so similar to networks that, by the time we finish, you'll have a much better understanding of how networking began. The first two technologies are SCSI and USB (Small Computer System Interface and the Universal Serial Bus, respectively). The third technology is Apple Computer's *FireWire*, which is the same as Sony's *i.Link*. The formal name for this technology is the Institute of Electrical and Electronic Engineers (IEEE) 1394 specification.

Chaining Devices

We've mentioned how IRQ controllers were daisy-chained, and we've seen how memory chips can be chained together on modules. When peripheral controllers began taking on more intelligence, it became possible for several devices to access a single controller. Rather than add more and more sockets to the controllers, a "pass-through" connection was added to the device. This allows a downstream device (added afterward) to send and receive data to or from a host, usually the PC.

In other words, instead of the PC (host) connecting to only one device, the host can connect to one device, and a second device can be connected to the first device. By connecting to the first device, the second device does not have to connect directly to the PC. We see something similar to this with an IDE controller and master/slave drives.

An IDE or EIDE disk must be mounted inside the computer. There is no standard provision for an IDE ribbon cable to run to external devices. For a while, kits were available on the market that allowed a connection to an external IDE drive using the parallel port, but the wide acceptance of Iomega's Jaz and Zip drives have relegated these kits to novelty status.

For example, if an Iomega Zip drive connects to the host computer through the parallel port controller, a pass-through connector on the back of the Zip drive allows a printer to be connected in a chain. Cue the music! "The printer's connected to the Zip drive; the Zip drive's connected to printer port. The printer port's connected to the motherboard, and they all go singin' along."

When devices are chained to a single controller, the controller handles the prioritization of the data stream. It then sends appropriate information to either the drive or the printer. The port controller is the host, and both the drive and printer are chained devices. The problem with pass-through connectors, is that only two devices can be connected to the host, much like an IDE controller.

Typical floppy drive controllers for IBM PCs and clones allow a maximum of two floppy drives to be connected with a single cable. On the exam, you'll likely be tested on how many devices can be attached to certain types of cable interfaces. For example, SCSI allows a total of up to 8 devices—one host adapter and seven peripherals. A floppy disk, IDE, or EIDE controller allows two devices. Always remember that a SCSI interface requires a host; therefore, only 7 additional devices can be connected to the interface.

SCSI Interface

The SCSI interface (pronounced "scuzzy") is one of the occult mysteries of "computerdom." Like any of the PC technologies, the interface could take up an entire chapter, but our purpose here is to help you understand SCSI enough to pass the exam. (See Chapter 9 for more on SCSI connectors and other cables.). The SCSI interface was originally developed so that Apple computers could take advantage of some of the emerging drive technology being developed for IBM computers.

SCSI is used by many manufacturers and supports a mixture of drives and devices within the same system (for example, disk drives, RAID arrays, tape backups, and scanners). With the modern ATA interface and USB ports (discussed in a moment), SCSI has moved to a less dominant role in the home consumer market. However, because of certain throughput and speed advantages, we often see SCSI devices in networking environments. Aside from a mandatory host adapter, there can be up to seven additional devices on a SCSI chain. SCSI is available in three versions: SCSI-1, 2, and 3.

The SCSI bus also allows computers that aren't IBM compatible to use hard drives that were developed specifically for IBM-type PCs. An important thing to remember about the SCSI interface is that the bus allows not only hard drives but also other devices to be connected to an external cable.

The IDE and EIDE controller also uses drives and other devices, but only allows two devices in a chain and does not support external devices.

The SCSI Chain—8 ID Numbers

SCSI is completely different from IDE in the sense that it isn't restricted to disk drives. SCSI is not a controller/adapter like the IDE; it is a complete and separate bus. The bus connects to the system bus on the motherboard through a host adapter. This is how you can see references to a PCI SCSI adapter. In that case, the host adapter fits a PCI slot on the motherboard bus. In the old days, the same reference would apply to an ISA SCSI adapter.

A single SCSI bus can hold up to eight devices, each with a unique SCSI identification (ID) number from 0 through 7. These numbers are called the *Logical Unit Number* (LUN). For instance, LUN 0 might be assigned to a SCSI hard drive and LUN 4 might be a CD-ROM. LUN 7 might be the host adapter. *Be sure to remember that hexadecimal counting begins at zero*. The host adapter takes up one of the ID numbers, leaving seven IDs for the other hardware devices.

The main thing to remember about configuring a SCSI device is that the host adapter and every device must have a SCSI ID number. The ID number is almost always between 0 and 6 (seven choices), with the host adapter usually set to 7 at the factory. ID 7 is the highest priority, and the adapter is critical. If the adapter ID is 7, that means it's the eighth device—leaving room for seven more devices.

Don't be confused by the 8 ID numbers and 7 devices on the overall SCSI bus. Remember that the host adapter automatically takes up one ID number. The remaining seven hardware devices take up the remaining seven identification numbers.

A trick question on the exam might focus on the number of devices, but will ask you how many unique SCSI ID numbers are possible.

The ID is set in much the same way that master/slave jumpers are set on an IDE hard drive. For no reason at all, and instead of making it simple, SCSI manufacturers use binary numbers represented by three jumpers. One SCSI manufacturer might have binary 000 as SCSI ID 0 (LUN 0) and binary 100 as SCSI ID 4. Just to be diabolical, another SCSI manufacturer might reverse the jumper settings, so that ID 4 could just as easily be 001.

A SCSI cable must be terminated at both ends, just like a network bus. We discuss terminators later in this chapter, but they're essentially a way to absorb signals and prevent bounce-back interference. Because the host adapter is usually at one end, it typically has a built-in terminator. If you put the host adapter in the middle of the chain, you'll need to remember to remove the terminator mounted on the controller and install terminators at both ends of the cable.

SCSI-1

The first set of standards, SCSI-1, was finalized in 1986 and included 18 commands, but the interface could send only one command at a time. Sometimes called Narrow SCSI, the 8-bit bus required a host adapter and used a unique SCSI ID number for each drive. It introduced the seven-device limit to a daisy chain—setting aside the host adapter—where the remaining devices could *only* be different types of hard drives. SCSI-1 was very strict about termination and used a 132-ohm (impedance) passive terminator. The terminator didn't work well with high-speed transfer rates, sometimes causing data errors when more than one device was on a chain. Another problem with SCSI-1 was that the cable length was limited to 6 meters, which is approximately 19 feet.

A meter is slightly longer than three feet (a yard). The number of feet is about three times the measurement in meters—"three and change," as we say. (3.28 is the actual multiplier, but you can more easily use 3 in your head, for approximations.) One inch is 2.54 centimeters, but once again, you can estimate that the number of centimeters is about two-and-a-half times the inch measurement.

SCSI-1 cables use a 50-pin ribbon connector with an 8-bit data path for internal drive controllers. External peripherals such as scanners and tape drives, use a 50-contact Centronix connector (see Chapter 9). The maximum cable length is 6 meters (19.6 feet).

SCSI-2

Release 2 of the specification lowered the terminator resistance and used an active (voltage-regulated) terminator. The lower impedance (ohms) helped improve reliability. SCSI-2 included the original 18 commands (rewriting some of them) and added new commands, including specific support for drives *other than hard drives*, (e.g., CD-ROM; DAT; floptical; removable disk; standard QIC tape; magneto-optical; WORM drives; and scanners). Some drives still required third-party software drivers, but the seven-device limit stayed.

SCSI-2 also introduced support for a bus-mastering controller (onboard CPU/DMA controller), and support for multitasking environments. Up to 256 commands could be sent at one time to a device, which stored them in a buffer and reordered them for better efficiency. However, increased throughput and speed led to problems requiring a reduced cable length with a maximum of 3 meters.

Although we list SCSI cable lengths and connectors here, Chapter 9 is focused more on the many other types of connectors used in a PC system. The principle connector to know for SCSI is the 50-contact Centronix and the 50-pin ribbon cable for drives.

The SCSI-2 specification brought about a change in the width of the bus. As the bus made the changeover from 8 bits to 16 bits, each minor variation led to the many names of SCSI, as follows:

- *Fast SCSI, or Fast-10 (8-bit)*—Capable of 10Mbps transfers, with a maximum cable length of 3 meters, used a 50-pin connector for internal drives, and a 50-pin connector (DB50) for external host and peripheral drives.
- *Ultra SCSI, or Fast-20 (8-bit)*—Capable of 20Mbps transfers, with a maximum cable length of 1.5 meters, used the same connectors as Fast-10.
- *Ultra2 SCSI (8-bit)*—Capable of 40Mbps transfers, with a maximum cable length of 12 meters (39 feet), also used the same connectors as Fast-10.
- *Fast Wide SCSI, Fast-10 (16-bit)*—Capable of 20Mbps transfers, with a maximum cable length of 1.5 meters (4.9 feet), used a new 68-pin internal and external connector (half-pitch DB68) for newer hard drives.
- *Ultra Wide SCSI, Fast-20 (16-bit)*—Capable of 40Mbps transfers, with the same cables and connectors as Fast-10.

Bus-Mastering

When a controller has more than one device attached to it, bus-mastering is where the single controller can directly communicate with all the attached devices. In the past each device had to communicate with the CPU. Bus-mastering skips the "middle man" and speeds up the flow of information moving through the controller.

The original DMA provided control over devices from the motherboard, and was sometimes called "third-party DMA." The CPU was primarily in control of transfer requests, communicating with the device controller, and the DMA channels controller acted as a third-party "helper" by off-loading work from the CPU (see Chapter 5 "Direct Memory Access").

Bus-mastering is also called "first-party DMA," given that the device does all the transfer work without using a separate DMA controller. In other words, the device takes control of the transfer bus, becoming the master of the bus, so to speak. With the development of the PCI bus and bus-mastering (UltraDMA or UDMA), modern IDE hard drives began to catch up with the SCSI interface. You can check the Settings tab in the Device Manager, under the Properties for an IDE drive, to see if Windows (98 or later) DMA is enabled for a particular hard drive.

Warning: Incorrect settings can lead to a complete reinstallation of the system! Don't experiment unless you know what you're doing.

SCSI-3 (Ultra SCSI)

SCSI-3 is actually a collection of evolving specifications for device operation, using the same 16-bit bus width as SCSI-2, but increasing cable lengths and throughput. Because of increasing throughput speeds, cable lengths were initially reduced. Part of the changing specification was aimed at increasing length, while keeping the speed improvements of better bus transfers. There are a number of subsets to SCSI-3, referred to as the *SCSI Parallel Interface* (SPI). In fact, we no longer refer to SCSI-1, 2, or 3, but rather reference the specific subsets as follows:

- *Ultra2 Wide (U2W) SCSI, or Ultra2 LVD SCSI, or Fast-40 (16-bit)*—Capable of 80Mbps transfers, with a maximum cable length of 12 meters, used low-voltage differential (LVD) DB68 cables for some drives, or very high density (VHD) Centronix 68-pin connectors for RAID controllers and file servers.
- *Ultra3 SCSI, or Ultra160/m (16-bit)*—Capable of 160Mbps transfers, with a maximum cable length of 12 meters, uses the same DB68 and Centronix 68-pin connectors as Fast-40, but also an 80-pin Single Connector Attachment (SCA) connector for RAID controllers and SCA drives. SCA drives could be connected to DB68 connectors with an adaptor.

SCA and Hot-Swapping

You won't have to know the many versions of SCSI on the exam, which is primarily concerned with how many devices can be attached to the interface and how many data lines a basic cable uses. However, with CompTIA making various changes, we wanted to include a brief overview of the many specification names. Ultra3 SCSI increases throughput and added support for SCA drives.

The SCA specification (or subspecification) introduced hot-swapping. This meant that instead of having to shut down a file server and network whenever a drive went bad, the drive could be exchanged (swapped) while the system was still running. Networks have many disks in a redundant array of inexpensive disks (RAID), designed to protect valuable data at all times. Bringing down a RAID array to swap out a faulty disk was contrary to the basic concept of real-time backups, and SCA drives avoid those shutdowns. This idea of hot-swapping peripherals was an important aspect of the developing USB specification.

Storage Area Networks (SANs) and iSCSI

Although people sometimes think that computers are expensive, valuable pieces of equipment, the data stored on computers is far more valuable. If you run a business and someone steals your computers, you can replace the hardware and software applications. It may be expensive, but at least they can be replaced. The data, on the other hand, is irreplaceable unless it has been backed up. Data backups and the need for accessibility from anywhere on the planet has led to the development of wide area networks devoted almost entirely to data storage.

Multinational corporations and research universities can have storage needs up into the thousands of gigabytes or more. Backing up such a database requires high-speed transfers, very large disks, and various other evolving equipment. The Storage Networking Industry Association (SNIA) has launched the Storage Management Initiative (SMI) to develop a storage management standard for these types of storage networks. (SAN may also stand for *Server Area Network*, connecting many file servers, or System Area Network.)

On a regular LAN or WAN, most of the data transfers taking place are file access events, meaning that someone opens or saves a file, or accesses an application such as MS Word. Storage networks usually process block transfers, where large blocks of information are moved from one place to another over fiber optics, or fibre channel networks. The Fibre Channel protocol (FCP) is a serial SCSI command protocol used on these networks.

Storage area networks take advantage of the Internet to move large blocks of data across many different types of file servers. The Internet Small Computer Systems Interface (iSCSI) protocol defines the rules for transmitting block storage applications over TCP/IP networks. This leads to yet another set of acronyms, Fibre Channel over TCP/IP (FCIP), and the Internet Fibre Channel Protocol (iFCP). iSCSI interfaces can be directly connected to standard Gigabit Ethernet switches and/or IP routers, and provide for SCSI-3 commands to be encapsulated in TCP/IP packets and reliably delivered over IP networks.

Universal Serial Bus (USB)

The old COM (RS 232) and LPT ports are far too slow for modern processors, and although parallel transfer is faster than serial transfer, parallel bits get out of synch when they have to travel too far. This is known as *signal skew* or *jitter*, and is why both parallel and typical SCSI interfaces require fairly short cables. Serial cables can be much longer than parallel cables, but the COM port is very slow, transferring data at only 115,000 bits per second

(0.014MB/s). If we could boost the speed of serial transfers, we'd get the best of both—faster transfer and longer cables.

This problem of signal skew at high-speed parallel transfer rates shows up at the microscopic level in DDR memory modules. Rambus memory used a serial configuration, leading to latency (waiting) problems. DDR uses a parallel system, but has problems with skew.

Another problem is that, for a long time, too many devices were available for the limited number of basic I/O ports on IBM-compatible PC motherboards. A modem took one of the COM ports, regardless of whether it was internal or external. The mouse became as critical as a keyboard, but although the back panel added two new PS/2 connectors, the mouse was still using one of the serial controllers on the board. If anyone used two printers, they were either on a network, or they used an A/B box, so the back panel eliminated all but one LPT port.

Printer Switching Boxes

An A/B box is a device by which two printers can be used on one PC, simply by changing a switch. Switch boxes are usually found in any store that sells peripheral devices, and typically provide connections for two, three, or four printers (A/B/C/D). Windows uses a different printer driver for each type of printer (e.g., HP Laserjet, Epson Inkjet, Cannon Bubble Jet, etc.), and each printer is configured in the Printers dialog box.

To install a new printer driver, navigate the Start|Settings|Printers menus, or choose the Control Panel and double-click on the Printers icon. (This may require a Windows installation CD.) Simply picking a different printer in Windows is not the same as actually changing the physical printer. An HP Laserjet won't print in color, no matter how the job is sent from Windows.

Ordinarily, to use a different printer, you have to shut down the system and detach the printer from the parallel port. You then attach a different printer and restart the machine, reopening the application and sending the print job to the different printer. A switch box allows changing printers without shutting down the system, almost like having a small print network attached to a the LPT port.

On top of all this, when you added an expansion card to an internal bus slot, you'd have to reconfigure the system to deal with IRQs and DMA lines. Plug-and-Play went a long way toward making cards and devices more intelligent, but even today, internal modems can lead to mysterious screen freezes or disconnects, due to the vagaries of configuration settings. To get around the limited I/O ports and the need to configure add-on device cards, the industry developed two new serial transfer architectures: IEEE 1394, and the Universal Serial Bus (USB).

From the start, Apple Computers had developed the Apple Desktop Bus (ADB) as a way of connecting several simple devices (e.g., keyboard, mouse) to a single serial bus. This same concept was carried forward to the Macintosh and NeXT machines, and companies like Sun Microsystems and others were including the idea in their machines. IBM-compatible PCs didn't have this capability. At the same time, Apple was developing a much faster serial bus for high-speed transfers involving more complex and more expensive devices. Apple FireWire was eventually certified as the IEEE 1394 standard, and was designed for video conferencing, multimedia productions, and other applications requiring large throughput.

Intel and Microsoft got together with Compaq, DEC, IBM, NEC, and Northern Telecom, and decided to bring the concept of a multidevice serial bus to PCs, developing the USB specification. Although USB is faster than ADB, with added hot-swapping capabilities, most of the technology comes from the IEEE 1394 standard—Apple's FireWire. Intel worked alongside of Apple, and USB was originally intended to bring together PCs and Macs, or at least make them more complementary to each other.

FireWire was already developing into a high-speed communication standard for multimedia and video, so Intel developed USB with slower, less expensive devices in mind. The USB port was supposed to take over from the Apple ADB. To boost the USB performance up to the level of FireWire would make it cost-prohibitive, as well as less reliable. Back then, the company often said that USB was going to be complementary to the IEEE 1394 standard, and not intended to replace FireWire.

USB works primarily by putting a really cool magical symbol on a wire, shown in Figure 8.1. The symbol then moves data into another dimension, which speeds up...no, we're kidding. The main advantages of USB are that it provides fast data transfers over a serial bus, sometimes called *fast serial transfers*. Partly because serial transfers allow longer cable lengths, another advantage of USB technology is that additional devices may be connected to a PC through the use of hubs (discussed in a moment).

USB 1.0 and 1.1

When USB is used in conjunction with Plug-and-Play on a PC, it removes the need for dedicated cards and slots, and allows for hot-swapping peripherals. The operating system (Windows) understands USB peripherals as if they were installed in an expansion slot. This means (presumably) that configuration problems associated with a limited pool of memory addresses and IRQ lines should vanish. USB has done a very good job of doing just that, and manual configurations are becoming a thing of the past. A special symbol, shown in Figure 8.1, marks a device, cable, or connector as being part of the USB family.

The Universal Serial Bus has an important advantage of allowing hot-swapping. Ordinarily, plugging in or unplugging a device requires that the machine be powered down (to avoid power surges). USB and PnP allow device changes without powering down the PC.

Figure 8.1 The USB mark on cables, connectors, hubs, and peripheral devices.

Version 1.0 of the USB specification was released in January of 1996, and provided for data transfers on both a low and a high channel. The low-speed channel could transfer data at rates of 1.5 megabits per second (Mbps), or 0.1875 megabytes per second (MB/s), ten times faster than the COM port.

You'll most likely be tested on values in terms of bits per second. If you remember those, all you have to do is divide by 8 in order to calculate the bytes per second. Divide 1.5 megabits by 8 bits, and the result is 0.18 megabytes per second.

The high channel could transfer data at what was originally called a "high speed" rate of 12Mbps (1.5MB/s). When USB 2.0 entered the market, "high speed" had to be redefined to fit the new 480Mbps transfer mode, and so the original high speed was changed to "full" speed. Version 1.1 was released in September of 1998, with clarifications as to how USB ports would work and problem solutions to version 1.0.

USB 1.0 and 1.1 provide for a transfer rate of 1.5Mbps (1,500,000 bits) using a low channel, or "slow" channel, and 12Mbps (12,000,000 bits) using the high channel.

The important things to remember about both USB versions 1.0 and 1.1 are that:

- The topology is tiered star.
- 1 USB controller can sustain up to 127 devices.
- There are two channels: High and Low
- The high channel transfers at 12Mbps.
- The low, subchannel (e.g., pointing devices and keyboards) transfers at 1.5Mbps.

Powered USB Hubs

The first USB specification was released in January 1996, and was supported by the Pentium II chipsets. Windows 98, Windows Me, Windows NT (4.x and later), Windows 2000, and Windows XP include full support for USB. Version 1.0 also pioneered a way for PCs to daisy-chain more than two peripheral devices to a single USB controller, called a *hub*. We will discuss hubs and networks later in this chapter, but for the moment, you should understand levels and tiers as part of the USB specification.

USB hubs provide both connectivity and power. Most peripheral devices are powered through the devices' cables. This can overload power circuits, particularly in portable laptops where battery life is limited. To overcome this, USB hubs include a power supply, allowing the hubs themselves to provide power to their devices.

A maximum of 127 devices can be chained to a universal serial bus in a tiered star topology. Star means that all devices are linked to a central point with the wires radiating outward like a star. Tiered means that within the star, devices can be plugged into additional hubs—one after another, in several levels (tiers). Figure 8.2 shows the way this is done; in the figure, the tiers are numbered 1 through 5. The rules for USB hubs are as follows:

- Hubs can be plugged into the cable, and multiple devices can then be plugged into each hub.
- A hub can also be plugged into another hub, leading to a new, or lower level (tier) of devices
- You can have as many as five tiers of hubs.

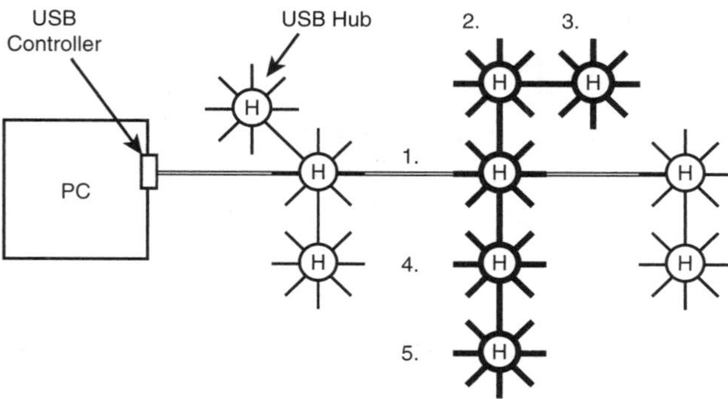

Figure 8.2 USB tiered-star topology.

USB 2.0

USB 2.0 introduces a new high-speed mode, offering transfer rates of 480Mbps, or 60MB/s. Notice that the new mode is 60 megabytes per second, or 40 times faster than the version 1.1 high-speed mode.

The new revision keeps the previous low channel and high channel, but there is a tremendous difference between the two lower-level channels and the new mode. If you look at Table 8.1, you can quickly see the different data rates of all three versions.

Table 8.1 USB signal transfer rates.

Version	Mbps	MB/s
1.0 (low)	1.5	0.1875
1.1 (high)	12	1.5
2.0	480	60

Two data signals (packets) can't exist in the same space at the same time. This is true in all of reality, with anything, and so a problem arises in a USB cable when a very high-speed device sends information at the same time as a slow-speed mouse, for instance. We mentioned (in Chapter 6) that when a fast and slow drive is connected to the same IDE controller, the controller will set to the lowest speed. This is much like what happens in USB 2.0. The transfer speed of the entire bus can be held back by data coming from a low-channel device.

USB 1.1 was often unable to transfer at 12Mbps if it was using any low-speed devices at the same time. Note that an Ethernet 10 card transfers data at middle-channel speeds. The difference between 12 and 1.5 isn't all that much of a difference. On the other hand, the difference between 480 and 1.5 is huge! Not only that, but if a mouse slows down just a tiny bit while an Ethernet card is sending information, it isn't all that important—we don't really notice.

USB 2.0 was designed to take on high-speed video and multimedia. How the intent changed from the original is anyone's guess, but the fact remains that if you hear a bump in a quality music file, you notice it. If three devices are transmitting at the same time, then (simplistically) each channel takes a third of the bandwidth. 480 divided by three, means that the so-called high-speed transfer would be taking place at an effective 160Mbps (actually less) with a 60% reduction. With many slower speed devices and only one or two high-speed devices, (e.g., one video conferencing camera), the problem becomes even more severe.

In order for USB 2.0 to take advantage of advances in hard drive technology, and to bring the bus back into alignment with things like UDMA /166, music jukeboxes, and Web cams, it will have to transfer data at better than 166MB/s. In the example above, you can see how quickly the transfer speeds degrade with multiple low-speed USB devices on a system. Then there are also 100BaseT network cards and plans for broadband Internet access to consider.

USB is the most popular serial technology on the market. Perhaps the fact that there are no royalty fees associated with the standard has something to do with it, but for whatever reason, the popularity and low cost of USB is leading to the elimination of the COM and LPT ports completely. USB support is being built into the South bridge of motherboards, and these so-called legacy-free machines are moving the industry towards true plug-and-play simplicity. Any device you buy can simply be plugged into a USB port and off you go. In fact, a secondary specification to USB is "On-the-Go," or USB OTG. This will (theoretically) make it possible to connect handheld devices (e.g., PDAs, digital cameras) to other devices without a proprietary data-transfer cradle.

Supplementary Information

In Chapter 4, we mentioned that AMD created faster throughput by using a change in state of the clock. You may recall that it wasn't the clock tick itself that was used for timing, but rather the change in voltage state as the clock went from a pause to a tick. The increasing voltage was one state, with the tick itself being a separate event. As the clock returned to its pre-tick condition, the reducing voltage was a second state. This allowed for two instructions per clock tick, rather than only one instruction being linked to the tick.

The "pause" condition, where zero voltage is being applied to the clock, constitutes a *reference point*. When the voltage goes up in order to generate a tick, that event is distinct from when the voltage returns to zero. Up until USB, this was how many digital processes worked with voltage changes. The speed increases in the USB specification were developed using a process called *Non-Return-to-Zero-Inverted* (NRZI) encoding.

NRZI Encoding

NRZI encoding means that only the variation of the voltage produces a change in state. A steady voltage represents a 1, and any change at all in voltage represents a 0. The change could be a drop in voltage or a return to zero voltage, but with NRZI, the return to zero is no longer required—no reference point is necessary. This works both ways. If the voltage changes a lot, it causes a string of 0s. If the voltage stays steady, it causes a string of 1s. On the other hand, a string of 1s or 0s can set the voltage to a steady state or a varying state, respectively.

NRZI is one of the ways that USB can generate much higher throughput than earlier serial transfer protocols. NRZI encoding is unique to USB.

USB Hubs

There is a small bus inside a USB hub with terminators at both ends and wires leading to connectors on the outer casing of the hub. Devices connect to a hub, and the hub then connects to a cable. Other cables then connect the hub to the computer. When a hub can be connected to another hub, which in turn connects to a main USB cable, this is called a *tiered-star topology*.

Later in this chapter we will be discussing networking, speaking of buses, hubs an topologies. You should be very careful in your understanding of USB technology, that you don't confuse the serial bus with a network. USB is not a networking protocol. It is a serial interface that allows for chaining devices through the use of special USB hubs.

Hubs also provide a bi-directional repeater. A repeater receives a signal, rebuilds it, and sends it out again. This is important because a USB cable has a limit of 5 meters (approximately 15 ft.). If you want to go any farther than 5 meters, you need a repeater to rebuild (and re-time) the signal.

Version 1.1 hubs were fairly simple devices, designed to move only two channels of information at closely related speeds. Version 2.0 is designed for very high transfer speeds, but comes with the price of delays and wasted bandwidth if slower devices take up that bandwidth. One solution is to provide more sophisticated (and more expensive) hubs.

Consumers can opt to replace their simple and low cost USB 1.1 hubs, with complex, higher cost and higher speed USB 2.0 hubs, which can then step up the speed from the slower speed, USB 1.1-compatible device. Data packets from earlier USB device can be sped up, but if a USB 1.1 hub is between the device and the computer, everything slows back down to the version 1.1 standard, including USB 2.0 hubs.

Like an IDE drive controller, if you mix 2.0 and 1.x hubs, any device downstream from the 1.x hub will be limited to the lower speed of the 1.x hub. We've mentioned how early CD-ROM drives used buffering to transfer information more quickly, and USB 2.0 hubs use a similar process. USB version 2.0 brings about improvements in three areas:

- Speed
- Power
- Buffering

Plug 'n' Play (PnP)

PnP comes from the expression plug-and-play (spoken as plug 'n' play). It was first introduced in Windows 95, but the concept originates with the old EISA bus. PnP is shorthand for a process in which the operating system works with the underlying hardware in an attempt to automatically configure peripheral devices.

The PnP standard is an agreement among hardware, software, and operating systems developers regarding how to "plug" (install) something into the system and have it "play" (work) automatically. Keep in mind that a truly workable auto-configuration process involves more than just the operating system.

PnP is both a hardware and a software solution. Not only do PnP devices have to be built according to the specification, but they also require a compatible operating system and a compatible BIOS. The three aspects described in the PnP industry specification are:

- PnP-compatible hardware
- PnP BIOS
- PnP operating system

After a device has been configured, the PnP operating system assigns various system resources (such as memory and time slices) as long as the computer is running. The interactivity of the PnP technology allows the device to tell the operating system what it needs, and the OS gives the device those resources.

Older (non-PnP) devices installed in a PnP system have their expansion cards configured manually. In that case, the operating system can't work with the device to manage system resources. As far as the operating system is concerned, it doesn't "see" the device, and may end up assigning those resources to some other card—a PnP-compliant one. This could shut the older card out of the resource pool, leaving the device that it controls dead.

A PnP operating system does not *require* PnP hardware. Older hardware won't be auto-configured by a PnP operating system, but this means only that it must be configured manually. Non-PnP hardware can still run on a PnP system.

Although the technical standard describes only the three major components, Microsoft also includes a fourth component. You may find a question on the exam concerning PnP-aware application software. PnP-aware applications refer to this fourth specification.

IEEE 1394

We said earlier that FireWire and i.Link are both part of the IEEE 1394 standard. For anyone who cares, IEEE stands for the Institute of Electrical and Electronic Engineers, and they set the technical standards for these kinds of things. The other group of people who set standards, are the American National Standards Institute (ANSI), and neither group can agree on anything for sure. That's why the nice thing about standards is that there are so many of them.

IEEE 1394 was designed around video applications, particularly video cameras and video software. Motion video requires extremely high processing speed and bandwidth, and although the architecture is also designed for linking many devices together, we typically see an IEEE 1394 cable used to connect a camera or video-editing equipment to a PC.

IEEE 1394 is faster than USB technology, and Apple Computers was not part of the USB consortium. The current standard calls for three signal rates of 100Mbps (12.5MB/s), 200Mbps (25MB/s), or 400Mbps (50MB/s). Although most cards support the 200Mbps rate, most of the devices on the market run at up to only 100Mbps. FireWire and i.Link, like SCSI and USB, will allocate bandwidth to the speed of the designated device. To that end, not all the connected devices are required to run at 400MB/s.

A proposed modification to the current specification indicates an upgrade to gigabits per second (Gbps) bandwidth.

IEEE 1394 uses what's called a *daisy chained and branched topology*, where each adapter card allows for up to 63 nodes, with 16 devices chained from each node. IEEE 1394 provides a performance improvement over ultra-wide SCSI and costs significantly less. However, the devices all use power from the computer, unlike the powered hubs of USB. IEEE 1394 is fully PnP-compatible, including a capability for what's called "hot swapping," which allows for connecting or disconnecting a device without shutting down the PC.

FireWire and i.Link transfer information from device to device, while the USB specification moves information through the computer. Aside from this detour through the box, USB was designed to incorporate very slow devices that can easily slow down any higher speed devices on the cable system. One way to see the real-world implications of this is to run benchmark tests on a USB hard drive.

In an IE 1394 constellation, if a 200Mbps and a 100Mbps device are on the same cable, the difference is 2:1. On a USB system, a high-speed video camera running with a 1.5Mbps device leads to a difference of around 320:1. Additionally, the farther from the computer a device is located in a USB chain, the higher the latency (delay) in signals reaching the CPU. Typically, a PC attaches many slow-speed devices (i.e., mouse, keyboard) close to the computer with higher speed devices farther away.

The likelihood that USB will ever run as fast as IE 1394 is fairly low. On the other hand, the gradual elimination of COM and LPT ports makes it highly probable that USB will become the only peripheral connection bus on PCs. You should be aware, though you won't be tested for the knowledge on the exam, that installing USB 2.0 devices on a system using both 2.0 and 1.1

hubs and other devices has its own complexities. We would encourage you to explore the way USB devices and hubs operate in a combined environment.

Summary—Bus Transfers

You're going to encounter questions having to do with cable connectors (see Chapter 9), transfer rates, the USB and the SCSI acronyms, and serial versus parallel buses. One approach to choosing the correct responses is to memorize the raw numbers and facts. Another approach is to understand why all this stuff (technical term) was invented in the first place. If you can imagine yourself out in the field, using and resolving problems with USB devices and SCSI cables, answering one or two questions about how they work may not be as worrisome. The main points to remember in the preceding section are as follows:

- ➤ Daisy-chaining devices means connecting one after another in a configuration of some kind. Know the names of the various ways hubs and devices can be strung together in a chain. Pay attention to tiered topology in relation to the USB interface.
- ➤ The SCSI interface is complex and filled with too many numbers. Stay focused on the idea of a controller and the number of devices that can be attached to the controller. Know what ID numbers refer to and (from the next chapter) remember that a typical cable uses a 50-pin connector.
- ➤ Be sure to understand the three versions of the USB specification and the three channels used for data transfers. Know the difference between a hub and a port, and use the question responses as an aid to remembering the transfer rates of each channel.
- ➤ You already know what PnP means, but you'll be tested on the formal definition of Plug-and-Play. Remember what is and isn't technically required for devices and a PnP operating system.
- ➤ One way or another, memorize the fact that IEEE 1394 (as opposed to 802.3) is associated with FireWire and i.Link systems.

Networking Overview

Networks typically connect both computers and peripherals together. USB and IEEE 1394 are designed to connect peripherals to a single computer. Networking is done to share resources, either for convenience or to save money. Connecting computers together in a network requires three things: a network interface card (NIC); a Network Operating System (NOS)—technically called a *redirector*; and a medium for transmitting data from one computer to another (usually some type of wire). We will focus most of our attention on wire (cable) transmission mediums.

Categories and Types

Networks fall into two broad categories: peer-to-peer and client/server. We can also divide each category into two types: Ethernet and token passing (often referred to as "token ring"). All computers are equal in a peer-to-peer network (think of a "jury of your peers"), and you can choose what data and resources you want to share. Client/server networks are configured in such a way that one or more computers act as file servers (or just servers), with the rest acting as clients. Servers, which control the overall network, are usually dedicated to storing data. A file server is like a lawyer, serving clients with filing, applications, and processing.

There are five different types of token rings, but all of them are token passing.

Peer-to-peer networks don't have dedicated servers, and therefore are less expensive to set up. Instead, each PC shares its own resources with the other PCs connected to the network. For example, you might access Sue's hard drive to retrieve a spreadsheet, and she might choose to print a document using a printer connected to your PC. Although security is provided to determine who can use what resources, peer-to-peer networks don't have the same level of security as client/server networks.

Peer-to-peer is where each computer is a peer (equal) to the other. Client/server is where a central file server provides services to many clients. Windows 95, 98, and ME provide built-in, peer-to-peer networking. Windows NT and 2000 (in their server versions) can also provide client/server networking.

Both peer-to-peer and client/server networks use software that performs the redirector function, but that software is called different things depending on the category. Beginning with Windows for Workgroups (version 3.11), Microsoft provided a peer-to-peer redirector as part of the operating system. Because of this, we rarely talk about redirectors in peer-to-peer networking, but refer to whether the feature is activated or not. Reference to a redirector usually means client/server networking.

Network Interface Card (NIC)

A network interface card plugs into the expansion bus of a motherboard and provides several necessary networking features. Initially, a NIC (pronounced *nick*) provides a unique network address for the PC. This address is stored in ROM on the card, and is a unique code assigned by the manufacturer. Secondly, the NIC provides a connection to the media or cable used for the network. Finally, it provides the processor and buffers required to send and receive packets of data over the network cable.

The NIC provides the network address for the PC. If you change the NIC, you change the address of the PC on the network. This can have interesting repercussions, depending on the network's configuration and security.

The Redirector

File servers run on a network operating system, which includes a redirector. The redirector monitors the CPU and determines whether data requests are local (in the server setup) or remote (outside). If the data is on a local hard drive, the request is routed to the drive. If the data isn't on the server's drives, the request is "redirected" to the NIC for transmission over the network.

All the machines running the operating system's client software also have a redirector as part of that software. When the file server broadcasts a signal, the redirector on the individual PCs checks to see whether or not the request is meant for that local setup.

Media

All networks communicate over some kind of media. This can be as simple as a pair of twisted wires, or as exotic as fiber optics and radio transmission. For the purposes of this discussion, we'll refer to the central media cable as the *backplane*. This isn't technically correct, but we're using it to refer to the main network "highway" where signals move around to various terminals. Ethernet is one of the first network types and one of the most popular, so let's start there.

Ethernet (IEEE 802.3)

Ethernet was originally developed as an experimental coaxial cable network in the 1970s by Xerox Corporation. Ethernet is a baseband network, meaning that only one signal can be on the network at a time and that the signal takes up the entire bandwidth. Originally, Ethernet ran at 3Mbps over a thick coaxial cable, and by 1980, the experiment was deemed a success. Xerox, together with Digital Equipment Corporation and Intel Corporation, developed version 1.0 of 10Mbps Ethernet specification. In 1985, the original Ethernet Version 1.0 specification was approved, and subsequently published as an official ANSI/IEEE Std. 802.3. The cable was named 10Base5, and the exact meaning of 10Base5 is discussed in the next chapter (Chapter 9).

Since the original standard was approved, ongoing developments and faster transmission rates have continued. Fast Ethernet, using Category 5 wiring, runs at 100Mbps. The Gigabit Ethernet standard (1,000Mbps) includes two primary additions: 1000Base-T for UTP (see Chapter 9) copper cable and 1000Base-X STP copper cable. Gigabit Ethernet also specifies standards for single and multimode fiber optic cable.

Network transmission speeds take place with frequencies well into the radio range, and the shielded coaxial wire prevented the cable from becoming an antenna, interfering with data transmissions. The cable was terminated by a resister at each end (called a *terminator*), which prevented signals traveling along the wire from reflecting back onto each other from the cable ends. All devices on the network attached to this cable using a tap and shared the cable as a transmission media.

See Figures 9.6 and 9.7 in Chapter 9 for an illustration of coaxial cable and terminators.

In an Ethernet network, the NIC "listens" to the cable, checking to see if anyone else's PC is talking. If no other PCs are transmitting at that moment, your card sends out a data transmission. As more terminals come online (join the network), each new card waits for a quiet moment (when no signal voltage is on the line) before transmitting data. If data signals moved instantaneously, each card would know when any other card was sending. Because data signals don't move instantaneously, there is a time delay over the length of wire, from one end of the network to the other.

When two network interface cards transmit at the same time and the signals meet in the middle somewhere, we have what's known as a *collision*. A collision creates a spike, or bump, in the voltage. The transmitting NICs detect this spike and send out a jam signal, which is nothing more than a stream of 0s and 1s designed to fill up the network. This causes all the cards on the network to stop transmitting, and a random number generator on each of the transmitting cards picks a time to begin transmission after an initial silence. This is why Ethernet is often called a *carrier sense, multiple access, collision detection (CSMACD) network*.

Terminators

Any electronic media or cable that carries a signal of any type, must be terminated properly at each end. To maintain error-free data travel along the bus, terminating resistors absorb any signal that reaches the end of the cable. This prevents the signal from "bouncing back" along the cable and crashing into other signals traveling along the bus (collisions). In a long backplane, it isn't unusual for a PC to transmit from one end, while a PC at the other end still hears silence and transmits at the same time.

Remember that electronic cables or media that carry data or signals are essentially a bus. To prevent errors caused by signals bouncing back along the bus from the ends of the cable, a terminating resistor must be at both ends. These are called *terminators.* Terminators absorb signals to keep them from reflecting back along the cable. SCSI devices also use terminators.

Throughput and Bandwidth

We introduced throughput in Chapter 2, saying that it's essentially how much data we can move through a bus. If you think of a byte as eight horses at the racetrack, then an 8-bit bus would be like the starting gates, where each horse (a bit) has its own gate. Suppose you have 100 rows of horses, and the gates only open and close for each row. Each time a row of horses goes through the gates, that's 1 cycle. The bus clock tells the gates when to open and shut. The number of times that the gates open and shut in a given time period is the frequency for that cycle.

If you think of bus throughput as bits per cycle, then you can begin to think of frequency as something like cycles per bit. Let's suppose that it takes 5 cycles to describe 1 bit. If each cycle takes 12 seconds, then it would take 60 seconds (1 minute) to produce one bit (5 cycles * 12 seconds per cycle = 60 seconds). The number of cycles in a given second is the frequency of those cycles, and this frequency is expressed in Hertz (Hz).

If you could make the cycles go faster, you could describe more bits. By "compressing" the frequency to 5 cycles per second, it would take 1 second to describe 1 bit. If 1MHz is 1 million cycles per second, that would allow for 200,000 bits, or 25,000 bytes (25KB or 0.25MB).

Bandwidth is a measure of the "capability" (or capacity) something has to move data. (Don't confuse bandwidth capacity with electrical capacitance.) For instance, our racetrack is only capable of handling a burst of 8 horses going through the gates. Part of that capability is defined by the dirt on the track, the weather, and the nature of the track. The "something" through which the data is moving could be a bus, an Ethernet cable, or even air.

Although the throughput is the actual data being moved, the bandwidth is the total potential data capacity of a medium. We almost never refer to bandwidth in conjunction with moving data through a bus. Usually we're referring to radio or a cable of some kind.

Baseband Ethernet bandwidth has the capacity to move only one signal at a time, with that signal taking up the entire bandwidth.

Technically, bandwidth is the difference between the highest and the lowest frequency being transmitted. High bandwidth allows for the transmission of a lot of information in a high frequency. Low bandwidth is a lesser capacity, allowing for less information to move at a lower frequency.

Broadband allows many different frequencies to travel over the transmission medium. Until recently, the most common example of broadband technology was radio, where many different signal frequencies (radio stations) could transmit at the same time. Amplitude Modulation (AM) radio is broadband technology, so when you hear about WAEC at 890 on your dial, the station is transmitting at a frequency of 890MHz. Fiber-optic cable allows for broadband data movement.

Baseband (time-division multiplexing) allows many signal frequencies, but each signal gets only a tiny slice of time for itself, and that signal uses the entire bandwidth. Broadband (frequency-division multiplexing) has a broad range of frequencies moving continuously, but any given signal gets only one frequency.

Token Ring (IEEE 802.5)

Ethernet networks using transmissions and quiet times are called *probabilistic*, in that moving data is a matter of probably avoiding a collision. IBM wanted to develop a deterministic way of making sure data would avoid a collision, and so it invented the token-ring network.

A token is a sort of placeholder for something that it represents, like a token of appreciation. A token ring network connects PCs in a ring and then passes an empty data packet from one PC to another. This symbol (the empty data packet) of what could become data is the token. When a terminal requires data from another terminal, it waits for the token to come around and then places its request (along with the NIC address of the PC from which it wants information) in the token. The token then becomes an actual data packet, and it passes around the ring to the appropriate PC.

Token ring networking is like a group of people sitting around a dinner table. If someone wants mashed potatoes, they wait for a pause in the conversation and then pass a note with their request to the person nearest the potatoes. That person reads the note and hands the potatoes to whomever is near them in the ring, and everyone passes the mashed potatoes along. When the person who sent the request gets the bowl, they dish out some potatoes onto their plate—the local hard drive. With every resource waiting for the token before it transmits, there are no longer any collisions.

Bus and Star Topology

Ethernet is a little like an old telephone party line. Regardless of how many people are talking on the phone, each person can hear every other person. The trick is to listen for the specific voice of the caller who's addressing you and ignore all the rest. Networks are a little more sophisticated than that, as we'll see in this section.

An Ethernet backplane is one long, heavy piece of coaxial cable that snakes its way through an office suite. This type of topology, which has only one wire, is called a *bus topology*. The cable can transport only one signal at a time, which means that only two devices can "talk" back and forth at any given time. All the PCs share that one cable, and any given PC can transmit when the bus isn't moving someone else's signal. All PCs on the bus can hear the transmission, but only the addressed PC copies the transmission into its buffer for processing.

In many cases, we use twisted-pair cables with modular connectors to connect several devices (e.g., terminals) to a hub. The hub is a box containing a small internal bus. When you connect a twisted pair cable to a hub, you are actually connecting it to a bus. The cables branching out from the hub look much like the legs of a starfish. Because of these hubs and branches, we call this type of installation a *star topology*. Figure 8.3 shows a linear bus topology (top), and a hub and star topology (bottom). Note the terminator resistors at each end of the linear bus.

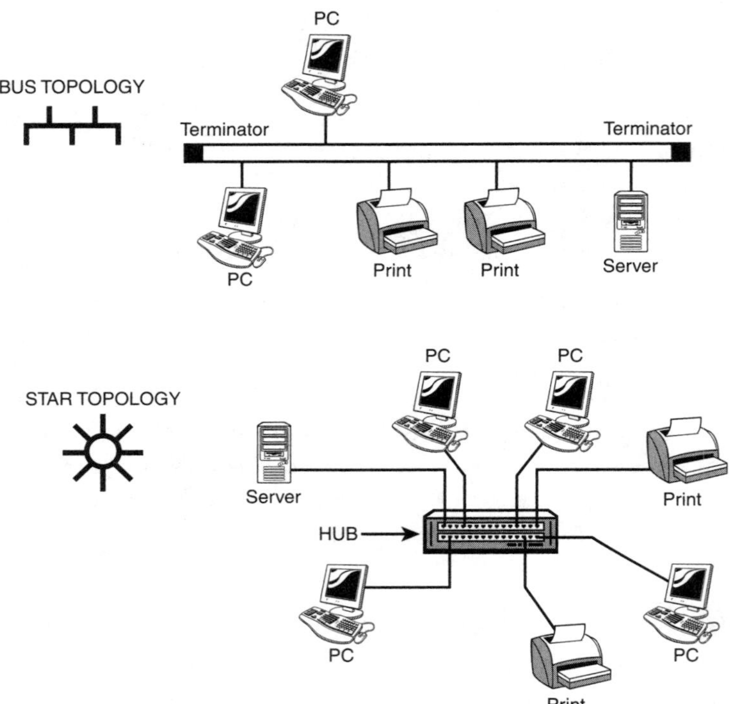

Figure 8.3 Outline of bus and star topologies.

Bridges and Routers

As networks became larger and larger, various limits began showing up. Signal strength and quality would decay with distance, and people wanted to add more computers to the network. Keep in mind that more transmissions lead to more signals, which in turn increases the probability of jam signals and slowdowns. A bridge is a way for a large network running at full capacity to be broken into smaller groups of segments.

Bridges work with only the addresses of the network cards on a specific network. When a bridge is installed in the middle of a network, it logs all of the NIC addresses on either side of it, only passing traffic if that traffic has a destination address on the other side of the bridge. This is how a bridge segments a network and allows for more PCs to be connected without creating traffic bottlenecks.

However, even with bridges, there is a limit to how many network addresses can be maintained and processed by a given device. Because of this, another level of addressing was established at the network level, and routers (rhymes with "shouters") were developed to operate at the network level (not at the individual resource level).

A bridge segments a network. It does not create two networks. This is a key point to remember.

The Router

With the introduction of the bridge, networks became so huge that individual NICs began running into trouble trying to figure out how to address a specific machine. If you think about it, the phone system (network) had a similar problem. At first, only four digits were used (NIC address) because only a couple of thousand phones existed. Then, each town began having enough phones that three additional exchange numbers (segment address) had to be added, making up our familiar, seven-digit number.

As more towns began interconnecting, we began to run out of exchange numbers. The country had to be broken down into separate networks comprised of several towns (and their internal exchange numbers). Three-digit area code numbers (routing address) were added to the system.

If you're calling someone nearby, you generally don't need to use an area code, unless you happen to live on the border of a separate area code. However, once you travel outside your neighborhood, you do have to dial an area code (then the exchange number, then the four-digit phone number).

A routing number is somewhat like the area code. Understand that this is an entire network to which a local machine is connected, not a segment. Routers direct traffic to whole networks, using a list of each network address. A router is like a phone book that holds only area codes.

The OSI Model

Networking was becoming so complicated that the Open System Interconnection (OSI) committee was formed to create the OSI model for networking—yet another set of standards. Seven layers are defined in the OSI model. We don't need to go into detail on each layer, but their names and basic functions are as follows:

7. *Application layer*—Program (e.g., spreadsheet), network (e.g., file transfer), and Internet (e.g., online email) applications

6. *Presentation layer*—Sound, video, graphics, text, and data
5. *Session layer*—Communication sessions; establishes, manages, and terminates these
4. *Transport layer*—End-to-end connection; sends segments from one host to another
3. *Network layer*—Network services and logical address specifications for "best path" connection (routers)
2. *Data link layer*—Physical (not logical) addresses for NICs, and related addressing within segments (bridges)
1. *Physical layer*—Electrical, mechanical, and transmission functions, along with specifications for wire (e.g., voltage, connectors, and data rates)

Look at the numbers assigned to each of the OSI layers. Each layer is often referred to by only its number. You will probably run into this on the exam, so know what number goes with which layer.

When a router is installed between two networks, it passes traffic with a network address to that network. Routers don't care about each NIC address because they're only concerned with networks as a whole. This is how many networks can be connected together to form one big inter-network like the Internet.

The Internet uses a protocol called *Transmission Control Protocol/Internet Protocol (TCP/IP)*, which establishes the format for addressing networks and stations on the network. In this environment, every PC has two addresses: The NIC has its built-in address, and the card is assigned a second TCP/IP address.

Under this format, every station is assigned a multidigit network address that is broken into four blocks. This is the IP address. For example, a specific PC may have the address 192.168.001.115. Some of these digits represent the network address, and the others represent the PC itself. A subnet mask determines what the digits represent. A Domain Name Server (DNS), which cross-references numeric addresses with names, is usually somewhere on the network to make addresses easier to remember.

A firewall is a router that can be programmed to accept or reject traffic based on IP addresses and content, such as packet contents. A firewall can also be set up to accept or reject certain protocols.

Summary—Network Overview

We were surprised to see networking added to the A+ exam, until we realized that simple networking is built into all the recent versions of Windows. What used to be a complex field of corporate PC management is now often found in residential homes and small businesses. You won't need to know the low-level details of the OSI model, but you should understand that an OSI model exists, and that it has seven layers. Some of the concepts to remember from this section include:

- The difference between Ethernet and token ring, and the difference between peer-to-peer and client/server
- Terminators and packet collisions
- Network cards (NICs) and the concept of a redirector
- Bus and star topologies, and how to recognize a simple drawing of each
- The difference between a bridge and a router.
- The names of the seven OSI model layers.

In the following section, pay attention to the concept of the TCP/IP protocol, domain names, and an IP address. You should be able to recognize an IP address from your own Web browsing experience, but you'll have to be able to identify the individual components making up an email address.

The Internet

Although you don't need to know the details of TCP for the exam, you should know that an IP address is typically 12 digits long and difficult to remember. Domain names are a way to cross-reference the address number to an actual name. A DNS server keeps track of these references, allowing people to use address names that are much easier to remember.

When you type a Universal Resource Locator (URL) into your Web browser, the DNS server translates it to an IP address and then passes the request along to the Internet. One of the subdivisions of the overall Internet is the World Wide Web (WWW). The HyperText Markup Language (HTML) was created to preserve nicely formatted documents, instead of typing plain old text files. The HyperText Transfer Protocol (HTTP) was invented to transmit those HTML documents over the World Wide Web.

This is why a typical URL is written as **http://www.*symbolics*.com**. The ***symbolics*** is the domain name, and the "com" is the type of domain. The periods ("dots") are separators, as are the colon and two forward slashes. In 1985 symbolics.com was assigned as the first registered domain name. Until recently, a limited number of domain types—for example, com (commercial), net (network), org (organization), edu (education), gov (government)—were available.

HTML and XML

Most of us have seen the http:// preface to an Internet URL. We've mentioned that the hypertext transfer protocol was designed to transfer hypertext markup language (HTML) documents back and forth from Web sites. HTML is a way of formatting text, producing fonts, typefaces, lines, paragraphs, bullets, and all the other formatting we're used to seeing in modern word processors. HTML is a language that tells a Web browser how to show you a document.

XML is an extended markup language, designed to handle information formatting. In other words, HTML formats the characters and blank space of a document, but we also want a way to format the actual information in a document. If you want to put the characters "Bob Smith" on a Web page, HTML can make those characters bold or italic; large or small; put a bullet in front of them, or put them in a table.

Bob Smith is a name, and that name can be conveyed in different ways, depending on the associated information. For instance, Bob might be Jane Smith's husband or Kelly Smith's father. Bob might be the CEO of a corporation or a boat owner. Bob might also be a male human being, or he could be the owner of an insurance policy. The information about Bob can be categorized in many ways, depending on context. XML is a way to design tags that will tell the system how to use additional information. Tags are somewhat like field types and names in a database form.

In the URL **http://www.jamesgjones.com**, the James G. Jones domain is a *com*mercial domain and therefore has a com suffix. The URL **http://www.comptia.org** indicates that CompTIA is an *org*anization because it has the org suffix. *Gov*ernment agencies typically use gov as their suffix, and *edu*cational institutions use edu.

With the explosive popularity of the Web, we started running out of addresses. The Internet Network Information Center (InterNIC), funded by the National Science Foundation, came together to coordinate a whole series of new extensions—for example, bus (business), co (country), tv (television), ws (Web site). We now have enough addresses to last until at least next week.

Email Addresses

An email address requires an additional user name to go along with the domain name. The separator between the two is the @ sign. The user name is to the left of the separator, and the domain name is to the right. A typical email address would be **aplus@jamesgjones.com**. In this case, the user name "a-plus" comes first, then the @ separator, then the "jamesgjones" domain name, then the dot separator, and finally the "com" to signify the type of domain.

An email address has a user name and a domain name, with the user name to the left of an @ sign, and the domain name to the right of the @ separator.

Supplementary Information

Very few people accessing the Internet have routers, networks, or assigned IP addresses, so how do they get online? In most cases, when you access the Internet through a dial-up telephone line and modem, you're actually calling an Internet Service Provider (ISP) over an analog line. The ISP connects your call, assigns a TCP/IP address to your PC for that session, and routes your data (using its router) to the Internet. Even with a 56.6Kbps modem, this is a slow task, so many people and small businesses are moving to faster broadband service, such as cable modems, Integrated Services Digital Networks (ISDN), digital subscriber lines (DSL), satellite wireless connections, or multichannel multipoint distribution services (MMDS).

Broadband connections are changing constantly, where any kind of transmission system could be used to connect a PC to the Internet. We already know about fiber optic connections, but there are cellular towers, laser beams, microwaves and even electrical power lines. Even broadband itself is pointing a way to the next *ultraband* step for even faster connections.

Cable

Remember the first Ethernet networks and the coaxial cable? Your cable television service uses a big, thick cable to connect from the wall to your TV or video cassette recorder (VCR). There's no reason a digital signal can't be transmitted across the cable. Everyone's got cable. (You are on cable, aren't you?). The cable provides a bus network, much like Ethernet, and your PC connects to a special cable modem that becomes the tap (see Chapter 9).

The coaxial cable connects to a node (intersection point) in your neighborhood, and from there the cable changes to fiber optics. Information travels at very high speeds from the node to the cable company and then out to the Internet. Cable modem connections are "always on," with typical speeds in the 1.5Mbs range. Note that cable connections tend to use a fixed IP address, making the PC vulnerable to possible security breaches.

Integrated Services Digital Network (ISDN)

ISDN is a set of standards that can provide up to 128Kbps of digital transmission over an ordinary phone line going into homes and small businesses. The service is provided over one of the pairs of wires already installed at your location. Unlike modems, which are affected by the vagaries of analog phone lines, ISDN uses a special adapter in place of the modem. An adapter must be installed at both your end and your provider's end of the transmission.

The throughput in an ISDN line is exactly as rated; however, in the case of ISDN, you need an inexpensive router or bridge at your location. This is often provided by the telephone company, and connects using a NIC with a straightforward and easy installation. After the service is operational, you don't have to wait for dialing, and you are permanently connected directly to the Internet.

Essentially, ISDN allows analog data to travel along with digital data over the same network. Broadband ISDN (BISDN) is expected to use fiber optic and radio media, along with something called *frame relay services*, for large bursts of high-speed data. The Fiber Distributed-Data Interface (FDDI) and the Synchronous Optical Network (SONET) are expected to produce transmission rates well beyond 2Mbps.

Digital Subscriber Line (DSL)

DSL is provided in many variations and speeds. Although the local telephone company provides the service, many individuals contract through an ISP for a total service. As with ISDN, you need a local router or bridge (often provided by the ISP). This special "modem" uses an existing pair of wires, if they're available at the location, but unlike ISDN, if a pair of wires is not available, the signal can be transposed over your active telephone line.

A DSL connection is always on, meaning that you're always connected to the Internet, and typically provides download speeds (reading a Web page) of 1.5Mbps and upload speeds (sending a file) of 128Kbps. To be eligible for a DSL connection, the PC must be within three miles of a central telephone office, otherwise the signal begins to degrade beyond the value of the specialized connection. Unlike a cable connection and its neighborhood node, the phone line is a direct connection to the home or business, so speeds aren't subject to how many people are using the line at any given time.

Satellite Wireless

A broadband wireless connection to the Internet works like a satellite television account, using a small satellite dish to send and receive signals. The satellite relays signals through to a service provider with a connection to the

Internet. Once again, a specialized modem handles the encoding and decoding of signals between your PC and the satellite, and the connection is always on. Also, like some DSL and cable connections, your service can be one way only where surfing the net (downloading) takes place through the satellite connection and uploading is done with the regular phone line.

Current satellite wireless isn't as fast as other types of connections, with a typical transmission rate of around 395Kbps. Even so, this is about seven times faster than a dial-up modem, and the system doesn't rely on any ground wires between the computer and the ISP. On the other hand, you have to have a clear view of the sky in the direction of the satellite, and there's a small amount of delay time as signals pass through the satellite relay.

MMDS

One of the newer technologies appearing on the scene is based on a line-of-sight transmission from a digital transceiver at the PC location to a tall transmission tower. Signals from the tower are decoded through a wireless modem with speeds of up to 5.6Mbps. Although this is an exciting possibility, signals can't pass through or around solid objects. The transceiver must be within 35 miles of a tower, and because the system uses wireless transmission frequencies, speeds can be affected by how many people are using the connection at any one time.

Internet2

Once again, the following information is not on the exam, but it's worth noting. Understanding information in context—where something came from and where it's going—can often help you to better retain the details of that information. By January of 2002, approximately 30 percent of the Internet's total available address space was in use. Since 1995, the number of users and addresses was doubling on almost a monthly basis. Concerns began to grow as to when the Internet would run out of 32-bit IP addresses.

The Internet Protocol Next Generation (IPng) group is part of the Internet Engineering Task Force (IETF). These organizations began working towards a new set of protocols to replace the existing Internet Protocol version 4 (IPv.4). A draft of Internet Protocol version 6 (IPv.6) was put in place near the end of 1998. Although China and other parts of Asia are having some problems with new IP addresses, the growth of the Internet has slowed significantly. Europe is having some problems, due to the rapid increase in mobile phone technology, and the many areas where land service will probably never be installed. However, the fear of running out of addresses has abated.

Aside from a potential address crunch, the tremendous growth of the World Wide Web, along with its completely open architecture, has produced an amazing flow of all kinds of information across the Internet. Originally developed for research and governmental purposes, such things as e-commerce and multimedia streaming are taking up more bandwidth. The existing Internet cannot handle the extremely large file transfers (e.g., an entire movie or a large university's research database).

Internet2 began in 1996 as a way to experiment with new technologies designed to make the best use of broadband and digital technology. The project was started by various corporations, universities, and nonprofit organizations, and it provides a sort of a laboratory for companies and researchers. There are now over 200 organizations joined together in the Internet2 project, including Intel, IBM, Microsoft, Cisco, and other large technology companies. The project is designed to plan the future of the Internet.

Qwest runs the U.S. high-speed optical network (Abilene) that connects many of the member organizations. The Canadian counterpart is called the *Canadian Network for the Advancement of Research, Industry, and Education (CANARIE)*. The Canadian system is working with a sort of virtual disk drive, built out of the entire network, with information being stored on parts of the network in much the same way a hard drive uses sectors and clusters. The "Wavelength" as it's called, is a virtual disk drive 5,000 miles in diameter.

In this case, the data transmission itself is used as a storage medium, with transfer rates of approximately 50 ms, at 5,000Mbps (5MB/s). Because the CANARIE system is an optical network, the information is converted to photons, which travel around the network in a never-ending flow. Any information on the system is immediately accessible, as it continually flows around the "drive," sort of like a hard drive's random access capabilities.

The latest Internet2 conference attempted to bring the entire member audience together, from all over the world, in a real-time video conferencing environment. There were some problems, but the technology worked. This makes it likely that online education and real-time remote medical attention will arrive in the not-too-distant future. Instead of sending photographic images or .AVI files as email attachments, a high-speed broadband Internet would allow anyone (or everyone) to connect with a live video feed. The project has already been able to transmit HDTV over the network on a small scale. Instead of today's halting and pause-laden video and sound, the new technology was broadcast quality.

P2P Networking

Another interesting development in Internet technology is point-to-point connectivity. (Don't misread P2P as PnP.) Two examples, inspired by the Napster music-sharing system, are the Gnutella and FreeNet systems. The idea is similar to using a peer-to-peer network within the larger TCP/IP environment of the Internet. Individual PCs running specialized software can access specific computers directly. The original purpose was for file sharing, but the implications for the future are that any set of individuals can set up an actual network to mirror their personal "network" of friends, business contacts, or any other group based on related interest.

Practice Questions

Question 1

What are two major benefits of using a USB?

- ❑ a. Ability to use Plug-and-Play components external to the PC
- ❑ b. Speed of transmission
- ❑ c. Ability to connect many computers together with a single cable
- ❑ d. Ability to fully use parallel transmission

Answers a and b are correct. USB uses high-speed serial transmission to connect peripheral devices to a PC. USB does not use parallel transmission, and it is not designed for connecting multiple PCs.

Question 2

The IEEE 1394 standard made home networking practical.

- ❍ a. True
- ❍ b. False

Answer b, false, is correct. IEEE 1394 technology, also called *FireWire or i.Link*, is used primarily to interface video equipment with PCs and to connect many devices to a single PC. Networking connects many PCs together.

Question 3

What are the two major types of network architecture?

- ❑ a. Broadband
- ❑ b. Peer-to-server
- ❑ c. Bus
- ❑ d. Token ring

Answers c and d are correct. Bus and token ring networking are two very general categories of networking, not to be confused with bus and star topologies. Broadband is a description of transmission capacity. "Peer-to-server" doesn't exist, although client/server networking uses a file server.

Although both peer-to-peer and client/server could also be two major categories, the inclusion of the false peer-to-server as an option points to the c and d combination.

Question 4

How many simultaneous signals can travel on an Ethernet network without error?

- ❍ a. One
- ❍ b. Two, when early token release is implemented
- ❍ c. 1,024
- ❍ d. Up to 10, on a 10MHz network

Answer a is correct. An Ethernet bus (wire) allows only one signal at a time to use the network. More than one signal can easily create an error condition known as a *collision*. Ethernet and token ring are two different kinds of networks. In a token ring network, the token is the only thing that travels across the wire, managing signals from each PC so as to avoid collisions. That being said, when you see a reference to Ethernet networking, it will almost never refer to a token ring system.

Question 5

Which device is most typically used to assign IP addresses to subnetworks?

- ❍ a. A router
- ❍ b. A bridge
- ❍ c. A NIC
- ❍ d. A TCP/IP

Answer a is correct. A bridge is used to break a network into segments, gathering the addresses of every resource in that network. A router is used to gather addresses for an entire network. The network interface card is abbreviated as NIC. TCP/IP is a packet addressing protocol (not a noun) and uses various IP addresses in order to ensure that information packets arrive at their correct destination.

Question 6

A SCSI card can have up to how many storage devices attached to it?

- ❍ a. 2
- ❍ b. 8
- ❍ c. 7
- ❍ d. 5

Answer c is correct. The SCSI bus requires that every device has a unique ID number. The card itself will take one identifier for the host adapter ID, leaving 7 numbers to be assigned to other devices. In this case, the devices are separated from the host adapter by the question asking about storage devices. SCSI cards can have eight ID numbers, but a host adapter is never a storage device.

Need to Know More?

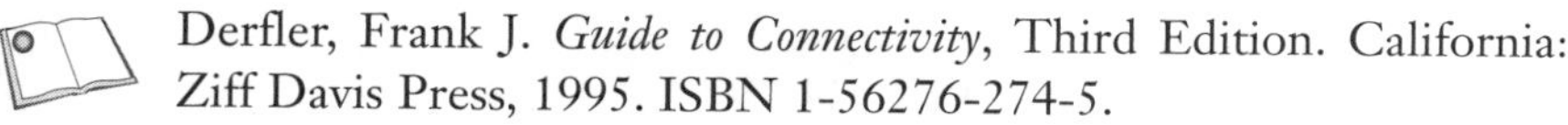

Derfler, Frank J. *Guide to Connectivity*, Third Edition. California: Ziff Davis Press, 1995. ISBN 1-56276-274-5.

Derfler, Frank J. and Lee Freed. *How Networks Work*. Indianapolis, IN: Que, 2000. ISBN 0-7897-2445-6.

Freedman, Alan. *Computer Desktop Encyclopedia*, Second Edition. AMACOM, 1999. ISBN 0-814-479-855. This is great for a fast look-up or a refresher.

Minasi, Mark. *The Complete PC Upgrade and Maintenance Guide, 11th Edition*. San Francisco, CA: Sybex Network Press, 2000. ISBN 0-782-128-009. This is considered one of the best reference books available. In fact, Minasi's book was instrumental in the formulation of the first A+ exam.

Mueller, Scott. *Upgrading and Repairing PCs, 12th Edition*. Indianapolis, IN: Que, 2000. ISBN 0-7897-2303-4. This is one of our favorites. If you are only going to have one reference book, give this one serious consideration.

http://www.whatis.com—A technical Web site resource with short articles describing many aspects of information technology

http://www.webopedia.com—An online encyclopedia devoted to technical terms, featuring additional links to other Web-based articles, research, and white papers.

Cables and Connectors

Terms you'll need to understand:

✓ Interface and port
✓ Input/output (I/O) bus
✓ COMmunications (COM) port and Line Printer Terminal (LPT)
✓ Serial and parallel
✓ Operating system device names
✓ DIN, mini-DIN, PS/2 and USB connector
✓ RJ-11 and RJ-45 modular connector

Concepts you'll need to master:

✓ Plug (male) and socket (female)
✓ Connector, cable, back panel (of the PC)
✓ Serial and parallel data transfer
✓ Coaxial cable naming conventions
✓ Categories of twisted-pair wire
✓ Shielding and insulation

When we turn on a computer by pressing the power switch, the monitor lights up; drives begin to whirl; lights blink; speakers beep; until, eventually, a bit of music plays, and the computer system is ready to go (you hope!). Beginning with the AC power connector that plugs into the wall outlet, everything connected to the CPU uses a particular type of wiring scheme and connector. The point where something meets something else is the interface, and in a computer system, there is an interface between every different hardware component. An interface is often called a *port*.

The spaghetti mess of cables around a computer can be sorted into various wires and connectors, grouped by the plugs and sockets at either end. A plug has pins that stick out, just like an electrical plug that goes into a wall, and we refer to it as a *male* connector. A socket, like a wall socket, has holes for seating pins, and we refer to it as a *female* connector. This has nothing whatsoever to do with gender; they are merely technical terms. Cables cannot reproduce on their own, regardless of what they may seem to be doing at night behind a desk.

Certain interfaces have been on computers from the very start, and are directly responsible for input and output (I/O) operations. These I/O ports constitute our first group of interfaces. The second group is made up of those connections that have changed through the years, and that mostly move data to or from a device. For the third group, we touch briefly on various connections used for connecting two or more computers together--networking. A more thorough discussion on networking is found in Chapter 8.

Basic I/O Interfaces

The XT motherboards, on through the AT and Baby AT form factors, used a basic set of data connections to move data in and out of the processors. This basic input and output system is known as the BIOS, and includes the rudimentary instruction programming that tells the CPU how to work with the hardware. The keyboard and mouse (input) connected through the serial ports or through dedicated interface cards. The video console and printers (output) used the video and parallel ports. Some printers used interface cards, as did tape backups and scanners. Older printers could use either a serial port or the more familiar parallel port.

Because the original XT machines used a DB25 connector as a serial port, a 25-pin serial plug is sometimes called an *XT connector.* The introduction of the AT form factor brought a second, 9-pin serial port. A DB9 serial connector is sometimes referred to as an *AT serial plug.*

You may never see an LPT3 port, but the operating system still reserves the name. The device names used for basic hardware interfaces are:

- *Serial ports*—COMmunications (COM)1, COM2, COM3, COM4
- *Legacy serial port*—AUXiliary (AUX), rarely used for anything anymore
- *Parallel ports*—Line Printer Terminal (LPT)1, LPT2, LPT3, LPT4, and PRiNter (PRN)
- *Video monitor*—CONsole (CON)
- *System Clock*—CLOCK$

There is also the NUL device, used as a sort of black hole in space. Any data sent to the NUL (printer) device simply vanishes, making this a place to send text messages that you don't want the person using the computer to see. For example, the PAUSE command in a batch file outputs "Press any key…" to the screen. A "Pause > NUL" line in a batch file will send all output from the Pause command into oblivion, leaving only a paused screen with a blinking cursor.

BIOS programming continues to change with advances in technology, and we spoke about ways to upgrade a BIOS chip in Chapter 3. Two additional interfaces have been added to most modern systems:

- *USB ports*—Universal Serial Bus fast serial transfers
- *AGP*—Accelerated Graphics port connector on the motherboard.

Most computers today also provide for CD-ROM drive recognition at a BIOS level.

Each I/O connection uses a specific plug or socket on the back panel of the computer, along with a controller interface to the motherboard. The connector joins the device to the computer housing (box), and the controller interface connects the data coming from the device to the motherboard. Early machines used separate controller boards, some of which occupied various bus slots.

Today, many of these basic I/O device controllers are built right onto the motherboard, eliminating the need for a specific adapter slot. Usually, these include a primary and a secondary IDE controller, a floppy controller, the two serial ports, and the parallel port. This joining together and mounting on the motherboard, created a single chip called the *Super I/O chip*. Some systems add other peripherals, such as a SCSI host adapter, a video adapter, an integrated mouse port, and/or a network interface card (NIC).

We'll remind you here that the floppy drive controller, having been one of the very first devices installed on early PCs, is still assigned to IRQ 6 by default. (See Chapter 5 for a complete listing of the IRQs.)

Although these controllers and ports are built in, they act just like cards that plug into an expansion slot. A potential problem with this type of convenience is that it can limit the "upgradability" (*scalability*) of a system, because the original devices can't be removed. Some motherboards allow for disabling the built-in devices, but many motherboards, such as Compaq's, do not.

Floppy and Hard Disk Controllers

These controllers, due to their many variations, almost always used an expansion slot in the past. However, when IDE and EIDE drives finally became standardized, the controllers were integrated onto the motherboard. Today, most IDE and EIDE (as well as some SCSI) controllers are on a Super I/O chip. Almost every disk drive has two connectors: one for electrical power and one for control/data signals. These connectors are fairly well standardized across the industry and across drives.

Typically, the control cable connector uses either a 34-pin edge or pinhead connector. Obsolete 5 ¼-inch drives used the larger edge connectors, while 3 ½-inch drives use smaller, pinhead connector. Because these cables have so many wires running through them, they're designed to be flat and flexible to save space. They're usually called *ribbon cables* because of their similarity to ribbons.

Don't confuse a smaller floppy drive ribbon cables with the typical 50-pin SCSI ribbon cable.

15-pin VGA

At the moment, most PCs have a built-in 15-pin standard VGA connector, used to connect an analog monitor with the system board and onboard graphics. The VGA connector and onboard graphics of a typical system do not support digital video signals. We mentioned in Chapter 7 that add-on graphics cards often provide specialized connectors to be used with digital and flat panel LCD monitors. The DVI-A connector is used only for analog monitors. A DVI-D connector is used for digital video monitors. Although there is no final standard for flat panel displays, a DFP connector is used to transmit signals to a digital flat panel monitor.

The exam will present you with a standard VGA video connector on a stylized back panel (see Figure 9.4). You should be able to recognize the video port (connector) as the only one with 15 pins. Keep in mind that the VGA connector on the computer is a female one, but the cable coming from the monitor uses a 15-pin male connector.

Parallel (LPT) Ports: 8 Bits Across

The majority of printers connect to a computer using a 25-pin parallel interface (excepting various network printers). The parallel port, using the LPT device name, transfers information in a sort of wave front, eight bits across, in which each bit goes in the same direction at the same time. You can think of parallel transfer as an army of British soldiers in a gun battle. They would line up in rows of eight, and the first row would stand up to shoot at the opposition. When the bullets were transferred, the first row would kneel down and the row behind them would stand up and fire. This cyclical process continued until the back row had fired their rifles, after which, the first row was reloaded and ready to fire again.

In the above example, you can imagine that by increasing the numbers of soldiers in each row, more bullets could be fired across the battlefield. The British learned this technique from the Romans, who used it with archers to shoot arrows. Computers use the same process in the parallel interface, to transfer data across a bus. An 8-bit bus is like eight riflemen firing at the enemy. A 16-bit, 32-bit, 64-bit, or 128-bit bus increases the "front line," so to speak, and moves more data (arrows or bullets) across the line of fire.

Parallel wiring is where a circuit provides alternate conducting paths (more than one) for electric current. A string of lights wired in parallel is somewhat like a ladder, where each bulb and socket is a separate rung. If one bulb burns out, current still travels up the sides of the ladder through the terminals in the sockets, and the rest of the lights continue to glow.

Serial wiring (discussed in a moment) is where an electric circuit provides only one conducting path for electric current. A string of lights wired in series is like a string of Christmas tree lights. If one bulb burns out, the entire chain goes dark.

You might think that since a parallel cable transfers eight bits at a time, it would have eight pins and be wider than a serial cable. You might also think that a serial cable uses one pin, because it transfers one bit at a time. Neither of these suppositions is true. Parallel data transfers move bytes of information, and serial transfers move bits. Other than that, the width of the connectors bears no relation to the number of data bits being transferred.

DB25

An IEEE-1284 cable, commonly called a *parallel printer cable*, uses a male DB25 connector on the computer end and a Centronics 36-pin (C36) male connector on the printer end. Although the correct name is either a DB25S or DB25P ("S" for socket, and "P" for plug), the exam will most assuredly drop the "S" and "P," leaving you to figure out from a graphic whether a question refers to a printer or serial connection. Both the parallel and serial forms of the DB25 connector use 25 pins. The female parallel port found on the back panel is sometimes called a *Type A connector*.

The port on the back panel of the computer is a *female* DB25 connector, meaning that it has twenty-five little holes. However, you may find a 25-pin *male* connector in an exam graphic. Not long ago, computers came with a 25-pin female parallel port, a 25-pin male serial port, and a 9-pin male serial port--one parallel port and two serial ports. Modern computers removed the DB25 serial connector and replaced it with a second DB9 serial connector. Today, you'll most likely find one 25-pin LPT connector and two 9-pin COM port interfaces.

Originally, the DB25 serial connector was used for serial printers and modems. Nowadays, a typical serial cable uses a female DB9 at the computer end and a male 25-pin connector at the modem end. Figure 9.1 shows each type of DB25 connector found on a back panel. The female parallel port is on top, with the male serial port on the bottom. You should remember that the printer *cable*--not the motherboard port--uses a 25-pin male plug.

When we set up a system, one of the last steps is to "plug in the printer." If you remember that phrase, it may help you to remember that the printer cable has a plug that connects to the computer, meaning it has pins and is a male connector. This is one of those last-minute facts you'll want to write down on the scratch paper you'll be given when you enter the exam room. Another immediate list should be the COM port addresses.

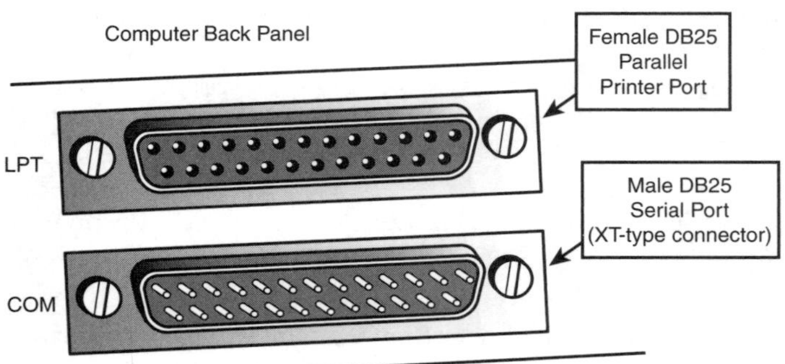

Figure 9.1 The two types of DB25 connectors.

RS-232 and DB9

Serial connectors on PCs come in two flavors: a 9-pin DB9 or a 25-pin DB25. This makes life very confusing, as parallel cables also use a 25-pin DB25 connector. Back before computers, electronics and radio standards were set by existing organizations. The serial connectors on PCs would eventually be standardized by the Electronic Industries Association (EIA), but before that happened there was a "(r)ecommended (s)tandard." The RS-232C was the recommended specification for PC serial connectors until a "D" version was released in 1987. In 1991, the EIA joined with the Telecommunications Industry association (TIA) to release the EIA/TIA-232-E standard. Most people refer to the connectors as RS-232C or just RS-232.

The EIA-232 standard provides for the two types of serial connectors we see in most computer systems today. There are two COM ports on a typical back panel, each using a 9-pin male DB9 connector. Older machines used a 25-pin male DB25 connector as the serial printer connector, which eventually disappeared. Apple Macintosh computers often used an RS-232C port.

The RS-232 standard has been updated to the RS-422 and RS-423 standard, which supports higher data transfer rates and is less susceptible to EMI. Apple Macintosh computers use an RS-422 port, which is backwards compatible with an RS-232C connector. RS-422 allows for multiple connections in a chain, whereas RS-423 supports only point-to-point connections.

We still see the male 25-pin connector on serial modem cables, connecting at the modem end. One way to distinguish a serial cable is that the cable is thinner than a parallel cable. Figure 9.2 shows a standard parallel cable. The DB25 plug is on the left side, with a male RS-232 (or DB25P) serial connector below it.

Be very careful that you read a question correctly. A printer port is a female connector found on the back panel of a computer. A parallel cable connector is a male, 25-pin plug used at the computer end of the cable. If you find a 25-pin male connector on the back panel of an older PC, it's almost always a serial connection.

External modems connect to the back panel with a female DB9 connector on the computer end of the cable. The male port connector on the back panel uses 9 pins, and the female cable connector has 9 sockets. You must remember that the parallel port on the back panel is always female.

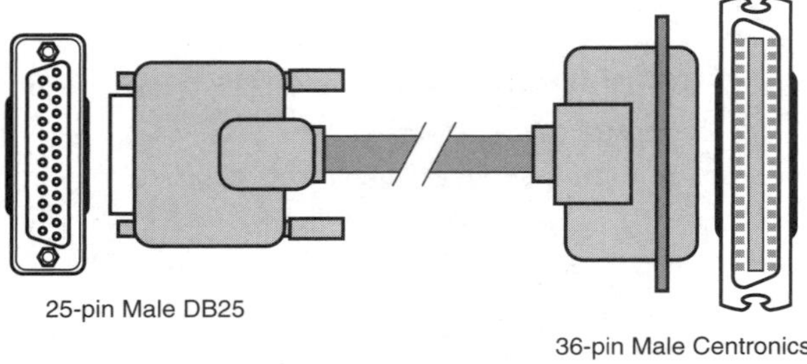

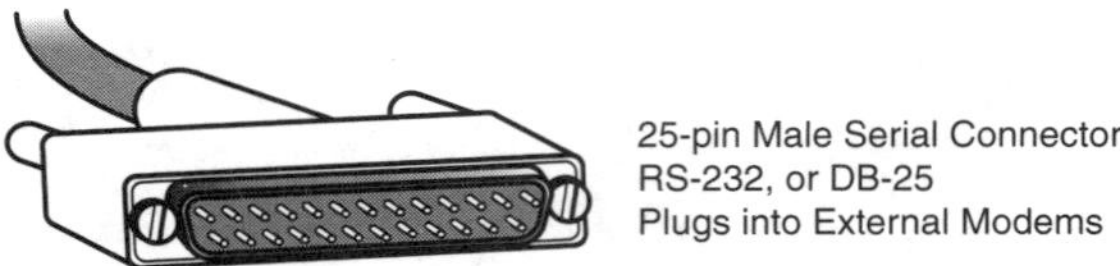

Figure 9.2 A typical parallel cable connecting a PC to a printer.

36-pin Centronics Connector

Centronics Corporation was one of the original printer developers. At the time, it created a parallel interface for its dot matrix printers that became the standard connection. A typical printer cable connects to the printer with a Centronics male connector that is 36 pins wide. A Centronics 36-pin connector (C36) is shown on the right side of the cable in of Figure 9.2.

On the exam, Centronics is used only for printer connectors. Don't confuse a 36-pin Centronics connector and a 50-pin SCSI connector.

SCSI Connectors

SCSI devices can be connected to the computer either internally or externally. When a SCSI device is an external one, it can be mounted in an individual box. Many SCSI devices may be mounted together in larger, tower enclosures. Newer devices use what is considered the preferred connector according to the SCSI-2 standard: a smaller 50-pin SCSI connector with two rows of 25 pins, frequently referred to as a 50-pin mini D shell (MDS50) connector. Figure 9.3 shows a typical SCSI connector. Note that it looks somewhat similar to a Centronics plug, but with 50 pins.

There isn't any easy way to remember the number of pins in the various connectors. You'll be tested on the 9-pin serial, 15-pin video, 25-pin parallel, 36-pin Centronics connectors, and the 50-pin SCSI cable, so do whatever you can to remember them.

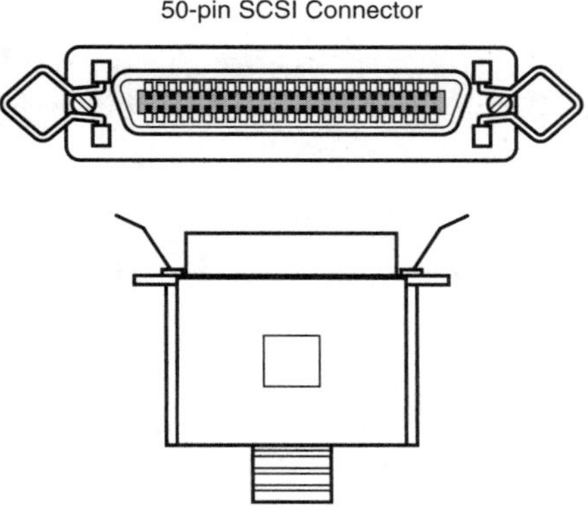

Figure 9.3 A standard 50-pin SCSI connector.

Types of Parallel Ports

Because we know that 8 bits equals 1 byte, we can see how parallel wiring puts 1 byte through the interface at a time (8 bits across). Depending upon how fast those bytes move through the interface, the throughput goes up in terms of kilobytes, megabytes, or gigabytes per second. Parallel ports are available in the following types:

- *Unidirectional (original parallel port)*—Data flows out, but can't come back in. (Printers could not communicate with the CPU.)
- *Standard bi-directional*—Peripherals can send status messages back to the CPU for action.
- *Standard Parallel Port (SPP)*—This is a setting often found in laptops and notebooks.
- *Extended Capabilities Port (ECP)*—ECP ports are about 10 times faster than the standard bi-directional port.
- *Enhanced Parallel Port (EPP) (also called fast mode parallel port)*—EPP ports are also about 10 times faster than the standard bi-directional port.

Serial (COM) Ports: 1 Bit After Another

As we've said, serial ports transfer information in a line, one bit at a time, much like ants following one another. Because only one bit (instead of an eight-bit byte) moves through the interface, serial ports are much slower than parallel ports. If a parallel port is like an army of ants marching eight abreast in columns, the serial port can be thought of as "the ants go marching one by one."

Bits, Bytes, and Baud

Microprocessors work with bytes (8-bit units). Serial devices work with bits (1-bit units). Bus connections are often involved in converting bytes to bits, or bits to bytes. Bits are binary digits (0s and 1s). Eight bits make up one byte, which typically corresponds to one character (i.e., a letter or number).

Today, data rates are measured in kilobytes per second (KB/s) and megabytes per second (MB/s). The term *baud rate* refers to the number of discrete signal events per second in a data transfer, not bits per second. The term *baud* has fallen out of use. In the early days of 300 and 1200 baud modems, the baud rate equaled the kilobytes per second. The term remained until 14.4KB/s modems entered the market, even though it was no longer technically correct to refer to the modem speed by its baud rate.

Newer computers almost always have a dedicated PS/2 connector (Mini-DIN) for the mouse and keyboard, and two 9-pin serial male ports. The top panel in Figure 9.4 shows how closely the serial and parallel ports on some computers resemble each other. The DB25 connectors are either next to or above each other, and the only way to remember which is the printer port is that it has a female connector. The lower panel is a more typical back panel, seen on today's computers. Note that the parallel port is now the only 25-pin connector.

Remember the relative sizes and shapes of the connectors. You may have to recognize them by their outlines.

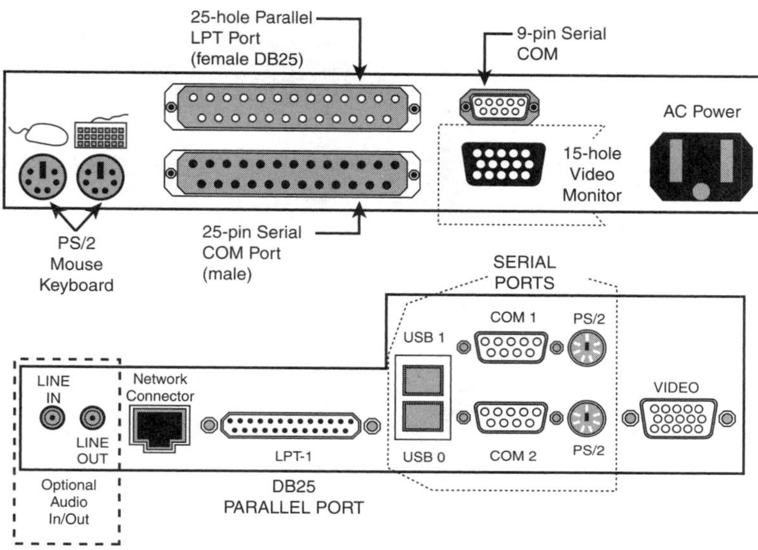

Figure 9.4 Typical back panels.

Keyboard or Mouse Connector: PS/2

The original AT motherboards used two types of connectors for keyboard cables: either a five-pin DIN, or a six-pin Mini-DIN (generally known as a PS/2 connector). The bigger 5-pin connector, known as an AT connector, gave way to the smaller PS/2 connector developed by IBM. Eventually, AT keyboards switched to the PS/2 style connector, and until recently, both keyboards and mice routinely used the smaller connector. Today's motherboards often come with two PS/2 connectors and two USB connectors. In Figure 9.5, you can see the relative size differences between the AT DIN connectors and PS/2 Mini-DIN connectors, along with the different shape of USB and FireWire cable ends.

5-pin DIN connectors may still be used for Musical Instrument Digital Interface (MIDI) connections to musical equipment. A PC back panel will probably never have an AT-style DIN connector (the MIDI connection requires an adapter), but you may find the cable out in the field.

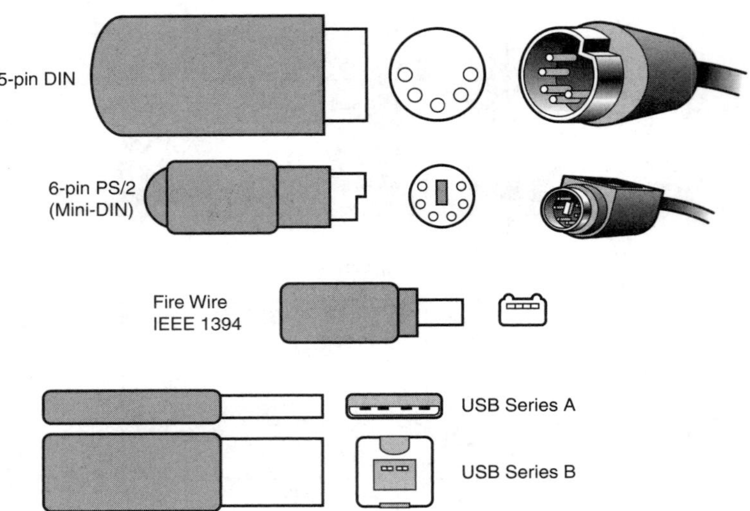

Figure 9.5 Keyboard, mouse, and USB connectors.

The difference in all these connectors is in both the number of pins and their shape. Keep in mind that the keyboard/mouse connection is often still configured as a COM port, even though it's installed as a PS/2 connector. (A USB mouse uses a separate I/O bus and does not take over a COM port.)

If a motherboard does not have serial ports available or a direct motherboard mouse port, you can install a mouse that uses an expansion slot. This type of mouse is generally referred to as a *bus mouse*. In the past, when older software used both the COM1 and COM2 ports, it was often necessary to use a bus mouse. The mouse then had to be configured to use COM3 or COM4 (logical ports).

Consistency has never been a strong point in the computer industry, so you can't just assume that a serial connector has nine pins. Neither can you assume that serial connectors are always used for modems. Serial connectors can be:

- DB9 (nine-pin)
- DB25 (25-pin, male [RS-232])
- Keyboard or mouse (6-pin Mini-DIN)
- AT keyboard or MIDI connectors (5-pin DIN)

Although USB devices use a serial transfer process, we don't commonly call them serial devices in the original sense. Nor are they networking devices. USB devices are simply that--USB devices--and they use USB connectors, not "serial" connectors. The bus may be referred to as a fast serial bus.

Summary—Standard Cables

The back panel of a computer box has various types of interface connectors called *ports*. Each of these ports uses either a male or female connector. The associated cable uses the opposite gender connector. On modern computers you'll generally find:

- 1 parallel port (LPT), using a female DB25 connector with 25 holes
- 2 serial ports (COM), using male DB9 connectors, each with 9 pins
- 2 Mini-DIN connectors, using female PS/2 style connectors, each with 6 pins
- 2 USB ports
- 1 VGA connector, using a female 15-pin connector with 15 holes. (The monitor cable has 15 pins.)

You'll be tested on several common cable connectors. Although you won't need to know the exact pin-outs, you should remember the following cables:

- Parallel printer cable--uses a male 25-pin DB25 connector at the computer end
- Centronics printer connector--is a male 36-pin (C36) connector developed by the Centronics corporation, and is at the printer end of a typical printer cable.
- External modem cable--uses a female 9-pin DB9 connector at the computer end, and a male 25-pin RS-232 (also called a male DB25, or DB25P) connector at the modem end.
- SCSI cable--the only SCSI cable we saw on the exam was a 50-pin ribbon cable, usually used to connect a device to an internal controller.

The original DOS device names for the various I/O ports were named: LPT (1 and 2), COM (1, 2, 3, and 4), CON (video console), AUX (auxiliary), PRN (printer), and NUL (a black hole throwaway device). The printer typically uses an LPT port, but you can also send printer output to the PRN device.

Network Cables and Connectors

We said that the wires around a computer could be sorted by groups, depending on their connectors. Networking wire can also be sorted by groups, but in this case, the grouping is more often the physical structure of the wire and/or the transmission rate for data. The three groups we discuss here are coaxial cable, twisted pair, and fiber optics. We also touch on wireless networking, which doesn't use wire (obviously).

Coaxial Cable

The first coaxial (abbreviated as coax) cable was quite thick and heavy, and was standardized at 10Base5 Ethernet (Thicknet). Breaking this down, it means that 10 megabits can travel across a baseband piece of cable to a maximum distance of 500 meters (i.e., the "5" × 100), or approximately 1,500 feet. This naming convention continued forward, so remember that Name = Megabits per second (Mbps) + "Base" + Distance (in hundreds of meters the signal can travel).

Originally, each terminal connected to a 10Base5 cable with a tap (sometimes called a *vampire tap*). These connectors ($65 to $95 apiece) look like tiny jaws with a pair of long, sharp teeth. The teeth drive right through the insulation and into the core wire.

Thicknet gave way to a thinner wire called *10Base2 (Thinnet)*. The reduced thickness was easier to handle, but meant a subsequent reduction in the maximum transmission distance. Although the wire could still move a single 10Mbps baseband signal, the maximum distance dropped to 200 meters (approximately 600 feet). Taps gave way to the bayonet nut connectors (BNCs), and terminal connectors or *T-connectors* ($1 to $3 apiece). Figure 9.6 shows the shielded core of coax cable. Figure 9.7 shows a standard T-connector and two terminators at the end of a short bus.

Both 10Base5 and 10Base2 require terminators at the end of the cable. If the cable breaks or a terminator isn't installed, the entire network can perform erratically and fail.

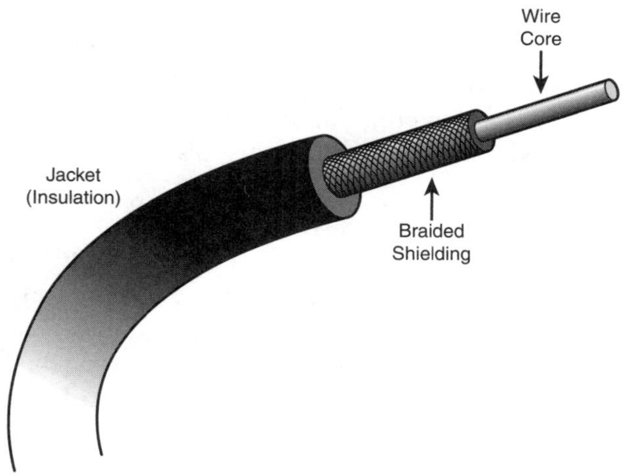

Figure 9.6 Coaxial cable with shielding and insulation.

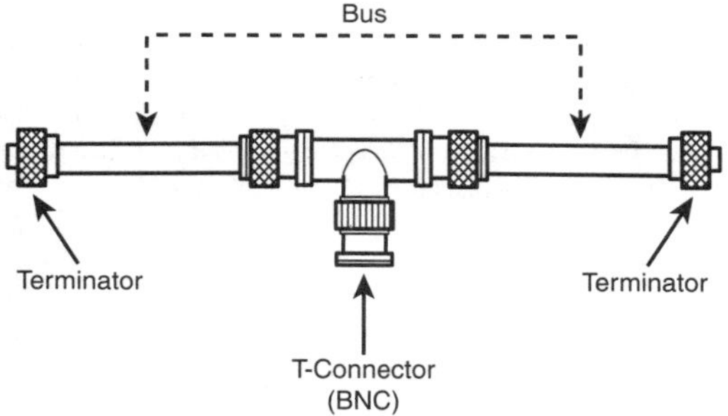

Figure 9.7 Coax with T-connector and terminators.

Twisted Pair

Because of cable-length limits and the difficulty of installing stiff coax cable, most Ethernet networks today use a type of wire called *10BaseT.* The "T" in 10BaseT stands for twisted-pair wiring, which is exactly what it sounds like--pairs of wires twisted together. Twisted-pair cables are short and connect several terminals to a hub.

Wire carries some amount of electricity. In this case, the wire carries fragile data signals made up of very small changes of voltage and frequencies. We've spoken of electromagnetic interference (EMI) and electrostatic discharge (ESD), and the first level of defense against them is the insulation wrapped around the metal core of a wire. The core can be many thin strands braided together, or it can be solid metal.

Insulation wraps around the outer layer of the wire. We can put a second line of defense between the insulation and the core, called *shielding*. Shielding (see Figure 9.6) is a braided metal or foil that, together with an underlying insulator, wraps around the wire core, intercepting radio and electromagnetic energy. Shielding is often used with coax cable, but may also be used with twisted-pair wire.

STP and UTP

10BaseT cable comes in two basic groups: Shielded Twisted Pair (STP) and Unshielded Twisted Pair (UTP). Both are still 10Mbps baseband cable, but UTP uses four pairs of wire (eight wires), where each wire spirals around its partner and then all four pairs are twisted together. Unshielded Twisted Pair is frequently used in both the telecommunications (telco) industry, and the computer industry. If we're speaking of telephone wire, we usually say twisted pair. To distinguish the same wire in networks and data transmission, we'll use 10BaseT.

A so-called drop ceiling (acoustical tile suspended on a frame) is called a *plenum-type ceiling*, and allows air to circulate. Twisted-pair wire can have regular insulation or Teflon insulation. Regular insulation gives off toxic fumes when it burns, so the U.S. Fire and Safety Code requires Teflon insulation for all plenum ceiling installations. Therefore, twisted-pair wire comes in either plenum-type or nonplenum.

STP 10BaseT, used mostly in token ring networks, uses an expensive IBM data connector, and is different from unshielded twisted pair. In this type of wire, each pair of wires is twisted and then shielded with foil. After the individually shielded pairs are twisted together, more foil wraps all four pairs. Finally, insulation is wrapped around the outer shielding.

Twisted Pair Categories

We use five categories to distinguish the gradation in quality (grade) of what looks like the same wire. Category 1, 2, and 3 (C1, C2, and C3, also referred to as *CAT1*, *CAT2*, etc.) are used almost exclusively for analog telephone signals. Category 4 (C4)is good enough for digital data signals, and can be used in either industry. C4 introduces some errors, but Category 5 (C5) is data grade wiring. C5 wiring is used almost always in networking situations where reliable data transmission is required.

Twisted pair cable is available with both a solid core and a stranded core. Solid C5 cable supports longer runs, whereas stranded wire is more flexible and better suited for patch cables. Patch cables typically have stranded core wire, and are used to connect a device to the wall, or a device to another device. Stranded-core wire is flexible, flatter, and more "forgiving" than solid-core wire. "Forgiving" means a more relaxed tolerance, where signals don't have to be as exact. Solid wire is rounder and more efficient at transferring data, but is stiffer and harder to work with. Solid-core twisted pair is usually used for the wiring inside the walls. When a length of cable is used in a network, we refer to the length of the "cable run."

Wiring Problems

UTP 10BaseT wiring pairs are not connected in a pins 1 to 8 series. Rather, the first pair connects to pins 1 and 2, while the second pair connects to pin 3 and 6. This "skipping" is used to maintain better data integrity. Cross-wiring the pairs to the wrong pins produces an unusable cable, or patch cord.

Two standards for wiring are used within a building where patch cords connect to the wiring inside the walls. Northern Telecommunication, Inc. created the 568-A standard, and American Telephone and Telegraph (AT&T) created the 568-B standard. The difference between the two standards is in the pairs that are used to transmit data after the signal reaches the wall. Because the standards are incompatible, only one may be used throughout the installation site.

RJ-45 Modular Connectors

At the end of a C5 patch cable, you'll find two RJ-45 modular connectors that look very much like the RJ-45 connectors used for phone cords. Figure 9.8 shows the outline of a modular connector with flat, stranded wire attached to the back. However, data modular connector plugs are wider than nondata RJ-11 four-wire phone connectors, and are designed to a much higher specification. RJ-45 data connectors use eight wires and gold contacts to eliminate tarnish. Network connectors are more expensive (55 to 80 cents) than RJ-45 phone connectors (8 to 10 cents).

Low-bidding network installers will sometimes use the RJ-45 phone connectors to cut costs. The only way to tell the two connectors apart is through the manufacturer's label, if there is one. The real difference, from an operational standpoint, is that the less expensive telephone RJ-45 connectors tarnish over time. When they do, they can drop below specified minimums, causing an increased number of errors and reduced throughput.

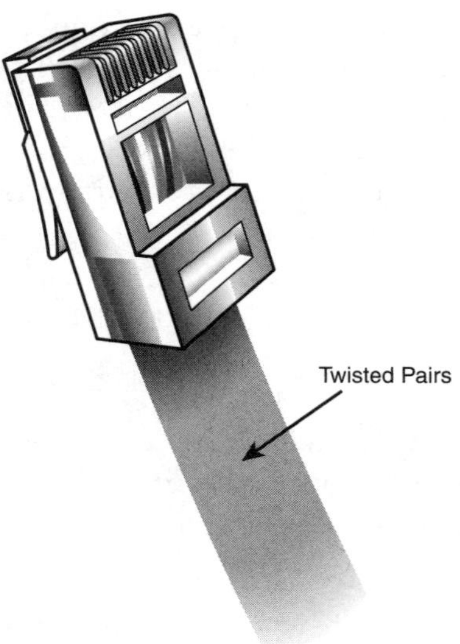

Figure 9.8 A typical modular connector.

Supplementary Information

Twisted pair wiring joins three concepts together into four different naming conventions, depending upon the transmission rate, how the data is being transmitted, and signal encoding. The "Base" in the name refers to baseband transmission. While there are as many variations as there are manufacturers, you will most often run into one of the following twisted pair configurations:

- *10Base-T*—10Mbps, baseband, over two twisted-pair cables
- *100Base-T2*—100Mbps, baseband, over two twisted-pair cables
- *100Base-T4*—100Mbps, baseband, over four-twisted pair cables
- *1000Base-LX*—100Mbps, baseband, long wavelength over optical fiber cable

Today's network wiring continues to build on the original categories. There is still CAT3, CAT4, and CAT5 wiring. As networks reach ever-higher transmission rates, the wiring specifications are being updated to handle the changes. The following is a list of the various standard specifications:

- *CAT3 Standard (1988)*—UTP cable and hardware must be able to maintain a transmission rate of 16MHz.

- *CAT4 Standard*—UTP cable and hardware must be able to maintain a transmission rate of 20MHz.
- *CAT5 Standard (1992)*—UTP cable and hardware must be able to maintain a transmission rate of 100MHz. Cable contains four pairs of copper wire, supporting Fast Ethernet (100Mbps) and comparable alternatives such as ATM. Fast Ethernet communications only utilize two pairs. As with all other types of twisted pair EIA/TIA cabling, CAT5 cable runs are limited to a maximum recommended length of 100m (328 feet). CAT5 performance is only possible when cable, connector modules, patch cords, and all electronics carry the same C5 rating.
- *CAT5e Standard (Enhanced Category 5)*—Cable and hardware must be able to maintain a transmission rate of 400MHz. Found in 155Mbps ATM, 100Mbps Fast Internet, 100Mbps TP-PMD, 100VG-AnyLAN, 550MHz Broadband Video.
- *CAT6 Standard*—Categories 6, 6e, and 7 represent the latest capabilities of UTP cable and equipment. Cable and hardware must be able to maintain a transmission rate of 550MHz . Support for 155Mbps ATM, 100Mbps Fast Ethernet, 100Mbps TP-PMD, 100VG-AnyLAN, and 550 MHz Broadband Video
- *CAT6e Standard (Enhanced Category 6)*—Cable and hardware must be able to maintain a transmission rate of 550MHz and standards under development, such as Gigabit Ethernet (1000BASE-T) and ATM at 622Mbps, 1.2Gbps, and 2.4Gbps.
- *CAT7 Standard (emerging)*—Cable and hardware should be able to maintain a transmission rate of 600MHz. Support for Gigabit Ethernet (1000BASE-T) and ATM at 622 Mbps, 1.2 and 2.4 Gbps.

Fiber Optic

Fiber optic cable (or simply *fiber*) is a bundle of at least two fiber strands (one for send, and one for receive). The strands are made of glass, and each strand is wrapped in a plastic shield. The entire bundle is then wrapped in an outer jacket. Fiber cable looks like wire, but conducts light instead of electricity. "Long-haul" fiber optic uses a laser beam as the light source, which has a very low skew factor and stays coherent (straight line) over longer distances than light-emitting diodes (LEDs). The two main types of fiber optic cable are:

- *Single mode*—Uses a laser source and can travel 22 kilometers (km) before requiring a repeater. Its transmission path is 5 microns wide.

➤ *Multimode*--Uses an LED source and can travel only 6 km. Its transmission path is 62 microns wide.

A fibre (same thing as fiber optics, but spelled differently for no apparent reason) channel requires two fibers. Light is unidirectional, meaning that one beam can send (transmit) information, but another beam must return (receive) information. Synchronous Optical NETwork (SONET) is a protocol based on multiples of a base rate of 51.84Mbps--called *Optical Carrier* (OC)-1--going up to 9.6 gigabits per second (Gbps) (OC-192). Typically, fiber optic cable runs in excess of 10 times the speed of its copper counterpart.

As is true of optical disks, dirt smudges and other interference can stop the transmissions. Although some people think a fiber cable cannot be repaired, this isn't true. A break can be fixed using a *fusion splicer*, and certain instruments can tell a technician how far away a break has occurred.

Wireless Networking

A wireless network uses radio frequencies, and has been finalized as IEEE 802.11. A device uses an access point (bridge) and a network interface card with a transmitter and receiver. Often, these NICs are very small and can fit on a PC card. Signals move at 11Mbps and can typically travel 100 to 200 yards. Special antennas can extend the transmission distances to more than a mile (used in corporate networking).

Infrared (IR) wireless uses light frequencies and also works with a transmitter and receiver. A wireless mouse uses IR technology, as do common television remote controls. Many printers also have an infrared port. The transmitter and receiver are often built into modern motherboards and devices, using a small plastic window to radiate the infrared light. Infrared Data Association (IrDA) specifications indicate that data can be transmitted from 0 to 3.3 yards. Speeds range from .9 to 1.1Mbps.

Summary--Network Cables

You'll be tested on a limited understanding of the basic principles of networking and the wiring used in networks. The common naming convention for network wire is to use the Mbps + "Base" + Distance (in hundreds of meters). The main types of wiring you'll want to remember include the following:

➤ *Thicknet* (10Base 5)--Ethernet coaxial cable capable of 10Mbps over a maximum distance of 500 meters

- *Thinnet* (10Base 2)—Ethernet coaxial cable capable of 10Mbps over a maximum distance of 200 meters
- *Coaxial cable* uses T-connectors (BNC) and terminators at the open end of a bus.
- *Twisted Pair* (10BaseT)—Ethernet wire with either a stranded or solid core; usually found in pairs; uses RJ-45 modular connectors.

Twisted pair wiring comes in several categories. Category 3 (CAT3) is usually insufficient to carry digital signals over any great length of wire. As far as the exam is concerned, most networks use CAT5 (Category 5) wiring. A C5 installation must use devices, connectors, and cable that are all rated Category 5.

The two main types of twisted pair wiring are Unshielded and Shielded. Unshielded twisted pair wire is known as UTP wire. Shielded twisted pair wire is known as STP wire.

Practice Questions

Question 1

A DB25 _______ connector is used to connect the _____ port to a printer.

- ❍ a. male, COM
- ❍ b. female, COM
- ❍ c. female, LPT
- ❍ d. male, LPT

Answer d is correct. The "25" in DB25 references the number of pins on the cable connector or back panel connector. When the cable has 25 pins, it fits into an LPT socket with 25 holes and is called a *DB25 parallel cable*. This question is ambiguous because the connector can refer to the cable connector or the back panel connector. We believe CompTIA will always mean the cable connector.

Question 2

A modem connects to the serial COM2 port using a ________ connector.

- ❍ a. DB15
- ❍ b. DB9
- ❍ c. Centronics
- ❍ d. DB25

Answer b is correct. The COM port serial cables use a 9-pin DB9 connector. Video connectors are usually 15-pin connectors, and the Centronics connector is used to connect a 25-pin DB25 cable to a printer at the printer end.

Question 3

Which of the following two designations do not apply to parallel interfaces?

- ❑ a. ECP
- ❑ b. EPP
- ❑ c. ECC
- ❑ d. UTP

Answers c and d are correct. Answer a is incorrect because ECP is the Extend Capabilities Port. Answer b is incorrect because EPP is the Enhanced Parallel Port. Answer c is correct because ECC is a type of parity and does not apply to parallel interfaces. Answer d is correct because UTP is a type of twisted-pair wiring (unshielded) and does not apply to the parallel interface.

Question 4

A Centronics printer cable uses a _______ pin connector, and a typical SCSI-2 cable uses a _______ pin connector.

- ❍ a. 25, 36
- ❍ b. 36, 50
- ❍ c. 50, 25
- ❍ d. 25, 9

Answer b is correct. A Centronics cable is a 36-pin connector. A SCSI cable is usually a 50-pin mini D-shell connector. Parallel cables are 25 pins, and serial cables are 9 pins. You'll have to remember these in whatever fashion suits you.

Question 5

10Base2 Ethernet coaxial cable is sometimes referred to as _______, and has a distance limit of _______ meters.

- ❍ a. Thinnet, 200
- ❍ b. Thinnet, 500
- ❍ c. Thicknet, 500
- ❍ d. Thicknet, 200

Answer a is correct. 10Base2 Ethernet coaxial cable, sometimes referred to as *Thinnet*, has a distance limit of 200 meters. 10Base5, the original coaxial cable, was thicker than 10Base2. Thicknet and Thinnet refer to the relative thickness of the cable wire. The 10 refers to the megabits per second transmission rate, and the last number is how many hundreds of meters the signal can travel. 10Base5 is 500 meters, while 10Base2 is 200 meters.

Question 6

In a wireless networking environment, data is transmitted using which medium?

- ❍ a. Infrared light
- ❍ b. Radio frequencies
- ❍ c. SONET protocols
- ❍ d. UTP

Answer b is correct. The clue in the question is both "networking" and "data." Wireless networking is done with radio frequencies. Mice and remote control units use infrared light to transmit simple commands. SONET refers to the Synchronous Optical NETwork protocols used in fiber optics, and UTP is Unshielded Twisted-Pair wire.

Need to Know More?

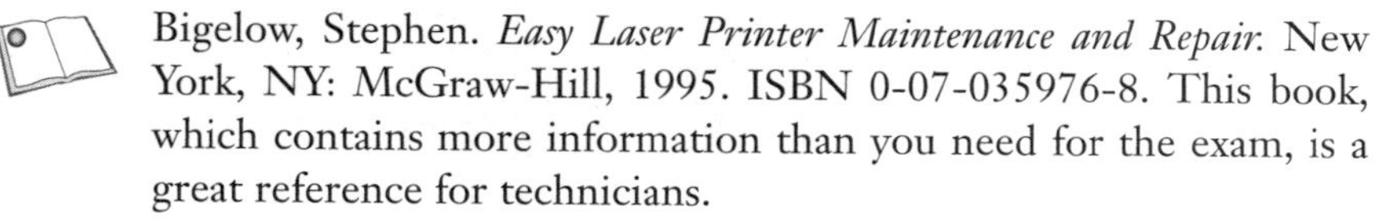

Bigelow, Stephen. *Easy Laser Printer Maintenance and Repair.* New York, NY: McGraw-Hill, 1995. ISBN 0-07-035976-8. This book, which contains more information than you need for the exam, is a great reference for technicians.

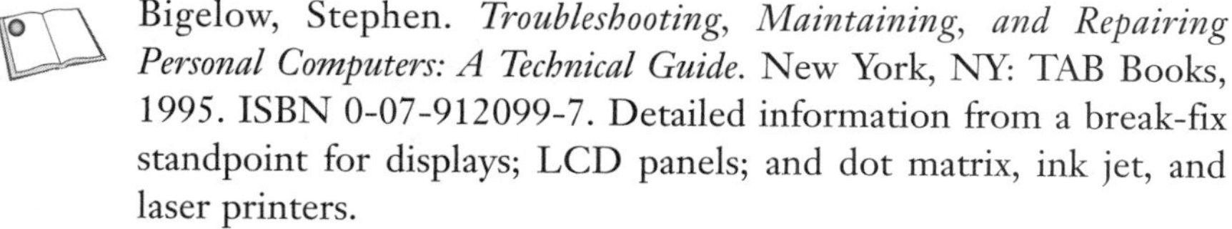

Bigelow, Stephen. *Troubleshooting, Maintaining, and Repairing Personal Computers: A Technical Guide.* New York, NY: TAB Books, 1995. ISBN 0-07-912099-7. Detailed information from a break-fix standpoint for displays; LCD panels; and dot matrix, ink jet, and laser printers.

Messmer, Hans-Peter. *The Indispensable PC Hardware Book.* Reading, MA: Addison-Wesley, 1995. ISBN 0-201-87697-3. This book contains much information, in great detail, about monitors and displays.

Minasi, Mark. *The Complete PC Upgrade and Maintenance Guide.* San Francisco, CA: Sybex Network Press, 1996. ISBN 0-7821-1956-5. This resource is a great source of information on peripherals from a repair standpoint.

Rosch, Winn. *Hardware Bible.* Indianapolis, IN: Sams Publishing, 1994. ISBN 0-672-30954-8. This book contains everything you'd want to know about computer hardware.

DOS

Terms you'll need to understand:

- ✓ Command interpreter, command line, switch
- ✓ Hidden and system file attributes (ATTRIB.EXE)
- ✓ Environment memory
- ✓ Search path, parent and child directories
- ✓ File allocation table (FAT)
- ✓ File fragmentation (DEFRAG.EXE)
- ✓ Wild cards, variables
- ✓ Shells

Concepts you'll need to master:

- ✓ Command interpreters and operating system kernels
- ✓ Partitions and logical drives versus physical disks (FDISK.EXE)
- ✓ Directories (folders) and subdirectories (subfolders)
- ✓ File systems, file management, file names
- ✓ Tracks, sectors, and clusters (SCANDISK.EXE)
- ✓ File searches (DIR)
- ✓ Operating systems versus shells

DOS is the underlying operating system for the Windows 9x family. Even the newer members of the Windows family (i.e., Windows NT, Windows 2000, and Windows XP) include troubleshooting utilities based on DOS commands. There's no doubt that if you want to understand Windows, you must know something about DOS—the Disk Operating System.

The scope of the A+ Operating Systems Technologies exam is so broad that you cannot memorize all of the variations. The best way to get a sense of how these systems work is to understand how they were developed. We're going to refer to DOS and Windows 3.x as a 16-bit concept. We'll refer to Windows 9x—which includes Windows 95, 98, and Me—along with Windows 2000, Windows XP, and Windows NT, as a 32-bit concept.

Windows 9x actually fits into both categories, but the overall division is between 16-bit (Chapter 11) and 32-bit Windows (Chapters 12 and 13). Yes, this seems complicated at first, but when you've seen the essential differences, you'll understand the basis for the groupings.

Why Read This Chapter?

One of the ways we'll be tracking the gradual elimination of DOS and the evolution of Windows into a true operating system is by keeping tabs on what happened to the system files and the use of an OS kernel. Windows 2000 still installs a file called COMMAND.COM on the hard drive. Opening a DOS window with this file produces a notice that you are now running Windows 2000 DOS.

In the world of PCs, everything started with DOS, and every time you use the Find tool in the Windows Explorer, you're dealing with DOS (e.g., *.* wild cards, extensions, associations, and file types). Aside from the historical context, three additional reasons for knowing about DOS come to mind:

- Preparing a disk for an operating system—any PC operating system—requires using FDISK (partitioning software) and FORMAT (logical drive software). Both of these programs are discussed in this chapter, together with the concepts of file space allocation and file naming.
- Windows 3.x, 9x, and Me all start by loading the files IO.SYS and MSDOS.SYS, which are DOS files.
- Key troubleshooting utilities you will be using for network and PC diagnostics are based on DOS, even the Windows 2000 and Windows XP Recovery Console.

ATTRIB and Windows

Here's an interesting problem you might easily encounter in modern-day Windows, where the only way to fix it seems to be through the use of DOS and the ATTRIB command. MS Word creates a number of temporary files when a document is open and in use. When you're working in a document file, you can use the File | Open menu to look at the folder containing the opened document, and see these files with their .TMP extensions.

Windows doesn't have a chance to remove temporary files when a system crashes. This is partly what we mean when we say that the system was improperly shut down (and runs SCANDISK.EXE prior to the next startup). An open MS Word document also leaves behind all its temporary files following a crash. What makes this interesting is that Word tracks the temporary files in its own application software. If a document is open, Word sends a notification to Windows to lock the document, meaning that only the one file may be open. If you try to open the file in a second instance, Word responds by telling you that the document is in use, and asks if you want to open a copy.

Following a crash, if you open Windows Explorer and look in the folder containing the previously opened Word document, you'll find the leftover, orphaned temporary files. These files are hidden, but with the View | Folder Options | View, "Show All Files" option enabled, you can easily find them. When you try to delete the orphaned .TMP files, Windows will inform you that they are locked, and will not allow you to remove them. If you are in Word and try to open the original document—the one you were in when you crashed—you'll get the MS Word message. If you come to an agreement with MS Word and open the proposed copy, but try to save it with the original file name, Word will tell you that you cannot overwrite an open file.

One idea would be to restart Windows in MS-DOS Command mode and then delete the document. Here is where you can see the difference between a clean version of DOS and the so-called command mode. When you try to delete one of these orphaned Word files from (what you think is) DOS, you'll get the same Windows error message; informing you that the document is in use and that you may not remove it.

ATTRIB and DOS

The only way to successfully remove the orphaned file(s) is to start the machine in a clean iteration of DOS and use the ATTRIB command. You can use either the **DIR /A:H /S** command or the **ATTRIB *.* /S** command to find the files, always remembering that they have their Hidden attribute turned on. Once you get a listing, you can navigate to the proper folder using

CD commands. After you've arrived at the folder, you'll have to use the **ATTRIB -H *.TMP** switch to unhide the file so you can delete them. The **DEL** command cannot find hidden files.

DOS and Long File Names

In many cases, you also will have the experience of seeing the underlying DOS file names, not the convenient Long File Names. If you have one folder named **C:\Program Files\Microsoft Office\Microsoft Word** and another folder named **C:\Program Files\Microsoft Office\Microsoft Excel**, you'll have to figure out which **micros~1** folder you want to get to. You'll also have to know how to use the CD command to change to the Program Files directory (listed as **progra~1**).

Starting Windows

When you've finally completed the repair, you should also know what command will start Windows. Typing "EXIT" won't do anything, since you're no longer in a DOS Window. If you used the Restart option on the Shutdown menu, you won't be able to remove the files in the first place. So you see, even such a simple problem as recovering a document name involves a number of DOS-related skills.

You might think that a file name isn't all that important, so why not just rename it? Imagine a multinational corporation at the end of their fiscal year. That one document might contain important financial information gathered from hundreds of sources, with document and file name references in countless memos, booklets, instructions, and so forth, not to mention network paths. If the file no longer exists, think of the interesting chaos that might create.

You should be seeing by now that solving this single problem involves a good working knowledge of the command line; a number of internal DOS commands; at least one external command; and the foundational understanding of directories and subdirectories. This is only one example of everyday problems that can crop up in Windows. Setting aside the fact that you'll be required to correctly answer a number of DOS-related exam questions, there is little doubt in our minds that you'll encounter DOS on a regular basis, even if you think you're "only" running Windows.

Operating Systems

A software program is a set of instructions put together in an organized way that tells a microprocessor what to do. When a program is written in

English, a human being can understand it. A programming language is a special way of using human language so that the instructions written by the developer (programmer) can later be turned into machine language—that is, compiled. COBOL, Basic, FORTRAN, Pascal, C++, Java, and Assembler, are examples of programming languages.

Compilers and Machine Language

What are compilers? Programs must spell out, in excruciating detail, every single instruction to the microprocessor. No matter how short a speech-based language might be, it still takes far too much space to write even a simple program. Therefore, computer languages use shorthand words to cram as much information as possible into the smallest amount of space. Move becomes **MOV**, Jump To becomes **JMP**, Delete or erase becomes **DEL**, Remove Directory becomes **RD**, list a directory of files becomes **DIR**, and so on.

After a program has been written so that a human being can understand it, the result can be reduced even further into something that a machine can understand—machine language. Machine language is composed entirely of 1s and 0s. The process of final reduction is called *compiling the program.* After the program has been compiled (using a separate application called a compiler), the instructions are run as fast as possible. Compiled (binary) programs in DOS have either one of two extensions: .COM (command program) or .EXE (executable program).

Batch programs, with .BAT extensions, are not compiled and are entered as plain English lists of commands. AUTOEXEC.BAT is a batch file, and the name is a reserved name used from within COMMAND.COM.

We usually divide software programs into two categories: operating systems and applications. Applications are groups of program files that make up a tool of some kind and that create user data (files). Human beings use application tools to produce documents, spreadsheets, databases, mailing lists, new airplane designs, virtual realities, and test scenarios (simulations), to name a few. America Online is an application, as are the component applications (pieces) that make up Microsoft Office. MS Word is part of the MS Office suite (a group of related applications), and MS Word is made up of many different program files.

Here's an example of how an application borrows part of an operating system. When you choose the Edit|Copy command from an application's main menu, you're using the graphical interface to access the COPY command from the underlying operating system.

In many cases, smaller programs have been created for the purposes of augmenting primary programs. These smaller programs are referred to as software tools, utilities, or simply tools. ScanDisk, Defrag, SYSEDIT, and HwDiag are examples of utilities.

FORMAT.COM and FDISK.EXE are command programs, whereas REGEDIT.EXE is more of a utility program designed for the specific purpose of editing a Windows Registry (sometimes called the *system registration*). WP.EXE is an application program that runs a word processor and borrows part of the operating system whenever it copies a paragraph or file from one place to another.

Utility programs were originally created as stand-alone software designed to do a single thing. Over time, and with the necessity of using many of these utilities on a regular basis, we began to see smaller programs joined together under a common interface. Most of the diagnostics utilities found under Windows 2000 and XP are these types of utility suites. Two good examples are the Administrative Tools and selective startup dialog window (MSCONFIG.EXE).

DOS

We believe that you'll find it easier to remember some of the details of DOS if you have a mental picture of how it came into existence. The history of DOS is somewhat hazy because of the amounts of money and the various egos that have been involved, but this section should give you a good idea of how it all came about.

A long time ago, in a place far away, a young girl suggested to her father that a new toy for electronics hobbyists should be called the *Altair*, after a star system named in a *Star Trek* episode. The Altair, released in 1970, was based on the Intel 8080 chip and was the first computer a person could take home. It had 256 bytes of memory, could hold about four lines of text instructions, and was operated by flipping switches on and off. Even though it had no keyboard, Bill Gates and Paul Allen were fascinated with it and spent long nights writing a version of Beginner's All-purpose Symbolic Instruction Code (Basic), a computer language that would work with the Altair. They called it *Altair Basic*.

When a switch was flipped to either on or off, the computer circuitry could use that information in some way. A series of switches taken together could form a binary number. When the computer looked at a number of switches to find a number, they were called the first *registers*. Registers have now become very small transistors on a microprocessor, and they continue to store binary numbers.

Gates decided that Altair Basic should have some sort of file management and disk storage capability, so he upgraded the original system. This was the first conceptual hint of the File Manager, which went on to become the Windows Explorer. Gates' and Allen's interest in operating languages and their belief that microprocessors would change the world led them to incorporate Microsoft in 1975 (to market a traffic-counting machine) and—as early as 1976—to start complaining about software piracy. At the time, software was stored on cards by punching holes in them.

CP/M

The Intel 8080 processor found its way into another computer called the *Imsai 8080*, which came with a floppy drive and was targeted at small businesses. The floppy drive circuitry was controlled by an operating system called *Control Program for Microcomputers* (CP/M), designed by Gary Kildall.

Kildall was working for a company called Intergalactic Digital Research and wanted a scaled-down language that would work with microprocessors rather than mainframe computers. Perhaps because of a government cover-up or something else, the company eventually dropped "Intergalactic," leaving only the name Digital Research. Intel didn't think there was much use for CP/M, so it granted Kildall full rights to it. Features of CP/M included the following:

- Used only 4KB of memory space.
- Introduced a 64KB command file and used a dot (period) plus three-letter (.COM) extension to signify the type of file. (COM files, short for COMmand files, still have a maximum size of 64KB.)
- Used a command interpreter, or command processor program, called *CCP* (short for console command processor).
- Used two fundamental files called *Basic DOS (BDOS)* and *BIOS*, to handle files and I/O processing.

Apple

Back in 1974, the most popular microprocessors were the Intel 8080 and the Motorola 6800. One of the 6800's inventors, Chuck Peddle, quit Motorola in 1975 and started a new company called *MOS Technologies*. MOS began manufacturing the 6501 microprocessor, which resembled Motorola's 6800. In 1976, Steve Wozniak and Steve Jobs took some MOS 6502 chips and built the first Apple computers—the Apple I.

At the time, Charles Tandy, who had been unsuccessful buying Imsai computers, created his own Tandy TRS-80 product line based on another chip—the Zilog Z-80. Both the TRS-80 and the Apple I computers came fully assembled and, to help keep costs down, used only uppercase letters. Neither Radio Shack nor Apple Corporation could keep the computers in stock. An immediate problem that began to crop up between the Apple and the CP/M systems was that:

- Operating systems don't necessarily work on all microchips.
- The Apple MOS-6502 was an 8-bit processor and couldn't run CP/M.

The Apple II model upgrade added an optional floppy drive and ran a program called *VisiCalc*—the first real spreadsheet application—created by Dan Bricklin, Dan Fylstra, and Bob Frankston. Businesses could use small PCs to create spreadsheets, and suddenly the PC market came alive. Meanwhile, Gates and Allen were writing Basic and other programming languages that worked on Intel and Zilog chips. Eventually, Apple turned away from the MOS chips and went to Motorola chips.

CP/M was a hot programming language, and some very exciting software applications based on the language were arriving on the market. However, these programs would run only on Intel and Zilog chips. Therefore, rather than spend the long hours necessary to translate Basic into a form that would work with the Apple computers, Gates and Allen chose to license CP/M from Kildall. They began selling CP/M, along with an add-on board that had a Zilog chip, so that Apple customers could put the Microsoft card into their computers and run CP/M-based programs.

86-DOS

Meanwhile, in Seattle, Tim Patterson was making motherboards for a company called Seattle Computer Products. Intel had just produced its first 16-bit 8086 chip, and Patterson needed a 16-bit operating system to go with the 8086. Kildall was saying that he would soon be finished with the CP/M-86 (the first vaporware). Patterson decided that he couldn't wait, so he wrote his own operating system.

In 1980, Patterson created a quick and dirty operating system (QDOS). QDOS soon became 86-DOS (for the 8086 processor), then SCP-DOS (after the company), and then simply the disk operating system (DOS). In polite company, though, we refer to the "D" in DOS as standing for disk.

To simplify matters for the growing number of programmers who were writing for the CP/M operating system, Patterson kept the basic CP/M file management structure, the way CP/M looked, and the way it loaded itself and programs into memory. This compatibility is often referred to as the "look and feel" of an operating system. Along the way, he added something called a *file allocation table* (FAT), which he found in Gates' Altair Basic.

Keep another eye on the FAT, because it too carried all the way into Windows 9x. FAT32 and all the other file management systems started here.

PC-DOS

At about the same time, in 1980, IBM approached Microsoft about a possible 8-bit PC (microcomputer) that IBM was considering manufacturing. IBM was making mainframes for the most part and looked to young Microsoft as one of the leading (if not only) businesses creating computer languages for microcomputers. IBM thought that PCs were mainly a passing hobby, but Gates and Allen were convinced that the microprocessor and the so-called *personal* computer would change the world. They convinced IBM to change its design to a 16-bit processor, and when IBM asked who had a 16-bit operating system, Gates is said to have replied "Gary Kildall." At that point, history gets a bit fuzzy, but somehow Kildall either wasn't available or chose not to sell IBM the rights to CP/M.

Gates and Allen purchased Patterson's 86-DOS for around $50,000 and suggested to IBM that Microsoft become the vendor for Basic, FORTRAN, Pascal, COBOL, and the 8086 Assembly language. They also proposed to license 86-DOS to IBM as the operating system for IBM's new PC. IBM agreed (another historical blunder), and in 1981, released the first personal computer with Microsoft's DOS 1.0, which IBM called PC-DOS. (Patterson became successful in his own right and eventually went to work for Microsoft.) It wasn't until the release of DOS 5.0 that Microsoft finally started selling its own generic version of MS-DOS on the open market.

PCs using IBM's PC-DOS still continued to use COMMAND.COM (the command interpreter), along with IBMDOS.COM and IBMBIO.COM. PCs using Microsoft's MS-DOS went on to use the COMMAND.COM interpreter, and changed the two other system files to IO.SYS and MSDOS.SYS.

Keep an eye on MSDOS.SYS, because it carried through all the way into Windows 98 and Windows Me.

CP/M into DOS

Without applications, few people would be interested in computers. At the time of the first IBM PC, the most popular applications were dBase II and WordStar, both of which ran on CP/M. Because IBM didn't have much in the way of interesting software, it pushed very strongly to make DOS similar enough to CP/M that it could run those other applications. Among the changes that DOS brought to CP/M were the following:

- Variable record lengths
- Large EXEcutable (.EXE) format files, along with smaller 64KB CP/M-style .COM files
- Terminate-and-stay-resident (TSR) programs that could end (terminate), but stay (reside) in memory and snap back onto the screen without reloading
- A FAT, short for *File Allocation Table*, which could keep track of all the pieces of files on a disk
- The ability to use device names to perform I/O operations on peripheral devices (e.g., screens and printers) the same way that it worked with files

Even today, we can use the **DOS COPY** command to copy a file to the screen (CONsole) and show the results on the monitor (**COPY CON FILENAME.TXT**). Likewise, we can copy a file to a printer and have the hardware device produce a printed output (**COPY FILENAME.TXT PRN**).

DOS kept the CP/M-style file names of eight characters, followed by a period, and then a three-character extension. DOS also kept the C> prompt format at the command line. Compatibility also meant keeping the CP/M-style file control blocks (FCBs), program segment prefixes (PSPs), and the way in which CP/M used memory addresses for loading.

Although Windows apparently bears little resemblance to DOS, the continued use of the C:\ annotation for the root directory (folder) of Drive C: traces all the way back to CP/M.

DOS also kept the CP/M representation of a directory as a *dot* and the parent directory (the directory one step above) as two dots, or *dot-dot.* We discuss the two dots in more detail later in this chapter when we look at directories and subdirectories, which are exactly the same as folders and subfolders. DOS also introduced the ability to use a specially reserved extension for files that contained plain English scripts that a user could write. These special batch files, with the .BAT extension, use rudimentary reserved words and need not be compiled into machine language.

MS-DOS and PC-DOS

Beginning with the release of DOS 5.0, two versions of DOS were sold in the consumer market: the IBM version and the Microsoft version—PC-DOS and MS-DOS, respectively. Any DOS questions on the exam will use the MS-DOS version.

The **VER** command (internal) is used to discover which version of DOS is running on a PC. At the command prompt, type "VER" and press Enter. The screen returns the version number and tells you whether the computer is using PC-DOS or MS-DOS (or some other variation). This command continues into all versions of Windows, although you must go to a command prompt to run it.

A fundamental difference between the IBM and the Microsoft versions of DOS is that they use two system files with different names. MS-DOS uses IO.SYS and MSDOS.SYS, and PC-DOS uses IBMBIO.COM and IBMDOS.COM.

IO.SYS and MSDOS.SYS are the two hidden system files that combine with COMMAND.COM (not hidden) to form the fundamental DOS operating system.

From DOS to Windows 9x

Windows 3.0, 3.1, 3.11, and Windows for Workgroups (3.11) are *not* operating systems. Windows is a GUI using a shell, which, theoretically, makes the daily operation of an IBM-compatible computer somewhat easier than using the DOS command line. However, Windows 3.x and Windows 9x still require DOS to run.

The release of Windows 95 included DOS 7, which made a real break from all prior DOS versions. Windows 95 isn't a true operating system either, but more of a hybrid of DOS and Microsoft's New Technology (NT). Nevertheless, many people have accepted Microsoft's claim that Windows 9x is an operating system. Windows 98 was a minor release of Windows, and included DOS 7.1 as the underlying OS. Windows 2000 narrowed the gap between DOS and Windows NT, as we'll see in Chapter 13, and Windows XP was the final integration of a 32-bit network operating system with the home computer and consumer market.

The Command Interpreter

An operating system includes many individual component programs, each of which tells a computer how to work in various ways. Therefore, either an operating system (OS) or an OS kernel makes all the computer hardware work. The point where human beings meet the operating system is the user interface. DOS is a text-based interface, in that you type words and letters. Windows is a graphical user interface, in that you use representational graphics and a pointer.

CompTIA proposes that an operating system (software) is made up of two things: a *command interpreter* that works with program and system files, and a *user interface* that allows a human being to instruct the command interpreter what to do. In our opinion, an operating system requires a file system and several other critical components, but we'll focus your attention on what CompTIA calls an operating system.

For the exam, remember that an operating system may be referred to as three components: system files, a command interpreter, and a user interface.

We issue commands at the user interface command line (discussed in a moment). The next part of an operating system is the command interpreter (a program). COMMAND.COM is the DOS command interpreter, which is also used by both Windows 3.x and 9x to control the computer. With so many separate files making up an operating system, there must be an oversight manager of some kind, to distinguish a letter you're typing to your mother from a string (line or group) of characters you're typing to instruct the computer to do something.

In Windows 2000, COMMAND.COM continues to open a so-called Windows 2000 DOS window. This can be done by selecting the Start|Run option and typing "COMMAND." However, a command line is now run from a program file called *CMD.EXE* and generates a command line window. Note that depending on which of these options you choose, you get different results. (When you are in DOS, remember to type "EXIT" and press Enter to return to Windows.)

The DOS Command Line

Being text-based, DOS uses a series of letters, entered in a row, as commands. These character strings contain reserved words, which are the starting points for a set of instructions that "command" the computer to do something. An example of a reserved word is "copy." An example of a reserved character is the colon (:). The colon is used by DOS to mean the word "drive."

The text that you enter to spell out commands is called a *command line*—a line of typing. The A> or the C> next to a blinking cursor is called the *prompt*, or *DOS prompt*. The command prompt is the blinking cursor that shows you where on the monitor screen the next character you type will appear. After you've typed out a character string at the command prompt and pressed the Enter key, the command interpreter looks at the string and decides what to do about it.

The DOS prompt is a combination of symbols at the left-most column of a plain screen, together with the blinking cursor, or insertion point of the command prompt. The default prompt is the A> or the C> symbol from CP/M, but you can change the way the prompt looks (with the **PROMPT** command).

The blinking bar in Windows is called the *insertion point,* descended from the old command prompt. Windows installs a simple AUTOEXEC.BAT file, which runs during the start-up process and executes a prompt command. PROMPT=pg changes the DOS prompt from C> to an indication of the drive and path (discussed later in this chapter), making the familiar C:\ prompt.

Parsing

When you enter a command, DOS breaks up the letters, symbols, and numbers into units that match internal patterns of characters. Breaking apart a line of characters into a particular pattern of meaningful pieces is called *parsing* the line. The patterns of characters are commands, and the commands are part of either the DOS system files or a program file. When news analysts would break apart former President Clinton's sentences in order to understand what he actually meant, they would be parsing his sentences.

Syntax

The dictionary defines *syntax* as follows: "The way words are put together in order to form sentences, clauses, or phrases." A DOS command line is an instruction to DOS to do something, and DOS reads it much like you or I read a sentence.

The conventional standard for listing the syntax of a command is to begin with the command, followed by square brackets ([ ]) that enclose each and every possible switch. Italicized words that come after the command usually refer to some additional characters that you're supposed to enter to replace the word. For example, **DIR [d:] [*path*] [*file name* [.*ext*]] [/P] [/W] [/S]** means that the **DIR** command can (but need not) be followed by any of the items listed in square brackets.

Switches

A command line uses words, numbers, and symbols to produce specific results. The words represent program files that DOS can find along the search path (discussed later in this chapter). Switches are certain symbols that call on variations of the specific command. The important things to remember about switches include the following:

- Switches almost always start with a single forward slash (/) and are immediately followed by a letter or a character.
- Some programmers use the dash (-) as a switch indicator. This is not the same as using a plus or minus (+/-) to turn an attribute on or off.
- A space separates the command word from the switch.

When you use the DIRectory **(DIR)** command to list a large directory, you see the entire directory go flying up the screen, shooting out of the top of the monitor and making a mess all over the floor. To prevent this from happening, use one of the following switches:

- **DIR /p**—Tells DOS to stop the list every 23 lines, which make up a screen page. ("P" is short for "by the page.")
- **DIR /w**—Tells DOS to show the files in a "wide" format (that is, across the screen).
- **DIR /s**—Tells DOS to show not only the current directory's files but also all the files in every subdirectory (now called a subfolder) below the current one.

Switches can often be combined to provide combined variations of any command that supports multiple switches. In the case of **DIR /s /p**, you're asking DOS to show you all the files in this directory and any subdirectories, and also to stop the display every 23 lines until you press any key.

The /? Switch

DOS versions 5 and later, as well as most command-line programs, include a rudimentary built-in Help feature that acts as a quick reminder of how a command can be used. As far back as version 3, MS DOS provided a complete help file with an expanded Help feature on how to use commands. This Help utility is still available on the Windows installation CDs (Browse, Tools, OldMSDos, HELP.COM). PC-DOS didn't include the expanded Help feature until later versions.

At a DOS prompt, you can almost always enter "[*command*] /?" (without the quotation marks) to obtain a cheat sheet on how to use that command. For example, **DIR /?** or **ATTRIB /?** gives you all the switches and a brief explanation of what each does.

File Mask (Specification)

We discuss wild cards (i.e., * and ?) under the "DIR Command" heading later in this chapter, but you should know that most DOS commands use modifier switches. Each switch modifies the action of the command, but the file mask, or file specification, defines the grouping of files that will be affected by the command. In other words, most commands are used to either list file information or modify file information. The DIR command with no switches and no file mask will list every file. The DIR command with no file mask and the /P switch will still list every file, but will pause the listing.

When you issue a command with a file specification, the command will only operate on the specific files matching that specification. If you specify a file that doesn't exist, you'll get a "File not found" error message. The file specification may include the full pathname for a file, allowing a command to operate on files found in a different location from the default (logged) directory.

An example of a file specification used with a full path name mask would be where you want to list the .SYS (driver) files in the Windows I/O Subsystem folder. Suppose you're logged onto the root directory of the D: drive, and you issue a DIR command. The result will be a listing of all the files in D:\. To use a file mask for the system files, you would type DIR C:\WINDOWS\SYSTEM\IOSUBSYS*.SYS and press Enter.

Error Messages

People sometimes forget that a computer doesn't have a conceptual mind, and that it can't actually harbor a grudge or get angry—at least not yet. Everything that happens on a computer is created by a human being. When something goes wrong and a message of some kind shows up on the screen, that message—called an *error message*—isn't simply a casual expletive that the computer thought up on the spur of the moment!

The actual text of the error messages must not only be written into a program, but it also ought to have some kind of connection to an underlying event. Within a program, connecting an error message to an event is sometimes called *trapping* an error. The programmer uses what's called an **IF…THEN** logic statement to display an error message on the screen.

For instance, the following statement might be used to trap for a missing file error: **IF** *filename* X on the command line doesn't match *filename* X in the directory allocation table (DAT), **THEN** type the message "File not found" to the screen. A much more frightening error message can appear when the boot-up BASIC routine cannot read anything from an installed hard drive: "Invalid media."

A message referring to invalid media means that something is seriously wrong with the hard drive. In some cases, a virus has wiped out the entire disk, including partition tables and everything else. In other cases, a hardware component has failed or the CMOS settings have told the machine that no hard disk is installed.

Error messages can often be either misleading or completely wrong, in terms of the error being reported. We'll take another look at errors messages in Chapter 14, "Troubleshooting." The text itself is not the computer scratching its head and dreaming up a statement, but rather a specific line of text that a programmer told the operating system to write to the screen when an explicit set of circumstances occurs. (A proposed error message we've seen recently as a candidate to be written into the Windows interface is "Closing current Windows session. Would you like to begin another game?")

The "Any Key" (PAUSE)

The most common way to allow time for a user to read an error message is to temporarily *pause* the screen until the user provides further input. Remember that the keyboard processor is constantly scanning the keyboard for status changes and key-press activity. When the error message reads, "Press any key to continue," it literally means that you can press any key on the keyboard. The most common keys to press are the spacebar, the Enter key, or the ESCape (ESC) key. In DOS, one of the internal batch file commands is **PAUSE**.

Commands and Programs

When you issue a command, you're using one of the operating system program files to gather computer-related instructions and apply them. A command is somewhat different than a program, in that the command is what a user types (often a program file's name) onto a command line. A program, on the other hand, is the set of instructions the computer actually uses to execute a sequence of events. Developers compile a program; users type a command.

A command is usually a word followed by several additional switches (e.g., **FORMAT A: /U**). A program is contained within a file (e.g., FORMAT.COM). The command interpreter must have the programming instructions to be able to keep all the letters in the word "FORMAT" together, and parse the A: and /U as separate command modifiers.

A personal computer can only do *exactly* what it's told to do. A human being creates every single detail of what a computer knows how to do. The human being using a computer is either a programmer or an operator (user). An operator relies on what the programmer told the computer to do, by using special instructions built into a program. Those special instructions are the commands.

Loading and Running a Program

One of the fundamental (and often confusing) principles of using a computer is the idea that a program "loads" into memory in order to "run." Program files are a way to store instructions on a computer without needing a constant supply of power. We've seen how RAM loses data when the power is turned off. We've also seen how disks store data without requiring a constant power supply. Running a file is when the system executes the instructions contained in a program—the command interpreter "runs" through a list of instructions.

Windows NT uses the word *initialize* to distinguish between loading a device driver and running it at a later time. This concept was carried forward into Windows 2000 and Windows XP (e.g., services).

The computer must load a file before it can be run. A program is *executed* (run) either when we type something on a command line (and press Enter), or when another program *calls* (programming word) the first program. Upon execution, the instructions that the computer needs at any given moment are copied (not moved) into memory from the program file. This is what we mean by loading a file. The original file remains stored on the disk, untouched and unchanged unless certain instructions make a change to the stored file.

Viruses often copy themselves into RAM and use programming instructions to change the original file on the disk. Understand that the file itself doesn't go into memory, but that a copy of the programmed instructions goes into memory.

The entire process of saving data on a computer revolves around the basic fact that data is always changed in memory, but the changes are only retained if the data is stored back to a storage media of some kind (for example, a disk). Memory is not the same thing as storage, even though many novices use the terms interchangeably.

COMMAND.COM

DOS is really a package of many programs and utilities that take up a lot of space in a default directory called C:\DOS (C:\WINDOWS\COMMAND in Windows 9x). When we talk about DOS, we're referring to the whole package and all the various subprograms—the Disk Operating System. However, the essence of the operating system is the command interpreter (COMMAND.COM) and the two hidden system files that handle basic I/O.

COMMAND.COM is usually loaded into RAM when a computer boots up, and parts of it stay in system memory during the entire session (the time during which the computer is turned on). COMMAND.COM uses a number of routines almost constantly, and they can be accessed faster if those parts of the program stay in fast RAM. The parts of the interpreter that stay in memory are called the *resident* parts. The parts of COMMAND.COM that move back and forth between the disk and memory are called the *transient* parts.

When a computer is running, we call that a *session*. Windows opens up a DOS session as a virtual machine. Keep an eye on how a real machine works, because you'll have a lot easier time understanding what Windows is doing when it creates the Virtual Machine (VM), or you run a 16-bit application under Windows 2000.

A fundamental part of COMMAND.COM is its ability to read a command line and pass the information contained in the characters back to MSDOS.SYS and IO.SYS for processing. If the command line fails to match exact patterns, COMMAND.COM contains a number of error messages that it sends to the screen. Command lines are still an important part of troubleshooting a computer. Although we're speaking here of COMMAND.COM, the concepts also apply to CMD.EXE and the Recovery Console.

The Recovery Console is an administrative tool found in Windows 2000 and XP, which essentially provides a way to bring up a nontransient DOS environment. CMD.EXE is transient, meaning that once the program or command you run from this command line terminates, the command window disappears, and you're returned to the Desktop.

Internal and External Commands

COMMAND.COM includes a number of internal commands and instructions on how to use batch files. Batch files are simple programs using plain text language to execute a series of events. Some examples of internal commands are **COPY**, **DEL**, **DIR**, and **ECHO**. These are called internal commands in order to differentiate them from external commands. External commands are the other program files included in the overall operating system. Examples of external commands in DOS include **ATTRIB**, **FDISK**, **FORMAT**, **SCANDISK**, or **DEFRAG**.

The command interpreter literally interprets keyboard or mouse input and makes decisions as to whether to change the computer or pass the input on to an application program.

Keep in mind that in an open operating system, the command interpreter is directly associated with a number of low-level system files. DOS uses two critical system files and keeps them hidden from the casual user. There is a specific attribute assigned to system (S) files, and SYS.COM is a utility command written to specifically operate on those system files. (We'll discuss SYS.COM and ATTRIB.EXE later in this chapter.)

The Environment

The environment is an area of memory that DOS keeps aside to store system settings. Because the information being stored changes, we call them environment *variables*. **PROMPT**, **PATH**, and **COMSPEC** are both environment commands and environment variables. The common way to set the environment variables is with the AUTOEXEC.BAT file. This batch file is discussed in its own section later in this chapter, as well as in Chapter 11. To list the environment to the screen, type **SET** and press Enter.

Variables

A mathematical or computer variable is an interesting device, and one that you already know how to use—you just don't know that you know it. As is often the case, confusion can arise when someone uses a formal word to describe a common event.

Variables are placeholders that are written down somewhere, and that act as stand-ins for something real that will happen later. You probably took algebra in high school and used the symbol "X" in equations as a variable. The "X" stands for "whatever I'm supposed to find to get the right answer on the test, later."

A classroom containing a number of desks is a variable situation. Suppose that 15 desks are in the room. Each semester, those 15 desks sit in the same place. If you were asked what those were, you would say, "Those are desks." However, each semester, 15 students enroll in the class and sit at the desks. The desks are the *variables,* and the students are the *data being held by the variable.*

Depending on which semester it was, if you were asked what those desks were, you would say, "That's Bill's desk" or "That's Sharon's desk." Bill and Sharon are the data being assigned to the variables (desks) at a particular moment in time. The next semester you would point to the same desks and say, "That's Donna's desk" or "That's Phillip's desk."

If you number each desk 1 through 15, you're *naming* the variables. Therefore, a computer programmer could say "Go get the data in '12.' **IF** '12' is empty, **THEN 'ANSWER'** = 0. **IF** '12' is not empty, **THEN** 'STUDENT' = '12.'" The number 12 is a variable representing desk number 12, which is either empty or contains a student. ANSWER and STUDENT are additional variables that also hold information that can change.

By providing the computer with a list of student names and their desk numbers each semester, the computer can tell you whether the desk is empty, whether the student is present, and what the student's name is.

The DOS environment is a small, 256-byte area of memory set aside to store configuration settings for the operating system to use. One way to use up the 256 bytes is by a path containing that many characters. Another way is by running several instances of COMMAND.COM at the same time.

16-bit Windows created its own little area of environment memory called *resources.* Windows resources can run out of room just like the DOS environment could run out of room. The evolution of Windows into 9x and 2000 was directly linked to how Windows took over memory management and the environment.

SET [variable]

The important variables to note are **COMSPEC=**, **PATH=**, **PROMPT=**, and **TMP=**. All of these are set manually, except for **COMSPEC=**, which tells DOS where COMMAND.COM is located. When we say *manually*, we mean either that the user enters a **SET** command at the command line, or that the **SET** commands can be listed in the AUTOEXEC.BAT batch file. For instance, **SET Temp=c:\dumb** assigns temporary files to the "dumb" subdirectory in the root of Drive C:. Applications will look for a **TEMP** variable in the environment to find the location for their temporary files.

When you install an application on your machine, Windows and the operating system use an environment variable to keep track of the many files that are opened and then closed during the process. These are temporary files, in that they aren't part of the final application you find listed on the Start|Programs menu option, and are deleted (hopefully) at the end of the installation routine.

An environment variable can be manually set by typing "SET [*variable name*]=[*value setting*]" (without the quotes) at the command line. To change the **PROMPT** variable at any time, type "SET PROMPT=Hello World" at the command line and press Enter. This means that instead of the DOS command line starting with C:\WINDOWS>_, it would start with Hello World_. Typing "PROMPT=$p Hello World$g" and pressing Enter would cause the command line to start with C:\WINDOWS Hello World>_.

To change the search path to only the \Windows and the \Exam directories, type "PATH=C:\WINdows;c:\eXAm" and press Enter. Note that it doesn't matter how you mix uppercase and lowercase letters, DOS will change all the letters to uppercase.

The **COMSPEC=** environment variable is automatically set by COMMAND.COM during the boot process. The default value for this variable setting will always be the drive containing the boot disk and the name of the command interpreter file (almost always COMMAND.COM).

Warning! COMSPEC can be changed, but you should know exactly what you're doing before you change it. In the past days of dual-floppy machines, power users would create a virtual disk in system memory, using RAMDRIVE.SYS. COMMAND.COM could then be copied to the RAM disk and COMSPEC set to point to that virtual disk as the location of the command interpreter. RAMDRIVE.SYS is still available in Windows 9x.

Both DOS and Windows can work with the environment. COMMAND.COM looks in the environment for a number of variable settings, whereas DOS batch files move information in and out of the environment in a rudimentary programming capability.

Batch files are plain ASCII text files containing DOS commands on separate lines. Batch files must have a .BAT extension, and are considered executable program files. COMMAND.COM contains a number of internal commands that can be used by batch files. Some of the internal commands include the **ECHO**, **@**, **ERRORLEVEL**, **PAUSE**, **FOR**, **CHOICE**, and **IF** commands.

The exam sometimes refers to COMMAND.COM as a "batch command processor," although the proper name is "command interpreter."

The only time that the **SET** command itself is required is from within a batch file. Otherwise, entering only the variable's name and a DOS character separator is sufficient at the command line. However, it's good practice to always use the **SET** command when changing environment variables. Another example at the command line would be to type "SET PATH=C:\;d:\Utils;E:\windows\ComMaND" Note again, that in the **PATH** variable, the case of the letters is ignored.

The semicolon is the formal separator used to separate out multiple "requests" (as in requesting different directories in a search path). The equal sign or a space is the formal character separator following a command (in this case, the variable name).

Typing the **SET** command and pressing Enter at a DOS command prompt produces a report of the current settings. For example, a typical environment **SET** report shows the following:

```
TMP=C:\WINDOWS\TEMP
winbootdir=C:\WINDOWS
COMSPEC=C:\COMMAND.COM
WINPMT=$P$G
PROMPT=Type EXIT to$_Return to Windows$_$p$g
PATH=C:\WINDOWS;C:\WINDOWS\COMMAND;C:\;C:\DOS;D:\UTILS;D:\BATCH;
    D:\WINUTILS
```

An interesting property of the DOS environment is that the names of the environment variables are automatically converted to uppercase in all instances. After you've passed the certification exam, you might be interested in researching how the **winbootdir=** and **windir=** variables can show up as lowercase.

PROMPT=

PROMPT is a reserved word for an internal DOS command, and is known as an *environment command* in that it affects the way that DOS looks on the screen when you're not doing anything. The prompt to the left of the blinking cursor simply exists, waiting for you to do something. The prompt command does not require the use of SET, even in an AUTOEXEC.BAT file.

PROMPT uses special symbols called *metastrings* in conjunction with the word prompt. When you type "PROMPT" with a dollar sign ($) and a metastring, DOS sends the information you entered to ANSI.SYS (an auxiliary system file that comes with DOS) and changes the environment. The **PROMPT** command and switches are case insensitive, meaning that you can enter them in uppercase, lowercase, or any combination of the two.

DOS uses the .SYS extension in both system files and device driver files. Check the possible responses to any question asking you about these files or the extension.

The case-insensitive command **PROMPT=PG** makes the prompt show the default drive, directory, and the > character, C:\DOS>_. The command **PROMPT=Type "EXIT" to$_return to Windows$_pg** (without spaces in Windows$_$p$g) produces a three-line prompt at a DOS screen as follows:

```
Type "EXIT" to
return to Windows
C:\DOS>_
```

The = character is used by DOS to signify a space. Therefore, you need not enter it, but it's good practice to use it so that you don't accidentally omit a space. The command **PROMPT=pg** works the same as the command **prompt Pg** because these commands are not case sensitive.

SET TEMP=

Both Windows and DOS applications use a temporary directory to store overflow files, swap files, and other temporary files. DOS and Windows know where to put those files by looking at the **TMP=** (DOS) or the **TEMP=** (Windows) setting.

The temporary directories are not required to be called \TMP or \TEMP. They can be called anything you like and can be located anywhere on any accessible drive. The important thing is that the **SET TEMP=** line of the AUTOEXEC.BAT file places the **TEMP** *variable* in the environment and names the variable's setting—in this case, a subfolder.

If you have enough RAM, you can locate a temporary directory on a RAM drive (a virtual drive created with the RAMDRIVE.SYS program). This is sometimes useful for storing temporary Internet files. The RAM drive vanishes when the computer is shut down, automatically removing everything stored to that virtual drive.

The Path

The path—a file's formal, full name (*pathname*)—is perhaps one of the most common causes of trouble at the software level. **PATH=** is an internal environment command. The path is also the true name of a file. When we tell someone about a file name, we imply the rest: the drive and the subdirectory chain. When you talk to DOS about a file, you must write out the entire file name, or you can make a specific subdirectory the default location. This is still true when you work with a command line in any version of Windows.

An example of using the DOS command line in Windows would be where you want to rename many files in one single action. Suppose you want to rename every file in a folder with a .DOC extension to the same name, but with an .OLD extension. Unless you have a third-party utility, you'll have to go to an MS DOS Window and use the REName command (REN). In this case, you would enter **REN *.DOC *.OLD**.

Directories can contain subdirectories, each of which can contain more subdirectories, each of which can contain more subdirectories, and so on down until the entire name of a subdirectory and file reaches a limit. DOS created this limit, setting it to 256 characters. The entire name of a file (including every directory needed to get to that file, and the drive where the file is located) is called its *full pathname*.

Windows' Long File Name limits are set by keyboard buffer and command-line character limitations. The default command line is 127 characters. Batch files and environment variables support up to 244 characters. To increase the default command-line buffer, place the following line in a CONFIG.SYS file: SHELL= c:\windows\command.com /u:255 (where /u: increases the environment space). If no other characters are necessary in a variable name or command-line statement, a long file name can be up to 255 characters.

DOS FAT16 directory names must follow the 8.3 (read "eight dot three") naming convention. DOS has no way of storing Long File Names, but Windows can go beyond the 8.3 convention. Special provisions were made to link a DOS name to a Windows file name. We'll discuss this in the "VFAT" section of Chapter 12.

Keep in mind that the maximum number of characters in the full name of all the directory levels and the file name is 256. (This is a different 256 than the default environment size.) If you have a file named C:\level2\level3\4thlevel\level5\onemore\yikes\holycow\MYFILE.DOC, there are 65 characters in the entire file name (the path). This example contains eight directories—one root directory and seven subdirectories. MYFILE.DOC is a data file in the directory at the eighth level.

Each directory is symbolized by the backslash at the right end of its name. The root directory—the highest, or topmost folder on the drive—is represented by a plain \ (backslash) to the right of a drive letter. C:\ shows that the backslash represents the root of Drive C:. In the previous example, "level2\" has a backslash at the end of its name, showing that level2 is a directory name. This continues all the way to MYFILE.DOC, which has no backslash, signifying that this is a data file.

Unix uses the forward slash (/)to represent the division in directories. Because the people who actually invented the Internet (not Al Gore) were familiar with Unix, Web addresses show the directory level on the computers hosting the Web site with these symbols. For instance, in **http://www.ibm.com/support/all_download_drivers.html**, you can see that "support" is a subdirectory of the main data directory for the overall site. The "all_download" folder is a subdirectory of the "support" folder. Finally, the data file containing the Web page for a listing of the various software drives is called "all_download_drivers.html."

Search Path

When you enter a word in a command line, COMMAND.COM parses the line and looks for a command file (program file) matching that word. If the command word is not found internally, COMMAND.COM looks elsewhere for a file with a .COM, an .EXE, or a .BAT extension—in that order. But where does DOS look? It looks in any directory listed in the search path.

Suppose that we've made the D:\JUNK directory the default directory by typing "D:" and then pressing Enter, then typing "CD\JUNK" and pressing Enter once again. Our current location, then, is D:\JUNK. Now suppose we type "FOURMAT A:" and then press Enter. What will happen? (Pay attention, and check the spelling!)

COMMAND.COM parses the line, finds A: to be a valid drive location, and expects FOURMAT to be a program file or internal command. DOS will attempt to execute the command through COMMAND.COM in the following order:

1. It first looks inside itself for the character string FOURMAT (which it won't find) and then in the current directory for a program file that begins with FOURMAT. Here, it will look first for FOURMAT.COM, then for FOURMAT.EXE, and finally for FOURMAT.BAT.

If FOURMAT.COM and FOURMAT.EXE both exist in the same directory, COMMAND.COM will execute the .COM file first and never know that the .EXE file exists alongside it. .COM files come first, then .EXE files, and finally .BAT files.

2. If FOURMAT.COM/EXE/BAT does not exist in the current directory, COMMAND.COM turns to the DOS environment and looks for an environment variable named PATH.

3. If PATH= exists, COMMAND.COM will start with the first directory listed and repeat Step 1.
4. If FOURMAT is still not found, COMMAND.COM will start with each directory after each semicolon and repeat Step 1.
5. If FOURMAT is not found in any of these places, DOS writes an error message to the screen that reads "File(s) not found". In this instance, the odds are that DOS wouldn't find FOURMAT.COM because the actual file name is FORMAT.COM and that command is located in the DOS subdirectory.

A search **PATH** is a list of directories that DOS can search to find a program name entered on the command line. The advantage of a **PATH** is that the command can be entered without being logged in to the specific directory containing the program file.

DOS Commands

The main thing to remember about DOS is that COMMAND.COM is the command processor (command interpreter) and that it uses MSDOS.SYS and IO.SYS to make up the trio of the DOS operating system. DOS comes with many other programs besides the main trio. As we've said, anything that comes with DOS but that isn't inside COMMAND.COM is an external command. If it can be entered on the DOS command line (MS-DOS prompt) or used in a batch or an AUTOEXEC.BAT file, it's a command.

Device drivers (.SYS files) could be called *commands*, but they're more accurately called *drivers*. The 16-bit device drivers are almost always loaded in a CONFIG.SYS file.

In Chapter 9 we mentioned the internal DOS device names. These can be used to instruct the basic devices that come with any PC. If you remember, some of these devices are PRN (printer), CON (video console), COM (communications), and LPT (line printer). When you type "COPY FILENAME.TXT PRN" and press Enter, you tell DOS to copy a file called filename.txt to the printer. The file will then be printed.

The right angle bracket (>) is also called a *redirector*. Issuing the **ECHO ^L >PRN** command will redirect a carriage return and line feed to the printer, causing a laser printer to eject a sheet of paper. Another example is where you issue a **TYPE AUTOEXEC.BAT** > [*somefile*]**.TXT** command and DOS will type out the contents of the batch file but redirect the output into a new file ([*somefile*]). If that new file exists, the contents will overwrite whatever was in it. If it doesn't exist, DOS will create it. Using the **TYPE AUTOEXEC.BAT** >> [*somefile*]**.TXT** command tells DOS to append (add) the contents to the redirected file.

ATTRIB.EXE

When data is created either in programs or as a result of program actions, the result is a file. Files, which are stored on disks, contain additional information that can be used by the operating and file management systems. For example, a file's header information generally contains identification data that other programs can read. This is how file-viewing applications (e.g., Quick View) can identify the correct viewer used to show the file.

Every file has another important piece of attached data: its attribute bit. The DOS and Windows basic file attributes come in four flavors: R (read-only), A (archive), S (system), and H (hidden). Additionally, folders have a D (directory) attribute, which can be seen with the **DIR /V** (for Verbose) switch in DOS 7.x. **ATTRIB** does not show the directory attribute.

Regardless of the extension a file uses, the header information remains the same. You might rename THISFILE.DOC to THISFILE.BMP but the header information maintains the fact that the file is a document file, not a Windows Bitmap image. MS Explorer will become confused and ask you what program you'd like to use to open the file (based on file association), but Quick View will correctly identify the file and present a document.

Network operating systems include several additional attributes for the purposes of rights and permissions.

Each standard attribute can be turned on or off using the plus (+) or minus (-) sign associated with the external **ATTRIB** command. If an attribute is turned on, it shows in the results of issuing the command with no switches (e.g., **ATTRIB**). The syntax for ATTRIB.EXE is:

```
ATTRIB [+R ¦ -R] [+A ¦ -A] [+S ¦ -S] [+H ¦ -H] [[drive:]
    [path]filename] [/S]

  +   Sets an attribute.
  -   Clears an attribute.
  R   Read-only file attribute.
  A   Archive file attribute.
  S   System file attribute.
  H   Hidden file attribute.
  /S  Processes files in all directories in the specified path.
```

The results of using the **ATTRIB** command show the current attribute of a given file or set of files specified in the file mask. DOS 6.x added several switches to the **DIR** command, where specific files could be shown on the basis of their attribute. For example, **DIR /A:H** shows a listing of all hidden files in a directory. Another switch added to **DIR** is the **/S** for subdirectories. Prior to these changes in **DIR**, the only way to see every file in every subdirectory was to use **ATTRIB**, **CHKDSK**, or **TREE**.

DOS 7.x modified the /V "verbose" switch to include all attributes, including (D)irectories (also known as folders). To see this, open an MS DOS window or command line, and type **DIR /A:H /V /P.** The resulting report will show you how the /V switch provides an Attributes column where you can see the Directory attribute. The /V switch also displays the Long File Names version of the files and folders. The /A:H "attributes:hidden" switch selects only hidden files for display. Finally, the /P "page" switch pauses the screen every 23 lines until you press a key. Type **DIR /A /V /P** to see the entire listing with the attributes for all the files. Type **DIR /A /P** (without the /V switch), and the attributes are no longer presented.

The ATTRIB command is used primarily to change file attributes. One example of this is when a computer cannot start in Safe Mode, and you want to manually back up the Registry. Typing **ATTRIB -H -R C:\WINDOWS\SYSTEM.DAT** will unhide the file and remove the Read-Only attribute. Without this step, the COPY command will not find the file. (Note that you should only do this if you know what you're doing.) Look at the following example of the **ATTRIB** command:

```
    SHR     IO.DOS        C:\IO.DOS
    SHR     MSDOS.DOS     C:\MSDOS.DOS
A    H      BOOTLOG.PRV   C:\BOOTLOG.PRV
      R     COMMAND.DOS   C:\COMMAND.DOS
      R     WINA20.386    C:\WINA20.386
A           CONFIG.DOS    C:\CONFIG.DOS
A           AUTOEXEC.DOS  C:\AUTOEXEC.DOS
     HR     SUHDLOG.DAT   C:\SUHDLOG.DAT
     H      MSDOS.--      C:\MSDOS.--
     H      SETUPLOG.TXT  C:\SETUPLOG.TXT
A           COMMAND.COM   C:\COMMAND.COM
```

In this case, IO.DOS is a system, hidden, read-only file. The **DIR /A:[*option*]** command lists only those files with the specific attributes you state. In both the **DIR** and the **ATTRIB** command, the /S "subdirectories" switch is used to show files you've specified in both the default folder and any of its subfolders.

In older, as well as modern PCs, issuing the **ATTRIB *.* /S >PRN** command is one method of getting a full printout of every file on the disk. The

> redirector sends the results of the command to the printer. Another method is to type DIR *.* /S >PRN.

If you want the listing saved to a text file, type **DIR *.* /S >**[*filename*]**.TXT** (where [*filename*] can be any allowable file name). The screen will pause while DOS redirects the listing to the file and then presents you with a prompt. A new text file, with whatever name you assigned to it, will now be available in the folder you named (or the current default folder if you did not include a path). You can open this text file in any word processor and use it like a standard document.

The **TREE** command in versions prior to DOS 7.0 could be used to produce a full listing of files or a graphical report of all directories on a logical drive. Microsoft removed the **TREE** command in DOS 7.0, leaving shareware utilities as the only way to meet this need. Strangely enough, the TREE command also makes a reappearance in Windows 2000.

Hidden Files

Certain files on a drive are so important that if they don't exist, the system will fail to boot. On the other hand, the DEL command makes it very easy to delete the files. One of the more dangerous aspects of Windows File Manager and Windows Explorer is that files can be easily deleted, regardless of whether they are hidden or otherwise protected.

The R (Read-only) attribute means that a file can be opened and read, but not changed. Read-only does *not* protect the file from being deleted. The hidden and system attributes make the file undeletable by a normal DEL command. If you type "DEL IO.SYS" and press Enter, the result will be "File(s) not found." IO.SYS is hidden, and you can't delete a file unless DOS can see it.

Remember that a hidden file is only more difficult, but not impossible, to delete. Using Windows Explorer or File Manager, or changing the attribute to -H will make the file visible to DOS, after which it can be easily deleted.

The DIR Command: File Searches

One of the commands used almost routinely in DOS and Windows is the **DIR** command, which shows a directory listing. You may think that Windows doesn't use this command, but every time you call up the File Manager or Explorer, Windows is using the **DIR** command properties to get a listing of the files you're seeing.

If you try to find a file using the Search or Find options in Windows, you're presented with a field in the dialog boxes where you enter some parts of a file name, and something having to do with asterisks (also called the "star"). If you've ever used the Save As or Open command in almost any application, your options for the type of file include the DOS names. For example, the default in Microsoft Word is to open all Word documents (*.doc).

In the following section, we'll look at the DOS wild cards, but for now, just remember that the **DIR** command does two things. It shows a listing of files on a drive or in a directory, and it is used to search for files on a drive or in a directory.

Wild Cards

If you've ever played poker, you know that in certain games, the dealer can make a card "wild." The wild card can represent any other card. The wild card becomes a variable just like the blank tile in a Scrabble game, or one of our previously mentioned student's desks. You can use the card, and it can represent whatever you'd like it to.

DOS has two reserved symbols that represent this sort of variable: the asterisk (*) and the question mark (?). You can use the wild cards in the Explorer's Find: All Files | Named: dialog box, exactly the way they've always worked in DOS. The asterisk and question mark each have a slightly different way of working, though, which works out in the following manner:

- The asterisk symbol represents one or more characters to the right of the point where the asterisk is used. Its results can be limited to the first eight characters in a file name by placing a single dot (period) after the asterisk (i.e., *.).
- The question mark symbol can represent only a single character. If more than one character is needed, more than one question mark must be used. When the question mark is used, it means one character must be available for every question mark typed.

There will most likely be at least one question on the exam involving wild cards. Be sure you understand that a question mark (?) represents a single character and that the asterisk (*) represents multiple characters.

Perhaps the easiest way to demonstrate wild cards is to show various ways they would be used with the **DIR** command. Let's suppose we have a number of files with a .WKS extension in a directory and another set of files that have an .XLS extension. The main part of the file name can be anywhere from one to eight characters; however, a number of the files start with REP for report, followed by a date (e.g., REP1998, REP1999, REP00).

Let's further suppose that this directory has a number of files with many different extensions. There might be a THISONE.TXT, THATONE.MIS, NEWFILE.DLL, OLD.BAK, REAL.DOC, RUSS.DOC, and MY.WRK.

If we were to try and find every file that was an Excel spreadsheet (.XLS extension), we would have to use one of the wild cards. The way that we look specifically for every file with the .XLS extension is to use **DIR *.XLS** as the command. Note that the default in MS Explorer 4.x is to search for all subdirectories. This can be limited to a single directory by deselecting the Include subfolders check box. The DOS command to search subdirectories would be **DIR *.XLS /S**.

If you were to use **DIR ????????.XLS** under the assumption that you would find anything in the main name, it wouldn't work. The reason is that the question mark doesn't just represent any single character, but it means that some character *must* exist as well. In this instance, you would be telling DOS to look for a file that must have eight characters, a period, and the .XLS extension. Although there may be a few files with both an eight-letter name and an .XLS extension, there may also be many files with seven, five, or four characters to the left of the dot.

If you were to use **DIR ?.***, you would have to have a file with at least one character in the name, along with an extension. There might be 200 files in a directory, but if none of them had only one character and an extension, DOS would return the "File(s) not found" message.

If you wanted to find every file that was a report file, you would use **DIR REP*.*** because all these files begin with the letters REP and the company's naming standards require that all reports begin with the letters REP.

Developing a consistent way to name your files allows you to use the DOS wild cards to search for those files in a logical manner.

To find all the temp files on Drive C:, you would have to know that almost all Windows temp files end with .TMP. Another form of temporary file has the ~ (tilde, pronounced "till-dee") as the first character. You can't use the command-line **DIR** to find two different types of files. For instance, you can't use **DIR ~*.* ; *.TMP**. The semicolon isn't allowed on the command line. However, you *can* type ***.TMP; ~*.*** in Explorer, using the semicolon as a separator.

Using DOS in the situation just described, you would have to issue two **DIR** sequences. The first would be **DIR C:\~*.* /S** to find any file that began with a tilde, starting from the root directory of Drive C: and looking in every subdirectory on the drive. The second would be to use **DIR C:*.TMP /S** to find any file in any subdirectory on Drive C: with a .TMP extension.

Saving Search Results

There is another use for the > symbol. Whenever you issue a command, that command performs an action. Many times the command also outputs some type of result. The result can be in the form of messages or, in the case of the **DIR** command, the listing of your directory.

If you use the > redirector, you can send the output results from **DIR** to either a printer or another file. Using **DIR C:*.TMP /S > PRN** would redirect the results of searching for every .TMP file on the entire Drive C: to the printer, where you could go over the list at your leisure. Another way would be to use **DIR C:*.TMP /S > C:\SOMEFILE.TXT** would create a file called SOMEFILE.TXT in the root directory of Drive C: that would contain all the files listed in the search result. Later, you can open C:\SOMEFILE.TXT with Microsoft Word, Notepad, EDIT, or any other application that can read a plain, ASCII text file.

What's sad about Windows is that it's extremely difficult to save the search parameters (file names and types) as an icon on your desktop. Windows says it will save the search, but it won't save the *.TMP or A*.EXE parameters in the shortcut.

Web browsers routinely cache Internet site information such as graphics, cookies, and pages. This sort of caching (as opposed to L-1 or L-2 memory caches) downloads a page from a Web site under the assumption that you'll want to go back to it. However, "cleaning out the cache" is a manual process in most cases. If the cache isn't emptied, it can grow to thousands and thousands of files. Additionally, temporary files aren't always deleted as an application cleans up after itself. This, too, can lead to thousands of files slowing down the system.

To clean out a cache is a fairly simple thing. Find the cache directory (folder) assigned in the Preferences of your Web browser. Do a search of that folder for *.* files (every file with any name). Select them all with either

Ctrl+A (Select All) or "Shift Select." To use the Shift key to select every file between one file and another, highlight the first file, hold down the Shift key, scroll to the last (or other) file, and click to highlight it while still holding down the Shift key. Then press the DEL key.

Windows 2000 and Windows XP provide the Disk Cleanup utility tool to help clean out some of these types of files. Windows 9x users can have a similar option with third-party commercial software, such as Norton Utilities (Symantec, Inc.).

Finding temporary files is where knowing wild cards comes in handy. From the Search dialog box, you can enter ~*.* ; *.TMP to find all files that begin with the tilde and all files that end with .TMP. When they've been found, you can delete them all.

Vanilla ASCII (Plain Text)

Batch files, AUTOEXEC.BAT, CONFIG.SYS, and many generic reference files require that only characters from ASCII 0032 through 0126 be in the file. These basic characters are called *plain*, or *vanilla*, ASCII characters (from plain, good ol' vanilla ice cream). Books often mention using a text editor or your favorite word processor to create these files.

A text editor is a word processing program that allows only plain ASCII characters and no formatting whatsoever. A text editor might allow you to use the Tab key, but when you save the file, the tabs are converted to a number of spaces. The original text editor that came with DOS was called *EDLIN.COM* (for "edit lines") and drove most early DOS users insane.

Most upscale word processors allow you to choose the File | Save As feature and pick a *.TXT file type. This combination gives you all the search-and-replace, copying, moving, macros, formatting, and other features of a powerful word processor to create a document; a plain ASCII TXT file is the result. Common text editors include EDIT.COM (introduced with DOS 5.0 and higher), NOTEPAD.EXE (the Windows 3.x text-editing utility), and WORDPAD.EXE (the Windows 9x replacement for Notepad).

If you have a copy of it, you can copy NOTEPAD.EXE to the Windows 9x Send To folder, after which it will show up as an option on the Properties Send To menu. If you highlight a file in MS Explorer and right-click for the properties, you can send that file to the Notepad, oftentimes getting an idea of contents of that file. This is particularly useful if a file extension isn't registered in the Explorer's File Types option.

Summary—DOS

DOS is an important part of understanding computers, whether you're looking at a folder listing in the Explorer, or using an MS DOS Window to run a game. Before you take the exam you should have a clear understanding of the following points:

- The command interpreter and underlying system files (COMMAND.COM, MSDOS.SYS, and IO.SYS
- Wild cards and searching for files with the DIR command
- The Path and search path, and how DOS uses environment variables to keep track of file locations
- The difference between internal and external commands, and what it means to load a program into memory.
- File attributes and the ATTRIB.EXE program, used to locate files that have been modified, or to hide files from a directory listing.

Keep in mind that although DOS was disconnected from Windows NT, Windows 2000, and Windows XP, the Recovery Console operates in a traditional DOS-like environment. One way or another, you're going to encounter the command line, and you should know what it is and how it works before you go for an A+ certification.

Logical Formatting and Partitions: FDISK

Before we get into this topic, let's make sure we all understand that a physical disk is a bunch of machinery with platters that store magnetic information. Up until now, we've used the word "drive" interchangeably with "disk," but in this segment, it's critical that you understand the difference. A disk is not a logical drive.

In Chapter 6, we said that many people refer to the disk in a mechanical housing as a drive. In this discussion, you must understand that a drive is a logical designation created by an operating system! For instance, a floppy disk is a physical item that you insert into a floppy disk mechanism. For the operating system to recognize the disk, that mechanism must be given a symbolic name. DOS and Windows designate a mechanical disk subsystem by the letters A through Z.

Partitions

A partition is an area on a disk: just that—an area. If that area has been formatted by an operating system, it becomes a *logical drive*. Logical drives are assigned both a drive letter and a volume name. Low-level formatting is where a manufacturer actually magnetizes the tracks on a disk. Logical formatting is where an operating system installs its file management system.

The Installable File System (IFS) in Windows 3.x uses a helper program to load into memory. That helper program is a device loaded through CONFIG.SYS and is called *IFSHLP.SYS*.

Volumes and Terms

Logical formatting means that some amount of space is set-aside on a physical disk (what we've previously called a "hard drive") as a discrete area in which to store data and program files. These areas are the partitions, but they are routinely referred to as *volumes* and must be given a volume name during the partitioning process. (You see this name next to the drive symbol in the Explorer.) Each partition must have a volume name, and after a volume is formatted, it becomes a [logical] drive. Effectively, and for the sake of clarity, partition and volume mean the same thing in this section.

The volume name is used to explicitly designate a partition, and is assigned during the FDISK "Create a Partition" procedure. As a safety measure, to avoid accidentally deleting a partition and wiping out any information on that area of the disk, you must enter the volume name of the partition before you delete it. The **FORMAT** command allows you to create a volume name on a floppy disk. Windows Explorer uses the **FORMAT** command when you right-click on the floppy drive icon and select Format.

The Windows 9x Explorer will not let you format a hard drive containing files. To partition and format a hard drive, you must use a DOS command line. Format is also one of the commands available in the Windows 2000 Recovery Console.

A physical disk can contain a number of partitions that DOS recognizes as logical drives. Almost all PCs have a physical hard drive (disk) and at least one logical drive (partition). An exception would be a diskless network terminal, from which the hard disk is removed and from which the terminal is booted up with a floppy disk. Microsoft created certain names for the various conceptual areas of a fixed disk as follows:

- *Fixed disk drive*—The actual set of platters attached to a drive controller. Disk drives are listed with numbers.

- *Partition or logical drive*—An area set-aside on a disk for storage. Logical drives are assigned the letters A through Z by the operating system.
- *Volume label*—The actual 11-character name of a logical drive.
- *Primary partition*—A bootable area of a fixed disk, assigned a drive letter (C:, D:, etc.). Primary partitions may not be subdivided. The maximum number of primary partitions in Windows 9x is three.
- *Extended partition*—A nonbootable area of a disk. Extended partitions are not assigned a drive letter. Extended partitions may be subdivided into logical drives, which are then assigned a drive letter.
- *Status*—The letter used to show which partition is active (A). The Active partition defines which Primary partition is being used to boot the system.
- *Type*—The term used to list either a Primary (PRI), Extended (EXT), or Non-DOS partition
- *System*—The term used to list the type of file system being used. DOS partitions are FAT16. Other types include FAT32, HPFS, and NTFS.

Number of Volumes

The absolute and technical maximum number of logical drives is 26 (A through Z). However, the A: and B: drive designators are built into DOS, and are always considered floppy disk drives. The letter C is always the first letter assigned to a hard disk, so Drive C: is considered the first bootable logical drive (Active Primary partition) on a hard disk. That makes three letters being used in almost every situation. A printout of an FDISK information report shows how each word is used.

```
                      Display Partition Information

Current fixed disk drive: 1

Partition  Status   Type    Volume Label  Mbytes   System   Usage
    1        A     Non-DOS                     2                %
    2              Non-DOS                   250              24%
 C: 3              PRI DOS   W95_5-8-97      300   FAT16      29%
    4              EXT DOS                   478              46%

Total disk space is  1030 Mbytes (1 Mbyte = 1048576 bytes)

The Extended DOS Partition contains Logical DOS Drives.
Do you want to display the logical drive information (Y/N)..?[Y]
----------------------------------------------------------------
                      Display Logical DOS Drive Information

Drv Volume Label  Mbytes  System  Usage
D:  ALL-DATA         300  FAT16     63%
E:  DATA             178  FAT16     37%
```

```
Total Extended DOS Partition size is   478 Mbytes
    (1 MByte = 1048576 bytes)
```

In Windows 2000 and Windows NT, the FDISK.EXE program became part of the Computer Management utility. This provided a graphic, interactive way of partitioning a disk, much like the Powerquest Partition Magic utility program.

Primary and Extended Partitions

Partitions are categorized as either *primary* or *extended*. Now here's where it gets tricky. If you have a PC with a fixed disk (hard drive) that means it *must* have a set of platters for storing information. One way or another, a useable computer will boot up from either Drive A: or Drive C: (or a bootable CD-ROM). That means three letters are taken, because A and B are built into COMMAND.COM, and C is automatically assigned to the fixed disk.

When you lay this all out, it means that a hard "drive" can technically have a maximum of 24 logical drives. To make things even more confusing, a logical drive (in the real world) often refers to either the Primary or Extended partitions. If you have a Primary partition (required to boot a machine) *and* an Extended partition, the Extended partition can have a maximum of 23 logical drives. The floppy disk drive takes up 2 drive letters, and the Primary partition takes up 1 drive letter (A:/B: floppy; C: Primary), leaving 23 letters in the alphabet.

Formatting a disk (technically called *logical formatting*) means that the DOS file system is used to create the FAT, the DAT, and the root directory. Formatting also defines the number and size of clusters on the volume.

Be sure to remember that COMMAND.COM can recognize 24 drives beyond drives A: and B:, but that an extended DOS partition can contain a maximum of only 23 logical drives. Drive C: is almost always a Primary partition.

Because the volume (logical drive) might be smaller than the physical disk, the names "volume" and "drive" are not interchangeable with "disk."

You can partition a disk into logical drives or volumes, but you can't partition a drive into logical disks.

Partitioning and Multiple Physical Disks

We were asked if, on a multi-disk system, a physical disk could be partitioned as one, single extended partition. Initially, we thought that a disk must have at least one Primary partition in order for the operating system to recognize the structural organization. In fact, and working with various operating systems on multi-disk systems, we found that a second physical disk can be partitioned as a single extended partition. Obviously, one disk in the system must have a Primary, Active partition in order to boot the OS, but secondary disks or any additional disks may be set up entirely as extended partitions. The additional disks can then be logically formatted into various drives, and assigned drive letters.

When multiple Primary partitions have been created, along with extended, logical drive partitions, MS Explorer will present the Primary partitions first, in the Folders view (left pane), in the order in which they're found on the drive controllers. Non-Primary drives are listed following (below) the Primary partitions, also in the order of the drive controllers. For example, a two-disk system with a Primary partition on both disks and an Extended partition on each, will show as C: for Disk 0 (Primary), and D: for Disk 1 (Primary). Explorer will then show Drive E: on Disk 0, and finally, Drive F: on Disk 1. This can lead to some confusion if you install a second fixed disk and decide to include on it both a Primary and Extended partition (for example if you wanted two separate operating systems, separated by physical disks). In this case, drive references will likely change if the Explorer can see every disk. We tested this on both Windows NT (XP) and Windows 9x systems.

The external DOS program used to partition a physical disk is FDISK.EXE. The external DOS program used to format a logical drive is FORMAT.COM. Partitioning a disk completely destroys not only all the data on a disk, but any logical formatting on that disk as well.

LASTDRIVE=

Certain DOS settings are automatically set to a default value. As mentioned previously, this is done in the environment with an environment variable. The DOS environment shell is 256 bytes by default, and the prompt is C> or A> by default. **LASTDRIVE** is the environment variable that contains the last letter of the alphabet you will allow DOS to use to assign recognition to a logical drive. The default number of logical drives is set to five. Drives A: and B: are automatically set as floppy drives, and the first nonremovable disk (drive 0) is set to C:. For example, **LASTDRIVE=K** increases the number of logical drives that DOS can "see" to 11, with Drive K: being the last.

The default setting of 5 drives for **LASTDRIVE** leaves D: and E: open as additional, available logical drives following drives A:, B:, and C:, which are found on a system with a hard disk.

LASTDRIVE is set in the CONFIG.SYS file in a DOS and Windows 3.x machine. The directive still exists in MSDOS.SYS on a Windows 9x machine (the default is still 5 drives), but in Windows 9x, LASTDRIVE can be increased only by creating an optional CONFIG.SYS file in the root directory of the boot partition.

We said there was a limit to how many logical drives a fixed disk could contain. There's also a limit to the number of logical drives **LASTDRIVE** will recognize. The reason for the limit of 24 logical drives, in this instance, is that drives A: and B: always exist in the system, even if they don't physically exist on the PC. There are 26 letters in the alphabet, so 26 minus 2 (A: and B:) leaves 24.

An interesting fact to keep in mind is that Novell uses the default drive F: to search for the **LOGIN.EXE** command. However, during the installation of the client software, Novell requires that the **LASTDRIVE** be set to Z: (usually done in a CONFIG.SYS file). Note that whereas drives are always accessed by using the drive letter and a colon, the **LASTDRIVE=** statement doesn't require a colon, as in LASTDRIVE=K.

LASTDRIVE is an important (though not required) CONFIG.SYS file directive for networks and is important when many partitions exist on a big hard drive. If no line for **LASTDRIVE** exists, DOS assumes that only five logical drives exist on the system.

If a disk is partitioned into 12 logical drives—two Primary partitions and an Extended partition with 10 logical partitions—you must create a CONFIG.SYS file (with a text editor) and include the **LASTDRIVE=N** line. Whether you use DOS, 16-bit Windows, or Windows 9x, the extra drives can be made visible only by using a CONFIG.SYS file.

In the 12-drive example, the actual value for **LASTDRIVE=** can be any letter from N to Z. However, if it appears earlier in the alphabet than N (e.g., L), DOS won't see whatever drives exist that would have had the letters you forgot. In this case, the last drive is N (the fourteenth letter) because A: and B: are the floppy drives; therefore, 12 logical drives exist in addition to the floppies.

SET in AUTOEXEC.BAT

Some of the environment variables are set after the system has booted up. Others are set during the boot-up process (covered in Chapter 11). If the variable controls how COMMAND.COM understands the system, it has to be set in a CONFIG.SYS file, which loads before the command interpreter. **LASTDRIVE** and **SHELL** are examples of these variables, and when they are set in a CONFIG.SYS file, they are called *directives*. Directives do not use the **SET=** prefix.

If a variable applies to a session, it must be set in either the AUTOEXEC.BAT file or from a command line. **PROMPT**, **PATH**, and **TEMP** can all be changed during an active session. When the variable is set in this fashion, it is called a *SET* command. The **SET=** prefix is only required from within a batch file.

FORMAT.COM

Partitioning a disk tells the operating system only how the disk is divided into potential drive space. No matter which operating system (e.g., DOS, OS/2, or NT) you choose to install on any given partition, you need to set up the partition as a logical drive with some kind of file system. The DOS **FORMAT** command prepares the drive's file system in the following manner:

- Creates a boot sector, two copies of the FAT, and the root directory
- Performs a low-level check for bad sectors, marking any that it finds as unusable
- Provides an optional single-step system files transfer to make a disk bootable
- Allows the user to label a disk with a volume name at the end of the **FORMAT** process

During a *quick format* (**FORMAT [*d:*] /Q**), the program changes only the FAT on the disk and tells DOS that every sector on the drive is now available for data. The data still resides on the disk, but DOS has been told that it can write over anything and put a new entry into the FAT. Unconditional formatting (**/U**) erases data from the entire disk. Safe formatting places a hidden file on a floppy disk, reducing the entire storage area of the disk.

To completely format a disk and have FORMAT.COM examine the entire disk, use the **FORMAT [d:] /U** switch (for Unconditional).

LABEL.EXE

Oddly enough, a DIR listing (since the time of DOS 1.0) includes a line that states "Volume in Drive X:" and possibly a label of up to 11 characters. However, there was no way to label a disk other than running a format on it and putting the label on at the end. DOS 3.0 introduced the **LABEL** command, which allowed a volume label to be put on a disk without formatting it.

SYS.COM

When a working hard drive suddenly produces an error at boot-up that reads "Nonsystem disk or disk error. Replace and press any key when ready," it may mean that the system files have become corrupted. It could also mean that someone forgot to take a data floppy out of Drive A: when he or she shut down the system the last time. SYS.COM is the first step to try to fix the problem (after you check to see if there's a floppy in the drive).

The boot sector includes the Master Boot Record (MBR). You can't just copy the DOS system files using the **COPY** command because of the specific location of both the files and a special bootstrap loader (discussed in Chapter 11). Additionally, both IO.SYS and MSDOS.SYS are hidden files, and **COPY** won't see them.

SYS.COM is a special DOS program that has one purpose only: to copy the system files to another bootable disk. The destination disk must first have been formatted as a bootable disk. SYS.COM replaces corrupted system files on a hard drive by copying clean versions of the system files from a working, virus-free bootable floppy.

SYS.COM is indicated when a hard drive stops (following the POST) and the message "Bad or missing command interpreter" appears. The command to copy the system files from Drive A: (bootable disk) to drive C: (with corrupted files) is **SYS C:** or **SYS A: C:**.

An even more frightening message following the POST is "Nonsystem disk or disk error" when you're booting from a hard drive. Boot from your emergency boot disk and see whether you can log on to drive C:. If you can, try SYS.COM.

A bootable floppy will start the operating system and provide a way to test for access to the hard drive. If the system boots and you type "C:" and press Enter, you should log on to drive C:, regardless of whether that drive is bootable. If you can't log on to drive C:, a more serious problem exists.

Logical Block Addressing (LBA)

When DOS 1.0 was released, the hard drive wasn't available for PCs. Version 2.0 was released partly to support the introduction of the newly developed 10MB and 20MB hard drives. Through version 3.3, the maximum amount of space that DOS could handle was 32MB. Although larger hard disks were available, the only way to use them with DOS was to partition them into logical drives of 32MB or less.

DOS 4.0.1 broke the 32MB barrier, allowing for 256MB partitions. Hard disks were beginning to enter the range of gigabyte capacity and could now be broken up into larger logical drives. When DOS 5.0 finally arrived, it included support for 2GB logical drive partitions. However, the BIOS for the drive controllers in many computers (e.g., the 80486 chip) couldn't always support the large drives.

The original IDE specification handled logical drive space up to 512MB. The IDE controller-addressing model didn't allow addresses large enough to work with larger drives. Logical block addressing (LBA) allowed an older IDE controller to access logical drives up to 8.4GB as long as the computer's ROM BIOS included LBA support.

File Systems

Many people think of day-to-day file management as saving, copying, deleting, moving, and modifying files. For clarity, we'll use the term "maintenance" to mean what a user does with files. We'll use the term "management" to mean fundamental operating system processes.

An operating system must include a file system to make sense of the bits of magnetized coating on a disk. The file system keeps track of where all the parts of files are located; the directories and file names; and the used and unused space on a disk—allocated space and free space, respectively. The file system continually updates the cluster locations of all the parts of a file. When we speak of DOS, we'll use the term "directory." When we speak of Windows, we'll use the term "folder." Both terms mean the same thing, but understanding a directory will show you why a command line uses the Change Directory (**CD**) command.

The Windows 9x Long File Names feature uses the DOS file system to actually store the data on the physical disk. However, Windows controls how the FAT is used.

The original disks were able to store only 160KB of information, and programs and PCs were using only 64KB of RAM at that time. Engineers had to make a decision regarding how much space to set aside on a disk to hold all the information in a file structure (the FAT), as well as the directory allocation table used for the directory structure. They needed to strike a compromise between the expected size of future disks and the amount of space to take away from programs and data files.

DOS was set up to work with 16 bits worth of addresses, allowing for 65,525 clusters. Back then, no one ever imagined that PCs would be important or useful enough to need more than this 32MB of space. The original 16-bit FAT continues to this day, and Windows 9x still relies on it. The FAT32 system is an actual change to the basic 16-bit file allocation table, and uses 32-bit addressing along with adjustable cluster sizes. We discuss FAT32 in Chapter 12.

Directories (Folders)

A DOS directory is a special type of file. Directories and their subdirectories are used to keep together files having a common purpose—to organize a disk. For example, C:\DOS usually contains all the DOS operating system files, and C:\MSOFFICE contains the files that pertain to Microsoft Office. Today, we speak of folders and subfolders, but many of the routine operations involving running a computer are still linked to the concept of directories.

All files have names. All files also contain data. Commonly, a file contains data, so we use a directory name to contain file names. These are fundamental principles of files, and DOS uses one way (the file allocation table) to keep track of the data, and another way (the directory allocation table) to keep track of the file names.

Directory Tree

A directory and all its subdirectories are an example of a hierarchy. The original designers thought it looked like a tree, and the first part of a tree is the root. If you suppose that a directory tree looks somewhat like a root system, then smaller and smaller roots branch off of a larger root. The left pane of the MS Explorer shows the directory tree, while the right pane shows both the files and the subdirectories contained within a highlighted directory.

The FAT uses one directory—the root directory—as the starting point for all the files on a given drive (volume). The root directory can contain only a limited number of files, including both data and program files and subdirectory names.

The root directory, with its representative backslash (\), is at the top of the tree (level 1). The root directory is still a file, containing both data files and other directory files—subdirectories. When a subdirectory contains files, it becomes a lower level in the hierarchy. Level 2 is represented by an indented line coming down from the root, and there are smaller horizontal lines "branching" to the right. This stepladder design of lines and branches unfolds when you click on the little + or – sign to the left of a directory name in Explorer.

Every FAT16 volume must have its own root directory on the first track and sector of the Active, Primary partition. The maximum number of directory entries in the root directory is 512. To have more than 512 file and directory names, you must use at least one subdirectory. Subdirectories can have as many directory entries as there is room on the disk.

An interesting problem on some hard drives occurs when DOS prevents the user from creating a new file. An error message referring to insufficient disk space appears, but the user knows that he or she has a 500MB partition available. This might happen when users have put all their files into the root directory. With no subdirectories, the directory table has run out of room for a new file name and issues the out-of-space error.

Directory Management

To create a directory, DOS uses the command **MD** (Make Directory). To create a directory called "example" branching from the root directory, the command is **MD\EXAMPLE** (note the backslash). To create a directory one level below whichever is the current (default) directory, the command is **MD EXAMPLE** (note the space). In the first example, the backslash explicitly names the root directory as the directory that will contain the new "example" subdirectory.

To delete a directory, the original command was **RD** (Remove Directory). If there were files in the directory, the files had to be removed first (**DEL *.***). Only then could the directory be removed (**RD C:\EXAMPLE**). DOS 6.0 introduced the **DELTREE** command, which could take out a whole directory and all its subdirectories in one step.

To change from one directory to another, DOS used the **CD** (Change Directory) command. Used with an absolute name, **CD** would take you to that exact directory. Used with a space before another directory name, the command would take you down to the next subdirectory from the current location.

Relative and Absolute Locations

If we all are facing the same direction to begin with and someone yells, "Turn left!", we'll all end up facing the same way. On the other hand, if we're all facing different directions and someone yells the same thing, we'll end up facing different directions. However, no matter how many of us are facing in different directions, if someone yells, "Turn north!", then we'll all end up facing one way (assuming everyone has a compass and understands basic geography).

North, south, east, and west are absolute directions on the planet Earth. No matter which direction you're facing, north is always in a specific direction. Left and right, on the other hand, are relative directions. When someone is talking about "left" or "right," you need to know which way they're facing to determine what absolute direction they're talking about.

If you issue the command **CD\WINDOWS\SYSTEM**, you'll be taken to the root directory (the first backslash) and then moved down through WINDOWS to SYSTEM. However, if you issue the command **CD**

SYSTEM (using a space after the **CD**), DOS starts from wherever you are and tries to go down one level to a subdirectory called *System*. If you happen to be in the Windows directory, this command will work. If you happen to be in some other directory and there isn't a SYSTEM subfolder in that folder, you'll get a "File(s) not found" error.

A space after the **CD** command is a relative "down" designation. Before issuing such a command, be sure there is a location to go down to; if there isn't, DOS returns an error message. The **CD . .** command always moves up toward the root. Even at the root, DOS will *not* return an error message.

Dot, Dot-Dot, and Dot-Dot-Dot

The **CD** command (also known as ***CHDIR***) is used to change the default directory to another directory. The default directory is the directory where COMMAND.COM first looks for any referenced program entered on a command line. If you type "CD" (without the quotes) and press Enter, DOS returns the name of the default directory.

If you type TRUENAME, an undocumented DOS command, DOS will also return the actual drive and path of the current location. This can be used on networks and where long folder names have been "mapped" to a substitute drive letter (using the SUBST command).

If you are logged in to the C:\WINDOWS\SYSTEM directory, you have made that directory the default directory. If you then type "CD.." (two dots in a row), DOS changes the default to the directory immediately above the existing one—the parent directory.

When you type the full pathname to a file, you're giving DOS an absolute name. If you say "Change directories (**CD**) to the C:\WINDOWS\COMMAND directory," DOS knows exactly where that is. On the other hand, you can use what's called the "dot-dot" (. .) to tell DOS "**CD** to the next directory up from here." The dot and the dot-dot are still there from CP/M.

From the C:\WINDOWS\SYSTEM directory, you could type the absolute location by issuing the command **CD** <space> **C:\WINDOWS**. This would change the default location to one step above where you are, but it means typing a lot more characters.

Typing two dots after the **CD** command moves you up one level from where you are to the parent directory.

The single dot represents "here" to DOS. You can use it as a shortcut with a program command such as **XCOPY** when you want to copy all the files in a single directory of Drive A: (floppy disk) to the current directory. Instead of typing out the whole location, you can enter **XCOPY A: .** with the single dot after the A: to tell DOS that you want the files to arrive "here." This is handy if you're copying a lot of files from Drive A: to a network location like J:\pdj16\US\station5\1998\edu-work\process\managers\march. In this instance, you can log in to the network location and use the single dot rather than retyping the entire path.

In Windows 9x (DOS 7.x) the "dot" navigational tool was extended to include three dots. Typing **CD ..** moves up to the immediate parent folder. Typing **CD ...** moves up to the parent of the immediate parent (i.e., up two levels instead of one).

Subdirectories (Subfolders)

Subdirectories are symbolized by the name of the parent (containing) directory, followed by a backslash. For instance, in the case of C:\WINDOWS, the parent directory is the root directory of Drive C:. The first backslash follows to the right of the drive name. Therefore, WINDOWS is a subdirectory of the root directory.

The DOS word for "drive" is the colon (:). Therefore, the C drive is written as C:.

C:\WINDOWS\SYSTEM is the name of a subdirectory called *SYSTEM*. (It could also be the name of a file called *System*.) The SYSTEM subdirectory is under its parent, the WINDOWS directory. WINDOWS is under the root directory.

Directory or File Name?

In the name C:\WINDOWS\SYSTEM, "SYSTEM" can be either a file name or a subdirectory name. The last name in a path, or complete file and directory listing, is somewhat ambiguous. You can see this uncertainty when using the **XCOPY** command to copy a series of files to a different subdirectory. **XCOPY** will ask you whether you want the destination to be a file or a directory.

Even though subdirectories can have an extension, convention has it that file names use from one- to three-character extensions, whereas subdirectories stay with just the eight main characters of typical file names. This helps keep subdirectories and files separate. Additionally, because subdirectories are files (albeit of a special type), DOS provides angle brackets (< and >) and the DIR abbreviation (<DIR>) to indicate that something is a subdirectory.

Because subdirectories are files, they can also have one- to three-character extensions. However, many applications programmers forget to consider this, and those applications can't show the 8.3 type of subdirectory names in their File|Open dialog boxes.

File Management

We've said that, technically, an operating system includes a file management system and a command processor. File management involves controlling file names and keeping track of the files on a hard disk. The file management system must have a way to write to, read from, and locate tracks, sectors, and clusters. DOS and Windows use some version of a FAT, along with a root directory, as part of its file management system.

We saw in Chapter 6 that disk manufacturers perform a low-level format on brand-new hard drives, whereby they divide the disks into tracks and sectors. A sector is almost always a 512-byte piece of a track—a half of a kilobyte. The manufacturer's physical formatting creates many circular bands of magnetic strips on the platters of the disk called *tracks*. Each platter has a set of concentric tracks stepping outward from the center, and each platter is vertically aligned. All of the vertically aligned tracks (one above the others on every lower platter) taken together are called a *cylinder*.

Tracks are divided into sectors. Sectors can contain 512 bytes of data. Some number of sectors is used to make up a cluster.

In Figure 10.1, we've taken the top platter of a typical hard drive (disk) and outlined the tracks, sectors, and clusters. Note that the black ring in the drawing is a cylinder. Below this platter is another platter, and if you could see the black ring on that platter, it would be exactly the same distance from the spindle motor. Note also that in this example, 1 cluster is made up of 4 sectors (2048 bytes).

Observe that in the center of this platter is the spindle motor. The very first track next to the motor is track 0. The adjacent track outward from 0 is track 1, and so on. In Figure 10.1, the example track is the fourth out from the spindle. This is the top track of cylinder 3, track 3.

Each platter has its own set of tracks, each beginning with track 0. During the FORMAT process, all the tracks of a given number (for example, cylinder 1) are formatted at once, and the screen shows you which cylinder is being worked on. Moving down from (read/write) head 0, the next platter would have head 1, then head 2, and so on. Head 2 would be the third set of read/write heads down, working on the third platter of the hard disk.

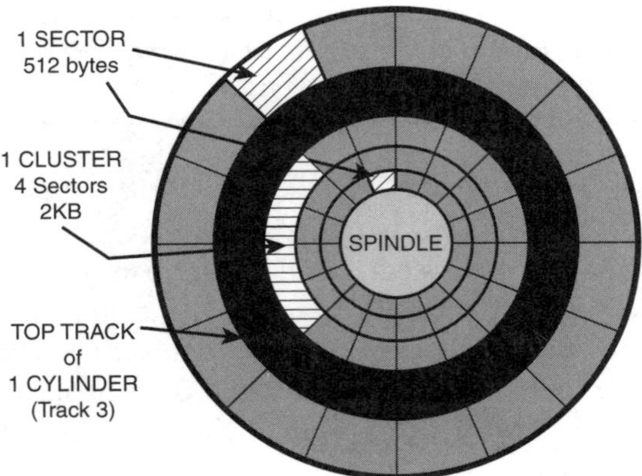

Figure 10.1 The basic division of a hard drive into sectors, clusters, and tracks.

If a hard drive is manufactured to have read/write heads on both the top and bottom sides, then head 0 would be the top read/write heads on platter 0, head 1 would be the bottom read/write heads on platter 0, head 2 would be the top read/write heads on platter 1, and so on.

Logical Formatting: Clusters

The next step in the process is to prepare the disk for an operating system of some kind. In this case, we'll discuss and work with DOS. Windows uses the same set of basic principles.

A logical (as opposed to a physical [low-level]) formatting process creates a FAT (discussed shortly) and defines the *minimum* number of sectors a cluster can use to store data on that drive volume. If any group of sectors has been allocated (reserved and set aside) for use by file data, that group is called a *file allocation unit*. If there is actual data stored in file allocation units, we call that group of sectors a *cluster*. Depending on how a disk is formatted, clusters can contain a varying number of sectors.

Today, when you buy a computer from a store, the low-level formatting has already been done by the original equipment manufacturer (OEM). Typically, the logical formatting has also been done by the dealer. Most dealers format a hard disk as one logical drive—a single partition. The larger the partition, the larger the clusters needed to fill up that space. Large clusters mean wasted space when a small 2,000-byte file takes up 1 cluster composed of 16 sectors (8,192 bytes).

The file allocation table (FAT) keeps track of the clusters. Always remember that clusters consist of a specific number of sectors, and that clusters can contain more sectors as the volume grows larger. A volume is the formal name for a logical drive. In the "FDISK" section, we discuss the absolute difference between a volume and a disk.

The formatting process determines how many sectors will be inside each cluster, depending on the size of the logical drive (volume), not the physical disk.

Let's review the differences between tracks, sectors and clusters. Clusters are made out of sectors, and sectors are half-kilobyte pieces of tracks as follows:

- Tracks are divided into sectors of 512 bytes.
- Sectors are combined into clusters, starting at 2KB (2,048 bytes), or 4 sectors.
- Clusters must fill the entire volume from beginning to end.
- The size of the volume (logical drive) dictates the size of the clusters. Clusters will grow larger in order to fill the entire logical drive.
- The largest cluster DOS can make is 32KB, making 2GB the largest logical drive that DOS can address with FAT16. (Larger disks must be partitioned.)
- The maximum number of FAT16 (DOS) clusters is 65,525.

Sectors are the basic storage unit on tracks; they are not clusters. Sectors can hold 512 bytes (not kilobytes) of information. Tracks are divided into sectors, and drives are divided into clusters.

File Allocation Table (FAT)

The formatting process creates a root directory (folder) that must be at a specific physical location on a logical drive. The FAT is designed for a maximum number of entries (file names) in that root directory, which limits the maximum number of clusters (not sectors) in the root directory. The directory allocation table (DAT), along with the FAT, keeps track of the directory structure. DOS uses a particular format for making directories on a disk.

The file allocation table is literally a table with bits of information about files. The first piece of data is the name (address) of the cluster that holds the beginning 2KB of a file—about one page of typing.

The FAT is absolutely critical to the maintenance of all the data on a given disk. Without an allocation table, there's no way to know where anything is on that disk. For this reason, DOS maintains two copies of the FAT in case one of the copies becomes corrupted. Some third-party software tools can recover a disk through the use of the second copy of the FAT. However, this assumes that the second copy isn't corrupted, which usually is not the case.

Time and wear and tear eventually affect the magnetic layers used to store data on disks. Even if no outside interference (e.g., speaker magnets or frigid cold) wipes out data, physical properties of magnetism can cause a loss of data. When this happens and the drive heads can't read or write data to the sector, the DOS **FORMAT** command marks the sector as bad and, from that point, as unavailable. If the boot sector goes bad, the disk is no longer usable. If the FAT becomes corrupted, most often it's because the entire area where both copies of the FAT are stored has failed.

The 16-bit FAT (FAT16) addressing structure has a maximum of 65,525 clusters, each limited to a maximum size of 32KB. Therefore, the largest drive using a FAT16 partitioning and formatting scheme is 2GB. LBA (discussed in its own section later in this chapter) provided a way to work with newer BIOS to support up to 8GB of physical disk space. With a combination of FAT16 partitioning, formatting, and Windows 9x, the largest physical disk can be greater than 8GB, but the largest logical drive is still limited to 2GB.

FAT32 Clusters

Clusters are fixed at a minimum of 2KB (four 512-byte sectors), meaning that even a 3-byte file would take up a 2,048 bytes worth of space on a small logical drive. As the size of the volume grows larger, the formatting process increases the size of the clusters. FAT16 tries to fill up a volume with clusters, meaning that on a 2GB disk, each cluster will have expanded to 32KB in size. That same 3-byte file would now take up 32,768 bytes of storage space. When a small file on a large disk uses up a whole cluster, the unused portion is called *slack space*. It isn't at all unusual for a large volume with many small files to have many megabytes of slack space.

FAT32 uses a different cluster size adjustment, and can work with a volume 2TB (terabytes) in size. The same 32KB cluster created by FAT16 uses only 4KB of space on a 2GB volume formatted with FAT32. FAT32 makes more efficient use of a disk by cutting down on slack space. Additionally, the smaller cluster size on large hard drives shortens the amount of time needed by the read/write heads (seek time) to find a file.

SCANDISK and CHKDSK (Check Disk)

From the beginning (DOS 1.0), there had to be a way to reconcile the FAT with what was actually on the disk. One of the external programs that came with DOS was the program CHKDSK.EXE (Check Disk) that checked the disk for discrepancies between the allocation table and file clusters.

CHKDSK looked at the FAT for a beginning and ending cluster address for a file. Then DOS went to that address on the disk (the cylinder, track, and sector) and checked to see whether any readable information was in the cluster. DOS didn't read the file for news about how Granny was doing in Oshkosh; rather, it used the drive's read-write heads to copy the information into RAM and write it back again. It then checked the directory listing and name against the records in the FAT. If all went well, CHKDSK went on to the next entry in the FAT and did it all over again. CHKDSK has been completely replaced by SCANDISK (SCANDISK.EXE).

CHKDSK is an obsolete program and can wreak total havoc on a Windows 9x computer. Never run this program! Always use SCANDISK or a proven third-party utility.

Having said the above, Check Disk (a revised version) makes its reappearance as one of the available commands under the Windows 2000 and Windows XP Recovery Console.

If a cluster address in the FAT does not match the data on the disk, SCANDISK returns a message to the user that there are lost clusters or cross-linked files. Lost clusters are areas of the disk that have been allocated to a specific file when the file itself wasn't closed correctly (maybe because of a crash or a lockup). Cross-linked files are scarier. Cross-linking means that, according to the FAT, two files occupy the same space somewhere in a group of clusters. Possibly, either the FAT or the DAT has been corrupted. This can sometimes happen when the power goes out or is turned off while the computer is running an application.

CHKDSK was the only way (without third-party utilities) to validate the FAT and the DAT prior to DOS 6.0 when ScanDisk was introduced. One of the first utilities provided by Symantec's Norton Utilities was Disk Doctor, which allowed a user to check a disk for sectors that were either bad or becoming bad. If bad sectors were found, Disk Doctor would attempt to move any data within them and mark the sectors as bad. CHKDSK does not check for bad sectors in which the physical disk is damaged or unusable.

ScanDisk finally allowed a way for DOS owners to attempt to fix cross-linking, lost clusters, and bad sectors. You don't have to reformat a hard drive just to set aside bad sectors anymore. ScanDisk can't be used on a network drive, but it can be used under Windows. We will discuss DEFRAG (defragmenting) in the following section.

ScanDisk is a way to scan a disk for problems and then work toward repairing some of those problems. DEFRAG is a way to speed up disk access by combining parts of files from all over a disk into organized, continuous blocks of clusters.

DEFRAG.EXE

If you write a two-page letter and save it as NAME1.DOC, the file system notes the name of the file and puts the two pages onto the hard drive in a set of clusters. Suppose that you then write another two-page letter and save it as NAME2.DOC. Again, the file system keeps track of the name and the clusters containing the second file. How does the file system know which clusters have which data in them?

Keep the picture of your two letters in mind. Suppose that you decide to make some additions to the first letter. You open your application (say, a word processor) and load NAME1.DOC into memory. You add another two pages of text and then re-save the letter. It still has the same name, but now you have two additional pages of data.

If the file system tries to store the added two new pages next to the original two pages, there isn't any room. Your second file, NAME2.DOC, has taken the neighboring set of clusters. Therefore, the file system skips the two pages of NAME2.DOC and puts the additional pages of NAME1.DOC after the end of NAME2.DOC. If you look at Figure 10.2, you can see how your files can eventually end up in pieces and scattered all over the hard drive. When many files are scattered over a drive, we say the drive is fragmented and is in need of defragmenting, or "defragging."

DEFRAG.EXE was added to DOS 6.0 as a way to put all the parts of files into one continuous group of clusters. This is a typical maintenance chore and should be done on a regular basis. Prior to DOS 6.x, the only way to defragment a file was to use a third-party software utility tool. Because DOS originally included almost no utilities, an entire industry of utility companies sprang up around this void. The Norton utility was called *Speed Disk*.

The revenues from the utilities eventually reached high enough numbers that, for DOS 5.0, Microsoft contracted with some of the largest companies to add scaled-down versions of a few of its utilities into DOS itself. For example, MEMMAKER.EXE was a subset of Helix Corporation's memory manager. SCANDISK and DEFRAG are other examples of utilities. Before DOS 6.0, most people either didn't know that you should defragment your disk periodically, or they used the Norton SPEEDISK.EXE utility.

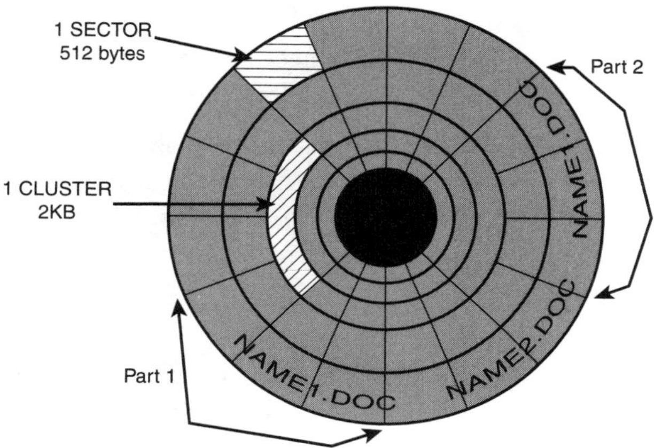

Figure 10.2 Stylized disk showing a file splitting up another file.

The nice thing about third-party utilities is that they're not tied to the operating system's command interpreter. DEFRAG.EXE could run only if it was the correct version, based on a matching version of COMMAND.COM. Even copying DEFRAG.EXE from Windows 95 OS/R-A to OS/R-B wouldn't work. Norton Utilities' SPEEDISK could be run on any system, regardless of what version of COMMAND.COM was installed.

The DOS version of DEFRAG.EXE is run from the command line. DOS 7.0 (Windows 95) includes DEFRAG.EXE in the C:\WINDOWS subdirectory, but could also run it from within a window. Following Windows 95, DEFRAG became a graphics-only application, meaning it could be run only in a window, not from the command line. In each ensuing discussion of specific operating systems, we'll focus on the different maintenance utilities that were added to help troubleshoot a problem.

Defragmenting a disk means that parts of files are brought together into contiguous sectors. ScanDisk (SCANDISK.EXE) is used to check the validity of the FAT and the integrity of the sectors. DEFRAG uses the valid FAT to find all the parts of a file and bring them together.

The DEFRAG process is automatic and requires a perfect FAT and a perfect disk. If, at the beginning of the process, DEFRAG finds an error in the FAT, the program halts, and the user is given a message to run ScanDisk.

File Names

Information can't be saved without a name. Certain file-naming conventions were developed in the DOS world, and computer people are often judged on the elegance of their procedures. You can create an archive file with something like WinZip or PKZip and call it *ARCHIVE.698* (instead of ARCHIVE.ZIP). However, if another technician needs to conduct research into which type of file it is, you'll probably be considered ignorant (at best).

This system has carried forward to the extent that many applications routinely assign a specific extension to their data files. You can override the process if you know how, but most people haven't learned how. Even in the Explorer, the default installation is to hide the "type" extensions, and you must choose a specific option to unhide file types.

Some file names are absolute in their names—for instance, AUTOEXEC.BAT, CONFIG.SYS, SYSTEM.DAT, and USER.DAT. If you spell these in any way other than the required way, they won't work in the expected manner. The best policy is to learn the common extensions and stick with the program. Computers are hard enough to deal with, and you don't need to spend extra time decoding someone else's surrealistic file-naming ideas.

Nondisplayed Periods

One confusing aspect of DOS is that when a DIR listing of files in a directory is sent to the screen or printed, no periods appear. It looks like the file names are split into one to eight characters, a big empty space, and then one to three characters, or the <DIR> notation. You can see the periods in Windows Explorer if a folder has an extension, but not in an MS DOS window.

Although the screen or printer doesn't print the periods in the file names, DOS needs those periods. If you try to find a file name without using the period, you will receive a "File not found" response.

Characters Allowed in DOS File Names

We've spoken about the 8.3 file name format. Which characters, then, can you use for file names? These characters are found in the ASCII character set. The original set was 126 characters until IBM added another 126 characters (high-bit) for the extended ASCII character set. DOS allows any character between ASCII decimal number 33 and 255.

Windows 95 (borrowing a Macintosh and networking idea) wanted to overcome the limits of DOS characters, particularly the space character. Long File Names can be seen in any 32-bit version of Windows, but DOS (7.x) keeps track of the files through the use of a tilde (~) and consecutive numbers to truncate the long file name into its first eight characters (i.e., prior to the extension). We'll discuss how this happens when we describe the VFAT in Chapter 12. The allowed characters in DOS are:

- The letters A through Z
- The numbers 0 through 9
- ', ~, ", !, @, #, $, %, ^, &, (,), -, _, {, }
- High-bit characters from 127 through 255

The lower the scan code number of a character, the higher the file name will be on a directory listing sorted by name. This is confusing to some people who expect a list sorted by name to have all names beginning with "A" at the top and all names beginning with "Z" at the bottom. Because 1 is a lower number than 2, all files beginning with 1 will move to the top of a directory listing. For example, 11NOV98.DOC will appear directly below 1JAN98.DOC, and 2FEB98.DOC will be third.

To force a file name to the top of a directory listing, begin the name with something like !, @, or # because these have very low scan codes.

By convention, temporary deletable files often start with a tilde (~), an underscore (_), a percent sign (%), a dollar sign ($), or an ampersand (&). Table 10.1 shows common file name extensions in DOS.

The use of the tilde (~) is a configuration option in the Windows 9x setup, and can also be changed by modifying the Registry.

Table 10.1 Common DOS file name extensions.

Extension	Type of File
.COM	64KB compiled command file
.EXE	Large, compiled executable file
.BAT	ASCII plain-text batch file

Table 10.1 Common DOS file name extensions *(continued)*

Extension	Type of File
.SYS	System driver software/instruction file
.GRP	Windows program group file
.BAK, .OLD	Backup file
.TMP	Temporary file (usually deletable)
.INI	Initialization file (DOS and Windows)
.DLL	Windows Dynamic Link Library
.INF	Windows 9x autoscript setup program
.VXD	Windows and DOS 7.x virtual device driver file
.DRV	Driver software file
.TXT	Plain ASCII file created by text editor
.HLP	Windows HELP hypertext file
.DOC	Document file (full character sets, formatting)
.WRI	Windows 3.x MS Write file
.HTM	Internet HTML (Hypertext Markup Language)
.BMP	Windows bitmap graphics file
.WMF	Windows metafile graphics file
.PCX	MS Paint raster image
.ICO	Windows icon file
.LNK	Windows Shortcut file
.TTF	TrueType font file
.OVL	Program overlay file
.BAS	BASIC program file
.SCR	Script file or screen-saver file
.DAT	Data file
.ZIP	Archive file
.EX_, .CO_	Microsoft expand/extract archive
.DIZ	Internet shareware description text
.WAV	Waveform sound file
.MID	MIDI sound file
.CB, .CAB	Windows 9x cabinet file

Summary—Disk Management

We've covered a variety of complex topics in this segment. Formatting a drive and assigning it a logical drive letter is different from partitioning a disk and assigning it a volume name. Be sure that you understand the following concepts before moving on to the next chapters:

- Partitions and drives, with a particular emphasis on the difference between primary and extended partitions.
- The number of logical drives that may be assigned to any system of disks. A computer may have more than one physical hard drive and multiple operating systems. Each operating system can only understand a maximum number of drive letters—26.
- The difference between FDISK (partitioning) and FORMAT (logical drive letter assignment)
- SYS.COM, the specialized utility used to replace system files on a damaged boot disk
- File systems and the FAT, including the difference between FAT16 and FAT32 (discussed further in Chapter 12) and file allocation units
- Naming conventions used in DOS, even with Windows 2000 and XP, and how DOS file names allow only certain characters as opposed to Long File Names
- Common file extensions and the way extensions are used as file associations in Windows Explorer
- Directories and subdirectories, folders and subfolders, and navigating the search path
- Sectors, clusters, tracks, and cylinders and how clusters may vary in size, depending upon the size of the volume
- Fragmented disks and how to use DEFRAG to bring files into contiguous clusters; Scan Disk and repairing a hard drive

Operating Systems vs. Shells

For many years, people were marketing menu programs and shells for the text-based DOS, hoping to make using computers one thing (user interface) and configuring them another. A computer menu is a list of options (choices) written to the screen. The user selects one of the options and presses keys or clicks a mouse button to pick one of the options. Menu choices are essentially the same as program items in 16-bit Windows and shortcuts in 32-bit Windows.

Even today, when you run CMD.EXE or choose Start|Run and enter "COMMAND.COM", you are creating a DOS shell. It appears to you as a DOS or text-based window, but it is, in fact, a small shell.

In time, menu programs became more sophisticated. Some companies included security features in their menu programs where a user could access the command processor only through the menu. By controlling how the menu program passed commands to the command processor (the file's properties), menu programs began to become more and more like shells.

File Properties

These days, the defining characteristics of a menu choice are often included in what we call *properties*. Borland's Quattro Pro spreadsheet introduced the idea of using the mouse's right button to call up a menu for changing the properties of whatever the mouse was pointing to. The idea quickly caught on, and now most Windows-based applications access a properties menu from the right mouse button.

On the main Program Manager menu in 16-bit Windows, File | Properties lists the essential properties of a program. 32-bit Windows incorporates the right-click of the mouse (alternative mouse click) to create a context-sensitive properties menu, meaning that the properties will change depending upon the context of what the mouse is pointing to.

Shells

A shell is where the command processor (COMMAND.COM) loads another instance of itself, resulting in two or more separate command processors being "resident" in RAM. Both Windows File Manager and the Windows 9x Explorer are programs that pass a user's intentions to the underlying DOS command processor. They place a layer between the user's actions and the underlying operating system. This layer is what we mean by the term *shell*.

In a DOS session, the resident part of COMMAND.COM sitting in conventional memory, intercepts keystrokes from the keyboard and then passes them on to the CPU. Strictly speaking, COMMAND.COM is creating a shell around the operating environment where any instruction that enters the environment is tracked by COMMAND.COM before the instruction can move out of the environment.

Another way to think of a shell is that it acts like an executive secretary screening calls to the boss. Anyone (i.e., the program instruction) who wants to contact the executive must first go through the secretary. The secretary has a list of high-priority people who get passed through immediately. Other people are directed to someone else, depending on their business. Network operating systems often use a shell that works alongside the COMMAND.COM interpreter. Both shells look at incoming program instructions to see which operating system should take the call.

A CONFIG.SYS file uses an optional directive (statement) called **SHELL=** to tell COMMAND.COM to increase the size of the environment space in memory. **SHELL=C:\COMMAND.COM /E:1024 /P** increases the environment to 1,024 bytes and keeps it permanent (the P). The **SHELL=** directive also sets an environment variable that tells the operating system where to find its command processor. In this case, DOS always knows that COMMAND.COM is in the root directory of Drive C:.

The memory environment is still a configuration option for 16-bit DOS sessions under Windows 9x. To see this, locate the DOSPRMPT.PIF shortcut to COMMAND.COM and examine the properties (right-click). On the Memory tab, each type of memory can be configured, along with the environment size. Types of memory are discussed in Chapter 11.

The word *shell*, like many words in the language of computers and operating systems, has been modified to include menus. Remember that when someone talks about making a computer more "user friendly," this can be done by either changing the way an operating system works, or by changing the words used to describe the computer. It's a lot cheaper to change a word than it is to change a basic operating system installed on hundreds of millions of computers.

To create a transparent (unnoticed) interface with the computer, Microsoft introduced a Windows applet called *File Manager* (WINFILE.EXE) as a replacement for the **DIR**, **COPY**, **MOVE**, **RENAME** (**REN**), **DELETE** (**DEL**), **MD**, **CD**, and **RD** commands. An applet is a self-contained program application that works from within an overseeing parent application. For instance, in the overall "application" of your kitchen, a can opener would be analogous to an applet. In time, the distinction between an application and an applet has become blurred.

The Windows 3.x File Manager is an applet under the Program Manager (PROGMAN.EXE) domain, its companion interface program. PROGMAN.EXE runs first and then offers the opportunity to run the File Manager interface from within it.

Windows Explorer (EXPLORER.EXE) creates the Windows 9x Desktop interface (folder) and runs constantly during a Windows session. On the other hand, File Manager must be explicitly run and closed from within PROGMAN.EXE. To see this, press Ctrl+Alt+Delete in a Windows session from a plain desktop. Task Manager (TASKMAN.EXE) runs, and Windows Explorer is one of the tasks. Both 16-bit and 32-bit Windows have the Task Manager utility program.

SYSTEM.INI and SHELL=

The **SHELL=** line in the SYSTEM.INI file defines the interface program that Windows presents to the user at startup. In Windows 3.x, the two shells are Program Manager and File Manager. By default, the line reads **SHELL=PROGMAN.EXE**, which loads Program Manager as the user interface for Windows 3.x.

By editing the SYSTEM.INI file and changing the line to **SHELL= WINFILE.EXE**, Windows 3.x starts with File Manager as the primary interface. However, File Manager doesn't include a desktop area for creating program groups and icons. The Microsoft Web site still offers MSDOS.EXE (the old MS-DOS Executive from Windows 2.x) for use as a shell interface.

Windows 95 first extended the File Manager's capabilities to include the desktop, icons, and program groups (folders). File Manger became EXPLORER.EXE.

SHELL=

Ordinarily, 256 bytes is enough to handle the few configuration settings DOS uses during a session. In some cases, a larger environment is used for tweaking the speed of the machine (enhancing performance by experimental settings changes). The DOS environment is technically called the DOS *shell*. The line that changes the environment size is:

```
SHELL=C:\COMMAND.COM /P /E:1024
```

The **SHELL=** environment variable can be set only from within an optional CONFIG.SYS file or from the Properties menu of a .PIF file (Program Information File) used to run a Real Mode DOS session under Windows. In this case, the shell is set to the COMMAND.COM interpreter. The **/P** switch loads COMMAND.COM and keeps it permanent. The **/E:** switch tells COMMAND.COM to change the environment, and 1,024 is the value for the number of bytes. The environment has been increased from the default of 256 bytes to 1,024 bytes.

Batch Files

The underlying programming and operations of a menu control how an option is executed. Some menus include the ability to combine the selection and key-press process into a single event. Simple menus can be created by using batch files. Menus reduce the number of keystrokes necessary to run a program and store complicated configurations used in running certain programs.

A batch file is a file containing a list of commands, one on each line of the file. Naming the file with the .BAT extension tells DOS that this file is an executable program file. DOS then reads each line of the file as though a user were entering that line. DOS menus use file names such as 1.BAT, 2.BAT, A.BAT, B.BAT, WP.BAT, and LOTUS.BAT, and the files are usually saved to a subdirectory in the search path. When the user turns on the computer, the last command in the AUTOEXEC.BAT file might call, for example, MENU.BAT, which draws a menu on the screen.

For the exam, remember that when statements are put into a text file that can be interpreted by COMMAND.COM (a command processor), we refer to that file as a batch file. AUTOEXEC.BAT is a batch file. CONFIG.SYS is a configuration file. Both files can also be called *startup command files.*

By storing complex configuration switches, batch files are used to automate the process of running a program. Some programs require configuration switches to be entered at a command line. Batch files allow the computer to literally type commands to itself in exactly the same way a human being uses the command interface. Other programs can be configured only from within a CONFIG.SYS file.

AUTOEXEC.BAT

If you ever look inside COMMAND.COM, you'll find a reference to a file with a specific name: AUTOEXEC.BAT. This is a batch file and is just like any other batch file that can be created using a text editor. If the file has this name, spelled this way, and it resides in the root directory, DOS processes any instructions in this file as the final step in the boot process. Like CONFIG.SYS, AUTOEXEC.BAT is not required to boot the computer. If

AUOTEXEC.BAT does exist, COMMAND.COM processes it as the last step in the boot process.

Observe the way a programming sequence in the command processor looks for a specific file in a specific location. This example of "hard coding" a set of events will show up again during the boot process, and later with Windows NT and Windows 2000.

The AUTOEXEC.BAT file is used to run commands that you want to have processed every time you start the computer. Typically, you want to set a **PATH** each time you use the computer to tell DOS and Windows to use the TEMP and TMP directories for various overflow files.

AUTOEXEC.BAT files may still be necessary on a Windows 9x or even NT machine. They're particularly useful in configuring 16-bit device drivers that require a CONFIG.SYS file. These configuration switches might be for nonPnP-compliant 16-bit devices, such as CD-ROM drives and sound cards. The character strings following a command name can be exceptionally complicated and arcane. A batch file is a good way to store this kind of complexity within a file with a simple one-word name to enter.

AUTOEXEC.BAT files were routinely used to configure networking connections, search paths, and sound cards in DOS and Windows 3.x machines. They are still useful for various configuration settings that you want to carry over into Windows. An example would be where the SUBST command can create a drive icon in the Windows Explorer for a substituted drive.

After the last command line in the AUTOEXEC.BAT file has been processed, control returns to COMMAND.COM, and the computer is ready to begin a working session. If an application's startup program file is the last command, the last thing AUTOEXEC.BAT does is start the application, placing the user at whatever startup location that application normally provides.

A Sample Batch File

A batch file is a plain-text file composed of command lines and saved with the .BAT extension. Using DOS's Edit or the Windows Notepad, you can create a new file with the following lines:

```
@ECHO OFF
DIR C:\ /P
ECHO This is a test line
PAUSE
REM I don't want this line to show
DIR C:\ /W
```

When you are finished entering these lines, pressing Enter at the end of each line, save it as some file name with the .BAT extension—for example, C:\TRYTHIS.BAT. Remember that it *must* be plain ASCII text. Open a DOS window by choosing Start | Run and typing "COMMAND" as the program you want to run.

When you type "C:\TRYTHIS" and press Enter, this batch file gives a directory listing of the root directory on Drive C:, pausing every 23 lines for a keypress (**DIR C:\ /p**). When the DIR is finished, it displays the on-screen message "This is a test line".

The **ECHO** command is a batch file command that tells DOS to type to the screen whatever follows **ECHO** and a space. The @ command (@ ECHO) tells DOS to turn off any text typed to the screen unless the ECHO command is used at the start of a particular line. Output results of a command are not affected by the ECHO or REM commands.

The **PAUSE** command (internal to COMMAND.COM) pauses the process and places the generic message "Press any key to continue…" at the next line below the test-line row. When you press a key, the batch file skips the following line:

```
REM I don't want this line to show.
```

REM (short for *remark*) is an internal DOS batch file command that must begin in the first column of a new line. **REM**, followed by a space, causes COMMAND.COM to bypass the line and move processing to the next line.

REM is often used to *remark out* a line in the AUTOEXEC.BAT or CONFIG.SYS file in a test situation where you might want to keep the commands in the line, but bypass them for a number of sessions until you've figured out some particular problem. Then you can delete the REM from the file.

Windows allows this type of "commenting out" in the WIN.INI and SYSTEM.INI files by using a semicolon (;) followed by a space in the first column of the line. **REM** won't work in a Windows INI file, and a semicolon won't work in a DOS batch file.

Because the line following the **PAUSE** command has been "commented out" and won't be processed, you won't see "I don't want this line to show" on the screen. The next thing you *will* see is another DIR listing of the root directory, but this time in wide format and without the pause (**DIR C:\ /w**). When the DIR is finished listing, the batch file turns control back over to COMMAND.COM and returns the DOS prompt.

This is exactly how the AUTOEXEC.BAT file works, and you can edit the file with DOS's Edit, the Windows Notepad, WordPad, or any other word processor that creates .TXT files. Be sure that you save the file in plain ASCII, because it's not unusual for someone to edit the CONFIG.SYS file or AUTOEXEC.BAT file with Microsoft Word and then save it as a .DOC file, which contains all kinds of extended, non-ASCII characters. When this happens, the computer either throws up and dies when it hits the non-ASCII file, or bypasses the file completely. If the AUTOEXEC.BAT file contains network login commands, the user can end up mystified as to why he or she can't log on to the network.

Always make a backup copy of the latest working CONFIG.SYS and AUTOEXEC.BAT files before editing them so that you have a current, uncorrupted version in case of emergencies.

Practice Questions

Question 1

Which files does MS-DOS require to be present on a disk in order for it to boot? [Choose all that apply]

- ❑ a. IBMBIO.COM
- ❑ b. IO.SYS
- ❑ c. COMMAND.COM
- ❑ d. DOS.SYS

Answers b and c are correct. MS-DOS requires IO.SYS and MSDOS.SYS as the two basic system files, with COMMAND.COM being the fundamental command interpreter. Answer a is incorrect because IBMBIO.COM was a system file from IBM's version of DOS. Answer d is incorrect because DOS does not use a file called DOS.SYS.

Question 2

Files with which of the following extensions can be executed from the DOS command prompt? [Check all that apply]

- ❑ a. .TXT
- ❑ b. .EXE
- ❑ c. .COM
- ❑ d. .BAT

Answers b, c, and d are correct. Executable (.EXE), command (.COM), and batch (.BAT) files can be executed from the command prompt. Answer a is incorrect because text (.TXT) files contain text data and must be accessed by another program application.

Question 3

The following **DIR** command would find all files that begin with "A" and are device drivers:

- ❍ a. DIR *A.SYS
- ❍ b. DIR A?????.SYS
- ❍ c. DIR A.*
- ❍ d. DIR A*.SYS

Answer d is correct. The asterisk (*) wild card overrides anything to the right of the symbol in either the main file name or the extension. Answer a is incorrect because it would find all files with a .SYS extension, regardless of what letter they started with. Answer b is incorrect because it would find only files that begin with A and contain six characters in their main file names. There may be some files with fewer or more characters than six. Answer c is incorrect because it would find any file beginning with "A" regardless of what extension it had (such as .EXE or .DOC).

Question 4

DEFRAG.EXE is used to scan a disk for bad sectors, mark them as unusable, and bring all files into contiguous sequence.

- ❍ a. True
- ❍ b. False

Answer b, false, is correct. Defragmenting a disk brings files into contiguous blocks, thereby improving the efficiency of the system. SCANDISK.EXE is used to check for disk-level problems, such as bad sectors, cross-linked files, or corrupted FAT listings.

Question 5

A hard drive can have up to _______ logical drives, and an extended partition can have up to _______ logical drives.

- ❍ a. 24, 23
- ❍ b. 26, 24
- ❍ c. 1, 26
- ❍ d. 23, 1

Answer a is correct. Note the reference to a hard drive, meaning a fixed disk not including a floppy drive. A: and B: are reserved drive names for floppy disk mechanisms. A single fixed disk can take all the remaining letters of the alphabet (24). An Extended partition can be created only after a Primary partition has been created, and the Primary partition takes up one letter. If the Primary partition uses the C: designation, that leaves 23 letters in the alphabet remaining. Answer b is incorrect because the floppy disks take two letters. Answer c is incorrect because it's possible for a fixed disk to have many more than just one logical drive. Answer d is incorrect because in addition to any logical drives contained within an extended partition, a Primary partition is considered a logical drive.

Question 6

DOS system files must be located in the _______ partition, and that partition must be set to _______ for the computer to start DOS.

- ❍ a. first, Primary
- ❍ b. Primary, Active
- ❍ c. current, initialize
- ❍ d. Extended, DOS

Answer b is correct. The DOS system files must reside in a Primary partition, and that partition must be made Active. Answer a is incorrect because the Primary partition does not have to be the first partition on the disk. Answer c is incorrect because, until the system boots up, there is no "current" or default partition or drive. Answer d is incorrect because DOS cannot be booted from an extended partition.

Question 7

A sector is located on a _______ and contains _______ bytes of information:

- ❍ a. cluster, 512
- ❍ b. track, 512
- ❍ c. platter, 16
- ❍ d. track, 16

Answer b is correct. A cylinder is formatted by a manufacturer to contain tracks and sectors. Each cylinder is the vertical stack of tracks at the same distance from the spindle motor. Tracks are divided into sectors of 512 bytes. Answer a is incorrect because a cluster is composed of some number of sectors, defined during the formatting process. Answer c is incorrect because, although a track is on a platter, it does not contain 16 bytes of information. Answer d is incorrect because a sector contains 512 bytes of information, not 16 bytes.

Need to Know More?

DOS books are getting harder to find, and they all cover this operating system in far more depth than required by the A+ exam. However, if you really want to get into it, here are three in particular that we like:

http://www3.sympatico.ca/rhwatson/dos7/commandintro.html
Webmaster: Bob Watson, 2001
A comprehensive listing of all the commands and utilities found in DOS 7.x (Windows 95, 98, 98SE), and links to additional DOS-related sites. Most of the commands are the same in Window Me, but this page has not tested them.

Gookin, Dan. *Batch Files and Beyond: Your Path to PC Power*. Blue Ridge Summit, PA: Windcrest, 1993. ISBN: 0830643850.

Minasi, Mark. *Inside DOS 6.2*. Upper Saddle River, NJ: Prentice Hall, 1993. ISBN 1-56205-289-6.

Norton, Peter. *Peter Norton's Complete Guide to DOS 6.22*. Indianapolis, IN: Sams Publishing, 1994. ISBN 0-67230-614-X.

Booting, Windows 3.11, and Memory

Terms you'll need to understand:

- ✓ Bootable disk
- ✓ Virtual, emulate, and simulate
- ✓ WIN.COM
- ✓ Program information files (.PIF)
- ✓ SYSTEM.INI and WIN.INI
- ✓ Conventional memory and extended memory
- ✓ Swap files
- ✓ HIMEM.SYS and EMM386.EXE
- ✓ System resources

Concepts you'll need to master:

- ✓ Booting and system files
- ✓ CONFIG.SYS
- ✓ Starting 16-bit Windows
- ✓ Virtual Real Mode and the virtual machine (VM)
- ✓ Initialization (.INI) files
- ✓ Virtual memory
- ✓ Virtual device drivers (VxD)
- ✓ Windows 3.x global heap

In Chapter 10 we spoke about how DOS was the underlying Windows operating system up until Windows versions 2000 and XP. We discussed the fact that DOS and the Windows 3.x shell were part of a migration path towards a 32-bit operating system. Everything Microsoft has been doing over the past decade can be linked to the problems of backward compatibility with DOS. We also understand that some readers may be encountering both DOS and 16-bit Windows for the first time.

Windows 95 brought a more subtle change to the computer industry than a new interface and 32-bit applications. For the first time, computers began to take on individually specific configurations. It became much more difficult for support personnel to speak with an end user, knowing most of the settings on that user's machine. Tech support began to fall back on reformatting or reinstalling a machine, rather than being able to fix a problem machine. In a similar fashion, it's almost impossible to describe a universal boot sequence for modern-day computers. For this reason, we're going to take the time to discuss the original boot-up process in detail, in the hopes that you'll better be able to see how to diagnose Windows startup problems—an important part of the A+ exam.

We'll track the original boot process as it follows the power-on self-test (POST). We'll also follow the startup process for Windows 3.11 as it loads itself, creates a virtual DOS machine, and takes over some of the underlying DOS chores. Remember that Windows 95 and Windows 98 were modifications of Windows 3.11, where code was added on an as-needed basis, in order to move the customer base over to a true, 32-bit operating system (Windows NT).

Booting and System Files

Everything about starting a PC revolves around something called the *Master Boot Record* and the process of joining the motherboard BIOS to the operating system. DOS works with the IO.SYS file and an optional CONFIG.SYS file before passing control to MSDOS.SYS, the third of the three critical system files (COMMAND.COM and IO.SYS being the other two). We've tried to focus your attention on important points by using Exam Alerts, but you should also work with a computer and pay attention to everything that goes on when you turn on the power.

When the PC's power switch is turned on, the POST routine in a ROM BIOS chip initializes the system and runs a test of all the components built in to the computer. Prior to Plug-and-Play, you had to physically turn off the computer in order to plug in a new peripheral. Even with the Windows

Device Manager, you'll often be required to shut down and restart Windows. Remember that hot swapping means that you can add or remove a device while the machine is running. However, installing a device for the first time still requires an explanation of that device to the operating system.

The POST is run only when power to the CPU is turned off and then turned on again. A system reset (accomplished with the Reset button) or a warm boot (accomplished with Ctrl+Alt+Del) does not always include the POST.

The Three-Fingered Salute

When an irreversible error occurs in memory, the CPU freezes up and the computer won't accept input. Sometimes, the mouse pointer moves around, but clicking won't do anything. Other times, the system won't even recognize keystrokes. In either case, if this happens to you, you're experiencing a computer crash. We've heard that in the business world, problems are considered opportunities. If you keep reminding yourself that a computer crash is really an opportunity, perhaps you'll feel better about it.

In any event, if the computer's display is frozen or locked, but the system accepts keyboard input, the universal key combination of pressing and holding the Ctrl key, then pressing and holding the Alt key, and then pressing and holding the Del key—keeping all three keys pressed simultaneously—generates a restart, or system reset command from ROM BIOS. This three-key combination—a *warm boot*—is abbreviated Ctrl+Alt+Del.

If the computer is so locked up that even the keyboard can't access the system, the only way to restart the computer is either to turn the power off and then back on, or to use the Reset button on the face of the casing. This type of lockup is called a *hard crash*, and it requires a *cold boot* to restart the computer. Until recently, pressing a Reset button would not call a POST routine, even though a cold boot includes the routine. However, modern systems usually do call the POST from the Reset buttons, making no distinction between a system reset and a cold boot.

There are a few of ways of telling whether the machine has just entered a cold boot, or whether it's going through a warm reboot. One way is to watch the monitor during the startup process. A cold boot almost always runs a simple memory diagnostics routine (parity checking), and you'll often see a count of the available memory on the screen. Another way is by seeing the CMOS settings display for a moment, or the notification of which key to press to access the settings. Finally, a POST operation will always access the built-in speaker, generating one of the beep codes discussed later in this chapter.

The cold boot, not a warm boot or reset, calls the POST, although some third-party software utilities can call the cold boot instruction set from ROM BIOS. Windows often generates a cold re-boot during certain installation procedures.

Booting Overview

There's an old saying that relates to pulling yourself up by your own bootstraps. The reference is to bettering your position in life by relying completely on your own talents and capabilities, not waiting for someone else to lend a hand. Because DOS loads itself (sort of by its own bootstraps), the startup process has come to be known as the *boot* process, or *booting up* the computer. It does not have anything to do with the number of people who put their foot through the screen, back when PCs were just entering the market.

Following the test for what's connected, the POST looks to the ROM BIOS on the motherboard and begins a parity-checking program to test the main memory chips. The parity program writes information to each chip and then reads the information and compares it. Sometimes, you can see this parity-checking process take place by the rapidly incrementing numbers at the top of a black startup screen. We discuss parity in Chapter 3.

Each succeeding version of DOS and the BIOS contains *fixes*, or *patches*, for problems. The system moves some of these patches to lower memory, so they won't have to be constantly read from the ROM chip. This is the reserved motherboard BIOS area of memory (how DOS uses memory is discussed in the "Memory" section later in this chapter). Patches routinely overwrite ROM instructions.

Finally, the BIOS looks for the first sector (track 0, sector 0) of a floppy disk in Drive A: for a bootstrap loader built into the operating system. If it finds the bootstrap loader there, it transfers control to the bootstrap loader to load the operating system. Otherwise, depending on the CMOS settings (in newer computers), BIOS looks at the first sector on Drive C:, a SCSI disk, or even a CD-ROM for the bootstrap loader.

ROM BIOS Looks at the Boot Sector

Formatting divides the disk into two specific areas: a system area for DOS system files and a files area for data and programs. The system area is called the *boot sector*. Formatting also sets up two copies of the FAT and creates the root directory. If the disk is to be made bootable (able to start the operating system), COMMAND.COM and the two system files must be in the root directory of that disk. The boot sector is:

- ➤ Always the first sector (sector 0) of the first track (track 0) of the first cylinder (cylinder 0) of the disk
- ➤ 512 bytes long, just like any other sector
- ➤ Contained on all disks, regardless of whether they are bootable

In a moment, we'll discuss the partition loader. The Master Boot *Record* is the first available track and sector of a partition. The boot *sector* is the first sector on the disk.

The FAT (and directory table) comes directly after the boot sector, and takes up different amounts of room, depending on how large the drive is. There are two copies of the FAT, to protect against one being corrupted. A boot-sector virus is where the boot sector of the disk has become infected (corrupted). We discuss viruses in the "Viruses" section of Chapter 14.

The root directory (symbolized by the backslash, as was said in Chapter 10) comes after the FAT. In FAT16 systems, the size of the root directory is 16 kilobytes. The 16KB limit on a FAT16 file system format is what makes the 512-name limit in the root directory. The general file storage area comes after the space set aside for the root directory. Make a note that Virtual FAT (VFAT) uses the FAT as a vector table. Vectors are discussed in the "Memory" section of this chapter.

You may only have 512 file names—including folder names—in the root directory of a FAT16 partition. This limit is set by the 16KB storage area of the File Allocation Table. Regardless of how large a hard drive may be, if a partition is formatted to FAT16 and you try to save a file beyond the limit, DOS will generate an "unable to create file" error message. The files themselves can be as large as you want, but there can be only 512 names for those files.

BASIC Bootstrap Loader

If the disk has been formatted to be a bootable disk running DOS, Windows 3.x, Windows 95, Windows 98, or Windows Me, the system area must contain the DOS system files. These files can be installed during formatting by using the command **FORMAT [drive:] /S**, where **[drive:]** is the bootable drive, or they can be copied over using the external SYS.COM command. In this case, the command is either **SYS A:** or **SYS C:**. (The **SYS** and **FORMAT** commands are discussed in Chapter 10.)

The boot sector also contains a very small program written in BASIC. This program calls a small part of IO.SYS called the *bootstrap loader*, which either copies (loads) the so-called DOS *kernel* (system files) into memory at start-up, or writes the message "Nonsystem disk or disk error. Replace and press any key when ready," to the screen. The MS-DOS system files IO.SYS and MSDOS.SYS must be in a root directory for the DOS kernel to be loaded.

The bootstrap loader work in conjunction with the system files and must be in the boot sector. Simply copying COMMAND.COM and the two hidden system files to a floppy disk won't extract the bootstrap loader. The only way to install the bootstrap loader into the boot sector is with FORMAT.COM or SYS.COM.

The bootstrap loader contains a BIOS parameter block *(BPB)*, which contains information about the physical structure of the disk. If it's a hard disk, the BPB is read only once because the disk won't be removed. If it's a floppy disk, every time the disk is accessed, DOS works with the change-line process (see the "Change Line Jumper" section of Chapter 6) to read the BPB if a new disk is in the drive.

An interesting problem occurred when DOS was loaded from a floppy disk in dual-floppy computers. COMMAND.COM, the command interpreter, would partially load into RAM and would keep track of where the rest of the interpreter was stored (using the **COMSPEC** environment variable). A user would replace the COMMAND.COM disk with a word processor or other application disk and use the computer. At the end of the application session, the user would exit the application and discover an error message: "Missing or bad system files." COMMAND.COM was trying to find itself on the now-removed boot disk.

Partition Loader

If the boot disk is a fixed disk, the boot sector also has a small partition loader program with 16 bytes of information per partition, identifying the operating system, the starting and ending sector of the partition, and which partition is bootable. The partition loader points the process toward the Active Primary partition for that fixed disk. The Active partition is what makes the hard disk bootable.

The BPB and partition loader, taken together, are what is properly called the *Master Boot Record (MBR)*. An undocumented switch for FDISK can sometimes re-create the MBR. In some cases, this may be a way to eliminate a boot-sector virus if a virus protection program isn't available. To use the switch, type "FDISK /MBR" from a DOS screen (not from a DOS window running within the Windows shell or Explorer). You should be extremely careful using the **/MBR** switch with a suspected virus because certain viral infections can cause the total loss of an entire partition and all its data.

The boot sector, sometimes improperly called the *Master Boot Record* (MBR), is found on cylinder 0, head 0, track 0, sector 0. The boot sector is the absolute first sector on a disk. Whether a disk is bootable or not, all disks have a boot sector. The boot sector contains the partition loader.

Technically, the Master Boot Record is the BPB and partition loader. On the exam, though, the Master Boot Record probably refers to the entire boot sector.

Bootstrap Loads IO.SYS

ROM BIOS runs the bootstrap loader, which loads the I/O device management system, IO.SYS and MSDOS.SYS. IO.SYS is the device driver file where you'll find the original DOS devices, such as COM, LPT, and PRN ports, to name a few (discussed in Chapter 9). The DOS kernel manages system-level functions, such as file management and memory management. For the computer to understand itself and for the kernel to be loaded, the two DOS system files must be present in the root directory of the boot disk, either A: or C:, of a formatted drive.

The two DOS system files have their attributes set to Hidden, Read-Only, System. ATTRIB.EXE is the DOS program used to change file attributes: Archive (A), Hidden (H), Read-Only (R), and System (S). In DOS 7.x, Windows 9x uses MSDOS.SYS and IO.SYS differently.

Windows 9x continues to use both MSDOS.SYS and IO.SYS. The files have been modified to perform slightly different operations, but IO.SYS is still the low-level input-output manager.

IO.SYS Checks for CONFIG.SYS

Following the bootstrap loader, IO.SYS loads first. Once again, IO.SYS contains generic device drivers for the basic peripherals used on the computer, such as the monitor, disk drives, keyboard, communications and printer I/O ports. It also contains a module called ***SYSINIT***, which runs through a startup procedure and device driver initialization. **SYSINIT** (inside IO.SYS) calls the CONFIG.SYS file (if it exists) to initialize 16-bit devices.

IO.SYS always loads first, *no matter what.* Whether it's DOS, Windows 3.x, Windows 9x, or Windows Me, IO.SYS is always the first program file that loads following the POST and bootstrap routines. In Windows 9x and ME, IO.SYS contains a hard-coded device driver loading instruction for HIMEM.SYS.

SYSINIT

We just said that IO.SYS takes care of the generic instructions involving hardware devices. After IO.SYS is loaded into memory, the computer begins to wake up a bit and discover what it is. Up until this point, the motherboard and ROM BIOS have, for the most part, controlled the startup process. This is like when you first realize you're starting to wake up in the morning, but haven't opened your eyes yet. All you know is that you're alive—you're not sure yet who you are (depending on what kind of night you had).

Part of the **SYSINIT** module is a set of instructions that looks for a file named \CONFIG.SYS (with the backslash). This name, which is explicitly written into the program, is spelled exactly that way and contains a specific reference to the root directory (\) of the boot disk. The following are true of CONFIG.SYS:

- It is *not* a required file for booting up.
- It contains references to the location and configuration of software programs. These programs contain additional instructions on how to run hardware devices (such programs are called software *device driver files*, or *drivers*).
- It must be a plain ASCII text file created by the user or sometimes by an installation routine.
- It uses reserved command words called directives to configure various system options.

The CONFIG.SYS File

If CONFIG.SYS exists, IO.SYS reads the file line by line. DOS specifies the way in which each line of the CONFIG.SYS file is written. The file is much like a batch file, in that DOS has the capability to examine each line of text as a line of instructions. Because this is a .SYS file and not a program, we use the term *directives* rather than *commands* to refer to the reserved words used in the CONFIG.SYS file. The CONFIG.SYS file is discussed throughout this chapter.

Windows 95 joined a generic CONFIG.SYS file to the IO.SYS. Most of the directives were moved into the updated file, and CONFIG.SYS (theoretically) went away. However, compatibility issues with legacy systems (older systems) forced knowledgeable users to create a configuration file on their own, and to often create a subsequent AUTOEXEC.BAT file.

IO.SYS only began loading device drivers with Windows 95. The initial programming for HIMEM.SYS and other directives can be seen in IO.SYS all the way back in DOS 6.x, but it wasn't activated until Windows 95.

Many people have discovered that CONFIG.SYS may still be necessary, even with Windows Plug-and-Play. CONFIG.SYS is not required by 32-bit Windows; however, the implication for people learning about operating systems is that CONFIG.SYS was required by earlier versions of DOS and 16-bit Windows. This is not true.

Although WIN.INI is a necessary file in the Windows startup process, it does not have to exist prior to starting Windows. If the file does not exist, Windows will create a generic version. CONFIG.SYS, AUTOEXEC.BAT, and WIN.INI are unusual in this respect of being nonessential in an absolute sense.

A computer can be started without a CONFIG.SYS and an AUTOEXEC.BAT file. If there are CD-ROM drivers or sound card drivers in the file, those devices won't operate unless the ROM BIOS recognizes a bootable CD-ROM, but the basic computer will start and run. Read any exam questions about CONFIG.SYS very carefully.

The only files absolutely required to boot a computer into DOS are IO.SYS, MSDOS.SYS, and COMMAND.COM. The CONFIG.SYS file is optional.

The DOS F5 Key

Beginning with DOS 5.0, the boot process could be interrupted by pressing the F5 function key at the point where the message "Starting MS DOS..." appears on-screen. This interruption allows the user to choose from a menu on the monitor's screen. The menu provides choices such as:

- Bypass the CONFIG.SYS and AUTOEXEC.BAT files completely.
- Pause at each line of the CONFIG.SYS and AUTOEXEC.BAT files and choose whether to execute the program line.
- Choose different types of configurations based on specific formatting within the CONFIG.SYS text file.

For those of you who are familiar with the DOS F5 key, the exam room can be a confusing place to try to remember which key does what across all the environments of DOS, Windows 3.x, Windows 9x, and 32-bit Windows. We've created a table of all the startup function keys in Chapter 14.

You should know how to arrive at the Safe Mode text menu in Windows 9x. Pressing F8 between the "Starting Windows 9x..." message and the Windows 9x logo splash screen interrupts the boot process and allows you to choose various options from a Startup menu. (A *splash screen* is jargon for anything that appears on the screen prior to the actual program environment. This can often be a corporate logo, a shareware registration screen, or simply a notification screen that the program is still being prepared to run.)

CONFIG.SYS and MSDOS.SYS

The DOS system files attempt to find each device driver listed in CONFIG.SYS and to execute the instructions in that driver file (in the order in which they're found). Remember that a software driver is a special file that contains instructions from a manufacturer, regarding how to operate its piece of hardware. PnP specifications generally allow for new devices to be folded into the operating system through Internet downloads. However, prior to PnP (and in some cases, even with PnP), device drivers were often required for 16-bit devices.

CONFIG.SYS is examined before the full operating system has loaded. There has been no opportunity to issue a **PATH** statement, so each device must be listed by its full pathname.

In a DOS machine, after all the device drivers have worked out their differences, found one another, and settled down into RAM, control passes to MSDOS.SYS, which loads into a lower area of DOS memory. (We discuss the divisions of memory in the "Memory" section at the end of this chapter.) The MSDOS.SYS file contains all the support functions necessary to run programs and to allow program development. Prior to Windows 9x, this is where the interrupts listing was held, along with various patches, fixes, and updates to DOS.

When DOS runs through the lines in the CONFIG.SYS file, the files referred to are either found or not found. Assuming that all the device drivers are found and loaded into memory, the CONFIG.SYS file eventually ends, and control returns to IO.SYS.

IO.SYS Runs Twice

Let's take a moment to mention HIMEM.SYS here; we'll discuss it in greater detail later in this chapter. HIMEM.SYS is technically a software driver designed to allow access to any memory beyond the first 1MB. It originally loaded from a CONFIG.SYS file, back when all device drivers were being installed from this file. When the market reached a point where nearly every machine had more than 1MB of memory, HIMEM.SYS became a critical file. DOS 7.0 (Windows 95) folded the loading directive into IO.SYS, thereby ensuring it would be always installed and eliminating the possibility of accidentally failing to load it from an optional CONFIG.SYS file.

IO.SYS runs *once* to determine whether a CONFIG.SYS file should be read. If a configuration file exists, then IO.SYS drops out to allow the CONFIG.SYS file to load any existing Real Mode device drivers. After the CONFIG.SYS file has completed, IO.SYS then returns *again*, to read MSDOS.SYS for the rest of the startup process.

As we've said, this quick pass into CONFIG.SYS can lead to some confusion on the exam. Our information comes from the Microsoft technical description of the Windows 95 startup process, although it was difficult to find. In our opinion, the exam makes an assumption that this first look at CONFIG.SYS doesn't take place.

Before loading hardware device drivers from a CONFIG.SYS and an AUTOEXEC.BAT file, try commenting them out to see whether the Windows 9x auto-detection capabilities can run those devices with VxDs. (VxDs are discussed in the "Virtual Device Drives" section of this chapter.)

DOS 7.0 changed the basic system files, using the hidden IO.SYS to read configuration information from either the MSDOS.SYS hidden file, a CONFIG.SYS file (if one is present), or *both*. IO.SYS must still be in the boot sector of the bootable partition, and MSDOS.SYS (also hidden) is still placed in the root directory. COMMAND.COM is also carried forward in DOS 7.0 and installed in both the root directory and the Windows folder.

Technically speaking, IO.SYS reads CONFIG.SYS, then MSDOS.SYS, and then passes control to MSDOS.SYS. After MSDOS.SYS, control passes to COMMAND.COM, which reads CONFIG.SYS *again* before passing control to AUTOEXEC.BAT.

Although, technically, CONFIG.SYS is read twice, we believe the exam expects CONFIG.SYS (if it exists) to process following COMMAND.COM. This is one of those ambiguous, imprecise questions where Microsoft says what happens, but the proper response isn't listed on the exam.

Windows 9x looks in the boot sector, where it finds IO.SYS. Windows NT and OS/2 can be booted from a *boot track,* making it possible to boot them from a different partition than the Primary, Active one. In Windows 9x, the "Starting Windows 9x..." message is displayed on the screen following the initial POST and parity check, and is written into IO.SYS.

IO.SYS and 16-bit Device Drivers

IO.SYS in Windows 9x and ME does the same thing as in DOS. It sets up segment addressing in conventional memory, and loads low-level Real Mode device drivers into the first segment of memory (low memory). IO.SYS then reads MSDOS.SYS or an existing CONFIG.SYS file. We'll discuss Real Mode, low memory, and other aspects of memory addressing later in this chapter.

Windows 9x uses a preliminary hardware profile from the hardware detection phase to attempt to start the computer (for example, interrupts, BIOS serial and parallel ports, and CMOS or BIOS system board identification). After the computer is started for the first time, the Registry tells Windows 9x which settings to use at startup. IO.SYS reads both the MSDOS.SYS file (to process specific devices) and the Registry (SYSTEM.DAT) for the device settings.

If a CONFIG.SYS file, an AUTOEXEC.BAT file, or both are supposed to run, IO.SYS loads the COMMAND.COM command interpreter to run the two files. Depending on which lines are found in these files, COMMAND.COM runs various Real Mode commands and programs.

Remember that whatever is loaded into the DOS environment at this point descends to any DOS sessions run from within Windows. The Properties option of COMMAND.COM allows you to configure the DOS session environment.

MSDOS.SYS

Whether or not CONFIG.SYS, AUTOEXEC.BAT, or both exist, IO.SYS reads the MSDOS.SYS file first and then reads it again for VxDs (virtual device drivers) and other configuration settings. MSDOS.SYS is a plain ASCII text file that can be edited by DOS's EDIT.COM, the Windows Notepad (NOTEPAD.EXE), or Microsoft's WordPad. The important point is that all attributes are set on the file, making it hidden, system, and read-only. Before you can edit MSDOS.SYS, you're expected to know what you're doing and how to change the file attributes.

The MSDOS.SYS file tells Windows 9x about multiple booting options, Startup menus, which mode to start in, and whether the Windows GUI is supposed to start at all following boot-up.

If you press and hold the Shift key, instead of the F8 key, before the Windows splash screen, MSDOS.SYS is bypassed and not read at all. MSDOS.SYS can also be edited so as to force Windows 9x to start in plain DOS. To start Windows from the command prompt then requires typing WIN and pressing Enter.

MSDOS.SYS Passes to COMMAND.COM

If no CONFIG.SYS file can be found, IO.SYS hands off to MSDOS.SYS, which looks for COMMAND.COM in the root directory of the boot disk. COMMAND.COM must be from the same version of DOS as the system files are, or the process comes to a screeching halt with the message "Incorrect DOS version". The DOS kernel (system files) loads COMMAND.COM into memory following any device drivers from IO.SYS and CONFIG.SYS.

Beginning with DOS 5.0, COMMAND.COM could be loaded into conventional memory or upper memory, depending on whether a memory device manager (HIMEM.SYS) was run from CONFIG.SYS. However, regardless of the area of memory, COMMAND.COM is run and installs into some part of the first 1MB of RAM (conventional memory).

After all the device drivers have been accounted for, the last step in booting up a DOS machine is to load the command interpreter itself. COMMAND.COM moves its resident portion into RAM and checks to see if an AUTOEXEC.BAT file exists (spelled exactly that way) in the root directory. If AUTOEXEC.BAT is there, COMMAND.COM runs the batch commands in that file.

When the last command in the AUTOEXEC.BAT file has been run, COMMAND.COM returns a prompt on the screen, and the machine is ready to work. If the last command of the AUTOEXE.BAT file is WIN.COM, the process continues and loads Windows 3.x.

Summary—The Boot Process

The preceding section is one of the most complex in this book. Don't feel bad if you don't immediately understand everything we've talked about. Watch your computer, the next time you switch it on, and see if you can follow some of the on-screen cues to what's going on. Shut down the machine and restart in MS-DOS Mode. This isn't a completely clean DOS session, but it will allow you the opportunity of examining your hard drive for IO.SYS and MSDOS.SYS. Avoid using the Explorer, but try to find the files with DOS commands.

The boot process is how a box full of plastic, silicon, wire, and metal links up with a bunch of letters and characters (the OS) to become a useful computer. Yes it's complicated! That's why it took a couple of weeks to invent computers in the first place. The main things to remember are:

- The motherboard ROM BIOS chip contains a tiny routine, written in BASIC, which reaches out to look for certain files on the hard drive.
- The two system files, IO.SYS and MSDOS.SYS, work to load very low-level instructions into memory (e.g., the Interrupt Vector Tables), which the operating system uses to access hardware devices, memory, and the CPU.
- COMMAND.COM contains program code with references to the AUTOEXEC.BAT file and a listing of startup error message.
- IO.SYS contains coded language that explains to the operating system how to handle certain device operations. The file also calls to an optional CONFIG.SYS file.
- If a CONFIG.SYS file exists, each line in the file is used to load device instructions into memory. In many cases, additional configuration settings are "SET" in an AUTOEXEC.BAT file.
- The order in which file loads and runs is critical.

Keep in mind that neither the CONFIG.SYS nor AUTOEXEC.BAT are required, but if they exist, they run at the points we've listed above. Windows 9x still uses the same steps, and although most of what used to be in the CONFIG.SYS file has now been coded into IO.SYS, the process still follows the same steps.

If you're not sure of the order in which each file runs, go back and scan the subheadings we've used. Re-read the text under any heading where you aren't sure of what's going on. All this happens quickly, but it takes a lot of words to explain. Try to extract the essential points, and list them in whatever way is most comfortable for you.

Beep Codes

We've seen that the POST routine resides in ROM BIOS and executes when power is supplied to the motherboard at startup. During the time the POST runs and completes, no operating system is loaded, and no device drivers have been put into memory. Therefore, the PC has no way of working with a disk, a monitor, floppy drives, or any other device that requires a driver, including a keyboard. There's only one way for the POST to communicate with you—the system speaker.

The POST produces a pattern of sounds, depending on the exit condition it finds on completion of the program. These sounds access the motherboard's speaker and produce a *beep*. Most programs use error codes (also known as *exit codes*) to provide a way to tell the world what happened when the program finished. In DOS, the **ERRORLEVEL** batch command uses these error codes. An error code can include a code for successful completion with no errors.

The CHOICE command, used in batch files, uses ERRORLEVEL, the GOTO command, and Labels to provide interactive options. If you create a simple batch file using the CHOICE command to write one of three messages to the screen, you'll get a strong understanding of how batch files work. (The messages can be anything: Hi, I'm number 1, This is hard, I hate computers, and so on.)

Table 11.1 lists some of the main beep codes associated with a POST exit. The PC's speaker beep is a DOS bell control signal (decimal .007, or ^G). *Bell* refers to the old teletype machine bells.

Table 11.1 The main AMI BIOS beep codes.

Number of Beeps	Meaning
None	There must always be at least one beep. If you don't hear a beep when the POST has completed, then the PC speaker may be bad. Otherwise, the motherboard has failed, or the power supply is bad.
1	Successful. The POST has completed successfully. If you can see everything on the monitor, then the system started okay. The most common problem for a successful POST, but no monitor, is lack of power to the monitor. Check the monitor's fuse and power supply. If the monitor still has no picture following a 1-beep successful POST, then the video card may have a bad memory chip.

Table 11.1 The main AMI BIOS beep codes *(continued)*

Number of Beeps	Meaning
	To check the video memory, try reseating the SIMMs and rebooting the machine. If the SIMMs are in tightly and there's still no image, then you'll probably need to buy a new video card, because the SIMMs are usually soldered onto the IC board.
2, 3, or 4	Memory. The POST checks the first 64KB of main memory. If you hear 2, 3, or 4 beeps, then either video or main memory has a problem. If the video is working, then there was a parity error in the first 64KB of system memory (low memory). Try switching SIMMs between memory banks. If a reboot generates 1 beep, then you have a bad memory module in the switched bank.
4	Clock. 4 beeps can also mean a bad timer oscillator. If you hear more than four beeps at startup, you have a precarious situation. The motherboard could be smoking, or the CMOS could have lost its mind. Generally, a repeating series of beeps indicates that a network configuration file or user's logon script is failing to find various devices and drivers. Another possible cause, not related to the POST, is that following a successful startup, something is resting on the keyboard, and the keyboard buffer is sounding an alert.

The Bootable Disk

Back when every PC used DOS, making a bootable disk was a simple process. You would insert a disk into Drive A: and format it with system files (**FORMAT A: /S**). You would copy over a few useful DOS utilities, and from that point on, you could access just about any machine that could spin the floppy drive. Today, bootable disks have different purposes, and they're created in different ways, depending on the operating system and the user interface.

You're sure to encounter questions on the exam having to do with how to create a boot disk, an emergency startup disk, or an emergency repair disk (ERD). Chapter 14 covers Windows startup disks, but this is where we talk about how to make a simple, bootable, DOS startup disk.

DOS Bootable Disk

Making a disk bootable means that the three system files (IO.SYS, MSDOS.SYS, and COMMAND.COM) are copied to the disk. Along with the system files, the bootstrap loader is placed in the boot sector. If the disk can start the operating system, the disk is bootable. The steps to make a bootable DOS disk are:

1. On a working PC, insert a 1.44MB standard floppy disk into Drive A:. Exit all applications, or otherwise set the system to a DOS prompt (command line).
2. Type "FORMAT A: /S /U" and press Enter to format Drive A: and transfer the system files, formatting the disk unconditionally. Allow the process to complete.
3. Leave the new disk in Drive A: and restart the machine. If the machine successfully boots up, you are asked for the date (press Enter) and the time (press Enter), and you then arrive at an A> prompt. Note that there is no PROMPT command, which is why you do not see an A:\> prompt.

Making a DOS-Bootable Disk from Windows Explorer

Creating a bootable disk in Windows is a fun way to work in the graphical environment, but you don't have the opportunity to choose the /U (unconditional) switch, nor do you have as much control over the process as you do in DOS. To make a bootable DOS disk from Windows Explorer:

1. Insert a disk into Drive A:. Execute the EXPLORER.EXE program or select Start|Programs|Explorer. Windows 9x won't allow you to format a hard drive, and the Format Disk option does not appear unless you have a disk in Drive A:.
2. With a disk in Drive A:, right-click on the Drive A: icon. In the Properties dialog box, select Format. Make sure that you click on the Copy System Files radio button.

Remember that you can create an emergency startup disk in Windows 9x by selecting Start|Settings|Control Panel|Add Remove Programs and by clicking on the Startup Disk tab.

Neither Windows 3.x nor Windows 9x allows you to format a disk unconditionally (completely wiping out any pre-existing information). Windows Explorer won't allow the format option when you right-click on a nonremovable disk drive. Fortunately, we still have the option of either going to an MS-DOS prompt in a window, running a command line, or restarting the machine in DOS Mode. As long as you can get to a command line, you can still format any disk unconditionally.

The technical term for *right-clicking* (on the exam) is *alternative-click*. Don't confuse this with Alt-click or the Alt key. Another way of calling up the context menu is to highlight an object and press Shift-F10.

Bootable Disk Utility Files

You can assume that the only time you'll need a bootable disk is in an emergency, in which case you'll need to do some detective work and probably some repair work as well. The repair work could simply be editing a CONFIG.SYS file, or it could be as drastic as performing an FDISK re-partitioning of the hard drive.

In Windows 2000 and XP, FDISK operations take place under Disk Management.

A Windows 9x emergency startup disk isn't quite the same as a DOS bootable disk. The emergency disk boots the system using IO.SYS, MSDOS.SYS, and COMMAND.COM. However, it includes a number of utility programs that the process automatically copies to the emergency disk. If Windows 9x is workable and the problem involves accessing the hard drive, the emergency startup disk boots the system and tries to load Windows.

When you run FDISK and partition a hard disk, you totally and irrevocably wipe out all information on the disk. You remove not only applications and data, but also the logical drives themselves.

FDISK is used *only* to view the existing partition setup of a hard disk, or to completely destroy all information on the hard disk; there is no in-between. If you can think of *any* other option for solving a problem, you should attempt that before using FDISK to completely reinstall the disk.

If Windows 9x can be loaded at all, the emergency startup disk attempts to load in Safe Mode if it can't load normally. The emergency disk contains a number of programs that can be run only from within Windows (e.g., ScanDskW).

If Windows 9x can't load, IO.SYS still produces a "Starting Windows…" message, but the start sequence ends at a plain DOS prompt. In this case, no text-based F8-type Startup menu appears, and you'll need to know DOS commands to continue solving the problem. The message is hard-coded into IO.SYS, and is not Windows talking with you in a self-conscious fashion.

Some of the utility files that should be copied to the DOS bootable disk include: FORMAT.COM, FDISK.EXE, EDIT.COM (for editing ASCII startup files), SYS.COM, SCANDISK.EXE (the DOS version), ATTRIB.EXE, and DEBUG.EXE (for destroying a boot sector).

DEBUG.EXE is a program for creating Assembler (.COM) files. In very special cases, the only way to ensure that a boot sector virus has been totally destroyed is to use Assembler language. Also note that if you use EDIT.COM on any system prior to Windows 95, you *must* include QBASIC.EXE as the support file for the editor (or it won't run). EDIT.COM can be found on the installation CD-ROM if it isn't in the \Windows\Command folder.

Bootable Disk Configuration Files

A specific PC should have its own dedicated bootable disk. That disk should include up-to-date copies of critical startup files used to start the PC in a normal condition. Check to see if the machine has a CONFIG.SYS and AUTOEXEC.BAT file. If the PC has a CD-ROM drive, but no BIOS to support it, a device driver must load in the CONFIG.SYS file. References to the device driver might exist in the AUTOEXEC.BAT file as well (e.g., MSCDEX.EXE).

Place the PC's emergency boot disk in that PC's system binder along with a current printout of MSD.EXE, HWDIAG.EXE, or System Information. If you had to back up driver files in subdirectories, put those disks in the system binder as well.

A system binder is a three-ring binder containing configuration printouts, unusual instructions relating to a PC, and a number of vinyl disk-sized pocket pages. These vinyl pages hold critical installation disks for drivers, the operating system, and other important devices. The system binder is a good place to keep current backup copies of the SYSTEM.DAT and USER.DAT Registry files, along with CD-ROMs.

If the PC has a sound card, scanner, mouse, printer, or any peripheral that isn't absolutely critical, the device drivers can probably be replaced in the event of an FDISK-type catastrophe. You should examine the system for SCSI device drivers and other driver files that will be necessary when the problem is fixed.

Make sure that you have copies of any device drivers that reside on the hard drive (if you can access the drive). If you can't find original installation disks for SCSI devices, a sound card, a mouse, or other devices, back up copies of any subdirectories with driver files to disk.

Important configuration files to include on a PC's bootable emergency disk include CONFIG.SYS, AUTOEXEC.BAT, CD-ROM device drivers (manufacturer specific) or MSCDEX.EXE (generic CD driver), and WIN.INI and SYSTEM.INI (if necessary).

There's no point in making a backup copy of the Registry because the entire disk will have to be reinstalled. A "disk image" program is very useful in situations like this. We mention disk images in Chapter 13.

Supplemental Information

At this point, you might choose to skip ahead to the "Windows" section. With the success of PCs, everyone was looking for a better way to network them. Unix and Macintosh systems use a different file structure, and were designed from the ground up to be a network operating system (NOS). On the other hand, DOS was never designed for real networking. IBM and Microsoft were urgently trying to create a new version of an operating system that would handle more files, larger disks, and better networking. OS/2 (the new, "second" OS) was going to be that messiah of the IBM PC world.

We've seen that a 16-bit FAT limits the number of clusters on a single logical drive and that those clusters increase in size, depending on the size of the drive. OS/2 was going to feature a completely redesigned 32-bit file management system and better control over cluster size. Additionally, the new operating system was going to be designed for networking.

At the time, Microsoft and IBM were partners, and they noticed that they were losing customers who wanted something called *task switching*. Microsoft was looking at how many customers were buying into the easy-to-use graphical environment of the Macintosh, and they wanted something to lure those customers away from Apple computers. IBM promised to provide an operating system for the so-called multitasking 80286 chip and, in 1984, released Top View, a text-based task switcher.

IBM was also working on a multitasking environment for the new 80386 chip that Intel was researching. The 386 would correct the protected memory problems of the 286, and both IBM and Microsoft wanted an operating system that could take advantage of this, both for multitasking and for the user-friendly interface of the Mac's graphics. Both companies wanted safe multitasking, network capabilities, large disk- and memory-handling abilities, and a user-friendly graphical interface.

Windows requires a 386 or better processor to install. DOS 7.x (Windows 9x) includes an error message in COMMAND.COM that specifically addresses the need for a 386 processor on the machine.

The two companies decided that an idea Microsoft was developing for something called "Windows" would be the front-end interface of this new, second-generation operating system (OS/2). The Windows interface had some memory management functions built into the overall menu. IBM would take care of changing the underlying operating system, and provide a way for software to use *threads* for multithreaded preemptive multitasking. The two companies agreed to release individual products, but for compatibility and to save costs, they also agreed to share their underlying work, research, and code.

IBM and Microsoft began rewriting DOS to run in both Real and Protected Mode when software developers were slow to write programs for the 286. The results of these projects were OS/2 v1.0 and Windows 286, which could run most DOS programs in Real Mode just as they had run before, but in multiple instances.

In Protected Mode, OS/2 provided true multitasking (as opposed to task switching) as well as access to 1GB of virtual memory and 16MB of physical memory address space. This word "virtual" means temporarily simulated, and is similar to "emulate," which means to imitate.

Virtually Real

Existence can be broadly divided into physical and metaphysical reality. Metaphysical (from *meta*) is literally greater than physical. In physical reality, all things have attributes, or characteristics. When we point to an object and define it, we're taking out and using the single, unique attribute that distinguishes it from any other object in existence. Physical objects are accessible through our senses (perceptions) and can be touched, smelled, heard, seen, or tasted.

A virtual object is a thing that exhibits all the attributes of the same objects in its class (or set) except for one: physical existence. Virtual objects are not "sensible" to physical perceptions (yet). A virtual machine is a machine that works and acts exactly the same way as a physical machine, except that you can't reach over and pick it up with your physical arms.

Virtual reality (VR) can provide you with virtual arms. In this situation, your nonphysical arms work the same way as your physical arms. The difference is that you can use virtual arms to pick up a virtual machine. The end result is then reflected in the virtual reality as having consequences just like in the physical world. For instance, you could end up with a virtual hernia.

Microsoft Windows took advantage of something called *page frame switching* in both the 80286 and the 80386 chips to provide high-speed task switching. The better protection built in to the 386 helped make Windows more stable. (We discuss page frames in the "HIMEM.SYS and EMM386.EXE " section of this chapter.)

Windows 3.0, in Standard Mode, used the page frame memory-swapping capability of the 286 to switch among several running programs (tasks) without being able to run the programs concurrently. By the time software arrived on the market for Windows 3.0 Standard Mode, the new 386 chip was rapidly replacing the 286 chip.

Both 16-bit Windows and Windows 9x continue to use page frame task switching. Windows NT is Microsoft's true multitasking operating system, and Windows 2000 is the place where 16-bit and 32-bit Windows finally come together. We discuss Windows NT and 2000 in Chapter 13.

Multitasking

Computer multitasking is the ability to run multiple programs at the same time. In other words, if you download a file from America Online (AOL) and then switch to Microsoft Excel and print a spreadsheet, both tasks should happen simultaneously—at exactly the same time—and have no effect at all on each other.

If the download crashes in the middle of the process and AOL halts, the spreadsheet shouldn't even notice that anything has happened. AOL should be dropped out of memory with no fuss, and any gaps in RAM should fill in as smoothly as the ocean covers a sinking ship. If you're playing a musical CD at the same time, you should hear the music as smoothly as if you were playing it on a home stereo system. There should be no jerky pauses—indications of *time slices*—in the music.

Time Slices

Something like recalculating a spreadsheet can force the CPU into full-time work. In that case, the CPU can give only a few *time slices* to a CD, every other couple of microseconds if you're playing music while you're working on your spreadsheet. If controlling the data passing from a modem through a UART chip is also taking up the CPU's time, you begin to see something like a picture of a harried mother trying to control four young children in the middle of a mall during the Christmas rush. The CPU's attention can only rotate among all the tasks in some fraction of time—a time slice.

Microsoft Windows is a management software program that takes advantage of Virtual Real Mode, and programs designed for Windows can run alongside multiple DOS programs in multiple virtual machines. Because the processor can service only one application per clock tick, Windows manages the amount of time the CPU gives to each program in time slices, usually measured in milliseconds. Because the chip is so fast and time slices are so small, the multiple applications running under Windows appear to be running concurrently.

Processes

As instructions move back and forth between software, hardware, and the CPU, we say that they all have a *process* of some length of time (time slices). A program file is a complete set of instructions. When that program runs, we can think of the process as complete. It begins and ends, and it expects not to have any interruptions in memory addresses.

If a user wants to run two or more programs at the same time, a way must be set up to overcome a program's expectation of having the whole world of RAM to work with, and no unexpected memory gaps. Putting part of a program in base memory (the 640KB of the first 1MB of conventional memory) and another part in expanded memory leads to confusion, lockups, and crashes. Memory can become fragmented, just like a disk full of files can be fragmented. Although DOS includes DEFRAG.EXE for disks, it doesn't include a way to defragment memory itself.

Some third-party software utilities can defragment the area of memory used for Windows resources. This can sometimes be helpful when many applications have been opened and closed in a session. Sometimes, Windows reports there is enough memory to run an application, but the application returns an "insufficient memory" error. Defragmenting, or compressing, the Resources area may fix the problem. This problem continued through Windows 9x and Windows Me.

We see a similar problem when hardware or software runs a process and calls for work from the CPU. In this case, interrupts are sent to the CPU to interrupt whatever it's doing and reorder the priorities of action. If a process in the CPU hasn't finished, a snapshot of the whole process is switched into a *stack* and is retrieved when the new process has run its course.

Threads

Threads are a way for an application process to be divided into precise subprocesses that happen at the same time. You can think of a thread as the smallest amount of time required by the CPU to complete a single set of instructions. Threads operate very fast because they're very small pieces of code. Because threads are written into an application, they have full access to the entire program. They also share address space, file access paths, and other system resources associated with the application.

You can also think of a thread as a kind of interrupt written into an application by the programmer. The programmer decides, thread by thread, what the smallest piece of code is. The program can then send only the necessary instructions at a given moment. Threads also allow different areas of the same overall application to use only the instructions specific to those areas (e.g., to recalculate while redrawing the screen).

Threads can be moved into RAM at the same time, carrying with them (within the thread) a piece of code that tells the CPU how important that piece of code is in the overall scheme of things. This provides some help to the CPU as it moves processing in and out of the stack and allows one thread to interrupt (preempt) another thread.

The importance of a given thread is therefore prioritized, allowing one thread to preempt the time that is being called for by another thread from the CPU. This capability is called *preemptive multithreaded multitasking*. True preemptive multitasking requires that software be written with threads and that the operating system be written to understand threads.

Tricky Semantics

Because Windows decides (on the basis of time slices) whether and when a DOS application will have access to the CPU, the term *preemptive multitasking* for DOS applications crept its way into the language with the arrival of Windows 3.x. Because DOS applications aren't written in a threaded format, this use of the term isn't really accurate. It's true that Windows is literally preempting the DOS application's access to the CPU, but that doesn't mean that Windows is using preemptive multitasking in the way that it's formally defined.

Microsoft tends to advertise Windows 3.x as having preemptive multitasking capabilities. This is true semantically, but not in the generally accepted meaning of the term. In terms of the exam, you should think of Windows 3.x, Windows 9x, and Windows Me as offering real multitasking (without reference to its being preemptive).

Windows

In 1987, IBM released OS/2 version 1.0, which included the text-based Presentation Manager front-end interface. IBM designed this version to run hardware-based (chip) multitasking to take advantage of the 80286, but had the much better 80386 in mind. IBM deferred the development of the graphics to Microsoft, and Windows 2.0 arrived on the market with the ability to create so-called virtual 8086 computers (virtual machines) out of 640KB snapshots of memory.

Virtual Real Mode

IBM was having serious trouble developing its operating system, and Microsoft was becoming impatient because of Apple Corporation's constant increase in computer sales. Windows used MS-DOS Executive as its user interface, and version 2.x offered the ability to create a virtual 8086 memory environment called *Real Mode.*

Memory addressing in Real Mode is done directly, in the same way that original memory addressing was handled by the 8088/86 processors using conventional memory. Windows 2.x also introduced the concept of Dynamic Data Exchange (DDE), whereby applications running together under Windows could communicate with one another.

DDE led to Object Linking and Embedding (OLE), which eventually led to an incredibly confusing world of ActiveX and DirectX, none of which is part of the exam.

Using *Virtual* Real Mode, the CPU can simulate the way an actual 8088/86 does real operations with real memory addresses. At the same time, Windows can run hardware-based (80386) memory protection. This allows a true multitasking operating system to load multiple copies of DOS, while making the CPU think it's working with only one machine. There is only one physical machine present, but each copy of the DOS command processor is running in its own simulated world—a virtual machine.

If the system is using appropriate memory management software, the 386 chip could create several memory partitions. Each of these memory partitions can have its own copy of DOS and use the full range of DOS services, thereby functioning as if it were a stand-alone PC. When this type of organization is in place, the computer is often said to be running virtual machines. As we examine Windows, we see how the Virtual Machine (*VM*) Manager is a basic component of all versions of Windows. We'll also see how virtual machines can use virtual device drivers, called *VxDs* (files).

A virtual machine is a simulated PC. It "comes with" an 8088/86 CPU that can address only 1MB of RAM. Session configuration settings can "install" more memory in that virtual (fake) machine, making the configuration of a DOS session under Windows an exercise in the history of PCs.

The System VM (Virtual Machine)

A VM is an executable task. It's an actual program that combines application, support software such as ROM BIOS and DOS, memory, and CPU registers. Running COMMAND.COM or CMD.EXE at the Run line under a Windows Start menu creates a generic virtual machine. The properties in the DOSPRMPT.PIF (program information file) file in the Windows subfolder (the MS-DOS shortcut) allow you to configure a VM.

The DOSPRMPT.PIF file is a shortcut, located in the \Windows folder. You can configure the DOS session properties here, or in the context menu for COMMAND.COM. The target program for the .PIF file is COMMAND.COM.

Windows uses a single virtual machine called the *System VM* to run the Windows kernel, its other core components and extensions, as well as all Windows-based applications. Each time a DOS application is run, it creates a separate VM that exists for only the length of time that the DOS application is running—a session. Windows 3.x used an applet called the *PIF Editor* to control how each session's VM ran. These configuration settings are now controlled by the Properties option of the context menu.

Program Information Files

Windows provides memory to a DOS application in the same way that any PC comes with base memory to run programs. The amount of DRAM memory on a real PC is determined by chips and buyer choices. The amount of virtual memory on a virtual PC is determined by the requirements of the application asking for a VM (virtual machine). If no one does anything, the default settings are created by the _DEFAULT.PIF file that comes with Windows 3.x and the DOSPRMPT.PIF file that comes with Windows 9x. COMMAND.COM has its own properties in Windows 9x, and this property menu works much like the original .PIF files did.

Originally, a program information file was stored in a proprietary format, and couldn't be edited using a typical ASCII text editor. The PIFEDIT.EXE applet was used to edit .PIF files, much like REGEDIT.EXE is a specialized editor for the Windows 3.x Registration database and the Windows 9x Registry.

The PIF Editor dialog box asks for information about the program, including its full pathname and command file name, along with any startup switches that you want to use for that program. The **PROGRAMS=** line in the WIN.INI file (in the "WIN.INI" section) specifies that .EXE, .COM, .BAT, and .PIF file extensions are to be considered executable by Windows. Note that a .PIF file is an executable file in the Windows environment.

Rather than pointing a shortcut to an .EXE or .COM file, the properties can be used to point to the .PIF file associated with the actual executable file (as in the case of **DOSPRMT**). A .PIF file can also tell Windows how much time (in time slices) to give to the processes generated by the DOS application. Windows 9x properties can't do this.

Windows Resources

Windows uses something called *resources* that are called for by a program. These resources are the amount of memory a program or screen item needs at any given time it's active. The resource instructions to Windows were originally contained within .EXE files and dynamic link library (.DLL) files. Rather than leaving the moment-by-moment control of memory to DOS, Windows took over the management tasks. (Resources are discussed in more detail later in the "The Windows 3.x Environment: Global Heap" of this chapter.)

Dynamic Link Libraries (.DLL Files)

Along with the Windows kernel and core files, Microsoft provides the Windows *extensions* that are meant to standardize many Windows functions, including the look and the feel of the interface. COMMDLG.DLL is a generic way for a programmer to work with Windows to create standardized dialog boxes. DDEML.DLL is a library of management tools for DDE (Dynamic Data Exchange), and MMSYSTEM.DLL is a library of management tools for sound and multimedia.

The Windows extensions are designed to make the Windows environment as flexible as possible. .DLL files are Windows-executable files that allow applications to share program code and necessary resources. A programmer can extend the basic Windows environment by writing a .DLL to make it available to other Windows applications. Dynamic link libraries commonly have the .DLL extension, but they can also have an .EXE or other extension. KERNEL.EXE, USER.EXE, and GDI.EXE are Dynamic Link Libraries that have an .EXE extension.

The SHELL.DLL library provides the drag-and-drop capabilities used with File Manager. Such routines can be used by other applications without needing to rewrite the code. The programmer calls up the routines from the SHELL.DLL file (which installs with Windows by default).

Windows 3.0 and New Technology (NT)

Microsoft released a Windows 2.01 incremental upgrade shortly after releasing version 2.0. The main reason for the upgrade seems to have been that Windows took on IBM's System Application Architecture (SAA) standard for how a program looks to the user. This standard for a "look" describes how windows, menus, and dialog boxes should look for any and all programs running in a graphical environment. The idea was that, as with Macs, users shouldn't be required to relearn the skills they acquire from one program when learning a new one. The SAA standard became the standard for all IBM-type computers running a graphical, Windows-style interface.

The SAA for the "look and feel" of an application is not the same as the applications program interface (API). The API is how a program developer works with an operating system to develop new applications.

Another important aspect of Windows 2.x was that, after it was loaded, it took on some of the underlying DOS operations. In other words, while Windows was looking like a menu system and acting like a shell, it was also reaching down into the basic operating system to control how memory addressing and management was being done.

For a while, Microsoft and IBM were working together to improve both the OS/2 operating system and the Windows interface. IBM was primarily focusing on an operating system that communicated directly with the CPU. Microsoft was focusing more on the way in which the user was working with the computer. IBM has always tended to pay more attention to hardware (how things work), while over the years, it seems as if Microsoft has been more interested in appearances (how things look to the user).

OS/2 version 1.x was a whole new way of programming, and the API was difficult to learn. However, even in that version, OS/2 changed the FAT to support much larger drives. In 1989, IBM released OS/2 1.20, which had an improved Presentation Manager. Shortly thereafter, version 1.2 EE introduced something called the *High Performance File System* (HPFS).

HPFS is much more efficient and faster than FAT, and it keeps track of data on disks with fewer errors and better security. HPFS would eventually grow to be a true 32-bit file management system that could be located anywhere on a logical drive, not exclusively in the root directory. HPFS is not the same thing as the Windows NT File System (NTFS) or Windows 9x FAT32, however.

Although IBM's HPFS is a true 32-bit file management system, the Windows 9x Installable File System (IFS) is a virtualized 32-bit FAT (virtual FAT, or VFAT) that relies on the DOS 7.x 16-bit FAT for actual file management. Chapter 12 discusses the VFAT in greater detail.

IBM had begun work on two new OS/2 products: OS/2 2.0 and 3.0. Version 2.0 was going to be the first 32-bit operating system for PCs. It was designed specifically for the Intel 80386 and later chips, and would no longer be compatible with the 80286 processor. Version 3.0 was going to be a network server version of the operating system. It was also intended to be platform independent, meaning that the same operating system could run on PCs using different types of chips. Version 2.0 would focus on the individual user—the consumer market—whereas version 3.0 would focus on the business world and networks.

Because OS/2 was going to be built on top of something called a *microkernel*, it wouldn't matter what type of hardware it was running on. Therefore, it could run on Intel processors and on other types of chips made by Sun, Digital Equipment Corporation (DEC), and Motorola. Everything was fine, except that IBM was way behind in its work, and Microsoft was ready to go with an interface that looked almost exactly like a Mac screen.

In 1990, Bill Gates decided to release Windows 3.0, without IBM's agreement, in a move to lure customers away from the Macintosh to the Intel-based operating systems. DOS was *the* operating system in this market, and Microsoft wanted the Mac customers. IBM decided to step in to try to keep Microsoft from dominating the entire operating system market, and a great divorce battle ensued.

When the dust settled, an agreement had been made that IBM would continue to develop OS/2 2.0 for personal computers and Microsoft would take over development and funding for OS/2 3.0 (the network server version). Microsoft renamed the experimental network operating system Windows New Technology (NT), and gave it a version number of 3.0.

Program Manager and File Manager

One of the fundamental differences between Windows 2.x and 3.0 was the way they showed themselves to the user. The MS-DOS Executive was like a two dimensional version of File Manager. It had no colors, and it looked very similar to the results of a **DIR** command printed on paper. The difference between the directory command and MS-DOS Executive was that you could double-click on an application file's name, and the program would actually run. Windows 3.0 allowed running a mixture of Windows and DOS programs at the same time. It had its bugs, but it was progressing.

Another basic change in the look of Windows 3.0a and 3.0b was the introduction of icons and program groups. A program group is much like a subdirectory, but it looks almost exactly like the folders and subfolders of the Macintosh operating system (Mac OS). Icons incorporate a program item properties dialog box, where information is entered about the location of a program and how it starts—a graphic menu option. In Windows Explorer, the "look and feel" came so close to that of the Macintosh that Apple Corporation sued Microsoft in a legendary court battle. Microsoft won, so today's folders and subfolders continue to look and work the way they do.

Windows 3.1

Windows 3.0 and OS/2 2.0 included TrueType fonts (another war was being waged about who had the best way to draw letters on a screen and print them to printers). The idea of What You See Is What You Get (WYSIWYG) became a reality as Windows took on the ability to display characters the way they would actually look on the printed page. Microsoft wanted everything to connect to everything, and its new rallying cry became "Windows everywhere!"

In 1992, Windows 3.1 was released with all the improvements that were needed as a result of the somewhat rushed release of 3.0. Windows 3.1 improved the File Manager shell/applet interface and added internal fonts. Another improvement was the Object Linking and Embedding technology for interconnecting data produced by different applications.

The instructions and connections used in OLE were moved to a special database called the *Registration database* (REG.DAT). To prevent unsophisticated users from accidentally breaking links between programs, this database took on a proprietary form and could be edited only with a program call REGEDIT.EXE.

The Windows 3.x Registration database was the precursor to the 32-bit Windows Registry. REG.DAT eventually became SYSTEM.DAT and USER.DAT. The editing program is still called *REGEDIT.EXE*.

Windows 3.1 featured many improvements, making it more of a full version upgrade than the minor point revision implied by the number. The stability was significantly improved, and the way in which programs were isolated in memory became much more secure. Windows 3.1 finally took on the ability to shut down a frozen window without rebooting the entire computer (some of the time).

Another preview of the standardization to come was the common dialog box (COMMDLG.DLL) programming library so that the programmer didn't need to "re-create the wheel" every time they needed a dialog box. It's important to note that these common dialog features are held in certain files that change with various versions of Windows.

The 16-bit files were COMMDLG.DLL, VER.DLL, SHELL.DLL, DDEML.DLL, and LZEXPAND.DLL. Although you won't be tested on these names, keep in mind that 32-bit and 16-bit Windows applications might use different versions of these files and that, therefore, they aren't interchangeable.

Starting 16-Bit Windows

We've discussed the basic loading of the operating system, ending with the DOS command prompt. Typically, on a computer set up to run Windows 3.x, the last line of an AUTOEXEC file is WIN. This means that a program must be somewhere on the disk called WIN.* (using a DOS wild card). It just so happens that Windows has such a program, called *WIN.COM*, and it's located in the C:\Windows directory.

SETUP.EXE

DOS programs often included a separate installation routine (program) to make sure that every step of the installation was followed correctly. You can usually tell whether you're looking at a DOS- or Windows-based application by the name of its installation program. DOS programs continue to use INSTALL.EXE as the first file to run in setting up the program. Windows programs use SETUP.EXE.

Windows itself uses a SETUP.EXE program, which goes farther than the DOS installation routines. SETUP.EXE not only copies (and expands) files to various locations on the disk, but it also examines the hardware and software in the system. The theory behind this examination is that users shouldn't need to know how their computers run. Following the Microsoft lead, most modern installation programs attempt to identify the existing system before installing their application.

Most installation and setup programs make a number of assumptions about the destination computer—the default setup—and offer the computer owner a way to take only some control over the installation. Typically, the installation routine offers a somewhat misleading Express and Custom pair of setup options.

You should always choose the Custom or Advanced option if the setup routine offers one. In every case we've ever seen, there is a default setting for any steps in the program where you're given a choice. In situations where you don't know what you're looking at, you can choose the default. However, in places where you do know what you're looking at, you may often disagree with what some faraway programmer has decided to do to your system.

The Windows 3.x SETUP.EXE does a rudimentary examination of the type of hardware and memory available on the computer. It offers some basic configuration options, such as the directory to install Windows in and which kind of display, keyboard, mouse, and network configuration to use.

The key file used by SETUP.EXE is SETUP.INF (information file). SETUP.INF contains entries that determine which files will be copied during the installation. Note that Windows and other applications still use .INF setup files.

SETUP.EXE also uses EXPAND.EXE to decompress the files on the Windows installation disks. Because the files are stored in a shrunken (compressed) format, the **DOS COPY** command isn't enough to fully install Windows from original disks.

You can usually tell that a file has been compressed by Microsoft by looking at the last character in the file's extension. Microsoft's proprietary archive process usually makes this last character an underscore (PROGRAM.EX_). Another archive format used by Microsoft creates the .CAB files we see on an installation CD-ROM. .CAB files are a different form of .ZIP files (created with PKZip, or WinZip).

The initial options offered at the beginning of the custom installation can be changed later from within Windows by the Win Setup applet in the Main program group. If the automatic (default) setup is chosen, Microsoft decides which files to install and where to install them. Windows 3.0 didn't offer a choice, providing only automatic installation. Windows 3.x returned some control of the setup process to the user. Windows 9x pretty much removed that control (excepting script files used in network installations), and it was never seen again.

All the way back in DOS 5.0, Microsoft began installing a program in the root directory of the primary, active drive that tells Windows that the computer (processor) can support 386 Enhanced Mode. That file is WINA20.386, and it is located in the C:\ root directory (read-only). After SETUP.EXE determines that Windows can be installed on the computer and determines if there's enough room on the disk, it copies the core files and many of the required files to the hard drive.

SETUP.EXE creates a \WINDOWS subdirectory (typically on Drive C: at the root directory). It also creates a \WINDOWS\SYSTEM directory that Windows searches, regardless of which other subdirectories are listed in the **DOS PATH=** environment variable.

Windows 3.x SETUP.EXE allowed various switches at startup. You could always get a quick reminder of the switches by using the **SETUP /?** switch for DOS online help.

Three of the switches that you might need to know for the exam are:

- **/N**—Sets up a shared copy of Windows for Workgroups from a network server
- **/O:file**—Specifies the SETUP.INF file
- **/A**—Places Windows for Workgroups on a network server (administrative setup)

WIN.COM

MS-DOS 4.0 introduced something Microsoft called the *DOS Shell*, which was really a rudimentary graphic file maintenance and menu program. This complicated menu system was run from DOSSHELL.BAT, which used a very small stub program loader (SHELLB) to push the main program (SHELLC) into memory. SHELLB was about 3.5KB, whereas SHELLC was 150KB. This began the process of using a loader program.

WIN.COM is the next iteration of that loader stub. It calls into memory USER.EXE, GDI.EXE, and KERNEL.EXE—the core Windows files.

The three core Windows 3.x files are USER.EXE, GDI.EXE, and KERNEL.EXE.

During the setup process, SETUP.EXE combines VGALOGO.LGO and VGALOGO.RLE (the Microsoft logo screen) with WIN.CNF and creates WIN.COM, which loads the Windows program into memory and continues forward in graphical mode. Depending on whether an automatic or custom installation was chosen, the routine pauses at various points to allow further choices in terms of which applets will be installed.

VGALOGO.* are the two files Windows uses on systems with VGA graphics capabilities. Where the system used a CGA or EGA monitor, Windows had two files each for CGALOGO.* and EGALOGO.*, which it could compile into WIN.COM.

Typing "WIN" at the command prompt, or having the AUTOEXEC.BAT file enter it for you, runs WIN.COM that does some preliminary checking before it begins to search for the necessary core files for the Windows program. WIN.COM checks to see what type of computer, CPU, and memory are installed. The memory might be real, extended, or expanded.

Next, WIN.COM checks to see which device drivers have been loaded—especially virtual memory devices (HIMEM.SYS)—and then makes a decision regarding the mode in which Windows should start. WIN.COM also allows switches on its command line to force certain ways of loading. These different ways of running are called *modes* of operation. Depending on the amount of memory, the type of processor, and whether an extended memory device driver is present, 16-bit Windows' WIN.COM could use:

- **/R**—Real Mode
- **/S** or **/2**—Standard Mode
- **/3**—Enhanced Mode
- **/B**—To keep a boot log text file of any problems encountered during startup

Additional switches can be used, but the details of these are beyond the scope of this book. Typing "WIN :" (note the space before the colon) starts Windows 3.x without the Microsoft logo screen (or splash screen) during the startup process.

Real Mode (WIN /R)

Real Mode Windows 3.0 was designed to run on 8086-based computers. Microsoft offered this mode, but those computers were so limited that Windows ran too slowly for all practical purposes. Real Mode was a 100 percent compatible mode for running pure DOS. Some games that run under DOS environments had a problem running under Windows 3.0. DOS programs, especially these kinds of games, often write directly to the screen, and with Windows trying to handle device operations, the confusion caused lockups and crashes. Real Mode required at least an 8088/86 processor and 640KB of conventional memory. Real Mode was used mainly for running Windows 2.x applications that hadn't been converted to Windows 3.0, and was eliminated in Windows 3.1.

Standard Mode (WIN /S)

We saw that Windows grew out of changes in the way in which the processor manages memory. In a way, Windows does send instructions directly to the CPU. Remember that 286 Protected Mode is really what started everything. WIN.COM transfers control to other programs that take over management of expanded memory, extended memory, or both.

If WIN.COM finds the extended memory manager HIMEM.SYS in memory, and at least 256KB of conventional memory and 192KB of extended memory, Windows can start in Standard Mode. Windows uses Standard Mode when the computer has an 80286 chip with 1MB or more of memory or a 80386 processor with more than 1MB, but less than 2MB of memory.

If the computer has more than 2MB of memory and a 386 CPU or later, Windows uses Enhanced Mode by default. Because this is almost universally true on modern machines, HIMEM.SYS became a fundamental and critical file and is now called from IO.SYS.

One of the main differences between the 286 and the 386 chips was that although the 286 could switch into Protected Mode during a session, it required a system reset to switch back to Real Mode. This may be the reason that Bill Gates called the 80286 chip "brain-dead" and tried to push IBM into skipping development efforts to the 80386 rather than wasting time with the 286. IBM's corporate policy of always keeping its promises is what set back the development of OS/2 and eventually led to the split between the two corporations—yet another legendary management decision.

386 Enhanced Mode (WIN /3)

The 386 Enhanced Mode is usually referred to simply as *Enhanced Mode*. Its startup sequence is the same as the one for Standard Mode, except that Windows switches the 386 chip into 32-bit Protected Mode. Instead of calling the 286 kernel, WIN.COM loads KRNL386.EXE, which then loads the rest of Windows. Windows Enhanced Mode requires a 386 or faster processor and can, therefore, switch between Protected Mode and Real Mode without the problem of resetting the computer.

The 80386 processor chip introduced virtual memory by creating an illusion for DOS that 1MB of memory stayed constant. The chip would change the addresses to point to extended memory (vectoring) and report back to DOS that nothing was different—the memory was the same as it was a minute ago. Each new 1MB of memory is placed in front of DOS, page by page, using the page-frame segment of conventional memory.

In the same way that the 386 chip was fooling the old DOS into thinking that only 1MB of RAM was present, it fools Windows into thinking that many virtual 8086 PCs are running in the same place. The 386 Enhanced Mode also takes better control of DOS programs that bypass BIOS with video functions and intercepts those function calls (e.g., games). This allows most DOS programs that use a Graphics Mode to be run under Windows in Enhanced Mode.

The 80386 and all later chips protect both memory areas and hardware process operations by intercepting all memory addressing and hardware calls. Windows and the CPU get together and intercept *everything* an application tries to do. When two applications try to access the same device at the same time, Windows arbitrates and decides which one gets access first.

Windows 3.x Core Files

After WIN.COM has defined a running mode, it transfers control to DOSX.EXE and WIN386.EXE, which then load the Windows core programs into memory. Windows also loads its own device drivers from the SYSTEM.INI file, just as DOS uses the CONFIG.SYS file to load device drivers. The core Windows files are as follows:

- *USER.EXE*—Creates and maintains windows on the screen and handles requests to create, move, size, or close windows. Also controls the user interaction with icons and other interface components, including input devices such as the keyboard and mouse.
- *GDI.EXE*—Controls the graphics device interface, which is responsible for graphics operations that create images on the monitor or other display devices.
- *KRNL286.EXE or KRNL386.EXE*—Controls memory management, program loading, program code execution, and task scheduling. KRNL286.EXE is specific to the 80286 processor, and KRNL386.EXE applies to all later chips.

Initialization (.INI) Files

The so-called Windows operating system environment includes a number of support files, just like DOS does. Windows was designed to succeed DOS and become the main (and only) interface between the computer and the user. As a result, Microsoft tried to gather as many device drivers as possible and pull them together under a single umbrella. Additionally, as program files became larger, some of their supporting code was moved outside the .EXE or the .COM file to additional files. These files are required to run the application because the main executable file contains internal references to those files. Generally, these support files are located in a specific directory called a *working directory*.

For various reasons, PC users found that it was useful to locate the main program files in one place and some of the auxiliary files somewhere else. Not only that, but the data files created by an application are often placed on completely different drives (as in networks). To make some sense out of all this, certain types of configuration files were created to hold information regarding how the main executable file was supposed to run. These particular configuration files are called *initialization files*, and almost always have a .INI extension (read "eye-en-eye" or "in-nee").

We've seen that in a menu or shell, properties describe important information about the location of the main executable file and how to run it. Initialization files, on the other hand, describe to an *executable file* important information about how that program should run and where to find external support files.

The two fundamental .INI files used by Windows 3.x are the WIN.INI file and the SYSTEM.INI file. Both files are plain ASCII text files located by default in the \WINDOWS directory. New sections can be added to .INI files either by other program installations or by the user. Sections are enclosed in square brackets (e.g., [restrictions]) with a unique name.

SYSEDIT.EXE

SYSEDIT.EXE, located in the \WINDOWS\SYSTEM directory, is a small editing utility applet that opens and cascades the primary configuration files for Windows 3.1x and Windows 9x. In 16-bit Windows, the main files are CONFIG.SYS and AUTOEXEC.BAT for DOS, and SYSTEM.INI and WIN.INI for Windows. All four files are opened and arranged (cascade style) and can be viewed and edited. If Windows for Workgroups is installed, SCHDPLUS.INI is included in the editor for Schedule Plus (a workgroup schedule management program). Windows 3.x and Windows 9x also include PROTOCOL.INI for Real Mode networking protocols and configuration settings.

SYSEDIT can be set up in any program group window by using the File|New|Program Item dialog box in Program Manager. Likewise, you can drag the SYSEDIT.EXE program onto the Start button to put it into your Programs menu.

SYSTEM.INI

Anyone who installs a new piece of hardware or a new software application under Windows 3.x is touching the SYSTEM.INI file. This is the initialization file that Windows looks at after all the necessary and core system files have been installed. The SYSTEM.INI file contains the controls for the interface between Windows and DOS and, as we just saw, is where Windows VxDs are loaded into memory.

The SYSTEM.INI file is a plain ASCII text file that can be edited by WORDPAD.EXE, NOTEPAD.EXE (Windows applets), the DOS Editor (EDIT.COM), SYSEDIT.EXE, or any word processor that saves files in plain ASCII low-bit format.

WordPad is capable of saving to file types other than TXT (plain text). Be sure you choose the text format, or SYSTEM.INI becomes unreadable to Windows.

SYSTEM.INI is divided into sections, each of which has a heading enclosed in square brackets ([ ]). The most common areas of user interest are the [386Enh] section for 16-bit device drivers and the [boot] section, where the **SHELL=PROGMAN.EXE** line points to the shell file that runs the Program Manager at startup. This shell statement was moved into MSDOS.SYS for Windows 9x and calls the Desktop. The Program Manager still runs just fine under Windows 9x, and you can see a miniature version of how it used to look by right-clicking on the Start button and choosing Open.

Changing **SHELL=PROGMAN.EXE** to **SHELL=WINFILE.EXE** causes Windows 3.x to start up with the File Manager as the first window.

The only unusual thing to remember about the SYSTEM.INI and WIN.INI files (or any other Windows .INI file) is that **REM** (Remark) isn't the way to comment out a line in the file. To skip over the line in an .INI file, you must use a semicolon (;) in the first column of the specific line, followed by at least one space. **REM** is used for DOS batch files.

SYSTEM.INI can run alongside the Windows 9x Registry (SYSTEM.DAT and USER.DAT), and in Chapter 12, we discuss the differences between the three files. Until there are no more 16-bit legacy devices, there may still be a need for this particular file.

Remember that SYSTEM.INI installs device drivers and VxDs. Windows 9x continues to use the SYSTEM.INI file to load certain types of 16-bit device drivers, so even Window 9x machines may often have a SYSTEM.INI file.

WIN.INI

The second basic initialization file that Windows looks through at startup is WIN.INI. WIN.INI isn't required, but if it doesn't exist, Windows creates a default version. The WIN.INI file is where all the information about the overall user environment for Windows is stored. Whereas SYSTEM.INI is similar to the CONFIG.SYS file in the DOS startup process, WIN.INI is similar to the AUTOEXEC.BAT file at the end of the booting process.

WIN.INI contains the [windows] section, where programs can be set to run automatically without putting them in the Startup group window. **LOAD=** tells a program to run minimized on Windows startup, and **RUN=** tells a program to run normally at Windows startup.

When you can't find a reference to some program that seems to run from the Startup program group, you'll almost always find it referenced in either the **LOAD=** or **RUN=** line at the top of the WIN.INI file. Screen savers and antivirus programs typically use this line, as do mouse configurations.

The WIN.INI file also contains a listing of all the fonts installed into Windows, along with associated extensions for programs—file associations. For example, the [extensions] section of the WIN.INI file might have the line

```
bmp=C:\windows\ mspaint.exe ^.bmp
```

which tells Windows that, any time it sees a DOS file with a .BMP extension, it can make an assumption that the program MSPAINT.EXE will be used to open that file.

What Happens if Certain Files Are Missing?

There may be some peculiar scenarios on the A+ exam, and one of the more unusual ones that you may encounter is a situation in which either the SYSTEM.INI or WIN.INI file is missing. If the SYSTEM.INI file is missing, Windows simply won't start at all, and it produces an error message to that effect. If the WIN.INI file is missing, Windows starts in a default VGA Mode (assuming Enhanced Mode is possible). This is the precursor to the

Windows 9x Safe Mode (discussed in Chapter 12), where Windows starts with a basic configuration. When Windows can't find a WIN.INI file, it creates one when it starts. Any environmental customization (e.g., colors, icon spacing, or mouse configurations) will be missing, but you will at least be in Windows.

File Associations

Have you ever used the F2 key or the Properties menu to rename an executable file in the Windows Explorer? If you change the extension (assuming it's even visible) you'll get an Alert! message telling you that you may be unable to run the program and that the file naming police have been dispatched to arrest you immediately. Why is there an alert message at all?

Files are *associated* in the [extensions] section of the WIN.INI file by selecting File|Associate in File Manager. This used to be a simple process in Windows 3.x and has typically become far more complex under Windows 9x. Associating a program means that you can double-click on a file name in either File Manager or Windows Explorer, and Windows runs a program that can work with the file. But how does Windows know which program to run?

Here's where you really need to know all about file extensions, those three letters to the right of the period in a filename that we talked about Chapter 10. A common association is that any file ending with a .DOC extension automatically opens Microsoft Word. Both Windows 3.x and Windows 9x install certain pre-defined associations. Typically, .INI files, .BAT files, and .TXT files are associated with the Notepad or WordPad text editors. Many shareware programs (try before you buy) include a .DIZ description file. If you download a lot of shareware, you can easily associate the .DIZ extension with Notepad, thereby making it easy to double-click on the description and read it.

A default installation will typically hide the extensions in Windows Explorer. Whether or not you unhide the extensions, the associations are what produce the icon and description in the Explorer window. The Windows 3.x File Manager shows all file extensions by default, and choosing File|Associate immediately calls up a dialog box. Windows 9x, on the other hand, requires that you either do some detective work to find out what program is already associated with an extension, or fill out a nearly incomprehensible description form.

PROGMAN.INI

The poorly documented PROGMAN.INI file is a configuration file that controls the way the 16-bit Windows Program Manager appears to the user. The default .INI file contains a list of the program groups and very little other data. However, this file can be used to provide basic security on a system by removing certain options from the shell.

Usually, the last line under the [Groups] section begins with **Order=**, specifying the order in which Program Manager loads various groups. An optional section can be added by editing the PROGMAN.INI file and typing "[Restrictions]". The ***xxxx*=** lines added to this section can tell Program Manager whether to allow a user to run a program (**NoRun=**), change settings (**NoSaveSettings=**), or use the File menu (**NoFileMenu=**), among other things. Using the [Restrictions] section is a way to prevent someone from accidentally deleting (and/or creating) program groups.

The rapid onset of corporate networking and computer crime produced an industry-wide boom in security programming. Microsoft began including various security functions in Windows with the PROGMAN.INI file, but quickly moved into a full-featured set of security options. Typically, the person controlling computer security is a systems administrator or network administrator.

Group (.GRP) Files

Within the Program Manager, a number of additional windows are installed by default and can be added by the user. Each of these smaller windows is a program group. Each program group contains graphic symbols (icons) representing individual program items. Both program groups and program items can be created with the File | New option of the Program Manager menu. Windows Explorer works the same way, but choosing File | New offers an option for either a new file or a new folder (program group).

In almost the same way that a directory contains subdirectories and files, program groups contain icons pertaining to related programs (shortcuts), or they act as a sort of bucket to hold programs the user wants easy access to. Either way, Windows stores the information about which icons are in any given program group, along with each icon's properties. The files where this information is stored generally use the first eight letters of a window's title (found on the title bar) and a .GRP extension.

Group files were the precursor to the shortcut link (.LNK) files and are normally stored somewhere in the \WINDOWS directory. During the creation process, program groups offer the user an opportunity to name a specific location and file name, but most people don't use this option. The properties menu on a .LNK file continues to provide information about the actual executable program being pointed to.

A common problem found on Windows 3.x systems occurs when a user has accidentally highlighted a program group icon and deleted it. Although the group file has been deleted, the underlying programs are not affected at all. Create an \INIBACK directory (or some other name) and copy the group files and .INI files to it. In the event a .GRP file is accidentally deleted, you can restore the program group by simply copying it back to the \WINDOWS directory.

For the exam, remember that before you upgrade a Windows 3.x system to a Windows 9x environment, you should back up all .GRP files, along with all .INI files (*.GRP and *.INI). Windows 9x can interpret both types of files and carry the previous configuration through the upgrade.

The DOS commands **DIR** [d:]***.GRP /S** and **DIR** [d:]***.INI /S** will find all .GRP and .INI files on a drive (where [*d*:] is the drive letter). The *.GRP and *.INI can also be used within File Manager (File|Search) and within the Windows Explorer (Tools|Find).

Summary—Windows 3.x

We've talked about the way 16-bit Windows gathered together bits and pieces of older programs, DOS, and chip-based memory management so as to create a graphic user environment. We went into the history of Windows, and how IBM and Microsoft tried to work together to create a 32-bit operating system. This history, and their combined work, is what we see in the development of Windows NT and, eventually, Windows XP.

The reason for such a lengthy discussion of how Windows 3.x came into existence is that you're going to have to know about resources, Real Mode, and the Virtual Machine. These concepts are fundamental to how Windows 9x, 2000, and XP function. Keep in mind the following points, as you continue on into how Windows uses memory:

- Real Mode is where the operating system works with real hardware, real memory chips, and real addresses.
- Virtual Real Mode is where the system creates a sort of imitation of a computer—a virtual computer. The way Windows works with virtual machines changed with Windows 9x and 2000, so you should understand the initial concept of a "fake" machine, so to speak, running in memory.

- Windows 3.x introduced the first Registration database, which eventually became the Registry. This is where object linking was born, the original idea behind Windows shortcuts (.LNK) files.
- Windows 3.x also introduced file associations, whereby double-clicking on a file name would open an associated application (e.g., MS Word). Be sure you understand file extensions, otherwise go back and scan Chapter 10.
- Learn the basic system files used by Windows 3.x, in order to have a basis to remember the similar files used in Windows 9x. There will be questions on the exam about these basic files, particularly the USER.EXE, GDI.EXE and KERNEL.EXE core files.
- Keep track of the various startup modes used by Windows 3.x. We don't think you'll see related questions on the current exam, but we can't promise you that you won't.
- Understand how .INI files work, and the SYSEDIT applet used to display the startup files. SYSEDIT evolved into MSCONFIG.EXE, which became part of the Selective Startup dialog box in Windows 2000 and XP.

Memory

An operating system is software and, as such, loads into memory. It's important to understand the memory environment and how DOS, Windows, and any other software lives in that environment. In this context, the three main types of memory are:

- Conventional memory
- Expanded memory (EMS)
- Extended memory (XMS)

Basic Memory Divisions

You can think of memory as divided into two basic worlds: the world of what used to come with 8088/8086 PCs and the world of everything that was invented later. Remember that computers still face day-to-day limitations that are based on the way in which the first XT worked. These limitations have been forced on the manufacturers by the entire concept of backward compatibility. Windows 2000 was the first break from that backward compatibility and walking away from these limitations.

The Costs of Doing Business

Technical people sometimes forget that a computer is a tool that often is used in business to earn profits. A fundamental principle of business is that everything must pay for itself and that whatever remains is profit. Imagine a company using 30,000 computers with Windows 95 as the operating system.

Say that the price of a single copy of Windows 2000 is $50 (taking into consideration volume discounts, upgrade discounts, and so on), and then multiply $50 by the 30,000 computers. Simply purchasing the software would cost $1.5 million, which doesn't include shipping, taxes, and other incidental charges.

This company has an entire information systems (IS) staff and can assign five full-time employees the task of installing the upgrade on every computer. The rest of the staff must handle day-to-day problems and questions. Suppose that these five employees each make a salary of $16 per hour.

If it took only 30 minutes per computer to back up the original machine and install the upgrade, each computer would cost $8 in labor for one IS employee and possibly an additional half-hour of the person whose desk had the computer. Considering only the IS staff, 30,000 machines at $8 each would cost $240,000 in time and labor. With no problems, no errors, and a perfect first-time installation, it's already costing the company $1.74 million. We haven't even looked at the downtime of every salaried employee whose computer is unusable during the upgrade, from the $8-per-hour clerk to the $175,000-per-year executive (assuming $84 per hour with a loss of $42 of computer time). Nor have we looked at the time costs that the mailroom uses to process all those incoming copies of Windows 2000.

Those 30-minute-per-machine upgrades mean 15,000 work hours divided by the 5 IS employees, or 3,000 hours per IS employee. Assuming an 8-hour workday, it would take each IS employee 375 days to accomplish the upgrade. Naturally, with time off for weekends and sleep, you can see that it would take more than a year simply to change the company from Windows 95 to 2000. Then, think of what this would mean if the main spreadsheet program didn't work on the upgrade—if Windows 2000 wasn't backward compatible.

Microprocessors have many switches on their silicon layer and something called *microcode*, which is an extremely small machine language that is designed to process basic logic, arithmetic, and control signals. In addition to the switches, there are data banks that keep track of calculations in progress and registers that keep track of control data. The registers have a tiny amount of memory capability, allowing them to store only 2 bytes of information at a time.

If you recall that a byte is 8 bits, then 2 bytes would be 16 bits. A byte is something like the letter "G" or the number "5," and a register can contain 2 bytes. When the two bytes are put together, the combination is called a *word*.

A CPU has 14 registers, each of which is 2 bytes long, or 16 bits. The largest number that all these registers can hold (if every one of them had a hexadecimal F) would be 65,536. If you divide 1,048,576 (1MB) by 65,536, you get 16. Coincidentally, the first megabyte of RAM, as we'll see shortly, is divided into 16 segments.

The BIOS contains tables of interrupts, copyright information, testing routines, error messages, and some instructions to put characters on the screen in color. The ROM chips also hold a scaled-down version of Basic that the chip can use to execute instructions on how to move all the stored information into lower memory. Because DOS doesn't start running until after startup, this Basic code in the ROM chips controls the lights and beeps and initializes the printer and the keyboard.

Conventional Memory

ROM BIOS assigns and keeps track of specific locations in memory. These memory addresses are constantly being attached to bits of data and shuttled across buses and through the system. If the CPU can move 16 bits of information around in its own registers (internal bus), it stands to reason that it should be able to pass 16 bits of information to everything around it (external). Reason, however, has never been a strong point in the computer world.

The 8088 could keep track of a bit more (no pun intended) than a million separate addresses in memory, or 1MB (1,048,576 bits). Almost everything involved with moving data around a computer is done by its address. This is like mailing a picture of your new car to a friend. The post office has no interest in the picture, only in the address on the envelope. Imagine that you were a single mail carrier and had a million addresses to work with *every day*.

To make it easier to keep track of the first megabyte of memory, the 8088/86 CPU used 16 "regional ZIP codes," so to speak, called *segments*. Each segment of memory is 64KB long. Because the 8088/86 could address only 1MB of memory, this was fine. Newer chips have the capability to address far more than 1MB of memory and to do so more directly.

Memory segments are numbered, and the smaller numbers are said to be lower than the larger, higher numbers. For this reason, data stored in the first segments of RAM is said to be in *low memory*.

The original addressing scheme of the 8088/86 chips, using 16 segments of 64KB of memory, is the foundation of all later memory organization. This 1MB of RAM, divided into segments, is referred to as *conventional memory*. Memory addresses are expressed in hexadecimal numbers.

If you use binary math to calculate the number of addresses available to a 16-bit processor, you'll see that the number is less than the actual number available. Binary math alone won't go the whole distance (it would take 20 bits) because of the two-part address involving the segment and the offset. Without going into the details, you should know that memory error messages are reported using both parts of the address.

The segment address is one of the 16 regional segments of the 1MB. The offset address is the specific address within the 64KB length of the segment. The combination of segment and offset addresses is how a 16-bit processor can address 20 bits of addresses, or 1MB.

Although you might not be tested on this low level of detail, if you plan to work on computers, you should at least know what a segment address and an offset address look like. A typical example presented on the screen would be SEGMENT:OFFSET and appear as 30F9:0102.

80286 and Real Mode

The 8088/86 chips used single addresses for each segment:offset location in memory. The registers in the chip hold the actual hex number of the address as it directly relates to a real address in 1MB of memory. This direct, real, one-to-one relationship is known today as the *Real Mode* use of memory. The need for compatibility has kept Real Mode, along with the original 1MB of directly addressable memory, alive to this day (in 16-bit virtual machine windows).

The 286 chip changed from segment:offset addressing to something called *selector:offset addressing*. Instead of using a real segment, the registers held a pointer, or vector, to some other segment. Because the selector pointer is a smaller number than the full segment address, more selectors can fit into the same number of registers. This concept of using one address to refer to another address is used throughout the computer world. The words that describe this process are *mapping* and *aliasing*.

Aliasing and Mapping

When you rent a box at the post office, you're telling the post office that instead of putting an address on your big house, you want to put your address on a small box that will *refer* mail to your house. Instead of having to walk all the way to your house, the postal service can immediately move an envelope into your box, and you can then come pick it up. The box is vastly smaller than your house, and the distance from the incoming mail dock far shorter.

A cooperative venture between the post office (the CPU), which could deliver all the way to your house, and you (the hardware), who walks to the post office, results in faster processing and access to a larger storage area—the whole post office. In a nutshell, this is how expanded memory works.

The external **DOS SUBST** command (for *substitute*) is a way to shrink a long path of many subdirectories (with many characters) into the two characters of a drive letter. If you substitute C:\WINDOWS\SYSTEM\VBRUNS\100 with G:, instead of entering the full path, you can refer to it by using the aliased drive letter, G:. This is called *drive mapping*.

The 286 chip used part of its register group to provide an indicator to a real segment in additional sets of 1MB of memory. In other words, instead of a real address in a single megabyte of real memory, the register holds a sort of P.O. box number that refers to a whole new megabyte of memory. When the address is called, the CPU is pointed to this new megabyte and gets the segment:offset address of that new megabyte. Using this scheme, the 286 could address up to 16MB of memory.

Aliasing and mapping are used in expanded memory, interrupt vector tables, and most importantly, in the pseudo-32-bit FAT of the Windows 9x Installable File System (IFS) and VFAT. It is also used in networking, where very long path names (which include volumes and drives) are mapped to single drive letters.

If you think of air-traffic control as assigning a vector to an airplane, the controller is essentially pointing the pilot in a certain direction. The interrupt vector tables tell DOS where to look to find a particular set of interrupts. An undocumented command in DOS is the **TRUENAME** command, which returns the formal name of a subdirectory, regardless of how it may masquerade as a mapped or substituted drive letter.

Mapping is commonly used to create network drive letters out of specific subdirectories. Aliases are commonly used in Windows shortcuts (.LNK files), which are iconic representations of pointers to executable files somewhere on the drive.

Low Memory (Segment 1)

When DOS begins to load, even before the system files are hauled up by their bootstraps, BIOS installs its main I/O tools, tables, and instructions in the area of conventional memory that IBM originally reserved for it. The DOS system files "kernel" is also put into low memory—the first segment of the conventional 1MB of RAM (0000h to 9000h). Remember, this first megabyte is conventional memory and is addressed in the old, 8088/86 *real* way—Real Mode.

DOS uses a low-memory control process to map out the first megabyte of memory and stores this map in a location within the first segment of RAM. The first segment can easily be very crowded, containing device drivers, parts of COMMAND.COM, pieces of TSRs, disk buffers, and environment and file controls. The first segment of memory goes to:

- The interrupt vector table and DOS BIOS low-memory control
- IO.SYS and MSDOS.SYS
- Device drivers, such as MOUSE.SYS and ANSI.SYS
- Disk buffers
- Stacks (the way the CPU prioritizes and keeps track of tasks that were interrupted by more important tasks)
- The environment and file control blocks (FCBs)
- The resident part of COMMAND.COM, which is always in memory and produces the message "Abort, Retry, Ignore, Fail?"
- Pieces of the transient part of COMMAND.COM, which periodically drops out of memory to disk and then returns when it's needed
- The stack and data parts of programs, which are running but lurking in the background waiting to be called on (e.g., the **MODE** or **PRINT** commands from DOS or Borland's Sidekick)—TSR programs

When an event needs to interrupt the CPU, whatever generated the interrupt first checks the interrupt vector table for directions on where to look for the actual interrupt instructions. This table is in the first segment (low memory) from 0000h to 1000h. The interrupt vector table is used by BIOS, DOS, the interrupt controller chip, the main CPU, and any software programs that are running.

COMMAND.COM is a fairly large file, and for efficiency's sake, it doesn't load completely into RAM and remain there using up space. You need some parts of COMMAND.COM only rarely, whereas other parts must be available constantly. For example, the part that watches for a missing disk must be in memory all the time because the event causing the missing disk can happen at any time. This part of COMMAND.COM is *resident* because it's always resident (living) in memory.

The resident part of COMMAND.COM is like a sentry. It keeps an eye out for a commanding officer while the rest of the command is taking a break.

When you exit an application and go to a DOS command line, the resident part calls the *transient* part of COMMAND.COM, which hurries back from the disk and jumps into memory just in time to produce the C:\> prompt and begin parsing the command line.

Upper Memory (Segments 10–16)

Passing over the 640KB of applications memory, the very top segment of memory, from F000h to FFFFh, is also grabbed at the beginning of the start-up process. The motherboard's system BIOS installs to this segment to run the self-tests generated at the time the power is turned on (the POST). This is also where the ROM-level BIOS instructions are stored for drive controllers, keyboard polling, the system clock, I/O ports (serial and LPT), and a map of the addresses of the memory itself. System ROM (motherboard) and Basic go to segment 16.

IBM originally left a small 64KB gap directly above the area set aside for running programs. This area occurs at segment A000h and was quickly grabbed by enterprising memory management software utilities or was sometimes configurable by DIP switches. Instead of 640KB of user memory, this allowed for an additional 64KB, making 704KB available. Because this extra segment has always been there and has always been unclaimed, 32-bit operating systems routinely provide 704KB of usable memory for a virtual PC running in a DOS window.

Video RAM (B000)

The 64KB block after A000h was intended for EGA and VGA video extensions. IBM's common monochrome adapter (CMA)—also known as *monochrome display adapter* (MDA)—also laid claim to this area. However, as soon as CGA and color monitors arrived on the market, B000h to B800h became available to be stolen. Early memory managers could grab the 32KB between B000h and B800h for extra RAM on top of the previous 64KB.

Working with a CGA monitor was like looking through a screen door through silk underwear at a pine tree blowing in the wind without your glasses on. Not that it was a badly crafted monitor—it just turned the user's eyes into coffee cups. Aside from a resolution problem, the adapter card didn't have enough memory, and any scrolling would cause the screen to go black before it redrew itself. CGA vanished as soon as it could, leaving its IBM-reserved memory area free for memory management software.

The most commonly used DOS command with a CGA monitor was the **CLS** (clear screen) command. This command not only clears all text from the screen but also converts any residual color back to black-and-white. **CLS** is an internal DOS command that is built into COMMAND.COM.

Shortly after the failed CGA attempt, IBM introduced EGA, VGA, and the 8514/A color monitors. EGA and VGA demanded memory and went back to the A000h block to start high-resolution memory processing.

The 640K Barrier

DOS functions take up the first 64KB segment of the basic 1MB of conventional memory. ROM BIOS, the motherboard, COMMAND.COM, and other parts of DOS take an additional set of segments at the top of the conventional memory. Below these upper functions, video adapters, network cards, and certain drive controllers take up even more space. Because the top and the bottom of the 640KB user area is locked in by these other memory tenants, with most of the space taken at the top, people refer to the 640KB limit as the "640K barrier" or as hitting the "640K wall."

The base memory is whatever memory from the 640KB of user memory is left to the user after everything has loaded and all drivers and TSRs are in place. DOS 6.2 included a memory optimization software utility (MEMMAKER.EXE) that could provide close to 600KB of base memory. This optimization process took advantage of every unused piece of memory in the 1MB of conventional memory.

Virtual Memory

When Windows runs an application, that application looks at what it *thinks* is DOS and works with various memory addresses. In fact, Windows intercepts every addressing call from the program and hands the program an address based on Windows' own memory decisions. If a lot of memory has been used, Windows starts using disk space as additional, virtual memory.

When Windows puts an application's memory addresses on the disk, it uses 4KB chunks, and it doesn't tell the program that the apparent memory is somewhere on a disk. The application thinks it's addressing a continuous set of addresses in a RAM segment. When the application calls for memory addresses that aren't in actual RAM, it generates a page fault request, telling Windows to go to the disk and find those addresses. Windows then *pages* (loads) those addresses back into RAM and hands them to the application as though everything were completely normal.

Swap Files

Windows has two ways to set aside space on a hard drive to handle page overflow: temporary and permanent swap files. Windows 3.x could manage a maximum of only 16MB of installed RAM, but it could use far more virtual memory by saving 4KB pages (chunks) of memory to the disk as a swap file.

The default location of the swap file is the root directory of the drive where Windows was installed, usually Drive C:. This is true of Windows 9x as well as Windows 3.x.

The difference between a permanent and temporary swap file is mostly speed of access, leading to system performance issues. If Windows is going to swap out memory to the disk, it has two options: It can create a file somewhere on the disk and put memory there, or it can go to an already existing file. If it has to create the file at the moment; then it's a temporary swap file and is deleted when the session ends. You can create a permanent swap file out of contiguous sectors and save some time by not making Windows have to create the file when it needs it.

Windows 3.x created two files when it set up the drive's swap file. The first file, SPART.PAR, was a small read-only file in the Windows subdirectory. The sole purpose of this file was to tell Windows the location and size of the other file (the actual swap file). The swap file is usually in the root directory of the installation drive, but it can be on another, larger drive.

In Windows 3.1x, the permanent swap file is called 386PART.PAR and can be seen with File Manager if the View (by file type) options are set to show hidden files. The temporary swap file is usually called *WIN386.SWP*. A disadvantage of the temporary file is that it grows or shrinks depending on Windows' needs. The permanent swap file is fixed and doesn't grow to take over your disk.

If Windows is running in Standard Mode, a third type of temporary swap file—an application swap file—is created whenever a DOS application is started from within Windows.

Controlling Swap Files

Windows recommends a file size for the virtual memory swap file, and this recommendation can be changed. Windows 9x decided to drop the "swap file" name in favor of the more sophisticated-sounding "virtual memory." Either way, the file calculates all available space on the Windows installation drive, together with the largest block of contiguous, unfragmented space, to recommend a file 2.4 times the size of the physical memory installed on the computer.

User control over the type and size of the swap file is handled by the Control Panel applet (in the Main program group of Program Manager for Windows 3.x, or in Start|Settings under Windows 9x). Control Panel is run by the CONTROL.EXE program in the \WINDOWS directory. Any changes are stored in the CONTROL.INI file and in the \WINDOWS directory.

You can always get to the Control Panel quickly by clicking on the Start button (or pressing Ctrl+Esc), choosing Run and typing "control", and then pressing Enter. By the way, if you right-click on the Start button, you can quickly go to the Explorer or the Find (Explorer|Tools|Find|Files or Folders) option. To get a fast Desktop (Program Manager Window), click on Start, choose Run" and type a period (dot), and then press Enter.

The Control Panel (Windows 3.x)

The Control Panel icon opens to the Control Panel window, which contains icons for the internal subroutines held within CONTROL.EXE. In 16-bit Windows, one of the available icons is the Enhanced icon (a graphic picture of a CPU) through which virtual memory settings can be changed. The Enhanced option in the Control Panel is used to change virtual memory settings, swap file size and type, and device contention between I/O ports. The Enhanced option also provides for configuring task scheduling and Windows foreground, background, and exclusive processing.

In Windows 9x, virtual memory is accessed through the Control Panel's System icon, by double-clicking the My Computer icon and opening Control Panel, or by right-clicking to the Properties menu on the My Computer icon. At the System Properties dialog box, the Performance tab has a button for virtual memory. This is only slightly more sophisticated than the original Windows 3.x swap file. Allowing Windows to manage memory (recommended) is merely giving Windows a temporary swap file (which can take over the entire logical drive). Permanent swap file configuration is under the Let Me Manage… check box.

Because Windows would like to take total control of the user's system, the alert message following a reconfiguration to permanent swap file status is terrifying. It speaks of the end of the world and total collapse of civilization, as we know it. Instead of a button labeled OK, the button actually says, "A pox on you and yours!" Disabling virtual memory on this tab window merely disallows Windows from creating swap files.

A permanent swap file is a bit faster than a temporary swap file because it contains contiguous clusters and need not be created before Windows can use it. A temporary swap file must be created and saved before Windows can transfer the first 4KB memory block to the disk. It's better to defragment (DEFRAG.EXE) the disk before loading Windows and changing virtual memory to make the swap file permanent.

HIMEM.SYS and EMM386.EXE

Properly speaking, any memory beyond the first 1MB of conventional memory is extended memory. However, because there was no way to use this memory until the Lotus/Intel/Microsoft (LIM) specifications and hardware cards arrived on the market, the residue of expanded memory still exists. Even under Windows 9x, extended memory can be configured so that a part of it is used as expanded memory.

For any kind of memory beyond the conventional 1MB to be accessible by DOS, a memory manager device driver must be loaded from the CONFIG.SYS file. Originally, the device was only an expanded memory manager. With DOS 5.0, Microsoft began selling DOS directly to the customer. This generic DOS used HIMEM.SYS as a doorway manager to extended memory. Part of HIMEM.SYS is its ability to access unused parts of the conventional 1MB, which it calls *upper memory blocks (UMBs)*.

HIMEM.SYS does not provide expanded memory configuration. EMM386.EXE is the expanded memory device drive and will not run unless HIMEM.SYS has been loaded first. In DOS and 16-bit Windows, all this was done in the CONFIG.SYS (Configure the System) file. Windows 95 incorporated the loading of HIMEM.SYS into the IO.SYS system file. If an old legacy program requires expanded memory, then EMM386.EXE still loads from a CONFIG.SYS file, and one will have to be created. Windows 9x did away with creating this file automatically, along with the AUTOEXE.BAT file. That doesn't mean the CONFIG.SYS and AUTOEXEC.BAT aren't still necessary in some instances, however.

Do whatever you need to do to separate the correct names and characteristics for *expanded* (EMS) and *extended* (XMS) memory from conventional memory. The exam will contain questions about how each type of memory works and their correct names. You might use the *386* in EMM386.EXE to think of the old days, back when the 80386 processor was a hot item. Today, practically nothing uses expanded memory, so perhaps you can associate *expanded* with *old* and *386*. Another way might be that the "X" in XMS is the Roman numeral "TEN" and X-TEN sounds a lot like extended.

Upper Memory Blocks (UMBs)

DOS and Windows 3.x machines want to have as much base memory (640KB application memory) as possible for running DOS applications. DOS 5.0 introduced a change to COMMAND.COM that allowed it to use high memory and upper memory blocks to store parts of itself.

Upper memory blocks are managed by EMM386.EXE, which can run only after HIMEM.SYS has opened the door to extended memory. Therefore, the only way the **DOS=UMB** directive can be used is if the HIMEM.SYS driver is used first.

After HIMEM.SYS opens access to all memory above the 1MB of conventional memory, COMMAND.COM can be loaded into the High Memory Area (HMA). **DOS=HIGH** places most of the command processor into the HMA (above A000h). To use even more extra memory, the UMBs can be made accessible only through the expanded memory driver (EMM386.EXE).

EMM386.EXE allows high memory and UMBs to be used for applications and drivers. High memory can hold programs by using **DEVICEHIGH=** (in CONFIG.SYS) and **LOADHIGH=** (in AUTOEXEC.BAT).

Translation Buffers

Windows still requires DOS to handle certain functions, such as reading or writing a file to disk. To do this, Windows switches the CPU back to Real Mode so that DOS can run in Real Mode and read the conventional memory for instructions. To communicate with DOS, Windows places translation buffers in the upper memory 384KB area.

Translation buffers act as a kind of vector table for Windows to hand addresses to DOS. Windows also uses translation buffers to make Real Mode networking calls to a network operating system. Windows allocates two 4KB translation buffers (8KB) for each virtual PC. Running an application creates a virtual PC, so each running application uses 8KB of real memory in the form of translation buffers.

Networked physical computers use six 4KB translation buffers per virtual PC, which is 24KB per application.

Because all adapter cards, including network interface cards, use some address space in upper memory, a physical computer with a number of adapter cards can eventually take up all the upper memory. In this event, Windows can be told to use base memory for translation buffers. Translation buffers can't be split between upper and base memory. If the translation buffers end up in base memory, every virtual PC that Windows creates will inherit the buffers, leaving less memory for the application to run.

Remember that Windows creates virtual PCs out of the existing environment when it loads. Therefore, when an application runs and Windows 3.x creates a virtual PC for it, the VM inherits the DOS environment that was in existence when 16-bit Windows was started.

System Resources

All free memory (not conventional memory) available from the first DOS prompt is referred to as *base* memory (640KB), the high-memory area (HMA) above A000h, and *extended* memory (beyond 1MB). After Windows (all versions) is up and running, it takes control of memory on the system and loads device drivers, program code, and data files into free memory. DOS is out of the loop except for file management at the disk level and hardware management at the interrupt level.

For the exam, remember that, although there is a formal distinction between base memory and conventional memory, questions will usually apply the term "conventional" memory to the 640KB used for applications, and will refer to high memory by name.

The names used for memory in a DOS session change after Windows is running. All of memory becomes the global heap, or simply "the heap."

The Windows 3.x Environment: Global Heap

The *global heap* in Windows 3.x is the entire amount of memory available at startup. Windows reads the existing environment created by CONFIG.SYS (if it exists) and HIMEM.SYS (if it was loaded). Whatever programs have been installed by DOS prior to running Windows are recognized by Windows, and whatever memory is actually available for programs is taken by Windows.

The global heap is all available memory that Windows 3.x can see at startup. The maximum amount of actual memory Windows 3.x can use is 16MB. The global heap is divided into three main areas:

- *Conventional memory*—This is the same as base memory in DOS real sessions, (i.e., segments above low memory and below A000h).
- *High memory*—If DOS has set aside areas above the A000h segment for use by applications, Windows takes control of that area and adds it to the global heap of memory.
- *Extended memory*—After Windows starts, it already knows how much memory you have in your system by reading the virtual memory driver (HIMEM.SYS), and it takes over control of that memory from DOS and accesses it directly.

After Windows has taken over the management of RAM, it makes no difference whether the memory is extended or conventional. Windows sees all memory up to 16MB as part of the global heap. The theoretical limit to extended memory available to Windows 3.x is 15MB: 16MB minus the 1MB of conventional memory.

Windows loads program code into the heap by putting it first into lower segments and then into increasingly higher segments. The global heap is divided into two areas: USER.EXE and GDI.EXE. Each smaller area also has a local heap of memory.

The local heap is reported as the system resources, some of which is used and some of which is freed up as code moves in and out of memory. In Windows 3.x, each area is limited to one 64KB segment for a total of 128KB for the heap. The following system resources (memory) are a special area set aside by Windows:

- The USER and GDI local heaps together make up the Free System Resources percentage seen under the Help | About | (System) menu option from any main menu in a Windows-compliant application.
- Everything in the Windows environment (both 16-bit and 32-bit) uses a percentage of the system resources, including icons, windows, programs, applications, data, menus, program tools, and screen savers.

- System resources are reported as a percentage available. Typically, between 50 percent and 85 percent of the resources should be available at any given time (taking into account all programs running in that session).

So-called memory doubler software does not double the amount of installed RAM; rather, it doubles the amount of system resources available from the two local heaps.

Programs are supposed to be written in such a way that resources are taken from the free system resources and given up again when the code for that program terminates. Unfortunately, not all programmers follow the rules, and not all programs work the way they were intended to work.

If something takes up resources, but fails to release them back to the heaps at conclusion, those resources never return to the Windows resources memory. This problem is sometimes referred to as a *resource leak*. Windows must be exited and re-started to re-create a new heap and start again with maximum free resources. This problem can occur as easily in Windows 9x as in Windows 3.x, although fewer programs written for 32-bit Windows steal resources.

An "Out of memory" error in Windows often refers to the lack of enough free system resources, not to the amount of total free memory on the computer.

LIM 4 Expanded Memory

By the time the AT-class computers were arriving on the market and the 80286 chip was getting organized, the hottest application driving the sale of PCs was the Lotus 1-2-3 spreadsheet. Lotus was getting tired of hearing complaints from its customers with big spreadsheets running out of memory, so it decided to do something about it. Lotus got together with Intel and worked out a process (bank switching) that they decided to call the Expanded Memory Specification (EMS) 3. No one knows what happened to specification 1 or 2, but eventually Lotus and Intel brought pressure to bear on Microsoft to join with them and release LIM (Lotus-Intel-Microsoft) EMS 3.2 memory.

LIM 3.2 expanded memory introduced access to 8MB of additional memory, allowing the 80286 to address up to 16MB of additional memory. LIM expanded memory required a special hardware expansion card, and software had to be written specifically to work with both the EMS memory and the cards.

Not long after the release of the EMS LIM specification, AST (a large motherboard manufacturer) got together with Ashton-Tate, one of the largest software companies and the maker of dBase. Together, these two companies released a far more flexible version of expanded memory specifications called Enhanced EMS (EEMS). Lotus, Intel, and Microsoft then one-upped the AST-Ashton-Tate group and enhanced their specification to version 4. LIM 4 EMS provided 32MB of addressable memory.

Think about it: Starting with the 80286, processors could address 2MB or more of memory, but DOS could address only the 1MB of real memory. There had to be a special way to work around that limitation. The workaround, once again, had to do with the selector:offset mapping process. One last segment of real memory was set aside and configured as the EMS page frame segment—a 64KB *block* that was set aside somewhere between C000h and E000h—above 640KB base memory, but below video RAM.

The 64KB page frame was divided into four 16KB blocks called *pages*. When a program wanted to put data into expanded memory, it assigned an address to the data and then assigned a pointer vector to that address, kind of like renting warehouse space. The program put the data in the warehouse, making a note of the warehouse's location in the EMS page frame segment.

When the application called the data, it looked up the storage bin's address (the page of memory) in conventional memory, and then switched DOS into thinking that the 1MB of memory it was looking at was one of the extended megabytes. DOS used the data while still thinking that it was in the original 1MB. When the data was sent back to memory, EMM386.EXE picked it up and drove it back to its remote storage bin in extended memory.

EMM386.EXE

In Chapter 10, we discussed how commands are used. The syntax of any command includes the command and the variables (switches) that can be used to set various configuration values. EMM386.EXE offers a good example of the convention used to describe a command's syntax. The complete syntax for EMM386.EXE is as follows, where each of the settings enclosed in square brackets ([ ]) can either have a value or represent a value:

```
EMM386.EXE [memory] [L=minXMS] [NOEMS] [RAM] [ON¦OFF¦AUTO]
[I=address-address] [X=address-address] [W=ON¦OFF] [Mx]
[FRAME=address] [/Paddress] [Pn=address] [B=address]
[A=altregs] [H=handles] [D=nnn] [N=path]
```

EMM386.EXE RAM (using the **RAM** switch) provides whatever expanded memory is needed for any DOS applications that require it.

Conventional memory technically refers to the full 1MB of RAM installed on almost every computer sold in the last 10 years. The lower 640KB of application memory is technically called *base* memory. The upper 360KB is technically called *high* memory.

DEVICEHIGH and **LOADHIGH** can take advantage of high memory and UMBs to store device drivers. **DOS=HIGH,UMB** can load parts of COMMAND.COM into high memory and upper memory blocks.

The certification exam generally uses the conventional memory designation to mean the first 640KB and the high memory designation to mean the upper 360KB, including UMBs.

Task Switching

The 80286 not only increased addressable memory to 16MB, but also introduced the concept of Protected Mode. In theory, Protected Mode keeps a given area of memory isolated from another area of memory. People using plain DOS were already coming up with ways to do more than one thing at a time on computers, and the most popular way for doing so was by task switching. Some commercial menu programs even provided a way for the user to do this. This integration of the menu program and the ability to do task switching made PCs easier to use and more versatile.

Task switching means that the loaded parts of a program and its data files are taken out of RAM and stored to the disk as a kind of photographic snapshot. All the program code for a word processor is saved out of RAM onto a special area of the hard drive called a *swap file.* The data or documents being worked on at the moment of the switch are also stored to the swap file.

Sometimes, the CPU is in the middle of doing something when an IRQ comes along with an interruption. Depending upon how important that interruption is, the CPU has to put down whatever it was doing and pick up whatever the IRQ needs. The "place" in memory where the CPU keeps track of what processing it puts down is called a *stack*. If there are too many interruptions, the CPU can generate a stack overflow error. Task switching uses a process similar to that of the stacks used by the CPU.

Because it takes a certain amount of time to spin the disk, move the read-write heads, and store the information on disk, task switching is relatively slow. Not only must the contents of memory be stored, but a new program must be loaded into RAM and prepared for the user. Each new task being loaded into RAM requires a new snapshot of RAM: a window.

A way was needed to keep every program in memory and go beyond the 640K barrier of conventional memory so that the slowness of disk swapping RAM could be overcome. Then, the page frame and expanded memory arrived. Now, a program could be saved into expanded or extended memory just as easily as it could be saved to disk, and the 286 Protected Mode would (theoretically) keep everything nice and separate.

Page Frame Memory and Page Swapping

The 286 chip's Protected Mode and a LIM expanded memory card gave users access to 16MB of memory for use by programs and data. The idea was that if something could keep track of those snapshots of conventional RAM and shift them up into expanded memory, several programs could be run at once in the same base memory area. The 80286's protection features would make sure (in theory) that each program in memory had its own specially protected area and that, if something went wrong, the program could be shut down only in that area while everything else continued to run.

If you think of expanded memory as a sort of warehouse on the second floor of a building, then you can imagine a loading dock on the first floor. When a program is running, it's like a truck being loaded from the dock. If another truck (program) has to be loaded (run), then in our imaginary warehouse, all the boxes (program code) from the first truck have to be sent back up to the warehouse (expanded memory) on an elevator. New boxes have to be sent down the elevator, and the second truck has to change places with the first. The elevator is like the page frame. (We discussed memory pages in Chapter 3.)

Task switching is like a Lazy Susan on a dining room table. Someone who wants an item spins the rotating platter until the choice comes around. However, instead of the other choices becoming available to the other side of the table, the other programs are spun through the page frame doorway into expanded memory or are saved to the disk.

Task switching to expanded memory was a nice idea, but it didn't work out quite as planned. DOS had a hard time keeping the various balls it was juggling in the air and tracking which parts of memory were supposed to be used for what. Aside from that, the 64KB page frame area was becoming a bottleneck because users had to move a 550KB process through it during a switch and another 612KB process back up into EMS memory.

The 286 had some internal problems as well. For example, when a program crashed in a so-called protected area, it usually brought the entire system tumbling down with it, regardless of how well the program area was protected. This led to a reboot, which would cancel whatever had been going on with any other programs. The swap file would be erased during the reboot, and any data that hadn't been saved would be lost.

Virtual Device Drivers (VxDs)

The lowest area of the global heap (memory) is set aside for Windows to load Windows-based device drivers that handle the interface between Windows, DOS, and hardware devices. We saw that the CONFIG.SYS file in DOS installs device drivers in the first segment of conventional memory prior to loading Windows. The Windows device drivers are loaded into the lowest segment of the global heap, which is usually just above the low-memory area set aside by DOS.

Windows has its own device drivers that handle the keyboard, mouse, printers, video monitors, sound cards, scanners, and anything else that connects to the motherboard. All these device drivers are listed in the SYSTEM.INI file with any additional information they might need during startup.

For the exam, remember that a virtual device driver (VxD) is a 32-bit Protected Mode .DLL that manages a system resource (i.e., a hardware device or installed software) such that more than one application can use the resource at the same time. The 32-bit Protected Mode comes from the 32-bit 80386 chip architecture and therefore is available only for a 386 or faster CPU.

The V*x*D abbreviation is used to refer to any (V)irtual *device* (D)river, where *x* is used as a stand-in variable. The specific device driver replaces *x* with a character or characters referring to the specific type of driver. For example, a V*D*D is a virtual *display* driver, where *D* represents *display*.

VxDs work together with DOS to support multitasking in that more than one application can access the device at the same time in an arbitrated (managed) way. The VxDs work together with Windows to process interrupts and to carry out I/O processes for a specific application without interfering in another application's use of the same device. All the hardware devices on a typical computer have a VxD, including the motherboard program interrupt controller (PIC), the timer oscillator, DMA channels, disk controller(s), serial and parallel ports, keyboard and input devices, math coprocessor, and monitor display.

A virtual device driver is generally written to hold code for specific operations of a device that might not be included in the basic Windows installation. However, a VxD is required for any device that can retain settings information from an application that might mess up a request from another application. VxDs can also be written for any driver software that was installed by DOS during the CONFIG.SYS process.

When a VxD is a software driver, it usually surrounds the existing device (or TSR) and provides a specialized environment coming from Windows. This fools the existing device into thinking that only one computer running one application is present and that only that application will be using the hardware device controlled by the real driver. Again, the VxD is acting as a liaison between the Windows control management system and the individual device that is looking for a secure set of memory addresses.

For the exam, remember that VxDs are installed from the SYSTEM.INI file, usually in the [386Enh] section of the file, and begin with **DEVICE=**, the same as they do in the CONFIG.SYS file. Windows 95 extended this process and tries to substitute a VxD for any device listed in a CONFIG.SYS file.

Summary—Windows Memory

Once again, we want to reassure you that this stuff (technical term) is complicated! If you think you don't need to know any of what we've talked about, consider that in order to make an informed decision about modern computers, you can no longer simply choose how much RAM to install and what kind of CPU to buy. System performance is being defined, more and more, by such things as bus speeds, clocking, cache memory and resource management—all of which are connected with principles of conventional and extended memory.

Programs and computers use memory all the time, and the way that memory is accessed and configured are pretty important concepts to remember. Go over the following list to make sure you have a good understanding of each point:

- The three basic types of main memory are conventional, expanded, and extended memory.
- Memory addressing is done with segments, and real memory uses 16 64KB segments. Depending upon the address number of a segment, it can be low or high memory.

- When we use one thing to point to something else, we're redirecting traffic. Web sites often use one URL to redirect the browser to another address. DOS uses vector tables to send instructions to other memory addresses. Network drive mapping and the DOS SUBST (substitute) command, redirect requests to a drive letter to a different path name.
- Conventional memory has a 640KB "barrier." This was the main reason Extended memory was developed. Windows uses HIMEM.SYS as an extended memory manager, and you should know the difference between Extended (EMS) and Expanded (XMS) memory.
- One of the most inelegant features of 32-bit Windows is in its use of swap files and virtual memory. You should understand how a swap file is a way for Windows to pretend it has more memory than installed memory modules.
- You don't need to remember all the technical details of how translation buffers work, and so on, but you must remember how HIMEM.SYS manages memory and system resources.
- Be sure you have a clear understanding of the Windows memory heap.
- Learn the basics of Virtual Device Drivers (VxDs) because you'll not only see more discussion in the following chapters, but you'll have lots of encounters with device problems and the Windows Device Manager when you troubleshoot a problem machine.

An Example CONFIG.SYS File

The following CONFIG.SYS file was processed by MEMMAKER, a DOS memory-optimization utility. Let's again discuss the fundamental directives and what they do using a real-world example.

Be sure that you don't get caught saying that MEMMAKER speeds up the overall system performance. MEMMAKER only increases the amount of conventional memory available to DOS applications by moving whatever it can into high memory and UMBs (if they're available). Technically, this can speed up some applications, but for the exam, MEMMAKER affects space, not performance.

```
DEVICE=C:\DOS\SETVER.EXE
DEVICE=C:\WINDOWS\HIMEM.SYS /TESTMEM:OFF
DEVICE=C:\WINDOWS\EMM386.EXE RAM I=B000-B7FF WIN=CD00-CFFF
BUFFERS=40,0
FILES=70
DOS=UMB
LASTDRIVE=K
FCBS=16,0
```

```
DOS=HIGH
STACKS=9,256
SHELL=C:\COMMAND.COM /P /E:1024
DEVICE=C:\BUSLOGIC\BTDOSM.SYS /D
DEVICEHIGH /L:3,19344 =C:\BUSLOGIC\BTCDROM.SYS /D:MSCD0001
DEVICEHIGH /L:1,22576 =D:\IOMEGA\ASPIPPM1.SYS FILE=SMC.
ILM SPEED=10
DEVICE=D:\IOMEGA\SCSICFG.EXE /V
DEVICE=D:\IOMEGA\SCSIDRVR.SYS
DEVICEHIGH /L:1,5888 =C:\DOS\RAMDRIVE.SYS 2048 /E
DEVICE=C:\WINDOWS\IFSHLP.SYS
```

A quick (but subtle) way to see that this PC is not running Windows 9x is the fact that EMM386 has no **REM** (remark) in front of it, and the existence of the line **DOS=UMB**. In Windows 9x, SETUP.EXE automatically removes any expanded memory drivers from an existing CONFIG.SYS file during the installation process.

Remember that Windows 9x requires HIMEM.SYS to access extended memory for virtual memory management. HIMEM.SYS has been hard-coded into the IO.SYS file, which took over configuration from CONFIG.SYS. Windows 9x also uses REM to cancel any reference to SMARTDRV or EMM386.EXE.

Points of Interest

Notice that the **DEVICEHIGH=** directive has been put in by MEMMAKER. The /L:# value is automatically configured when MEMMAKER optimizes the specific addresses. The BusLogic SCSI adapter driver controlling the CD-ROM has been moved to high memory, as has an Iomega driver.

EMM386.EXE (expanded memory) has been told that Windows 3.x is present and to include (**/I=**) a range of memory addresses for use by devices. This is the **I=B000-B7FF** switch on the EMM386 line.

A RAM drive has been installed using the following line:

```
DEVICEHIGH /L:1,5888 =C:\ DOS\RAMDRIVE.SYS 2048 /E
```

The **/L:1,5888** was added by MEMMAKER to put the device driver in high memory. RAMDRIVE.SYS loads the RAM drive device driver and creates a 2MB RAM drive in extended (**/E**) memory. A companion line in the AUTOEXEC.BAT file could then be used (**SET TEMP=G:**) to tell DOS to use the RAM drive for temporary files.

RAMDRIVE.SYS comes with both DOS 6.x and Windows 9x and can create a virtual disk drive out of RAM. Because a RAM drive moves at the speed of memory, it can sometimes be useful for temporary files. However, the drive vanishes when the system is powered off.

Finally, HIMEM.SYS is used with an unusual **/TESTMEM:OFF** switch. During boot-up, when HIMEM loads, it tests the memory in almost the same way that the parity check is done during the POST. This second memory integrity check can take enough time that it can be turned off. **/TESTMEM:ON|OFF** is the settings switch to either turn off the memory checking or force it (useful with nonparity memory).

Windows 3.x could address a maximum of only 16MB of memory. Even though DOS could recognize more than that, 16-bit Windows would show "3% Remaining Resources" and fail almost as soon as it loaded. An undocumented way around this was to borrow the HIMEM.SYS file from Windows 95 OS/R-B and install it in place of the version that came with DOS 6.x. This would fool Windows 3.11 into believing it could use more than 64MB of RAM.

DEVICE= and DEVICEHIGH=

The **DEVICE=** directive means that a device is attached to the system. In this case, the device driver (usually a .SYS file) can be found on Drive D: in the \IOMEGA subdirectory. The specific name of the device driver file is ASPIPPM1.SYS. With a little experience, we might guess that this refers to an Iomega Zip, Jaz, or Ditto (tape) drive. A typical statement in the above CONFIG.SYS file appears as follows:

```
DEVICE=D:\IOMEGA\ASPIPPM1.SYS FILE=SMC.ILM SPEED=10
```

Remember that the CONFIG.SYS file is executed prior to the AUTOEXEC.BAT file during the boot process. The **PATH** environment variable can be set only after the system is under the control of the operating system. The **PATH** command can be run only in a batch file or at the DOS command line. **PATH=** is always found in the first few lines of the AUTOEXEC.BAT file.

Because no search path has been set when the CONFIG.SYS runs, every device must have its full path and file name in the directive. Because no path has been set, DOS can look for the driver file only in the root directory of the bootable disk in the boot drive. This is the directory that DOS is logged in to as the current directory at boot-up.

If enough memory was available in high memory (above conventional memory, according to the exam), the **DEVICEHIGH=** directive (DOS 5.0 and later) would attempt to load the Iomega (device) driver above the 640KB of base memory. In this case, the **DEVICE=** directive means that the driver is intended to load into conventional (base) memory.

MEMMAKER automatically runs hundreds of configuration settings to see which programs can make the most efficient use of high memory, UMBs, or both. In this case, it determined that the Iomega driver should stay in conventional base memory.

DOS marks an intentional space between characters with an equal sign (=), a semicolon (;), or a space (spacebar or ASCII decimal .0032 scan code). An equal sign or a semicolon is used most often to ensure that a space is marked and to leave no room for misinterpretation. ".0032" can be entered using the Alt key at the same time as the digits are entered on the numeric keypad of the keyboard.

Again, the line we're examining is:

```
DEVICE=D:\IOMEGA\ASPIPPM1.SYS FILE=SMC.ILM SPEED=10
```

A space and more information follow the device driver. **FILE=SMC.ILM** probably refers to a data file in which either further configuration settings are stored through customer configuration or the device reads factory-configured values.

During SETUP.EXE (all Windows versions) or INSTALL.EXE (DOS) for a new device, a typical detection program uses simple tests to check for the existence of certain hardware and software. This is not the same as the POST looking at CMOS settings.

Depending on whether Yes or No returns from a setup test, the new device's installation routine often chooses one of several files containing factory-configured values. These files are usually taken from the installation disk that comes with the device. Some knowledgeable guesswork would indicate that SMC.ILM is one of these factory configuration files relating to some device made by Iomega.

The exam might ask you to explain why Windows 9x notices a particular device attached to the system but can't provide the manufacturer's information and settings. Windows 9x has a large internal database of many devices made by today's hardware manufacturers.

If Windows 9x can read settings information from a BIOS chip on a PnP-compatible device, it configures the device with its correct settings. If Windows 9x can recognize that a generic type of device is attached to an I/O port, it tries to use generic settings, which might work.

If Windows 9x notices only that a device exists at an I/O port, but can't even tell which general class (Registry) the device falls into, it tries to prompt the user for specific configuration settings by using the Have Disk option dialog box during installation.

If neither PnP processing nor generic device awareness takes place, the device is ignored in a full PnP-enabled configuration. If PnP is not enabled, Windows 9x resource management stops short of managing device resources.

MSDET.INF

Windows 9x uses detection modules called by MSDET.INF during setup. These .DLL modules contain general settings information about classes (general categories) of devices. The specific .DLL files that MSDET.INF calls, try to read information from a device through PnP BIOS chips on the device. If PnP won't work, the .DLL generates common settings for that class of device. The settings are stored in the Registry following completion of the setup routine. This so-called auto-detection became available starting with Windows 95.

The data resulting from the checking process is stored in the DETLOG.TXT file (detection log text file), and the device has either a manufacturer's name and settings stored in the Registry or a generic class name. To distinguish between true PnP compatibility and the best-guess capabilities built into Windows 9x, we use the term *auto-detect* here, although it is not the formal name of a feature in Windows 9x.

At the end of the SMC.ILM file name is yet another space and the **SPEED=10** setting value. Note that no internal way exists of knowing what this refers to beyond some sort of speed setting with 10 being the value. The **SPEED** setting is explained only in the device's technical reference documentation.

A classic way to troubleshoot a PC is to bypass every reference to any device from all configuration files. Inexperienced technicians tend to use the Delete key to delete the entire file or to delete a line in a configuration file. In this situation, if it should turn out that the device was a critical system driver (such as a SCSI controller), the technician is left with only his or her memory to replace the line.

Regardless of whether CONFIG.SYS supports the **REM** statement, typing "REM" followed by a space at the beginning of any line in CONFIG.SYS or AUTOEXEC.BAT causes DOS to bypass the line without executing any instructions. In Windows .INI files, use the semicolon (;) followed by a space to accomplish the same bypass.

If it should turn out that a configuration line is necessary, it can be reactivated by deleting the **REM** or the semicolon, removing the necessity of trying to remember what you've deleted at a later date.

Practice Questions

Question 1

When a PC is first powered up, COMMAND.COM, AUTOEXEC.BAT, and CONFIG.SYS files load in which order?

- ❍ a. AUTOEXEC.BAT, CONFIG,SYS, COMMAND.COM
- ❍ b. COMMAND.COM, CONFIG.SYS, AUTOEXEC.BAT
- ❍ c. CONFIG.SYS, COMMAND.COM, AUTOEXEC.BAT
- ❍ d. COMMAND.COM, AUTOEXEC.BAT, CONFIG.SYS

Answer c is correct. CONFIG.SYS initializes 16-bit Real Mode devices and sets the environment, and then the command interpreter, COMMAND.COM, loads. After the interpreter is loaded, commands contained in the AUTOEXEC.BAT batch file are processed.

Question 2

A Windows Me machine no longer uses either a POST or a command interpreter because the Registry controls the entire process for the machine.

- ❍ a. True
- ❍ b. False

Answer b, false, is correct. All computers use a boot process involving a power-on self test (POST), regardless of what operating system is installed. The Windows Registry manages system configuration for Windows 9x machines running a Microsoft operating system and can only begin to operate after the system files have taken charge of the system.

Question 3

Windows 9x uses SYSTEM.DAT and USER.DAT to run driver software. Which initialization file is used in the case of a 16-bit legacy device?

- ❍ a. WIN.INI
- ❍ b. SYSTEM.INI
- ❍ c. WIN.COM
- ❍ d. PROGMAN.INI

Answer b is correct. SYSTEM.INI must be present for certain 16-bit hardware devices to be recognized by any version of Windows 95, 98, or ME. Answer a is incorrect because WIN.INI stores user configurations in a 16-bit Windows (3.x) environment. Answer c is incorrect because WIN.COM is the loader program for Windows and doesn't store any settings. Answer d, PROGMAN.INI, refers to the Windows 3.x Program Manager desktop shell and was sometimes used for rudimentary security.

Question 4

Windows 95, 98, and ME all the load ____________ memory manager from the ____________ system file.

- ❍ a. EMM386.EXE, MSDOS.SYS
- ❍ b. EMM386.EXE, CONFIG.SYS
- ● c. HIMEM.SYS, IO.SYS
- ❍ d. HIMEM.SYS, MSDOS.SYS

Answer c is correct. Beginning with Windows 95, HIMEM.SYS was loaded from within the IO.SYS system file. In DOS and Windows 3.x, extended memory was accessed through the **DEVICE=** line in the CONFIG.SYS file. Answers a and b are incorrect because EMM386.EXE is an expanded memory manager, not extended memory. HIMEM.SYS accesses XMS memory. Answer d is incorrect because MSDOS.SYS is concerned with how Windows starts up, not basic system access.

Question 5

Virtual Real Mode creates a ______ based on an ______ chip.

- ❍ a. Virtual XT, 80286
- ❍ b. Command session, 80386
- ❍ c. Real machine, 80286
- ● d. Virtual machine, 8088/86

Answer d is correct. The Virtual Machine (VM) is a software-generated copy of the first XT machine that was based on the 8088/86 CPU. It addresses memory in a "real" way. Answer a is incorrect because a VM is not a virtual XT, and the chip emulation is not a 286. Answer b is incorrect because of the 386 chip and the improper term "command session." Answer c is incorrect because of the 286 chip and the improper term "real machine."

Question 6

The utility program most used in a preliminary diagnostics session in order to examine settings and startup problems is _______.

- a. PIFEDIT.EXE
- b. SYSEDIT.EXE
- c. REGEDIT.EXE
- d. WINEDIT.EXE

Answer b is correct. Running SYSEDIT.EXE produces a cascade of windows showing the various basic text files the system uses during startup. Answer a is incorrect because PIFEDIT.EXE is used to configure a .PIF file for a DOS application. Answer c is incorrect because REGEDIT.EXE is used to open the Windows Registry and reconfigure basic elements of the Windows 9x system, not to do a preliminary diagnostics on a faulty system. Answer d is incorrect because there is no system editor called WINEDIT.EXE.

Question 7

IO.SYS is loaded into the _______ memory area of _______ memory.

- a. low, conventional
- b. high, low
- c. base, conventional
- d. conventional, low

Answer a is correct. IO.SYS contains basic functions and tables required by the BIOS and motherboard. It loads into the low area of the first 1MB of conventional memory. Answer b is incorrect because the high and low areas of memory are contained within what's called *conventional* or (incorrectly) *base* memory. Technically, base memory is whatever memory is left to the user for applications. Answer c is incorrect because base and conventional memory refer to the overall first megabyte of memory. Answer d is incorrect because the terms are in reverse order of proper usage.

Question 8

Windows 98 creates a permanent swap file when you choose to specify virtual memory settings in the system's performance dialog box.

- ❍ a. True
- ❍ b. False

Answer a, true, is correct. The performance tab of the System properties dialog box under the Control Panel allows user configuration of temporary or permanent swap files. When Windows manages virtual memory, it usually uses a temporary swap file that can grow to take over all empty (contiguous) space on a hard drive. Specifying the virtual memory settings creates a permanent swap file, both limiting the amount of drive space Windows will take over and saving the time it takes to create the temporary swap file during each session.

Need to Know More?

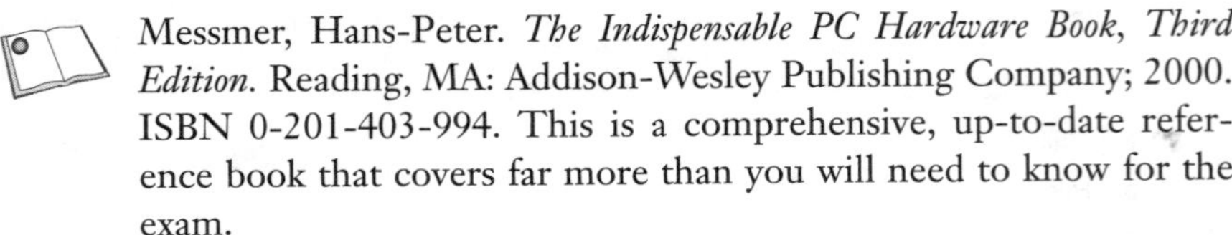

Messmer, Hans-Peter. *The Indispensable PC Hardware Book, Third Edition.* Reading, MA: Addison-Wesley Publishing Company; 2000. ISBN 0-201-403-994. This is a comprehensive, up-to-date reference book that covers far more than you will need to know for the exam.

Minasi, Mark. *The Complete PC Upgrade and Maintenance Guide, 11th Edition.* San Francisco, CA: Sybex Network Press, 2000. ISBN 0-782-128-009. This is considered one of the best reference books available. In fact, Minasi's book was instrumental in the formulation of the first A+ exam.

Rosch, Winn. *Hardware Bible, Fifth Edition.* Indianapolis, IN: Sams Publishing, 1999. ISBN 0-789-717-433. This is a well-organized reference book that covers software issues as well as hardware.

Muller, Scott. *Upgrading and Repairing PCs, 12th Edition.* Indianapolis, IN: Que, 2000. ISBN 0-7897-2303-4. This is one of our favorites. If you are going to have only one reference book, give this one serious consideration.

Freedman, Alan. *Computer Desktop Encyclopedia, Second Edition.* AMACOM, 1999. ISBN 0-814-479-855. This is great for a fast lookup or refresher.

Microsoft Windows 95 Resource Kit. Redmond, WA: Microsoft Press, ISBN 1-55615-678-2. This is the definitive resource for all Windows 95 questions. It assumes that you have a good working knowledge of Windows 95.

Windows 95, 98, and Me

Terms you'll need to understand:

- ✓ Version release number
- ✓ FAT32, FAT16, 32-bit, 16-bit, Virtual FAT (VFAT)
- ✓ Properties and Settings Tab
- ✓ File attributes (Hidden, System, Read-only)
- ✓ .INI files and log files (BOOTLOG.TXT and LOGVIEW.EXE)
- ✓ Safe Mode, Real Mode, Virtual Machine (VM) and VMM32, DOS command mode
- ✓ Vectors (pointers) and aliasing (mapping), truncated file names
- ✓ History log and version control

Concepts you'll need to master:

- ✓ The Registry (SYSTEM.DAT and USER.DAT)
- ✓ Configuration settings, CONFIG.SYS and AUTOTEXEC.BAT
- ✓ MS Explorer and the Windows Desktop
- ✓ HKey handles and keys
- ✓ The installation and startup process for Windows
- ✓ Static and dynamic Virtual device Drivers (VxDs)
- ✓ Long File Names (LFNs) and Installable File System (IFS)
- ✓ Network redirectors and IRQs
- ✓ Systems administration tools and utilities, applications suites

When Windows 95 was released (to much fanfare and rock-and-roll music), the world stood back to wonder at the final integration of DOS and Windows NT in a fully backward-compatible, 32-bit operating system. We were done! At last, there was a final Windows. So why do we still have Windows NT? And how come there's a Windows 98 SE, a Windows Me, a Windows 2000, a Windows XP; and why is Microsoft talking about the eventual release of something code-named *Longhorn*?

In this chapter we'll continue to refer to Windows 95, Windows 98, Windows 98 SE, and Windows Me as *Windows 9x*. In those instances where we use only the word "Windows," we mean 95/98/SE and Me. Otherwise, we'll refer specifically to the version names we're differentiating. We'll refer to Windows NT, Windows 2000, and Windows XP by their specific names.

A Word of Caution

The Windows Registry is arguably the most important, yet least understood change to the way modern machines are configured and maintained. You won't have to know the low-level details of the Registry for the A+ exam, but you must be able to visualize and remember various menu options, object names, and navigational pathways necessary for routine maintenance of a system. We'll discuss the Registry at some length in this chapter, but only from a basic perspective. Programs such as Tweak UI and X-Setup can modify nearly every configurable aspect of Windows, but they can also cause irreparable damage, necessitating a complete reinstallation. Many of today's home systems come with only an image file of the original installation on a CD-ROM—a so-called *Recovery Disk*.

Typical Recovery Disks, or original installation images, wipe out any and all user-created information. This information includes such things as documents, financial management data, business records, client histories, address books, favorite online places, personal photographs, email, and so forth. Be sure to have current, valid backups of the Registry files before making changes, and be sure to test your knowledge of the information we've provided before you take the exam.

In some instances, the only way to recover a machine is from the command line. If you think you don't need to know about DOS and command-line syntax, other than for the exam, you'd be well advised to explore Chapter 13 and the Windows 2000/XP Recovery Console, along with the information on Troubleshooting discussed in Chapter 14.

Windows 95 Introduced Changes

Windows 95 introduced a new interface, designed to be simpler to use. Along with the Windows desktop and new system management tools (discussed later in this chapter, and also in Chapter 14), Windows 95 also introduced several other basic features including:

- ➤ Pre-emptive multitasking
- ➤ Protected mode device drivers
- ➤ Multithreaded 32-bit application support
- ➤ Integrated email (Exchange; later to become Outlook) and dial-up networking
- ➤ Plug-and-Play, or Plug 'n' Play (PnP) support
- ➤ Enhanced multimedia and video support
- ➤ Long File names (LFN) and the Virtual FAT system (VFAT)
- ➤ Dynamic 32-bit Virtual Device Drivers (32-bit .VXDs)
- ➤ System Policies (and the Policy Editor) with User Profiles for better individual security management of the computer
- ➤ IO.SYS and MSDOS.SYS as the primary device-driver loader, with CONFIG.SYS and AUTOEXEC.BAT as secondary configuration files
- ➤ System settings and internal configuration going to a "Registry" as opposed to .INI files

Wizards

Windows 95 brought the concept of installation and administration "Wizards" to the home PC, for the purposes of making it easier to do system tasks. A Wizard is a set of software decision branches that produce related dialog boxes asking a user for input. In other words, if you don't know what you're doing or how to do it, the Wizard will take you through the process step-by-step. Depending upon what the user inputs, the underlying Wizard program makes a decision and presents the next dialog box in that decision branch. When all responses have been entered, the Wizard takes care of applying all the configuration information to the underlying system.

One of the benefits of the Windows 95 Installation Shield (which also uses a Wizard) is that it brought a rudimentary uninstaller into the operating system. If a program's installation routine was written to take advantage of the

Installation Shield, the user could uninstall the program at a later date, comfortable in the assumption that most of the ancillary files for that program would be removed, regardless of their location on the hard drive.

There are several commercial applications available, which do a much more sophisticated and complete job of tracking installations. These programs can usually keep track of installations and setups that have not been correctly written to use the Windows Install Shield.

The Desktop

Windows 9x came with many of the features found in Windows NT 4.0, making it superior in memory management and device control over Windows 3.x. In fact, the improved device handling of the new virtual device drivers (VxDs) made it more efficient to run almost any DOS program (including difficult game software) in an MS DOS window, or session—the DOS Virtual Machine (VM). We've mentioned that the primary shell, EXPLORER.EXE is an upgraded File Manager, incorporating elements of a desktop that once was unusable space sitting behind Program Manager.

The Windows 3.x desktop wasn't completely unusable. When an icon was minimized, Windows put it on the desktop. However, the Windows 3.x desktop was really only a place to store minimized icons rather than a place to organize work and applications. Windows 9x uses the Desktop as the main *metaphor* (representation) and the Start button, Taskbar, and Tray in place of the old Program Manager.

When several programs are open and running in Windows 9x and Windows 2000, the old Alt-Tab keystroke combination will still revolve around every program listed in the Task Bar.

When you start Windows 95, the new Desktop is nearly empty except for the My Computer, Network Neighborhood, and Recycle Bin icons. The Desktop uses a new technology called a *name space*, while the icons on the apparent desktop are called *objects*. To provide interactive help to a novice user, the Taskbar is at the bottom of the screen, and the Start button is prominently displayed. Rather than having Program Groups with icons sitting inside them, Windows 95 groups the programs in a cascading series of menus, growing from each menu item on a previous list, originating from the main Start menu.

Windows 95 can read .GRP files and .INI files from a Windows 3.x installation and convert all Program Groups to cascading menus. For this reason, you should back up the existing sets of these files before running an upgrade installation.

Right-Click for Properties (Shift-F10)

Almost every aspect of a Windows 9x object is always available by right-clicking the mouse. The right mouse button had been mostly useless in all the previous versions of Windows. A few pioneering companies (e.g., Borland) decided to use the right button to offer a shortcut to the main menu at the top of the screen. This was called a *properties floating menu.* The idea caught on, and Windows 95 compatibility required that all programs running under Windows 95 use the right-click of the mouse for properties. Nowadays, mice often have a middle button, scrolling wheels, and even fourth or fifth buttons that can be assigned various functions (e.g., the double-click).

CompTIA refers to clicking the right mouse button as "alternative click(ing)." This alternative click process has nothing to do with pressing the ALT key.

FAT32

It turned out that backward compatibility was not an easy thing to accomplish, and no one could afford to write off the millions of installed 16-bit PCs with their Real Mode applications. Although Windows 95 was described as an operating system, the technical fact remained that Windows 95 required an underlying DOS 7.0, and used a 16-bit FAT for its file management system, precisely for that backward compatibility with older DOS and Windows 3.11 systems. A second release of Windows 95 (Operating System Release 2, or B, known as *OS/R-B*) was only available as an original equipment manufacturer (OEM) version. OS/R-B included a new 32-bit FAT, or FAT32. In fact, Windows 95 was more of an interface than an operating system. DOS 7.0 was, and continues to be, the real operating system behind the entire Windows 9x family, with backwards compatibility being the driving force.

Windows 95 OS/R-B, Windows 98, and Windows Me, all included an option to format a logical partition for a 32-bit FAT called *FAT32.* This allows for multithreaded Protected Mode access to the disk through a Virtual File Allocation Table (VFAT) and a faster, more efficient method of disk caching. Windows 2000 supports both FAT32 and the Window NT File System (NTFS).

The Virtual File Allocation Table is not the same thing as a 32-bit File Allocation Table system. VFAT is part of the Windows 9x Virtual Machine Manager (VMM) and uses the existing FAT16 files structure. FAT32 is an actual enhancement to the underlying, disk-based file management system, being created through FDISK.EXE and taking place long before Windows ever loads. Keep in mind that FDISK is not interchangeable, and that you must use the program that applies to the operating system you're going to install. FDISK for Windows 9x is not the same as the FDISK for Windows 2000, even if they have the same name.

Because FAT16 uses 16-bit numbers for cluster addressing, the maximum allowable size for a FAT16 partition is 65,536 clusters, or 2 gigabytes. Current systems routinely come installed with huge hard disks far larger than that and so the FAT32 feature in Windows 9x allows for these single, large partitions. However, once a disk is setup with the FAT32 feature, it can't be easily changed back to a 16-bit FAT. Unfortunately, most new computer buyers haven't the slightest idea (or interest) in the underlying decisions being made for them by their system dealers.

The FAT32 works much the same way as FAT16, but uses larger 32-bit numbers in the data-addressing scheme. The larger numbers mean that FAT32 can manage more clusters on a disk. The maximum number of clusters a FAT32 partition will allow is 268,435,456, or 2 terabytes (TB). FAT32 requires that a disk have a partition table, so for that reason it cannot be installed on a floppy disk or any other removable disk having no partition table.

Drive Converter (FAT32)

Windows 98 provides "Drive Converter" as a conversion utility to convert an existing FAT16 to FAT32 without data loss. In Windows 95, a drive can be set up with either FAT16 or FAT32 during the FDISK process. Windows 98 allows for a conversion after the disk has been previously partitioned. Although the conversion utility allows a drive to be converted from FAT16 to FAT32 (or NTFS, in the case of Windows NT), the user is unable to revert back to FAT16 without reformatting the partition.

Viewing FAT32 partition information with a 16-bit FDISK will show that the partition is a non-DOS partition. This could mean that the partition is a FAT32 or NTFS partition, a UNIX partition, or some other partition that the 16-bit program cannot correctly describe. PowerQuest's "Partition Magic" is a much better tool for partitioning disks and for modifying those partitions without reformatting the entire disk.

Windows Versions

Beginning with Windows 95, Microsoft discontinued a custom of changing the name of its Windows versions to match the various incremental changes, fixes, patches, or service pack releases. In the past, Windows 3.0 was changed to Windows 3.1, then to Windows for Work groups 3.11, and everyone knew there were major changes. With Windows 95, one had do to some detective work to find out which version of the GUI was installed on a machine. Version numbers no longer reflected major changes.

Finding the Version

Windows 95 is version 4.00.950 in its first release. This makes sense, given that the previous version of Windows was version 3.11 (Windows for Work groups). Right-clicking on the My Computer icon on the Desktop, then choosing the Properties tab on the context menu, and finally looking at the General tab in the System Properties dialog window, one finds that Windows 9x was some version of Windows 4.x. Windows 98 SE will show a version number something like 4.10.2222 A.

Another way to see this, is to find EXPLORER.EXE in the \Windows subfolder and right-click (or press Shift-F10) for Properties. Under the Version tab; Product Version, we find a number something like 4.72.3110.1. Once again, this is Windows version 4.x.

The so-called *Windows Desktop* is actually something called a *Windows Name Space*. MS Explorer is the program used to create many of the features of the overall desktop model. In Windows 3.x, the Program Manager was PROGMAN.EXE, and it was loaded from the SYSTEM.INI file with the Shell=PROGMAN.EXE line. In Windows 9x, we see this in the still-existing SYSTEM.INI file with the line Shell=EXPLORER.EXE.

Microsoft released the first version of Windows 95 with FAT16 as the 16-bit file management system. When the File Allocation Table (FAT) was upgraded to FAT32 in Windows 95 OS/R-B, it was only released to computer manufacturing companies for pre-installation on new machines. Nobody told consumers about this. The second release of Windows 95 offered a choice, in terms of whether or not to change the organization of the hard drive to the more efficient FAT32. There was an OS/R-D release, but by that time there had been enough changes that Microsoft released Windows 98. (Nobody knows what happened to OS/R-C.)

Windows 95 OS/R-A had enough problems and missing features that a "Plus Pak" was released as an *add-on*. Installing the add-on package changed

Windows 95 at a system level, producing an oddly confusing semi-subrelease that wasn't version "A" anymore, but wasn't OS/R-B either. This idea of purchasing an optional Plus Pak, as opposed to downloading a service pack fix, continued into Windows 98. The SE version of Windows 98 was a clean installation of everything that had changed from the original release of Windows 98, including the updated MS Explorer 5.x World Wide Web browser.

Continuing on the path towards the ultimate realization of a fully integrated 32-bit DOS, Windows GUI, and network operating system (NOS), ongoing releases of Windows 98 showed up on the market, every so often, without any notice or fanfare. Windows 98 Professional had more changes and service pack releases, until the name was finally changed to Windows 98 SE (Second Edition). Rather than keeping track of an original installation disk and many service pack downloads, users could, if they wanted, buy a new copy of Windows 98 SE on CD-ROM. Of course, this came in either a full (new) install, or update install, depending on whether a previous version of Windows was on the machine.

Windows 98 was a major release update, again using the year in the name (1998) rather than a version number, but keeping the version numbering as a minor release (Windows 4.1.x). Windows 98 incorporated all the changes that had been previously put into the various versions of Windows 95, such as FAT32, USB support, disk-partitioning support, expanded Internet capabilities, and expanded hardware support. Meanwhile, the habit of naming the release after the calendar year was making it difficult to keep each Windows version from appearing outdated.

Windows 98 continued to take on modifications and service pack releases, with Microsoft gradually blending in the *new technology* (NT) of Windows NT 4.0. The first release of this combined attempt was called the Millenium Edition, or Windows Me, and was considerably unstable. The product acquired a bad enough reputation that Microsoft eventually abandoned it, choosing instead, to release Windows 2000 and distance itself from the Me version.

Windows 2000, as we discuss in Chapter 13, finally separated from DOS. The product name was still tied to the calendar year of the release date, but that ended with Windows XP. Windows XP is Windows 2000 with the ever-continuing incremental changes taking place as Microsoft moves towards whatever will be contained within "Longhorn" (scheduled for release sometime after 2005).

The old VER (Version) command is still available in any Windows environment, from Windows 95 to Windows XP. Running the command line prompt, either by double-clicking on an MS DOS Prompt; re-starting the machine in DOS mode; or by choosing Start | Run and typing "COMMAND" (without the quotation marks), opens up the command line where you can run the VER command.

The Registry

One of the primary ways Windows moved away from a text-based interface is in the way the user accesses a command line. Windows made this command line into a graphical adventure of dragging and dropping objects, clicking mouse buttons, working with toolbars, and puzzling out icons. Windows 95 began the basic changeover from a 16-bit operating system to a 32-bit OS. Many people tend to assume this change to 32-bit operation was the most important. Actually, the more important change was the final incorporation of the Windows Registry. Windows 3.x used a primitive Registry to keep track of objects, but from Windows 95 all they way through into Windows NT and XP, the Registry is what holds all the versions together.

The hidden SYSTEM.DAT and USER.DAT files make up the Registry, but they are only part of the overall Windows configuration system. Initialization files (.INI) continue to provide backwards compatibility for older applications, as well as necessary configuration data for current applications. Even the Registry Repair utility, which makes daily backups of the Registry (and should not be confused with the Registry Editor), requires a SCANREG.INI file. SCANREG was a manual utility in Windows 95, meaning that it was not run automatically at startup.

Registry Backup Files

Beginning with Windows 98, SCANREGW.EXE runs automatically during the Windows startup. This utility program is a somewhat simple Registry analysis program designed to check for problems in the Registry files. Those files include the two .DAT files, but also the SYSTEM.INI and WIN.INI files. The default number of five backups is configured in the SCANREG.INI file with the line MaxBackupCopies=5. This can be changed to any other number.

Each day, when Windows is started for the first time, the startup process (found by running MSCONFIG.EXE) includes a check of the Registry files for various problems. Once the files have been scanned, SCANREG uses Microsoft's compression utility (similar to PKZip, or WinZip) to create a .CAB file. These files are stored in the location described by the line BackupDirectory=[folder], where [folder] is, by default, C:\WINDOWS\SYSBCKUP.

After the files have been compressed, they're given an incremental name: rb000.cab, rb001.cab, rb002.cab, and so forth. Once the maximum number has been reached, according to the .INI file, the first .CAB file is overwritten by the next backup (number six).

To restore a corrupted Registry, you can use the **scanreg /restore** command, but only from a DOS command line. Because the program uses Expanded Memory, you cannot run it from the "Safe Mode Command Prompt Only" option. To extract only a single file, you can use WinZip or any other archive program that handles .CAB files. For more information, see the Microsoft support forum: **http://support.microsoft.com/default.aspx?scid=KB;EN-US;Q183887&**

An important component of the A+ exam has to do with understanding the way in which Windows loads, and the typical problems encountered during startup. We've covered those areas we found on the exam in Chapter 14 "Troubleshooting," but remember that this book is designed as a compressed review before you take the test. You should already have a solid, hands-on experience with the Registry and the command line by now. If you do not, we strongly recommend that you use additional preparation resources, some of which we've listed in the "Need To Know More" heading at the end of this chapter.

.INI Files

The Microsoft Windows 95 Resource Kit states that "the Registry simplifies the operating system by eliminating the need for AUTOEXEC.BAT, CONFIG.SYS, and .INI files (except when legacy applications require them)." This is about as true as saying that Congress simplifies the government of the country by eliminating the need for citizens to govern themselves. Initialization files are used routinely in Windows 9x, and both CONFIG.SYS and AUTOEXEC.BAT are alive and well. Yes, it's true that neither of the startup files are *as* necessary as before, and neither are .INI files the *only* way to configure Windows, but they still exist and are used regularly.

Computers are different from other types of machines, in that they remember things like settings, the color of a desktop, or the arrangement of icons. These settings, now stored in the Windows Registry (for the most part), were originally held in the CONFIG.SYS and AUTOEXEC.BAT files. There were a few data files (.DAT) and configuration files (.CFG), but the text-based initialization files (.INI) became the method of choice for storing configurations. Microsoft encouraged developers to use these .INI files, showing how it was done by using the Windows SYSTEM.INI and WIN.INI files to store basic Windows configuration information.

By the time Windows 3.x hit the market, problems with this idea were starting to crop up: There were too many .INI files being splattered all over the hard drives. Aside from the number of files, all these critical settings were in text files, making it too easy for anyone to modify them—even if they didn't know what they were doing. Microsoft, along with corporate information technology (IT) managers, decided that would never do.

Most, but not all, of the information that was once in .INI files is now stored somewhere in the Registry. In some cases, Windows itself creates new .INI files (e.g., TELEPHON.INI) that didn't exist under Windows 3.x. Most .INI files are stored in the WINDOWS folder.

The important .INI files used by Windows 3.x and Windows 9x include SYSTEM.INI, WIN.INI, PROGMAN.INI (Program Manager), and CONTROL.INI (Control Panel). PROGMAN.INI contains a listing of the Program Group files (*.GRP) used within Program Manager.

Editing Registry Files

The Registry combined most of the .INI files into a consolidated set of binary files (as opposed to text files), preventing people from casually changing settings. The operative word is "casual," meaning that less knowledgeable users could no longer open a critical configuration file in MS Word; saving it again in a proprietary Word format and causing a catastrophic system crash. This often happened, in the past, with CONFIG.SYS and AUTOEXEC.BAT files.

Windows 3.x used a combination of the SYSTEM.INI, WIN.INI, and REG.DAT files to keep track of device drivers, environment settings, and objects being controlled by Windows. REG.DAT was a binary file, requiring REGEDIT.EXE, a special editor program, to open it and make changes. When Windows 95 came along, the decision was made to (theoretically) remove the two .INI files and move as much as possible into a greatly expanded Registration database. That database was called the *Registry*.

REGEDIT.EXE continued to be the preferred editor for Windows 95, 98, and Me. Windows NT, 2000, and XP use REGEDT32.EXE as their own, preferred editor.

Windows 9x still uses both the WIN.INI file and the SYSTEM.INI file. If there's a conflict over two of the same devices, the device listed in the SYSTEM.INI file will take precedence over the one listed in the SYSTEM.DAT Registry file. A quick way to examine these two files, as well as the CONFIG.SYS and AUTOEXEC.BAT files, is to use the System

Configuration Editor (SYSEDIT.EXE) utility. This program opens a text-editing window with a cascade of each important file.

Objects and Shortcuts

Today's Registry is an outgrowth of the Windows 3.x Registration database. This original database was a little-known tool that managed Object Linking and Embedding (OLE) and the drag-and-drop features in Windows. OLE is a way to place (embed) a document (client) inside another document, using a kind of pointer to data (package) from an outside program's (server's) data. This kind of document is called a *compound document* because you can view or edit the data in the OLE connection (link) without knowing which application created it.

For example, the [Embedding] section in the WIN.INI file might contain the entry PBrush=Paintbrush Picture,C:\Programs\Access\MSPAINT.EXE,picture. This would indicate that a certain type of OLE picture object found in, say, an MS Word document should find MSPAINT.EXE in the specified location. Furthermore, the line tells Windows that it should use MS Paint to open the picture when the picture's OLE object is double-clicked.

When a program can embed a piece of itself in the form of an embedded object, that program is said to be an *OLE server*. It's called a server because it provides functional services to the program trying to open the object—the *OLE client*. If you're following all this correctly, you should also see that this is the primitive ancestor to something we're all familiar with today: *shortcuts*.

The original Registration database maintained information about the pathname and file names of OLE servers, the file names and extensions of data files and their associated programs, the class name of the objects that the OLE servers could edit (e.g., a picture), and protocols used by the objects. The Windows 3.x Registration database was held in a binary file called *REG.DAT*, which could be edited only by using a registration information editor called *REGEDIT.EXE*.

Be very careful that you don't buy into a response to a question that asks you whether REG.DAT is one of the current Windows Registry files. Only SYSTEM.DAT and USER.DAT are used in Windows 9x and later Registries.

Microsoft claimed that OLE would increase the amount of interconnectivity among computer applications, whereby compound documents would focus users more on the data and documents rather than worrying about how to open and use a particular program. To some extent, the World Wide Web's Hypertext Markup Language (HTML) superseded OLE, though not necessarily by using the same process. The technology behind OLE and Dynamic Data Exchange (DDE) is complex, but you should know what the acronyms stand for.

Microsoft has never given up on the idea that people want to simply click on either a picture or a simple description and go right to work with all the underlying files and data available. Part of the upcoming Longhorn will be a new application programming interface (API) framework, code-named *Avalon*. Avalon will be at the core of Longhorn's new information-access architecture, and something Microsoft is calling "the new "inductive" user interface (UI). This new interface is supposed to allow users to organize and share information more intuitively, most likely using some kind of "dock," somewhat like that found in Microsoft Office XP. Presumably, files will no longer be displayed on their physical location, being organized by context or in some other way defined by users or administrators.

Pointers

The Registry contains references to file locations (pointers) being used by hardware and software. For instance, if a scanner requires something like SCANNER.DLL in order to run, the Registry will hold the location of that .DLL file, along with the various configuration switches and options the file is working under. If an application uses a particular Windows system file, possibly COMDLG32.DLL, references to those file locations are also held in the Registry. These consolidated references are also used by utilities such as the Windows Update Manager, discussed under the Windows 98 section, later in this chapter, and Windows System File Checker (SFC), discussed in Chapter 13. Another way of seeing this is that Windows file associations are kept in a series of HKey locations with pointers to not only the opening application, but to other places in the Registry with descriptive information about the file extension.

The concept of using a pointer (vector) to another object, along with using an icon to represent the pointer, eventually led to the Windows "shortcuts" (.LNK) files. Shortcuts can be created in many ways, but the simplest is to highlight a program file name, hold down the right mouse button (properties button) and drag it onto the Desktop (or into another folder), and then release the mouse button. A short menu dialog will pop up with one of the choices being "Create Shortcut(s) Here."

From the first release of Windows 1.0, certain letters in a graphic menu option have always represented the use of shortcut keys. Pressing the ALT key will highlight the first option in any Windows menu. Pressing the underlined letter of an option will drop down that main options menu. With the options menu showing, pressing a combination of the ALT key and the underlined letter of an option, executes the specific choice without requiring an additional mouse click.

Components of the Registry

The Windows Registry has become one of the most obscure and complicated aspects of low-level work with Windows. Practically no one really understands the Windows Registry, but you should know how to identify some of its parts. The Windows 9x Registry is made up of two files, each of which is a Hidden, Read-only, System file (+H +R +S attributes) in the Windows folder. These files are:

- *USER.DAT*—holds user-specific customization setting to the way Windows looks, such as the Desktop, video resolution, and so on. These user settings were formerly held in the WIN.INI file, under Windows 3.x.
- *SYSTEM.DAT*—the largest of the two, stores all the hardware configurations, Windows internal settings, and application settings that were originally held in SYSTEM.INI.

SYSTEM.DAT and USER.DAT are both binary files, which cannot be edited with Notepad, Edit, or any other ASCII editor. The only way to edit the Registry is by using REGEDIT.EXE or a third-party program designed specifically for the purpose.

USER.DAT contains specific environment configuration (e.g., the Desktop) for the user, that is, the *session user*. If networking is enabled and a computer is configured for multiple users, a separate USER.DAT file is created for each user. This file can be accessed by capturing the User ID and password at the time the user logs into Windows. Typically, the User ID is part of the file's name. For instance, Bob Smith's User ID might be BSmith, which would lead to a BSMITH.DAT file. USER.DAT is the default user configurations file, but all of these user files are part of the Registry.

HKeys

MS Explorer lists folders in the left pane, using a + or - symbol to indicate any subfolders within (below) a given folder. The Registry looks the same, but calls each primary heading a *handle*, with *keys* as the underlying subdivisions. The Computer Management tool in Windows 2000 also looks like the

Explorer or Registry, but refers to *nodes* at the "folder" level and *branches* as the subdivisions.

The HKey is Microsoft's language for a program handle to a key that contains configuration information. Looking at the various HKeys in REGEDIT is essentially the same as looking at a drive in Windows Explorer. Each key is represented by a folder icon that can be expanded or collapsed just like folders and subfolders.

You may see a question that asks you what the little + sign is to the left of a folder. If you don't know that this is a one-click way to expand the folder, then we suggest that you postpone taking the exam until after you've installed Windows 9x and played around with it for awhile.

The Windows 9x Registry contains six primary HKeys. Each HKey is like a primary folder located in the root directory of a drive and has many levels of subkeys that descend like a directory tree. The root directory is called HKEY_CLASSES_ROOT. The six primary HKeys are:

- ***HKEY_CLASSES_ROOT***—file extensions and applications used for OLE
- ***HKEY_USERS***—data stored in USER.DAT that keeps network information and user configuration options
- ***HKEY_CURRENT_USER***—user information specific to the Windows 95 user at the moment (if networking is disabled, this is a duplicate of HKEY_USERS)
- ***HKEY_LOCAL_MACHINE***—the hardware and software configurations for a computer (multiple configurations can be stored for the same computer)
- ***HKEY_CURRENT_CONFIG***—printers and display settings
- ***HKEY_DYN_DATA***—dynamic data in RAM having to do with how Windows 95 is running (shown by the System Monitor applet)

The Windows 9x Registry is built around six master sections called *Hkey_[SectionName]* where *[SectionName]* is the name of each specific section. At the top of the Registry tree is Hkey_Classes_Root. The section used for hardware is Hkey_Local_Machine.

While we didn't see any questions asking for a list of all the main HKeys, there may be a reference to the Local Machine key as the location for all the device configurations. The odds are high that questions about the Registry keys will provide the correct names in the response or body of the text. You would be asked to choose or identify an HKey in terms of what it does, and we're fairly confident that you'll only have to know the Local Machine.

Most of the Registry is controlled by Windows during startup, within a work session, or is set up during installation. If problems occur during setup and some hardware device refuses to be recognized, editing the Local Machine key might help. However, the main problem is that removing software or changing a hardware device doesn't automatically change its entries in the Registry. Information about hardware and software is stored in *many* places within the Registry, and uninstaller programs have varying degrees of success in finding all occurrences and references.

Always make a backup of the Registry, particularly the SYSTEM. DAT file, before you make *any* changes to the system. This includes running an uninstaller program, since an incorrect guess on the part of the program can render the system totally inoperable.

Automatic Registry Copies

When Windows 9x is set up for the first time (from installation disks), a SYSTEM.NEW file is created as the first Registry. This file contains the hardware and software configuration information made during the detection phase of Setup. If everything works well and Windows starts successfully without crashing, SYSTEM.NEW is renamed SYSTEM.DAT.

After Windows is installed and working, the first successful Registry (SYSTEM.DAT) is renamed *SYSTEM.DA0* and held as a backup of the original Registry. The very first SYSTEM.DAT, used when Windows 9x starts from the hard disk, is also copied to SYSTEM.1ST in the root directory as another backup of the clean, first installation.

SYSTEM.1ST includes everything up to the first reboot of the system. If you replace SYSTEM.DAT with SYSTEM.1ST at any time and then reboot the computer, you'll get the "Starting Windows 9x For The First Time" screen, and Windows will go through the configuring hardware process, initializing the Control Panel, Start menu, and all the other aspects of a first-time start. Windows will then reboot and start up normally.

Every time Windows starts successfully, it backs up SYSTEM.DAT to SYSTEM.DA0 and USER.DAT to USER.DA0 (overwriting any existing .DA0 files). If something goes wrong, the .DA0 files are used automatically on restart, to return the computer to the successful previous startup. This is essentially the same process used in Windows NT/2000 as the "Last Known Good" hardware profile.

If Windows 9x is unable to start correctly, it will try to do so in Safe Mode. If the problem is something that Windows can recognize clearly enough to start the session in Safe Mode, the Registry files are *not* copied to the .DA0 names. By manually copying the previously good .DA0 files to .DAT names, Windows can start successfully again. However, not all problems are recognized by Windows's recovery capabilities.

To be safe and to provide the most convenient and speedy recovery from inadvertent or random corruption of the Registry, keep the following points in mind:

- Always keep a backup of the latest successful Registry: SYSTEM.DAT and USER.DAT somewhere other than in the WINDOWS folder.
- SYSTEM.1ST is a last-resort backup of the first configuration file, created following a successful first-time installation on a given computer. If this file doesn't work, you're probably going to have to reinstall everything on the computer (Windows, and all the software that's been added since the last installation).
- SYSTEM.1ST is located in the root directory of the bootable partition.
- SYSTEM.DAT and USER.DAT are located in the WINDOWS subdirectory.
- SYSTEM.DA0 and USER.DA0 are also located in the WINDOWS subdirectory (by default).

Backing Up the Registry

To copy Registry files from a DOS command line, you must use the ATTRIB command to turn off the hidden, system, and read-only attributes. From within Windows Explorer, the files can be copied without adjusting the attributes. If you use the Explorer (or File Manager) to copy the SYSTEM.DAT file, you must be sure to set the View Folder Options to show hidden files. From the main menu bar in the Explorer, choose View | Options | View tab and check the "Show All Files" button. From the main menu bar in File Manager, choose View | By File Type | Show Hidden | System Files.

You should also have the option check box of the Explorer "View" tab set to show that MS Explorer will *not* "Hide MS DOS extensions for file types that are registered." There are several files with the name SYSTEM.* and USER.* in the Windows folder, but only the SYSTEM.DAT and USER.DAT are the current Registry file.

Don't rely on the .DA0 files as a backup of the Registry. If you do, it's easy to start the computer and create a bad SYSTEM.DAT file, which copies to the SYSTEM.DA0 file along with the bad information. If the computer locks up and is rebooted, the bad SYSTEM.DA0 can copy over the bad SYSTEM.DAT and cause the same problem, leaving two copies of the bad Registry file. Then, your only recourse is the SYSTEM.1ST file, which has only original configuration information—no changes that have been made since the original installation.

The Emergency Recovery Utility (ERU.EXE) can be used to back up the Registry, but usually not to a floppy disk. SYSTEM.DAT is often larger than 1.4MB and, except for the most minimally configured computer, won't fit on a single floppy. However, ERU can copy specified system files to a different drive or directory, so using an Iomega Zip or Jaz disk will work, as will copying critical Registry files to a different directory on the hard drive and using a disk-spanning archive tool.

Something else to consider is that archiving programs like WinZip (Niko Mak Computing, Inc.) can spread a single file across multiple floppy disks. This is called "*spanning,*" and you can store a very large SYSTEM.DAT file on multiple floppies using this process. WinZip is available at **http://www.winzip.com**.

REGEDIT.EXE

REGEDIT.EXE (Registry Editor) runs from the command line or a custom icon. It combines the two files in a window that looks much like the Explorer, listing HKeys on the left side pane and the information within those keys in the right side pane.

Although a common procedure for making a copy of SYSTEM.DAT includes turning off all the attributes in order for DOS to see the file, the Explorer or File Manager will happily copy or move hidden files with only a brief dialog box asking for confirmation. Be sure that you check a question about SYSTEM.DAT for any reference to which environment is being used.

REGEDIT.EXE is installed into the WINDOWS folder during setup. The two Registry files are also stored in the WINDOWS folder, and have all their attributes set as Hidden, Read-only, and System. (ATTRIB.EXE and file attributes are discussed in Chapter 10.)

The data in SYSTEM.DAT can be exported (copied to another format) in an ASCII format, where it can be changed using an ASCII text editor. Once the changes have been saved, another feature of REGEDIT.EXE is that it can import (reabsorb information from another format) the ASCII file, thereby changing SYSTEM.DAT. However, REGEDIT.EXE is still required in order to perform the export and import process.

Making a copy of the two Registry files to another location is a way to back the files up, but in order for the files to actually function, they must be in their original locations with the file attributes properly set.

Although REGEDIT.EXE is installed to the WINDOWS folder during setup, Windows does not create a desktop icon or menu entry anywhere on the Start Menu. However, you can create a shortcut in the C:\WINDOWS\Start Menu\Accessories\System Tools folder, which will give you access to the editor from the menu. Keep in mind that this may not be such a good idea if novice users with an adventurous spirit have access to that computer.

Working with the Registry requires a serious amount of caution, as accidental changes can lead to a total reinstallation. Unlike word processors, changes in the Registry take place as soon as the Enter key is pressed. Some important points to remember about changes in the Registry include the following:

- The Registry is changed directly by changes to Control Panel or some other Windows applets.
- The 9x Registry is also changed directly by using REGEDIT.EXE or a third-party application specifically designed to edit the .DAT files. (Windows 2000 and NT prefer that you work with a 32-bit editor called REGEDT32.EXE.)
- Some installation routines use .INF (program information) files to write changes to the Registry automatically.
- Changes to the Registry take place immediately and are written to the SYSTEM.DAT and USER.DAT files without using a typical File|Save option.
- The *only* way to undo a change in the Registry is to either re-edit the line that was changed; copy a previous version of the .DAT file over the newly changed version; or import a previously-saved exported segment.

Unless you know exactly what you're doing, you shouldn't edit the Registry. Use the Control Panel interface to make changes to the system. As always, before you install any new software or any new hardware device, you should make a safe backup of the existing SYSTEM.DAT file and USER.DAT file.

Bizarre and amazing changes to Windows can occur with the installation of any new component. Sound cards and their drivers are a wonderful example of this. Sometimes, mystical gremlins can knock out a piece of hardware for no apparent reason whatsoever. Copying SYSTEM.DAT to another directory (e.g., REG_BACK) is simple to do from MS Explorer and can save you hours (if not days) of time recovering from a corrupted Registry.

Summary—Windows Registry

Most of the Windows questions we found on the operating system exam had to do with general concepts, critical files, and menu navigation steps to arrive at troubleshooting areas. You should understand the basic idea of the Windows Registry and the basics of FAT32. The most important points of the preceding section include:

- Understanding .INI files and knowing what the WIN.INI and SYSTEM.INI files do
- Remembering the two, critical Registry files (SYSTEM.DAT and USER.DAT) and knowing that they are hidden files
- OLE and .LNK files (Shortcuts)
- The main list of HKeys and the fact that the Registry looks a lot like the Explorer folder (or tree) view
- REGEDIT and REGEDT32, the two Registry editors. You should know why they exist, and their intended uses.

You should understand the way Windows makes backups of the Registry when it starts, and the various copies of SYSTEM.DAT. In most cases, if you know the main file name, the list of responses to exam questions will give you clues as to the other file names (see Chapter 1 for exam strategies). This also works with the Registry keys, for the most part. If you know the main HKey_Local_Machine and HKey_Current_User, the exam doesn't try to trip you up with phony names—at least not from what we saw.

Installing Windows 95, 98, and Me

Windows 9x provided two installation methods, as well as its several different versions—the *upgrade* and *full* version. The upgrade installation materials (disks or CD-ROM) required that the computer already had a copy of DOS and Windows 3.x installed, whereas the full installation disks required that no previous copy of Windows existed on the installation hard drive. Both formats required a logical partition with more than 32MB of free space.

Although the Windows 95 upgrade could be installed in such a way that the computer could boot up into either Windows 3.x or Windows 95, the documentation didn't really explain how to maintain the full integrity of DOS files earlier than version 7.0, along with all the existing Windows 3.x files. All the previous DOS and Windows 3.x files would ordinarily be removed from the hard drive.

Third-party books about Windows 95 often provide far clearer documentation and understanding of how to install an upgrade in such a way as to keep the Windows 3.x system safe and retain older DOS versions.

CD-ROM Device Drivers

Windows 95 often comes preinstalled on a hard drive, the installation being done at the retail point of sale. Usually, disk images are copied to the hard drive, and the user has the option of making floppies from these images. Otherwise, Windows 95 is available on CD-ROM. Disk images are special files that can be used to create an exact copy of a floppy disk, including bootable floppies.

Modern machines usually have a BIOS-compatible CD-ROM drive, meaning that the motherboard BIOS will recognize a CD drive during the POST. On older machines, the CD-ROM drive requires a device driver. On a system on which Windows 95 is running smoothly, the CD-ROM device is handled by Windows 95's internal list of device drivers. Many computer vendors don't include any external device driver for the CD-ROM drive, assuming that Windows 95 is a full operating system. If the hard drive becomes irrevocably corrupted and must be reformatted, how will the user use the CD-ROM drive to install Windows from a CD-ROM?

The full installation version of Windows 95 includes a bootable $3^1/_2$-inch disk for partitioning and formatting, but doesn't include the CD-ROM device drivers. It is good practice to maintain a separate DOS system disk with the CD-ROM device driver for the installed drive. Windows 98 provides for this problem when an Emergency Startup Disk is created. This disk uses generic CD-ROM drivers, and will generally provide access to most CD-ROM drives. In an emergency, if you have access to a Windows 98 machine, you can create a startup disk and use it to boot the older machine. From there, you can install whichever version of Windows is required.

Installation Phases

Nowadays, it's almost impossible to demonstrate a generic installation. For that reason, we'll present a Windows 95 installation with the caveat that the Windows 9x family installs, for the most part, in the same way. Most installations are done by the vendor, using a standardized disk image. These installations include Windows and all the included applications sold with the system. As an A+ technician, you'll mostly likely run a recovery from an original configuration CD-ROM.

With the trend towards removing any installation and configuration control from individual users, purchasing an installation copy of the Windows operating system is becoming increasingly more difficult. The operating system and recovery disks are sometimes included with a new machine, but in many instances the only way to buy a copy of Windows 98 is through the so-called gray market (OEM versions sold at flea markets and swap meets) or online.

The four phases for installing Windows 9x are as follows:

1. The startup and information-gathering phase
2. The hardware detection phase
3. The copying and expanding files phase
4. The final system configuration phase

Windows takes over more of the decision-making process from the user and provides more direct control over how the software will be installed on a given computer. Again, the idea is to make *using* the computer as far removed from the technical configuration of that computer as possible. Many potential problems arising from an installation can be traced to the fact that the computer is still under the control of the user, and not every computer is set up exactly as the Installation Shield expects to see it.

Startup and Information-Gathering Phase

When SETUP.EXE runs from a DOS prompt, the program searches all local drives for any previous version of Windows. If Setup was started from DOS, the program assumes that an existing copy of DOS is on the bootable hard drive. If a previous version of Windows is found, one of two things will happen, depending on whether this was an upgrade or a full installation version of Windows 95. If it was an upgrade version, Setup pauses; then it suggests running Setup from within Windows. With a full installation version,

Setup quits and then displays an error message that a previous copy of Windows was found. The suggestion to run Setup from within Windows can be bypassed.

It may come in handy to know that Setup only looks for WIN.COM and WINVER.EXE to determine if a previous version of Windows exists on the drive. If you need to reinstall an upgrade version of Windows 9x, it's less messy and you can save a lot of time by just copying these two files to a C:\WINDOWS directory and then running the Windows Setup.

If you need to reinstall a Windows 9x system and you only have the full installation version CD, you can just delete or rename WIN.COM to something like *WIN.CEM* and run Setup. The system won't detect the presence of the previous Windows installation. This comes in handy if you have Windows 95 on one partition and want to install Windows 98 on a second partition.

As Phase 1 continues, Setup runs the DOS version of SCANDISK.EXE (located on the installation disk). ScanDisk looks at the hard drive to make sure that it's running correctly and that it meets the minimum requirements for installing Windows 9x (e.g., enough memory, modern CPU, and disk space). If any of the setup requirements is missing, the installation quits.

The rest of Phase 1 checks for extended memory and runs an XMS memory manager if one isn't running. If you don't remember what an XMS manager is, go back and read Chapter 11. Setup installs HIMEM.SYS if no other extended memory manager is found. Setup then checks memory for any existing terminate-and-stay resident programs (TSRs) that are known to cause problems and then pauses to warn you before proceeding.

Please observe that you just saw an example of a test-taking strategy. In the preceding paragraph, you encountered the XMS acronym with no spell-out or reference. To introduce some confusion, we suggested that you go back and read another chapter in this book. Immediately following that suggestion, you were given the fact that HIMEM.SYS is an extended memory manager. Aside from the clue of eXtended Memory, the sentence stated that HIMEM.SYS is an "other" extended memory manager. If you use your head, you'll see that XMS is apparently referring to extended memory. This is how you can use some of the questions on the exam to respond correctly to other questions.

Windows 9x requires extended memory—XMS. If no other memory management program is loaded, Setup installs HIMEM.SYS, and IO.SYS loads HIMEM every time the system starts. Remember that XMS is different from EMS, which is expanded memory.

From a DOS startup, Setup installs the minimum files required to run Windows 3.1 and starts the kernel using the SHELL=SETUP.EXE in the SYSTEM.INI file. Until this point, Setup is running in Real Mode, and nothing is showing on the monitor. The system then starts the GUI.

Windows 2000 no longer supports Real Mode. We discuss Windows NT/2000 in the next chapter.

After the GUI starts, the Installation Wizard begins prompting the user for which components will be installed, and various networking options. It asks for user information, registration information, and in which directory to install Windows. When all the questions have been answered, the Installation Wizard moves on to the next phase.

Hardware Detection Phase

At this point, Plug and Play and the concept of VxDs come into effect. Setup checks the entire system for hardware and peripherals attached to the computer. It also checks the system resources for I/O addresses, IRQs, and DMAs. This is where Windows begins to build the first Registry.

PnP is a standards specification that attempts to remove IRQ and DMA conflicts among hardware devices. PnP data must be built in to both the ROM BIOS on a motherboard and a BIOS chip on the device. Finally, the operating system must be able to read the BIOS data and work with it for configuration purposes.

PnP devices let Windows know what they are, and which resources they need in order to run. For nonPnP devices, Windows looks at I/O ports and specific memory addresses, compares them against a database of known devices, and then makes a best guess. If the computer has PnP BIOS, Windows 9x queries the system board's CMOS for all installed devices and their configurations. This same hardware detection process is used from the Control Panel under the Add New Hardware option when any new hardware device is added to the computer.

If the Device Manger shows a question mark indicator for a particular device, that doesn't necessarily mean the device is having a problem. It may only mean that Windows was unable to find the specific driver information in its PnP database.

Copying and Expanding Files Phase

A number of archiving programs have been developed over time to pack as many files as possible onto a relatively small floppy disk. These programs (e.g., PKZip, Extract, and LHArc) change the form of a file to reduce its size (compression). Microsoft uses EXTRACT.EXE to expand these stored programs back to their original sizes. The DOS COPY command is not sufficient, and cannot be used to install any version of Windows because the files on the installation disks are in archived form.

The File Copy phase uses a list of files that has been created during the hardware detection phase, depending on which components should be installed. Windows then copies all necessary files to the destination directory and extracts them to their full executable size. While the files are in their compressed format, DOS is unable to read or execute the programs. Various Setup .DLL files are run after the files are copied, to create directories that might not exist and to install network capabilities.

Creating a Startup Disk

The Installation Wizard offers the user the option to make a startup disk during the files expansion phase of the installation. The disk can be made at this time, or the option can be bypassed. If the option is bypassed, a startup disk can be made at any time by using the Add/Remove Software applet in Control Panel. The startup disk requires a minimum of 1.2MB of storage.

Emergency Startup Disk

The so-called emergency startup disk is designed mainly for troubleshooting the Windows 9x program and system. Many users think that the disk is a way to start their computers in DOS Mode and to access the regular features and configuration of their PCs. However, the disk assumes that Windows is available on the hard drive, but is not starting for some reason.

The files on the startup diskette include the bootable system files (COMMAND.COM, IO.SYS, and MSDOS.SYS) along with FDISK, FORMAT, EDIT, SYS.COM, and a few other files for low-level access to partitioning and reformatting. Note that the copies of IO.SYS and MSDOS.SYS are the startup files for Windows 9x, and that these are not the same files that started DOS 6.x and earlier.

If Windows has become corrupted, the startup disk does not contain any device drivers or CONFIG.SYS or AUTOEXEC.BAT files to get the computer up and running. The computer will start, leaving the user at a plain DOS command line and with no device drivers loaded (e.g., CD-ROM driver).

Final System Configuration Phase

At this point, Setup makes irrevocable changes to any pre-existing Windows 3.x files and directories. Setup makes upgrades to files in the C:\WINDOWS and C:\WINDOWS\SYSTEM directories and installs DOS 7.x to the C:\WINDOWS\COMMAND directory. DOS 7.x replaces COMMAND.COM with a new version of COMMAND.COM.

Unless any files in the C:\DOS directory have been protected (by copying them to a different location), Setup removes them and prepares the computer for Windows 9x. To allow booting from a previous version of DOS, Windows must be set up in its own directory, and the older system must remain intact.

Keeping an Older Operating System

Some people actually prefer to keep an older operating system on their machine. The best way to do this is with a multiple-boot partitioning system, but in some cases this may not be the optimal choice. Because Windows has a tendency to insist on looking in the WINDOWS and WINDOWS\SYSTEM folders for files, it's usually best to rename a Windows 3.x C:\WINDOWS directory to something new (e.g., WIN3_1) and install Windows 9x into the expected WINDOWS folder. Likewise, to protect a previous version of DOS, it's best to transfer copies of everything in the DOS directory to something like OLD_DOS to avoid the high probability of losing them during Windows 9x installation.

Setup prompts the user to restart the computer to continue the installation from within Windows. Prior to restarting the computer, Setup:

- Modifies the boot sector of the boot drive and replaces the previous version of IO.SYS with the new Windows 9x version
- Replaces the old MSDOS.SYS with the Windows 9x version
- Renames pre-existing versions of the (hidden) DOS system files as IO.DOS and MSDOS.DOS
- Updates MSDOS.SYS with device drivers, startup mode notations, and any pre-existing CONFIG.SYS settings, along with any new configuration information that Windows will require at startup

First Restart

Windows 9x keeps track of the start and restart events, both during installation and with each new session. During an installation and following a successful restart of the computer for the first time, Windows makes further updates to the configuration of the system through the following process:

1. WINIT.EXE processes three sections of the WINIT.INI file (arial.win, user32.tmp, and logo.sys) to create a combined VMM32.VXD with all the VxDs needed by the specific computer.
2. SYSTEM.DAT is renamed *SYSTEM.DA0*, and SYSTEM.NEW is renamed *SYSYTEM.DAT*.
3. The Registry flag (indicator) is set to indicate that this is the first time Windows is being run following a new installation.
4. The "Run Once" module is run to configure printers, MIDI, and PCMCIA devices (on a new computer), and to run any new hardware manufacturer's custom setup program(s).
5. If the installation was done over a pre-existing Windows 3.x system, GRPCONV.EXE converts all Program Groups and Program Items from the previous version of Windows to Windows 9x format and renames the files to use Long File Names.

An installation may not necessarily install and configure a printer. If this happens, you can go to the Control Panel and open the Printers icon, and then choose "Add Printer." It's sometimes a good idea to install a Generic Printer and set the printer port (under Device Options) to FILE. This way, you can easily send a print job to a .PRN file and import the results into another application.

Installation Log Files

Windows uses a number of log files for tracking the state of applications and the way in which the applications load. These states are generated through error codes, and the log files contain messages written to the files by the error codes. A "good" or successful code can still be understood as an error code. During installation, even with custom choices and settings offered by the Installation Wizard, Windows still fails to install many of the additional utilities that come on the installation disks or CD-ROM.

The files in the root directory that Windows 9x Setup uses to track installation and successful configuration are:

- **SETUPLOG.TXT**—Setup sequence and pass/fail
- **DETLOG.TXT**—Hardware detection log file
- **NETLOG.TXT**—Networking setup log file

- **DETCRASH.LOG**—Hardware detection failure/crash log
- **BOOTLOG.TXT**—Success/fail boot sequence log

DETLOG.TXT keeps track of what hardware devices are found on the system. BOOTLOG.TXT keeps track of the first startup process and the success or failure of each step.

If the Startup Menu key is pressed (F8 or CTRL), BOOTLOG.TXT can be changed to reflect the current startup, and the previous version is overwritten. To keep a copy of the original installation startup sequence, copy BOOTLOG.TXT to another name (e.g., FIRSBOOT.TXT).

Windows Setup tracks each phase of an installation and makes success or fail notations in SUWARN.BAT (SetUp WARNings batch file). Setup also makes notations in the AUTOEXEC.BAT prior to a successful complete installation. Much of the moment-by-moment installation process is tracked in SETUPLOG.TXT and DETCRASH.LOG in case the setup crashes. If the installation and setup are successful, DETCRASH.LOG is deleted.

The Windows 9x Setup can fail at three points:

1. When insufficient, incorrect, or unavailable system resources are detected during SETUP.EXE in Real Mode
2. When a crash occurs during the hardware detection phase, creating DETCRASH.LOG
3. When a device stops working following hardware detection

Setup uses SETUPLOG.TXT to list information about the steps in the installation, including their sequence and the error information returned at the end of the step (whether it completed successfully or why not). In case of a failed setup, Windows uses SETUPLOG.TXT to bypass the steps that completed successfully, and continues only with the steps that failed.

If the installation fails, the process is designed to continue from a restart of the computer. Rather than reformat the drive and reinstall from the beginning, restart the computer and let Windows Setup pick up where it left off, trying to correct the installation problem itself.

Starting Windows 9x

Windows requires a minimum of 3MB of uncompressed space on the bootup partition (i.e., Active, Primary). Under DOS and Windows 3.x, the DOS system files were COMMAND.COM, MSDOS.SYS, and IO.SYS. The DOS command processor looked to the CONFIG.SYS file to load device drivers, and it also transferred control to AUTOEXEC.BAT to display recurring configuration commands at startup.

Windows 95 changed the basic system files, using the hidden IO.SYS to read configuration and device information from the MSDOS.SYS hidden file, a CONFIG.SYS file (if one is present), or both. IO.SYS must still be in the boot sector of the bootable partition; MSDOS.SYS is placed in the root directory, also hidden. COMMAND.COM is also carried forward in DOS 7.x and installed in the C:\WINDOWS directory.

IO.SYS runs first from DOS 7.x (just as it did in DOS 6.x), but contains a series of commands for processing device drivers out of both the MSDOS.SYS and the CONFIG.SYS file. CONFIG.SYS and AUTOEXEC.BAT are still required by some applications, which won't start without finding one of these files. The Windows emergency recovery utility (ERU) requires that a CONFIG.SYS and AUTOEXEC.BAT file exist.

POST and Bootstrap

No matter which operating system you use, the motherboard's ROM BIOS runs the POST routine when the computer is first turned on. Everything that applies to a plain DOS computer applies to a Windows computer. The bootstrap loader (discussed in Chapter 11) looks to the boot sector of the Primary, Active partition (the boot partition) for instructions on how to start whatever operating system is installed on that partition.

The boot sector and the master boot record (MBR) are technically two different things. However, the exam tends to confuse the two and may ask you to treat the MBR as though it were another name for boot sector.

Windows looks in the boot sector, where it finds IO.SYS. Windows NT and OS/2 can be booted from the boot track, making it possible to boot them from a different partition than the Primary, Active one; however, note that Windows NT/2000 still runs the NT Loader that looks in the boot track. In Windows 9x, the "Starting Windows 9x…" message is displayed on the screen following the initial POST and parity check, and is written into IO.SYS.

Pressing F8 between the "Starting Windows 9x…" message and the Windows logo splash screen will interrupt the boot process and allow you to choose various options from a Startup menu (more on this shortly).

DOS

If you remember the DOS boot sequence, you'll recognize IO.SYS as one of the system files in DOS startup trio. IO.SYS starts DOS in Real Mode. IO.SYS in Windows 9x does the same thing: It sets up the segment addressing in conventional memory, and loads Real Mode device drivers into the first segment of memory (low memory). IO.SYS then reads MSDOS.SYS (or an existing CONFIG.SYS file).

Windows 9x uses a preliminary hardware profile from the hardware detection phase to attempt to start the computer (e.g., interrupts, BIOS serial and parallel ports, and CMOS or BIOS system board identification). Once the computer is started for the first time, the Registry tells Windows which settings to use at startup. IO.SYS reads the MSDOS.SYS file to process specific devices, and reads the Registry (SYSTEM.DAT) for device settings.

If a CONFIG.SYS file, an AUTOEXEC.BAT file, or both are supposed to run, IO.SYS loads the COMMAND.COM command interpreter and runs the two configuration files. Depending on which lines are found in these files, DOS runs other Real Mode commands and programs. Remember that whatever is loaded into the DOS environment at this point will descend to any DOS sessions run from within Windows.

Technically speaking, IO.SYS reads CONFIG.SYS, then MSDOS.SYS, and then passes control to MSDOS.SYS. After MSDOS.SYS, control passes to COMMAND.COM, which reads CONFIG.SYS *again* before passing control to AUTOEXEC.BAT.

While technically, CONFIG.SYS is read twice, we believe the exam expects CONFIG.SYS (if it exists) to process following COMMAND.COM. This is one of those ambiguous, imprecise questions where Microsoft says what happens, but the proper response may not be listed on the exam.

MSDOS.SYS

Whether or not CONFIG.SYS, AUTOEXEC.BAT, or both exist, IO.SYS reads the MSDOS.SYS file first and reads it again for VxDs and other configuration settings. MSDOS.SYS is a plain ASCII text file that can be edited by DOS's EDIT.COM or Microsoft's WordPad. The important point is that all attributes are set on the file, making it hidden, system, and read-only. Before you can edit MSDOS.SYS, you're expected to know what you're doing and how to change the file attributes (see Chapter 11).

The MSDOS.SYS file tells Windows about multiple booting options, startup menus, which mode to start in, and whether the Windows GUI is supposed to start at all following bootup. If you press and hold the Shift key before the Windows splash screen instead of the F8 key, MSDOS.SYS is bypassed and not read at all.

WIN.COM

If MSDOS.SYS is configured to start Windows, it runs WIN.COM and loads Windows. Windows then looks for WINSTART.BAT and runs it if the file is found. MSDOS.SYS also contains path locations for important Windows files, including where to find the Registry. To enable the F4 shortcut key option (discussed shortly) to run a previous version of DOS, the directive BootMulti= must have the value 1 (BootMulti=1) in the [Options] section of MSDOS.SYS.

You can make changes to the MSDOS.SYS file so as to have a Windows 9x machine boot to DOS. This is a clean version of DOS, as opposed to a DOS session created by restarting in MS-DOS mode. Open a Web search engine and look up "edit MSDOS" if you're interested in the process. Use caution when you edit this file, as it must contain certain unreadable characters in order to start Windows.

Start Sequence

Remember that Windows 9x was an interim interface that's trying to keep compatible with 16-bit Windows 3.x and DOS Real Mode applications. Microsoft was also trying to induce programmers to write programs in the 32-bit Windows NT format. The resulting combination of 16-bit Windows, DOS, Windows NT, and 32-bit Windows 9x is confusing, which is why Microsoft changed the name of the operating system to Windows 2000. Following any Real Mode device drivers, Windows 9x loads any *static* VxDs required by Windows 3.1x programs.

Virtual device drivers were first introduced in Windows 3.1 by loading into memory and remaining there throughout the session, making them static (not moving). Windows 9x *dynamic* VxDs can be loaded into memory and then unloaded when a program terminates, if the VxD is no longer needed.

Just as in Windows 3.1x, the executable Virtual Machine Manager (VMM) runs, but this time VMM32.VXD includes both a Real Mode loader and the VMM as well as common, static VxDs from 16-bit format (in MRCI2.VXD).

VMM32.VXD is a combination file with many common VxD files bound up inside it. Typical VxD files are about 80KB, and typical VMM32.VXD files are about 650KB. The devices found inside this file were once loaded in the [386Enh] section of the SYSTEM.INI file. Windows 9x first checks the WINDOWS\SYSTEM\VMM32 directory for any 32-bit VXD files, rather than the VxDs bound in VMM32.VXD. If it finds any newer files, it loads them from that folder.

The Windows 2000 Help System includes the Update Manager (discussed later in this chapter) that can access Internet Web sites for updated .DLLs and .VXD files.

Assuming Windows finds no later version virtual device drivers in the VMM32 folder, VMM32.VXD loads static device drivers found in the DEVICE= line of the SYSTEM.INI file (which still comes with Windows 9x). The actual devices load from within VMM32, but show in the SYSTEM.INI file for backward compatibility.

The Registry contains entries for every .VXD file and, through its processing, controls VMM32.VXD. The Registry also contains entries for every virtual device driver that isn't directly associated with a piece of hardware. If two devices have a conflict at load time, the VxD in the SYSTEM.INI DEVICE= takes precedence over the one specified by the Registry. If the device can't be found, an error occurs.

As Windows starts up, the following three files are run in the sequence listed here (note the continued use of WIN.COM and SYSTEM.INI):

- **WIN.COM**—Controls the initial environment checks and loads the core Windows 95 components
- **VMM32.VXD**—Creates the virtual machine (VM) and installs all VxDs
- **SYSTEM.INI**—Is read for DEVICE= entries, which may differ from the Registry entries

Final Steps to Loading Windows 9x

Once device drivers have been loaded into memory and the Virtual Machine is up and running, Windows loads KERNEL32.DLL for the main Windows components and KRNL386.EXE, which loads Windows 3.x device drivers. GDI.EXE and GDI32.EXE load next, followed by USER.EXE and USER32.EXE. Notice the continued path from Windows 3.1x as the same files append a "32" to their names.

In order to ensure backward compatibility, Windows 9x loads in the same way that Windows 3.x loads. One of the primary differences is that Windows 9x runs DOS programming code under a *virtual* 8086 machine, rather than a Real Mode machine. Keep in mind that Windows NT/2000 ended all support for this Real Mode. Once the installation is complete and Windows 9x starts from the hard disk, it goes back and checks to see whether or not it has a matching internal 32-bit VxD for any static device drivers in memory. If it does, Windows comments out the original device's line in either CONFIG.SYS or AUTOEXEC.BAT.

When the startup process calls WIN.COM, the SYSTEM.INI file is read for Real Mode device drivers, and the SYSTEM.DAT file is read for the rest of the device configurations. In other words, Windows 9x reads both the Windows 3.x .INI files and the Registry .DAT files as it loads. Most of the devices and their configuration are installed from the SYSTEM.DAT file, but SYSTEM.INI is still read first.

Following the SYSTEM.INI and SYSTEM.DAT processing, WIN.INI is read for associated resources and environment values such as fonts, wallpaper, associated file extensions, and so on. Once WIN.INI has been processed, the USER.DAT file is read.

If networking has been enabled, Windows reads the USER.DAT file after the WIN.INI file, for Desktop configurations. Sometimes, USER.DAT and networking are used on stand-alone machines, in order to maintain consistencies throughout a corporate environment. At home, networking can be enabled in order to allow individual family members their own customized Desktop.

Finally, the SHELL= line in SYSTEM.INI is run in order to load EXPLORER.EXE, assuming that no other shell has been specified in a default installation.

Rudimentary security can be configured for the Windows 3.x Program Manager by making changes to the PROGMAN.INI file. These security measures (called *policies* at the time) have been enhanced with the Windows 9x Policy Editor, allowing for more complete security maintenance.

The concept of system policies acting as global templates for access rights has fallen into disuse. Windows NT/2000 mostly replaces policies with user profiles, group profiles, and domain administration, which we discuss in the next chapter.

Loading Device Drivers

We've said that Windows 9x continues to use IO.SYS to begin the startup process and initiate Real Mode. (If the computer is started using a previous version of DOS, IO.SYS is renamed *WINBOOT.SYS*.) Even in DOS 6.x, IO.SYS had rudimentary capabilities built into it to handle some of the basic directives (command lines) of the CONFIG.SYS file. However, the program wasn't ready to assume full control until Windows 95.

The Windows 9x IO.SYS finally took over from CONFIG.SYS and loads HIMEM.SYS, IFSHLP.SYS, SETVER.EXE, and DBLSPACE.BIN or DRVSPACE.BIN by default, if they exist (see Table 12.1). Additionally, the DOS 7.0 version includes defaults for all the old CONFIG.SYS directives, such as FILES, BUFFERS, COUNTRY, and SETVER.

Table 12.1 The common device directives that moved from CONFIG.SYS to IO.SYS.

DEVICE=	Description
DOS=HIGH	IO.SYS does not load EMM386.EXE (If this expanded memory manager is found in an existing CONFIG.SYS file, the UMB line is added.)
HIMEM.SYS	Real Mode memory manager to access extended memory; part of IO.SYS by default
IFSHLP.SYS	Installable File System Helper that loads device drivers and allows the system to make file system connections from within Windows to the DOS file management I/O
SETVER.EXE	To maintain backward compatibility with some older TSRs that won't run under newer versions of COMMAND.COM; optional and usually not necessary
FILES=	60 (default) Included for compatibility; specifies how many files can be open at any one time when running an MS DOS session; not required by Windows 95
BUFFERS=	30 (default) Specifies the number of file buffers; used by IO.SYS calls from DOS and Windows 3.x programs
STACKS=	9,256 (default) The number and size of the stack frames that the CPU uses during prioritization of incoming interrupts; used for backward compatibility; not required by Windows 95
SHELL=	C:\COMMAND.COM /p Indicates which command processor to use (e.g., NDOS or DRDOS); not the same as the SHELL= line in SYSTEM.INI (If the directive is used, but the /p switch is not used, AUTOEXEC.BAT is not processed. /p makes the command processor permanent in the environment.)
FCBS=	4 (default) A very old method of controlling open files (file control blocks); necessary only with DOS programs designed for DOS 2.x and earlier

CONFIG.SYS ordinarily doesn't use a SHELL= directive since the default assumption of the system is that COMMAND.COM is used and found on the boot disk. This directive is used primarily to increase the DOS environment space, and in that case, the /p switch must be included, as noted above. We discuss the DOS environment in Chapter 10.

Because of market pressures to maintain backward compatibility, IO.SYS still checks for a CONFIG.SYS file just as the older version did. If the CONFIG.SYS file is found and if it contains a DEVICE= line with the same directive as one found within IO.SYS, the one in CONFIG.SYS takes over.

To change a DEVICE setting from the default within IO.SYS, create a CONFIG.SYS file and use the same DEVICE= directive, but with a different setting. For example, FILES=100 would override the default FILES directive in IO.SYS and change the default from 60 to 100 possible open files. Some final thoughts to keep in mind regarding IO.SYS:

- IO.SYS cannot be edited (unlike MSDOS.SYS).
- Directive values in CONFIG.SYS must be set to the default or higher in IO.SYS to change their settings.
- EMM386.EXE can be loaded only in CONFIG.SYS for DOS, 16-bit Windows, and Windows 9x.

AUTOEXEC.BAT

Windows 9x specifically disables (with REM, or "remark") SMARTDRV, DBLBUFF.SYS, and MOUSE.SYS from any existing CONFIG.SYS, and disables any incompatible TSRs in an existing AUTOEXEC.BAT file by using an internal "known conflicts" list. It removes WIN and SHARE commands from an existing AUTOEXEC.BAT file, if they exist, and updates the PATH line.

Before making updates to an existing AUTOEXEC.BAT, Windows copies the file to AUTOEXEC.DOS.

Many of the older device drivers that were needed for DOS and Windows 3.x are handled by the loadable VxDs in 32-bit Windows. Microsoft says (in a technical white paper) that it will use 32-bit code in Windows 9x "wherever it significantly improves performance without sacrificing application compatibility, or where 32-bit code would increase memory requirements without significantly improving performance." To that extent, it's sometimes difficult to tell whether a given device would be better off using the Windows 9x 32-bit VxD or the 16-bit device driver loaded from within CONFIG.SYS.

Devices loaded from CONFIG.SYS often require command line-setting switches in the AUTOEXEC.BAT file. An AUTOEXEC.BAT file is usually required to set the path to something other than the Windows default search path (C:\WINDOWS; C:\WINDOWS\COMMAND). Likewise, an AUTOEXEC.BAT file is needed to change the Temporary (TEMP) directory to something other than C:\WINDOWS\TEMP.

Networking usually requires an AUTOEXEC.BAT file to run the command for NET START. However, because Windows is designed to handle many of the networking capabilities from within itself, it's usually better to create a separate batch file for starting the network and then place that file in the Windows Startup folder. Remember that along with .EXE and .COM, Windows considers files with a .BAT or .PIF extension as executable files. Generally, for everything except the most ornery DOS-based Real Mode programs, let Windows try to use one of its own VxDs.

Summary—Start Sequence

We'll remind you here that, nowadays, it's almost impossible to detail a common start sequence for every configuration of Windows. That being said, there is a common set of events that takes place on Windows 9x machines and Windows 2000 machines. You should have a fairly comfortable understanding of what takes place during the startup sequence, even if you don't know every single file and every single read-write operation. After you have a sense of the order of things, be sure to keep track of the following specifics:

- During the installation phase, Windows checks the machine and detects the hardware configuration. The important files to know are SCANDISK.EXE and DETLOG.TXT
- Windows has certain minimal installation requirements, and the Setup routine checks to make sure these requirements have been met. Remember that HIMEM.SYS is a critical operational file. You should also have a working knowledge of MSDOS.SYS.
- Remember how Windows provides for the optional creation of an emergency startup disk. Windows 9x uses one method of offering you this tool, but Windows 2000 works with an Emergency Repair Disk. We'll cover the ERD in Chapters 13 and 14, but be warned that understanding how these disks are created is important.

- Make sure you're comfortable with the first few times Windows starts, following an installation. Each restart generates certain files and modifies other files. Don't worry too much about the exact files, but be aware of them.

Testing for knowledge of 32-bit Windows isn't all that easy to do, especially at an entry level. One of the topics that makes for a good set of questions is the various log files created by Windows at varying times. We'll be discussing these log files again in Chapter 14, but as you review the startup sequence, be careful to note the references to these text files. You should also have a clear understanding of virtual device drivers. If not, then go back and review Chapter 11 and 16-bit Windows.

Windows and DOS

Many of the more powerful commands and utilities remained in DOS 7.0, being designed to work directly with the overhauled 9x GUI. As a result, some of the DOS 6.x executable programs were given DOS 7.x descendents, along with new Windows 9x counterparts. Some of the older programs could be run only from within Windows. Defrag (DEFRAG.EXE) is an important example of this. On the other hand, ScanDisk had both a DOS version (SCANDISK.EXE) and a Windows counterpart (SCANDSKW.EXE).

The fact that SCANDISK.EXE runs even before Windows 9x is set up, and that in OSR/B (version 2) a crash and improper close will automatically run ScanDisk, demonstrates how Windows 9x continued to depend on DOS.

Many DOS programs carried forward into the not-so-well-known C:\WINDOWS\COMMAND directory (now called a *folder*), but were given a 32-bit sibling. For example, XCOPY.EXE carried forward, but Windows 9s added XCOPY32.EXE. Some of the DOS 6.x programs were not automatically included during an installation, but remained available on the Windows installation CD-ROM. Examples included the DOS Editor (EDIT) and the Microsoft System Diagnostics tool (MSD.EXE), which, although they still run in plain DOS, require either an MS DOS window or a new option: "Restart in DOS Mode."

MSD.EXE was replaced with HWINFO.EXE, a much more sophisticated HardWare INFOrmation and diagnostics tool. Additionally, the Device Manager, found through the Properties option of the My Computer icon, provides in-depth system configuration and diagnostics options. The Device Manager is part of the System Properties menu, also found by double-clicking the System icon in the Control Panel (Start|Settings|Control Panel).

The MS Explorer

Another indication that DOS continued (and continues) to live on was in the way the user was presented with file names. Windows 9x introduced a change in terminology, where files were kept in folder and subfolders, rather than in directories and subdirectories. The Windows Explorer, or MS Explorer, replaced the old File Manager (WINFILE.EXE, which is still available in a standard Windows 9x installation), and a description column was added to the viewing pane. Previously, users were given the file name, the file size, the last modified date, and last modified time. None of this information was labeled until MS Explorer introduced column headings in the view pane.

DOS and Windows 3.x used file extensions, three characters to the right of a period, as a simple way to tell the operating system what kind of file information was being stored. These extensions could be associated with programs by using the Explorer's View | Folder Types | File Types menu option. When an extension is associated with a program, Windows can automatically open that program with the chosen file ready for modification. Windows 9x introduced the mixed blessing of hiding these file extensions and showing the user both a small icon and a "Type" column in the Explorer viewing pane.

In theory, any file created with MS Word will appear in the Explorer as a "Microsoft Word Document." Using file associations, the user could double-click on the file from the Explorer, and Windows would open up MS Word with the document in place for editing. Later versions of Windows (98/SE/Me), following a World Wide Web model, even provided the user with the option of single-clicking on a file name in order to open it.

In reality, not only could users easily rename files in the Explorer, simply by pressing the F2 key or slowly clicking twice on the name, but they could also add multiple extensions to the original file. If the extensions were hidden, there could be multiple files with what appeared to be exactly the same name. This separation of the apparent name from the "real" name—the name being stored by the underlying operating system—led to files with names like MyDocument.2001.txt.doc. Additionally, since many applications use the .DOC extension, users were unable to tell which application actually created the file. Finally, someone might tell a co-worker that important information was stored in a file called ThisFile.xls, but if the "Hide file extensions for known file types" option box was checked in the Explorer's View | Folder Options | View tab, the person would be unable to see the .XLS extension and think that the file had vanished.

Another mixed blessing of trying to hide the underlying DOS origins, was that any user who tried to use the MS Explorer file-searching tool (Tools | Find | Files or Folders) was presented with the old DOS system of wildcards, extensions, subfolders and so forth. Without understanding the concepts of extensions and wildcards, the "Find: All Files" window became a mystery.

Booting to DOS

Windows 95/98/98 SE, and Me (Millenium Edition) presented the user with a new "desktop" model, instead of the previous Program Manager. A "Start" button menu was added to a "Taskbar," and instead of simply allowing the user to turn off the machine, a list of "Shut Down" options was included on the Start button. Windows 95 took the first real steps towards controlling the hardware in the system, and if the machine were simply to be turned off, the resulting corrupted files became a problem. Users had to learn how to, or be taught to properly exit and close out of Windows before turning off the power.

In order to make computers easier for the average person to use, Microsoft has chosen to hide most of the management aspects of the operating system. This doesn't mean that a technical user can't access those functions, but that the tools, functions, and configuration options aren't as obvious. During the Windows 9x shut-down process, the user was presented with the option of completely shutting down the machine; restarting Windows; restarting without network connections; or restarting in DOS Mode. However, only by making certain obscure configuration changes could Windows be completely shut down and unloaded from memory.

"Restart in DOS Mode" gave the user the appearance of a plain command line, but was, in fact, a DOS window. If you were to type "exit" in this so-called DOS Mode, you would find yourself returned to Windows 9x. If you were to turn off the machine, Scan Disk would most likely run the next time the machine was turned on, indicating that the machine had been improperly shut down. It wasn't until Windows 2000 (discussed in Chapter 13) that this feature disappeared.

The DOS Mode option didn't actually disappear in Windows 2000. Instead, it was renamed to "Recovery Console," and stored on the installation disks as an option, or what some people refer to as a feature.

There is a hidden, system, read-only MSDOS.SYS file in the root folder (directory) of Windows 9x machines. Although it carries an .SYS extension (typically used for compiled software driver files), for those users who could figure out how to see the extension in the first place, this is a plain text file that can be edited in the Windows Note Pad (NOTEPAD.EXE). Changing the BootGUI=1 to BootGUI=0, causes Windows to start in an actual DOS Mode.

Windows 9x uses several graphics files on Startup, Shutdown, and to let the user know that it's okay to turn off their machine. The Startup graphic is called LOGO.SYS. The "Windows is shutting down" graphic is called LOGOW.SYS, and the "It is now safe to turn off your computer" graphic is called LOGOS.SYS.

Configuring the MSDOS.SYS file to boot the machine to DOS (not a GUI) will necessitate typing WIN and pressing Enter from a command prompt. This is still the old WIN.COM file from all the way back in Windows 1.0. However, shutting down Windows 9x will continue to produce the two graphic notifications that Windows is shutting down. An old DOS "mode" command, **mode co80**, can sometimes cancel the final graphic and return to a pure DOS command line. Renaming, or deleting, the LOGOS.SYS file will produce a text message: You may now turn off your machine or press Ctrl-Alt-Delete to reboot. So "restarting in DOS mode" is actually that—a mode, not really DOS itself.

Ultimately, it might help you to think of the Windows 9x versions as a transitional movement from DOS to NT. Windows 9x moved closer to the 32-bit GUI environment, but it was still composed of the two intertwined components of DOS and the graphical user interface. The important thing to know about the DOS component is that it controls the physical file locations on the disk and is required for disk partitioning.

In the event you think all this information about DOS is pointless, remember that the Windows 2000 command line (CMD.EXE), startup files, and Recovery Console are all based on DOS.

Useful Additional Components

Oddly enough, Windows 9x doesn't always install some of the more useful utilities that come on the installation CD-ROM. Among these extra utilities are the Accessibility options for people with disabilities, the LOGVIEW program mentioned earlier, and the Emergency Recovery Utility (ERU.EXE), which can back up the Registry files. Although the Accessibility options are important for people who need them, they can be useful for just about anyone. (The Accessibility options are routinely installed during an Express setup.)

Not all the extra utilities are listed in the Windows Setup Wizard. For example, the Emergency Recovery Utility is in the OTHER\MISC\ERU folder and must be manually copied to the hard drive. Remember that you can click once on the folder icon and press Ctrl+C to copy, and then Ctrl+V to paste the entire folder into a new location—perhaps a new folder called Registry Backup, rather than the obscure ERU name.

The Control Panel

Windows 95 introduced some important changes in how the machine was configured and fixed (if it ever broke). The Control Panel became much more sophisticated than the original applet in Windows 3.x, allowing for more control over the configuration of the machine at both hardware and software level. Changes to the overall look and feel of the system continued to be done in the control panel, and CONTROL.EXE was still found in the C:\WINDOWS folder.

The Windows 9x Control panel allows you to change many of the Registry settings from within a Windows session:

- Memory-related options are set in the System option of Control Panel.
- Hardware device options or parameters are set in the Device Manager option of Control Panel.
- Network and resource-sharing parameters are set in the Network option of Control Panel.
- Mouse and Keyboard options and parameters are set from the Mouse and the Keyboard option, respectively, of the Control Panel.
- All screen and display options are set either from the Display option of the Control Panel or by right-clicking on the Desktop and selecting Properties.

To install additional Windows components from Control Panel:

1. Insert the installation CD-ROM into the drive bay
2. Select Add/Remove Software
3. Select the Windows Setup tab on the dialog box
4. Check the new component's check box (leaving any previously installed check boxes gray). If you uncheck something that already was installed (showing as gray), Setup will assume that you mean to remove it.

Tweak UI

Microsoft technical support has had access to a collection of small utility programs ever since Windows 95 was released. Over time, those tools made their way onto many Internet sites and became known as "power toys." This collection is called *Tweak UI,* and it provides a graphical interface for changing various settings without going directly into the Registry. Some of these changes, such as turning off the ubiquitous animation and tool tips, can't be accessed through the Control Panel.

Tweak UI was finally included on the Windows 98 installation CD-ROM, in the \tools\reskit\powertoy\ folder. Note that each version of Windows has its own specific version of the program utilities, so don't use the Windows 95 version on a Windows 98 system.

Tweak UI can be downloaded from the Microsoft Web site, but the tools have gradually become less and less powerful. Windows 2000 incorporates a few of the most innocuous features from the old Tweak UI in the accessories area of the Start Menu. Too many unknowledgeable users were crashing their system, so while the Windows 95 version of Tweak UI is harder to find, some of the extra features will work on a Windows 98 system. Additional tools and utilities have been developed, many of which can be found on the **http://www.annoyances.org** Web site.

Note that Tweak UI has a bug in the installation routine, so to install this software, right-click on the .INF file and select Install. If you are prompted for the disk, point to the folder containing the files and click OK.

Startup Menu and Safe Mode

If you press the F8 key in Windows 95, or hold down the CTRL key in Windows 98/SE/Me, between the time the POST has ended and the Windows splash screen appears, you can halt the processing of MSDOS.SYS and call up the Windows 9x Interactive Startup menu. This menu allows you to start in DOS Mode, Safe Mode, or other options. Each of these choices offers different processes and results. The Startup menu offers the following choices:

- Normal
- Logged (BOOTLOG.TXT)
- Safe Mode
- Safe Mode with network support
- Step-by-step confirmation
- Command prompt only
- Safe Mode command prompt only
- Previous version of DOS

The message "Starting Windows 9x..." is written into IO.SYS, which means that if you make a bootable system disk and start the computer, you'll still see the message, even though you don't have the files available to start Windows. The text-based startup menu is also contained within IO.SYS, although you won't necessarily have access to all the options on the menu. For example, selecting Option 3 from an emergency boot disk will leave you at the command prompt because the floppy disk doesn't contain WIN.COM or a path to the Windows subdirectory.

Normal and Logged

Normal (Option 1) starts Windows normally and brings the user to the Desktop. If any networking configuration data is installed, Windows connects to the network and provides a Logon dialog boxes from within Windows (depending on the type of network). Don't confuse *logged* (writing to log files) with *logging in* to a network. Normal and Logged (Option 2) are the same thing, except that Logged writes the steps and status of the startup to the BOOTLOG.TXT file in the root directory of the bootable drive.

BOOTLOG.TXT is created following the first successful startup of Windows. The file contains lines for each step of the startup process and a notation regarding their successful or failed outcome. A new boot log is only created when you choose the option from the (F8) Startup menu.

Safe Mode (F5)

One of the critical concepts you need to know about 32-bit Windows is the use of VxDs (those first developed for Windows 3.1). In Safe Mode, Windows bypasses all network configurations, bypasses CONFIG.SYS and AUTOEXEC.BAT, and loads with only the most generic settings and minimal, static virtual device drivers.

Pressing F5 at the "Starting Windows 9x..." text screen is the same as selecting Option 3 from the menu to bypass all configuration files and start the session in Safe Mode. Safe Mode installs the minimum Windows setup, in VGA graphics Mode, with no network connections.

Safe Mode runs in VGA Mode, and it does not load any device drivers other than a keyboard driver, HIMEM.SYS, and the standard VGA device.

Safe Mode with Network Support (F6)

Safe Mode starts Windows without any network configuration or connections. Safe Mode with network support provides whatever networking connections are possible. Safe Mode is available in both choices, mainly to help troubleshoot when Windows doesn't start correctly. Sometimes, Windows will start in Safe Mode, but for some reason won't allow the network connection. Safe Mode is primarily a diagnostics tool, or the way in which Windows starts when a problem exists.

Step-by-Step Confirmation (Shift+F8)

Beginning with DOS 5, two keystrokes have been available to control the way in which the system starts up. You must be watchful and quick with your fingers, but if you use the keystrokes, you can bypass configurations or choose a line-by-line agreement for every configuration step. The following startup messages appear right after the initial BIOS startup messages:

- "Starting MS-DOS..." (DOS 5.0 and later)
- "Starting Windows 9x..." (DOS 7.x and Windows 9x)

Choosing the step-by-step confirmation option from the F8 Startup menu is the same as pressing Shift+F8 at the "Starting Windows 9x..." message in Windows 95. This combination of F8 and F5 and their shifted states can be confusing, but you should know the differences for the exam. Table 12.2 lists what happens if you press the keys as soon as you see the "Starting" messages for DOS or Windows.

Table 12.2 F8 and F5 "Starting" options in DOS and Windows.	
DOS Keystroke	**Result**
F5	Bypasses CONFIG.SYS and AUTOEXEC.BAT configurations
F8	Processes CONFIG.SYS and AUTOEXEC.BAT one line at a time
Windows Keystroke	**Result**
F5	Starts Windows in Safe Mode, bypassing CONFIG.SYS and AUTOEXEC.BAT
Shift+F5	Starts in Real (DOS) Mode
F8	Calls up text-based Startup menu
Shift+F8	Starts Windows and processes configurations line by line

If you press and hold the Shift key from the time you see the first Windows splash screen until you see the Desktop and the Taskbar, Windows will bypass anything in the Startup folder.

Command Prompt Only (Shift F5)

If you want to start the computer in plain, real DOS 7, you can either modify MSDOS.SYS to always start with the command prompt or choose Option 6 in the Startup menu. Certain commands (e.g., FDISK.EXE) can't be run from within Windows 9x, and this option gives you a plain DOS environment.

In spite of what everyone talks about, Windows NT and Windows 2000 provide a Recovery Console tool as an optional installation, which allows you to start at a plain command prompt.

To start Windows 9x from the command prompt, type "WIN" and press Enter. When you exit a Windows session after starting from the command prompt, you return to the DOS prompt rather than the "It is now safe to shut off your machine" final exit screen.

The final shutdown screen is actually one of two graphics image files and can be changed. These files are located initially in your Windows folder. LOGOW.SYS is the one that reads "Please wait while...," and LOGOS.SYS is the one that reads "It is now safe to...." Make backup copies of the files LOGOW.SYS and LOGOS.SYS in a safe place; then copy the two originals into a temporary folder.

These files are standard bitmaps, so rename the extensions of these duplicates to .BMP. You can use any graphics editor to edit these files, such as MSPaint, Photoshop, or Paint Shop Pro. The files are 256-color windows bitmaps (RGB-encoded, but not RGB color), 320 x 400. Since the aspect ratio (width / height) of these files are not standard 4:3, like most computer screens, the bitmaps will appear vertically elongated.

To make your new design conform to this aspect ratio, resize the bitmap to 534 x 400 while you're working on it. Make sure to resize them back to 320 x 400 when you're done. Save your changes, and rename the extensions of your new files back to .SYS. Last, copy the new files back into your Windows folder.

Safe Mode Command Prompt Only

This option is like pressing the F5 key in DOS 5.0 and 6.0, starting DOS with no networking. The startup bypasses the CONFIG.SYS and AUTOEXEC.BAT files, and stops at the command prompt. It probably would've made more sense to call this option "Command Prompt with No Configurations."

Previous Version of DOS (F4)

This option from the Startup menu can also be run by pressing the F4 key when the "Starting..." message appears. The option is a bit misleading because a default installation of Windows 9x deletes any previous version of Windows 3.x and DOS.

You'll need to remember that F8 and F4 are important Windows startup keys. F8 gets you the text-based Startup menu. F4 (may) get you a previous version of DOS.

The Installable File System (IFS) Manager

DOS has always had the 8.3 file name structure. Although the creative use of directory and subdirectory names can produce a lot of information about a file, Apple's method of using common English names has been easier for most users. Because of the way the DOS FAT works, the maximum limit for a file name, including all the directory information, is 64 characters. Windows 9x long file names allow up to 255 characters and can include previously illegal characters, such as <space> and the + symbol.

Novell's Netware NOS created something called the "OS/2 name space" feature, which was designed to resolve conflicts between DOS and Apple computers running on the same network. If an Apple user saved a file as "1997 Third Quart Annual Report" and a DOS user opened and saved that file again, the Apple user might see "1997thir.dqa" as the new file name. Netware and the OS/2 name space helped resolve the abrupt cutting off (truncating) of anything after 11 characters.

Windows 9x uses something similar to the OS/2 name space in that the Installable File System Manager (IFS Manager) works to convert long file names to the 8.3 names required by the underlying 16-bit FAT. IFS Manager works the other way as well, in that a request for a short file name goes out to retrieve the correct long file name in the directory listing. The IFS Manager is loaded through a "helper file" called IFSHLP.SYS (in the Windows folder).

File naming conventions are voluntary ways of naming files. File naming rules, on the other hand, are statements of what characters may or may not be used in a file name. The exam may confuse you by using the term "convention" to mean "rule."

Remember that in DOS file names, the <space>, plus, asterisk, question mark, and slashes are not allowed. Even though Windows 9x LFNs will allow some of these illegal characters, our feeling is that the exam will test your knowledge of allowable characters, rather than whether a certain file name is possible under the extended capabilities of the long file name feature.

The Windows 9x IFS is a way to store additional file information about LFNs, while allowing the DOS 16-bit FAT to control the location of the basic file clusters and sectors. Remember that part of a file system's job is to associate human names to a series of numbers that describe the cylinder, track, sectors, and clusters where data is physically stored. This new file system is made up of three parts:

- IFS Manager, which works out the problems and differences between different file system components
- File system drivers, which provide access to low-level disk devices, CD-ROM file systems, and network devices
- The block I/O subsystem, which deals directly with physical disks

People sometimes refer to FAT32, 32-bit FAT, VFAT, or even HPFS when discussing the Windows 9x IFS. "VFAT" stands for "Virtual FAT" and is part of the Installable File System. VFAT was first introduced in Windows for Work groups 3.11 and was tightened up in Windows 95. The IFSHELP.SYS driver reference in the Windows 3.x startup sequence refers to the prototype version of what went on to become the Windows 95 IFS Manager.

On the other hand, HPFS stands for *high performance file system*, which was engineered into OS/2. Neither Windows 95 nor Windows NT uses or currently supports the HPFS. NT uses the NT File System (NTFS). For simplicity, we refer to the underlying 16-bit FAT as the *base file system*, the Windows 95 modification as the *IFS*, and any other file systems by their own names. Windows 95 uses a 32-bit VFAT that works in conjunction with the 16-bit base FAT controlled by DOS 7.0. The "32" in FAT32 refers to this VFAT.

NTFS is the Windows NT file system, while WINS is a Windows Internet naming system used for certain type of network protocols. While we don't believe you'll see a question on the WINS, NTFS, or HPFS, you should make note of their names and abbreviations.

Network Redirectors

Usually, an application, operating system, or both use Interrupt 21 to access the disk and file system. Networking operating system redirectors (TSRs) and CD-ROM drivers keep an eye on Interrupt 21 and determine whether the file system request is for the base file system or for its own 32-bit systems. A redirector grabs a request for the base file system and redirects the request to a different file system. As we said in Chapter 8, a redirector is like the executive secretary, watching the phone and directing calls either to the boss or to someone else in the company.

One problem with this idea is that you must load different device drivers for each system watching over that ever-popular IRQ 21. Different networks have their own redirector devices, and they often argue about who gets to take the file home to Mom and Dad. Aside from that, PCs have a terrible time connecting to more than two different networks at the same time.

The Windows 9x IFS Manager controls all the network redirectors as though they were different file systems. This allows an unlimited number of 32-bit redirectors to be used at the same time, as well as allowing the system to connect with any number of different networks. On any given machine, including stand-alone machines, the DOS file system is used as though it were just another network file system.

For any software to work with any hardware, instructions must be stored somewhere, either in a ROM BIOS chip on an expansion card or in a software program—a device driver. One way or another, the device driver must end up in memory somewhere. Although memory isn't a hardware device per se, extended memory still requires an XMS device driver (e.g., HIMEM.SYS). Likewise, expanded memory requires an EMS device driver (e.g., EMM386.EXE) in conjunction with and following the extended memory driver.

The limitations of the FAT and the large storage capacity of new hard drives and CDs put an increasing strain on the capabilities of the old 16-bit FAT to keep up. If DOS could be magically turned into a network operating system, many of those problems would just go away. The IFS Manager is that interim magic wand, and acts somewhat like a network redirector to grab all the Interrupt 21 requests from applications that want to access the DOS file system. The DOS file system is still laying down bits of information in clusters, on sectors, in tracks, and on cylinders. However, instead of DOS making the decisions about names, IFS Manager is now doing that.

VFAT

Using long file names and improving disk caching required a way to connect newer network operating systems to the old DOS file system on the same computer. Because the required FAT couldn't be eliminated, a second FAT had to be developed—a *virtual FAT*. This new VFAT had to live side by side with the original, and that could work only if one of them was the boss. IFS Manager makes sure that VFAT is in charge.

When Windows starts up, the IFS waits for the system files to run all the Real Mode device drivers, and for the drivers to connect to the file system and hardware devices. Once DOS has the computer functioning, Windows steps in and takes control with VMM32. As we saw earlier, VMM32 uses its compiled library of internal VxDs to replace whatever Real Mode drivers it finds in memory.

The VxDs in VMM32 are designed specifically to communicate with the IFS Manager, so the DOS file system is mounted (connected) in the same sense that a network volume is mounted and recognized by a network operating system. This ability to communicate with the IFS is part of what it means to write a 32-bit application that's 100 percent Windows compatible.

Truncating to Short File Names

Windows 9x has an internal list of all the interrupts that DOS can use (a maximum of 71) and adds a few more. Among the extra interrupts is the way in which Long File Names can be recognized by the operating system. Because DOS itself can't recognize the long name, IFS Manager uses one of the extra interrupts to store the file name with an alias pointer (similar to a vector), and returns to tell DOS what to do with the file.

IFS Manager also takes what you enter as a long file name and splits it apart (parses it) so that part of it can be used as a corresponding short file name (regular DOS 8.3 name). The rest of the name is stored for later rebuilding, and the alias pointer is associated with all the pieces of the file name.

If you have a file called "*1998 Fooferaugh + My list of stuff*" and another file called "*1998 Fooferaugh and Dave's stuff,*" IFS Manager will truncate the two files to an 8.3 name. Theoretically, that would result in two files called *1998foof.era* at the same time—*totally* illegal by DOS rules, the United Nations Resolution 439 on International Tom Foolery, and a breach of the 1927 Zambian nuclear arms treaty!

When IFS Manager finds two files that will truncate to the same name, it uses the first six characters (minus spaces) and adds a tilde (~) plus incremental numbers (beginning with 1). If any periods are in the long file name, IFS Manager uses the first three characters after the last period as the DOS extension. Otherwise, it uses the next three characters it finds. In our example, the files would be named *1998fo~1.era* and *1998fo~2.era* for the short DOS name.

The default use of the tilde can be changed by editing the Registry.

Short Names and Aliases

A typical way for a file system to come calling on the disk is when a DOS VM is created to run a DOS application in Windows. Windows 3.x applications also make calls to the file system, and both use Interrupt 21. The file system works to find room on the disk, store a file name in the Directory Allocation Table (DAT), and help the disk controller move the hardware around. The DAT is an index for the longer FAT.

Along with the short name in the FAT, the parsed long file name is given the pointer to hang onto. When anything calls the file system, IFS Manager goes back to DOS and presents the request. DOS hands IFS Manager the file location information, and IFS Manager looks at the associated alias number to find the rest of the file name. IFS Manager then shows the user the long file name.

By the time the proposed Windows 9x long file name reaches the file system, IFS Manager has parsed it and added a pointer number. Meanwhile, DOS hasn't a clue that anything unusual is happening and still thinks it's running the same as it did back in 1981. DOS dutifully lays down the file, stores what it was told to store in the DAT, and goes back to sleep. The file is stored in clusters all over the disk, and IFS Manager makes sure that anything and everything in Windows sees the file name that it's supposed to see.

In certain circumstances, the VFAT and the 16-bit DOS FAT can become partly desynchronized. In this strange situation, Explorer (not the File Manager, though) can end up showing two files with exactly the same name in the same directory. This is rare, but it results from the fact that the names being presented in Explorer aren't the actual file names any more than the name being presented in any other Windows 9x application is the actual name.

The DIR command in a DOS window is stolen by IFS Manager and returns the DOS directory with the long file name set aside in the IFS name space (to the far right of the DIR listing). Restarting the computer in DOS Mode shuts down the entire Windows environment and eliminates the IFS and IFS Manager, along with LFN support. A DIR command at a plain DOS prompt (e.g., Option 6 from the F8 Startup menu) will show only the short name of the file as it's actually registered in the DAT.

From a DOS command prompt within Windows, you can still use a long name (if you know it) by surrounding the long name with quotation marks. For example if you type CD "Program Files" instead of CD PROGRA~1, Windows IFS Manager will put you in the right folder. This will also work for individual files on a command line. The second, or closing quote, isn't usually necessary.

Saving Long File Names

As you can see, the only thing keeping track of the long file names is IFS Manager. If you decide to store all the files from a Windows computer on a network, the long file names will be stored only if the OS/2 name space has been enabled. If name space isn't enabled, the long file names are lost in the river of history. This is the same problem if you store files on a floppy disk and copy them over to a 16-bit DOS or Windows machine.

There are two other places where Long File Names can fail, the one being in certain Internet transfers and the other being under the old File Manager (WINFILE.EXE). Sometimes, File Manager is easier to use than Explorer, but you can't see LFNs and if you rename a file from within File Manager, the next time you look at it under Explorer, it will have a DOS file name. The same goes for file transfers from a Windows machine to some other machine that doesn't support Long File Names.

A little-known (and hardly referenced) utility that comes with the Windows CD-ROM is the LFNBK.EXE utility (for "long file name backup"). LFNBK.EXE is found in the ADMIN\APPTOOLS\LFNBACK folder, along with LFNBK.TXT that describes the basic operations and switches. Perhaps the program is hard to notice because Microsoft says that it's for experienced users and shouldn't be relied on for day-to-day maintenance.

The most immediate problem with long file names is that they're stored within Windows. In addition, part of that storage is the alias map that connects the physical location of the file to its corresponding IFS long name. Suppose that you decide to use a 16-bit defragmenting utility from the DOS prompt. Part of the defragmenting process involves moving file clusters around. Naturally, the utility is in constant communication with the file system's DAT, which keeps track of the clusters, no matter where they end up. But who's telling all this to IFS Manager? No one!

Using a DOS-based file maintenance program can disassociate the short file name from the long file name, causing the long file name to be lost forever. Reformatting a hard drive and reinstalling Windows will not keep previous long file names associated with the short file names held by DOS. Keeping the original long file names requires a complete backup of the existing Windows environment.

An interesting problem arises when long file names disappear from the system. Certain program instructions that are internal to Windows 9x program files make calls to other files by their specific LFNs. The files exist on the drive but only in short-name form. Because Windows is looking for the exact file name of a program and expecting IFS Manager to have that name, it can't find the file because it can only see the short name. At that point, Windows fails to run.

Reports and Utilities

One of the less obvious ways in which the various versions of Windows differ from each other, is in an almost adversarial relationship between the computer user and the operating system. DOS was generally known as an *open system*, in that aside from allowing developers access to all the programming aspects, whoever was using the computer could make just about any configuration changes they wanted. Windows 95 began making user access to system-level configuration and repair tools more difficult. Sometimes, this was done by referencing the particular programs in thick books such as the "Windows Resource Kit," sold separately from the operating system. Other times, as with the Registry and REGEDIT.EXE, the user had to know where the file was located and how to work with the results of running the file.

The old Windows 3.11 Program Manager introduced policies, whereby a systems administrator could prevent the user from accessing certain parts of the underlying file system. Windows 95 increased this security with a Policy Editor feature, which allowed systems administrators and IT professionals an even more sophisticated way of locking less knowledgeable users out of the basic configuration features for the systems. This trend continues, and one of the ways Windows Me differs from Windows 95 and 98 is that it became much more difficult to use diagnostics tools and utilities.

When we discuss Windows NT and Windows 2000 in the next chapter, we'll focus more on what you'll be allowed to do, as opposed to what a fully authorized systems administrator can do. Windows NT is where the first real separation between the corporate and home-user market took effect. Windows 2000 is an attempt to reintegrate the entire PC market through the use of a single name for all versions of the Windows operating system.

Hardware Diagnostics

We've talked about how DOS came with several program files that weren't essential to the operating system, but that provided tools and utilities for managing files and disks. Tweak UI was a set of utilities like this. We've also spoken about how third-party developers—both commercial and shareware—created a market of ancillary tools and utilities, and Norton Utilities is an example of commercial utilities. In DOS 5.0, Microsoft began licensing some of these third-party technologies, and for the first time, DOS wasn't developed wholly "in house," so to speak.

Windows 95 began focusing more attention on the tools and utilities needed by system administrators to properly maintain and support the increasingly complex operating system and system configurations. Diagnostics tools continued to be left either on the installation disk (rapidly becoming a CD-ROM, rather than many floppy disks), or as obscure files somewhere in the Windows subfolder. However, Windows 95 introduced a consolidated reporting capability for a basic presentation of the hardware connected to a given system. The feeling seems to have been that a report wouldn't damage the functionality of the system, but having access to tools and utilities could be trouble.

Borrowing from the Apple MacIntosh, the "My Computer" icon made its first appearance on the Desktop. By right-clicking this icon and going to a standardized "Properties" option, Windows 95 provided a way for the user (or more likely an administrator) to *explore* the various devices and peripherals attached to the motherboard, along with their basic settings. This metaphor of exploring, or *browsing* a system, began with the Windows Explorer, and carries through in all subsequent versions of Windows. However, Microsoft frowns upon the use of the word "browsing," and has taken to using different words to describe what it would like you to do.

Building on the detailed reporting capabilities of MSD.EXE (Microsoft Diagnostics), HWDIAG.EXE (Hardware Diagnostics) is a much more sophisticated diagnostics tool, running a thorough analysis of the specific hardware devices attached to the system. HWDIAG.EXE works in conjunction with Plug-and-Play to report out such things as the manufacturer for a network card, the way the card is configured, and even the software version the card is using.

HWDIAG.EXE and MSD.EXE are both hardware and configuration diagnostics tools. Neither program was installed by default in Windows 95, remaining on the installation disk during the basic setup routines.

Windows 9x vs. Windows 3.x

Windows 95 provides many significant changes to Windows 3.1 and sets the standard for all of the Windows 9x systems to come. Obviously, this is a prime area for test questions, so let's do a quick review before moving on. Windows 9x differs from Windows 3.1x primarily by:

- Using IO.SYS and MSDOS.SYS as the primary device-loading programs rather than CONFIG.SYS and AUTOEXEC.BAT
- Using loadable, dynamic, 32-bit virtual device drivers alongside static, fixed, 16-bit VxDs
- Using OLE shortcut objects, with links to data and/or the programs that created the data
- Using a floating Properties menu accessed by right-clicking the mouse, or using a special Windows key on a "Windows keyboard" (not unlike the special command key used on Apple keyboards)
- Allowing Long File Names (LFN) through a virtual FAT (VFAT)
- Placing most of the system configuration details in the Registry files

- Showing the user a Desktop with a Taskbar and Start button rather than Program Manager, Program Groups, and Task Manager
- Including a more sophisticated and integrated Installation Wizard and Installation Shield for installing new software
- Improving the integration of networking and security within the Windows environment
- Improving system resource control with a larger memory heap
- Microsoft's becoming directly involved in controlling the Windows 9x compatibility certification and approval of software applications development

Windows 98

Windows 98 came in two basic versions: Windows 98 Original and Windows 98 Second Edition. Just as the version information in Windows 95 indicates that it's Windows 4.0.x, version information in Windows 98 indicates that it's Windows 4.1.x (e.g., 4.10.2222.A).

Windows 98 Original standardized the varying modifications of Windows 95 OS/R-1 and OS/R-2 (A and B), and it was very much like the mysterious Windows 95 OS/R-D. Because Windows 98 was the next in a line of many improvements, it could easily be said that Windows 98 was an improved version of Windows 95. The basic differences were the inclusion of FAT32 (from OS/R-2 of Windows 95), streamlined administration tools, and better remote connectivity. In the original release, Windows 98 included:

- *Accessibility Utility*—originally a barely documented feature in Windows 95, this feature allows users with certain disabilities to tailor the system.
- *Advanced Power Management*—allowing Windows to manage the Always On, Standby, or Hibernation status of the machine, and to turn off the entire machine following Shut Down.
- *Backup*—a much better set of utilities than those available from DOS 1.0, the Windows 98 utility comes from Seagate and uses a different file compression format based on the QIC 113 tape backup specification.
- *Hyper Terminal*—a 32-bit telephony API and unimodem subsystems for asychronous connectivity.
- *Internet Explorer 4.0*
- *USB support in the evolving Plug-and-Play capabilities*

- *Outlook Express 5.0*—a better email client than Exchange
- *Net Meeting 3.0*—a small application designed for audio/video conferencing over the Internet
- *System Agent*—A utility designed to automatically launch specific programs in scheduled system maintenance.
- *System File Checker*—a precursor to the Windows File Protection system for better file security and integrity.
- *Windows Media support*—for .MP3, .WAV, .AVI, and .MPEG multimedia file formats with "Windows Media Player 6.1"
- Broadband Internet access support

Windows 98 Second Edition, added updates that were included in Windows Me, and then went on to become part of Windows 2000. The Second Edition included:

- Improved USB support
- Pentium III 3D video support
- Internet Explorer 5.0 (5.0 is included on the CD-ROM for Windows 98 SE. Upgrades are available online.)
- Internet connection sharing—Multiple machines can share a single modem and Internet ISP connection.
- IEEE 1394 (Firewire) support—Hi-bandwidth for digital cameras and new storage device connections
- Support for the latest advances in hardware features—Such as multiple monitors, AGP video, and DVD drives
- *Better IRQ sharing*—In order to handle the increasing number of devices installed on computer systems such as printers, scanners, webcams, zip drives, and so on

Utilities

A primary change in Window 98 was the Internet integration features of the Active Desktop. An installation option allowed the user to view the Desktop as a Web page. The popularity of the Internet was making most users familiar with how a Web browser worked, and the Windows 98 Desktop included single-clicking on icons and programs (as opposed to double-clicking), as well as a bubble-help descriptive feature for icons and programs. These small help notations, often called *toolbar tips* or "*mouse-overs,*" make Desktop objects more understandable when the mouse pointer "hovers" over the object. This need for bubble help only goes to show that if we'd been meant to see things in pictures, we would be speaking hieroglyphs.

Windows 98 introduced the concept of using the original file management and browsing tool (Explorer) as a Web browser. The Web browser made the idea of browsing the Internet a commonly understood metaphor, so the File Manager, limited to moving and changing files, became MS Explorer. In Windows 98, one of the installation options gave the Explorer a way to present the contents of a local hard drive in a Web browser format.

As always, this Web View / Active Desktop was a mixed blessing, and the Explorer seemed unable to retain configured settings. In one Windows session, the user might choose to see files in the Explorer in one way, but that way would vanish in the next session. One way to force the Explorer to look a certain way seems to be to open any Explorer view and configure that view as to sort order, details, or icons, etc. Then choose View | Folder Options from the main menu bar and choose the View tab. Under the "Folder Views," click the "Like Current Folder" button, and Windows will, for the most part, hold that setting for all following session…for the most part.

This browser format, allowed for direct support of hypertext markup language (HTML) files with a .HTM extension, and also for common Web features, such as one-click transfers from one file to another. Windows 98 tried to bring the Internet to every user, and shipped with a wide array of Internet-related tools and features. MS Explorer added support for Dynamic HTML (DHTML), a way of making a typical HTML page (at a Web site) change according to different parameters. For example, a Web site might present different information to a user, depending upon their address or the time of day. Several of the technologies involved in dynamic page changes include: CGI, Java, Javascript, and ActiveX.

The technologies that brought about DHTML introduced a scripting language whereby plain text "commands" could be formed into a sort of combination macro and batch programming language. Explorer support for scripting on the local machine's Desktop allows virus-like scripts to be run in ways that were previously impossible. This is how email messages could run a destructive script that acts much the way a virus does without ever running an executable (.EXE or .COM) program.

Microsoft System Information Utility

Microsoft has historically tried to keep end users separate from developers, tech support people, and systems administration. Inevitably, the Internet has opened access to all sorts of specialized tools and utilities that people have developed to make supporting Windows easier. Over time, these in-house, undocumented programs have made their way into the open market, taking on growing status within the tech support community. Once a program has become a "must-have" utility for anyone involved with troubleshooting a system, Microsoft eventually comes around to formally putting it into a new release of their software, giving it a user interface, menus, name and some supporting help.

This utility provides a single interface for several of the older Windows 95 utilities, including the Device Manager and HWDIAG.EXE. The Windows 98 version gives you not only detailed information about the hardware, software, and system configuration, but will also provide a *configuration history* for each device. Much like the Update Manager history log, the configuration history keeps track of when and how each item in the system was changed.

The Microsoft System Information utility acts as a central control panel for several other troubleshooting and debugging tools. From the Tools menu option, you can check the Registry and make a backup copy to a .CAB file. Remember that in Windows 95, this was the almost undocumented ERU.EXE. There are also menu options for the System File Checker, the System Configuration Utility, Dr. Watson (a trap for system errors and system snapshot), the Version Conflict manager, ScanDisk, and more.

The utility runs out of MSINFO32.EXE, and can be found either through Start | Accessories | System Tools | System Information, or in the C:\Program Files\Common Files\Microsoft Shared\MSINFO subfolder. This utility is also a precursor to the Windows 2000 and Windows XP Computer Management tool, which opens the System Information applet.

If you purchase and install Norton Utilities, you'll find a System Information option on the context menu when you right-click on the My Computer Icon. This is the Norton System Information, not to be confused with the Microsoft System Information, and provides a comprehensive view of the machine's hardware, memory, and networking status. The utility has a Reports button for printing out any view.

Registry Checker

As with many utilities installed with Windows 98, the Registry Checker was a separate, downloadable program that was originally only available from the Microsoft Web site (or various shareware sites). This utility examines the Registry for various signs of corruption, such as invalid entries or empty data blocks. If there are no errors, the program makes a backup copy of the system files (SYSTEM.DAT and USER.DAT) with all the working Registry settings.

If the Registry Checker detects a problem, it tries to use the previous backup to restore the Registry. If no backup is available, Registry Checker will make a best-guess attempt to repair the Registry by examining the many separate locations configuration information is held for any hardware device or software application. While this is better than nothing, the Registry is so complicated that sometimes the attempted repair is worse than the original problem. The best insurance is always to maintain current backups of the Registry independently of all these utility backups.

We discuss the Registry Checker again in Chapter 14, "Troubleshooting."

System File Checker (SFC)

Windows 95 tech support people were able to use a Registry Checker utility, available for download from the Microsoft site (if you knew about it), to analyze a corrupted Windows Registry and to attempt to fix it. Windows 98 incorporated the System File Checker to work in a similar fashion on overall system files.

This utility checks through the critical system files on a machine by taking a snapshot of each file whenever a program calls any of the files. DOS used something called a check-sum to keep a database of how many bits a file should contain. Some of the original, simple virus checkers used a database made up of the file name, how many bits the file was made up of, and the time and date of the original file. SFC checks these system files against a similar database, each time a file is run.

If the System File Checker finds a difference between a current file and the description of that file in its database, it offers to either restore any file that has changed, or to update its database to reflect a new version of the file.

Version Conflict Manager

This utility tool tracks version numbers of important system files, providing reports and methods for updating older system files. This came from several attempted commercial programs that would immediately log onto the Web and download the files when you tried to access, upgrade, or install a program that wanted a particular version of a system file (e.g., WINSOCK.DLL).

Disk Cleanup

Somewhat similar to DeFrag, Disk Cleanup "cleans up" the hard drive by removing or compressing files you don't need. The program runs through the files on a hard drive, flagging those that are out-of-date, or that haven't been used in a long time, warning you when the drive is getting filled up. At that point, you can make decisions as to what you'd like to do with those files.

Help Desk

One of the biggest changes between Windows 95 and Windows 98 is the Help feature. The Help Desk takes all .HLP files and administrative Wizards and expands them through something that looks very much like a standard HTML window. Help, in Windows 98, provides four levels of tech support on the machine: Local Help, Microsoft's "Getting Started Online" book, Web Help, and System Troubleshooting.

Local (home-based) help is a help system that loads into a special help engine that displays HTML files. Another assumption Windows 98 makes is that everyone wants (or needs) to be connected to the Internet in an always-on connection. When you access a Web Help link, Windows automatically opens the MS Explorer browser and tries to move you to the Windows 98 Support Online page, either through a broadband connection or by having Windows 98 automatically run your modem. After you've completed an online registration from, you're given access to the Support Online databases, as well as a knowledge base (database of people's experience) of trouble shooting wizards and *frequently asked questions* (FAQs), as well as other resources.

If you don't have a direct connection to an Internet Service Provider (ISP), using AOL as a gateway, for instance, the automated online help feature fails. If you know you're going to need online help, and your machine is working well enough, you can first connect to the Internet with a standard dial-up procedure and then call up Help from the Start menu. In this situation, the automated process will most likely succeed.

MSCONFIG.EXE

The System Configuration Utility simplifies how you specify which processes you want to activate during startup. In this applet, you can view the CONFIG.SYS, AUTOTEXEC.BAT, SYSTEM.INI, and WIN.INI files from directly within the troubleshooting tool. Check boxes allow you to edit or disable individual lines in the various initialization files. You can also access which area of Windows you're making changes to. For instance, the "Startup" tab presents the various configuration files and the lines within those files that affect the Windows Startup—the programs that will automatically begin running once Windows finishes loading.

The General tab of the configuration utility provides button options for a Normal startup; for a Diagnostic startup, with an interactive processing of individual drivers and devices; or for a Selective Startup. Using the Selective Startup, you can disable each of the main tabs, one at a time, to quickly determine which area is causing the problem. Once you've determined that the Startup Group, for instance, is the culprit, you can then disable individual items until you find the specific problem.

This utility can be accessed through the Tools option of the System Information utility. It can also be run by pressing Start and choosing the Run option; then type MSCONFIG in the Run dialog box.

Exiting certain utilities will produce a dialog box asking you if you want to reboot your computer. If you choose OK, you'll most likely have a complete, cold reboot, restarting the entire machine. In most cases, you can choose to reboot later, or say No to the dialog box. If you then choose Start|Log Off (regardless of whether or not you have networking options installed, Explorer will shut down and restart, applying the changes you've made.

Another way to accomplish a reset of the Desktop is to click the mouse anywhere in an open area of the Desktop and press the F5 (refresh) key. Finally, you can press CTRL-ALT-DEL to bring up the Task Manager, click to select Explorer, and choose End Task. This will shut down the Explorer (and the Desktop shell). After a moment, the Explorer will restart, applying any changes you made.

If you choose to use the Shut Down option of the Start Menu, and you want to Restart your computer without going through a full reboot, you can hold down the Shift key while you click on OK. This will restart Windows without going through a cold boot.

Windows Update Manager

Through the help desk, you can access the Update Manager to keep the Windows operating system current with the latest software drivers, patches, bug fixes, and incremental release updates. Under the supposition that most computers would eventually be always connected to the Internet in some fashion, accessing the Update Manager produces an automatic attempt to access the Internet and go directly to the Web site for Windows updates.

The Update Manager examines the Registry, working through all the software and hardware configurations along with the associated files being used in those settings. The Update Manager then compares the files it finds on your hard drive with the information held in the update database on the Web site, downloading appropriate updated files into the locations pointed to in the Registry keys.

Once various files have been flagged (marked) for updating, the Web site provides links to various other locations on the site where these updated files can be found and downloaded. The Update Manager then helps install and/or uninstall various files. Following an Update Manager session, the program creates a history log (file) of the activities and file modifications that took place during the session. Through this history log, you can remove previous updates and return the machine to original configurations in the event it becomes necessary.

Maintenance Wizard

Windows 3.x introduced various macro language (automated series of steps) events, and third-party developers soon began to create small programs, making it easier (in theory) to use these macros. IBM created something called *REXX* in OS/2 as something more than a batch language, but less than a full-blown programming language. Microsoft did something similar in the Excel, Word, and Access (database) macro programming language and Visual BASIC.

Prior to Windows 9x, DOS users were versed at creating small batch files containing all the various programs, switches, and file locations involved in certain maintenance tasks. For instance, to copy any changed files from a directory to a floppy disk, a batch file would store the various switches used by XCOPY.EXE, along with whichever directories were to be examined. However, they were left to third-party developers to figure out how to time the batch files to the system clock.

Over time it became quite clear that the average user had no intention of, nor interest in learning a complex programming language for anything. To bring the ease of automated task steps down to earth, Microsoft introduced the Maintenance Wizard. The Maintenance Wizard stores not only the time of day, but also the number of times a particular maintenance task should be performed, and walks the user through such mundane tasks as defragmenting the hard drive, getting rid of old and unwanted files, and running ScanDisk.

This Wizard schedules routine tasks such as ScanDisk, DeFrag, Backup, or the Disk Cleanup utility. In order to run the Maintenance Wizard, the system must have the Task Scheduler installed and loaded. This can be annoying, as the icon for the scheduler sits in the Tray forevermore. Another way to get a consolidated view of the various maintenance tasks is to right-click on the drive icon in the Explorer. Choose Properties from the Context Menu; then choose the Tools tab. Finally, each of these tasks can be run by selecting Start | Accessories | System Tools and picking each tool from the resulting menu.

Windows Me

The year 2000 came and went, and the world didn't come to an end. With the release of Windows 95, Microsoft decided to stop using a version number in the name of the operating system, choosing instead to use a year reference. As Windows 98 continued to change through updates and fixes, it too eventually required a full version release, becoming Windows Millennium Edition (Me). This was where things really started getting confusing.

At one time, both Windows Me and Windows 2000 were fully-supported versions on the open market. Based on the logic of the names, one would think that Me and 2000 are essentially the same thing. In fact, Me and 2000 are very different systems. We'll discuss 2000 in the next chapter, but the release of Windows Me was based on a marketing assessment where Microsoft believed the home market was ready to abandon applications based on Windows 3.1 architecture and move to NT. Windows NT was still too restrictive, but a transition system moving towards NT could be very viable. That system would become Windows Me.

We discuss Me from a troubleshooting perspective in Chapter 14. This version of Windows was so unstable and filled with problems that Microsoft effectively stopped supporting it. We would encourage you to strongly advise anyone with a problematic machine running Me to either revert to Windows 98 SE, or upgrade to Windows 2000 or XP.

For the first time, Windows Me got rid of support for virtual machines running in Real Mode. If you remember, Real Mode is a reference to the original XT computers and addressing real memory with direct addresses. The CONFIG.SYS and AUTOEXEC.BAT configuration files, having always been necessary for any hardware or software expecting to find a basic, 16-bit DOS machine, vanished. Since Me eliminated support for this type of virtual machine, all references to the configuration files disappeared.

Windows Me no longer even processed a CONFIG.SYS or AUTOEXEC.BAT in any fashion during the Startup. Additionally, there was no longer any way to get to a DOS machine, under Windows Me, from a default installation. The only way to get to DOS was with an Emergency Boot Disk created after Windows Me had been installed.

Windows 95 had automated the process of checking for real device drivers to see if it could replace or substitute those drivers with virtual device drivers. If a VxD could do whatever the original driver was designed to do, a knowledgeable user could comment out the driver from the CONFIG.SYS file, reboot the machine, and see if the device still worked. Windows Me took more control over this process, going through any existing CONFIG.SYS file and assigning what it thought were the appropriate VxDs. Once the file was stripped of all its device drivers, Me went through the AUTOEXEC.BAT file and moved all configuration switches into the Registry.

Both the CONFIG.SYS and AUTOEXC.BAT files could continue to reside on the hard drive, and Me would leave them there in the event it found one of the pesky buggers during an update installation. However, once Windows Me was installed, it would modify the file names and their locations, keeping an eye on any new hardware installations. If an installation searched for either of the files, Me would intercept the search and hand off its own location to the installation routine. The device's installation routine commands were allowed to modify the older files and then Me would wait for a reboot.

The next time the Windows Me machine started up, Me went through the changed configuration files, placing SET commands in the AUTOEXEC.BAT file and adjusting the installation, according to what Microsoft thought the way things ought to be. In more than a few instances, Windows Me made the wrong choices and many programs, games, and devices the home computer user wanted very much to use, failed to run.

There is very little on the low-level specifics of Me in the current A+ exam, although the exam seems to be continually evolving. The primary change in Windows Me was the elimination of Real Mode support. Other than that, Windows Me is essentially the same as Windows 98, with many of the configuration utilities being better protected from the casual user.

Summary—Windows 98

For the most part, the exam folds together Windows 95, 98, and 2000, making no particular distinction between them at a low level. Questions relating to Windows 9x and Windows 2000 generally specify each of the two main families, and questions about Windows NT likewise indicate that they are specific. The preceding section focused more on the diagnostics and reporting utilities, which we'll discuss again in Chapter 14. However, you should keep track of the following points:

- Windows 98 introduced the Active Desktop, a way of seeing file and disk information in a World Wide Web format. You should understand the feature and how to activate or deactivate it from the Desktop Properties menu (Web tab).
- Microsoft System Information (MSINFO32.EXE) had its roots in the old Microsoft Diagnostics (MSD.EXE) tool. Understand how to run the program from the File|Run command line, as well as how to navigate to the System Tools accessories. Note that Windows 2000 uses the same concept in its Computer Management tool, discussed that in Chapters 13 and 14.
- Be aware of tools such as the Registry Checker, System File Checker (SFC), Hardware Diagnostics, Defrag, and Scandisk. If you remember their appearance in Windows 9x, it may help you to remember their locations and functions.
- MSCONFIG (The System Configuration Utility) has gone a long way toward making startup configurations and optional startup items manageable. You should understand the program, and run it on your own, using a Windows 9x. machine. Each version of Windows 95, 98, and Me had slight changes in the program, but if you've actually seen and used the program, you'll find that a picture (in your memory) is worth a thousand words.

We don't think you'll see many questions directly related to Windows Me, but you'll want to remember that the Millenium Edition was truly a hybrid release of 16/32-bitWindows and NT. The main thing to remember about Me is that if you encounter a machine with many problems and the installed OS is Windows Me, do whatever you can to convert the installation either forward to Windows 2000 or backwards to Windows 98 SE.

Practice Questions

Question 1

Windows maintains file names through which of the following? (Check all that apply.)

- ❑ a. LFNs
- ❑ b. VFAT
- ❑ c. FAT32
- ❑ d. DAT

Answers b, c, and d are correct. Choice a, the Windows Long File Names (LFNs), is not a maintenance process. Once names have been created, Windows uses the Virtual FAT (VFAT), the underlying 32-bit file allocation table (FAT32), and the Directory Allocation Table (DAT) to maintain the address locations for the data in the file's clusters.

Question 2

The Windows Registry is made up of which set of files?

- ❍ a. USER.BAT, SYSTEM.BAT, SYSTEM.INI, WINDOWS.INI
- ❍ b. SYSTEM.INI, WIN.INI, HKEY.DAT, REG32.DAT
- ❍ c. USER.DAT, SYSTEM.DAT
- ❍ d. SYSTEM.INI, WIN.INI

Answer c is correct. Although Windows 9x may still use the original initialization files from Windows 3.x, the SYSTEM.INI and WIN.INI files are not part of the Registry. Therefore, choices a, b, and d are all incorrect. A .BAT file is a batch file extension and the Registry files are in binary format.

Question 3

Where will Windows look before finding a 32-bit virtual device driver to replace a static VxD?

- a. SYSTEM.INI
- b. WIN.INI
- c. VMM32.DLL
- d. KRNL328.EXE

Answer a is correct. Note the use of "before" in the question, along with a reference to a static device driver. The first place Windows 9x will look for these static VxDs is in the SYSTEM.INI file. Answer b is incorrect because the WIN.INI file maintains user configuration settings, not device driver. Answers c and d are incorrect because Windows doesn't look in either .DLL or .EXE files for device drivers.

Question 4

The best way to back up the system registration files is with the ______________ utility:

- a. BACKUP.EXE
- b. ERU.EXE
- c. REGEDT32.EXE
- d. LFNBK.EXE

Answer b is correct. ERU.EXE is the Emergency Repair Utility program, specifically designed to back up the Windows Registry, sometimes called the *system registration files*. Answer a is incorrect because the DOS Backup program is designed to back up entire file areas. Answer c is incorrect because it refers to the 32-bit version of REGEDIT.EXE, the preferred Registry Editor for Windows 2000 and NT. Answer d is incorrect because it refers to a utility for backing up Long File Names.

Question 5

FAT32 has the advantage over FAT16 due to which of the following main reasons? (Check all that apply.)

- a. Files larger than 2GB
- b. Multiple 2GB partitions
- c. Variable cluster sizes
- d. The nonactive bootable file system

Answers a and c are correct. FAT16 is limited to a maximum file size of 2GB, either in one file or a single partition size. FAT32 uses larger, 32-bit addresses in the FAT, in order to provide access to partitions larger than 2GB. FAT32 also provides adjustable cluster sizes, making storage of smaller files more efficient. Answer b is technically correct but functionally incorrect in that although FAT32 can easily support many 2GB partitions, this is no more an advantage than FAT16, NTFS, or HPFS file systems. There is no such term as that referenced by answer d.

Question 6

Windows 95, 98, and Me all create a Real Mode VM during a DOS session.

- a. True
- b. False

Answer b, false, is correct. The primary distinction between Windows Me and all previous versions of Windows is that Windows Me terminated support for Real Mode. Windows 95 and Windows 98 both continued that support for backward compatibility reasons.

Need to Know More?

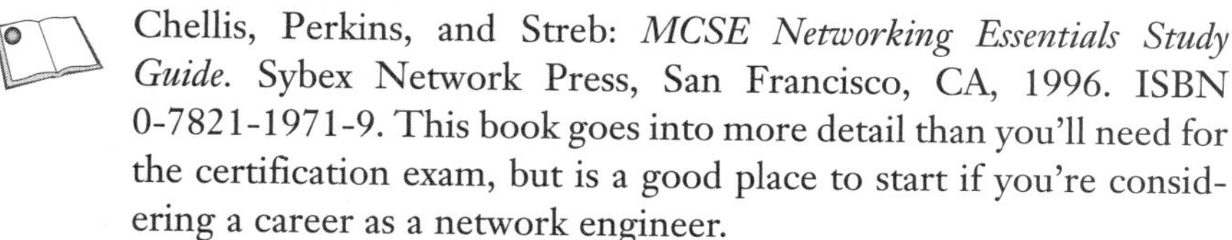

Chellis, Perkins, and Streb: *MCSE Networking Essentials Study Guide*. Sybex Network Press, San Francisco, CA, 1996. ISBN 0-7821-1971-9. This book goes into more detail than you'll need for the certification exam, but is a good place to start if you're considering a career as a network engineer.

Derfler, Frank J.: *PC Magazine Guide to Connectivity*. Ziff Davis, 1995. ISBN 1-56276-274-5. This book is easy to read and provides a good introduction to networking.

Microsoft Windows 95 Resource Kit. Microsoft Press, Redmond, WA. ISBN 1-55615-678-2. This is the definitive resource for all Windows 95 questions. It assumes that you have a good working knowledge of Windows 95.

Microsoft Windows 98 Resource Kit. Microsoft Press, Redmond, WA. ISBN 1-57231-644-0. This is the definitive resource for all Windows 98 questions. It assumes that you have a good working knowledge of Windows.

Norton, Peter, and Mueller, John: *Complete Guide to Windows 95*. Sams, Indianapolis, IN, 1997. ISBN 0-672-30791-X. This very good introduction to Windows 95 explains the "why" as well as the "how."

Tidrow, Rob: *Windows 95 Registry Troubleshooting*. New Riders, Indianapolis, IN, 1996. ISBN 1-56205-556-9. This book goes into more detail than you'll need for the certification exam, but if you really want to get into it, this is your source.

Windows NT, Windows 2000, and XP

Terms you'll need to understand:

- ✓ Multitasking and the Virtual Machine (VM)
- ✓ Network server and local machines
- ✓ End-user and network administrator
- ✓ Logging on to a network
- ✓ Load and initialize (a program)
- ✓ A network or machine event

Concepts you'll need to master:

- ✓ Modular programming and development
- ✓ Operating system layers surrounding a kernel
- ✓ Security, granting, and blocking access rights
- ✓ User and Group accounts and profiles
- ✓ Loader programs (NT Loader)
- ✓ Booting from multiple operating systems
- ✓ Volume sets, mirroring, and RAID
- ✓ The Control Panel

Windows NT was Microsoft's venture into large-scale, enterprise operating systems. Enterprise installations must have stability, security, scalability, and sophisticated networking capabilities. When we talk about scalability, we mean that a smaller system can grow to meet large-*scale* and more complex demands. Neither Windows 3.1 nor Windows 9x were originally designed to meet any of these requirements, having been primarily developed for the consumer market and individual computers. Although they did offer small-scale, peer-to-peer networking, it was more as an optional feature than a basic foundation for national and international business operations. Windows NT was Microsoft's competitive response to Novell's Netware, which dominated the corporate desktop networking market at the time.

If you remember, Windows 3.x provided a simplistic multitasking environment for 16-bit applications. It wasn't an actual operating system, but rather, an *interface*—a GUI—that ran on top of DOS. Remember, too, that each program was given its own process (session machine), and that all Windows applications shared a single virtual machine. This overall environment was called the *System Virtual Machine*, or *System VM*. With every application sharing this one VM, individually running session machines weren't isolated in any way. One badly behaved process could bring down every other running program, including Windows itself, causing a full crash.

Windows 9x ran a completely separate virtual machine for each application. You've seen how you can open an MS DOS window at the same time as you're working in a word processor and the Explorer. All three of these events are understood by Windows to be individual sessions. By isolating every session machine from each other, Windows 9x was able to provide much more stability, thereby reducing the chances of any single program causing an entire system crash.

Multitasking

Windows 3.x used cooperative multitasking rather than pre-emptive multitasking. In cooperative multitasking, the CPU has no control over a given program, and that program can completely take over the CPU. If the program doesn't give back that control, too bad. A single program can "steal" the CPU, along with all the memory resources, and keep other programs from getting any attention. In pre-emptive multitasking, the operating system stays in control of the way any individual program is allowed to access both the resources and the central processor.

Windows 9x retains control of the CPU, using its own decision-making procedures to give running programs access to the CPU. This control of the CPU is given on a conditional basis, meaning that at any given time,

Windows 9x can pre-empt a program from performing a function. By acting first and taking control of the VM, Windows 9x can suspend the program's operations, along with any access to resources that program had, including the CPU. This also prevents any individual program from hogging the processor.

In theory, if one Win32 program (32-bit program) crashes in a pre-emptive multitasking operating system, it won't affect any of the other virtual machines. For example, if a 16- or 32-bit program crashes within Windows 9x, the operating system can shut down that specific virtual machine, leaving the other processes running untouched. You've probably seen those error messages where you're told that a program has performed an illegal function. Windows 9x gives you the option of either shutting down that specific session, or getting more detail as to what happened. Windows has pre-empted any further operation of that program, but your overall system hasn't crashed.

Windows 9x supports multithreaded multitasking, as long as the program has been written with the appropriate programming threads. It went a long way towards stability, but was still far short of enterprise networking and security requirements. Because of its origins as a simple interface, as well as the need for backward compatibility in a mostly nontechnical home or office environment, Windows 9x could never become a large-scale networking OS. Windows NT, on the other hand, was developed from the ground up, specifically to meet enterprise requirements and with little concern for backwards compatibility.

Windows Versions

To many people, Windows NT may appear to have been built on the features and capabilities of Windows 95. Actually, it's the other way around. NT used a quite different interface, and Windows 95 was the first of the consumer market versions of Windows to take on the appearance of NT. Essentially, the Windows NT look and feel was the foundation for Windows 95, 98, and Millennium Edition (Me).

Remember the joint venture, where Microsoft was going to develop a user interface and IBM's OS/2 was going to be the underlying operating system. When Microsoft and IBM split up, each company took some of the shared technology and began developing its own complete version of an operating system and interface. Time passed, and Intel's Pentium processors entered the market with the capability of working together in a multiprocessor environment. NT had been designed, from the start, to support multiple processors on high-powered network servers. Windows 9x could work with only a single CPU.

Although there's no reason why you can't run Windows 9x on a multiprocessor system, what happened was that Windows 9x shut down the additional processors, returning the system to a single-processor environment. NT actually ran the different processors.

NT Versions 3.1 and 4.0

NT 3.1 was Microsoft's first release of its own version of the OS code. Presumably, versions 1.x, 2.x, and 3.0 were part of IBM's OS/2. The interface for Windows NT 3.1 looked almost exactly like 16-bit Windows 3.1, but when you opened up an object on the desktop, the menus were all different. This made for a nicely confusing situation.

NT 3.x was also an early example of how separating device drivers from their underlying hardware could cause serious compatibility problems. Because of this, Microsoft began publishing a book with lists of all the specific devices that had been tested successfully for compatibility with NT. This hardware compatibility list was routinely updated on the Internet.

Windows NT 4.0 began the real divergence between IBM and Microsoft. IBM's OS/2 Warp made a momentary splash on the market, but NT was starting to gain a foothold in corporate America. Keep in mind that Microsoft had been trying for a long time to convince the home PC market of the benefits of a full 32-bit operating system. Windows 95 was able to support 32-bit applications right out of the box, but at its core, was designed to also support 16-bit applications. However, it was supposed to be the product that would finally bring the consumer market over to NT. The main problem was that NT wasn't able to do a very good job with all those 16-bit applications home users continued to run.

Although Windows XP is not covered in the exam, there are questions about Windows NT and 2000. Hopefully, if you have a sense of how NT fits in with current versions of Windows, you'll find it easier to handle these questions.

NT Version 5.0, Windows 2000

So what happened after Windows NT 4.x? We've seen that the underlying version numbers in Windows 9x begin with 4. Minor numbers (those to the right of the first decimal point) are associated with Windows 95 OS/R-B, 98, or Me. Windows NT 3.x used the same graphic interface as Windows 3.1. Windows NT 4.0, on the other hand, provided the graphic interface for Windows 9x and later. There doesn't seem to be a version 5.0 for NT, but perhaps Windows 2000 has an underlying version number that begins with 5.0?

Back when there were only twenty or a million computers in the world, releasing a new version of an operating system was a relatively simple thing: you released the version; everyone installed it on their machines; and presto...done. Nowadays, with hundreds of millions of machines running applications designed for old or new operating systems, it's not so easy. Incremental version numbers, changing calendar years, problem fixes, and service packs—all these things make it very confusing for people to know what they have installed on their machine.

The naming problem came to a head when Microsoft reached the final phase of joining Windows NT with the home consumer market. "New technology" in 1992 seemed a bit more like "obsolete technology" in the year 2000. The convergence of home and enterprise Windows continued the convention of using the calendar year, but the name "NT" faded into history. Windows 2000 took over from NT as follows:

- Windows 2000 Professional is similar to Windows NT Workstation 5.0.
- Windows 2000 Server is similar to Windows NT Server 5.0.
- Windows 2000 Advanced Server is similar to Windows NT Server 5.0 Enterprise Edition.

Windows XP (Version 5.1)

When Windows 3.0 was released, it was a huge improvement over Windows 2.0, but it was fairly unstable. Version 3.0 was Microsoft's rush to the market with all the technology it had developed with IBM. (Actually, the release of Windows 3.0 as a separate product was partly to blame for the split with IBM). Windows 3.1 came out almost immediately thereafter, and although the decimal number seemed to indicate an incremental release, it was a fundamental change. Windows 3.1 was far more stable than 3.0, with enough changes that it could have been named 4.0.

Windows XP is more like Windows 5.1, and is as different from Windows 2000, in terms of stability, as Windows 3.1 was from 3.0. Rumor has it that Bill Gates (CEO of Microsoft, Inc.) wanted people to "experience" a computer, rather than simply "use" a computer. Tying the product name to the calendar year was apparently becoming tiresome, and so Windows finally became the Windows eXPerience, or Windows XP. Other Microsoft productivity applications will take on the XP name, with developmental tools being renamed with a .NET extension. Apparently, Microsoft believes that programmers will develop applications based on the sharing concepts of the World Wide Web (remember the Active Desktop in Windows 98). End-users will have no idea what the underlying technology is, knowing only that they can sit down and get to work—just like the Internet.

Bringing together the home consumer market with the international enterprise community was bound to generate an astronomical number of problems for Microsoft. With all the incremental upgrades, it made sense to change the name of Windows 95 to Windows 98. Of course, all the logos, packaging, marketing and promotional material, reference manuals, TV commercials, and everything else had to be changed, too, in order to reflect the new name—all because of a single digit. Microsoft needed a product name that wouldn't have to be changed every couple of years (or months).

NT Architecture

Internally, Windows NT is designed differently from DOS and uses a modular design, or modular architecture. DOS used separate program files, but NT uses separate components. Each component manages a separate conceptual function of the overall operating system. One of the problems with updating DOS was that the three basic system files all had to be modified in order to work with each other. Following any change to the system files, all the ancillary files had to be updated as well. Modular design is a way to upgrade separate parts of the operating system without the expense of having to upgrade the entire system and all of its extensions.

Modular Design

We know that a computer program is a series of very exact statements, where each statement leads to the next statement. A series of statements is often called a *routine*. No statement has to necessarily be the next line of code, because a computer can read very fast and find the next statement wherever it's located in the program (like the Find feature in a word processor). When a statement tells the computer to go to another statement that isn't next in line, we could say the program is making a *call*. The program calls system functions and memory functions, but when it asks the computer to run another whole set of instructions before it returns to where the program left off, we say the main routine is calling a subroutine.

Originally, programming was done in a long line of sequential statements. Whenever anyone had to modify the program, they would insert a call to a subroutine and write the entire modification somewhere else in the program. Sometimes, those subroutines had to be modified, in which case someone would insert another call to a new subroutine. Programs can often be hundreds of thousands, or even millions of lines long, and after a while, all the modifications calling other modifications became known as *spaghetti code,* referring to the total mess of tangled references.

Although spaghetti code calls up a reasonable image for the old way of programming, it became too expensive to continue the practice of inserting calls to subroutines in such a disorganized fashion. Modular design is a formal set of practices designed to make the individual components of a program easier to work with. Each module is a separate component that can be connected with other modules (routines). Any component, or module, can be added, modified, or replaced without affecting the rest of the components. Integrated design is where there is no clear distinction or separation between the parts of a program.

Modular software design was introduced as a way to keep the related parts of a program all in one area. Main routines were kept separate from subroutines, and modifications were done in an organized fashion. The programs are still very long, but at least they tend to follow an orderly progression of references.

Kernel Mode

Each module in Windows NT is entirely independent of every other module, with none of them sharing any specific program code. The way the modules work together is with system calls. Not only is NT a modular program, but the operating system is divided into two larger divisions: the Kernel Mode and User Mode.

A Kernel

DOS was known as an *open* operating system because any knowledgeable person could access the fundamental system files. Some people refer to IO.SYS as the DOS kernel, but this is not really consistent with the definition of the word *kernel* as it's used with NT. When the underlying system files of an operating system—the files that speak directly with the BIOS—are placed out of bounds by the OS developers, we refer to that operating system as being based on a kernel. A kernel uses *metadrivers*, created by the OS developers, as a way to connect third-party device driver software to the operating system and motherboard. The prefix "meta" comes from Greek, meaning after or beyond. Windows NT, 2000, and XP are differentiated from DOS, 16-bit Windows, and Windows 9x in that Microsoft terminated the use of an open OS and began using a kernel.

In Kernel Mode, certain critical components of the operating system give direct access to system hardware. We speak of the *privileges* of a given module, and Kernel Mode is more privileged than User Mode. When components of the OS are running in User Mode, they have no direct access to the system hardware. Therefore, we say they run in a less privileged mode. Applications and some of the NT subsystems run in User Mode.

The Hardware Abstraction Layer (HAL)

We can divide the Kernel Mode into two separate levels, or *layers*. At the lowest level is the hardware abstraction layer (HAL)—not to be confused with the fictional super-computer that Arthur C. Clarke wrote about. If you remember our networking discussion in Chapter 8, you'll remember we spoke about the OSI model, and how different layers of the network operating system are designed with different purposes. The Hardware Abstraction Layer takes a look at different kinds of hardware, disguising the actual (concrete) properties of each device and presenting an abstraction of that hardware (a symbolic reference) to the next layer.

The HAL presents a uniform, standardized interface to this next higher layer, which is called the Windows NT Executive layer. To make matters even more confusing, the Executive layer also contains two layers. Let's take a moment to look at the various divisions of Windows NT:

- User Mode is where applications and some of the NT subsystems run in a less privileged mode than Kernel Mode.
- Kernel Mode is where the system is given direct access to hardware.
- The Kernel Mode is divided into two layers: the lower layer being the hardware abstraction layer (HAL); the higher layer being the Executive layer.
- The Executive layer is divided into the micro kernel layer and the system services layer.

The Executive Layer Micro Kernel

The micro kernel, sometimes called simply the *kernel*, is the lowest level within the Executive layer. This could be considered the core component of Windows NT. The micro kernel is responsible for scheduling all jobs going to the CPU. It also controls every processor in a multiprocessor system. The NT micro kernel is somewhat like a command interpreter, in that it must reside in main memory. Because the microkernel is the fundamental control structure for the CPUs, it can never be removed from main memory in any type of memory paging (discussed in Chapters 3 and 10).

The Executive Layer System Services

Just above the micro kernel layer is the system service layer. Remember, both the micro kernel and the system services are part of the Executive layer. The system service modules are the components within the Executive layer that connect upward with the various applications and subsystems in the User Mode. The system services layer is made up of a number of modules, including:

- The Process Manager
- The Object Manager
- The Security Reference Monitor (discussed in more detail later in this chapter)
- The Local Procedure Call Monitor
- The Virtual Memory Manager
- The I/O Manager

Be sure to understand the system services. You'll be seeing references to when these services load during the startup process for Windows NT and 2000.

User Mode

NT applications run in the User Mode and have no direct access to either the micro kernel (kernel) or the hardware abstraction layer (HAL). For example, a 16-bit virtual machine is an application process. If a database application is running inside an MS DOS window (i.e., the DOS VM), the combination is also considered to be an application process. Unlike Windows 9x and DOS, you can see the many levels of underlying control NT is exerting to prevent that database application from ever having any access to the actual computer system.

Windows NT has both a User Mode and the Kernel Mode. The User Mode is divided into several additional modules, and the System Services communicate with these modules, each in their own fashion. Two of the more important components of the User Mode are the Win32 subsystem, and the Security subsystem.

An application connects to the operating system partly through the Win32 subsystem, which then interfaces with the Security subsystem. The Security subsystem then places calls to the Executive layer (running in Kernel Mode), which in turn places calls to either the system services or the HAL. Although this is complicated, it's not all that different from the way the networking OSI layers interact with each other. Then again, understanding the OSI model isn't all that easy, either.

NT Workstation and NT Server

We've mentioned client/server networking as a network where individual PCs act as clients to a central file server. The client machines are often referred to as *local* machines, and the file server (or servers) is often referred to as a *remote* machine because it's often quite a distance away from the local machines. We've also said that Windows NT was designed from its inception to be a networking operating system that could run on many hardware platforms (portability). As a result, Windows NT comes in both a server version (remote) and a workstation version (local).

Both versions of NT share the same, core operating system code (within modules). NT, like Windows 9x, also uses a Registry. During startup, NT checks with the system registration to learn whether the system should be run as either a workstation client or an NT server. The workstation is designed specifically to run as a secure, multitasking desktop client.

NT Server has many additional administrative tools, as well as disk-level enhancements, because it was designed as a full network operating system. Aside from the administrative tools, Windows NT uses a distinct disk and file management structure called the *New Technology File System (NTFS)*. We've seen how Windows 9x can use either a FAT16 (16-bit file allocation table) or a FAT32 (32-bit FAT) at the disk level. The NT File System, somewhat related to the OS/2 High Performance File System (HPFS), is a completely redesigned networking file management system.

The NT Registry

Windows 9x uses the binary Registry files to hold a consolidated configuration listing for the overall system. It requires the 16-bit REGEDIT.EXE program to make modifications to the Registry. Windows NT uses the 32-bit editor program (REGEDT32.EXE) to perform essentially the same thing on an NT machine.

We still see traces of the old DOS eight-letter file name with the dot and the three-character extension.

The Windows NT Registry is broken into five separate subtrees, like Windows 9x. Once again we can see how Windows 9x borrowed from the development efforts coming from NT with the NT Registry being:

- *HKEY_LOCAL_MACHINE*—Holds local hardware configurations, the Security Accounts Manager database, and software configurations.
- *HKEY_CLASSES_ROOT*—Holds file associations and application links that can be defined through the NT Explorer Options menu.
- *HKEY_CURRENT_CONFIG*—Holds the current hardware profile and configuration for the devices currently in use.
- *HKEY_CURRENT_USER*—Holds the current user profile for the person logged on to the machine (e.g., user preferences for Desktop and network privileges).
- *HKEY_USERS*—Holds every user profile for the machine, including the currently logged-on user, along with a generic user profile that acts as a template for new, first-time users.

NT Networking

Let's suppose we were to set up a computer in a building somewhere, and then we installed some kind of software on that machine. After we've configured a particular machine, we then deploy (spread out) a networking strategy. NT networking strategy is based on work groups (people) and domains (territories). Each grouping is considered to be a security definition. In other words, groups and domains make it possible to enforce security on the network by assigning access right to individuals, groups, or whole territories.

When a machine has been set up and all the software has been installed, it's ready to be used by a person. In the case of a file server, the machine is ready to be used by other machines; however, even file servers have to be managed (administered) by a person. As we talk about NT security, we refer to an *end-user* as the person doing day-to-day work on a local computer, and we refer to the *network administrator* as the person in charge of giving network access to end-users.

Microsoft designed Windows NT to be used in government installations, as well as multinational corporate environments. One of the reasons the following discussion of security is so complicated is that NT is a C-2 compliant operating system, as defined by the National Computer Security Council (NCSC). NCSC security levels are then specified in U.S. Department of Defense Trusted Computer Systems Evaluation Criteria, known as the *Orange Book*. C-2 allows NT to be used by the Department of Defense, along with other government agencies. That doesn't make the ensuing discussion any easier to understand, but we thought you'd like to know.

Security Account Manager (SAM)

In a small, work group deployment, each individual machine is considered an equal to every other machine, much like peer-to-peer networking. Each machine holds its own Security Account Manager (SAM) database (and Sam is not related to Hal!). With each computer using its own security administration, work groups are good in situations where it's feasible for someone to go around to each local PC and adjust who has access to what.

In larger environments, often covering many buildings, managing network security becomes a problem. Some corporate campuses can have thousands of employees, and it would be nearly impossible for the few IT professionals to be constantly running around to each PC when an employee needed different sharing access to network resources. This kind of environment calls for distributed applications, where central file servers hold various applications and distribute session copies to whoever needs that application at any given time.

Distributed applications are set up using the Windows NT domain structure. When NT is set up using domains, every participating computer in a domain uses a Central Domain SAM database. These domain Security Account Managers are coordinated by Windows NT file servers. An individual network administrator can go into one machine and assign such things as resource sharing, login names, and passwords. When we speak of how an operating system can be used for a range of deployments going from small to large, we say Windows NT is scalable.

User ID

Networks use a logon name as the user identification (User ID). The typical way to ensure that a given person is who they say they are, is for the end-user to invent a user password. First-time users are given a User ID and an initial password by the network administrator. The User ID stays the same, but the password changes periodically.

Making Up Passwords

Passwords are the only real protection you have in terms of keeping your identity secure on a network. In many corporate environments, your password allows you access to information that can have legal ramifications. Rather than making up something fairly logical as a password, such as your initials or birthday, a better password is a certain phrase you remember. For instance, you might like the phrase, "I'm a little teapot," so you can easily remember it. Why not make your password IALTP? This acronym makes no sense whatsoever on its own, but each letter stands for the words in a phrase you particularly like and can remember. This sort of password is extremely difficult to crack by an illegal user, yet very easy to remember (and type) as a phrase. If you like short phrases and your password must be longer, make a rule that you type your password twice in a row, as in IALTPIALTP.

The Logon Procedure

The first step anyone has to take in a networking environment is to log on to the network (with the *logon* procedure or **logon** command). This means the network computers have to recognize a human being in order to understand what that person will or won't be allowed to do. The list of these privileges is called a user *account*, and the end-user's account information defines which areas and resources on the network that person will have access to.

The logon procedure in Windows NT begins by pressing the Control, Alt (alternate), and Delete keys all at once (Ctrl+Alt+Del). Originally, this was the way to restart a machine with a warm boot (see Chapter 10). In Windows 9x, the keystrokes were reassigned to the Task Manager, calling up TASKMAN.EXE in order to show programs running in memory at that moment. Pressing Ctrl+Alt+Del on an NT machine calls up an NT Logon Information dialog box, generally called *WinLogon*.

Local Security Authorization (LSA)

Within the logon dialog box, you select the option indicating you want to log on to the network, and then enter your User ID and password. When you've entered your information, NT begins the Local Security Authorization (LSA) process, which runs the logon authentication package. The LSA is the software interface between the end-user, the User Mode, and the Kernel Mode.

Whether the logon is referring to a work group or a domain, the authentication package compares what you entered against the SAM. Understand that a work group will have a local Security Account Management database on the machine you're using, whereas a domain will transmit the authentication package to the Central Domain SAM database on a file server.

In large corporations, different User IDs can be assigned to seek out completely different sets of remote file servers.

Security Access Token (SAT)

If the information in the logon authentication package doesn't match the SAM, a dialog box pops up displaying a "Logon failure" warning. If the authentication package matches, NT creates a logon session and passes specific account information to the Local Security Authority. The software making up the LSA creates a security access token (SAT).

Session Logs

Windows NT provides a way for every logon session to be stored, much like any history log (as with the Windows 98 Troubleshooting log). This session log can then be audited, which means that a network administrator can review the log for information about what was done by the end-user.

Security Identification (SID)

Following a successful logon procedure, after the Local Security Authority has generated the security access token, this token has its own properties. The SAT contains the end-user's security identification (security ID, or SID), the SID for any groups to which the end-user belongs, and the various network privileges (user rights) assigned to that person.

The SID is a permanent account identifier, based on a hashing algorithm. Once the SID is generated, it stays the same even when the account name and/or password are changed. The only way to change the SID itself is to delete the user account and then re-create it.

The security access token (SAT) is only generated one time, following a successful logon procedure. Any rights or privileges the network administrator changes will not change the SID, but will take effect only after the end-user has logged off the network and begins the logon process the next time.

The User Process

Finally, the logon process calls the Win32 subsystem (in the User Mode module), and Win32 creates a user process. Win32 then connects the SAT to that user process. After this has been completed, the Win32 subsystem creates the end-user's Desktop from the person's profile (held in HKEY_CURRENT_USER). This may sound pretty complicated, but imagine the people who dreamed up all this stuff in the first place!

The reason for so much complexity just to sit down and type a letter focuses on the two basic philosophies of network security. Peer-to-peer networks have generally tended to begin with the premise that individual people should control their own machines, relying on honor and character in giving every user full access to the entire network. Client/server networks tend to be based on a more skeptical perspective, taking total control over the network and allowing individual users specific privileges. NT, much like NetWare, begins with the assumption that no one has access to anything, and then it creates user profiles where specific access is granted, little by little.

The Security Reference Monitor

When the LSA has generated the authentication package; created the security access token; and opened a session; the Local Security Authority logs *audit messages* generated by the *Security Reference Monitor* module. Referring back to the "Kernel Mode" section, we've indicated that the Security Reference Monitor is part of the System Services layer. Remember, too, that the System Services layer is just above the micro kernel, and that these two layers are held within the Executive layer. The Executive layer is just below the User Mode.

The Security Reference Monitor takes charge of verifying whether an access request (e.g., sending a document to a printer and accessing that printer) to an object is allowed, and whether the requesting process has permission to perform an operation on the object. In other words, part of your account profile gives you certain user rights. These rights grant you and your machine permission to initiate certain processes, such as saving a file (process) to a disk (object) somewhere. When you and your machine request access to disk space on a file server, the Security Reference Monitor checks to see whether you have permission to access that disk.

Entities, Attributes, and Masks

An *entity* is a single thing. That thing exists in some fashion, and we human beings understand its existence by observing its attributes. An apple is an entity and it has many attributes. Some of the apple's attributes include seeds, a core, leaves, red skin, sour or sweet taste, worms, and so on. A 2 is also an entity, but in this case the 2 is an *abstraction*. You can't point to a 2, but can only point to the influence of *two-ness* on other entities. For instance, two apples are not the same thing as the two-ness of the "pair" of apples. Pair-ness, is an attribute of 2.

A concrete entity is something you can perceive directly with your senses. An abstract entity is something you can perceive only with your mind. A 2 has attributes in exactly the same way that an apple or a file has attributes. Some of the attributes of a 2 include the actual symbol we use to describe the two-ness of things (2 or II), its even-ness, and the fact that it contains a 1 and a 1. The 1 is also an entity, with attributes of singleness, oddness, unit, and individuality.

In an object-oriented computer world, we try to consolidate various associated attributes into a single entity. Then we call the entity an object. An entity is the same thing as an object. Because attributes are often abstract, the entities themselves are even more abstract (high-level or low-level abstractions). The computer world is being created in an ongoing way, and each programmer or developer sees sets of attributes in his or her own way. NT is a world of abstractions, and Microsoft has chosen to assign names to things based on what it considers to be similarities. In one world, a description is a list of attributes assigned to an entity. In the NT world, Microsoft changed the word "description" to the word "mask," and proclaimed it good. This would be the philosophy of Microsoftism, or a Microsoftian way of understanding reality.

Access Control List (ACL)

The Security Reference Monitor generates the audit messages we just mentioned, and in order to come up with these particular messages, it looks in the access-control list (ACL). The access control list is made up of access masks. These masks are just a complicated way of saying that each object has a list detailing which end-users and work groups can mess with (technical term) the object. Remember how we said NT's hardware abstraction layer disguises an actual piece of hardware? In a way, the HAL is treating every piece of hardware like an object. Filled with an overblown sense of its own importance, NT chooses to call each entry on the access control list, an *access-control entry* (ACE).

There are three types of access masks: Specific (specific to an object), Standard (objects within a group), and Generic (pointers to both specific and standard masks). A specific access mask can have up to 16 properties used to describe a specific object. A mask is nothing more than a complicated way of saying the list of things that describe an object. Your driver's license is a specific access mask for you, the specific object. In this case, your driver's license could have 16 places to put some descriptive information, like your hair color, your weight, or the color of your eyes.

If you go along with this for a minute, you can see how NT also creates a sort of end-user object out of whoever is using an NT workstation. Part of the network operating system assigns attributes to the living, people-type objects, while another part of the operating system is busy assigning attributes to the hardware and file resource objects. Just like you would have an account profile that tells NT what you're allowed to do, so does every object have an access mask (description) that tells NT what groups of people can mess with that object.

In the NT world, an object might be a printer, a modem, a word processor application, a folder, or even a file within a folder. The network administrator builds an access mask for every object, and lists those masks in the access control list, the ACL we were just talking about. The Security Reference Monitor is like a hall monitor in school, constantly interrupting the flow of requests and asking to see a pass. When the security access token (SAT) shows its pass, the monitor checks its clipboard (the mask), looking at the ACL (the list) to see whether the next step is allowed. One thing for sure, the world of computers isn't a free democracy!

Blocked access takes precedence over *granted* access. NT always finds that a user has been blocked before it checks to see whether the user has permission to access an object. In other words, NT starts with the assumption that a user is blocked and then looks to see if there are access privileges. The thing that's interesting about this is that if an end-user has individual access rights to a folder, but that end-user is logged onto the network as part of a blocked group, the group rights take precedence over the individual rights (not unlike communism). In a situation where a group is denied access to an object, all the users within that group are denied access, regardless of their rights during an individual session.

To sum it all up in the simplest possible terms and to make all of this exceptionally easy to remember, we could say that the SRM from the LSA looks at the SAT for the SID. If the SAT compared to the ACL's ACE doesn't match, the SRM and ACL deny the SAT's SID access. See? Nothing could be simpler. Oh, and don't forget the User Mode working alongside the Kernel Mode, talking through the Executive layer with the Win32 subsystem in order to get the micro kernel to fool around with the system services. And just think—you don't even have to try to install an NT system.

The preceding paragraph was ironic.

Accounts and Profiles

User accounts and profiles are ways for the network to understand end-users and what kind of privileges they have. An account is basically another way of talking about a user profile. If you were to open a savings account, you would put money into your account. The bank would assign you an account number. At the same time, the bank could look at how you seem to be similar to other people, and create a profile of all people like you. The bank could try to tailor different kinds of accounts to every individual person in the world, or it could tailor its services to a lesser number of profiles.

Given the flagrant disregard for common understanding of language in the computer industry, networking reverses the way accounts and profiles are used. In a networking environment, an account is a generic category for all end-users who fit into a typical pattern. A profile is the specific services an individual end-user has access to. In the backward world of computer-speak, you go into a bank and open a checking profile. If you seem to be similar to lots of other people, the bank creates an account for groups of people like you.

Administrator

The Administrator account is a default account, meaning that it's been set up within the operating system and will always be there. Every installation of NT will have someone in charge of managing the networking events, and that person takes ownership of the Administrator account. The Administrator account cannot be removed, and it grants permissions to that person (or group of people) to make changes within the operating system itself.

User

Another generic account is the User account. The basic User account is more like a template because, when the network administrator opens a New User dialog box, the User account template forms the basis for whatever modifications the administrator will make. Saving that information creates a specific User account, and the next time a new account is opened, the template comes up with blank spaces to fill in.

User accounts, which can be used for groups or individuals, contain the varying information making up the profile for that user. Keep in mind that a "user" could mean more than one person. Each user account will have different rights, depending on what network resources the administrator assigns.

Guest

Finally, Windows NT comes with a third type of default account called the *Guest* account. It's not at all unusual for a corporation to have many file servers and applications, all designed to produce whatever work the company does. In all that specific technology, there will usually be a generic word processor and spreadsheet application. The files being created each day for those two applications are stored on various disks with more or less security and privacy. But what happens when a visiting person wants to borrow a computer to type a memo to his or her secretary back at the home office?

The Guest account provides a way for someone who isn't an end-user with a User account assigned to them to use network resources in a very restricted fashion. The network administrator has control over all accounts and all resources, and can set the default rights to the Guest account.

Windows NT provides three default accounts: Administrator, User, and Guest. After a user account has been set up, the administrator uses the operating system security features to grant rights and permissions to each account in terms of accessing network resources. Every account generates its own security access token (SAT), which identifies the account to every object at every access request.

Managing User Accounts

The Windows 9x Explorer is a dulled-down version of the NT Explorer. In Windows 9x, the Explorer is mostly used for file maintenance tasks, such as copying, moving, deleting, and creating folders and subfolders. The NT Explorer is used for folder and file maintenance, but also to view and set object permissions and to configure auditing on files and folders.

Beyond the basic file maintenance found in the NT Explorer, workstations configured as work groups use the User Manager Administration utility to manage User accounts. For those PCs configured as NT servers in a domain, the account management tool is the User Manager for Domains.

User IDs (account names) can be up to 20 characters in length, with both letters and numbers, and may contain certain special characters (e.g., asterisks, dashes, underlines, and so forth). Each User account can optionally be assigned a password of up to 14 characters in length, but there is a limitation on the minimum number of characters that must be used. The password may be blank, but the account policy must be configured to allow blank passwords. Passwords can use the same characters as the User ID names.

Remember that User ID names can be up to 20 characters long, and must be unique for each domain on a network. The names are not case sensitive and can include letters (both uppercase and lowercase), numbers, and certain special characters.

NT can also be configured to keep password lists with a history of up to 24 previous passwords. This is done to prevent end-users from using the same passwords each time the system goes through a change-password cycle. The required change for passwords helps to protect against a system invasion where over familiarity with a password has made that password pointless. The network administrator will often require a password change once a month.

Passwords can be up to 14 characters long, but the use of a password can be set to required or optional by an administrator. Unlike User ID names, passwords are case sensitive, meaning that if you created a capital letter in some position, you must type a capital letter in that same position the next time you use the password. Passwords can also be a combination of letters, numbers, and certain special characters.

Managing Groups

Windows NT, like the Novell operating system, provides a way to assign rights and permissions to many end-users at the same time. You can imagine what it would be like if you were setting up an NT network in a corporation with 5,000 employees and you had to create a User account for each person, and then assign rights and access to individual folders and files every time. To aid in this process, many end-users can be assigned to a single group.

After a group has been defined, all the profile information for that group is automatically assigned to any individual user joined to that group. Suppose you get a job in the IT department of the A+ Corporation. The network administrator has probably set up a Totally Cool Group for everyone in the IT department. One of the privileges of that group is that anyone assigned to the Totally Cool Group has the right to assign other users to groups, or to assign object access to end-users. All your boss has to do is enter you into the system and assign you to the group, and you take on all the rights and privileges of being Totally Cool. It's a lot like the cliques in high school, when you stop to think about it.

Another example would be where a group of real people in the real world is in charge of developing and writing a business course. Each person in this bunch (group) has his or her own User account, so a management person would have access to things that a temporary employee would not. By creating a related project group in NT, anyone involved in that particular project automatically takes on the rights and permissions allowed while that particular project is under way. Note that if the management person is logged into the project group, he only has whatever rights are assigned to that group. To regain his or her special management rights would require logging in under the personal User ID.

NT establishes certain groups at the time it's installed, giving those groups certain default permissions. These templates are the changeover point where policies began turning into profiles. Each of these groups has certain default rights and permissions. The default groups are:

- Administrators (NT Server)
- Operators—Based on operations defined as Account, Backup, Print, or Server
- Power Users
- Users
- Guests.

NT Workstation uses local groups. NT Servers use both local and global groups. A local group is specific to a local machine (your own PC), whereas a global group can be set up across an entire domain. Any end-user assigned to a global group can go to any machine on the network and log on under that group name, gaining access to all the resources assigned to the global group anywhere in the domain.

In addition to the default groups available on NT Workstation, NT Server also includes the Administrators group, but provides for additional groups based on Operators rights. These rights are assigned in terms of Account, Backup, Print, and Server operators. Once again, each group is given certain rights and permissions, with the Administrators having all rights and permissions. Also remember that group rights take precedence over individual rights, so someone who has many rights in their own User account, could lose some of those rights when they log on to the network as part of a group.

Policies vs. Profiles

Beginning with Windows for Work groups 3.11, various levels of networking were built into the system. WFW 3.11 used simple peer-to-peer networking. NT is much more sophisticated. In the old days, part of managing a network was to set certain policies, or general rules as to how people could interact with the overall network. The term "policies" has fallen into disuse, being replaced by the concept of group rights, domain management, and systems administration templates.

Windows 3.x introduced an almost undocumented feature, whereby the PROGMAN.INI file could be opened (in a text editor) and a [Restrictions] heading could be inserted at a blank line. These restrictions included **NoRun=**, **NoClose=**, **NoSaveSettings=**, **NoFileMenu=**, and **EditLevel=**. Depending on the numeric values (0–4) entered after the equal sign, an administrator could prevent users from running certain programs, saving modified settings, or even accessing the main menu's File option.

Windows 95 began making the restrictions more sophisticated, introducing the optional Policy Editor with the first release of OSR/A. *Optional* means that the Policy Editor (POLEDIT.EXE) was not automatically installed during Setup. This time the restrictions broadened to include restricted access to the Control Panel, customization limits for the Desktop, and restrictions on network access configuration changes. An example would be the administrator setting the policy for the MS-DOS environment where certain types of programs could not be run at all.

Policies are an exclusive authorization process, meaning that out of all possible ways an end-user might get into trouble, certain global areas can be excluded. Profiles, on the other hand, are more like an inclusive authorization process, meaning that the systems administrator has to figure out ahead of time what an end-user may need to accomplish. Given that work environments are constantly adapting to meet changing conditions, an inclusive process tends to carry with it a much greater burden (overhead) on the corporate network administrators as they run around adding rights and permissions they hadn't thought of previously.

Starting Windows NT

Windows NT is a portable operating system, meaning, as we've said, that it can be installed on systems using an Alpha CPU or an Intel CPU, among others. Because of this, the way NT starts up is different for each platform. We'll focus on the Intel environment, given that it's the most typical environment for an A+ technician to be working with.

If you understand the way NT starts up, you'll have a much better understanding of how Windows 2000 does almost exactly the same thing.

There are 17 steps in the startup process, and we're pretty sure that within the year, anyone shopping in a supermarket will be required to know all seventeen steps before they can purchase a pint of milk. The first step, as it is for any other computer, is the POST. At the end of the POST, the BIOS hands off to the bootstrap loader, which looks for something in the boot sector of a disk.

NT, like any other operating system, looks in the boot sector of a disk for the Master Boot Record (MBR). Instructions in the MBR tell the operating system to look for the Active partition and to load the NT boot sector from that partition. In DOS, the location of the boot sector was restricted to an Active, Primary partition. OS/2 didn't have this restriction and could load from a so-called nonbootable partition. NT must find its system files on an Active, Primary partition.

NT Boot and System Partitions

Windows NT creates a small boot partition at the front of the disk, and this boot partition contains the boot loader that tells the operating system where to find the NT system files. The system files are installed on a system partition, and this system partition is the volume that contains the required files needed to load NT. The system partition must be on a disk that the bootstrap loader can find directly through the BIOS. The boot partition can be on the same disk as the system partition, but it doesn't have to be.

In Windows NT, there can be a maximum of 4 Primary partitions (as opposed to 3 in DOS). In both NT and DOS (or Windows 9x), there can only be 1 Extended partition per disk. Remember that an Extended partition is then subdivided into formatted logical drives (volumes).

NT Loader (NTLDR)

After the information in the boot sector goes into memory, it loads the NT boot loader (NTLDR) into memory. The boot loader (or simply the NT Loader) switches the processor into 32-bit mode, and starts a mini file system to support either a FAT or NTFS volume. At that point, the system reads a BOOT.INI file, displaying the available operating system selections to the end-user. A specific configuration line in the .INI file defines how long the options list stays displayed.

The BOOT.INI file displays a list of any other operating systems available on the disk.

Following the BOOT.INI file and display, NT boot loader then runs NTDETECT.COM to detect and prepare a list (profile) of the currently installed hardware. This list of hardware is passed back to the NT Loader, which then asks whether or not you want to invoke the **Last Known Good** hardware profile. This assumes NT has been run before, and pressing the spacebar during this message accepts that last hardware profile.

Assuming you've chosen to use the previously known-to-be good hardware profile, NT Loader then brings the NT kernel (NTOSKRNL.EXE) into memory and passes the hardware profile to the kernel. At this point, the kernel loads, *but does not initialize* all the hardware device drivers associated with the hardware profile. The kernel then attempts to take control of the hardware devices, turning the monitor's screen blue only when it has successfully accomplished that control.

Loading a program into memory is not the same as running that program. We say that NT loads a program or device driver, but the initializing step is separate and begins running that program.

Following the NT blue screen, when all device drivers have been initialized and their companion devices are under control, the kernel loads and initializes a second group of drivers. (This is step 11, by the way, for anyone who's counting.)

Session Manager (SMSS)

Windows NT then runs the Session Manager (SMSS.EXE), which starts the high-level subsystems and services. When the SMSS is successfully in place, NT runs a boot-time Check Disk (not anything at all like the old DOS CHKDSK.EXE) on every partition, to verify partition integrity. Actually, this is much like ScanDisk; only it needed a different name because NT was way cooler than everything else.

NT then sets up a swap file, giving it a different (and cooler) name. This swap file is called the *paging file*, and is used pretty much the way that any other swap file is used for virtual memory disk swapping (paging). After the paging file has been set up, NT runs the Win32 subsystem to set up the User Mode and control user input at the keyboard and monitor.

Win32 and LSA

Win32 starts WINLOGON.EXE, which runs the Local Security Authority (LSASS.EXE) that pops up the Logon dialog box. This is the same as the Local Security Authority in Window 2000, and at this point, even though a logon process can begin, the startup process is still continuing with system services loading in the background.

When we talk about multitasking, one event is in the foreground, taking the computer's focus and interacting directly with the user. Other events are in the background, running on the system out of sight from the user and behind the window on the screen.

Last Known Good

Once an end-user has successfully logged on, the startup is considered to be "good," and the HKEY_LOCAL_MACHINE\System\LastKnownGood Registry subkey is updated to point to the particular key containing the hardware configuration that was just used to start NT.

Each time NT has a successful startup, the hardware profile and associated pass/fail error codes are recorded in a particular file. LastKnownGood accesses this file in the event of a crash on startup, and allows you to choose whether you want to use that last profile. This safety feature was carried over to Windows 9x, and we've seen how the Registry makes an automatic copy of itself, along with a first-time startup file, each time a successful startup takes place.

NT File System (NTFS)

Windows NT was designed to work with not only different hardware platforms, but with different file management systems. Novell's NetWare (operating system) was the clear market leader in the field, allowing IBM-type PCs to work alongside Macintosh machines on the same network. Because Apple computers use a completely different way of storing files, NetWare had almost no competition in its ability to work with both systems.

As we've said, the two file systems most commonly supported by NT nowadays, are the FAT and NTFS. Once again, the file allocation table systems came out of the original DOS environment. We saw previously how the original decision to create a 16-bit file allocation system created all the convoluted development efforts in Windows 9x. Most of these efforts were spent reconciling the operating system with multigigabyte disks, far larger than anyone had ever envisioned.

Windows NT continues to format all floppy disks using a FAT16 format, still the most widely used system in the world. FAT16 can be accessed by DOS, all versions of Windows, and OS/2. The file names in FAT16 retain the 8.3 format of a name and an extension, meaning that Windows Long File Names are truncated.

A problem with FAT16 is that individual files have no security protection. The only attributes available are the archive, hidden, system, and read-only (A, H, S, R) attributes. Network operating systems usually include additional attributes for assigning file access rights to individual users. However, the biggest problem with FAT16 is that file sizes are limited to 2GB.

In Windows NT and Windows 2000, only partitions formatted as NTFS volumes provide the local file security of network file attributes. FAT16 and FAT32 file systems do not provide this security.

NTFS is a completely different way of managing files. A FAT is essentially a simple (flat file) database. Each entry contains the cluster addresses for a file, and the entire volume is contained within a single table. NTFS works more like a relational database.

Relational vs. Flat File Databases

A so-called flat file database is where every record contains the fields and data used to capture information. Searching for data is done by looking at every record in a single file. Relational databases break up the database into many smaller files for faster processing of very large amounts of data. In a relational database, fields are not necessarily locked to every other field in a record of information. For example, one database might contain a person's name, address, and phone number. Another database might contain all the cars the person owns. The two databases are linked together through the related information of the phone number.

Transaction logs track each activity in and out of a relational database to re-create each of the small databases making up the overall system in the event of a problem. This activity can be anything associated in any way with any access to the many databases within the overall relational database system. Some of these activities include querying a file, reading or writing data to a record, storing the results of a query, and so forth.

FAT systems maintain a primary table and a single copy of that table. In some cases, the copy of the FAT can actually be useful following a system failure. NTFS, on the other hand, maintains a transaction log for file management operations. In a catastrophic system failure, NT can use this transaction log to rebuild the cluster addresses of almost every file on the volume. The specific differences between NTFS and FAT include:

- Local security at the volume, folder, and file level.
- Support for Long File Names up to 255 characters in length
- Support for files up to 16 exabytes (EB) in size (16 billion billion, or 16 quintillion bytes). That would be 16 to the 18th power, or a 16 with 18 zeros after it; 1 megabyte is a million bytes, and 1 exabyte is a billion gigabytes.
- Automatic generation of the DOS 8.3 format file names for compatibility.
- Support for case-sensitive file names for compatibility with the Portable Operating System Interface for Unix (POSIX) used in many government installations.

POSIX is a particular type of file management system.

NTFS uses 2MB of space on any disk where the system is installed, making it more appropriate for larger drives. Given the size of today's drives, this space overhead is no longer an issue; however, it can't be used on a floppy disk or small drives. Additionally, NTFS is currently available in only Windows NT, Windows 2000, and Windows XP.

NT Disk Administration

One of the important modules we listed in the System Services Layer was the I/O Manager. This module controls the disk subsystem, along with all input and output requests made through NT. Remember that we said the system services are part of the NT Executive layer (along with the micro kernel), and that the Executive layer acts as an interface between the high-level (User Mode) and low-level (Kernel Mode) components of the operating system.

The I/O Manager uses a series of layered software drivers that communicate with each other through the Executive layer. For example, for the file system driver to communicate with a disk drive, an I/O request is routed through the I/O Manager. The I/O Manager communicates the request to both the disk controller and the controller's device driver. Because each driver is kept separate and contained, NT (theoretically) makes it easier to replace devices or to update drivers without having to completely reinstall the system.

The Disk Administrator Tool

The disk subsystem's Disk Administrator utility is a graphical systems management tool that you can get to through the Administrative Tools menu. Disk Administrator has two views within the graphical presentation: the partition view and the volume view. (Refer to the "Logical Formatting and Partitions: FDISK" section of Chapter 10 for a discussion of the difference between a partition and a logical drive [also called a volume]).

Both NT Server and NT Workstation have the Disk Administrator utility. Both versions allow you to:

- Create or delete partitions
- Create or delete, format, extend, and label volumes
- Create or delete striped sets (discussed in a moment)
- Assign drive identification letters
- Adjust the access order of drives
- Save and restore drive configurations

The NT Server version of Disk Administrator also allows you to establish or break disk mirroring (or duplexing), and to create, delete, or regenerate striped sets with parity. We discuss volume sets and striped sets, along with mirroring and duplexing, in the next two sections.

The Disk Administrator is accessible only to members of the Administrator user group.

Volume Sets

One of the important ways NT differs from Windows 9x in its use of disk space is that several partitions can be joined together in a single, logical area called a *volume set*. These partitions can be on a single physical disk, or located on several physical disks running off different controllers. Another interesting thing about a volume set, is that it can include different types of disks.

➤ A volume set can have a maximum of 32 different partitions.

When data is written to the volume set, the process takes place in a sequential fashion. When the first partition in the volume set fills up, the data is written to the next partition, and so on down the line. Neither the system partition nor the boot partition can be part of a volume set.

Volume sets combine free space in partitions on 1 to 32 disks, writing data in sequential order.

Striped Sets

A striped set is somewhat like a volume set because data is written across different physical disks. The partitions on each disk are equal in size, giving rise to the term "stripes." Unlike a volume set, data can be written to whatever disk is sitting idle, making for a more efficient (and faster) I/O process. Much like random access read/writes take place on different platters of a hard drive, striped sets allow for something akin to random access read/writes to whole sets of disks.

➤ Striped sets can be set up on anywhere from 2 to 32 physical disks.

One of the problems with striped sets is that if any of the disks in the set fails, all data on that particular physical disk will be lost. This kind of setup is called *no fault tolerance* because the system has no tolerance at all for any faulty machinery.

Boot partitions can be mirrored or duplexed, but not striped. System partitions cannot be used in a striped set. Striped sets provide better read/write efficiency by writing to whichever disk is idle at the moment.

Striped Sets with Parity

Striped sets can be configured either with or without parity. Striped sets *with parity* can be set up on anywhere from 3 to 32 partitions and work in a fashion vaguely similar to the parity circuits used to test main memory (see Chapter 3). In this configuration, one of the partition stripes in the disk array (group, or set) is set up as a parity check. If any of the disks in the set fails, that data can be reconstructed using the parity information in the parity stripe. NT generates an error message, but it continues to function until the systems administrator has a convenient time to replace the failed disk. This requires shutting down the network, so a convenient time would be when network use is very low.

➤ Striped sets with parity can be set up on anywhere from 3 to 32 partitions

One of the problems with maintaining a parity stripe on a single partition is that a bottleneck forms at that parity stripe when many other disks are writing their data recovery information to the single stripe.

Disk Mirroring and Duplexing

With volume sets and striped sets, many physical disks are set up to act as a virtual, single entity. Different data is written to any of the partitions within the two types of sets. Disk mirroring, on the other hand, is where two partitions are mirrors of each other. Each partition contains an exact copy (not actually reversed like a real mirror) of every piece of data on the other, mirrored partition (also called a *mirrored set*). We call it *disk mirroring* because these two partitions are almost always on two separate disks.

The advantage of disk mirroring is that if one physical disk fails, no reconstruction is necessary. The network continues operating using the data from the mirrored (constantly-updated backup) copy of whatever information was on the failed disk. NT generates an error message, and once again, the failed disk drive can be replaced at a more convenient time for the systems administrator.

Disk duplexing is almost the same as mirroring, except each disk is connected to a different drive controller. One of the problems with both mirroring and duplexing is that any amount of data requires twice the physical resources. In other words, rather than having room for two files on two disks, this data redundancy means having one file on two disks, with an exact copy on each disk. On the other hand, this means less chance of losing any data.

Mirrored sets are set up on two physical drives using a single controller, as with an IDE or SCSI controller. If the two drives use separate controllers, this is called *duplexing* or *disk duplexing*. Mirroring is also known as *RAID 1*, and is available only in the NT Server version of Windows NT.

RAID

The word "redundant" means an unnecessary repetition. The word "array" means a lineup. A Redundant Array of Inexpensive Disks *(RAID)* is essentially where a network file server uses extra disks to keep multiple copies of data. In these situations, the data itself is more valuable than the cost of the disks. That's why the disks are termed inexpensive. Making repeated copies of the valuable data isn't actually unnecessary; still, that's what the computer people called it, using the word "redundant." The concept of RAID data protection has been around long enough that there are now six different levels of protection (0 through 5). Each level indicates a higher degree of protection.

RAID Level 0 (RAID 0) is the no fault tolerance process of using 64KB block storage areas in a striped set. Once again, the striped set means multiple partitions all of the same size. Both Windows NT Workstation and NT Server use RAID 0 in most instances. Even though the data protection is limited, read/write access is more efficient because data goes to whichever spindle motor is idle.

Striped partitions are partitions of equal size on one or more physical disks, joined into a logical area called a *set*. Striped sets provide no fault tolerance and can be set up using anywhere from 2 to 32 partitions on one or more physical disks. Striped sets are also known as RAID 0.

Striped sets with parity combine 3 to 32 partitions, where one of the partitions is used as the parity stripe. Striped sets with parity do provide fault tolerance, and are also known as *RAID 5*.

RAID 1 is the most common form of RAID at the moment and is often used in disk mirroring and disk duplexing. Level 1 provides positive fault tolerance, but at the cost of a 50 percent reduction in resources. This is that double disk problem we just spoke about, where two disks are used to store one set of data. RAID 1 is only available on NT Server machines.

RAID 2 is similar to striped sets, but the data is moved at a bit level, rather than in 64KB blocks. One of the disks in RAID 2 is set aside for data recovery. This method of data protection is currently unavailable through Windows NT.

RAID 3 is disk striping with parity, with data being moved at the bit level rather than the block level. RAID 4 is disk striping at the block level, with one disk reserved for parity recovery. RAID 5 is also block-level disk striping, but the parity information is evenly spread across all the disks in the array, as opposed to being on only one disk. This removes the typical, single-stripe bottleneck of parity writing.

Windows NT supports RAID Levels 1 and 5 on the Server version, along with RAID 0 on both the Server and Workstation versions.

Troubleshooting Tools

From the perspective of the A+ exam, CompTIA assumes you won't be involved in an NT installation beyond the point of following a list of basic instructions from a systems administrator. You'll most likely be presented with a scenario in which an NT machine has successfully started, and you've been called in to find out the nature of a problem involving day-to-day operations. This is where you'll need to know some of the basic tools and utilities.

The Event Viewer

An A+ technician is generally a first-tier tech support person, and will rarely have an administrator password or be involved in a large-scale network installation. A typical problem-solving situation might involve working with a network administrator to uncover what events took place prior to a problem, and how those events took place. First-tier support handles the basic detective work in terms of describing the "crime scene." After the specifics of the problem have been isolated, you will most likely hand the problem off to a network administrator for final resolution.

That being said, one of the important troubleshooting utilities you should know about is the Event Viewer. Like Windows 2000 and XP, Windows NT provided the Event Viewer tool in a graphic format, bringing together a consolidated set of underlying files gathered into a single presentation area. These files are log files, and although the tools may be fairly easy to use, interpreting the results of an Event Viewer session isn't always so simple. No special permissions are necessary to view the System and Application logs; however, only a member of the Administrator group can view the Security log.

Access to the Event Viewer takes place through the Administrative Tools menu. The viewer brings up the System, Application, and Security log files. The System log file holds event information generated by the operating system itself. The Application log contains both system and user information, such as which user tried to open a spreadsheet and what happened at that time.

The information in the Security log file is generated by the audit policy and audit messages managed through the Security Reference Monitor. Security events include such things as failed passwords, failed ID names, inappropriate access attempts, or any other breach of system security as defined by the network administrators. The Event Viewer logs the following information with each event:

- System date
- System time
- Application or component that logged the event
- Category of event
- An event number
- The User ID (who was logged on during the event)
- The computer name where the event took place (assigned during installation).

Typically, the Event log presents lines and symbols indicating that an application was started successfully. An exclamation point indicates a warning of a possible problem, and so on. The log files are very extensive, and if something crashes, the log files can often describe what happened. After NT has successfully started, the Event Viewer is one of the first places you'll go to find out what problem has taken place. Note that NT must have successfully started in the first place.

Bootable and Emergency Repair Disks

Two important hardware tools you'll want to understand are a bootable floppy disk and a so-called Emergency Repair Disk (often referred to as an *ERD*). The bootable floppy disk is far too small to hold the entire Windows NT operating system, but it can hold the key files necessary to begin a startup process. If NT will boot from a floppy disk, you'll at least have a general idea of the most likely next step. If all the workstations in an environment have been set up the same way, the bootable floppy disk can use a generic hardware profile to start all the machines.

If the bootable floppy disk can't start the machine, another tool you can try is the emergency repair disk. The programs on this disk can be used to repair some of the problems associated with Windows NT system partitioning, and for restoring the NT configuration. This repair disk cannot be used to start an NT session because it isn't a bootable disk.

The Emergency Repair Disk also differs from a bootable floppy disk, in that each repair disk is inextricably linked to the specific machine that was used to create it. If the network has 300 computers, and they've all been set up the same way, you can have a single, generic bootable disk, but you'll need 300 emergency repair disks.

Corporate network administrators rarely use an emergency repair disk, given how many disks it would entail. Instead, if a corporate machine has a serious startup problem, the administrator will wipe the entire system clean from the machine and create a new installation, often from a disk image.

Disk Images

One of the lost advantages of DOS and 16-bit Windows is that software installed on one of these machines was folder-specific as opposed to sector-specific. What this means is that any files, excepting the two DOS system files, could be copied from one machine to another, or from one location on the disk to another, without affecting how the operating system or applications would run. Certain **SET=** changes and .INI file lines might have to be updated, but if you installed Windows 3.x on a machine, you could do a complete system backup using the XCOPY.EXE program.

Windows 95 introduced sector-specific installations where the location of certain system files was tracked not only through folder locations, but also right down to specific sectors on the hard drive. When a file is copied from a hard drive to a floppy disk and then back to the hard drive, that file is assigned a track, sector, and cluster by the FAT in accordance with whatever free space is available. If the Windows Registry expects to find the start of a file on an exact disk sector, the copy procedure causes a fatal crash in the system.

A disk image is created using special software, and the image is an exact photograph of a partition or even an entire hard drive. The image is so exact that it includes the track, sector, and cluster information. Writing a disk image to a CD-ROM or network drive allows you to wipe a hard drive clean and then write the image back to the hard drive, or to a new hard drive with all the original address locations intact.

The Task Manager

All the way back in 16-bit Windows, Microsoft provided the TASKMAN.EXE program as a way of viewing what programs were running in memory. Windows 3.x offered the Switch To option to call up the Task Manager from a pull-down menu in the upper left-hand corner of any window. Additionally, information pertaining to the available Windows resources was on the Help|About menu of any Windows-compliant program.

Windows 9x removed the pull-down Switch To option, changing the entire concept into the new Taskbar. Access to the Task Manager became less obvious, but the information became more detailed. In Windows 9x, the Task Manager is accessed through the Ctrl+Alt+Del keystroke combination. System resources information was moved to the Performance tab of the My Computer properties dialog box.

In Windows NT, the Ctrl+Alt+Del keystrokes begin a logon procedure. However, once you're logged onto the NT machine, Ctrl+Alt+Del offers several choices, one of which is the Task Manager. You can also access the Task Manager by right-clicking on the Taskbar and then selecting the Task Manager option from the Properties menu.

The NT Task Manager combines a detailed report of every program running in memory, system performance in terms of resources and available memory, and a recent usage history. The recent history tracks what processes are taking place, and which resources are being assigned. It also offers a real-time graphic representation of a resource monitor, showing how the overall system is working.

Performance Monitor

The Task Manager reports on the overall status of the machine. Performance Monitor is similar, except that it can be set to monitor specific aspects of the machine either in a moving graphic or a tab format. A few of the many things you can assign to the Performance Monitor include the CPU, the percent of processor time, the percent of user time, memory, available bytes, page faults per second, logical disk usage, the percent of free space, average disk cue length, and so on.

Many of these low-level performance details are obscure and probably something you'll never use. You should know about the utility, though, because it's another way to get into the underlying set of events taking place on the machine. In its graphic-charting form, the items you've chosen to monitor show as a real-time change line in a small window.

Windows 9x systems also provided a graphic resource monitor by running System Monitor (SYSMON.EXE), usually found in the main Windows folder (C:\Windows). One of the configuration options was to show the stream of bytes uploaded or downloaded during an online session.

The Network Management Monitoring Agent

Net Watcher first appeared in Windows 95 and was designed to allow a network administrator to monitor the network in terms of usage load and traffic. Windows NT includes the Network Monitor, but in only the Server version of the operating system. The monitoring agent can track how the network is functioning at any given time and report out many statistics.

The Network Monitor initially displays in a window divided into four areas. These areas show a real-time graph representing: network use, total network statistics, session statistics, and station statistics. The full SMS management tool adds such features as: Find Routers, Resolve Address From Names, tracking local traffic, and more.

Network Monitor is essentially the same product as the optional NT Systems Management Server (SMS). The NT Server version has several of its functions disabled, indicating that SMS is really only the fully-functional monitoring agent.

NT Error Messages

At this point, you've probably sensed that Windows NT is a somewhat complex operating system. We've heard stories of people who've actually taken seminars lasting weeks in order to understand only a few of the intricacies of the system. Naturally, we fully expect you to have a complete and thorough understanding of everything involved with NT in 25 or 30 pages. No, we're kidding again. All we can do is give you a broad overview of the most likely way in which an A+ technician will come in contact with NT. You probably won't deal with NT Server, but will spend most of your time working with the Workstation version. Most of the errors we discuss in this section are related to the startup process.

Someone once told us about a young man who wanted to become one of the world's great writers. When he was asked to define what he meant by great, he said, "I want to write stuff that the whole world will read; stuff that people will react to on a truly emotional level; stuff that will make them scream, cry, and howl in pain and anger!" He now works as an operating systems developer writing error messages.

NT Detect

Of the thousands of error messages generated during Windows NT operations, certain messages are fairly common for workstations, and we'd like to at least reference them at this point. The first error message we'll mention is "NT Detect Failed."

NTDETECT.COM is responsible for the hardware detection phase of the startup process. The file is located in the root folder of the boot drive, and if it becomes corrupted or is missing, you can try booting from a bootable floppy. If this solves the problem, copy NTDETECT.COM from the floppy to the root folder on the hard drive. Another possibility would be to boot the system from an NT setup disk and then repair the problem with an emergency repair disk.

Missing Kernel

Another common error message is "The kernel file is missing from the disk." One way to solve this problem is to strike the machine repeatedly with a five-pound sledgehammer. This is not a recommended procedure for the corporate environment. A better strategy would be to understand that the NT loader (NTLDR.COM) file is missing or has become corrupted. Like NTDETECT.COM, this file is in the root folder of the boot drive and can be copied over from a bootable floppy disk or an Emergency Repair Disk.

Missing BOOT.INI

Sometimes, NT is feeling so poorly that it can't even give you an error message telling you what's wrong. An example of this is where the machine starts Windows NT, but does not display the operating system selection menu. This is the menu we mentioned previously, where you're asked if you want to use the Last Known Good hardware profile. In this problem scenario, neither the menu displays nor does the waiting time take place.

A likely cause of this kind of error is that the BOOT.INI file is missing from the root folder of the boot drive. You might recall that after the NT Loader has finished loading, the system reads the BOOT.INI file in order to display the available operating system selections. To recover from this, allow the system to start and then log on to Windows and copy the .INI file from the bootable floppy to the root folder of the bootable disk.

If NT or Windows 2000 can't find a BOOT.INI file, the system will load from the first partition on the first disk it finds, looking in the *winnt* folder for its files.

Missing Files

Another common type of error message comes up as "Windows NT could not start because the following file is missing or corrupt," with a listing of some particularly obscure file name. Below the allegedly missing file is the statement, "Please reinstall a copy of the above file." For some strange reason, people seem to make the assumption that when NT says a file is missing, a file must be missing. After all, the machine is a self-aware consciousness, right?

Many television shows have been written about the hilarious and zany antics of a group of happy-go-lucky network administrators joyfully copying file after file into some unknown folder, only to have the same error message come up time and time again. Each time, the name of the file changes, but NT blissfully doesn't seem to care. One of the critical lines in the BOOT.INI file is the line pointing to the location of the system partition. You would think that NT could figure out where to find its own files, wouldn't you? This is a classic instance of an error message that gives you all kinds of interesting information, none of which has any bearing on the actual problem.

Try to boot the machine from the bootable floppy, and if that works, replace the BOOT.INI file on the bootable hard drive. If the same error message keeps coming up, try using an NT setup disk or an emergency repair disk to resolve the problem.

Summary—Windows NT

In a very simplistic fashion, Windows networking can be split into two categories: enterprise and business installations, and home installations. The reason we're choosing this split is based on how CompTIA approaches A+ certification. The exam is designed around the entry-level skills associated with PC tech support. You should understand the design structure of these operating systems, but you needn't focus too deeply on the complex fashion in which they might be applied to a large corporate setting.

Given that Windows 2000 and XP (2K/XP) grew out of Windows NT, security and stability are at the foundation of how these systems work. If you understand the way the OS clamps down on security, you may be able to see where a home or small business network uses a reduced, or basic application of many configuration settings. Conceptually, you should understand the following points:

- NT and Windows 2K/XP are modular-design operating systems. Understand the essence of kernel mode and user mode, and how the kernel protects the OS from mistakes or attacks by the end user.
- Spend some time getting to know the hardware abstraction layer (HAL), and have a picture of how the operating system takes over much of the device management process.
- You should clearly understand the concept of Windows Services, although you won't be tested on specific services and how they load. You should know that the loading process is part of the overall startup process.
- Understand that the Registry is much like the Windows 9x Registry. If you're comfortable with the division of HKey handles, you should be able to choose correct responses to these types of questions.
- Have a fairly good idea of the main acronyms used by Windows NT, 2K/XP. Remember that the LSA is the *Local Security Authorization*. Note the Security Account Management (SAM) database, the Security Access Token (SAT), and Security Identification (SID).
- You should know about the Access Control List (ACL) and how a network grants "rights" to users. A home computer may have an administrative ID and password, or it may not. Depending on the level of security, you may or may not be able to access some of the administrative tools.
- Keep a working knowledge of the default user accounts. These are pretty much the same in Windows NT and 2K/XP. Remember the Administrator, User, Guest accounts and understand the concept of user groups.
- Be somewhat familiar with the startup process, following the logic of what ought to load before something else can load. Pay particular attention to the NT Loader, as the NTLDR file is a major troubleshooting villain in NT/2K/XP.
- Be sure you understand what a Last Known Good hardware profile means, and that it's different from the last known good Registry file.
- Make sure you know that the NT File System works on an NTFS partition. This should connect, in your mind, with the FAT16 and FAT32 DOS partitions. You should also recognize the High Performance File System (HPFS) created by IBM's OS/2.
- Have a working knowledge of RAID and the various levels (0–5), along with the term "fault tolerance." You won't necessarily have to know exactly how many volumes and sets are specified by each level, but you should

be able to recognize that the terms *striped set*, *disk mirroring*, and *duplexing*, for instance, refer to data backup and protection.

The bulk of the questions we saw pertaining to NT and Win2000 were related to system administration and how to access various diagnostics utilities. You should make a note wherever you see a reference to these tools in Chapters 12, 13, and 14. Memorize any menu navigational paths we've listed, because we chose them based on the likelihood of their being on the exam.

The more time and experience you've had actually getting around in Windows 2000, the better you'll be able to visualize the menu paths necessary to reach various tools. Keep in mind that given the format of the exam, you'll almost always be asked to choose a response where the navigation path is already listed. In other words, you should be able to read a response and visualize each cascading menu. You shouldn't have to create a path from memory.

You'll almost always find at least one question pertaining to bootable disks, ERDs, and emergency startup disks. If you can't visualize the differences, then skim back over Chapter 12 and the preceding section of this chapter. We'll discuss them again in Chapter 14.

Finally, the preceding segment was where we introduced most of the basic error messages associated with NT and Win2000. The exam is going to ask you about diagnostics utilities; how to find them; when you would need them; and which tool is most probably associated with a given type of error.

Windows 2000

The Windows 2000 graphic interface, like that of Windows 98, was very similar to Windows NT, with many of the underlying modules making their first integrated appearance. Windows 2000 is where the security, scalability, stability, and networking of NT merged with the usability of Windows 98, providing the beginnings of a universal operating system for both commercial and home users. Windows 2000 was released in four versions:

- *Windows 2000 Professional*—essentially the Windows NT Workstation version, packaged for the individual desktop machine
- *Windows 2000 Server*—an entry-level network server version, equal to Windows NT Server, with support for two-way symmetric processing (using two CPUs simultaneously) and designed for medium-sized deployments

- *Windows 2000 Advanced Server*--a mid-sized deployment with support for four CPUs in simultaneous processing and support for more physical memory
- *Windows 2000 Datacenter Server*--a large-scale deployment with support for 16 CPUs and 64GB of physical memory

Although we've mentioned Windows XP along the way, remember that the focus of the current CompTIA A+ Exam is Windows NT and 2000. For the most part, we refer only to Windows 2000 in this segment, to remain consistent with the exam.

In the same way that Windows 9x tried to use software intelligence (Wizards) to help users make configuration and setup choices, Windows 2000 applied those Wizards to help an NT user set up networking, work groups, and domains. It's almost as though Microsoft kept an internal corporate split, using two different project groups to develop the GUI and the operating system, like in its original joint effort with IBM.

We've also mentioned that Microsoft has always tended to believe that understanding how a computer works shouldn't be necessary when simply using a computer. Although this philosophy is all well and good for end-users, less and less information is available to the tech support community on how to repair current operating system problems. This applies to Windows 2000 and XP, particularly, where there is very little information on the underlying structure.

Although the entire Windows metaphor is designed for the lowest common denominator of understanding, almost every novice user will eventually become fairly proficient. Configuring Windows, or "tweaking the system," can make some things a little easier or better, in terms of daily use, but getting into the low-level problem-solving areas is becoming close to impossible. So much of today's "repair" methodology is based on wiping out a disk and reinstalling an image, that backing up user-created data files is becoming an absolute necessity.

Starting Windows 2000

We can simply tell you that Windows 2000 is essentially the same as Windows NT, but where you'll see the truth of the matter is in the loading process. We won't go into the detail we did with Windows 95 because computers have become so dependent upon their own, local configurations that it's almost impossible to describe a generic boot process.

As with NT, the basic landmarks in a boot process include the pre-booting events of the POST and the boot process itself. Following these two steps, there's a distinction between the *load* events and *initialization* events. This is Microsoftian for getting something into memory (loading). Once that something is in memory, it's connected to a piece of hardware or software and made to start running (initialized). Finally, there's the logon procedure, which, like NT, continues forward while the services load in the background. The short version of loading Windows 2000 Professional is as follows:

1. NTLDR.COM—Acts as a bootstrap loader for the basic operating system. This begins the NT hardware detection phase, switches the CPU into 32-bit mode, and loads a mini file system that can work with either a FAT or NTFS file management system.
2. BOOT.INI—Contains a pointer listing any other operating systems available, along with a configuration statement as to how long the options list will display.
3. NTDETECT.COM—Identifies current hardware components installed on the machine and prepares a list of that configuration. This is where the spacebar option takes place, allowing different hardware profiles to be loaded.
4. NTOSKRNL.EXE—Loads the operating system kernel and creates the current Registry hardware key. Along with the kernel, the file loads (not initializes) device drivers and loads (not initializes) the Session Manager.
5. HAL.DLL—A dynamic link library that generates the hardware abstraction layer, interfacing between the operating system and the specific hardware.
6. SYSTEM—Opens the Registry and reads the operating system configuration, initializing the device drivers loaded previously by NTSOSKRL.EXE, and then loads any additional device drivers found in the Registry.
7. SMSS.EXE—Initializes the Session Manager, executes any boot-time command files (like the old AUTOEXEC.BAT), and then loads basic services and sets up the so-called page file (swap file). The program creates links to the file system that can be used by DOS commands and then starts the Win32 I/O subsystem and begins the logon process.
8. WINLOGON.EXE—The specific program file that generates the logon process and starts the Local Security Authority (LSA).
9. LSASS.EXE—The program file for the LSA, providing all the security-checking done by the system.

Although we've listed the primary files in this startup process, Windows 2000 (like NT) uses countless other .DLL files, device drivers, helper files, and system files to load and run the system.

Multiple Boot Options

Back when IBM was developing OS/2 (which looked a whole lot like DOS), the company developed a little program that would allow a machine to have more than one operating system installed. This program gave the user a menu to choose which OS to boot from. The IBM Boot Manager was one of those rare moments of elegance where the program was designed to do one single thing and do it perfectly. You'll still find that program packaged with PowerQuest's PartitionMagic, but we should remember that Microsoft's Windows NT was originally part of the OS/2 joint development effort.

Windows NT and 2000 both provide a paused screen during the startup process, partly to ask you if you want to use the same hardware profile that worked the last time (LastKnownGood), but also to offer you a menu of any other available operating system you might want to boot from. This internalization of a multiple boot process began showing up in DOS 5.0, where you could boot to different configurations. At that time, you were still restricted to DOS as the operating system, but NT 3.x introduced an internalized multiple OS option.

A situation where the last known hardware profile might not be the appropriate selection could arise when a laptop computer connects through a docking station.

One of the optional files used during a Windows 2000 startup is BOOTSECT.DOS. This file allows you to start the machine with MS-DOS, Windows 95, 98, or some other OS. Keep in mind that a DOS or Windows 9x partition must be a Primary partition, and must be marked as Active in order to boot the machine. One of the installation problems with Windows NT was that the NT Loader must be in the very first tracks and sectors of a physical disk. This can conflict with the IBM Boot Manager, which uses a 2MB partition at the very front of the disk and then hides all the other bootable partitions. Boot Manager "unhides" a partition (depending on your OS selection) and marks that partition as Active. It seems odd that NT and the Boot Manager would struggle for the same bit of disk real estate—you'd think they would just get along—but there you have it.

We've also spoken about how prior to the development of USB ports, a number of devices started using the fast parallel port to connect a SCSI device. One of the more successful of these devices was the Iomega removable disk drive system—the Zip and Jaz drives. Many people wanted to use one of these removable drives as a bootable disk, where the size of the disks (greater than 100MB) would allow for all the system files. If you remember, an NT bootable disk can hold only the very few files used at the very beginning of the startup.

How do you make a removable drive bootable if the system sees it as a secondary disk drive? Windows 2000/NT provides the NTBOOTDD.SYS file (in the root directory of the boot partition) for just that purpose. Iomega also provides certain utility files for the same purpose. Note that NTBOOTDD.SYS will run only *after* the NTDETECT.COM hardware detection phase has been completed.

Safe Mode

For both Windows NT and 2000, you can return to the Last Known Good Registry by pressing the spacebar at the paused OS selection menu. Windows 2000 uses either an emergency repair disk or bootable floppy disk in the same way that NT does. Another option is to load Windows 2000 in Safe Mode (just like Windows 9x), where only the minimal default device drivers are loaded. We will discuss startup problems and Safe Mode in detail in Chapter 14, "Troubleshooting."

If dual-boot is installed on the local machine, meaning that more than one operating system is available during the BOOT.INI pause, then when the boot loader prompts for an operating system, pressing the spacebar will start Windows 2000 normally. When the Boot Loader prompts for an operating system, pressing F8 will present an options menu screen from which you can start Windows 2000 in Safe Mode.

Understand the function of the BOOT.INI file. This file is often the culprit in Windows startup failures.

Active Directory

Perhaps one of the most important differences between Windows 2000 and Windows NT is that Windows 2000 includes the new Active Directory feature. Active Directory is a component of the Windows Open Services

Architecture (WOSA), and provides what is called *Directory Service* to all the objects on a network, across the entire network. The Directory Service gathers up information on every object, such as users, computers, printers, hardware, and all the policies and permissions, and presents this information in a single, hierarchical view. A hierarchical view has headings with subheadings going down in levels. This is similar to the outlining you had to learn in school, where you start with a book of information that is divided into chapters, which is divided into topics and then into ideas, and you eventually end up with a specific paragraph of details.

Date warehouses use a concept called *drilling down* into information, and this too, uses the principle of outlining. The Windows Explorer works with drive letters at the top of the hierarchy, and below each drive is a root directory folder containing many subfolders, going all the way down to the last leaf on the last twig of the last branch—a file. The Registry uses handles (HKeys) to contain many subkeys, all of which end up with a specific configuration line. The Computer Management tools work with nodes and branches to arrive eventually at a specific event for a specific device.

We should mention here that in a very large network, each domain doesn't necessarily have to be running the same network operating system. In fact, one of the biggest problems Novell had to work out in the historic development of networks was that a single business location could easily have many IBM-type PCs running alongside Macintosh computers. Active Directory is one of the latest developments growing out of a long line of methods for joining together different operating systems.

Windows NT presents each domain to the systems administrators at the top level of the network hierarchy. This is all well and good, but you can easily have hundreds of domains in a network. That would be like opening up the Explorer and discovering that you had 100 separate drives to work with. In addition to the drives, the administrators would have to configure each "drive" (domain) separately, going in and adding all the resources to that domain, along with all the rights and profiles.

Novell and Microsoft eventually figured out a better way to do this, and Windows 2000 consolidates all the old NT domains into a single, higher-level called the *Active Directory*. In addition to the Directory Service hierarchical (outline) presentation, Active Directory gathers together and consolidates the security and authentication services across the network. These two features combine to make it easier for anyone on a Windows 2000 network to get to resources, while at the same time making it much easier for network administrators to control that access.

The Directory Service is actually integrated into the Domain Name System (DNS) concept we spoke about in Chapter 8. As we discussed, a DNS entry is a way of making a numeric IP address more user-friendly, by providing a descriptive name to the underlying address. Active Directory does somewhat the same thing, by taking the complicated resource names of objects on the network and turning them into something an average human being can understand. For example, an NT network might provide a printer somewhere and list it with a long line of symbols, characters, slashes, and colons. Windows 2000 can use Active Directory to call that printer “Bob’s printer in the Raleigh, North Carolina branch office.” The users don’t need to know what the underlying name for that printer is anymore.

Although the principle is similar to the DNS concept, Active Directory goes even further than merely cross-referencing names and building in security for each network object. Within an Active Directory database, access requests for a network object are handled with Lightweight Directory Access Protocol (LDAP) queries. DNS is essentially a very simple listing of an IP address and the cross-referenced name. Active Directory is more like a full-scale database.

With a complete database made up of many fields (categories of details), Active Directory can produce varying amounts of information about an object on the network. Some of these queries (questions) can return (answer) to a network administrator such information as a user name, contact information, administrative contact information, access permissions, ownership information, and object attributes.

When you go to an Internet search engine, you type in a query and the system goes out and gathers all the IP addresses of Web sites where it finds something related to your question. Before the search engine presents you with your results, it converts the IP addresses to domain names by using DNS entries. But that’s not what you see, right? The final presentation is a top-level (hierarchical) link with a descriptive title, together with a short description of what that titled link is all about. When you click on that link, you’re taken to the site location where you can begin to drill down into the site by clicking other links.

A DNS server doesn’t require the Active Directory feature, but Active Directory can work only in conjunction with DNS servers. For that reason, Active Directory can run only on one of the Windows 2000 Server versions.

Windows 2000 Diagnostics and Troubleshooting

Windows 2000 provides more diagnostics and troubleshooting tools than any of the previous versions of Windows. Following the NT philosophy of merging diagnostics tools into the graphical interface, Windows 2000 doesn't use an MS-DOS command-line mode for troubleshooting (excepting in the Recovery Console). In Windows 9x, if Safe Mode failed, you could always go to the underlying DOS prompt and rummage around in the system to run various utilities. Windows 2000 and NT don't rely on specific files as utility programs, relying instead on groups of associated files combined into a tool with its own interface, menus, and presentation. In most cases, you can't even find the underlying files used in an administrative tool.

A number of the questions on the exam will refer to navigation paths branching from the Start menu. For example, you may be given a list of responses asking you for the correct set of steps to arrive at the Control Panel or an icon within the Control panel. We've included many of those navigational pathways, along with other ways of finding various problem-solving and troubleshooting aids. (See Chapter 14 for more on troubleshooting.)

System Configuration Utility

This utility became available in Windows 98 and in Windows 2000, and you can find it through the following navigation route: Start | Programs | Accessories | System Tools | Systems Information. From the Systems Information option, you first select Tools and then the System Configuration Utility.

Another way to get to the System Configuration Utility tool is by going to the Start menu, choosing the Run option, typing "MSCONFIG" in the Open line, and then pressing Enter.

The MSCONFIG.EXE program first became available in Windows 98, where it was located under the same menu navigation route as Windows 2000, with the exception of choosing Diagnostic Startup as the last step.

The Windows 2000 System Configuration Utility presents a graphical interface with a number of tabs across the top area, just like any properties dialog box. Each tab is associated with a particular type of configuration, or an area within Windows where you can adjust specific settings. For example, the Startup window has been available as far back as Windows 3.0. By dragging a program icon or file name into the Startup window (or onto the Startup icon), you were able to change the underlying configuration of Windows without having to know the configuration details.

Windows 9x carried forward the idea of a Startup "group" where you could change the underlying Registry by dragging an icon or a program file name from the Explorer onto the Start menu, onto the Desktop, or into the \Windows\Start Menu\Programs\StartUp folder (in Explorer). The problems began when you had programs running during the Windows Startup that you didn't want to have running.

Unfortunately, the StartUp folder isn't the only place where Windows autoloads programs. Programs could be run from the WIN.INI file, with the LOAD= and RUN= lines, or even from within an AUTOEXEC.BAT file. In Windows 9x, you can run REGEDIT to examine the following location: HKEY_LOCAL_MACHINE/Software/Microsoft/Windows/Current Version/Run or Run Service. This is where you'll find *more* references to programs that will start with Windows, such as System Agent, NetMeeting, the active movie check, and so on.

For Windows 9x, startup programs may show up in the system Registry in four primary locations:

- HKEY_LOCAL_MACHINE\SOFTWARE\Microsoft\Windows\CurrentVersion\Run
- HKEY_LOCAL_MACHINE\SOFTWARE\Microsoft\Windows\CurrentVersion\RunServices
- HKEY_USERS\.DEFAULT\SOFTWARE\Microsoft\Windows\CurrentVersion\Run
- HKEY_CURRENT_USER\SOFTWARE\Microsoft\Windows\CurrentVersion\Run

You can see why the integrated System Configuration Utility in Windows 2000 is the first place to look for something as simple as a program you don't want to run during the Startup process. Additional tabs in the tool include General, System.ini, Win.ini, Static VxDs, Startup, Environment, and International. (Note the Static VxDs tab, showing the virtual device drivers we discussed in Chapters 11 and 12.) Each tab shows the current way Windows 2000 will start, and each tab has areas where specific configuration settings can be adjusted.

In Windows 98, the MSCONFIG.EXE System Configuration Utility tabs were General, Config.sys, Autoexec.bat, System.ini, Win.ini, and Startup.

In the previous chapter, we mentioned Tweak UI (where the UI stands for User Interface), and said that this is a set of more powerful tools used by in-house Microsoft tech support people. These tools worked in a similar fashion to the System Configuration Utility that came with Windows 98. The tool was an optional installation, and was not installed by default. If you chose to install it, it became available from Start | Settings | Control Panel, where you could double-click on the Tweak UI icon. In Windows 2000, the power tools went back into hiding, but a much more simplified "UI" option became available in a default installation.

Administrative Tools

The Windows 2000 Desktop is very similar to the Windows 9x Desktop, with a Start button that opens up a path to Programs, Accessories, and System Tools. From the System Tools option, you can then choose either the Administrative Tools option, which opens up the Control Panel series of tools, or the System Information option specifically. Figure 13.1 shows the Administrative Tools folder containing the various utility tools, including the Computer Management tool that opens up into the System Information area.

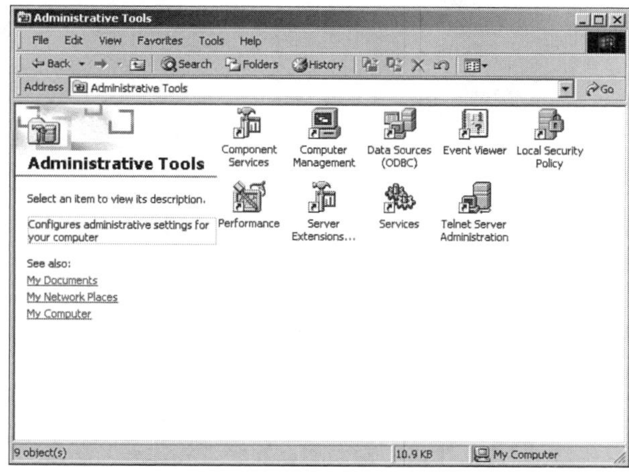

Figure 13.1 The Administrative Tools folder.

Figure 13.2 is the local Computer Management window, which looks remarkably like the Windows Explorer or the Windows Registry. The left panel is arranged in nodes and branches, and the right panel contains the specific lines of information pertaining to whichever local management tool you've highlighted. Note that the System Information section is only one of several tools. You can also see the System Tools section, Performance Logs and Alerts section, Shared Folders section, Device Manager section, and Local Users and Groups section.

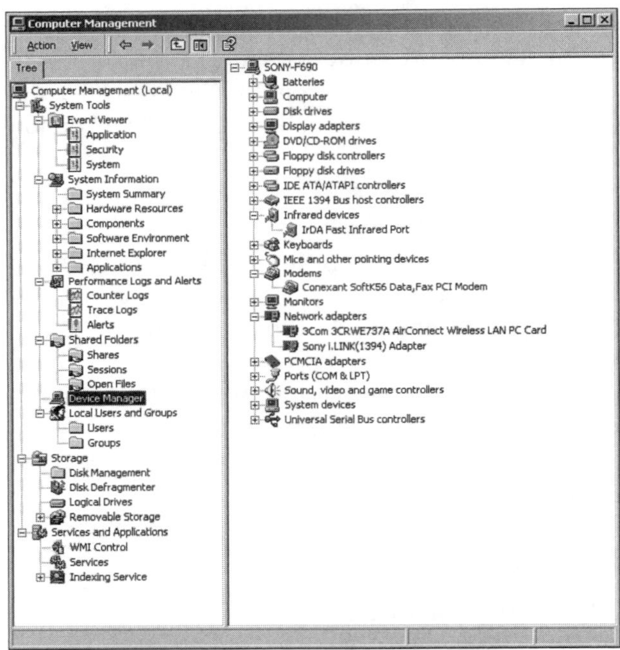

Figure 13.2 The administrative Computer Management tools window.

Each node has its branches, just like the Explorer and the Registry. For example, the System Information tool has a System Summary branch, which tells you all about the overall condition of the computer. You can run reports from these information tools, giving a detailed report of such things as available memory, percent of resources being used, and so on.

My Computer and Control Panel

Many court cases have proven that the Microsoft Windows Desktop bears little or no resemblance to the Apple Computer Macintosh Desktop. Any similarity of an icon representing the hardware attached to a specific computer is purely coincidental. Coincidentally, Windows uses an icon called My Computer (by default) to represent the computer you're working with. Double-clicking on the My Computer icon opens up a window listing all the accessible drives, along with a Control Panel icon and an Available Printers icon.

Right-clicking for the Properties menu on the My Computer icon opens a dialog box with several tabs, including the Device Manager. Whether you choose a pathway from the Start button or the My Computer icon, one way or another you'll have access to these system-reporting tools.

The Control Panel applet (tool) has been available since the first release of Windows, way back when. The only thing that's changed is how you get to the Control Panel and what new and interesting ways it offers for you to get into trouble…or rather, for troubleshooting. Part of the evolving security in Windows pertains to preventing an untrained user from accessing critical system components and whacking (technical term) the machine.

Windows 98 offered exceptional troubleshooting and diagnostics tools; however, those tools were readily accessible and made it too easy for end-users to cause problems. One of the main differences in Windows Me was that many of the configuration tools were hidden away from casual access. Windows NT and Windows 2000 can be set up to block access to some of the more critical configuration tools.

The Device Manager

We'll discuss the Device Manager again in Chapter 14, but you should know that, beginning with Windows 95, this was one of the tabs on the Properties dialog box arising out of the My Computer icon. As we've said, the Device Manager could also be accessed by navigating from the Start menu to Settings | Control Panel and then double-clicking the System icon.

The System icon gives you access to the specific device configurations for any device associated with the machine. The Windows 2000 Computer Management tool brings in the NT Event Manager and Local Security Policy tools, along with such things as Performance, Services, Server extensions, and other areas focusing on networking and dial-up connectivity.

The Device Manager is a graphic representation of all the hardware devices attached to the local machine. Aside from the various drives and controllers, monitors, and ports, one of the nodes in the Device Manager is the System Devices node. This is where low-level motherboard devices are listed, along with their configurations.

We'll be examining the Device Manager again in Chapter 14. Be sure you understand how to access any system device through the various navigational pathways you find in your reading.

Networking (My Network Places)

Another of the critical troubleshooting icons located in the Control Panel is the Network and Dial-up Connections icon. We'll follow a specific troubleshooting procedure in the next chapter, but we also want to mention this icon here. As you know, a local machine (your PC) can gain access to a network only when it has some way to physically connect to the wires and computers making up that network. Setting aside dial-up connections, the connection is generally accomplished with a network card (the NIC) plugged into an expansion slot on the motherboard. This is true for both cable-modems and DSL connections to the Internet.

Network cards come in many varieties and brands. However, each network card must not only be physically installed in a machine, but it must also be configured. We've said that a NIC has a specific address stored in ROM on the card, and that address must be initialized on the network. In order to make the card "visible" to the local machine, both the hardware and the operating system have to be reconfigured. This configuration process takes place in both the Device Manager and the Network icon in the Control Panel.

Interactive Partitioning

One of the interesting changes introduced with Windows NT and 2000 was the Storage section under the Computer Management tool (where System Information is also found). This graphic presentation of the physical disks attached to the system goes one step farther than simply presenting the partitioning information for the disks. Borrowing a good idea from PowerQuest, you can now manage partition chores, such as re-sizing or deleting, directly in the windows. On the one hand, this makes partitioning a drive a lot more intuitive, but on the other hand, it could lead to the total loss of any information on the system. This is another area where access rights can be assigned to allow or block the feature.

Some of these system tools make their first appearance in Windows 2000 and are unavailable in Windows NT.

System Agent

The System Agent was first available in Windows 98. You could begin at the Start menu and navigate a route through Programs and Accessories until you got to the last option, which was Maintenance Wizard. This tool provided a way to schedule tasks (date, time, and frequency), such as ScanDisk and defragmenting a drive. The same routing path held true in Windows 2000, except that the tool name was changed to Schedule Tasks.

Windows Update Manager

The Windows Update Manager is designed to provide automated access to changes and updates to the operating system. It first appeared in Windows 98 and continues in Window 2000 and XP. Ordinarily, Windows 98 installed an Internet shortcut to the Update Manager page located on www.microsoft.com. This icon was installed on the Start Menu during Setup. If the icon is missing or was removed, you can usually run the Update Manager by clicking Start; choosing Run; typing "wupdmgr.exe " (without quotes); and clicking OK.

Microsoft's Windows Update service assumes that everyone will eventually be connected to the Internet on a regular basis. If you are not using an always-on connection, you must first open a connection. The Update Wizard uses ActiveX controls, which are installed the first time you connect to the Update Manager page. As far as anyone knows, Microsoft does not use the Update Manager to gather any information other than what is necessary to check for updates.

Following the installation of the ActiveX controls, the Update Manager automatically compares device drivers installed on the computer with a database of updated drivers on the Microsoft server. If newer drivers are found on the server, you're presented with a list of these drivers. When a specific driver is selected, a new Web page opens, and the installation procedure takes place. The Update Wizard can also be run from the Device Manager, where choosing the Driver tab of any device will offer an option button to Update Driver.

After running the Update Manger, you can uninstall components added to the machine. This does not require an open online connection. From the System Information utility Tools menu, select Update Wizard Uninstall. The Wizard will step through the process of restoring the original file from the Windows\System\Reinstallbackups folder.

Windows File Protection (WFP)

Many times, installing a new program or application can lead to important files being overwritten. When the installation has completed, systems can begin acting strangely and become unstable. Typically, critical .EXE or .DLL files have been changed during the new installation, leading to mismatched file version or even completely different file contents. All .SYS, .DLL, .EXE, and .OCX files that ship on the Windows CD are protected. The True Type fonts; Micross.ttf, Tahoma.ttf, and Tahomabd.ttf, are also protected. Unfortunately, in many cases, neither the Uninstall Wizard nor a commercial uninstaller can fix the problem, given that the important system files had the same name.

Windows 98 and Me offered the System File Checker (SFC.EXE), and a feature called *System File Protection (SFP)*. Windows 2000 and Windows XP introduce the *Windows File Protection (WFP)* feature, designed to prevent this type of problem. WFP works similarly to SFP, by preventing automated installation and setup routines from replacing essential system files, but does it in a different way.

SFC is run manually; it then scans all protected system files and replaces incorrect versions with correct Microsoft versions. WFP, on the other hand, protects system files by running in the background and detecting attempts to replace protected system files. WFP is triggered after it receives a directory change notification on a file in a protected directory. Once this notification is received, WFP determines which file was changed. If the file is protected, WFP looks up the file signature in a catalog file to determine if the new file is the correct Microsoft version. If it is not, the operating system replaces the file with the correct version from the \dllcache directory or the original installation disk.

WFP logs an event to the system event log, noting the file replacement attempt. If the administrative user cancels the WFP file restoration, that causes an event to be logged, noting the cancellation.

The Windows XP core is much more protected than in Windows 2000. Essential system data cannot be overwritten by drivers or software installations, and .DLL files are now stored side by side on the hard disk. Each program uses its own Dynamic Link Libraries, almost guaranteeing much better reliability than Windows 2000.

System File Checker

The System File Checker is a command-line utility, meaning that it doesn't stay running in the background like WFP. SFC allows an Administrator to scan all protected files to verify their versions. System File Checker can also set the registry value SFCScan. On a Windows Me system, the program will also check and reinstall the \Systemroot\system32\dllcache directory. If the dllcache directory becomes corrupted or unusable, SFC can be run with various options that will try to repair the contents of the dllcache directory.

SFP on Windows Me

Most of the time, Windows Me became unstable following a setup application that either installed older versions of system files over newer versions, or that installed modified versions of system files without renaming them. In both cases, the newly installed application would cause failures in any other applications that depended on the later or unmodified version of the file.

System File Protection on Windows Me restored the original, correct version of a system file if a newly installed application replaced it with an incorrect version. SFP ran in the background on Windows Me, like WFP, monitoring all attempts to change protected system files. SFP could not be disabled on a Windows Me system.

One of the interesting things we see in Me is that the System File Monitor goes through the following procedure while protecting critical system files: It stores a copy of the original file, and then checks a database of catalog files to determine whether the new version of the file is a valid replacement. If the new version of the file is a valid replacement, Windows Me allows the new file to replace the old version; otherwise, it restores the original version of the file silently, *without alerting the end user*. The stored copy of the original file is deleted soon after the file is either replaced or restored. File corruption produced by something other than overwriting would not trigger SFP. If a protected system file becomes corrupted, the end user can replace the corrupted version of the file with a valid copy from the distribution media.

The Recovery Console

We remember when OS/2 Warp was first released on the market we asked how we could get to the "real" computer system, the black text-based screen with a DOS prompt. We were told we couldn't get there anymore, and that OS/2 was always in a graphic mode. It turned out that we could open an editor into the CONFIG.SYS file, which was a vastly expanded version of the old DOS file and contained all sorts of configuration options (much like the Registry).

Windows 2000 appears to be similar to OS/2 because it no longer provides an MS-DOS Mode command-line interface. You can run individual commands in the CMD.EXE line, but when the program or command terminates, you're returned to the Windows Desktop. We said that it appears to be this way, but in fact, Recovery Console is one of the utilities installed during a Windows 2000 setup.

Recovery Console gives you a way to run a nontransient command environment where almost all of the DOS commands continue to live on. Some of the more useful commands are **XCOPY**, **MOVE**, **CD**, **DEL**, and the good old **DIR** command. In many cases, a graphic environment requires so many mouse clicks that you can do the same thing a whole lot faster with a basic knowledge of DOS. In some instances, you can't do certain things in Windows.

The Recovery Console is one of the low-level troubleshooting utilities that comes with Windows 2000, but it may have its access blocked by a network administrator. On your own PC where you're given Administrator rights by default, you can still get to the old DOS-looking environment. See—there was a reason we talked at length about DOS in Chapter 10.

Windows XP

Once again, remember that Windows XP is not covered on the current A+ Exam. We described Windows 2000 as a blending of the usability of Windows 98 with the security, stability, scalability, and networking of NT. Well, that blending ended up more on the NT side of the house than the Windows 98 side of the house. Business users were delighted to trade some of the flexibility and interface options of Windows 98/Me for the benefits of Windows 2000. The home and small business consumer market was not nearly as delighted.

XP, like Win2000, comes in two versions: the Home and the Professional editions. Although both versions operate in the same way, XP Professional provides additional functionality required in corporate installations. Windows XP has a redesigned desktop, similar to Windows 2000, but much more intuitive. Internet integration and Microsoft Office integration is also carried to a whole new level in XP (a point some find disturbing), with additional enhancements to an already extensive suite of diagnostics and trouble shooting tools.

Windows Product Activation (WPA)

Windows XP is also the first operating system to feature a new Windows Product Activation technology, designed to cut down on software piracy. Microsoft estimates that close to eighty percent of the machines running Windows are doing so in violation of the licensing agreement. The new activation procedure will create a unique ID for a specific machine, based on an analysis of the hardware on that machine. The ID is then matched to the Product Key.

The user has 30 days to activate Windows XP, after which the system won't work. Once activated, Windows XP will only work with the exact computer defined by the identification code. This prevents the OS from being installed on *any* other computer. In fact, if you make a significant change in your system (adding new hardware), Windows XP may very well stop working until you go through other activation procedure. Activation can be accomplished over the Internet, where the authenticity of the license is checked and the copy of XP is unlocked. For buyers who are not connected to the Internet, Microsoft provides an Activation process via the phone.

Reduced Startup Time

Over the years, Windows has taken longer and longer to load all the various components and start the machine. In an age of microwave popcorn and always-on DSL connections, more and more people have complained about the slow startup time. Microsoft has put some serious effort into this complaint with Windows XP, and has dramatically reduced the waiting time. Previous versions of Windows could easily take two minutes or more to start. Windows XP now loads in less than 1 minute, although complex configurations of such things as SCSI cards can slow things down. Even so, it's a nice enhancement.

Summary—Windows 2000

Much of the preceding section was devoted to the similarities between Windows 2000 and its NT ancestor. Because this version of Windows was still quite new when the current exam was in development, most of the questions deal with diagnostics. We've indicated in many places where you should make a note as to a menu path or a diagnostics tool. In the next chapter we'll run through many of these tools once again, but you should be comfortable with the overall manner in which Windows 2000 is presented, and the working steps involved with getting around in the Desktop interface.

Practice Questions

Question 1

Which of the following two modules are contained in the Windows NT Kernel Mode?

- ❍ a. The Executive assistant and Security Options layer
- ❍ b. The Hardware Abstraction layer and Executive layer
- ❍ c. The User Applications layer and Hardware Abstraction layer
- ❍ d. The Executive layer and Local Security Authority layer

Answer b is correct. The Kernel Mode is divided into two layers. The lower layer is the hardware abstraction layer (HAL), and the higher layer is the Executive layer. Answer a is incorrect as there is no Executive Assistant or Security Options layer. Answer c is incorrect because it confuses a User Applications layer with the User Mode and the Applications layer. Answer d is incorrect because the Local Security Authority is part of the Security Reference Monitor module within the Executive layer.

Question 2

A Windows 2000 network can be divided into ______, ______, and ______.

- ❍ a. computers, stars, base topologies
- ❍ b. groups, profiles, accounts
- ❍ c. users, groups, domains
- ❍ d. domains, directories, profiles

Answer c is correct. NT and 2000 networks are commonly divided into individual users, groups of objects, and large domains of groups. Answer a is incorrect in the use of base topologies, and because star topologies are architecture types rather than network divisions. Answer b is incorrect because profiles and accounts are associated with both groups and users. Answer d is incorrect because networks aren't commonly divided into directories and profiles.

Question 3

Which two tools or utilities would you use to troubleshoot a Windows NT computer that failed to successfully boot?

- ❑ a. A bootable system disk
- ❑ b. The emergency repair utility
- ❑ c. A systems information disk
- ❑ d. An emergency repair disk

Answers a and d are correct. NT and Windows 2000 both provide an opportunity to create a bootable system disk and an emergency repair disk. The emergency repair disk is customized to a specific machine, but both disks can be tried with a machine that fails to boot. Answer b is incorrect because it refers to the ERU.EXE utility in Windows 9x that is used to back up a Registry. Answer c is incorrect because there is no such disk.

Question 4

What are the requirements for an employee to gain access to a printer in the Accounting domain? [Choose the two best answers]

- ❑ a. An access code
- ❑ b. A user identification
- ❑ c. A group password
- ❑ d. A guest account

Answers b and c are correct. User accounts can have a password that differs from the password given to that user as part of a group. The question refers to requirements and an Accounting domain, implying that some sort of password is required. NT and 2000 networks require a User ID (identification). Answer a is incorrect because an access code is usually applied to an entryway of some sort and is much too broad a term to be applied to the operating system. Answer d is incorrect because a Guest account is almost always assigned extremely limited rights and would rarely allow access to Accounting department information.

Question 5

WINLOGON.EXE is the program file that runs the ______ procedure and begins the ______.

- a. logon, Local Security Authority
- b. Windows splash screen, logon process
- c. Session Manager, security logon process
- d. logon, device loading process.

Answer a is correct. The WINLOGON program initiates the logon procedure, which then starts the Local Security Authority (LSA). Answer b is incorrect because no program runs the splash screen; the splash screen is called by a program. Answer c is incorrect because the Session Manager is part of the basic NT operating system and loads near the beginning. Answer d is incorrect because devices are loaded and initialized in several places prior to the logon process.

Question 6

Which of the following cannot be done in the Recovery Console?

- a. Run an XCOPY procedure.
- b. Access the Registry HKeys.
- c. Examine partition information.
- d. Format a system disk.

Answer b is correct. The Recovery Console allows all DOS command-line operations that do not require a graphical interface. The Registry Editor is a graphic editing environment run through REGEDT32.EXE and, as such, requires that you be in a Windows GUI environment. Answer a is incorrect because XCOPY is a commonly used file-copying utility program found only in DOS. Answer c is incorrect because FDISK is capable of reporting on partitions without necessarily re-partitioning a disk. Answer d is incorrect because formatting a floppy disk is a common option for a command-line interface.

Need to Know More?

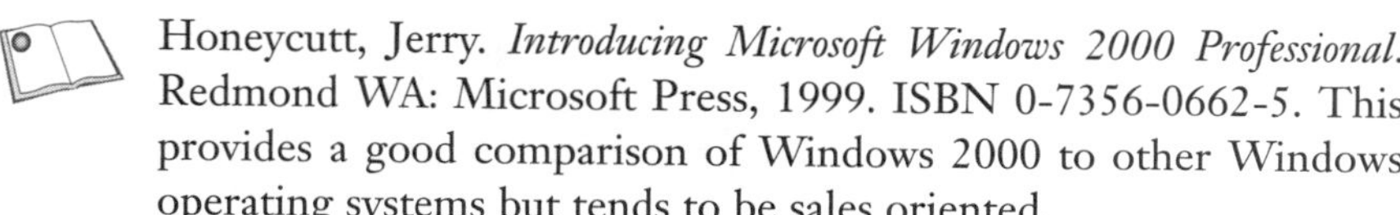

Honeycutt, Jerry. *Introducing Microsoft Windows 2000 Professional.* Redmond WA: Microsoft Press, 1999. ISBN 0-7356-0662-5. This provides a good comparison of Windows 2000 to other Windows operating systems but tends to be sales oriented.

Matthews, Martin S. *Windows 2000, A Beginners Guide*. Berkley, CA: Osborne/McGraw-Hill, 2000. ISBN 0072123249. This is the one "must-have" book for anybody new to Windows 2000 in a network environment. It simply covers it all.

Pearce, Eric. *Windows NT in a Nutshell.* Sebastol, CA: O'Reilly & Associates, 1997. ISBN 1-56592-251-4. This is a very good "how to" book for day-to-day operation of Windows NT.

Troubleshooting

Terms you'll need to understand:

✓ Startup function keys
✓ Safe Mode, Last Known Good configuration
✓ Emergency Repair Disk (ERD)
✓ ScanReg and Recovery Console

Concepts you'll need to master:

✓ Windows startup process and failures
✓ Last successful Registry files
✓ Command line operations and commands
✓ Network connectivity

In many cases, your first contact with a problem PC will be when the person using it says, "*I don't know what the problem is. Everything was working just fine yesterday, and now it* [fill in the exam question]." Startup problems are among the most common situations you'll encounter, where the system won't boot up, or the operating environment won't start. Another common problem is where an unknown system requires some sort of identification, repair, or optimization. Often, a written problem description will be taped to the box. If there is no information at all attached to the computer, don't worry: As you'll see in this chapter, a computer can be made to report almost everything about itself.

In the following discussion, we break out troubleshooting problems into three broad categories:

- *Startup problems*—Refer to events surrounding a failure to load the operating system.
- *Boot and hardware problems*—Refer to hardware and booting events taking place between the time the power is switched on and when the operating system takes control.
- *Connectivity problems*—Assume that a machine has booted up and an operating system is present. In this case, the machine is not connecting to an existing network.

Throughout the book, we've discussed various things that can go wrong and the typical ways they can be fixed. Once again, this is not a comprehensive book about computer technology, nor is it a technical repair manual; it is designed as a compressed review of PC technology. This chapter is meant to help with the types of troubleshooting questions you're likely to encounter on the exam, and the typical diagnostics tools used in repairing those problems.

For the most part, when we mention Windows 2000, you can include Windows XP. Windows XP is not covered on the current exam.

Startup Function Keys

By default, certain function keys are available in DOS, Windows 9x, and Windows 2000. Although each operating system uses the same set of keys, specific keys work differently at startup. System Administrators can disable access to these function keys, either by editing MSDOS.SYS or with customization utilities such as Tweak UI. Table 14.1 is a listing of the function keys and how they are used.

Table 14.1 The startup function keys.

Keys	OS	Description
F5	DOS	Bypass all the commands in your CONFIG.SYS and AUTOEXEC.BAT files when the text "Starting MS-DOS…" appears.
F8	DOS	Steps through each individual command in the AUTOEXEC.BAT and CONFIG.SYS files. To carry out all remaining startup commands, press ESC.
Ctrl-F5	DOS	Bypasses all the commands in your CONFIG.SYS and AUTOEXEC.BAT files and does not load DRVSPACE.BIN.
Ctrl-F8	DOS	Bypasses loading DRVSPACE.BIN and provides interactive Y/N for individual commands in CONFIG.SYS and AUTOEXEC.BAT files. To carry out all remaining startup commands, press ESC. To bypass all remaining startup commands, press F5.
F4	Windows 95	Starts the previous version of MS-DOS or Windows 3.1 if it was installed before.
F5	Windows 95	Starts in Safe Mode. Very few drivers are loaded and no backup of the registry is made to prevent using a corrupt copy. The screen resolution is VGA 640x480, 16 colors, and network is not supported.
F6	Windows 95	Starts in Safe Mode with network support.
F8	Windows 95, 98, SE, Me, 2000, XP	Displays the Windows Startup menu. In Windows 98 and Me, the F8 key is still functional, but there is no "Starting Windows…" prompt, so it's hard to know exactly when to press it. Use the CTRL key.
Ctrl	Windows 98, Me	Hold the CTRL key down while your computer is booting to pause at the Windows 98 and Windows Me Interactive Boot Menu.
Shift+F8	Windows 95, 98	Interactive start, where the system asks for confirmation for each line in CONFIG.SYS and AUTOEXEC.BAT.

(continued)

Table 14.1 The startup function keys *(continued)*

Keys	OS	Description
SHIFT	Windows 3x, 95	Holding the Shift key down during Startup prevents all programs in the Startup group from loading.
SHIFT (Restart)	Windows 98	If you choose RESTART during a Windows 98 Shutdown, holding the Shift key while clicking on Okay will avoid restarting the machine from a cold boot. This option restarts the Windows Explorer shell.
SHIFT	Windows 2000, XP	You can bypass the Startup folders during logon by holding down the Shift key. First, type your password at logon; then hold down the Shift key and continue holding Shift until the logon process completes.

Startup Problems

One of the most frequent causes of Windows problems involves changing a configuration or installing a new application. Invariably, the user will restart the machine, paying no attention to testing the post-installation stability of the system. The startup sequence was covered in Chapters 12 and 13, and the following section will focus on specific diagnostic and repair situations.

The initial strategy for fixing a machine with a startup problem is to begin with the last working Registry files. In their most basic attempts to safeguard the Registry files, Windows 9x and 2000 will automatically attempt to use a previous version of the files if the system crashes during startup. In some cases this is helpful, but in other instances, all that happens is that previously useful Registry files now become corrupted as well. If none of the available Registry files work, Windows will try to start in Safe Mode.

In Windows 2000, you'll also have the option of using a Last Known Good hardware profile. If the problem can't be solved, you'll have to try an emergency boot disk, an Emergency Repair Disk (ERD), or a software utility program. If the machine manages to get past the startup but is running erratically, Windows 9x, 2000, and XP all offer Safe Mode.

Realistically, the typical strategy for fixing almost any computer problems, these days, is to reformat the hard drive and reinstall an original disk image created by the computer vendor. These so-called recovery disks have been mentioned previously, and can be a menace to anyone who isn't aware of their function. They are not designed to recover anything, but are designed to reset the hard drive to its original state. In a way, these recovery disks are to applications, what a system reset (re-boot) is to RAM. Anything that hasn't been saved in a safe location is wiped from memory, and the machine is returned to the condition it was in when it was purchased.

Windows Crashes

Windows 2000 and XP are perhaps the most stable versions of Windows on the market. However, they still crash unexpectedly, or go through mysterious restarts from time to time. There are a number of good Web sites devoted to the increasingly complex issues of troubleshooting Windows 2000 and Windows XP. We've included some of the sites we found under the "Need To Know More" heading at the end of this chapter. Discussion forums, such as those found on Annoyances.org (**http://www.annoyances.org**), indicate that system crashes are most often caused by the following situations:

- *Corrupted Registry files*—Editing the Registry; installation routines; or changes to low-level configuration settings can cause a failure in the Registry. The machine will usually become unstable and attempt to start in Safe Mode with the next startup.
- *Power Supplies and Heat*—An insufficient power supply, especially on machines with multiple expansion cards, drives, or cooling fans, should be upgraded to at least a 350-400W power supply. If the power supply is faulty, it should be replaced (not repaired). Make sure the cooling fan or fans are working, and that there is adequate ventilation around the computer case. Temperature problems are very hard to diagnose. Some of today's computers provide a CPU temperature reading (see the computer's reference manual).
- *Sound Cards*—Even though most sound cards can be recognized by the Windows Plug-and-Play database, they continue to cause problems. Before you install drivers and files for an add-on sound card, be sure to back up the Registry.
- *USB Hubs*—These seem to be an important reason for system crashes, particularly hotsync cradles for handheld devices (e.g., Palm, Handspring, Sony, etc.). If the system crashes on a regular basis, try taking out the USB device. If that solves the problem, contact the manufacturer for possible driver updates.

- *Loose PCI Cards*—Another reason for continuing crashes may be loose expansion cards. All the way back to the original XTs, loose memory modules were causing trouble. The development of in-line memory modules solved the problem by hardwiring the chips to an IC board (SIMMs and DIMMs). Add-on cards are becoming less necessary, as integrated motherboards and USB devices become more prevalent. Reseat all the expansion cards and restart the machine. Use the Device Manager to remove the driver information, and Windows will rescan the system, reinstalling the devices.
- *Memory Modules*—Most machines will experience unusual stability problems if there's a bad memory chip or module in the system. Commercial hardware analysis software products, such as Smith Micro, Inc.'s *Check-It* (**http://www.smithmicro.com**) can do comprehensive tests of all the hardware in a system, including the memory. Otherwise, you'll have to remove each module, one at a time, to see if it's the cause of the problem. Keep in mind that some computers require that memory modules work in pairs. If this is the case (see the computer's reference manual), then be sure to remove and replace the modules in pairs.
- *File Management Systems*—There may be more than one nonremovable disk in the system. If one drive is using NTFS while another is using FAT32, the different file management systems can sometimes be the source of the problem. Try converting all the drives to the NT File System (NTFS) and see if that solves the problem.

Troubleshooting Strategies

Figuring out why a computer fails to start, or why it crashes in the middle of a session, is a large part of what makes being a tech support person such a joy. Windows 9x routinely throws up globs of error messages, offering you the option of choosing a "Details" button as an explanation for the error. The details are lines of hexadecimal addresses, none of which make any sense to most living human beings. There are, however, clues to be found in the particular kind of behavior associated with a crash. For example, foot-long flames shooting from the top of the monitor indicate a fire of some sort. In situations like this, the A+ Certified technician will generally run screaming out of the building, or call the fire department.

When the boot process fails, you'll probably be left with a complete lock-up, a blank screen, an automatic reboot, or a blue error screen (the so-called blue screen of death). For example, if the system boots to a blank screen, it often means there's a video problem, or a video driver set to the wrong resolution.

If the system boots to a blue screen, it's often due to an incorrect device driver or a failure with a piece of hardware. Each blue screen lists an error message, pointing to a specific problem. Grab a bottle of aspirin, then check the Windows 2000 Resource Kit, or go to the Microsoft Support Web site (**http://www.microsoft.com**) for the meaning of specific error messages.

We cannot guarantee that any of the Web sites referenced in this book will continue to be available online. We've tried to choose those sites that appear to have some longevity and stability. If a site is no longer accessible, use any search engine to query the Internet for specific problems.

Restoring a System

A complete restore, often called a *full restore*, is not the same thing as a Windows reinstallation (i.e., a reinstall). In most cases, a reinstall will fix corrupted system files or files that have been over-written by some program's installation routine. Afterwards, you may have to reinstall various applications, but the Windows reinstallation should keep any configuration files that were previously on the hard drive. This may be a bad thing, if one of those files is causing the constant crashing.

A full restoration means that you're about to reformat the hard drive and restore (or recover) everything from a backup of some kind. This will allow you to lose any data added to the system following that last backup. We say "allow," because so many of today's technical support personnel seem to think this is the very best option to start with. If it weren't such a good idea, then why do so many tech support calls end with a completely restored system and none of the user's data?

Okay, we're being a bit facetious here, but if you've tested everything you can test and the machine continues to crash, then a full restore may be your only remaining option. The restoration can be from either a vendor's original system disk, or from a backup of some kind—a disk image on a CD-R or DVD, a tape backup, or an image file on a network server.

The problem with a full restoration is that you can't restore a backup unless you have a running copy of Windows. For the most part, this will mean reformatting the hard drive. Install Windows to a different, temporary directory. When you finally can run the backup, Windows will go to its expected folder, preventing the just-installed version from being over-written. Windows is being reinstalled only in order to gain access to the backup and restore functions. If this solves the problem, you can then go back and remove the temporary Windows folder and leave the restored version in place.

The Device Manager

The Device Manager is used to manage the system hardware. If you find a problem device, you can remove, disable, or reconfigure the device, or update the driver. If the computer starts correctly, that particular device may be the cause of the problem.

When you install a new piece of hardware, Windows is supposed to be able to detect that something new has been connected to the system. It will scan the hard drive for a software driver and then try to find a driver on the original installation disk. Failing that, Windows will ask you if you have a disk with driver software, or allow you to connect to the Windows Update site on the Microsoft Web site. After the hardware is correctly installed, you can access the Device Manager in three typical ways:

- Move through Start | Settings | Control Panel to the System icon. Double-click the System icon and choose the Device Manager tab.
- Double-click on the My Computer icon, located on the Desktop, and choose the Control Panel icon. Double-click on the Control Panel; then double-click on the System icon. Choose the Device Manager tab.
- Right-click on the My Computer icon and choose Properties from the context menu. Choose the Device Manager tab from the System Properties dialog box.
- In Windows 2000, access the Device Manager using the following steps:
    - Right-click the My Computer icon and choose the Properties option.
    - Chose the Hardware Tab; then choose the Device Manager.

If a symbol is displayed next to a device (e.g., an exclamation point), there may be a problem with the device. To disable a device in the Windows 9x Device Manager, click on the device name and choose Remove. In Windows 2000, right-click on the device name; then click Disable. The following symbols indicate types of problems:

- A black exclamation point (!) on a yellow field indicates the device is in a problem state. Note that a device that is in a problem state can be functioning. There is usually also an associated problem code.
- A red "X" indicates a disabled device that is physically present in the computer and is consuming resources, but that does not have a protected-mode driver loaded.

- A blue "i" on a white field (found under the Computer properties) on a device resource indicates that the Use Automatic Settings feature is not selected for the device. The resource was manually selected; however, this does not indicate a problem or disabled state.
- (Windows Me) A green question mark "?" means that a compatible driver for this device is installed, indicating the possibility that all the features of the device may not be accessible.

If you disable a device in Windows 2000, check that the device is listed on the Windows 2000 Hardware Compatibility List (HCL), and that it is correctly installed. If the problem persists, contact the manufacturer to see about a possible version update or to report the problem.

Device Resources (Windows 2000)

To check for possible device conflicts, double-click the device name; then choose the Resources tab. If there is a device conflict, it should be listed under Conflicting Device list. If Windows successfully detects a device and the device is functioning correctly, the "Use Automatic Settings" check box will be selected. If the resource settings are based on "Basic Configuration," you may have to change the configuration. To do so, either click a different basic configuration from the list, or manually change the resource settings.

This procedure may require you to change the computer's CMOS settings, as well as the BIOS settings. If you make the wrong changes to these setting, you may be unable to start the machine at all.

If the computer starts correctly, the device that you disabled may be the cause of the startup problem. Check to see if the device is listed on the Windows 2000 Hardware Compatibility List (HCL), and that it is installed correctly. You may also want to contact the manufacturer.

Windows 9x Safe Mode

Windows 9x introduced Safe Mode as a way to start a bare-bones instance of the operating system. Safe Mode was one of the options in a text-based menu running from a DOS environment, just prior to loading WIN.COM. We discuss the Interactive Menu in Chapter 12, "Windows 95, 98, and Me."

Windows 95

To start Windows 95 in Safe Mode, press the F8 key when you see the "Starting Windows 95" message; then choose Safe Mode from the Startup menu. If you still can't start the computer, reinstall Windows 95 into a new, empty folder (as opposed to over the existing installation). This step helps to establish whether the problem is related to a remnant of the previous operating system (such as a configuration setting) or a hardware problem.

Because Windows 95 OS/R-B was designed to be preinstalled on new hard disks, booting to a previous operating system was unsupported. The Startup menu did not have this option. However, people were able to purchase OS/R-B on the gray market. They would install it on machines with a previous version of Windows and then try to boot the previous operating system. The system would hang and crash.

Windows 98 and Windows Me

To start Windows 98 or Me in Safe Mode, restart your computer; then press and hold down the CTRL key until the interactive Startup menu appears. You can then choose Safe Mode. If Windows 98 or Me won't start in Safe Mode, there may be a problem with the Registry. Run the Windows Registry Checker (Scanreg.exe) tool.

To start Windows Registry Checker, restart your computer, press and hold the CTRL key, and then choose Command Prompt Only. Type SCANREG and then press ENTER. To use SCANREG to restore a previous version of the Registry:

1. Restart your computer with the Startup disk in your floppy disk drive; choose the Minimal Boot option.
2. Type **scanreg /restore** at the command line and then press ENTER.

The Registry Checker requires extended memory in order to operate properly. It will not run if you start your computer with the Safe Mode Command Prompt Only option. The only exception to this is the **scanreg /restore** command. This is the only ScanReg function that can run without extended memory. This means you cannot use the Shutdown "Restart in MS DOS Mode" option to run other ScanReg options.

The Emergency Repair Utility (ERU.EXE) backup program was changed to the Registry Checker in Windows 98 and Me. Not only can SCANREGW.EXE be used to back up and restore the Registry files, but the Registry Checker attempts to go through corrupted system files and make a best guess as to how to fix them. The DOS version of the Registry Checker is SCANREG.EXE. This is the program used to run **scanreg /restore**, and is also used during the installation procedure.

The last good Registry is not the same as the Last Known Good *hardware* profile Windows NT, 2000, and XP choose when you press the spacebar during a boot process.

Windows 95 Emergency Recovery Utility (ERU.EXE)

We've discussed the fact that Windows attempts to use a previously existing version of the system registration files. We've also said that sometimes a corrupted hardware profile can cause previous system files to also become corrupted. Windows 95 provided the Emergency Recovery Utility (ERU.EXE) as a way to back up and restore the system registration files. You cannot mix and match Registry files, and the system will fail to start if Windows 95 Registry files are restored into a Windows 98 system.

Windows 2000 also has the ERU tool, along with the Emergency Repair Disk. You should know that in order to use the Emergency Recover Utility, Windows 2000 requires an Emergency Repair Disk and a repair folder located somewhere on the computer's hard disk. The Windows NT/2000 emergency disks were covered in Chapter 13, "Troubleshooting Tools."

Emergency Repair Disk

Windows 2000 (and XP) does not provide the option to create an emergency startup disk as you were able to do in Windows 95 and 98. If you remember, you could go to the Control Panel, in those versions, and choose Add/Remove Software. You could then choose the Startup tab and choose Create a Startup Disk.

Windows 2000 uses the following steps to create an Emergency Repair Disk:

1. From the desktop, choose Start | Programs | Accessories | System tools and then Backup.
2. You will be given three options: Backup, Restore, and Emergency Repair Disk.
3. Choose "Emergency Repair Disk," and a wizard will walk you through the process of creating the disk

The Emergency Repair Disk, otherwise known as an *ERD*, is created during the Setup process. It contains a backup copy of the BOOT.INI file, along with several critical Registry keys. The ERD must be kept up-to-date with any configuration changes you make to the machine; otherwise, it won't do a very good job of fixing an emergency problem.

If you have a current ERD, simply boot the system off the Windows 2000 boot floppies. When you reach the point at which Setup asks if you want to set up Windows 2000 or repair an existing installation, choose the repair option and follow the prompts. Before the repair process begins, you'll be asked if you want to use a fast repair or a manual repair.

A fast repair automatically updates some key system files, the Registry, the boot sector, and the startup environment. A manual repair is most useful when you already know what's wrong with the system, and you don't want to overwrite anything you don't have to.

The Emergency Repair Process

If you have created an Emergency Repair Disk (ERD), use it to troubleshoot and resolve the startup problem. Note that the emergency repair process is limited to repairing the system files, the partition boot sector, and the startup environment.

If a problem takes place after you click the **Microsoft Windows 2000** option on the boot loader menu, or when you receive the "Please select the operating system to start" message, operating system files may be missing or damaged.

Windows 2000 Safe Mode

Safe Mode helps you diagnose problems. If a symptom does not reappear when you start in Safe Mode, the default settings and minimum device drivers were not the cause. Many times, a new device was added or a driver file was changed. You can use Safe Mode to remove the device or reverse the change to the driver file. Remove any newly added hardware and restart the computer, and see if this fixes the problem.

To start Windows 2000 in Safe Mode, press F8 when you see the message: "Please select the operating system to start." In the Windows Advanced Option Menu, use the arrow keys to select Safe Mode and press ENTER. If you are running other operating systems on the computer, click Microsoft Windows 2000; then press ENTER.

In Safe Mode, Windows 2000 uses only basic files and drivers (mouse, monitor, keyboard, disks, base video, default system services, and no network connections). You can choose the Safe Mode with Networking option, which loads also the essential services and drivers to start networking. You can also choose Safe Mode with Command Prompt option, which is exactly the same as Safe Mode except it starts a command prompt instead of Windows 2000. The Interactive Start Menu for Windows 2000 is as follows:

- *Safe Mode with Networking*—Starts Windows 2000 using only basic files and drivers, plus network connections.
- *Safe Mode with Command Prompt*—After logging on, once again using only basic files and drivers, the system stops at a command prompt. The GUI is not loaded.
- *Enable Boot Logging*—Logs all drivers and services that were loaded (or not loaded) to the NTBTLOG.TXT file, located in the %windir% directory. Safe Mode, Safe Mode with Networking, and Safe Mode with Command Prompt use the boot log to list all drivers and services being loaded.
- *Enable VGA Mode*—Starts Windows 2000 using the standard VGA driver. This is useful if you have installed a new video driver and Windows 2000 is not starting properly. The basic video driver is also used when you start Windows 2000 in Safe Mode, Safe Mode with Networking, or Safe Mode with Command Prompt.
- *Last Known Good Configuration*—Starts Windows 2000 using the registry information saved at the last successful shutdown. Last Known Good does not solve problems caused by corrupted or missing drivers or files. Any changes made in the current session will be lost.
- *Directory Service Restore Mode (Not available in Windows 2000 Professional)*—This is used by Windows 2000 Server for restoring the SYSVOL directory and the Active Directory directory service on a domain controller.
- *Debugging Mode*—Starts Windows 2000 while sending debug information through a serial cable to another computer.

If you are using, or have used, Remote Install Services to install Windows 2000 on your computer, you may see additional options related to restoring or recovering your system using Remote Install Services.

Last Known Good

Every time Windows 2000 boots successfully, Windows copies its configuration settings to a set of System Registration files. During a normal boot process, Windows displays the message, “Press the Spacebar for Last Known Good Configuration.” Pressing the spacebar causes Windows to use the configuration it used during the last successful boot.

The Last Known Good Configuration starts the computer using Registry information saved at the last proper shutdown. Windows 9x did this automatically, if it detected a problem during Startup. However, there was very little the user could do from a startup menu, to specifically choose a previous copy of the Registry.

If you find startup problems after making a major configuration change to the computer, try using the Last Known Good Configuration feature. These kinds of changes might include installing a new device and software driver, or a new software application.

Remember that this last Registry is created during a successful and proper Shutdown event. When you start the computer using the Last Known Good configuration, the configuration will not contain any changes that were made since the last successful startup.

If you can start the computer with Last Known Good Configuration, then chances are that one of the last changes was the cause of the problem. Revert the change by removing or updating the driver; uninstall the program, and restart the machine. Contact the device or software vendor for compatibility information.

Selective Startup (MSCONFIG.EXE)

From the Start menu, choose the Run option and type **msconfig** in the "Open" dialog box. This is the Microsoft System Configuration utility, designed to gather all the startup information into one interactive dialog box. MSCONFIG was introduced in Windows 95, but was featured in a more obvious way with the release of Windows 98.

The General tab of the System Configuration Utility offers choices for a Normal startup, a Diagnostic startup, where you can selectively choose device drivers and software, and the Selective startup. The Selective startup has a set of check boxes that let you choose whether or not to process the CONFIG.SYS, AUTOEXEC.BAT, WIN.INI, SYSTEM.INI, or Startup Group. Windows 2000 is slightly different, and Table 14.2 demonstrates the four different boot options under Selective Startup. The table indicates the items each boot option verifies.

Table 14.2 Selective startup options of the System Configuration Utility.

Description	Boot A	Boot B	Boot C	Boot D
Process System.ini file	Yes	No	Yes	Yes
Process Win.ini file	No	Yes	Yes	Yes
Load Static VxD	Yes	Yes	No	Yes
Load Startup group items	Yes	Yes	Yes	No

If the Load Startup Group Item is grayed-out, the Startup Group has been customized at some point. Click the Startup tab at the top and record the startup items that are checked so you can return to this customized configuration after the installation.

MSCONFIG is available for Window 9x, Me, 2000, and XP. Windows 95 and Windows 2000 used a special version, but still called MSCONFIG.EXE. Windows 95 should have the file in the C:\Windows\System folder. Windows 2000 users should have it in the C:\WINNT\system32 folder.

Windows Me

The System Configuration Utility tool cannot disable a file that has the read-only attribute: Even so, it pretends that it did. To determine if the System Configuration Utility tool has replaced the file that you are trying to disable, open the file. If the System Configuration Utility did replace the file, you should see the following text at the beginning of the file:

```
rem
rem   *** DO NOT EDIT THIS FILE! ***
rem
rem   This file was created by the System Configuration Utility as
rem   a placeholder for your SYSTEM.INI file. Your actual
rem   SYSTEM.INI file has been saved under the name SYSTEM.TSH.
rem
```

This is reminiscent of how Windows Me would hide and change basic configuration files on its own, without notifying the computer user.

Windows Me and Fast CPUs

Your computer may stop responding (hang) during the boot process if the computer contains a processor that runs at 850 megahertz (MHz) or faster. When this occurs, the computer hangs before the Windows Millennium Edition (Me) bitmap is displayed. Computers with a Japanese BIOS may be more susceptible to this problem.

A supported fix is now available from Microsoft, but it is only intended to correct the problem described in this article and should be applied only to systems experiencing this specific problem. See the Microsoft Service Link: **http://support.microsoft.com/?id=kb;en-us;Q278844**.

Windows XP Advanced Startup

Use the Advanced Startup option to run Windows XP Professional in troubleshooting mode. Click Start and then click Shutdown. When you're asked, "What do you want the computer to do?" click Restart, and OK. When the list of available operating systems appears, press the F8 key. On the "Advanced Options" screen, select the startup option you want and then press ENTER.

System Information

The System Information tool displays a comprehensive view of the computer's hardware, the system components, and the software environment. Use this tool to help you identify possible problem devices and device conflicts. To do so, follow these steps:

1. Click Start and then click Run.
2. In the Open box, type **msinfo32** and then click OK. Check for problem devices or device conflicts.
3. In the console tree, click to expand Components and then click Problem Devices. Note any devices that are listed in the right pane.
4. In the console tree, click to expand Hardware Resources; then click Conflicts/Sharing. Note any resource conflicts that are listed in the right pane.

If no problem devices or conflicts are reported by the System Information tool, check for programs that start automatically when Windows starts. To do so, follow these steps:

1. In the console tree, click to expand Software Environment and then click Startup Programs.
2. Programs that start automatically when Windows starts are listed in the right pane.
3. Disable the programs, and then restart the computer.

For more information about how to disable the program, refer to the program documentation or contact the manufacturer. If you disable the startup programs, and the startup problem is resolved, enable the programs again, one at a time. Shut down and restart the computer each time you enable a program, and note if the incorrect startup behavior occurs. If the behavior occurs, the last program that you enabled may be causing the incorrect startup behavior.

LOGVIEW.EXE

Windows 9x includes the SYSEDIT.EXE program that came with Windows 3.11. System Edit examines initial configuration files, but doesn't open the Windows log files. Log files can be opened with any ASCII text editor (e.g., Notepad or WordPad) for viewing and printing.

Log files are plain ASCII text files (.TXT) that show when a program was last run and that report any problems encountered at the time. If they find no problems, the log file holds an exit-status report. The LOGVIEW.EXE program utility is similar to SYSEDIT, but shows all the log files on the drive.

LOGVIEW.EXE is found in the OTHER\MISC\LOGVIEW folder on the Windows 9x installation CD-ROM and must be copied from the CD-ROM manually to a destination on the hard drive.

BOOTLOG.TXT

The BOOTLOG.TXT file is a hidden ASCII text file located in the root directory of the primary active drive. This file keeps a record of the entire startup process for the first time Windows is installed successfully. The F8 option for an interactive Startup menu (pressed when the "Starting Windows 9x" message displays at bootup) allows you to create a new BOOTLOG.TXT file at any time. Additionally, you can create a new file by using the /B switch with WIN.COM (i.e., WIN /B) from a DOS command prompt in MS DOS Mode.

The details in the BOOTLOG.TXT file are written in sequence during the startup and generally break down to about five major sections. Although a line in the BOOTLOG.TXT file might indicate that something has failed, it doesn't necessarily mean that the startup process has aborted. For example, a loadfailed= line entry means that the specified VxD failed to load for some reason, probably because whatever the driver was referring to doesn't exist or couldn't be found.

Another reason for a "failed" line in the boot log may be that something was actually successful. Windows often loads a driver or file into memory and then unloads it again. Following the unloading, it will check to see if the removal was successful. When the check is completed, the device does not exist and may generate a fail notice.

It's usually wise to make a copy of the BOOTLOG.TXT file before creating a new one, just to have a copy of a successful installation and startup.

BOOTLOG.TXT and NTBTLOG.TXT

The Windows 9x "Start With logged" option used the BOOTLOG.TXT file. Windows 2000 and XP use NTBTLOG.TXT to do the same thing. If there are continuing startup problems, open the appropriate boot log file and make a note of the drivers and/or services that did or did *not* load when you started the computer. Use the list of drivers and services that failed to load at startup to help identify possible causes of startup problems.

The Windows 9x log file is located in the root folder of the installation drive, usually the C:\ folder. The Windows 2000 log is usually in the Winnt folder. This is a plain text file, and you can use any text editor, such as Microsoft Notepad (NOTEPAD.EXE), to open and view the contents.

Some startup problems may occur so early in the startup process that Windows may not save a boot log file to the hard disk drive. These are usually hardware-related problems, or problems involving BIOS or CMOS.

To determine the possible cause of the issue, perform a logged boot and look at the last entry in the Bootlog.txt file. The last entry should be the problem device or virtual device driver. It's either not loading, or loading incorrectly. To perform a logged boot:

1. Start the computer; then press and hold the CTRL key while the computer starts.
2. When the **Startup** menu appears, choose **Logged (\Bootlog.txt)**.
3. Restart the computer.

To review the log file, start Windows Explorer and double-click the **C:\Bootlog.txt** file. Look at the last entry in the file. If the machine cannot start windows but can arrive at a command line, you can use the DOS Editor (EDIT.COM) to open the file.

Event Viewer

View the event logs in Event Viewer for additional information that may help you to identify and diagnose the cause of the startup problem. To view events recorded to the event logs, follow these steps:

1. Click Start, point to Settings, and then click Control Panel.
2. Double-click Administrative Tools and then double-click Event Viewer.

Alternatively, start Microsoft Management Console (MMC) that contains the Event Viewer snap-in.

1. In the console tree, click to expand Event Viewer and then click the log that you want to view, for example, System log or Application log.
2. In the details pane, double-click the event that you want to view.

To copy the details of the event, click Copy, open a new document in the program in which you want to paste the event (for example, Microsoft Word), and then click Paste on the Edit menu.

To view the description of the previous event or the next event, press either the UP ARROW key or the DOWN ARROW key.

When Windows can boot to Safe Mode but not to Normal mode, it almost always indicates a bad device driver or a hardware conflict. The trick is to figure out which hardware device is causing the problem. Begin by looking in your event logs for a clue. If the event logs are no help, you can use the process of elimination. To do so, go into the Device Manager and disable every device that would normally be disabled in Safe Mode. Now, reboot the machine in Normal mode. If the machine boots properly, enable one of the devices that you disabled and reboot. Repeat this process, enabling one device at a time, until you find the device that is causing the problem.

If checking the devices doesn't cure the problem, you can try to use the System File Checker to test the integrity of your critical system files. To do so, go to a command prompt and enter the command **sfc /scannow**. Doing so will begin the process of testing your critical system files. To see other System File Checker options, type **sfc /?** and press Enter.

Task Manager

In Windows 95/98/Me you can bring up the Task List by pressing Ctrl+Alt+Del. In Windows NT4, 2000, and XP, you can bring up the Task List by right-clicking on the Task Bar and choosing "Task Manager." For a list of almost every loading task and description, visit the Answers That Work site, at **http://www.answersthatwork.com/Tasklist_pages/tasklist.htm**.

System File Checker

SFC allows a Systems Administrator to scan all protected files to verify their versions. SFC scans all protected system files and replaces incorrect versions with correct Microsoft versions. The System File Checker is a command-line utility, meaning that it doesn't stay running in the background like WFP. On a Windows Me system, the program will also check and reinstall the \Systemroot\system32\dllcache directory. If the dllcache directory becomes corrupted or unusable, SFC can be run with various options that will try to repair the contents of the dllcache directory.

Windows Me System File Protection (SFP)

Most of the time, Windows Me became unstable following a setup application that either installed older versions of system files over newer versions, or that installed modified versions of system files without renaming them. In both cases, the newly installed application would cause failures in any other applications that depended on the later or unmodified version of the file.

System File Protection on Windows Me restored the original, correct version of a system file if a newly installed application replaced it with an incorrect version. SFP ran in the background on Windows Me, like WFP, monitoring all attempts to change protected system files. SFP could not be disabled on Windows Me systems.

One of the interesting things we see in Me is that the System File Monitor goes through the following procedure while protecting critical system files: It stores a copy of the original file and then checks a database of catalog files to determine whether the new version of the file is a valid replacement. If the new version of the file is a valid replacement, Windows Me allows the new file to replace the old version; otherwise, it restores the original version of the file silently, *without alerting the end user*. The stored copy of the original file is deleted soon after the file is either replaced or restored. File corruption produced by something other than overwriting would not trigger SFP. If a protected system file becomes corrupted, the end user can replace the corrupted version of the file with a valid copy from the distribution media.

Windows File Protection (WFP)

Typically, critical .EXE or .DLL files can be changed during a new installation, leading to mismatched file versions or even completely different file contents. All .SYS, .DLL, .EXE, and .OCX files that ship on the Windows CD are protected, as are the True Type fonts; Micross.ttf, Tahoma.ttf, and Tahomabd.ttf. Unfortunately, in many cases, neither the Uninstall Wizard, nor a commercial uninstaller can fix the problem, given that the important system files have been replaced with files of the same name.

Windows 98 and Me offered the System File Checker (SFC.EXE), and a feature called *System File Protection (SFP)*. Windows 2000 and Windows XP introduce the Windows File Protection (WFP) feature, designed to prevent this type of problem. WFP works similarly to Windows Millenium Edition's SFP, by preventing automated installation and setup routines from replacing essential system files, but does it in a different way.

WFP protects system files by running in the background and detecting attempts to replace protected system files. WFP is triggered after it receives a directory change notification on a file in a protected directory. Once this notification is received, WFP determines which file was changed. If the file is protected, WFP looks up the file signature in a catalog file to determine if the new file is the correct Microsoft version. If it is not, the operating system replaces the file with the correct version from the \dllcache directory or the original installation disk.

WFP logs an event to the system event log, noting the file replacement attempt. If the administrative user cancels the WFP file restoration, that causes an event to be logged, noting the cancellation.

The Windows XP core is much more protected than in Windows 2000. Essential system data cannot be overwritten by drivers or software installations, and .DLL files are now stored side by side on the hard disk. Each program uses its own Dynamic Link Libraries, almost guaranteeing much better reliability than Windows 2000.

Diagnostics Utilities

We've discussed various diagnostics tools and utilities in previous chapters, but we'll pass over them one last time so they're fresh in your mind. Certain tools have either disappeared or have been modified as Windows has developed, including MSD.EXE. Microsoft Diagnostics was a command-line program that would generate a report of the configuration files used on the machine. MSD was superseded by Hardware Diagnostics.

Windows 95 Hardware Diagnostics (HwDiag.EXE)

Windows 95 offered HwDiag.EXE as a reporting and diagnostics utility, but it wasn't installed by default on a new machine. The program was available on the installation disks, and ran in a graphical environment. Hardware Diagnostics generated a detailed report of every device attached to the machine, as long as Windows could recognize the device. This file is no longer included with Windows 98.

Another way to generate a report of the many devices listed is from the Device Manager, located using the Properties menu of the My Computer icon. You can print either a System Summary Report or an All Devices And Summary Report. Although the HwDiag.EXE program seems to have vanished, the detailed report printed using the Device Manager is sophisticated enough to read manufacturer information, version numbers, and so forth.

If you choose to print any reports to a file, you should be aware that if the default printer is a typical laser printer, the file will be created using the printer control language (PCL) format the printer uses. It's always a good idea to set up (during installation) the *generic printer* and configure its port setting to print to a file. If you print with this printer, configured in this fashion, you'll always be asked for a file name and destination.

You can always set up a generic printer with the Add Printer option under the Printers icon of the Control Panel.

Administrative Tools

Windows 2000 has several other icons, and a machine set up as a networking machine will have options that are different than a stand-alone machine's options. To reach the Windows 2000 utility tools, double-click on My Computer, open the Control Panel, and double-click on Administrative Tools.

Another way is to navigate through Start|Settings|Control Panel| Administrative Tools and to look at the various selections under Administrative Tools. Some of the main icons to know are Component Services, Event Viewer, and Users and Passwords (refer back to Figure 13.1 in Chapter 13).

System Reports and My Computer

You can troubleshoot a failed system from within the operating system environment, viewing many of the logs and reports at the computer. Generally, you'll be better off if you print out reports of the various event logs, diagnostics tools, and configuration viewers. We've mentioned that the Device Manager in Windows 9x is a thorough reporting utility for the many hardware devices attached to the machine. Device Manager reports also provide sections on memory usage, IRQ, and DMA usage.

Windows 2000 provides several tools from the Start|Programs| Accessories|System Tools menu. At the System Tools option, you can access Backup, Disk Cleanup, Disk Defragmenter, Schedule Tasks, and System Information. The System Information Print option is similar to the old HwDiag.EXE with very detailed reports on all devices.

Make a note of these menu navigation routes because you'll likely be asked to recognize them during the exam.

When you right-click on the My Computer icon in a Windows 2000 environment, the Properties menu selection brings up a dialog box with the following tabs: General, Network Identification, Hardware, User Profiles, and Advanced.

Remember that double-clicking on the My Computer icon brings up a program window with the drives and the Control Panel icon.

The Advanced tab has a Performance button where you can set environment variables, along with Startup and Recovery options. The Startup and Recovery options include a series of check boxes that tell the computer what to do when it crashes.

The Hardware options tab offers choices to get to the Hardware Wizard and the Device Manager. The Windows 2000 Device Manager offers another two choices, one of which is Driver Signing To Ensure That All Drivers Are Digitally Signed By Microsoft To Validate Drivers. The other is Hardware Profiles, where you can create the different profiles offered at the BOOT.INI pause screen. Once again, hardware profiles might include a docking station, a Desktop profile, and so forth.

Registry Checker (Scanregw.exe)

Safe Mode provides a limited operating environment, but it gives you access to the various diagnostics tools and utilities within the operating system. REGEDIT is the Windows 9x Registry Editor. SYSEDIT opens the critical .INI files, along with AUTOEXEC.BAT, and CONFIG.SYS. LOGVIEW opens the various log files where crash information may be stored, including BOOTLOG.TXT.

To start the Windows 95, 98 and Me Registry Checker tool, click Start | Run, and type **scanregw** in the Open box. Click OK. As discussed in Chapter 12, ScanRegW (Scan Registry—Windows [version]) makes backups of the Registry files, SYSTEM.DAT and USER.DAT, along with the SYSTEM.INI and WIN.INI files. The default configuration is to keep five backups in .CAB files. To find Registry files from within a working copy of Windows, use the following steps:

1. Click Start, point to Find, and then click Files Or Folders.
2. In the Named box, type rb0*.cab, and then click Find Now.
3. Double-click the cabinet file that contains the file that you want to restore.
4. Right-click the file that you want to restore, click Extract, and then choose the folder where the new file is to be placed. Microsoft recommends that you place the file in the \Windows\Temp folder.
5. Restart the computer in MS-DOS mode (in Windows Me this requires that you restart with the Windows Me Startup disk).

6. Copy the file that you extracted to the appropriate folder. Note that registry .DAT files are hidden and read-only, so you need to use both the ATTRIB and the COPY commands to replace existing file with the newly extracted ones.

Windows 2000 Recovery Console

When you've tried a bootable disk and an Emergency Repair Disk, and you've tried to get into Safe Mode on a Windows 2000 machine, one of your last options before reinstalling the machine is to try the Recovery Console. The Recovery Console allows you to attempt to repair the boot sector and to create a new boot floppy or Emergency Repair Disk.

In most corporate settings, the Recovery Console will require an administrator password.

In Chapter 13, we said that you could run a transient command-line window by choosing the "Run" option from the Start menu. At the Run window, type "CMD" (to run CMD.EXE) and press Enter. Whatever program you run eventually terminates, and you're returned to the Widows Desktop. Recovery Console provides a DOS-like command-line interface used for repairing a Windows NT, 2000, or XP machine.

Recovery Console is started from the Windows 2000 setup disks (either CD or floppy) where, after booting from the disk, you follow the instructions to "Repair a Windows 2000 installation using the Recovery Console." If you have multiple partitions with different operating systems, you are asked to choose which drive you want to log on to by picking a number and then pressing Enter. You may then be asked to enter the Administrator password. If this password has not been enabled, you can simply press Enter to continue. At that point you are presented with a C:\WINNT prompt.

You may add the Windows Recovery Console to the Windows Startup folder by using **Winnt32.exe** with the **/cmdcons** switch. This procedure requires approximately 7 MB of hard disk space on your system partition, in order to hold the **Cmdcons** folder and files.

While you are using the Windows Recovery Console, you cannot copy a file from the local hard disk to a floppy disk. You can copy a file from a floppy disk or CD-ROM to a hard disk, and from one hard disk to another hard disk. From the Windows Recovery Console you can only use the following folders (if you try to access other folders, you receive an "Access Denied" error message):

- The root folder
- The %SystemRoot% folder and the subfolders of the currently logged Windows installation
- The Cmdcons folder
- Removable media drives such as CD-ROM drives

Available Commands

Some of the familiar DOS commands available at the Recovery Console include: **ATTRIB**, **CD**, **CHKDSK**, **COPY**, **DIR**, **DEL**, **FORMAT**, **MD**, **RD**, and **REN**. You can also type "HELP" and get a complete list of commands, just like at the DOS prompt, or you can use **COMMAND /?** for the typical short form of the command.

The Report and Fix program options include: **DISABLE** or **ENABLE**, to allow or disallow device drivers; **Partition** (DISKPART.EXE), to add or delete a disk partition; **FIXBOOT** and **FIXMBR**, to correct problems with the boot record and MBR; and **LISTSVC**, to list the device drivers and services available on the computer. Table 14.3 is a listing of all the commands available in the Recovery Console. You can use the HELP command to get a listing from within the application.

Table 14.3 Commands available in Recovery Console.

attrib	delete	fixboot	md	type
cd	dir	fixmb	rmkdir	systemroot
chdir	disable	format	more	
chkdsk	diskpart	help	rd	
cls	enable	listsvc	ren	
copy	exit	logon	rename	
del	expand	map	rmdir	

Supplemental Information

You should know how to work with file attributes from your experience with either the Windows Explorer properties context menu or through having read Chapter 10. The specific command line programs we most often found on the exam are covered in the DOS chapter. For your information, and as a way to demonstrate how important and understanding of DOS commands continues to be, we've listed the names and essential purpose for the Recovery Console commands in this segment. If you choose, you may jump to "System Maintenance" at this point.

ATTRIB

You can *view* the attributes of files such as BOOTLOG.INI using either the DIR or the ATTRIB command. However, you can only *change* the attributes of a file by using the ATTRIB command, as discussed in Chapter 10, "DOS." The four main attributes are Hidden (H), System (S), Read-Only (R), and Archive (A). At least one attribute must be set.

CHKDSK /p /r

In the Recovery Console, this command checks and repairs the drive, or it can be used to recover a drive. It also marks bad sectors and recovers readable information. Check Disk was used in the same way, back in the old days of DOS. It continued through Windows 3.x and then became unusable in Windows 9x. This version is designed specifically for the command-line environment of a Windows 2000 or XP machine.

The **/p** switch instructs CHKDSK to do a complete analysis (check) of the drive, even if the drive is not marked with problems. It then corrects any errors it finds. The **/r** switch locates bad sectors and recovers readable information. CHKDSK requires the AUTOCHK.EXE file, which it automatically locates in the bootup folder. This folder is usually the **Cmdcons** folder if the Command Console was preinstalled. If the folder cannot be found in the bootup folder, CHKDSK tries to locate the Windows installation CD-ROM. If the installation disk isn't found, the program prompts you to provide the location for AUTOCHK.EXE.

Listsvc

This command lists all available services, drivers, and their start types for the current Windows installation. This command may be useful when using the **disable** and **enable** commands. These are extracted from the %SystemRoot%\System32\Config\SYSTEM hive. Unpredictable results may occur if the SYSTEM hive becomes damaged or is missing.

Disable

This command can be used to disable a system service or a device driver. Use the **listsvc** command to display all services or drivers that can be disabled. **Disable** prints the original start type of the service and then resets the service to SERVICE_DISABLED. Record the old start type in case you need to re-enable the service. Start_type values for system services are:

- SERVICE_DISABLED
- SERVICE_BOOT_START
- SERVICE_SYSTEM_START
- SERVICE_AUTO_START
- SERVICE_DEMAND_START

Enable

This command is used to enable a Windows system service or driver. The **enable** command prints the old start type of the service before resetting it to the new value. The values are the same as for Disable, except that SERVICE_DISABLED is not an option.

Map

Use this command to list drive letters, file system types, partition sizes, and mappings to physical devices.

Diskpart

This command is used to manage the partitions on your hard disk volumes. This command is reminiscent of the FDISK.EXE command. If no switches are used, Diskpart displays a menu for managing the existing partitions.

Be very careful with this command. Diskpart can damage your partition table if the disk has been upgraded to a dynamic disk configuration. Do not modify the structure of dynamic disks unless you are using the Disk Management tool.

Fixboot

This command is used to write new Windows boot sector code on a boot partition. This command fixes problems where the Windows boot sector is corrupted. The Emergency Repair process also fixes the boot sector. This command overrides the default of writing to the system boot partition.

Fixmbr

This command is similar to an almost undocumented switch with the DOS FDISK command (FDISK **/mbr**). As a command in Windows 2000, it is used to repair the master boot record (MBR) of the system partition. This command is used in scenarios where a virus has damaged the MBR and Windows cannot start.

This command has the potential to damage your partition tables if a virus is present or a hardware problem exists. This command may lead to inaccessible partitions. Microsoft suggests running antivirus software before using this command.

Logon

The **logon** command lists all detected installations of Windows, and then requests the local administrator password for the copy of Windows you chose to log on to. If more than three attempts to log on do not succeed, the console quits and your computer restarts.

Exit

Use EXIT to quit the Recovery Command Console and restart the computer.

System Maintenance

One of the biggest problems with modern iterations of Windows and the Internet is the number of temporary files accumulated on the hard drive. In Windows 9x, the way you removed those files was to use the Explorer's saved search criteria to create shortcuts for ~*.* and *.TMP files. You could also create Desktop shortcuts for ScanDisk and Defrag. Otherwise, you were left to purchase commercial third-party software programs designed to clean up the hard drive. Windows 2000 offers a utility called *Disk Cleanup*.

MS Internet Explorer did offer an option of cleaning out temporary files, but it was a manual decision process. Utilities such as Tweak UI could configure Windows 98 to do some automated clearing of temporary files.

Windows 2000 Disk Cleanup

To reach the cleanup utility, choose Start | Programs | Accessories | System Tools | Disk Cleanup. One of the options under Disk Cleanup is "Select

Drive," which reads the drive you select and produces a menu. The menu options are check boxes asking you which types of files you want to delete. Among the types you can select are: downloaded program files, temporary Internet files, offline Web pages, Recycle Bin, temporary files, temporary offline files, offline files, or catalog files for the Content Indexer.

The Content Indexer is similar to the Windows 9x Find Fast utility, which would index an entire hard drive and provide speedier searches through the index rather than searching the drive directly.

Other option tabs in the Disk Cleanup utility include "Windows Components" and "Installed Programs." The Windows Components menu allows you to remove unused components. You're presented with a list of check boxes, and you then tell Disk Cleanup what you want it to get rid of. The Installed Programs menu is much the same as the Windows Components menu, in that it lists all the installed programs on the PC, along with how much space they take. To help you decide what you'd like to remove, the lists can be sorted in several ways, such as by frequency of use, date last used, and names and sizes.

Boot Problems

During the initialization process, a machine can't display anything to the monitor, and you can't enter anything from the keyboard. We discussed the power-on self-test (POST) in Chapter 11 and included a listing of the error indicators in the "Beep Codes" section. If the machine can't get past the initialization, the most likely problems involve either a bad power supply or a failed motherboard.

Sometimes, a machine has actually booted up okay, but the monitor is turned off or broken. In some instances, the monitor's image controls have been changed, dimming down the image to point where you can't see it. Check the brightness controls and monitor indicator lights, but in a worst case, you might have to try a different monitor. When we refer to the process of using a piece of equipment we know to be good, we speak of *switching out* the problem piece of equipment. After the machine has passed the initialization stage and before ROM BIOS hands off to the operating system, the most common area where you'll encounter problems is with the CMOS.

NTLDR Is Missing

When you start your Windows 2000-based computer, you may receive the following error message: "NTLDR is missing, Press any key to restart." This problem may occur if the machine is using an outdated BIOS, or if one or more of the following Windows boot files are missing or damaged:

- Ntldr
- Ntdetect.com
- Boot.ini

Verify that the machine is using a current BIOS, or repair the Windows 2000 installation. Microsoft recommends that you fully back up your data on a regular basis, as the best defense against losses. Backups are a fundamental part of any disaster recovery plan. (You do have a disaster recovery plan, don't you?)

Incorrect or damaged CMOS and BIOS settings can often cause startup problems. For information about the correct CMOS and BIOS settings for the computer, either refer to the system's documentation or contact the manufacturer. Contact the computer manufacturer (usually a visit to their Web site) to find out about the latest BIOS updates, availability, and how to install the latest BIOS on the machine.

CMOS Problems

A machine can have a hardware password stored in the CMOS, in which case it will prompt the user for that password upon completion of the POST. Some PCs offer separate passwords for the machine and general access to the operating system. The default option in the CMOS Password setting is to disable the password completely (with a None or Disabled selection). If the machine password is disabled, the POST automatically hands off to the operating system.

If the user forgets the password, the recommended way to recover the system is to remove the CMOS battery long enough for the loss of power to clear the chip, or to reconfigure a jumper on the motherboard to clear the chip. These steps clear all CMOS settings and require reconfiguring the CMOS when the battery is replaced. In the field, some technicians have been known to short-circuit the CMOS jumper to clear the chip. However, although this could be the only available option on the exam, the procedure is not recommended.

Another important setting in CMOS is the order in which the machine checks its drives for an operating system. Keep in mind that a *default* setting is the value that will be set if no manual configuration change takes place, or when a cleared CMOS receives power for the first time. The default in most PCs is that the system will search first in Drive A: and then Drive C:. Other settings include completely disabling the checking of Drive A:, checking for a bootable CD-ROM, or checking for a bootable SCSI drive.

In the event that drive C: becomes disabled, the operating system can often be booted from drive A:. If the CMOS has disabled the checking of drive A:, there will be no way at all to access the hard drive. If a CMOS password is enabled, the only way to change the CMOS is to remove the battery (or reset the jumper on those motherboards that provide a jumper).

CMOS Error Messages

If no operating system is found, CMOS returns an error message to the screen and pauses the system. The two typical messages about a missing operating system are "Bad or missing command interpreter" or "Nonsystem disk or disk error." These errors will show on any DOS or Windows machine, and indicate that you should try to reinstall the system files. On Windows 9x machines, you can try the SYS.COM utility. On a Windows NT or 2000 system, try using a bootable disk and an Emergency Repair Disk.

Remember that CMOS errors can often be generated after someone has changed the settings for the computer. This situation can lead to anything from an inability to boot the machine, to a simple pause at the POST screen. Some errors might allow the machine to continue booting after pressing a function key (often F1).

CMOS settings are stored in a sort of file, and checksum validation works with CMOS memory much the way it works with files. *Checksum validation* means that a number is read when the file is created and stored, and that number can be appended (added on to) to the file and stored for later checking. When the file is read, the same process runs and should generate the same number. If the new number doesn't match the stored number, a *checksum error* occurs. The settings file has a stored checksum, and when the CPU reads the CMOS internal file, the numbers should match.

There are many CMOS errors, but some of the important ones to know include:

- *CMOS display type mismatch*—This error indicates that the video settings don't apply to the actual monitor installed on the system. The first step is to re-enter CMOS and verify that the correct monitor has been selected.

- *CMOS memory size mismatch*—This error will appear on many machines when more memory has been added. Auto-detection will usually reconfigure the CMOS with a pause during the POST to make sure that what CMOS saw matches reality.
- *CMOS device mismatch error*—Displays and hard disks are considered devices, and any one of the attached devices can generate this error. Most likely, the wrong device is listed in CMOS for the physical device attached to the machine.
- *CMOS checksum failure*—A checksum failure indicates that corruption exists in the CMOS memory. Often this can happen with a bad battery or a loose connection to the battery. If changing and checking the battery doesn't solve the problem, it might be a motherboard going bad. Checksum errors may also indicate a virus.

Hardware Problems

One of the most common problems uncovered during the boot process is where a piece of hardware isn't recognized by the system. A bad keyboard will generate a beep code and often a message to the monitor. Keyboards are inexpensive enough that if you can't switch out the keyboard, replacing it should solve the problem.

If the machine seems to be running okay, you'll probably hear the cooling fan making some amount of noise, and some indicator lights should be showing on the faceplate. A bad monitor doesn't have a cooling fan, so without sophisticated testing equipment, the only way to test a video connection is to switch out the monitor.

Master/Slave Jumpers

Another problem is where a new drive of some kind has been added to one of the controllers on the motherboard. For example, you might have a hard drive attached to one IDE controller and then attach a second drive to the same controller. If you weren't paying attention to jumpers, you might discover that the system doesn't recognize the second hard drive.

Most drives have a configuration setting for Primary Only, Primary Second Available, and Second (or terminology to that effect). The typical default setting for a new drive is to make it the Primary Only (master) drive. If the original hard drive is configured as a Primary Only drive, then when you add a second drive, the controller won't even see it because it's being told there's only one drive on the controller interface. Additionally, even if the first drive was configured to see a second drive, the new drive is probably set to Primary Only.

The default IRQ for a primary IDE fixed disk controller is IRQ 14. The secondary controller takes IRQ 15 by default. Note that jumpering an additional drive on the same controller isn't generally an IRQ problem, but rather a jumper switch problem.

Jumper settings are the first thing to check when a new drive isn't being recognized. Make sure you've opened up access to the new drive by changing the first drive's jumper switches. You'll also have to set the jumpers on the second drive to make it a secondary drive (or slave). The second thing to look for is a bad power supply at the cable connections. When all else fails, switch out the new drive with a drive that you know is good, and verify that any power connectors are working and in good condition.

A good place to have electronic testing equipment is where you're having possible troubles with power connectors and cables. If nothing else, a multimeter can verify that a connection is providing a complete circuit between one location and another.

Circuitry Failures

It's not often that you'll come across a machine where the entire motherboard has been fried (technical term). It happens, though, and in those instances, it might be more cost-effective to buy a new computer. You should already know that integrated circuits are delicate and can be short-circuited with a blast of static electricity (electrostatic discharge [ESD]). Another way to fry a motherboard is when a bad power supply sends a high voltage discharge through the electronics of the entire system, melting many of the components.

Lightning is another source of high voltage, and when lightning discharges to a nearby ground point, it's called a *proximity strike*. If a powerful storm is moving through the area, it's a very good idea to disconnect all computers from the building's wiring structure. Not only should you disconnect the power cords, but you should also remember that any modems are connected to the building's telephone wiring.

In Chapter 8, we touched on hot swapping, one of the features of USB. You also know that a computer constantly polls a keyboard, waiting for any activity coming from that keyboard. Because of the constant interplay between the motherboard and the various devices attached to that motherboard, it's never a good idea to unplug a device or plug in a new device while the power is on. The universal serial bus is one of the first technologies that safely allows you to add and remove devices without turning off the main power supply.

Some computer reference manuals indicate that you don't need to turn off the machine to attach or detach a device. Laptop computers often use portable floppy drives or detachable CD-ROM drives. Desktop machines can run into trouble with keyboards, scanners, removable storage devices, and even a mouse. Anything that attaches to the motherboard can cause an electronic pulse to run through the motherboard and its components.

Although you would think the reference manual would tell you the truth about the machine, it's a rare instance where the machine will recognize a new device without a cold boot (machine reset). It may be possible to attach a new device with the machine running, but you can get into real trouble when you detach a device in this manner. Unless you're working with a USB device, the recommended method is still to turn off the machine before you plug in or unplug any piece of hardware.

Connectivity Problems

Up until this point, we've mostly discussed troubleshooting procedures for either a stand-alone machine or a network machine. However, one of the biggest headaches to deal with is when a machine has started successfully but won't connect to a network. In this scenario, the two possible causes are the network interface card (NIC) itself, or the way that the NIC is interfacing with the operating system.

You can use the Device Manager to go in and look at the type of card Windows thinks is installed in the machine. However, the only way to know for sure what type of card is installed is to open the machine and actually look at the card. Older cards had no way of telling you whether they were working or not, so unless the card has LED indicators, you'll have to first switch out the card in order to prove whether or not it's working. Keep in mind that when you install another card, you'll have to reconfigure most of the network settings.

Windows 9x introduced a Network Neighborhood icon on the Desktop, which became My Network Places in Windows 2000. Right-clicking on the Network icon and selecting properties opens up much of the configuration information, but the more thorough way to check the network configuration is through the Control Panel.

The Windows 2000 Control Panel includes a Network and Dial-up Connections icon, which includes a Make New Connection option. There can be more than one connection, and assuming networking has already been set up and there is an active connection, the Windows Taskbar displays a small icon that looks like two computers talking with each other.

Double-clicking the icon on the Taskbar brings up a status and activity dialog box that shows the connection status, duration, and speed of a good connection. A second box shows connection activity in terms of real-time packets sent and received. Right-clicking on the icon brings up a Properties menu of options, such as configuring the network and NICs, and includes a second button that allows you to disable a specific network connection.

Network Card Configuration Problems

Assuming you've been lucky and the NIC has onboard LEDs to indicate that the card is in good working condition, the second aspect of connectivity is how the card is configured within Windows. We're only going to touch lightly on the entire concept of installing a NIC and configuring connections, but you should know how to get to the places where you might be asked to find out any existing information.

Begin with the Start | Settings | Network and Dial-up Connections menus. You're given a choice of all available connections or networks that have been set up for that computer. When you highlight any of the available networks, you'll be given a screen with icons representing each network and a Make New Connections Wizard.

Double-click on any of the existing network connections to produce a window that tells you the connection, status duration speed, activity, and properties. The Properties option opens the Network Configure window, where you can add or configure a new protocol, NIC, or client. Note that these options are the same as when you double-click the icon on the Taskbar, which we mentioned a moment ago.

Another way to get to the same place is to right-click on My Network Places (Windows 98 and 2000) or Network Neighborhood (Windows 95). The Properties option takes you to the Network and Dial-up Connections window, where you can examine the configurations for the local machine's network installation.

Remember that one of the tools available in Windows 2000 is the Performance Monitor (discussed in Chapter 13), which can be set to monitor specific aspects of the machine either in a moving graphic or a tab format. Another tool is the Net Watcher that first appeared in Windows 95, which became the Network Monitor in the Windows NT and 2000 Server version.

Services Icon

According to Microsoft, services are those programs or routines that provide support for other programs, particularly at low or hardware levels. Network services are a specialized software-based functionality provided by network servers (such as Directory Service), which is like a phone book used for locating users and resources.

One of the icons in the Windows NT and 2000 Control Panel is the Services icon. There are a great many services, but some examples include Alerter (notifies selected users of computers of administrative alerts); Dynamic Host Configuration Protocol (DHCP) Client; Domain Name System (DNS) Client (resolves and caches domain names); Event Log; Network connections; Plug and Play; Print Spooler; Telephony; and the Utility Manager (accessibility tools to start and/or set up accessibility features).

Connection Validation

PING is an acronym for Packet INternet Groper, which is a protocol for testing whether a particular computer is connected to the Internet—or any Transmission Control Protocol/Internet Protocol (TCP/IP) network—by sending a packet to its IP address and waiting for a response. The name actually comes from the submarine's active SONAR where a sound is sent out and surrounding objects are revealed.

PING is a Unix protocol used to test whether a computer is connected to another computer through a network. To use the PING utility, you must know the specific IP address of that computer.

Access Denied

Another common problem with networked computers is that end users who attempt to use one of the network resources can be denied access. The resources could be a file folder, a printer, an Internet connection, or even their own computers. Typically, the cause is either a password problem, or an administrative authorization situation.

Before you can even begin to work with passwords and access rights, you must have an Administrator password. Although A+ technicians will most likely not have administrative rights, CompTIA indicates they will be asking questions about administrative areas.

Assuming that you have the Administrator password, navigate through the Start | Settings | Control Panel menu to the Users and Passwords icon. Double-click on the icon to bring up a dialog box with two tabs: User and Advanced. The User tab lists all the users available on the local machine. When you highlight any one of the listed users, you're presented with a list of check boxes. One of the check boxes states that the User Must Enter A User Name And Password To Use This Computer. If this box is checked, when you go to any user, you will see three buttons: Look At Properties, Remove, or Add A User.

On many new machines, Windows 2000 is preinstalled, and the purchaser is given a default Administrator User ID and password. In a home environment, the machine can be reconfigured to start up without a user name or password.

Below the three buttons is an option to change the password for that highlighted user. The Look At Properties button provides two additional tabs: General (information about the user) and Group Memberships. The Group Memberships tab provides choices for the level of access that user will be granted.

PROTOCOL.INI

We've discussed the SYSEDIT.EXE system files editor, saying that this was a utility program used in Windows 3.x and Windows 9x to call up the essential .INI files. We've also referenced the startup configuration tab in the Systems Tools accessories. One of the lesser known .INI files called up in the system editor for Windows for Work groups 3.11 and Windows 9x is PROTOCOL.INI, the Real Mode networking configuration file.

Information stored in this file is overwritten by information stored in the Registry, so although you can edit the PROTOCOL.INI file from SYSEDIT, the information won't necessarily stay there. Information in the files is created through the setup .INF files for any installed networking components. The best way to edit this file is through the Network icon in the Windows 9x Control Panel, used in conjunction with the setup software for the network hardware.

PROTOCOL.INI contains information about the I/O address, DMA access, IRQs, and separate sections for each network adapter and network protocol. If a network card develops a memory access conflict with a video controller, using a combination of error messages and the protocol information may sometimes help you to adjust one of the conflicting devices.

Viruses

A computer virus is a set of instructions (a program) that tells the PC to execute a series of actions without the owner's consent or knowledge. A virus can operate only by running the instructions held within a program. Even the modern macro and scripting viruses are a series of instructions. The difference between a program virus and a macro virus is that a macro virus uses an application—such as Microsoft Word, Microsoft Excel, or Netscape—rather than the operating system as the command interpreter.

Some versions of Windows and DOS offered the Microsoft Anti-Virus (MSAV) utilities as a primitive defense against viruses. Third-party virus protection programs are far better choices because they constantly upgrade their virus databases. Often, these third-party, virus-fixing updates can be downloaded from an Internet site. McAfee.com and Symantec's Norton Anti-Virus are two popular virus-fighting tools.

A virus program usually waits for an event to take place and then executes its instructions. The operative word here is "execute." A virus is a small program of some kind. One way or another, there must be some kind of executable code. The trigger event might be a specific date and time on the system clock, or a set of keystrokes, or it could be opening a macro virus in an autorun application. A virus may also work by attaching itself to a particular program. When the hosting program is executed, it runs the virus code. Each virus program has its own program code, called a *signature*.

Many email messages are clogging the Internet, warning of deadly email viruses. Opening and reading a text email message provides no opportunity to execute a binary program. Only the attachments that come with email messages can be potential virus carriers.

Types of Viruses

A virus is classified according to how the virus is transmitted and how it infects the computer. No matter which kind of virus is involved, it can't be spread by coughing on a machine or by placing a PC too close to another PC (or a VCR). Another common myth (with no basis in reality) is that viruses can enter a PC through some sort of sub-band channel of a modem connection.

The main categories of viruses are as follows:

- *Boot sector*—Overwrites the disk's original boot sector with its own code. Every time the PC boots up, the virus is executed.
- *Master boot sector*—Overwrites the master boot sector's partition table on the hard disk. These viruses are difficult to detect because many disk examination tools don't allow you to see the partition sector (head 0, track 0, sector 0) of a hard disk.
- *Macro viruses*—Written in the macro language of applications, such as a word processor or spreadsheet. Macro viruses infect files (not the boot sector or partition table) and can reside in memory when the specific application's document is accessed. Usually, the virus is triggered by an autorun feature in the application that runs a macro, much like an AUTOEXEC.BAT file. Otherwise, the virus runs by user actions, such as certain keystrokes or menu choices.
- *Scripted viruses*—Uses JavaScript, ActiveX controls, or other such scripting languages to introduce instructions to the machine through the operating system. Scripted viruses use Internet functionality as the command processor, and can be written as plain text commands that will run from email messages, graphics files, or any other area where the virus programmer hides them.

Macro viruses can be stored in files with any extension. Most modern applications can recognize their own files by information stored in the header of the file. A Microsoft Word document might have the default .DOC extension or an .XYZ extension. Regardless of the extension, it's still a Word document and is capable of running macros. Macro viruses are spread through file transfers and email. However, they can be executed only by the program that interprets the macro commands. Once again, until email programs include some sort of macro capability, plain email messages can't contain viruses.

Scripted Viruses

ActiveX controls allow Web developers to create interactive, dynamic Web pages. An ActiveX control is a component object embedded in a Web page. It can run automatically when the page is viewed, or most browsers can be configured to prompt the user whenever an ActiveX control is about to run.

People who write viruses may embed malicious or destructive programming code in an ActiveX control.

Java Scripts also allow Web developers to create interactive, dynamic Web pages. JavaScript provides a bit more general capability than ActiveX, running as small applications from the Web site. Java applets, much like the old Windows 3x applets, are small programs embedded in HTML pages. Remember that HTML stands for Hyper Text Markup Language, and is mostly a plain-text format language. Both ActiveX and Java scripts can be prevented by setting a Web browser's security configuration options.

VBScript (Visual Basic Script), or VBS, is a script written in a script programming language designed for local PCs. Where JavaScript is designed to be "pushed" from a Web site, Visual Basic is designed to be run as an application on a local hard drive. VBScript and JavaScript viruses both make use of Microsoft's Windows Scripting Host to infect a machine. Since Windows Scripting Host is available on Windows 98 and Windows 2000, these viruses can be activated simply by double-clicking on a file with a .VBS or .JS extension in the Explorer.

Stealth Viruses

Two common types of stealth viruses are the Trojan and the Worm virus. A Trojan is a destructive program disguised as a game or other useful program. Users download a program that looks like it will meet some particular need, but when they run it, the virus enters their system. In many cases, the program containing the virus actually does what the victim had hoped it would do. A *Worm*, coming from the Write Once, Read Many (WORM) acronym, propagates across computers by duplicating itself in memory, then duplicating itself again and again. The Worm writes itself to the infected machine one time and then copies itself again and again, eventually filling up an entire disk. Some Worms can even transfer themselves to other machines through links between the two machines' memory.

Example Script Trojan Horse

There was a virus not long ago that arrived in an email message. The Subject line read: Scene from last weekend, with the Message line reading: "Please do not forward!!" This email carried an attachment named: scenes.zip. The attached .ZIP file contained a Rich Text Format (.RTF) document named SCENES.WRI (an MS Write or WordPad extension). If the document was opened, there were two icons representing two embedded objects (remember OLE?). Both icons appeared to be placeholders for an image file, but the actual embedded object was an executable program detected by Sophos Anti-Virus as Troj/Senecs.

The object labeled SCENE2.JPG was an actual image. However, the object identified in the document as SCENES1.JPG was actually named "Copy of RESULT.EXE " and was an executable file. This file contained a number of files, including a JPEG image and a mass mailing script, along with other malicious programming code. Note that while it may seem as though an image file was carrying a virus, it wasn't an actual image file; only the extension was renamed.

If the embedded executable was opened, it inserted and ran a Visual Basic Script (VBS) file, which attempted to send the SCENES.ZIP file to all the contacts listed in the Microsoft Outlook address book on that machine. Troj/Senecs also inserted two additional Trojans horses: Troj/Optix-03-C and Troj/WebDL-E. Troj/Optix-03-C was a backdoor virus run in the background as a server process, allowing a remote user (using a client program) to gain access and control over the machine.

Firewalls

A firewall isn't really an antiviral program, so much as a way to prevent unauthorized programs from finding their way onto a computer. Firewalls can be either hardware based or software based, and are designed to put a security layer between computers. Most often, firewalls are installed on home computers with always-on connections (i.e., DSL or cable modems), or on networks. Network firewalls put the security layer between the local network and an ultranetwork like the Internet.

How Viruses Work

Viruses of different types work in different ways. Some viruses keep the same code and attach to programs or load into memory. Newer viruses are aware of antivirus programs, so they make an effort to change their code while continuing to do their damage.

Functional characteristics of viruses include the following:

- *Memory-resident viruses*—Load themselves in memory, take control of the operating system, and attach themselves to executable files (e.g., .EXE, .COM, and .SYS). These viruses often change the file attribute information and the file size, time, and date information.

Viruses can't attach to .BAT files because these files are text-based lists of commands. A virus may, however, be attached to a program file *called* by a batch file.

- *Nonresident file viruses*—Infect other programs when an infected program is run. They don't remain in memory, so they don't infect the system. These viruses often change the file attribute information and the file size, time, and date information. Like memory-resident viruses, nonresident viruses attach themselves to executable files.
- *Multipartite viruses*—Combine the characteristics of memory-resident, nonresident file, and boot sector viruses.

Remember that COMMAND.COM is a program. If a virus attaches itself to the main command interpreter, executing any of the DOS internal commands (e.g., **DIR**, **DEL**, or **MD**) will cause the virus to execute. Inserting a disk infected with a boot sector virus in drive A: and running a simple **DIR** command often causes the virus to be copied to the hard drive's boot sector.

- *Polymorphic viruses*—Modify their appearance and change their *signatures* (their program code) periodically (for example, by changing the order of program execution). This allows the virus to escape signature-scanning detection methods.
- *Stealth viruses*—Hide their presence. All viruses try to conceal themselves in some way, but stealth viruses make a greater effort to do so. This type of virus can infect a program by adding bytes to the infected file. It then subtracts the same number of bytes from the directory entry of the infected file, making it appear as if no change has taken place.

It seems that the exam capitalizes on the bizarre and complex names and acronyms used in the PC world. If you know only that polymorphic and multipartite are weird names that you don't hear much at all, you'll have a tool for deciphering any questions that throw these terms at you. Keep in mind that the most deadly viruses tend to affect the boot sector, Master Boot Record, and partition table.

Viruses in Image Files

As of 2002, it isn't possible to actually embed executable code in an image file. These image files are typically known as .JPG, .BMP, .GIF files, and so forth. Although representatives from the McAfee corporation say that it could happen in the future, it cannot be done at the moment. Something else to be aware of, the overall adventure of creating viruses is beginning to slow down, according to statistics.

Embedding a secret image within another image is sometimes called *spy code*. This can be done, these days, and that image can be password protected. Messages can be embedded within images in this fashion, giving rise to modern-day secret messages that can be sent as email attachments. These are not viruses, in that they do not contain executable code.

Spyware and Adware

Technically speaking, *spyware* is the jargon name given to any technology that gathers information about a person or organization without their knowledge. Spyware is typically a program that secretly gathers information about the user and relays that information to advertisers or other interested parties. Spyware is often attached to an interesting, useful, or entertaining piece of software or freeware that you download from the Internet. It might be a game, like Snood, or it might be a utility designed to make your desktop look pretty. Whatever application carrying the spyware, when the PC connects to the Internet, the spyware sends out whatever information it's been designed to gather.

In a most strict and formal use of the word, programs that are installed on a computer with the user's knowledge are not gathering information without that person's knowledge. To that extent, if the user fully understands that data is being collected and what that data is, spyware walks a narrow line between advertising and a virus. Spyware can gather information about email addresses, and even find and transmit passwords and credit card numbers.

Spyware is similar to a Trojan horse in that users unwittingly install the program when they install something else. Because these are independent, executable programs, they have the ability to monitor keystrokes, scan files on the hard drive, catalog applications like word processors, install other spyware programs, read cookies, change the default home page on the Web browser, or anything else a program can do. The problem is that there isn't an easy way to see that the computer is being controlled or affected. All that happens is that the spyware sends information back to the author, who then either uses it for marketing purposes, or sells it to someone else.

There are a number of free programs on reliable sites, such as the Zif-Davis (**http://www.zdnet.com**) Web site or CNET (**http://www.cnet.com**), designed to check your system for spyware.

Summary—Troubleshooting

We've reached the end of our overall review of personal computers. Each chapter has given you a series of representative practice questions, very similar to both the Sample Test and the actual exam. At this point, we would recommend that you leaf through the book, going back and checking yourself with all the previous practice questions. If you've forgotten the underlying knowledge captured by any of those questions, take the time to re-read the chapter or skim the headings.

If you feel good about your understanding of each topic we've covered, then by all means proceed to the next chapter. We haven't provided a listing of the main points in this chapter because *everything* in the chapter is important. You should know all the topics, and each of the techniques discussed under each section.

Finally, we'd like you to remember two of the most widely-used system errors in the entire computer industry: the IATC error, and the id10t error. Many tech support people have encountered these problems, falling victim to the same errors themselves from time to time. Idiot At The Controls (IATC) indicates that what appears to be a system error, is actually the result of some dumb set of operator actions. The closely related ID10T error is found in situations where a caffeine-frazzled support person slaps himself (or herself) on the forehead and realizes that something obviously and totally self-evident has been missed.

Everyone has to start somewhere, and regardless of how advanced your understanding of computers may be, you too, were once a beginner. Never forget that, to the person whose computer you're working on, the data is far more important than the machine and application software. If it's at all possible, repair the system before you reinstall the hard drive.

Practice Questions

Question 1

Exchanging a portable floppy drive is best done when it is connected to which of the following interface connectors?

- ❍ a. PS/2
- ❍ b. DB9
- ● c. USB
- ❍ d. DB25

Answer c is correct. The question makes no mention of the machine's power status, and exchanging any hardware components is best done either with the power turned off or with a USB device. Answers a and b are incorrect because a floppy drive uses neither a PS/2 mouse connector nor a DB9 serial port. Answer d is incorrect because the DB25 interface connector is almost always used as a printer connection or a SCSI pass-through for removable hard drives, scanners, and so forth.

Question 2

Which two of the following are indications that a virus has possibly infected the computer?

- ❑ a. CMOS memory size mismatch error
- ■ b. CMOS checksum error
- ■ c. Insufficient space on Drive D: error
- ❑ d. GUI image failure error

Answers b and c are correct. A checksum failure indicates that a file has changed between the time it was read into memory and written back to disk, a common first indicator of a virus. Another common indicator is when files begin to unexpectedly fill up a disk. Answer a is incorrect because this is an indication that physical memory has been changed by the addition or removal of memory modules. The error listed in answer d doesn't exist.

Question 3

Which menu would you choose in order to connect a user to a different printer on a network?

- ❍ a. Start|Programs|Accessories|System Tools
- ❍ b. Start|Settings|Accessories|Printers
- ❍ c. Start|Programs|Settings|Control Panel
- ● d. Start|Settings|Control Panel

Answer d is correct. Although the faster way to access this menu would be through the Start|Settings|Printers option, you can also get to the Printers icon through the Control Panel under the Start|Settings menu route. Answer a is incorrect because printers are not configured or added from the System Tools menu. Answer b is incorrect because the Settings menu does not include an Accessories option. Answer c is incorrect because the Programs menu does not include a Settings menu.

Question 4

Of the following options, which two would fail to uncover a bindings problem with the network card on a local machine?

- ❑ a. Selecting Start|Settings|Control Panel|System
- ■ b. Right-clicking on the Network Neighborhood icon in Windows 2000
- ❑ c. Double-clicking on the My Computer icon
- ■ d. Selecting Start|Programs|Accessories|SystemTools|Connection Manager

Answers b and d are correct. Answer b is correct because Windows 2000 does not have a Network Neighborhood icon (it uses a My Network Places icon instead). Answer d is correct because no version of Windows has a Connection Manager menu option. Answer a is incorrect because the System icon in the Control Panel provides access to the Device Manager, where you can do some initial detective work about a network card. Answer c is incorrect because double-clicking on the My Computer icon is another way to access the Control Panel and network configuration information.

Question 5

An employee has called with a problem where he or she cannot print to the Customer Service line printer. What are two areas you would explore to see where the problem might lie?

- [x] a. Select Start|Settings|Control Panel|Network and Dial-up Connections
- [x] b. Click on the Local Area Connection icon
- [ ] c. Right-click on the NIC LED icon in the System Tray
- [ ] d. Edit the PROTOCOL.INI file through SYSEDIT.COM

Answers a and b are correct. The Network and Dial-up Connections option of the Windows 2000 Control Panel offers a connections status report under the Local Area Connection icon. The responses to this question are tricky in that response b is the next step after going to the menu listed in response a. Answer c is incorrect because although the Taskbar may have a Connections icon showing, there is no NIC LED icon, and the System Tray is not used for this purpose. Answer d is incorrect because the PROTOCOL.INI file is a listing of any Real Mode networking hardware configurations and does not show any status problems with network cards.

Question 6

Which of the following utility programs is used to check the structural integrity of the system registration files?

- ○ a. Emergency Recovery Utility
- ○ b. Emergency Registry Recover
- ● c. Registry Checker
- ○ d. Registry File Monitor

Answer c is correct. The Registry Checker (SCANREGW.EXE) can back up the system registration files and also do a simple structural test of the Registry. Answer a is incorrect because the Emergency Recovery Utility provides only backup and restore capability. Answer b and d are incorrect because the utilities listed in those options don't exist.

Need to Know More?

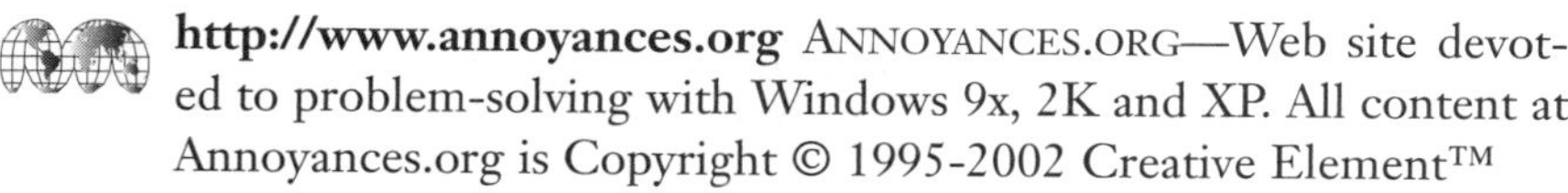

http://www.annoyances.org ANNOYANCES.ORG—Web site devoted to problem-solving with Windows 9x, 2K and XP. All content at Annoyances.org is Copyright © 1995-2002 Creative Element™

http://www.labmice.net/troubleshooting/boot_problems.htm *Labmice.net*—wholly owned, operated, and edited by Bernie Klinder

http://www.labmice.net/windowsxp/default.htm Windows XP Resource Center

http://aumha.org/index.htm *Windows Support Center*, James A. Eshelman, Proprietor & Webmaster.

http://aumha.org/kbstrtup.htm Startup Problems

http://www.pacs-portal.co.uk/startup_content.htm Using MSCONFIG.EXE and the various Start Group options: *"A central resource for PC users and Tech Support staff alike who are concerned about the poor performance of their PCs due to the number of programs that run at system start-up."*—Paul Collins, Webmaster

http://www.pacs-portal.co.uk/startup_pages/startup_full.htm An alphabetic listing of the more than 1,400 item that can run at startup in the various versions of Windows.

http://support.microsoft.com/default.aspx?scid=fh;EN-US;faqs Microsoft's Product Support FAQ page

http://support.microsoft.com/default.aspx?scid=/support/win2000/tshooters/tshoot.asp Microsoft's Windows 2000 Online Troubleshooter

http://www.microsoft.com/windowsxp/pro/using/howto/gettingstarted/guide/troubleshoot.asp *Troubleshooting Windows XP Professional*: Microsoft Knowledgebase

http://www.symantec.com/avcenter/vinfodb.html Symantec Security Response: Virus Search & Threats encyclopedia © 2000 Symantec Corporation, 20330 Stevens Creek Boulevard, Cupertino, CA 95014 USA. All rights reserved.

http://vil.nai.com/vil/default.asp McAfee Security AVERT (Anti-Virus Emergency Response Team) virus listings © 2002, Networks Associates Technology, Inc. All Rights Reserved. McAfee is a business unit of Network Associates, Inc.

Aspinwall, Jim. *IRQ, DMA and I/O*. New York, NY: MIS Press, 1995. ISBN 1-55828-456-7.

Bigelow, Stephen. *Troubleshooting and Repairing Computer Printers*. New York, NY: TAB Books, 1996. ISBN 0-07-005732-X.

Freedman, Alan. *Computer Desktop Encyclopedia, Second Edition*. AMACOM, 1999. ISBN 0-814-479-855. This is great for a fast look-up or refresher.

Karney, James. *Upgrade and Maintain Your PC*. Indianapolis, IN: MIS Press, 1996. ISBN 1-558-28460-5.

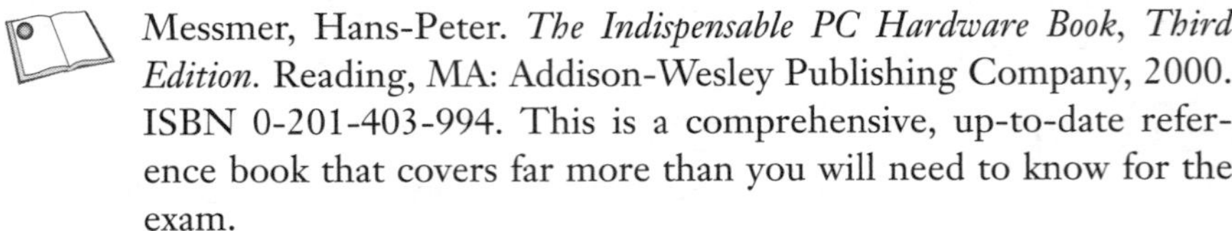

Messmer, Hans-Peter. *The Indispensable PC Hardware Book, Third Edition*. Reading, MA: Addison-Wesley Publishing Company, 2000. ISBN 0-201-403-994. This is a comprehensive, up-to-date reference book that covers far more than you will need to know for the exam.

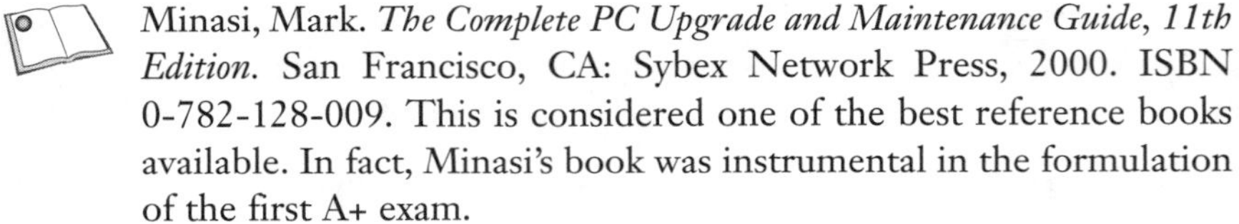

Minasi, Mark. *The Complete PC Upgrade and Maintenance Guide, 11th Edition*. San Francisco, CA: Sybex Network Press, 2000. ISBN 0-782-128-009. This is considered one of the best reference books available. In fact, Minasi's book was instrumental in the formulation of the first A+ exam.

Minasi, Mark. *The Complete PC Upgrade and Maintenance Guide*. San Francisco, CA: Sybex Network Press, 1996. ISBN 0-782-11956-5.

Mueller, Scott. *Upgrading and Repairing PCs, 12th Edition*. Indianapolis, IN: Que, 2000. ISBN 0-7897-2303-4. This is one of our favorites. If you are only going to have one reference book, give this one serious consideration.

Rosch, Winn. *Hardware Bible, Fifth Edition*. Indianapolis, IN: Sams Publishing, 1999. ISBN 0-789-717-433. This is a well-organized reference book that covers software issues as well as hardware.

Sample Test

Do you have a countdown timer? It's time to take the exam! In the Introduction and Chapter 1 of this book, we covered many test-taking strategies. Although you'll be taking the exam on a computer, we've made the following test an accurate representation of the questions. Before taking this sample test, you should feel very comfortable about your knowledge. Once you're done, Chapter 16 provides the answers. Remember, if you cheat, you're only hurting yourself!

Give yourself 90 minutes to complete this exam. Sit at a table or desk, and try to make the surface as empty and clean as you can. Lay down a piece of paper and a pencil and spend 5 minutes writing down the things you most want to have handy (from the Cram Sheet and your notes). Remember, you'll be allowed a blank sheet of paper and a pencil in the exam room, but you will not be allowed to bring anything else in with you. This paper can hold last-minute cram points you scribble down, or it can be used to break apart complex lists of possible responses to questions.

The Questions

No matter how much you might want to go back and pretend, you only get one chance to be surprised in a book like this. You can read the end of a novel, then go back and experience some excitement by finding out how the story arrived at that ending, but it isn't the same with a sample test. If you skim the answers and take the test again, it won't be an accurate assessment of your knowledge.

Keep in mind that we've already developed careers in the PC industry, and we aren't going in to take your exam for you. We're trying to prepare *you* for a career, and only you can create an accurate simulation of the test environment. Try to re-create the exam rooms you remember from school, or from other times in your past. The more accurate your simulation, the easier you'll feel when you're faced with the real thing.

Single Choice and Multiple Choice Responses

Every question on the current exam is supposed to be a multiple-choice question with only a single correct response. Previous tests have had what are called "scenario" questions, where you're asked to fill in a sentence, or pick a likely set of options. These types of questions aren't supposed to be on the final exam, and we saw none on the final beta versions.

The way the current exam gets around the forbidden scenario questions is to provide a paragraph with a number of blanks. Each response has a list of words that can fill in the blanks in the order they appear. Be careful! It only takes misreading one set of orders to produce an incorrect response.

If you haven't yet, you might want to read through Chapter 1, where we speak about the test environment and adaptive testing. If you already read Chapter 1, we'll remind you that we've chosen to continue the now-discontinued practice of allowing multiple answers. This is so that we can use a printed sample test to vary the complexity level and difficulty of the questions. As we said in the beginning, "If you can get through our test, you'll have no trouble with the real exam."

Picking the Right Answer

Go back and refresh your memory with some of the strategies we discussed in Chapter 1, and think about some of the types of questions you're about to encounter. Keep in mind that the people creating these kinds of tests (ourselves included) take a sort of twisted pleasure in trying to screw you up! We've been where you are, and we made it through, so we think it's only fair that you should have to sweat a little.

Oh come on…lighten up! We're not trying to ruin your life. What we want you to do is to go into the test with your eyes wide open, and all your senses on full alert. This is war! Look at each question as though it were a possible bomb. Keep your eyes peeled for the following:

- Words like "best," "required," "most appropriate." These are red flags telling you that there are multiple possibilities, based on how an unstated industry standard might apply.
- Long lists of commands. These can easily be read in the wrong order if you don't have your eyes focused. Write them down on your scratch paper, and put numbers next to them to ensure the proper order.
- Questions that try to draw images in your mind. Let the image come and try to see it clearly. Add in sounds and action. These questions are often troubleshooting steps involving step-by-step menu choices.

Confusing Questions

By the time this test reached your hands, many people read it through, reviewed it, made suggestions, and researched every single word and punctuation mark. The test has been designed with psychology in mind, and with a full knowledge of many other tests. If there's confusion about a particular question, you can pretty much bet your next paycheck that the confusion was specifically factored into that question!

We found a number of questions on the exam that really *were* confusing! To that end, we've tried to highlight those areas of knowledge throughout the book, and to give you our thoughts as to how we analyzed the questions. In our own version of the exam, we've tried to cause you some confusion as well, but in a very specific manner.

Part of our preparation methodology is based on the idea that you've read the book and you're feeling fairly confident. You should also have a fair amount of intuition going for you, based on your hands-on experience with computers. Using those assumptions, we still want to throw a few curve balls at you so that you'll be somewhat familiar with the "Yikes!" feeling when it hits you in the real exam (and it will!).

Remember—trust your instincts! If you get some of our most confusing questions right, then you'll probably do extremely well on the CompTIA exam. If you get them wrong, don't feel bad. The questions are *designed* to be difficult. Once you get the answers from Chapter 16, you'll be more likely to remember where you tripped, and we'll have crammed that much more information into your head.

The Exam Framework

The questions you're about to see have not been organized in any specific order. We've made no attempt to follow the progression of this book, or to follow any other sort of logical progression. This is a general test of your overall knowledge of microcomputers.

The real world comes at you from every direction at once, and frequently you'll have to juggle many important problems at the same time. This test has also been designed with possible job interviews in mind, where you're taken back to a repair or service environment and turned loose for an hour or so.

Many of the questions use jargon phrasing and shortened versions of terminology. Throughout the book we've tried to highlight the many different ways of saying the same thing. We've used different words to refer to various terms, and inter-mixed acronyms with the full spelling of the terms. Repeatedly, we've tried to prepare you for the varying ways that technical professionals refer to the problems and tools of the trade.

The A+ exam was created by a committee of professionals, each of whom has a different way of talking about computers. We've tried to extract as many of those styles as possible, and to jumble them together in a similar way as to what we found on the exam. Life is rarely simple, and the exam (in our opinion) is actually quite difficult.

Begin the Exam

From the time you complete your notes on the blank sheet of paper, you have 90 minutes to complete the test. Take your time, and imagine you're shipwrecked on a desert island, having all the time in the world. Read every word carefully, and then read the whole question a second time before you look at the responses.

Read each response on its own, and don't try to fit it in with the question. When you've read each response as though it were a random fact, go back and read the question one more time.

A common flaw in the human mind is to immediately attempt to make sense out of incoming data. This flaw is often used against you on various exams. By reading the question on its own, and then reading each response without thinking about the question, you overload the "surprise circuit." Once your mind stops trying to puzzle over the question, you're ready to actually read the question as it stands.

Start your timer, and begin the exam now.

Question 1

Your primary controller is connected to a disk, with one active partition and one extended partition formatted as one logical drive. You connect a second disk drive to the secondary controller and create two partitions. Which drive letter will be assigned to the first of the new partitions?

❍ a. C

❍ b. D

❍ c. E

❍ d. F

Question 2

How many devices can be attached to a SCSI chain?

❍ a. 5

❍ b. 6

❍ c. 7

❍ d. 8

Question 3

If you use IRQ 2 in an AT system, which IRQ cannot be used?

- ❍ a. IRQ 13
- ❍ b. IRQ 5
- ❍ c. IRQ 9
- ❍ d. IRQ 8

Question 4 

You are upgrading Windows 3.1 to Windows 95. What should you do with regard to SMARTDRV?

- ❍ a. Expand its size to speed loading.
- ❍ b. Disable SMARTDRV.
- ❍ c. Change the settings for SMARTDRV to Protected Mode.
- ❍ d. Activate the write-through option for SMARTDRV.

Question 5 

A user complains that he has connected his Windows 2000 workstation to the network, but cannot find any other devices on the network. What would be the best thing to do first?

- ❍ a. Remove the NIC and start over.
- ❍ b. Replace the patch cable with a known good cable.
- ❍ c. Check the card link status light.
- ❍ d. Reload the drivers for the NIC.

Question 6 

What function key stops the automatic loading of Windows 95 and provides you with a menu of options for loading?

- ❍ a. F1
- ❍ b. F8
- ❍ c. F9
- ❍ d. F3

Question 7

Which of the following would aid system cooling?

❍ a. Removing the expansion covers in the back of the system case for increased airflow

❍ b. Attaching covers to any open expansion slots on the back of the system unit

❍ c. Placing the system unit against a cool inside wall

❍ d. Opening windows to increase airflow in the room

Question 8

Which is the common default IRQ used for LPT2?

❍ a. IRQ 5

❍ b. IRQ 9

❍ c. IRQ 7

❍ d. IRQ 14

Question 9

When a piece of paper comes out of a laser printer almost completely black, the primary corona wire has failed to properly charge which of the following things?

❍ a. The separation pad

❍ b. The heating roller

❍ c. The EP drum

❍ d. The paper

Question 10

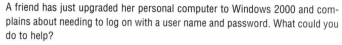

A friend has just upgraded her personal computer to Windows 2000 and complains about needing to log on with a user name and password. What could you do to help?

- ❍ a. Nothing. Windows 2000 security requires a user name and password.
- ❍ b. Disable networking if it is a stand-alone computer.
- ❍ c. Log on as Administrator and uncheck the password requirement Users Must Enter A Username And Password To Use This Computer box in the Users and Passwords dialog box.
- ❍ d. Change the password to blank.

Question 11

A user of a Windows 98 peer-to-peer networked computer has loaded one of his favorite DOS-based programs but cannot print from it to the network printer. What is the most likely reason?

- ❍ a. The DOS print drivers are not loaded.
- ❍ b. DOS program support has not been enabled.
- ❍ c. The printer is not supported in DOS.
- ❍ d. The printer port has not been captured for DOS applications.

Question 12

The thermal fuse fails in a laser printer. What is the most probable cause?

- ❍ a. The fuser overheated.
- ❍ b. The corona wire shorted.
- ❍ c. The drum overcharged.
- ❍ d. The laser diode needs changing.

Question 13

How would you deactivate the infrared port on a laptop computer running Windows 2000?

❍ a. Go to My Computer|Control Panel|Add-Remove Hardware, select IrDA, and select Remove.

❍ b. Go to the Device Manager, expand the Infrared Devices node, select IrDA, and select Disable.

❍ c. The infrared port is a system board component and must be deactivated on the system board.

❍ d. Infrared ports are autosensing and do not need to be deactivated.

Question 14

The print from a dot matrix printer is erratic, with some characters only partially printed. What needs to be done?

❍ a. The ribbon needs to be replaced.

❍ b. The print head needs to be aligned.

❍ c. A lighter weight paper needs to be used.

❍ d. The tractor feed needs adjusting.

Question 15

HIMEM.SYS is reported missing or corrupted as Windows 98 loads. What will happen?

❍ a. Nothing. Windows 98 does not require HIMEM.SYS.

❍ b. Windows 98 will load in Safe Mode.

❍ c. Windows 98 will fail to load.

❍ d. Windows 98 will load, but will have access to only the first 1MB of RAM memory.

Question 16

Windows 98 recognizes a new modem as a Standard Modem and does not identify the type and manufacturer. Why?

❍ a. Windows 98 does not have a driver for this modem.

❍ b. The modem is not PnP.

❍ c. The SYSTEM.DAT does not have a listing.

❍ d. The modem is not seated correctly.

Question 17

Windows Safe Mode loads which of the following display drivers?

❍ a. SVGA

❍ b. VGA

❍ c. EGA

❍ d. CGA

Question 18

How would you start a Windows 2000 computer in Safe Mode if no other operating systems were present?

❍ a. Press an arrow key immediately following the POST and select Safe Mode.

❍ b. Hold down the Ctrl key during the logon screen.

❍ c. Press F6 during the POST.

❍ d. Select Start|Run, type “CMD” to enter Command Mode, and then type “Safe”.

Question 19

A consultant recommends you enable RAID Level 4 on your NT server for reliability. How would you do this?

- ❍ a. Go to the Disk Administrator utility to remove the existing partitions and then select Tools|RAID|Level 4|Initialize.
- ❍ b. Delete all partitions using the Recovery Console and then reinitialize the drives as a RAID array.
- ❍ c. RAID Level 4 is not supported in NT Server.
- ❍ d. Enable block striping with parity blocks in the Disk Administrator.

Question 20

ATTRIB C:*.SYS /S /-H will cause which of the following to occur?

- ❍ a. Archive all .SYS files on Drive C:.
- ❍ b. Hide all .SYS files in the root directory.
- ❍ c. Unhide all .SYS files in the root directory.
- ❍ d. Unhide all .SYS files on Drive C:.

Question 21

The CONFIG.SYS file contains the line **LASTDRIVE=F**. The system uses a CD-ROM, one primary partition, and three logical DOS drives. A loaded CD-ROM disk will do which of the following?

- ❍ a. Install a program.
- ❍ b. Become the G: drive.
- ❍ c. Become the F: drive.
- ❍ d. Do nothing at all.

Question 22 

To bypass the execution of a line in a configuration file, which two of the following choices are used?

- ❑ a. **REM**
- ❑ b. :
- ❑ c. ;
- ❑ d. //

Question 23

What device would best protect a PC against erratic power and blackouts?

- ❍ a. A line conditioner
- ❍ b. A surge protector
- ❍ c. The UPS
- ❍ d. The ATA

Question 24 

Which files are required by Windows 98 to load? [Choose the two best answers]

- ❑ a. IO.SYS
- ❑ b. AUTOEXEC.BAT
- ❑ c. MSDOS.SYS
- ❑ d. CONFIG.SYS

Question 25

What is the default interrupt and address for COM1?

- ❍ a. IRQ 4 and 27F8h
- ❍ b. IRQ 5 and 03F8h
- ❍ c. IRQ 4 and 03F8h
- ❍ d. IRQ 3 and 02E8h

Question 26

What does the small "h" following an address indicate?

❍ a. The address should be read in hexadecimal.

❍ b. The address uses a high-order bit.

❍ c. The address is a default address.

❍ d. The address uses hard coding.

Question 27

Which of the following resolutions apply to a standard VGA monitor? [Choose the two best answers]

❑ a. 640 pixels

❑ b. 480 pixels

❑ c. 600 pixels

❑ d. 800 pixels

Question 28

What is a monitor called when it draws every other line on the screen and then returns and draws skipped lines?

❍ a. Interfaced

❍ b. Noninterfaced

❍ c. Interlaced

❍ d. Noninterlaced

Question 29

A cable in a 10BaseT Ethernet network breaks. What is the most likely result?

❍ a. The entire network crashes.

❍ b. Only the PC attached to that cable loses connectivity.

❍ c. The network operating system forces a system shutdown.

❍ d. Nothing.

Question 30

What is the default networking protocol used on the Internet?

❍ a. IPX/SPX

❍ b. DNS

❍ c. TCP/IP

❍ d. MIME

Question 31

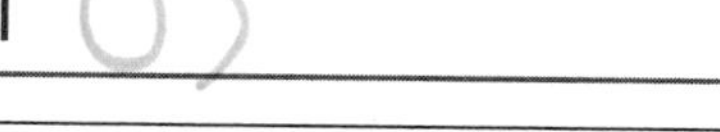

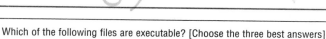

Which of the following files are executable? [Choose the three best answers]

❑ a. .EXE

❑ b. .BAT

❑ c. .INI

❑ d. .COM

Question 32

How can you verify what services are running under Windows 2000?

❍ a. Go to My Computer|Control Panel|Administrative Tools|Computer Management and select the Services icon.

❍ b. Go to My Computer|Control Panel|Administrative Tools|Computer Management and select the Event Viewer.

❍ c. Hold down the Ctrl, Alt, and Del keys and select Task Manager.

❍ d. Go to Start|Settings|Control Panel and select the System icon.

Question 33

Which command will list all files in the directory where the third character of the extension is the underscore (_)?

❍ a. DIR *._

❍ b. DIR *.*_

❍ c. DIR *.?_

❍ d. DIR *.??_

Question 34

The Windows REGEDIT.EXE program is used to edit which of the following files? [Choose the two best answers]

- ❑ a. USER.DAT
- ❑ b. CLASSES.DAT
- ❑ c. MSDOS.SYS
- ❑ d. SYSTEM.DAT

Question 35

Which file is used to control the boot process in Windows NT and Windows 2000?

- ❍ a. NTOSKRNL.EXE
- ❍ b. NTLDR.COM
- ❍ c. SMSS.EXE
- ❍ d. NTBOOTDD.SYS

Question 36

Which of the following cannot be changed by a polymorphic virus?

- ❍ a. The boot sector
- ❍ b. The master boot record
- ❍ c. The master cylinder
- ❍ d. The partition table

Question 37

How many DMA controllers and DMA channels are on an ATX system board?

- ❍ a. 2 controllers and 8 DMA channels
- ❍ b. 1 controller and 16 DMA channels
- ❍ c. 1 controller and 4 DMA channels
- ❍ d. 2 controllers and 16 DMA channels

Question 38

What is the preferred editor for changing the Registry entries in Windows NT and Windows 2000?

- ❍ a. REGEDT32.EXE
- ❍ b. REGEDIT.EXE
- ❍ c. SYSEDIT.EXE
- ❍ d. NTEDIT32.EXE

Question 39

Which commands can be run from the Recovery Console? [Choose the two best answers]

- ❑ a. FIXBOOT
- ❑ b. FIXREG
- ❑ c. FIXDSK
- ❑ d. FIXMBR

Question 40

A user has set a password in CMOS and then forgotten it. What would you do to gain access to the system?

- ❍ a. Use one of the password-breaking programs available on the Internet.
- ❍ b. Remove battery power to CMOS to clear it, reconnect the battery, and then reconfigure the CMOS.
- ❍ c. Go to Start|Settings|Control Panel|Users and Passwords, and check the No Password Required option.
- ❍ d. Run the FIXBIOS.EXE program to reinstall the master password.

Question 41

There is no beep code at system startup. What is the most likely problem?

- ❍ a. The speaker is disconnected.
- ❍ b. There is no beep code for a normal system start.
- ❍ c. The system clock is not working.
- ❍ d. A memory module failed the POST.

Question 42

What is the best cleaning solution to use on a dirty system case?

❍ a. Alcohol

❍ b. Carbosol

❍ c. Mild soap and water

❍ d. Diluted muratic acid

Question 43

Which of the following are not used to connect a CPU to a motherboard? [Choose the two best answers]

❑ a. Socket 7

❑ b. Socket B

❑ c. Slot 1

❑ d. Slot 4

Question 44

Which electrical component commonly found in computers can hold an electrical charge even when disconnected from power?

❍ a. A resistor

❍ b. A capacitor

❍ c. A diode

❍ d. A transistor

Question 45

A good fuse will give what kind of reading when tested with a standard multimeter?

❍ a. High DC volts value

❍ b. Low ohm value

❍ c. High ohm value

❍ d. High capacitance value

Question 46

To reduce possible ESD damage while repairing a PC, what is the most effective way to ground yourself?

❍ a. With a copper strap attached to the workbench

❍ b. With a copper strap attached to the PC

❍ c. By touching the chassis while replacing components

❍ d. None of the above

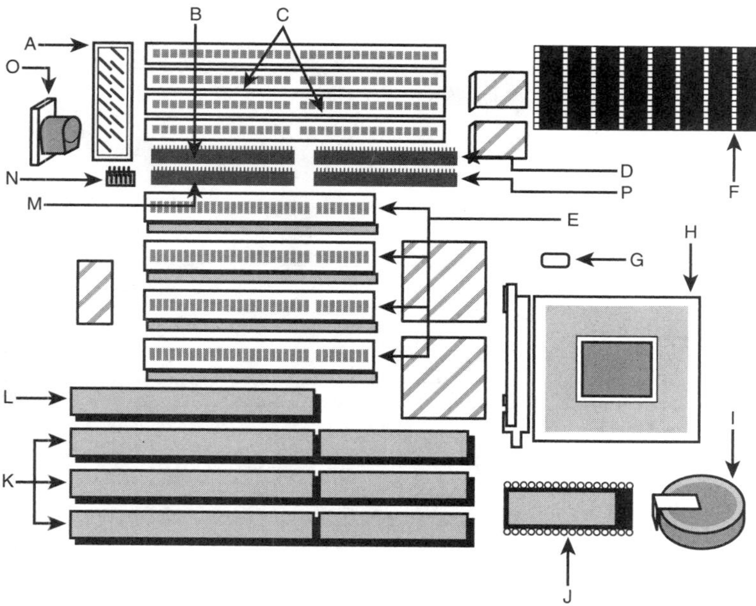

Exhibit 15.1 Use this motherboard diagram to answer questions 47 through 51.

Question 47

What are the two items that the letters "D" and "P" point to?

❍ a. IDE controllers

❍ b. ISA bus slots

❍ c. L-2 cache chips

❍ d. SIMM banks

Question 48

What is the item that the letter "H" points to?

- ❍ a. Modem
- ❍ b. Battery
- ❍ c. CPU
- ❍ d. Parallel interface

Question 49

What are the three items the letter "K" points to?

- ❍ a. PCI slots
- ❍ b. 8-bit ISA slots
- ❍ c. Memory banks
- ❍ d. 16-bit ISA slots

Question 50

What is the letter "C" labeling?

- ❍ a. PCI bus
- ❍ b. SIMM slots
- ❍ c. ZIF socket
- ❍ d. BIOS chip

Question 51

What does the letter "A" point to?

- ❍ a. AT keyboard connector
- ❍ b. Orientation chip
- ❍ c. Power connector
- ❍ d. LPT connector

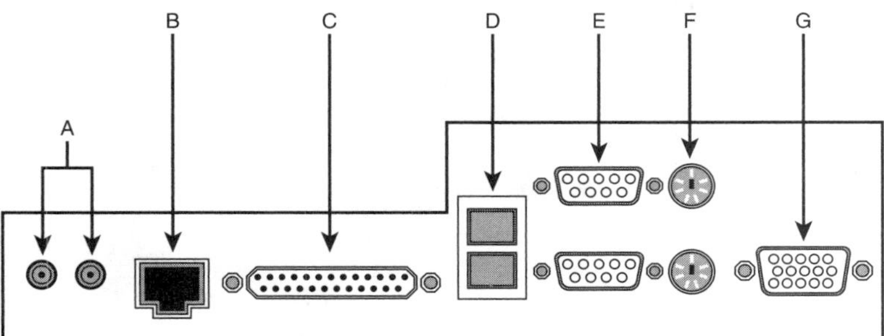

Exhibit 15.2 Use this chassis back panel diagram to answer questions 52 through 54.

Question 52

A parallel printer cable connects to which item (designated by a letter)?

❍ a. C

❍ b. D

❍ c. E

❍ d. F

Question 53

What items does the letter "E" point to?

❍ a. Video interface connectors

❍ b. USB interface connectors

❍ c. Serial interface connectors

❍ d. PS/2 interface connectors

Question 54

A USB port is shown in the diagram by which letter?

❍ a. B

❍ b. C

❍ c. D

❍ d. E

Question 55

How would you change the drive letter assigned to the CD-ROM in a Windows 2000 system?

- ❍ a. Change the load order in the SYSTEM.INI file so that the proper drive letter is assigned.
- ❍ b. Change the drive assignment in CMOS.
- ❍ c. Use REGEDIT.EXE to open the Registry. Highlight the HKEY_LOCAL_MACHINE and select the CD-ROM subkey.
- ❍ d. Select the CD-ROM drive properties on the Device Manager|Settings tab. Set the Start Drive Letter and End Drive Letter.

Question 56

A user wants to change his default printer on an NT workstation. How would you do this?

- ❍ a. Go to Start|Programs|Accessories|Printer Tools and select the Print First check box.
- ❍ b. Select the properties for the printer that the user wants in the Printer window and choose Set As Default.
- ❍ c. Configure the existing default printer as Secondary and set the desired printer as Primary.
- ❍ d. Provide the desired printer with a lower IP address.

Question 57

What is the best and simplest solution for resolving Ethernet congestion?

- ❍ a. Add another hub to the network.
- ❍ b. Segment the network with a router.
- ❍ c. Segment the network with a bridge.
- ❍ d. Set up a secondary IP network token.

Question 58

What are the first two files called when Windows NT and 2000 begin to boot?

❑ a. NTSYS.DLL

❑ b. NTOSKRNL.EXE

❑ c. WINNT.SYS

❑ d. NTDETECT.COM

Question 59

When a PC is powered on, the POST routine completes with one beep. What does this mean?

❍ a. The system is testing the PC speaker.

❍ b. The system has a nonsystem disk in Drive A:.

❍ c. The system has completed the POST with no errors.

❍ d. The system CMOS has a bad battery.

Question 60

Windows 98 can use all of the following files during boot-up, except which one of the following?

❍ a. WIN.COM

❍ b. MSDOS.SYS

❍ c. PROGMAN.INI

❍ d. LOGO.SYS

Question 61

When you save a file to a disk, where is the information about which sectors and clusters the file is using placed?

❍ a. PAT

❍ b. FAT

❍ c. MBR

❍ d. HTFS

Question 62 

The Windows Me default installation process removes which file reference from a CONFIG.SYS file?

- ❍ a. EMM386.EXE
- ❍ b. MSCDEX.SYS
- ❍ c. SMARTDRV.EXE
- ❍ d. MSDOS.SYS

Question 63

Which device can be connected to the computer and recognized while the computer is running?

- ❍ a. A keyboard
- ❍ b. A monitor
- ❍ c. A serial joystick
- ❍ d. A USB mouse

Question 64

Which type of connectors do the AMD Athlon and Duron processors use? [Choose the two best answers]

- ❑ a. Socket 1
- ❑ b. Slot A
- ❑ c. Socket 370
- ❑ d. Socket A

Question 65

IRQ 14 is the default IRQ assigned to which of the following?

- ❍ a. Secondary disk controller
- ❍ b. Primary disk controller
- ❍ c. Master slave disk controller
- ❍ d. XT drive controller

Question 66

A cable has a 25-pin male connector at one end and a Centronics 36-pin male connector at the other end. A common use for this cable is best described by which of the following choices?

❍ a. A parallel printer connection

❍ b. A modem connection

❍ c. A serial printer connection

❍ d. A SCSI device connection

Question 67 

Which of the following keys are displayed by the **REGEDIT** command? [Choose the three best answers]

❑ a. HKEY_USERS

❑ b. HKEY_CLASSES_ROOT

❑ c. HKEY_LOCAL_SECURITY

❑ d. HKEY_CURRENT_CONFIG

Question 68

The number 5 in the 10Base5 standard refers to which of the following?

❍ a. The maximum length of the cable in hundreds of meters

❍ b. The width of the cable in centimeters

❍ c. The width of the center conductor in millimeters

❍ d. The maximum number of connections per meter

Question 69 

A user is assigned proper user permissions in Windows 2000, but still cannot access a shared resource. Why?

- ❍ a. The user is a member of a group that does not have access to the resource.
- ❍ b. User permissions are not activated.
- ❍ c. The resource is already in use.
- ❍ d. The resource ACL has not been set to Active.

Question 70

Which of the following connectors are not used in a typical networking situation? [Choose the two best answers]

- ❑ a. Mini DIN
- ❑ b. RJ-11
- ❑ c. RJ-45
- ❑ d. DB15

Answer Key

1. c

2. c

3. c

4. b

5. c

6. b

7. b

8. a

9. c

10. c

11. d

12. a

13. b

14. a

15. c

16. a

17. b

18. a

19. c

20. d

21. d

22. a and c

23. c

24. a and c

25. c

26. a

27. a and b

28. c

29. b

30. c

31. a, b, and d

32. a

33. d

34. a and d

35. b

36. c

37. a

38. a

39. a and d

40. b

41. a

42. c

43. b and d

44. b

45. b

46. d

47. a

48. c

49. d

50. b

51. c

52. a

53. c

54. c

55. d

56. b

57. c

58. b and d

59. c

60. c

61. b

62. a

63. d

64. b and d

65. b

66. a

67. a, b, and d

68. a

69. a

70. b and d

Question 1

Answer c is correct. Drives A: and B: are automatically installed on a PC. The primary controller has one fixed disk with Drive C: as the Active partition and Drive D: as the extended partition. The second disk will start with the letter E, regardless of how many logical drives are installed on that disk. The one active partition is bootable because it is active. For that reason, it becomes Drive C:. The one extended partition is formatted as one logical drive; therefore, the entire extended partition on the first disk is a logical Drive D:. The C and D letters are being used, so any new disk (or change in the Extended partition) will begin with E, the next available letter. In this scenario, LASTDRIVE= does not need to be changed because the system recognizes five drive letters by default.

Question 2

Answer c is correct. This is a tricky question because the question specifically uses the word "devices." The automatic host adapter for a SCSI card takes up one of eight possible ID numbers. That leaves room for up to seven devices to be daisy-chained to the SCSI controller, each with a unique ID number. Answers a and b are technically correct, but the implication of the question itself is that you're being tested on the limits of a SCSI chain. For that reason, answers a and b are incorrect in this context. Answer d is incorrect because the host adapter takes up the eighth ID number.

Question 3

Answer c is correct. The AT BIOS cascades IRQ 9 to IRQ 2. If the system is using IRQ 2, then it must also be using IRQ 9, and you cannot use it for anything else. IRQ 13 is a red herring, and is typically set-aside for a math coprocessor. IRQ 5 is the default line assigned to LPT2, and IRQ 8 is the default line set-aside for the system clock.

Question 4

Answer b is correct. Windows 95 doesn't use SMARTDRV. If you don't remove or comment out the SMARTDRV line from your CONFIG.SYS file, SETUP.EXE does it for you. Answer a is incorrect because you can't expand the SMARTDRV program; you can only increase the size of the cache. Answer b is incorrect because whether SMARTDRV runs in Real Mode or Protected Mode is irrelevant to an upgrade installation. The installation process will halt and ask you to disable the program. Answer d is incorrect because SMARTDRV has no "write-through" option.

Question 5

Answer c is correct. A link status light on the NIC would indicate that the physical connection to the network is okay and that the card is functioning. Absence of a link status light could point to a physical problem with the card or cable, or a missing driver. Answer a is incorrect because without a network interface card, the user will never connect to a network. Although physically reinstalling the card might be useful, this is not what you would do first, given that response c offers you the link status LED. Answer b is incorrect because although the next step in the process may be to replace the patch cord, the question asks "What would be the best thing to do first?". Answer d is incorrect because reloading drivers is a much more complex process than simply checking the link status light.

Question 6

Answer b is correct. The F8 key, pressed between the time the "Starting Windows 95..." message and the Microsoft Windows 95 logo appear, interrupts the load process and produces the text-based Start menu. Pressing the F1 key, the F9 key, or the F3 key at this point will do nothing to interrupt the startup process. Although you can still use the F8 key in Windows 98, the way to arrive at Safe Mode is to hold down the Ctrl key while Windows 98 is starting.

Question 7

Answer b is correct. The expansion slot covers are part of the engineering design to allow for optimal airflow within the case of any PC that uses expansion slots and covers. Removing unused slot covers causes cooling air to flow out of the case and generally increases the temperature inside the case. Answers c and d might provide minimal aid in cooling the overall environment, but they are incorrect in the context of the "system cooling" referred to in the question.

Question 8

Answer a is correct. LPT2 uses IRQ 5. Answer b is incorrect because IRQ 9 is generally redirected to IRQ 2. Answer c is incorrect because LPT1 is assigned to IRQ 7 by default. Answer d is incorrect because IRQ 14 is normally assigned to the primary disk controller. (See the "IRQs, DMA, and I/O Ports" section of Chapter 5 for a complete listing of the default IRQ assignments.)

Question 9

Answer c is correct. The primary corona wire is used to place a negative charge on the electrophotographic (EP) drum. This removes toner from those areas that will not produce an image. The secondary corona wire places a charge on the paper to attract toner to the correct locations. If the paper fails to charge, no toner will stick to the paper for fusing. If the drum fails to charge correctly, the entire drum will take on toner and transfer it to the whole piece of paper. The separation pad, in answer a, prevents more than one sheet of paper from entering the printer at any given time. Answer b is incorrect because the fusing assembly contains the heating roller and is used to fuse the image toner particles to the paper. Answer d is incorrect because if the paper is completely black, something failed to move an image to the paper. The transfer corona wire charges the paper, not the primary corona wire.

Question 10

Answer c is correct. Windows 2000 provides a check box in the Users and Passwords dialog box so that the user name and password function can be bypassed in stand-alone situations where security is not an issue. Answer a is incorrect because although Windows 2000 is designed as a network operating system, it does not require a user name and password. Answer b is incorrect because Windows 2000 passwords are a separate issue from networking capabilities. Disabling networking does nothing to resolve the password problem. Answer d is incorrect because configuring a blank password will not remove the initial logon dialog box, which is the original complaint.

Question 11

Answer d is correct. Windows 98 asks if the printer will be used for DOS applications during setup. If you respond yes, all of the settings are made automatically. However, if the printer was not configured for DOS initially, you must go back to the Printer|Properties|Detail dialog box and select Capture Printer Port to enable DOS printing. Answer a is incorrect because although applications use printer drivers and DOS has a printer device driver, nothing uses "print drivers." Answer b is incorrect because the program is apparently working and the complaint is only that the user cannot print. Answer c is incorrect because it is Windows printer support that is the issue, not DOS printer support. The program is running in a virtual DOS machine, and Windows 98 is controlling the surrounding peripherals, including the printer.

Question 12

Answer a is correct. The fuser step of the printing process involves high amounts of heat to melt the toner and to fuse it to the paper. For safety, a thermal fuse is inserted in the circuit to prevent possible fire hazards. Answer b is incorrect because a short circuit at the corona wire would shut down the printer or cause a fire. The corona wire does not have a thermal fuse. Answer c is incorrect because the EP drum does not use heat, and answer d is incorrect because the laser printer contains no such thing as a laser diode.

Question 13

Answer b is correct. Selecting a device from the Device Manager display and choosing Disable will deactivate the device driver instructions for any device showing in the listing. The question refers to deactivating a device, not removing a device. Answer a is incorrect because the Control Panel has an Add New Hardware icon, but no Add-Remove Hardware icon. Answer c is incorrect because activation and deactivation are almost always Windows choices, not system board events. Answer d is incorrect because although autodetection is a feature in Windows, autosensing is not.

Question 14

Answer a is correct. The clue is that some characters are only partially printing. The immediate diagnostic test would be to replace the existing ink ribbon. Print head alignment is not a common cause of partial character printing. The weight of the paper has no direct connection to the print quality. The tractor feed could cause misalignment of characters, but would be unlikely to cause partial printing.

Question 15

Answer c is correct. Windows 98 requires HIMEM.SYS and a minimum of 4MB of extended memory. HIMEM.SYS is a memory manager that allows access to all memory above the first 1MB of conventional memory. If HIMEM.SYS is missing or fails, Windows cannot access anything more than 1MB of memory and will fail to load. Answer b is incorrect because in order to reach Safe Mode, Windows must have been able to access extended memory in the first place. Answer d is incorrect because Windows cannot load at all without HIMEM.SYS.

Question 16

Answer a is correct. If Windows 9x can access the device and understand that the device is a modem, it attempts to find an internal device driver for the specific modem. Windows will use PnP BIOS to read the manufacturer's name and the model of the modem, if available. However, whether or not the device is PnP, Windows understands it is a modem. If an internal device driver is not named, Windows assigns a generic device driver and calls it a Standard Modem. After the name and settings are assigned, they are written to the SYSTEM.DAT file. Answer b is incorrect because although the modem is not PnP, Windows still recognizes it enough to assign resources and a device name. Answer c and d are incorrect because the device must be listed and correctly seated if it shows up in the Device Manager.

Question 17

Answer b is correct. The Windows Safe Mode installs a keyboard driver and a standard VGA display driver, and bypasses network connections without loading network drivers. Safe Mode is a diagnostic mode designed to reduce configuration problems to their absolute minimum. CGA and EGA graphics modes are obsolete standards, so answers c and d are incorrect. Answer a is incorrect because SVGA graphic modes have numerous configuration options, making it an inappropriate mode for troubleshooting possible display problems.

Question 18

Answer a is correct. If the Windows 2000 computer is not set up for dual booting, pressing any of the arrow keys after POST will bring you to a menu where you can select Safe Mode booting. Answer b is incorrect because Safe Mode does not initialize network connections and a logon screen is part of networking. Answer c is incorrect because you do not have access to the keyboard during the POST. Answer d is incorrect because neither DOS nor Windows has a **SAFE** command.

Question 19

Answer c is correct. A Windows NT file server must be running the Windows NT Server version of the operating system, which supports RAID Levels 0, 1, and 5. Level 4 is not supported in Windows NT Server. Answer a is an option made up entirely of nonexistent terms and features. Answer b is incorrect because Recovery Console is a Windows 2000 feature. Answer d is incorrect because although disk mirroring and striping is done through the Disk Administrator, the system will still be unable to support RAID Level 4.

Question 20

Answer d is correct. The **/S** switch tells **ATTRIB** to operate on all subdirectories. The **C:*.SYS** tells **ATTRIB** to operate on all .SYS files on Drive C:, beginning at the root directory. The **-H** switch tells **ATTRIB** to turn the hidden attribute off or to unhide the file. Answer a is incorrect because the archive attribute is set with the **/+A** switch. Answer b is incorrect because the **/-H** switch uses the minus sign not the plus sign (hide). Answer c is incorrect because the **/S** switch extends the reach of the command beyond the root directory.

Question 21

Answer d is correct. If no CONFIG.SYS file existed, or if an existing file did not contain a **LASTDRIVE=** statement, DOS would be able to read only the default maximum of five drives. In this question, CONFIG.SYS exists and contains a **LASTDRIVE=F** statement telling DOS to recognize a maximum of six drives. The system has the default Drive A: and Drive B:; a Drive C: Primary partition; and Drives D:, E:, and F: as three additional logical DOS drives. The CD-ROM would become the seventh drive with Drive G: assigned to it by default. To make seven drives visible, the **LASTDRIVE=F** statement would have to be modified to **LASTDRIVE=G**. Unless the modification were made, an additional CD-ROM drive would fail to be recognized and none of the events in answers a, b, and c would take place.

Question 22

Answers a and c are correct. **REM** (an abbreviation of remark) is used in DOS to bypass a line (comment out or remark out) in batch files and configuration files. Windows uses the semicolon (;) to bypass lines in .INI file. Answer b is incorrect because the colon is used to signify drive letters. Answer d is incorrect because paired forward slashes are commonly used as a directory statement in networking operating systems.

Question 23

Answer c is correct. An uninterruptible power supply (UPS) contains a battery backup to provide power to the PC during power interruptions and blackouts. The UPS also provides line conditioning, meaning that erratic power events are stabilized before reaching the computer. Answer a is incorrect because the line conditioning is a feature of the UPS, not a separate device. Answer b is incorrect because a surge protector provides no protection from a blackout. The ATA referenced in answer d is the AT Attachment bus specification associated with an IDE controller, and has nothing to do with protecting a computer.

Question 24

Answers a and c are correct. Only IO.SYS and MSDOS.SYS are required by Windows 98. CONFIG.SYS and AUTOEXEC.BAT can be used to install Real Mode device drivers and applications, but the two files are not required to load any version of Windows.

Question 25

Answer c is correct. COM1 uses IRQ 4 and address 03F8h for the default installation. (COM1 is odd and uses even IRQs.) Answers a and b are not COM addresses. Answer d is the default address for COM4. COM ports 1 and 3 use IRQ 4, whereas COM ports 2 and 4 use IRQ 3.

Question 26

Answer a is correct. A common indicator that a number or address is a hexadecimal unit is either a lowercase or an uppercase h before or after the unit.

Question 27

Answers a and b are correct. A standard VGA monitor has a resolution of 640×480. Although an SVGA monitor can be configured to a 640x480 resolution, 600×800 is a more common configuration. Pixels (picture units) is a designation for graphic resolution in displayed images such as monitors or graphics. Dots per inch (dpi) is a designation for printed or scanned resolutions.

Question 28

Answer c is correct. Monitors are either interlaced or noninterlaced, not interfaced or noninterfaced. When the electron gun at the back of a CRT monitor draws every odd line and then returns and draws every even line, it is interlaced (like lacing up shoes). If the electron gun draws every line in a single pass (no skipping lines), the monitor is a noninterlaced monitor.

Question 29

Answer b is correct. 10BaseT is a twisted-pair wiring configuration. Twisted pair allows each PC to connect to a hub directly. If the wire breaks, only the specific PC connected by that wire will be affected. The overall network connection is designed in such a way that each PC has its own connection, and the wiring integrity is not dependent on a functional connection between all the PCs.

Question 30

Answer c is correct. The Internet is a Unix-based network using Transmission Control Protocol/Internet Protocol (TCP/IP) networking protocols. Internet Packet Exchange/Sequenced Packet Exchange (IPX/SPX) is typically used in a local area network (LAN) running NetWare.

DNS is a service that converts host names to IP addresses. Multipurpose Internet Mail Extensions (MIME) is an email protocol.

Question 31

Answers a, b, and d are correct. Files with a suffix (extension) of .BAT, .EXE, and .COM are all considered executable. Although Windows considers .PIF files to be executable, files ending in .INI are Windows configuration files and cannot be executed (run) from a command line.

Question 32

Answer a is correct. Windows 2000 provides many services that help other programs run. The status of these services is listed under the Services icon in Computer Management. The action in answer b would be used to view each event associated with a specific situation that is taking place on the computer, to find out why something failed to work properly. The action in answer c would be used to find out what programs were currently in memory. Answer d is incorrect because the System icon is used to check the devices installed on the system and to check the percentage of Windows resources remaining.

Question 33

Answer d is correct. The ? wild card is used to represent a single, unknown character. The question indicates a three-character extension, so **DIR *.??_** is correct. **DIR *._** will find all files with only the underscore character following the period. **DIR *.*_** will find any file with any extension. **DIR *.?_** will find any file with a two-character extension ending with an underscore.

Question 34

Answers a and d are correct. The REGEDIT.EXE program is used to edit the USER.DAT and SYSTEM.DAT files making up the Windows 9x Registry. MSDOS.SYS is a text-based system file and can be edited with any text editor. Answer b is incorrect because although CLASSES.DAT may be a file, it is not one related to the Registry.

Question 35

Answer b is correct. The Window NT Loader file (NTLDR.COM) controls the boot process for Windows NT and Windows 2000. NT Loader then loads NTOSKRNL.EXE, the operating system kernel. NTBOOTDD.SYS is a special file used to make NT bootable from a removable hard drive. SMSS.EXE is the Windows NT or Windows 2000 Session Manager.

Question 36

Answer c is correct. A polymorphic virus or any other type of virus cannot make changes to the master cylinder, because a cylinder is a single track located in the same place on every platter making up a hard drive. A virus is a set of program instructions and, as such, can make programming changes anywhere on a system where other program or instruction data can be stored. The boot sector, Master Boot Record, and partition table all contain data. Although a cylinder is made up of tracks and each track contains sectors and clusters, a virus program can affect only one of those sectors or clusters, not the whole cylinder (in this context).

Question 37

Answer a is correct. XT motherboards contained one DMA controller with four channels. The AT system board added a second controller and four more channels, making a total of two DMA controllers with eight channels (four channels per controller). The ATX (as well as the LPX and NLX) form factor is an outgrowth of the AT motherboard, continuing the use of two controllers and eight channels.

Question 38

Answer a is correct. REGEDT32.EXE is the 32-bit version of REGEDIT.EXE, and is the preferred editor for Windows 2000 and Windows NT. REGEDIT.EXE was the Registry Editor included in Windows 9x, and originally designed to edit the Windows 3.x REG.DAT file. SYSEDIT.EXE is a utility program that opens the main DOS configuration files and Windows .INI files. Answer d refers to some fictitious file, unrelated to the Windows Registry.

Question 39

Answers a and d are correct. The Windows 2000 Recovery Console allows the **FIXBOOT** and **FIXMBR** commands, along with a number of other DOS-like commands. The fictitious red herrings referred to in answers b and c do not exist in the Recovery Console.

Question 40

Answer b is correct. The CMOS chip cannot be accessed by any program that requires d an operating system to be loaded, because operating systems work only after a PC has been configured. As such, answers a, c, and d are incorrect because they all refer to a program or a program (Window) option. There is no generic, master password for CMOS, and the password is contained within the chip itself. The only way to clear the password is to clear the CMOS by removing all power to the chip.

Question 41

Answer a is correct. Beep codes are always generated by the POST. Regardless of the number of beeps generated, there will always be at least one. If no beeps are heard, the most likely problem is that the speaker is disconnected or broken.

Question 42

Answer c is correct. Mild soapy water is noncorrosive and provides the best cleaning solution for plastic, vinyl, or metal cases. Alcohol is used mainly where no residue should be left, such as certain internal metal or plastic parts. Carbosol is a fictional term, and muratic acid (diluted or otherwise) is a form of hydrochloric acid used to clean concrete.

Question 43

Answers b and d are correct. Note that this is a tricky question because it asks you to choose what does not do something. If you aren't paying attention you can easily choose the wrong answers based on what you know will work.

Neither Socket B nor Slot 4 is associated with microprocessors and their packaging, making them the correct choices for this question. Socket 7 is a flat design used to install a CPU on the motherboard. Slot 1 is a vertical design, using a small circuit board with a single edge connector and a special processor slot on the motherboard.

Question 44

Answer b is correct. Capacitors store electricity for later release. Resistors, diodes, and transistors are other electronic components often found on a motherboard, but all three of these components require a constant flow of electricity in order to function.

Question 45

Answer b is correct. A fuse is a breakable part of a circuit line. Ohms are used to measure resistance. If the circuit enters a condition beyond a specified tolerance, the fuse breaks, and the circuit line is interrupted. If the fuse is unbroken, it appears as a normal part of the circuit line and has no more resistance than any other part of the circuit line. A high ohm value would mean there is a great deal of resistance in the circuit coming from somewhere else on the circuit. A low ohm reading at the fuse would indicate that current is flowing through the fuse with no interruption, and the fuse is good.

Question 46

Answer d is correct. Ground straps must have a resistor placed in the line to avoid electrocuting the technician in the event of a short. All the other answers offer ways to ground yourself, but none of the options offers protection against an electrostatic discharge. The question asks for the most effective way to reduce ESD damage, and none of the listed options interferes with an electrical discharge.

Question 47

Answer a is correct. A good approach to this question is to first eliminate what you know to be incorrect answers. ISA bus slots are usually long and divided, and are typically located near the edge of a motherboard, as in the case of K. Level 2 (L-2) Processor cache chips are located very close to the CPU and are very small, as in the case of G. SIMM banks are typically the same size, much smaller than ISA slots, and narrower than PCI slots, as in the case of C. When you've eliminated most of the expansion slots, the remaining connectors in the area close to D and P are probably interface controllers. IDE controllers are usually paired, one above the other (not side by side).

Question 48

Answer c is correct. Typically, the CPU is the largest chip on a motherboard and, up through the Pentium Pro, is usually large and square. An internal modem is a separate expansion card and not part of the motherboard. The CMOS battery, offered as answer b, is almost always round or cylindrical and either clips or is soldered onto the motherboard. H points to something square. Parallel port interfaces are small, narrow connectors, longer than floppy controllers but smaller than memory banks. Most modern PCs have only one parallel interface.

Question 49

Answer d is correct. Although the diagram does not show 16 connector points, the general shape of an expansion slot is fairly accurate. 16-bit slots are longer than 8-bit slots, and ISA slots (if they exist) usually were offered as three 16-bit connectors and one 8-bit connector. The 8-bit ISA slot is pointed to by L and the three 16-bit slots are pointed to by K. Four PCI slots are pointed to by E, with PCI slots tending to be in the middle of the motherboard. The memory banks are pointed to by C.

Question 50

Answer b is correct. The SIMM (or DIMM) memory banks are usually closer to the outer edge of the motherboard, narrow, and observably smaller than ISA slot and PCI slots. The letter E points to a PCI bus, which is often closer to the center of a motherboard. A zero-insertion-force (ZIF) socket is a CPU socket and will always have some kind of handle (like a paper cutter) connected to the socket. This handle is pictured on the left side of the square CPU socket pointed to by H. The BIOS chip, pointed to by J, is usually preinstalled on a motherboard and is smaller than the CPU socket. This motherboard is using socket technology, as opposed to slot technology, to mount the CPU.

Question 51

Answer c is correct. The main power supply almost always connects to the computer near the edge of the motherboard with a large pin-connector. The AT keyboard connector (not interface) must be at the edge of the motherboard in order for the keyboard to plug into it. "Orientation chip" is a fictitious term, and "LPT" is a DOS device name, not a connector. Between answers a and c, the keyboard connector should look round and small, but the power supply connector should look large and rectangular and be a one-of-a-kind connector.

Question 52

Answer a is correct. Most modern PCs have only one printer port and that connector is a DB25 female connector. When there are two serial ports, one of them is almost always a 9-pin connector and the other a DB25 male connector. This panel shows only one 25-pin connector, so C is pointing to the parallel port. D points to the USB connectors, E points to a pair of 9-pin serial ports, and F points to a pair of 6-pin PS/2 connectors.

Question 53

Answer c is correct. The video connector is a 15-pin connector, and you can count on the fact that there will only be one video connector on an exam exhibit. If you know that the parallel port is a DB25 connector, and if you remember that PS/2 connectors are round, the choices reduce to either answer b or answer c. USB connectors are square and about the size of a PS/2 connector. E is pointing to a 9-pin cable connector, making it a serial port interface.

Question 54

Answer c is correct. USB ports are square and typically come as a vertical pair, as pointed to by D. Network connectors (if they're built in) are almost always RJ-45 connectors with the recognizable clip-slot at the bottom (like a modular phone jack). B points to a network connector. C is the parallel port, and E is a 9-pin serial port.

Question 55

Answer d is correct. Drive letters are assigned by the operating system during the boot process. Answer b is incorrect because CMOS only controls the order in which the system will look at drives. Windows 2000 provides a way to reassign drive letters from within the operating system by selecting the device (in this case, a CD-ROM drive) in the Device Manager and then choosing the appropriate start and end drive letters. Answer a is incorrect because SYSTEM.INI has no control over assigning drive letters. Answer c is incorrect because the Registry contains configuration settings for the hardware device, not drive letter assignments.

Question 56

Answer b is correct. Setting the default printer for a Windows NT workstation is done in the same way as in Windows 2000 and Windows 9x. Right-click on the printer in the Printers folder and select Set As Default. Answer a presents a fictitious menu path, and there is no "Print First" check box in Windows. Answer c is incorrect because changing a printer involves making a printer the default, not the primary or secondary printer. Answer d is incorrect because although a network printer may have an IP address, the relative priority of a network resource has nothing at all to do with the many-digit IP address number and the IP address has no bearing on whether a printer is the default printer.

Question 57

Answer c is correct. A bridge was specifically designed to reduce network traffic congestion by segmenting an existing network. Routers move traffic between networks, and hubs provide a way to add additional resources to a network (increasing possible congestion). Answer d, "Set up a secondary IP network token," is purely fictitious. A token, in a token ring network, uses an Internet Protocol (IP) address to correctly transfer data packets.

Question 58

Answers b and d are correct. NTDETECT.COM identifies hardware for the hardware abstraction level (HAL) and NTOSKRNL.EXE loads the core operating system. The files referred to in answers a and c may exist somewhere, but they have nothing to do with loading Windows NT or Windows 2000 (or any other version of Windows, for that matter).

Question 59

Answer c is correct. If a POST routine completes with one beep, it means that the system has completed the POST with no errors. There is no provision on a computer to self-test the PC speaker (how would the computer hear it?). Answer b is incorrect because it refers to a CMOS error generated by a disk in the floppy disk drive. Answer d is incorrect because the POST is a low-level hardware validation routine and beep codes tell you only if the fundamental connections have been made with the basic system components. A bad CMOS battery may cause the loss of all configuration settings, but it has nothing to do with the POST.

Question 60

Answer c is correct. Windows 3.x used the Program Manager as its primary shell interface. Program Groups and Program Items were maintained partly through the PROGMAN.INI file. Although an upgrade installation from a Windows 3.x machine can make a one-time conversion of the .GRP files referenced in the PROGMAN.INI file, the question asks about files Windows uses for booting. MSDOS.SYS is one of the DOS system files used to boot the operating system. WIN.COM is the small loader program used to start Windows. LOGO.SYS is the graphic file that produces the Windows splash screen.

Question 61

Answer b is correct. The FAT is the file allocation table used for storing addresses of file clusters on a disk. The partition allocation table (PAT) stores information about the location of each partition on a disk and is not used for file storage information. The Master Boot Record (MBR) is used to store information pointing the system towards the location of an operating system. The High Performance File System (HPFS) is a file management system used by OS/2.

Question 62

Answer a is correct. EMM386.EXE is an expanded memory manager, and Windows 95, 98, and ME do not use an expanded memory manager. Following Windows 3.x, all versions of Windows require the HIMEM.SYS extended memory manager, and will load the file from either a CONFIG.SYS file or from MSDOS.SYS. Windows Me will automatically place a **REM** and a space before any line in a CONFIG.SYS file containing EMM386.EXE and SMARTDRV.EXE references. Smart Drive is a DOS file-caching program, and is not used by Windows Me. MSDOS.SYS is a system file, and no references to it are ever used in CONFIG.SYS. MSCDEX.SYS is the generic Microsoft CD-ROM drive device driver and may be a required reference in a CONFIG.SYS file on machines where the BIOS cannot recognize a drive.

Question 63

Answer d is correct. USB devices are designed to be safely attached or detached from a running computer (hot swapping) and, at the same time, recognized by the operating system. Monitors, serial devices, and keyboards are checked at the POST and can actually damage the system board if disconnected or connected during operation.

Question 64

Answers b and d are correct. Athlon and Duron processors were produced in both the Slot A and Socket A configuration. They are not pin compatible with Intel-designed Slot 1, Slot 2, Socket 7, Socket 8, or Socket 370 architectures. There may have been a Socket 1 at some point in time, but if there was, it has long since disappeared. Athalon and Duron processors are modern processors.

Question 65

Answer b is correct. IRQ 14 is assigned to the primary disk controller. IRQ 15 is assigned to the secondary disk controller. There is no such thing as the master slave disk controller. IRQ 2 was originally assigned to the XT drive controller, but now contains cascaded instructions from IRQ 9.

Question 66

Answer a is correct. The clues here are both the 25-pin male connector and the Centronics connector. Because there can be serial cables with DB25 female connectors, the Centronics connector indicates that in this case, the question is referring to a parallel printer cable. If the cable had a DB25 female connector on one end and a 9-pin serial connector at the other, it could be a modem connection. The 36-pin male Centronics specifies that this is not a serial printer connection, and the DB25 connector specifies that it is not a SCSI cable. SCSI cables often use 50-pin ribbon cables.

Question 67

Answers a, b, and d are correct. HKEY_USERS, HKEY_CLASSES_ROOT, and HKEY_CURRENT_CONFIG are three of the six keys displayed in REGEDT. There is no HKEY_LOCAL_SECURITY.

Question 68

Answer a is correct. Originally, the last digit in network wiring referred to the maximum length of a cable in hundreds of meters. 10Base5 refers to a cable with 500 meters maximum length. 10Base2 is a thinner cable, with a maximum length of 200 meters. When 10BaseT wiring was introduced, the last character changed to reflect the type of wiring. T refers to twisted pair.

Question 69

Answer a is correct. Even though a user may be given individual rights, restrictions on a group that the user belongs to will supersede the assigned rights if they conflict. User permissions are not a feature that needs to be activated or deactivated, and neither does the resource ACL have such a feature. Networks provide shared access to resources, making answer c incorrect. The user may have to wait until the resource is free, but in this context the question refers to permissions and rights, not queues and hardware problems.

Question 70

Answers b and d are correct. Mini DINs are used in Apple Computer networks and RJ-45, or, more properly, "modular data connectors," are extensively used in 10BaseT networks. RJ-11 is a modular telephone connector, and DB15s are often used for monitors.

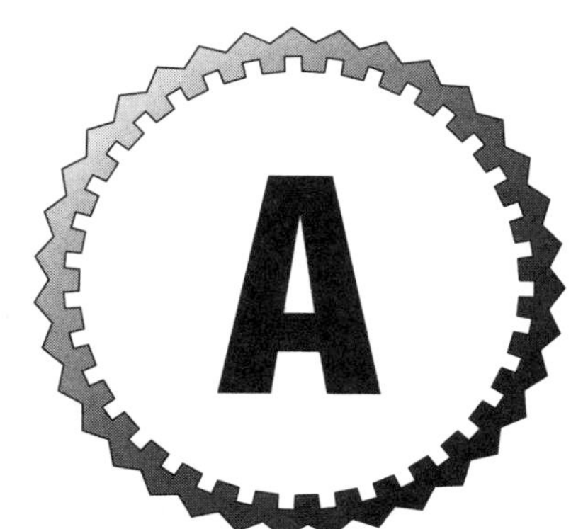

What's on the CD-ROM

This appendix is a brief rundown of what you'll find on the CD-ROM that comes with this book. For a more detailed description of the *PrepLogic Practice Tests, Preview Edition* exam simulation software, see Appendix B, "Using *PrepLogic, Preview Edition* Software." In addition to the *PrepLogic Practice Tests, Preview Edition*, the CD-ROM includes the electronic version of the book in Portable Document Format (PDF), several utility and application programs, and a complete listing of test objectives and where they are covered in the book. Finally, a pointer list to online pointers and references are added to this CD. You will need a computer with Internet access and a relatively recent browser installed to use this feature.

PrepLogic Practice Tests, Preview Edition

PrepLogic is a leading provider of certification training tools. Trusted by certification students worldwide, we believe PrepLogic is the best practice exam software available. In addition to providing a means of evaluating your knowledge of the Exam Cram material, *PrepLogic Practice Tests, Preview Edition* features several innovations that help you to improve your mastery of the subject matter.

For example, the practice tests allow you to check your score by exam area or domain to determine which topics you need to study more. Another feature allows you to obtain immediate feedback on your responses in the form of explanations for the correct and incorrect answers.

PrepLogic Practice Tests, Preview Edition exhibits most of the full functionality of the *Premium Edition* but offers only a fraction of the total questions. To get the complete set of practice questions and exam functionality, visit `PrepLogic.com` and order the *Premium Edition* for this and other challenging exam titles.

Again, for a more detailed description of the *PrepLogic Practice Tests, Preview Edition* features, see Appendix B.

Exclusive Electronic Version of Text

The CD-ROM also contains the electronic version of this book in Portable Document Format (PDF). The electronic version comes complete with all figures as they appear in the book. You will find that the search capabilities of the reader comes in handy for study and review purposes.

Easy Access to Online Pointers and References

The Suggested Reading section at the end of each chapter in this Exam Cram contains numerous pointers to Web sites, newsgroups, mailing lists, and other online resources. To make this material as easy to use as possible, we include all this information in an HTML document entitled "Online Pointers" on the CD. Open this document in your favorite Web browser to find links you can follow through any Internet connection to access these resources directly.

Using the *PrepLogic Practice Tests, Preview Edition* Software

This Exam Cram includes a special version of PrepLogic Practice Tests—a revolutionary test engine designed to give you the best in certification exam preparation. PrepLogic offers sample and practice exams for many of today's most in-demand and challenging technical certifications. This special *Preview Edition* is included with this book as a tool to use in assessing your knowledge of the Exam Cram material, while also providing you with the experience of taking an electronic exam.

This appendix describes in detail what *PrepLogic Practice Tests, Preview Edition* is, how it works, and what it can do to help you prepare for the exam. Note that although the *Preview Edition* includes all the test simulation functions of the complete, retail version, it contains only a single practice test. The *Premium Edition*, available at `PrepLogic.com`, contains the complete set of challenging practice exams designed to optimize your learning experience.

Exam Simulation

One of the main functions of *PrepLogic Practice Tests, Preview Edition* is exam simulation. To prepare you to take the actual vendor certification exam, PrepLogic is designed to offer the most effective exam simulation available.

Question Quality

The questions provided in the *PrepLogic Practice Tests, Preview Edition* are written to the highest standards of technical accuracy. The questions tap the content of the Exam Cram chapters and help you to review and assess your knowledge before you take the actual exam.

Interface Design

The *PrepLogic Practice Tests, Preview Edition* exam simulation interface provides you with the experience of taking an electronic exam. This enables you to effectively prepare yourself for taking the actual exam by making the test experience a familiar one. Using this test simulation can help to eliminate the sense of surprise or anxiety you might experience in the testing center because you will already be acquainted with computerized testing.

Effective Learning Environment

The *PrepLogic Practice Tests, Preview Edition* interface provides a learning environment that not only tests you through the computer, but also teaches the material you need to know to pass the certification exam. Each question comes with a detailed explanation of the correct answer and often provides reasons the other options are incorrect. This information helps to reinforce the knowledge you already have and also provides practical information you can use on the job.

Software Requirements

PrepLogic Practice Tests requires a computer with the following:

- Microsoft Windows 98, Windows Me, Windows NT 4.0, Windows 2000, or Windows XP
- A 166MHz or faster processor is recommended
- A minimum of 32MB of RAM
- As with any Windows application, the more memory, the better your performance
- 10MB of hard drive space

Installing *PrepLogic Practice Tests, Preview Edition*

Install *PrepLogic Practice Tests, Preview Edition* by running the setup program on the *PrepLogic Practice Tests, Preview Edition* CD. Follow these instructions to install the software on your computer:

1. Insert the CD into your CD-ROM drive. The Autorun feature of Windows should launch the software. If you have Autorun disabled, click the Start button and select Run. Go to the root directory of the CD and select setup.exe. Click Open, and then click OK.
2. The Installation Wizard copies the *PrepLogic Practice Tests, Preview Edition* files to your hard drive; adds *PrepLogic Practice Tests, Preview Edition* to your Desktop and Program menu; and installs test engine components to the appropriate system folders.

Removing *PrepLogic Practice Tests, Preview Edition* from Your Computer

If you elect to remove the *PrepLogic Practice Tests,, Preview Edition* product from your computer, an uninstall process has been included to ensure that it is removed from your system safely and completely. Follow these instructions to remove PrepLogic Practice Tests, Preview Edition from your computer:

1. Select Start, Settings, Control Panel.
2. Double-click the Add/Remove Programs icon.
3. You are presented with a list of software currently installed on your computer. Select the appropriate *PrepLogic Practice Tests, Preview Edition* title you wish to remove. Click the Add/Remove button. The software is then removed from you computer.

Using *PrepLogic Practice Tests, Preview Edition*

PrepLogic is designed to be user friendly and intuitive. Because the software has a smooth learning curve, your time is maximized, as you will start practicing almost immediately. *PrepLogic Practice Tests, Preview Edition* has two major modes of study: Practice Test and Flash Review.

Using Practice Test mode, you can develop your test-taking abilities, as well as your knowledge through the use of the Show Answer option. While you are taking the test, you can reveal the answers along with a detailed explanation of why the given answers are right or wrong. This gives you the ability to better understand the material presented.

Flash Review is designed to reinforce exam topics rather than quiz you. In this mode, you will be shown a series of questions, but no answer choices. Instead, you will be given a button that reveals the correct answer to the question and a full explanation for that answer.

Starting a Practice Test Mode Session

Practice Test mode enables you to control the exam experience in ways that actual certification exams do not allow:

- **Enable Show Answer Button**—Activates the Show Answer button, allowing you to view the correct answer(s) and a full explanation for each question during the exam. When not enabled, you must wait until after your exam has been graded to view the correct answer(s) and explanation(s).

- **Enable Item Review Button**—Activates the Item Review button, allowing you to view your answer choices, marked questions, and facilitating navigation between questions.
- **Randomize Choices**—Randomize answer choices from one exam session to the next; makes memorizing question choices more difficult, therefore keeping questions fresh and challenging longer.

To begin studying in Practice Test mode, click the Practice Test radio button from the main exam customization screen. This will enable the options detailed above.

To your left, you are presented with the options of selecting the pre-configured Practice Test or creating your own Custom Test. The pre-configured test has a fixed time limit and number of questions. Custom Tests allow you to configure the time limit and the number of questions in your exam.

The *Preview Edition* included with this book includes a single pre-configured Practice Test. Get the compete set of challenging PrepLogic Practice Tests at `PrepLogic.com` and make certain you're ready for the big exam.

Click the Begin Exam button to begin your exam.

Starting a Flash Review Mode Session

Flash Review mode provides you with an easy way to reinforce topics covered in the practice questions. To begin studying in Flash Review mode, click the Flash Review radio button from the main exam customization screen. Select either the pre-configured Practice Test or create your own Custom Test.

Click the Best Exam button to begin your Flash Review of the exam questions.

Standard *PrepLogic Practice Tests, Preview Edition* Options

The following list describes the function of each of the buttons you see. Depending on the options, some of the buttons will be grayed out and inaccessible or missing completely. Buttons that are accessible are active. The buttons are as follows:

- **Exhibit**—This button is visible if an exhibit is provided to support the question. An exhibit is an image that provides supplemental information necessary to answer the question.
- **Item Review**—This button leaves the question window and opens the Item Review screen. From this screen you will see all questions, your answers, and your marked items. You will also see correct answers listed here when appropriate.
- **Show Answer**—This option displays the correct answer with an explanation of why it is correct. If you select this option, the current question is not scored.
- **Mark Item**—Check this box to tag a question you need to review further. You can view and navigate your Marked Items by clicking the Item Review button (if enabled). When grading your exam, you will be notified if you have marked items remaining.
- **Previous Item**—This option allows you to view the previous question.
- **Next Item**—This option allows you to view the next question.
- **Grade Exam**—When you have completed your exam, click this button to end your exam and view your detailed score report. If you have unanswered or marked items remaining you will be asked if you would like to continue taking your exam or view your exam report.

Time Remaining

If the test is timed, the time remaining is displayed on the upper right corner of the application screen. It counts down the minutes and seconds remaining to complete the test. If you run out of time, you will be asked if you want to continue taking the test or if you want to end your exam.

Your Examination Score Report

The Examination Score Report screen appears when the Practice Test mode ends—as the result of time expiration, completion of all questions, or your decision to terminate early.

This screen provides you with a graphical display of your test score with a breakdown of scores by topic domain. The graphical display at the top of the screen compares your overall score with the PrepLogic Exam Competency Score.

The PrepLogic Exam Competency Score reflects the level of subject competency required to pass this vendor's exam. While this score does not directly translate to a passing score, consistently matching or exceeding this score does suggest you possess the knowledge to pass the actual vendor exam.

Review Your Exam

From Your Score Report screen, you can review the exam that you just completed by clicking on the View Items button. Navigate through the items viewing the questions, your answers, the correct answers, and the explanations for those answers. You can return to your score report by clicking the View Items button.

Get More Exams

Each *PrepLogic Practice Tests, Preview Edition* that accompanies your Exam Cram contains a single PrepLogic Practice Test. Certification students worldwide trust PrepLogic Practice Tests to help them pass their IT certification exams the first time. Purchase the *Premium Edition* of PrepLogic Practice Tests and get the entire set of all new challenging Practice Tests for this exam. PrepLogic Practice Tests—Because You Want to Pass the First Time.

Contacting PrepLogic

If you would like to contact PrepLogic for any reason, including information about our extensive line of certification practice tests, we invite you to do so. Please contact us online at **http://www.preplogic.com**.

Customer Service

If you have a damaged product and need a replacement or refund, please call the following phone number:

800-858-7674

Product Suggestions and Comments

We value your input! Please email your suggestions and comments to the following address:

feedback@preplogic.com

License Agreement

YOU MUST AGREE TO THE TERMS AND CONDITIONS OUTLINED IN THE END USER LICENSE AGREEMENT ("EULA") PRESENTED TO YOU DURING THE INSTALLATION PROCESS. IF YOU DO NOT AGREE TO THESE TERMS DO NOT INSTALL THE SOFTWARE.

Acronym Glossary

AC (alternating current)
Changes from a positive voltage to a negative voltage during one cycle. The most common example is household electricity, which is 110 volts at 60 hertz in the United States.

ADC (analog-to-digital converter)
An electronic device, usually packaged in a chip, that converts analog signals, such as speech, to a digital bit stream.

AGP (accelerated graphics port)
Provides the video controller card with a dedicated path to the CPU. Found on newer PCs.

AM (amplitude modulation)
A type of radio transmission.

AMD (Advance Micro Devices)
A corporation specializing in microprocessor chip manufacturing.

ANSI (American National Standards Institute)
One of several organizations that develop standards for the information technology industry.

AOL (America OnLine)
An international private networking system that provides online services to paid subscribers.

API (application programming interface)
Provides a set of uniform building blocks that many programmers can use when building an application. *(See MAPI.)*

ASCII (American Standard Code for Information Interchange)
Specifies a seven-bit pattern used for communications between computers and peripherals.

ASPI (Advanced SCSI Programming Interface)
A protocol for a program or device to interface with the SCSI bus. *(See SCSI.)*

AT (Advanced Technology)
IBM's name for its 80286 PC form factor, which it introduced in 1984.

AT&T (American Telephone and Telegraph) Corp.
One of the world's largest communications providers, originally Bell Telephone Co. (1878).

ATA (Advanced Technology Attachment)
The ANSI standard for IDE drives.

ATAPI (ATA packet interface)
A specification for attaching additional drives to an ATA connector. The ANSI standard for EIDE drives.

ATX (Advanced Technology Extensions)
A system board form factor that incorporates an accelerated graphics port. It is designed for the Pentium II and is mounted vertically.

Basic (Beginner's All-Purpose Symbolic Instruction Code)
A popular programming language developed in the 1960s at Dartmouth College.

BBS (bulletin board service)
Online access locations where users post information and where other users can read or download information.

BDOS (Basic DOS)
One of the original system files in CP/M, the other being BIOS (not the same thing as the ROM BIOS chip on a motherboard).

BIOS (Basic Input Output System)
A set of detailed instructions for PC startup, which usually are stored in ROM on the system board.

BNC (bayonet nut connector)
A type of connecting hardware used with network cables and interface cards.

CAD (computer aided design)
Drawing programs used in engineering and architectural settings.

CAV (constant angular velocity)
One of the ways in which an optical disk maintains a correct speed by using a small data buffer.

CCD (charge-coupled device)
A semiconductor that is sensitive to light and is used for imaging in scanners, video cameras, and digital still cameras.

CCP (console command processor)
The original command interpreter used in CP/M.

CD (compact disk)
A plastic disk measuring 4.75 inches in diameter that is capable of storing a large amount of digital information.

CDC (Control Data Corporation)
One of the original developers of the IDE specification.

CD-RW (compact disk, read-write)

A compact disk that can be written to and read from. Technically, the RW does not stand for re-writeable.

CGA (Color Graphics Adapter)

An IBM video standard that provides low-resolution text and graphics.

CGI (common gateway interface)

An Internet scripting language.

CLV (constant linear velocity)

One of the ways in which an optical disk maintains a correct speed by adjusting spindle motor speed.

CMA (common monochrome adapter)

IBM's original PC monitor, also known as *monochrome display adapter* (MDA).

CMOS (Complementary Metal Oxide Semiconductor)

The type of chip commonly used to store the BIOS for a PC. It is usually backed up with a small battery for times when the PC's power is off.

CMY (cyan, magenta, yellow)

The three primary colors of reflective light used in paint, ink, and other indirect sources of color. CMY is used in LCD color monitors.

COBOL (Common Business Oriented Language)

A high-level programming language commonly used on mainframe and minicomputers.

CompTIA (Computing and Industry Trade Association)

A nonprofit organization made up of over 6,000 member companies that developed the A+ certification program.

CP/M (Control Program for Microcomputers)

The first operating system developed for microcomputers.

CPU (central processing unit)

The main chip where instructions are executed.

CRC (Cyclical Redundancy Check)

A method used to verify data.

CRT (cathode ray tube)

The picture tube of a monitor.

CSMACD (carrier sense, multiple access, collision detection)

Another name for an Ethernet network.

DAC (Digital-to-analog converter)

An electronic device that converts digital signals to analog.

DASD (direct access storage device)

The technical name given by the IBM PC Institute for a disk drive subsystem.

DAT (digital audio tape)
Used in small cassettes for storing backup information. (Also used to refer to as a *Directory Allocation Table*.)

DC (direct current)
Electricity that flows in only one direction. The power supply in a PC converts alternating current from the wall socket to direct current at voltages needed by PC components.

DDE (Dynamic Data Exchange)
A message protocol within Windows that allows applications to exchange data automatically.

DDR (double data rate)
Usually associated with DDR SDRAM.

DEC (Digital Equipment Corporation)
One of the original corporations involved with the development of PCs.

DHTML (dynamic hypertext markup language)
Like HTML except that information can be changed, based upon data gathered at a Web site. For example, user location can be captured to change the contents of a Web page.

DIMM (dual inline memory module)
A popular form factor for RAM in which each side of the edge connector has separate connections.

DIMM (dual inline memory module)
A narrow printed circuit board that holds memory chips. This module uses DRAM chips on both sides of the board.

DIN (Deutsche Institut fur Normung)
The German Standards Institute, which developed standards for many of the connectors used in PCs.

DIP (dual inline package)
A common rectangular chip housing with leads on both of its long sides.

DMA (direct memory access)
Specialized circuitry, often including a dedicated microprocessor, that allows data transfer between memory locations without using the CPU.

DMF (distributed media format)
Microsoft's proprietary 1.7MB formatting method for distribution disks.

DNS (domain name system)
A DNS server works to convert numeric IP addresses to readable format.

DOS (Disk Operating System)
The most widely used single-user operating system in the world.

dpi (dots per inch)
Written in lowercase, a measure of resolution mostly applied to printers and scanners.

DRAM (dynamic RAM)
The most common type of computer memory.

DS (double sided)
Description of a storage method used with disks. *(See HD.)*

DS/DL (double sided, double layer)
A storage format for DVDs.

DS/SL (double sided, single layer)
A storage format for DVDs.

DSL (digital subscriber line)
A high speed Internet connection system.

DVD (digital versatile disk)
An optical storage disk much like compact disk (CD), using a different method for storing. DVDs have storage capacities approaching 10GB.

DVD-R (digital versatile disk, recordable)
An optical storage disk that can be written to by the consumer.

EB (exabyte)
1,024 petabytes, 1-million terabytes. 5 exabytes would store every word ever spoken by all human beings.

ECC (error correction code)
Tests for memory errors, which it corrects on the fly.

ECP (electronic control package)
Not the same as the enhance capabilities port for parallel interfaces, the electronic control package is the circuitry used by a laser printer to communicate with its CPU and control panel.

ECP (Enhanced Capabilities Port, or IEEE 1284)
The standard for enhanced parallel ports that are compatible with the Centronics parallel port.

EDO (extended data output)
A type of memory that approaches the speed of SRAM by overlapping internal operations.

EEMS (Enhanced EMS)
An enhancement of the Enhanced Memory Specification. EEMS was developed by AST, Inc. together with Ashton-Tate, Inc.

EEPROM (electrically erasable programmable read only memory)
Holds data without power. It can be erased and overwritten from within the computer or externally with an electrical charge.

EGA (Enhanced Graphics Adapter)
A medium-resolution IBM text and graphics standard. It was superseded by today's VGA standard.

EIDE (Enhanced Integrated Drive Electronics)
An extension of the IDE interface that is compatible with more devices and offers increased transfer rates.

EISA (Extended Industry Standard Architecture)

Expands the 16-bit ISA bus to 32 bits and provides bus mastering.

ELD (electro-luminescent display)

A type of video display used in notebook computers.

EMI (electromagnetic interference)

An adverse effect caused by electromagnetic waves emanating from an electrical device.

EMS (Expanded Memory Specification)

The expanded memory specification developed by Lotus, Intel, and Microsoft prior to the development of extended memory (XMS).

EP (Electrophotographic)

The EP drum in a laser printer is sensitive to light.

EPP (Enhanced Parallel Port, or IEEE 1284)

A high-speed ECP capable of bi-directional speeds approaching 2MB per second.

EPROM (erasable programmable read only memory)

A type of ROM that can be erased and reprogrammed.

ESD (electrostatic discharge)

Electrical current moving from an electrically charged object to an approaching conductive object.

ESDI (Enhanced Small Device Interface)

An interface specification for hard drive controllers. *(See IDE.)*

FAT (file allocation table)

The part of DOS that keeps track of where data is stored on a disk.

FC PGA (flipped chip pin grid array)

A configuration of CPU connector pins where the chip is turned upside down.

FCB (file control block)

Used in the CP/M file management system.

FDDI (Fiber Distributed-Data Interface)

Used in fiber optics for transmission of large bursts of high-speed data.

FH (firmware hub)

(See GMCH.)

FIFO (first in, first out)

Applied to buffering, usually in a modem buffer.

FM (frequency modulation)

A type of radio transmission.

FORTRAN (*for*mula *tran*slator)

Designed by John Backus for IBM in the late 1950s, FORTRAN is the oldest, high-level programming language.

FPM (fast page memory)

A type of memory using addressing pages.

FPU (floating-point unit)
Commonly called a *math coprocessor*, it was available as an optional chip for Intel CPUs up to and including the 80386. The unit was internally integrated in the 80486 and Pentium processors.

FTM (flat technology monitor)
A monitor with a flat face in front (not the same as a flat panel display used in notebooks).

GB (gigabyte)
1,024 megabytes, 1 million kilobytes.

GIF (graphics interchange format)
A file format for bitmap graphics made popular by CompuServe (online service), often used in Web page designs.

GMCH (graphics and memory controller hub)
Part of the 800 series chip set hub architecture, along with the I/O Controller Hub (IOCH) and the Firmware Hub (FH).

GUI (graphic user interface)
Implemented with Windows, it incorporates icons, pull-down menus, and the use of a mouse.

HAL (hardware abstraction layer)
One of the foundation layers of Windows NT and Windows 2000.

HAZMAT (hazardous materials)
Chemical compounds that can cause public health dangers. *(See MSD.)*

HD (high density)
Description of data density on a disk (DS, HD).

HDTV (high definition television)
A standard for displaying high-resolution television images.

HMA (high memory area)
A term that refers to the random access memory (RAM) between 640K and 1024K (or 1Mb).

HPFS (high performance file system)
The preferred file management system for OS/2.

HTML (Hypertext Markup Language)
A standard for defining and linking documents on the World Wide Web.

Hz (Hertz)
A unit measuring cycles per second (MHz is millions (mega) of cycles per second).

I/O (input/output)
An acronym used to reference any place where data is moving into or out of something.

IBM (International Business Machines)
The corporation that developed the first personal computer (PC).

IC (integrated circuit)
An arrangement of circuit traces and electronic components often placed on a so-called integrated circuit card or board.

IDE (Integrated Drive Electronics)

A popular hardware interface used to connect hard drives to a PC.

IEEE (Institute of Electrical and Electronic Engineers)

An organization with an overall membership of over 300,000 members that is highly involved in setting standards.

IFS (installable file system)

Windows file management component. (IFS can also mean the image formation system in a laser printer.)

InterNIC (Internet Network Information Center)

A committee funded by the National Science Foundation to provide specifications for the Internet.

IOCH (I/O controller hub)

(See GMCH.)

IP (Internet protocol)

An IP address is a series of numbers and periods, and many networks use the address. The protocol is the set of rules for that addressing.

IR (infrared)

A frequency of light in the short wave spectrum.

IRQ (interrupt request)

A hardware interrupt generated by a device that requires service from the CPU. The request is transmitted through one of 8 to 16 physical lines on the system board, with one device typically allowed per line.

ISA (Industry Standard Architecture)

An expansion bus commonly used on PCs. It provides a data path of 8 to 16 bits and is sometimes referred to as an AT bus because of its use in the first IBM AT computers.

ISDN (Integrated Services Digital Network)

A specification for digital transmission of data over analog phone lines.

ISO (International Organization for Standardization)

An umbrella group for many of the international standards committees, such as ANSI.

ISP (Internet service provider)

Usually a business involved in providing Internet connections and Web hosting.

JPEG (Joint Photographic Experts Group)

A compression format used for graphic image files, resulting in a common .JPG extension.

KB (kilobyte)

1,024 bytes.

LAN (local area network)

Standard acronym for most networks. *(See WAN.)*

LBA (logical block addressing)
Used to overcome early BIOS and IDE controller limitations in recognizing hard drives larger than 512MB.

LCD (liquid crystal display)
A type of computer display panel using liquid crystals to pass or block light.

LDAP (Lightweight Directory Access Protocol)
A query language used by Windows NT and Windows 2000 to manage access requests.

LED (light-emitting diode)
A small electrical device that generates light when current passes through it.

LIM (Lotus/Intel/Microsoft)
Three companies that jointly developed a standard for memory management above 640K.

LPX (Low Profile Extensions)
An AT system board form factor used in small desktop cases.

LSA (Local Security Authority)
A module in Windows NT and Windows 2000 acting as the interface between User Mode and Kernel Mode.

LUN (Logical Unit Number)
The identification (ID) number assigned to a device on a SCSI interface.

MAPI (messaging application programming interface)
Built into Windows as a way for different email programs to work together.

MB (megabytes)
1,024 kilobytes, 1 million bytes.

MB/s (megabytes per second)
A data transfer rate of 1 million bytes per second.

Mbps (megabits per second)
A data transfer rate of 1 million bits per second.

MBR (Master Boot Record)
The first sector on a bootable partition.

MCA (Microchannel Architecture)
A 32-bit expansion bus developed by IBM. The bus requires specially designed cards that are not interchangeable with other popular bus designs.

MDA (Monochrome Display Adapter)
The first IBM standard for monochrome video displays for text.

MDRAM (multibank dynamic random access memory)
A type of video memory that uses many 32KB DRAM chips to form an interleaved array of graphics memory banks.

MICR (magnetic ink character recognition)
Used in some scanners to capture magnetic pattern information.

MIME (multipurpose Internet extensions)

A specification used to translate binary files to the text-based email messaging protocol used by the Internet.

MIPS (millions of instructions per second)

A unit of measure to gauge the speed of a CPU.

MMDS (multichannel multipoint distribution services)

A form of broadband Internet connection using line-of-sight transmission towers.

MMU (memory management unit)

A component of a microprocessor (CPU).

MMX (Multimedia Extensions)

An expanded CPU instruction set optimized for multimedia applications.

Modem (MOdulator-DEModulator)

A device for sending data over telephone lines.

MPEG (Moving Picture Experts Group)

Pronounced m-peg, a type of video compression.

MSCDEX (Microsoft CD Extensions)

The MSCDEX.EXE generic software driver for CD-ROM drives.

MSD Sheet (material safety data)

Usually written as MSDS: A required description of each and every hazardous material used in a business location. (Not to be confused with MSD.EXE, the Microsoft Diagnostics program utility.)

NCSC (National Computer Security Council)

A government agency that defines levels of security for computer systems. Windows NT is C-2 compliant.

NIC (network interface card)

Provides the physical connection of a PC to the cable of a local area network.

NLX (InteLex form factor)

A trademark of the InteLex Corporation, the NLX was a form factor designed to follow the LPX motherboard form factor. NLX is a standard supported by Intel and IBM.

NOS (network operating system)

An operating system used to connect many computers together.

NRZI (non return to zero)

A signaling process using voltage changes to generate binary numbers in a USB cable.

NT (New Technology)

Windows NT is a multitasking operating system that became Windows 2000.

NTFS (New Technology File System)
The preferred file system used by Windows NT.

NTSC (National Television Standards Committee)
The committee responsible for setting video standards in the United States. NTSC signals are composite signals used with television and VCRs, and they are different than RGB signals on a computer monitor.

OEM (original equipment manufacturer)
An OEM version of Windows means that it was created specially for the original maker of the computer, to be sold by that vendor as part of a package.

OS/2 (Operating System 2, second generation)
IBM's single-user, multitasking operating system for PCs.

OSI (open systems interconnection)
The OSI layer is the way various parts of the network operating system work with hardware and software.

PAL (Phase Alternating Line)
The predominant television specification used in Europe.

PARC (Palo Alto Research Center)
The Xerox development center where laser printers, the mouse, and the GUI were developed.

PAT (partition allocation table)
The first sector on a fixed disk, containing partition information for that disk.

PB (petabyte)
1,024 terabytes, 1 million gigabytes, 1 billion megabytes. 2 petabytes would hold the contents of all U.S. academic research libraries.

PCB (printed circuit board)
A board where electrical paths are etched on the board, as opposed to connected with wires.

PCI (Peripheral Component Interconnect)
A popular expansion bus that provides a high-speed data path between the CPU and peripherals.

PCL (printer control language)
Formatting commands used by a printer during the print process.

PCMCIA (Personal Computer Memory Card Industry Association)
A nonprofit industry association that standardized the 16-bit socket, allowing portable computers to utilize credit-card-size expansion cards.

PDP (plasma display panel)
A type of video display sometimes used in notebook computers (also referred to as *gas plasma panels*).

PGA (pin grid array)

An arrangement of connection pins on a microprocessor. When the pins are in a set of staggered rows, they are called a *staggered pin grid array* (SPGA).

PIC (programmable interrupt controller)

An improvement added to the second series Pentium chips.

PIF (program information file)

A proprietary format file used by Windows to store configuration settings for a Real Mode virtual machine session.

PIO (programmed input/output)

Five modes used in the ATA specification. *(See ATA.)*

PnP (Plug 'n' Play, Plug and Play)

An Intel standard that allows components to be automatically configured when added to a PC. The standard requires support from the BIOS, the expansion card, and the operating system.

POSIX (Portable Operating System Interface for Unix)

An operating system used in many government offices.

POST (power on self-test)

A series of built-in tests that are performed at system startup.

PROM (programmable read only memory)

This ROM requires a special machine to write instruction to a chip one time only, and the chip cannot be changed. *(See EPROM.)*

QDOS (quick and dirty operating system)

The original version of the disk operating system (DOS).

QIC (quarter inch cartridge)

A format used in tape backup machines.

RADAR (Radio Detecting/ Detection And Ranging)

Radio waves generated by a source to bounce back from an object for the purpose of revealing the object's shape.

RAID (redundant array of inexpensive disks)

Used in networking as a form of data protection. There are six levels of RAID (0 through 5).

RAM (random access memory)

The computer's main workspace. Data stored in RAM can be accessed directly without having to read information stored before or after the desired data.

RAMDAC (Random Access Memory Digital-to-Analog Converter)

A component used with graphics cards and video subsystems to convert binary information to analog images.

RDRAM (Rambus dynamic random access memory)

A special type of DRAM memory chip developed by the Rambus Corporation.

Rexx (Restructured Extended Executor)
A batch language developed for OS/2, with many more powerful commands than those in DOS.

RGB (red, green, blue)
The three primary colors of light used in color monitors.

RIMM (Rambus inline memory module)
A memory module composed of Rambus memory chips on a printed circuit board.

RISC (reduced instruction set computer)
Computers using processors designed to run limited numbers of instructions very fast.

RLE (run-length encoding)
A compression format used for graphic image files, commonly used to compress Windows logo files. These files have an .RLE extension.

ROM (read-only memory)
A memory chip that permanently stores instructions and data.

RPM (revolutions per minute)
The speed at which a disk revolves around a spindle.

SAA (System Application Architecture)
A user interface standard developed by IBM.

SAM (security accounts manager)
A security module in Windows NT and Windows 2000.

SASI (Shugart Associates Systems Interface)
Developed by Alan Shugart as part of the original floppy disk drive system.

SAT (security access token)
A token created for each user on a Windows NT or Windows 2000 network. The SAT carries identification information across the network.

SCSI (Small Computer System Interface)
A hardware interface that allows the connection of up to seven devices.

SDRAM (synchronous dynamic random access memory)
SDRAM is a DRAM chip with an internal synchronizing clock designed to reduce interrupt requests to the CPU.

SEC (single edge connector)
A chip packaging design where chips (often memory chips) are placed on a printed circuit board with a single edge connector.

SECAM (SEquential Couleur Avec Memoire)
A French video standard adopted by the Eastern block countries of the former Soviet Union.

SEP (single edge processor)
A type of packaging for a microprocessor with a single edge connector.

SGRAM (synchronous graphics RAM)

A type of video memory that uses an internal clock to synchronize graphics memory to the motherboard clock.

SID (security identification)

The Security ID is part of the security access token in Windows NT and Windows 2000.

SIMM (single inline memory module)

A narrow printed circuit board that holds memory chips. The connector is integrated into the edge of the board so it can easily be added to sockets on the system board. This module uses DRAM chips on one side of the board.

SMI (system management interrupt)

Used for power conservation and management.

SONAR (Sound Navigation and Ranging)

Sound signals generated by a source to bounce back from an object for the purpose of revealing the object's shape.

SONET (Synchronous Optical NETwork)

A protocol used for fiber optics cable data transfers.

SPARC (Scalable Processor Architecture)

A 32-bit and 64-bit microprocessor architecture created by Sun Microsystems, Inc., designed to run on RISC chips; usually used on Unix systems or the Sun Solaris operating system.

SPGA (staggered pin grid array)

Microprocessor connection pin configuration. *(See PGA.)*

SPI (SCSI parallel interface)

Pronounced "spy," a subdivision of the SCSI-3 specification.

SPP (standard parallel port)

The original parallel port controller, assigned the LPT or PRN device abbreviation name.

SQL (structured query language)

A query language used to request information from a database.

SRAM (synchronous RAM)

A memory chip with an internal clock that synchronizes the memory to the motherboard clock. Requires power to hold content, but does not need refreshing like other types of RAM. Because of this, it is very fast. (Sometimes referred to as *static RAM.*)

SS (single sided)

Description of a storage method used with disks. *(See DS.)*

SS/DL (single sided, double layer)

A storage format for DVDs.

SS/SL (single sided, single layer)

A storage format for DVDs.

SSFDC (Solid State Floppy Disk Card)
The original name for the SmartMedia flash memory card.

ST (Shugart Technology, Inc.)
The ST-506/412 interface was the accepted standard for all PC hard disks and stood as the basis for the ESDI and IDE hard drive controller interfaces.

STP (shielded twisted pair)
A type of shielded twisted-pair wire used in networking and telephony.

SVGA (Super Video Graphics Array)
The SVGA video standard provides a higher resolution than VGA, providing 16 million colors and resolutions up to 1600×1200 pixels.

TB (terabytes)
1,024 gigabytes, 1 million megabytes, 1 billion kilobytes. 10 terabytes would hold a printout of the entire U.S. Library of Congress. Estimates indicate that the human mind can hold approximately 15 terabytes of information.

TCP/IP (transport control protocol/Internet protocol)
Formerly named transport control *program*, the transport protocol coordinates packet information for the many IP packets and addresses in an online transmission.

TIFF (tagged image file format)
A compression format used for bitmap image files, resulting in a .TIF extension that can be read by both PCs and MacIntosh systems.

TSR (terminate, stay resident)
A type of program that stays in memory (resident), even when it has stopped running (terminate). A TSR can be called up using a "hot key," and runs in its own DOS window.

UART (Universal Asynchronous Receiver Transmitter)
A semiconductor device that transmits and receives data through the serial port.

UDMA (Ultra DMA)
The way Direct Memory Access (DMA) was speeded up in the Ultra ATA specification. Also called *UDMA/33*. *(See ATA.)*

ULSI (ultra large-scale integration)
A type of manufacturing for microprocessor chips.

UMB (upper memory block)
An area of the first megabyte of memory.

UPS (uninterruptible power supply)
Provides backup power when the main power fails or moves to an unacceptable level.

URL (universal resource locator)
An Internet address, typically presented as a domain name.

USB (Universal Serial Bus)
A new standard that allows 128 devices to be daisy-chained to a cable running at 1.5MB per second.

UTP (unshielded twisted pair)
A type of twisted-pair wire used in networking where there is no special shielding against electromagnetic interference.

UV (ultraviolet)
A frequency of light in the long wave spectrum.

VCR (video cassette recorder)
A device used to record NTSC signals from television inputs.

VDT (video display terminal)
Any video device used to display video information.

VESA (Video Electronics Standards Association)
An organization composed of PC vendors that is dedicated to improving video and multimedia standards.

VFAT (virtual file allocation table)
A 32-bit file system used in Windows for Work groups and Windows 95. The VFAT is faster than the DOS FAT and provides for long file names.

VGA (Video Graphics Array)
The IBM video standard that has become the minimum standard for PC displays. It provides 16 colors at 640×448 resolution.

VHD (very high density)
Found in SCSI connectors providing high data transfer rates.

VID (voltage identification)
The voltage ID pins that work with a voltage regulator module (VRM) to control voltages on a microprocessor.

VL Bus (VESA Local bus)
A type of VESA bus interface.

VLSI (very large-scale integration)
A type of manufacturing for microprocessor chips.

VM (Virtual Machine)
Windows uses software to create a representation or emulation of a Real Mode 8086 PC.

VMM (Virtual Machine Manager)
The Windows software that manages the Real Mode VMs.

VRAM (video RAM)
Differs from common RAM in that it utilizes two ports (dual-ported) to simultaneously refresh the video screen and receive data for the next screen.

VRM (voltage regulator module)
An electronic component that can provide varying levels of voltage to another component.

VxD(virtual device driver)
Runs in the most privileged CPU mode and allows low-level interaction with hardware and internal Windows functions.

WAN (wide area network)
Typically used for very large networks, often where multiple geographic locations are included. *(See. LAN.)*

WORM (write once, read many)
Usually, a compact disk that can be written to one time and then read from many times. WORM is sometimes associated with a "worm" virus.

WOSA (Windows Open Services Architecture)
Part of the Windows technology used in conjunction with Active Directory.

WRAM (windows RAM)
Windows RAM bears no relation to Microsoft Windows, and it is a type of dual-ported video memory with large block addressing.

WWW (World Wide Web)
A subdivision of the Internet that uses HTML formatting.

WYSIWYG (What You See Is What You Get)
Refers to the ability to display text and graphics on a monitor using the same fonts and size relationships as will be printed in the final document.

XGA (extended graphics adapter)
The first IBM video adapter to use VRAM.

XMS (extended memory specification)
Any physical memory beyond the first 1MB of conventional memory.

XT (Extended Technology)
The first IBM PC with a hard drive. It used the same 8088 processor and 8-bit expansion bus as the original PC.

YB (yottabyte)
1,024 zettabytes.

ZB (zettabyte)
1,024 exabytes.

ZIF (zero-insertion force)
A socket that uses a lever to grasp the pins of a chip once it is inserted. This eliminated bent pins and became very popular for mounting CPUs.

Index

Symbols and Numbers

! command, 147
+++ command, 147
, (comma) command, 147
/ (forward slash), Unix directory names, 331
/2, 410
/3 (Enhanced Mode), 410
3DNow!, 103-104
8-bit addressing, 152
10BaseT wire (twisted-pair cabling), 295-296
15-pin VGA connectors, 284-285
16-bit device drivers, IO.SYS, 388
24-bit resolution, 152
24-bit scanners, 151
25-pin serial plugs, 282
32-bit processing, 107
36-pin Centronics connectors, 288
64-bit processing, 107
86-DOS, 314-315
386 Enhanced Mode (WIN/3), 411-412
640K barrier, 426
640x480 pixesl, 198
8086 processors, 92-93
8088 processors, 92-93
8250 UART, 146
8514/A, 204
16450 UART, 146
16550A UART, 146
80286 processors, 93-94
80386 processors, 95
  coprocessors, 96
  SX versions, 95-96
80486 processors, 97

A

A+ certification tests, 2-3
  adaptive testing, 9-10
  answers, 633
  certification, 5
  core hardware, 3
  design, 10
  exam requirements, 7
  exam site, 5-9
  framework, 634-635
  linguistics, 10-11
  operating systems technologies, 3
  preparation, 6-7, 13-14
  qualifications, 2
  questions, 10-14, 632-634
  resources, 7
  sample exam, 632
    answers, 658-679
    questions, 636-656
  scheduling, 4-5
  scoring, 6
  signing up for, 4
  testing, 6
A/ command, 147
/A switch (SETUP.EXE), 409
A/B boxes, 249

absolute file names, 360
absolute locations, 350
AC (Alternating Current), 120, 693
AC/DC power supply, 228
Accelerated Graphics Port (AGP), 72
Accelerated Graphics Port. *See* AGP
Access Control List (ACLs), 534-535
Accessibility Utility (Windows 98), 503
accounts, 536
  Administrator, 536
  Guest, 537
  User, 536
    groups, 538-539
    managing, 537-538
ACLs (Access Control Lists), 534-535
Active Desktop, 504
Active Directory, 562-564
active matrix, LCDs (liquid crystal displays), 214
adaptive testing, 9-10
ADB (Apple Desktop Bus), 250
ADC (analog-to-digital converter), 693
addresses
  grids, 51
  I/O, 138
  memory, 65
administrative tools, Windows 2000 System Configuration Utility, 567-568
Administrator account, 536
Advance Micro Devices. *See* AMD
Advanced Power Management (Windows 98), 503
Advanced Startup option (Windows XP), 596
Advanced Technology Attachment. *See* ATA
Advanced Technology Extensions. *See* ATX
Advanced Technology. *See* AT
adware, 624
AGP (accelerated graphics port), 37, 41-42, 72, 205-207, 283, 693
  buses, 30
  frame buffers, 206
  modes, 208-209
  pipelining, 207
  queuing, 207
aliases (Windows 9x file names), 498-499
aliasing, 422-423
Allen, Paul, 312
Altair Basic, 312-313
Alternating Current (AC), 120, 693
alternative clicks, 453
AM (amplitude modulation), 693
AMD (Advanced Micro Devices), 24, 90, 693
  chipets, 40
  processors, 104-105
    Athlon, 105-106
    Athlon XP, 108
    Duron, 105-106
    K-6, 105
America OnLine (AOL), 693
American National Standards Institute (ANSI), 160, 257, 693
American Telephone and Telegraph (AT&T), 297
AMI BIOS beep codes, 391-392
amplitude, 123
  amplitude modulation (AM), 693
amps, 122-123
analog information, compared to digital information, 119-120
analog-to-digital converter. *See* ADC
ANSI (American National Standards Institute), 160, 257, 693
answers
  A+ certification test, 633
  sample A+ certification test, 658-679
anti-aliasing, 199
AOL (America OnLine), 693
APIs (Application Programming Interfaces), 404, 693
Apple, 313-314
  Computer FireWire. *See* FireWire
  Desktop Bus (ADB), 250
applets, PIF Editor, 402
Application layer (OSI model), 268
application programming interfaces, 404, 693
architecture, Windows NT, 524-525
  kernel mode, 525-527
  User mode, 527-528
archive files, 360
ASCII (American Standard Code for Information Interchange), 339, 693
ASPI, 694
AT (Advanced Technology), 694
  form factor, 19-21
  serial plugs, 282
AT&C command, 148
AT&Fn command, 148
AT&T (American Telephone and Telegraph) Corp., 297, 694
AT-class computers, 93

ATA (Advanced Technology Attachment), 694
  command, 147
  DataFlash, 187
  packet interface (ATAPI), 694
  specification, 171
ATA-2 specification, 171-172
  burst transfer rates, 173-174
  fast ATA, 173
  PIO modes, 172-173
ATA/ATAPI 4, 174-175
ATAboy2, 176
ATAPI (ATA packet interface), 694
ATD <string> command, 147
ATE command, 148
ATFn command, 148
Athlon processor, 41, 105-106
Athlon XP processor, 108
ATI command, 148
ATLn command, 148
ATMn command, 148
ATTRIB command, 309-310, 333-335, 607
attributes, 533-534
ATX (Advanced Technology Extensions), 23, 694
  form factor, 23-25
ATZ command, 148
AUTOEXEC.BAT, 367-368, 483-484
AUTOEXEC.BAT file, 385
Avalon, 461

B

B000, 425-426
B800h, 425-426
Baby AT boards, 19
backside bus, 62
backups
  Backup (Windows 98), 503
  system binders, 395
  Windows Registry, 465-466
  Windows Registry backup files, 457
ballast, 124
bandwidth, 263-264
base file system, 496
base-2 numbering, 133
base-10 numbering, 132
base-16 numbering, 133-134
Basic, 312, 694
  bootstrap loader, 381-388
Basic DOS (BDOS), 694
Basic Input Output System. *See* BIOS
.BAT extensions, 311
batch files, 367
  AUTOEXEC.BAT, 367-368
  samples, 368-370
batch programs, 311
baud rates, 290
bayonet nut connector. *See* BNC
BBS (bulletin board service), 54, 694
BDOS (Basic DOS), 694
beat waves, 203
beep codes, 391-392
Beginner's All-Purpose Symbolic Instruction Code. *See* BASIC
binary numbers
  base-16, 133-134
  base-2, 133
BIOS (basic input/output system), 53, 694
  Flash, 53-55
BIOS parameter block (BPB), 382
BISDN (Broadband ISDN), 272
bit rates, scanners, 151
bitmap fonts, 224-225
bits, 30-31, 290
block access, 535
BNC, 694
/B boot log text file, 410
BOOT.INI file, 542, 555, 560
BOOTLOG.TXT, 476, 597-599
bootstrap, Windows 9x startup, 477-478
bootstrap loader
  BASIC, 381-382
  IO.SYS file, 383
    16-bit device drivers, 388
    CONFIG.SYS, 383-387
    HIMEM.SYS, 387-388
    SYSINIT, 384
bootups, 378, 390-391. *See also* startups
  boot sector, 381
    BASIC bootstrap loader, 381-384
    partition loader, 382-383
    viruses, 620
  cold boots, 379-380
  crashes
    Ctrl+Alt+Del, 379-380
    hard, 379
  disks, 392
    configuration files, 395-396
    DOS, 392-394
    troubleshooting Windows NT, 551-552
    utility files, 394-395
  to DOS, 487-488

IO.SYS file, 383
16-bit device drivers, 388
CONFIG.SYS, 383-387
HIMEM.SYS, 387-388
SYSINIT, 384
MBR, 378
MSDOS.SYS, 388-389
parition loader, 382-383
POST, 378
process overview, 380
ROM BIOS, 381-382
troubleshooting, 610
CMOS, 611-613
hardware problems, 613-615
NTLDR, 611
Windows 2000 options, 561-562
Windows NT partitions, 541
BPB (BIOS parameter block), 382
Bricklin, Dan, 314
bridges, 266-267
broadband, 264
Broadband ISDN (BISDN), 272
broadband wireless, Internet access, 272-273
bubble jet printers, 216
buffers, command turnaround time, 178-179
BUFFERS=, 482
bulletin board service (BBSes), 54, 694
burst transfer rates, ATA specification, 173-174
bus-mastering, 246-247
buses
AGP (accelerated graphics port), 30, 41-42
architecture, 28-30
backside, Level 2 cache memory (L-2), 62-64
clocking, 59-60
data paths, 29
DMA channels, 135-136
EISA, 31-32
front side, 61-62
internal, 64-65
ISA, 29-31
MCA, 31-32
memory, 60-62
narrow channel, 77-78
PCI, 29
processor speed, 29, 91-92
rider cards, 25
structure (motherboards), 18
topology, 265
transfers, 259
USB, 248-250, 254-255
hubs, 252, 255-256
NRZI encoding, 255
release 2.0, 253-254
releases 1.0 and 1.1, 250-252
VESA, 32-33, 37
VL Bus, 709
wide channel, 77
bytes, 30-31, 290

C

cables, 293-294
coaxial, 294
Internet access, 271
networking
fiber-optic, 299-300
twisted-pair configurations, 299
parallel ports, 285
36-pin Centronics connector, 288
DB25, 286
RS-232 and DB9, 287
SCSI connectors, 288-289
types, 289
ribbon, 284
serial ports, 290-293
twisted-pair, 295-296
configuration, 298-299
quality gradation, 296-297
RJ-45 modular connectors, 297
STP, 296
UTP, 296
wiring problems, 297
cache memory, 60-64
block, 65
Extended Data Out (EDO) memory, 66-67
FPM, 66
range, 65-66
speed, 67-69
hierarchy, 63
primary (L-1), 64-65
secondary (L-2), 64-65
CAD, 694
calling functions, 524
CANARIE (Canadian Network for the Advancement of Research, Industry, and Education), 274
capacitance, 128-130
capacitive switches (keyboards), 143-144

capacitors, 127-130
card readers, 188
CardBus, 43
carrier sense, multiple access, collision detection network (CSMACD), 263, 695
cartridges, 102
cascading IRQs, 132
CAT3 Standard (1988), 298
CAT4 Standard, 299
CAT5 Standard (1992), 299
CAT5e Standard (Enhanced Category 5), 299
CAT6 Standard, 299
CAT6e Standard (Enhanced Category 6), 299
CAT7 Standard (emerging), 299
cathode ray tubes. *See* CRTs
CAV, 694
CCDs (charge-coupled device), 149-150, 197, 694
CCP, 694
CD (Change Directory), 348, 351
CD-ROMs, 181
  device drivers, 469
CD-Rs, 181, 183
CD-RWs, 181, 695
CDs, 181-183, 694
Celeron, 104
cells, DIMM, 61
certification tests (A+), 2-3
  adaptive testing, 9-10
  answers, 633
  certification, 5
  core hardware, 3
  design, 10
  exam requirements, 7
  exam site, 5-6, 8-9
  framework, 634-635
  linguistics, 10-11
  operating systems technologies, 3
  preparation, 6-7, 13-14
  qualifications, 2
  questions, 10-14, 632-634
  resources, 7
  sample exam, 632
    answers, 658-679
    questions, 636-656
  scheduling, 4-5
  scoring, 6
  signing up for, 4
  testing, 6
CGA (Color Graphics Adapter), 204, 695
CGALOGO.*, 409
CGI (common gateway interface), 695
chace memory, 63
chaining devices, 242-243
  cable interfaces, 243
  daisy-chaining, 132
  SCSI, 243-248
Change Directory (CD) command, 348, 351
change line jumpers, floppy drives, 165
channels, DMA, 135-136, 141
characters, DOS file names, 360-361
charge-coupled device. *See* CCD
checksum errors, 613
chips, 90-91, 106
  32-bit processing, 107
  64-bit processing, 107
  8086, 92-93
  8088, 92-93
  80286, 93-94
  80386, 95
    coprocessors, 96
    SX versions, 95-96
  80486, 97
  AMD, 104-105
    Athlon, 105-106
    Athlon XP, 108
    Duron, 105-106
    K-6, 105
  Enhanced Mode, 96
  integration, 97
  internal bus, 64-65
  manufacturing masks, 64
  manufacturing technology, 110
  memory modules, 73, 76, 81
    continuity, 78
    DDR SDRAM, 79-80
    DDR-II, 80-81
    DIMMs, 74-75
    DIP, 73
    narrow channel bus, 77-78
    RIMMs, 75-76
    serial and parallel transfers, 76-77
    SIMMs, 74
  names, 108-109
  Pentiums, 97-98
    Celeron, 104
    clock multiplier, 100
    first series, 98
    over-clocking, 100-101
    P6 family, 101-104
    second series, 99
    third series, 99

- performance, 108-109
- protected mode
  - compared to real mode, 94
  - switching to real mode, 94-95
- real mode, 92-94
  - compared to protected mode, 94
  - switching from protected mode to, 94-95
- scalability, 97
- speed, 91
- upgrades, 97

chipset (motherboards), 18, 38-41
- ALi, 41
- AMD, 40
- FC-PGA (Flipped Chip Pin-Grid Array), 40
- North bridge, 60
- Nvidia, 41
- SiS, 41
- South bridge, 60
- VIA, 41

CHKDSK
- clusters, 357-358
- command, 607

circuits, 122
- boards, 68-69
- troubleshooting, 614-615

cleaning
- IFS (Image Formation System), 229-230
- printers, 220-221

client/server networking, 260-261

clients, OLE, 460

clocks
- multipliers, Pentiums, 100
- speed, 22-23
- ticks, 119

clusters, 354-355
- CHKDSK, 357-358
- compared to sectors, 169
- FAT, 354-356
- FAT32, 356
- SCANDISK, 357-358

CLV (Constant Linear Velocity), 182, 695

CMA, 695

CMOS (Complementary Metal Oxide Semiconductor), 21, 53, 695
- settings, 53-54
- troubleshooting, 611-613

CMY (cyan, magenta, yellow), 695

coaxial cable, 294

COBOL, 695

code, spaghetti, 525

cold boots, 81, 379-380

Color Graphics Adapter. *See* CGA

colors
- LCDs (liquid crystal displays), 213
- monitors, 196
- pixel resolution, 198

COM ports, 139-140

comma (,) command, 147

command prompt, 493-494

COMMAND.COM, 318, 324
- DOS command line, 318-319
- error messages, 321-322
- external commands, 325
- file mask, 321
- internal commands, 325
- MSDOS.SYS, 389
- parsing, 319
- programs, 322-323
  - loading, 323-324
  - running, 323-324
- switches, 320-321
- syntax, 319-320

commands
- batch files, 367
  - AUTOEXEC.BAT, 367-368
  - samples, 368-370
- CD (Change Directory), 348, 351
- COMMAND.COM. *See* COMMAND.COM
- DEL hidden files, 335
- DIR, 320, 335-336
- DIRectory, 320
- DOS COPY, 316
- ECHO, 369
- ERRORLEVEL, 391
- FORMAT, 341
- FORMAT.COM, 345-346
- interpreters, 318
  - DOS command line, 318-319
  - error messages, 321-322
  - file mask, 321
  - parsing, 319
  - programs, 322-324
  - switches, 320-321
  - syntax, 319-320
- LABEL command, 346
- logon, 531
- MD (Make Directory), 349
- modem, 147-148
- PAUSE, 322, 369
- PRINT, 234
- Print Screen, 54

Recovery Panel, 606
ATTRIB, 309-310, 333-335, 607
CHKDSK, 607
disable, 608
diskpart, 608
enable, 608
EXIT, 609
fixboot, 608
fixmbr, 609
listsvc, 607
logon, 609
map, 608
SET, 328
SMARTDRV /S, 64
Start menu, Settings, 249
turnaround time, 178-179
VER, 317
commercial color-separation printing, 196
Common Business Oriented Language (COBOL), 695
common gateway interface (CGI), 695
common monochrome adapter (CMA), 695
compact disk, read-write. *See* CD-RWs
CompactFlash, 187
compilers, 311
Complementary Metal Oxide Semiconductor. *See* CMOS
components
Windows 9x, 489-490
Windows Registry, 462
copies, 464-465
HKeys, 462-464
compound documents, 460
CompTIA (Computing and Industry Trade Association), 4, 695
Computer Management tool (Windows 2000), 462
Computing Technology Industry Association, 7
COMSPEC= variable, 327
CON (CONsole), 195
condensers. *See* capacitors
conditioning, IFS (Image Formation System), 230-231
CONFIG.SYS file, 365, 383-385, 482-483
F5 key, 385-386
HIMEM.SYS, 387-388
MEMMAKER sample file, 439-441
DEVICE= directive, 441-443
DEVICEHIGH= directive, 441-443
MSDOS.SYS, 386-387
configurations
bootable disks with, 395-396
floppy drives, 164
change line jumper, 165
media sensor jumper, 164
write protection, 165
hard drives, 178-179
twisted pair cable, 298-299
Windows 9x installation, 474
connections (network), 615
scanners, 150-151
troubleshooting, 615-616
access, 617-618
NICs, 616-617
PROTOCOL.INI, 618-619
Services icon, 617
validation, 617
connectors, 294
coaxial cable, 294
female, 205
keyed, 24
keying, 130
networking, 299-300
PS/2, 93
T-connectors, 294
twisted-pair cable, 295-296
configuration, 298-299
quality gradation, 296-297
RJ-45 modular connectors, 297
STP, 296
UTP, 296
wiring problems, 297
CONsole (CON), 195
Constant Linear Velocity (CLV), 182, 695
consumable printer components, 222
continuity modules, 78
continuous feed printer, 218
continuous-form paper, 221
contrast ratios, monitors, 200-201
Control Panel, 338, 428-429, 489-490, 568-569
Control Program for Microcomputers (CP/M), 313, 316-317, 695
controllers, 165-166
DMA, 134-135, 141
channels, 135-136
motherboards, 135
floppy drives, 284
hard drives, 169, 284
IDE, 169-175
SCSI, 169-170
IRQs, 131-132

conventional memory, 421-422
cooperative multitasking, 520
copying files, Windows 9x installation, 473
core files, Windows 3.x, 412
core hardware test, 3
CP/M (Control Program for Microcomputers), 313, 316-317, 695
CPUs, 90-91, 106, 695
  32-bit processing, 107
  64-bit processing, 107
  8086, 92-93
  8088, 92-93
  80286, 93-94
  80386, 95
    coprocessors, 96
    SX versions, 95-96
  80486, 97
  AMD, 104-105
    Athlon, 105-106
    Athlon XP, 108
    Duron, 105-106
    K-6, 105
  Athlon, 41
  Enhanced Mode, 96
  integration, 97
  IRQs, 130
  manufacturing technology, 110
  names, 108-109
  Pentiums, 97-98
    Celeron, 104
    clock multiplier, 100
    first series, 98
    over-clocking, 100-101
    P6 family, 101-104
    second series, 99
    third series, 99
  performance, 108-109
  protected mode
    compared to real mode, 94
    switching to real mode, 94-95
  real mode, 92-94
    compared to protected mode, 94
    switching from protected mode to, 94-95
  registers, 61
  scalability, 97
  slots, 33-34, 42-43
  sockets, 33-34
    7, 34
    A, 34
    indexing, 35
    SEC, 35-37
    SEP, 35-37
  speed, 29, 91-92
  upgrades, 97
  Windows Me, 595
crashes
  Ctrl+Alt+Del, 379-380
  hard, 379
  troubleshooting Windows 2000/XP, 585-586
CRC (Cyclical Redundancy Check), 174, 695
CRTs (cathode ray tubes), 195-196, 695
Crucial Technology Web site, 56
CSMACD (carrier sense, multiple access, collision detection network), 263, 695
cyan, magenta, yellow (CMY), 695
cycles, 123
cyclical processes, 120
Cyclical Redundancy Check (CRC), 174, 695
cylinders (heads), 161, 168, 353
Cyrix, 90

D

DAC, 696
daisy-chaining, 132, 258
DASD (Direct Access Storage Device), 166, 696. *See also* hard drives
DAT (Digital Audio Tape), 180-181, 355, 696
Data link layer (OSI model), 268
data output buffers, 66
data paths, 29
data warehouses, 563
databases
  flat file, 544
  relational, 544
daughterboards. *See* IC boards
DB25 connectors, 286
DB9 connectors, 282, 287
DC (direct current), 696
DDE (Dynamic Data Exchange), 461, 696
DDR SDRAM (Double Data Rate SDRAM), 79-80, 696
DDR-II memory, 80-81
debouncing, 143
DEBUG.EXE, 395
DEC, 696
decimal numbering, 132
default printer ports, 140
DEFRAG.EXE, 358-359
defragmenting, 358-359

DEL command, 335
density, floppy disks, 161
design, A+ tests, 10
Desktop
    Windows 95, 452
    Windows 9x, 452-453
DETCRASH.LOG, 476
DETLOG.TXT, 475-476
developing IFS (Image Formation System), 231-232
device drivers
    16-bit, IO.SYS file, 388
    CD-ROMs, 469
    loading, 482
    virtual, 479
    VxDs, 437-438
Device Manager (Windows 2000), 569
    troubleshooting hardware, 588-589
Device Resources, troubleshooting hardware, 589
DEVICE= directive, MEMMAKER CONFIG.SYS file, 441-443
DEVICEHIGH= directive, MEMMAKER CONFIG.SYS file, 441-443
devices
    chaining, 242-243
    hot swapping, 379
    input, 118
    logical, 139
    output, 118
    peripheral. *See* peripheral devices
    physical, 139
    SCSI, 243
        LUN, 244
        SCSI-1, 245
        SCSI-2, 245-247
        SCSI-3, 247-248
    troubleshooting
        Device Manager, 588-589
        Device Resources, 589
        System Information tool, 596-600
    virtual, 139
DHTML, 696
diagnostics, 602
    Administrative Tools, 602-603
    hardware, 501-502
    HwDiag.EXE, 602
    My Computer, 603-604
    Scanregw.exe, 604-605
    system reports, 603-604
    Windows 2000, 565
        Control Panel, 568-569
        interactive partitioning, 570
        My Network Places, 570
        Recovery Console, 573-574
        System Agent, 571
        System Configuration Utility, 565-569
        System File Checker, 573
        Windows File Protection (WFP), 572
        Windows Update Manager, 571
dialectrics, 127
Digital Audio Tape (DAT), 180-181, 355, 696
Digital Flat Panel (DVP), 211
digital information, 118-120
digital subscriber lines. *See* DSL
Digital Video Interface. *See* DVI
Digital-to-analog converter (DAC), 696
DIME (Direct Memory Execute), 207
DIMMs (Dual Inline Memory Modules), 61, 74-75, 696
DIN, 696
diodes, 197
DIP (Dual Inline Package), 73, 696
DIR command, 320, 335-336
DIR listings (DOS), 360
Direct Access Storage Device (DASD), 166, 696. *See also* hard drives
direct current (DC), 696
direct memory access. *See* DMA
Direct Memory Execute (DIME), 207
direct thermal printers, 216
directories, 349
    absolute locations, 350
    compared to file names, 352
    DIR listings, DOS, 360
    FAT, 349
    FAT16 directory names, 330-331
    management, 350
    relative locations, 350
    root, 381
    subdirectories, 352
    tree, 349
    Unix forward slash (/), 331
directory allocation table (DAT), 180-181, 355, 696
DIRectory command, 320
Directory Service (Windows 2000), 563
DirectX 8.1, 209
disable command, 608
discharges, 122
Disk Administrator Tool, 546
Disk Cleanup (Windows 2000), 508, 609-610

Disk Cleanup, 177-178
Disk Operating System. *See* DOS
diskpart command, 608
disks. *See also* Recovery Disks
  bootable, 392
    configuration files, 395-396
    DOS, 392-394
    utility files, 394-395
    Windows NT, 551-552
  caching
    SMARTDRV.EXE, 64
    SMARTRV.SYS, 64
  Emergency Repair Disk (ERD), 551-552
  emergency startup disk, 473
  floppy, 160-161
  formatting, boot sector, 381-382
  hard, 166-167
    controllers, 169-175
    PCI specification, 176-177
    random access, 168
    sectors, 168-169
    tracks, 168-169
  mirroring, Windows NT disk administration, 548
  partitions, 340-341
    extended, 343-345
    FORMAT.COM, 345-346
    LABEL command, 346
    LBA (Logical Block Addressing), 347
    primary, 343-345
    SYS.COM, 346-347
    terms, 341-342
    volumes, 341-343
  Windows NT, 545-546
    Disk Administrator Tool, 546
    disk mirroring, 548
    duplexing, 548
    RAID, 549
    striped sets, 547-548
    volume sets, 546-547
Distributed Media Format (DMF), 161
DLLs, 403
  HAL.DLL, 560
  SHELL.DLL, 403
DMA (direct memory access), 39, 134, 141, 696
  channels, 58-59, 135-136
  controllers, 134-135
DMF (Distributed Media Format), 161, 697
DNS (Domain Name Server), 268, 697
documents, compound, 460
Domain Name Server (DNS), 268
DOS, 308, 312-313, 340, 697
  86-DOS, 314-315
  Apple, 313-314
  ASCII text, 339
  ATTRIB command, 309-310, 333-335
  boot sequence, Windows 9x startup, 478
  bootable disks, 392-393
    configuration files, 395-396
    creating with Windows Explorer, 393-394
    utility files, 394-395
  command interpreters, 318
    command line, 318-319
    error messages, 321-322
    file mask, 321
    parsing, 319
    programs, 322-324
    switches, 320-321
    syntax, 319-320
  COMMAND.COM. *See* COMMAND.COM
  Control Program for Microcomputers (CP/M), 313, 316-317
  DEL command, 335
  DIR command, 335-336
  DIR listings, 360
  DOS COPY command, 316
  environment, 325-326
    COMSPEC= variable, 327
    LASTDRIVE= variable, 344-345
    paths, 329-331
    PROMPT variable, 327-329
    search paths, 331-332
    SET TEMP= variable, 329
    SET <variable>, 326-328
  F5 key, 385-386
  FAT16 directory names, 330-331
  file names, 310
    characters, 360-361
    extensions, 361-362
  FORMAT.COM, 345-346
  LABEL command, 346
  MS-DOS, 315, 317
  PC-DOS, 315, 317
  saving searches, 338-339
  starting Windows, 310
  VER command, 317
  wild card searches, 336-338
  Windows, 485-486
    booting to, 487-488
    MS Explorer, 486-487
  Windows 9x, 317-318

DOS COPY command, 316
DOS prompt, 319
DOS Shell, 409
DOS=HIGH, 482
DOSSHELL.BAT, 409
dot matrix printers, 218-220, 223
dot pitches, 199
dots per inch. *See* dpi
double data rate (DDR), 696
Double Data Rate SDRAM (DDR SDRAM), 79-80
double-sided (DS), 161
double-sided double density, 161
dpi (dots per inch), 198, 697
  printers, 216
DRAM, 56-57, 70, 697
drilling down (data warehouses), 563
Drive Converter (Windows 98), 454
drives, 177-178
  fixed disk, 341
  floppy, 161-162
    configuration, 164-165
    controllers, 284
    head actuators, 163
    logic boards, 163
    read-write heads, 162
    spindle motor, 163
  hard, 166-167
    configuration, 178-179
    controllers, 169-175, 284
    PCI specification, 176-177
    random access, 168
    read/write heads, 354
    sectors, 168-169, 354
    tracks, 168-169, 354
  logical, 340-341
    extended partitions, 343-345
    FORMAT.COM, 345-346
    LABEL command, 346
    LBA (Logical Block Addressing), 347
    primary partitions, 343-345
    SYS.COM, 346-347
    terms, 341-342
    volumes, 341-343
DS (double-sided), 161, 697
DS/DL, 697
DS/SL, 697
DSL (digital subscriber lines), 271-272, 697
Dual Inline Memory Modules (DIMMs), 74-75
Dual Inline Package (DIP), 73
dual scans, LCDs (liquid crystal displays), 214
duplexing, Windows NT disk administration, 548
Duron processor, 105-106
DVD-Rs, 697
DVDs, 181, 184-186, 697
DVI (Digital Video Interface), 210-211
DVP (Digital Flat Panel), 211
Dynamic Data Exchange (DDE), 461, 696
dynamic VxDs, 479

E

EB, 697
ECC (error correction code), 83-84, 697
ECHO command, 369
ECP (extended capabilities port), 289, 697
editing Registry files, 459-460
EDO, 697
EEMS (Enhanced EMS), 434, 697
EEPROM (electrically erasable programmable ROM), 54-55, 698
EGA, 204, 698
EGALOGO.*, 409
EIA (Electronic Industries Association), 287
EIDE, 698
  disk, 242
EISA (Extended Industry Standard Architecture), 31-32, 698
ELD (electro-luminescent display) monitors, 211, 698
electrical components
  capacitors, 127-130
  dialectrics, 127
  multimeters, 126-127
  power supplies, 130
  resistors, 126
electrically erasable programmable ROM (EEPROM), 54-55
electricity, 120
  amps, 122-123
  circuits, 122
  cycles, 123
  EMI, 124
  ESD, 124-126
  frequencies, 123
  negative electrons, 121-122
  positive electrons, 121-122
  resistors, 126
  signal traces, 29
  volts, 122-123
  watts, 122-123

electro-luminescent display (ELD), 211, 698
electromagnetic fields, 124
electromagnetic interference (EMI), 124, 295
Electronic Industries Association (EIA), 287
electrons, 120
- interlaced mode, 202-204
- negative, 121-122
- noninterlaced mode, 202-204
- positive, 121-122
- redraws, 201

electrophotographic (EP), 227
electrostatic discharge (ESD), 124, 295
email addresses, 270-271
Emergency Recovery Utility (ERU.EXE), 591
Emergency Repair Disk (ERD)
- troubleshooting Windows NT, 551-552
- Windows 2000, 591-592

emergency startup disk, 473
EMI (electromagnetic interference), 124, 295, 698
EMM386.EXE, 429-430, 434-435
- global heep, 431-433
- LIM 4, 433-434
- system resources, 431
- translation buffers, 430-431
- UMBs (upper memory blocks), 430

EMS, 698
enable command, 608
encoders, 144
end of cycle process, IFS (Image Formation System), 233-234
end-users, 529
Enhanced EMS (EEMS), 434
Enhanced Mode, 96
enhanced parallel ports (EPP), 289
Enhanced Small Device Interface. *See* ESDI
entities, 533-534
environment, DOS, 325-326
- COMSPEC= variable, 327
- LASTDRIVE= variable, 344-345
- paths, 329-331
- PROMPT= variable, 327-329
- search paths, 331-332
- SET TEMP= variable, 329
- SET <variable>, 326-328

EP (electrophotographic), 227, 698
EPP(enhanced parallel port), 289, 698
EPROM (erasable programmable ROM), 55, 698
erase lamp assemblies, 228
erasing, IFS (Image Formation System), 230
ERD (Emergency Repair Disk), 551-552, 591-592
error correction code (ECC), 83-84
ERRORLEVEL command, 391
errors
- codes, 391-392
- messages, 321-322
  - CMOS, 612-613
  - troubleshooting startups, 586
  - Windows NT, 554-555
- trapping, 322

ERU.EXE (Emergency Recovery Utility), 591
ESD (electrostatic discharge), 124-126, 295, 698
ESDI (Enhanced Small Device Interface), 169, 698
Ethernet (IEEE 802.3), 260, 262-263
Ethernet token-ring networks, 264-265
even parity, memory, 82-83
Event Viewer, 550-551, 599
events
- initialization, 560
- load, 560

exam simulation, PrepLogic Practice Tests, 686
exam. *See* certification tests (A+)
Examination Score Report, 690
executable files
- LSASS.EXE, 560
- MSD.EXE, IRQ usage, 136-137
- NTOSKRNL.EXE, 560
- SMSS.EXE, 560
- WINLOGON.EXE, 560

Executive Layer
- micro kernel, 526
- system service, 527

EXIT command, 609
exlectricity, 141
expanding files, Windows 9x installation, 473
expansion buses, 42-43
- AGP (accelerated graphics port), 30, 41-42
- architecture, 28-30
- backside, Level 2 cache memory (L-2), 62-64
- clocking, 59-60
- data paths, 29
- DMA channels, 135-136
- EISA, 31-32

front side, 61-62
internal, 64-65
ISA, 29-31
MCA, 31-32
memory, 60-62
narrow channel, 77-78
PCI, 29
processor speed, 29, 91-92
rider cards, 25
structure (motherboards), 18
topology, 265
transfers, 259
USB, 248-250, 254-255
hubs, 252, 255-256
NRZI encoding, 255
release 2.0, 253-254
releases 1.0 and 1.1, 250-252
VESA, 32-33, 37
VL Bus, 709
wide channel, 77
expansion cards. *See* PCMCIA
Explorer, 486-487, 505
creating bootable disks with, 393-394
EXT (Extended), 342
extended capabilities ports (ECP), 289
Extended Data Out (EDO) memory, 66-67
eXtended Graphics Adapter. *See* XGA
Extended Industry Standard Architecture. *See* EISA
extended memory, 429-430
EMM386.EXE, 434-435
global heep, 431-433
LIM 4, 433-434
page frame memory, 436-437
page swapping, 436-437
system resources, 431
task switching, 435-436
translation buffers, 430-431
UMBs (upper memory blocks), 430
extended partitions, 342-345
eXtended Technology. *See* XT
extensions
.BAT, 311
DOS file names, 361-362
external commands (COMMAND.COM), 325
external memory, 64-65

F

F4 key, 583
F5 key, 583
DOS, 385-386
F6 key, 583
F8 key, 583
fast ATA, 173
Fast Page Mode (FPM), 66
Fast SCSI, 246
fast serial transfers, 250
Fast Wide SCSI, 246
FAT (file allocation table), 315-316, 348, 356, 381, 698
clusters, 354-356
directories, 349
FAT16, 454
directory names, 330-331
root directory, 381
volumes, 349
FAT32, 348, 453-454
clusters, 356
FC-PGA (Flipped Chip Pin-Grid Array), 40, 698
FCB (file control block), 316, 698
FCBS=, 482
FCIP (Fibre Channel over TCP/IP), 248
FCP (Fibre Channel protocol), 248
FDDI (Fiber Distributed-Data Interface), 272, 698
FDISK, 340
partitions, 341
extended, 343-345
FORMAT.COM, 345-346
LABEL command, 346
LBA (Logical Block Addressing), 347
primary, 343-345
SYS.COM, 346-347
terms, 341-342
volumes, 341-343
female connectors, 205
FH (firmware hub), 699
Fiber Distributed-Data Interface (FDDI), 272
fiber optic cable, 299-300
Fibre Channel over TCP/IP (FCIP), 248
Fibre Channel protocol (FCP), 248
fields, electromagnetic, 124
FIFO, 699
file allocation table. *See* FAT
file control blocks. *See* FCBs
File Manager, 365, 405-406
file systems, 342, 348
base, 496
directories, 348-349
absolute locations, 350
management, 349-350

relative locations, 350
tree, 349
file allocation table. *See* FAT
HPFS (high performance file system), 496
NTFS (NT file system), 496
subdirectories, 352
files
archive, 360
AUTOEXEC.BAT, 385
batch, 367
AUTOEXEC.BAT, 367-368
samples, 368-370
BOOT.INI, 542, 555, 560
bootable disks
configuration files, 395-396
utility files, 394-395
CGALOGO.*, 409
CONFIG.SYS, 365, 383-385, 482-483
F5 key, 385-386
MEMMAKER, 439-443
MSDOS.SYS, 386-387
copying, Windows 9x installation, 473
DOSSHELL.BAT, 409
dynamic link libraries. *See* DLLs
EGALOGO.*, 409
error message of missing files, 556
expanding, 473
GRP, 417-418
HIMEM.SYS, 387-388, 429-430
global heep, 431-433
LIM 4, 433-434
system resources, 431
translation buffers, 430-431
UMBs (upper memory blocks), 430
.INI, 458-459
initialization, Windows 3.x, 412-418
IO.SYS, 383, 482-483
16-bit device drivers, 388
CONFIG.SYS, 383-387
HIMEM.SYS, 387-388
SYSINIT, 384
LSASS.EXE, 560
management, 353
clusters, 354-358
DEFRAG.EXE, 358-359
masks, 321
names, 360
absolute, 360
characters, 360-361
compared to directories, 352
DOS, 310, 329-332
extensions, 361-362
Windows 9x, 495, 498-500
NTOSKRNL.EXE, 560
.PIF (Program Information Files), 402-403
PROGMAN.INI, 481
properties, 364
PROTOCOL.INI, 618-619
sawp, 194
searches
DIR command, 335-336
saving, 338-339
wild cards, 336-338
SMSS.EXE, 560
swap, 427-428, 435
SYSTEM.DAT, 457, 462, 481
SYSTEM.INI, 480-481
USER.DAT, 457, 462
VGALOGO.*, 409
VMM32.VXD, 480
WIN.COM, 480
WIN.INI, 385
Windows Registry, 459-460
WINLOGON.EXE, 560
FILES=, 482
fill rates, graphics accelerator cards, 210
final output, 194-195
Fine Pitch Ball Grid Array (FPBGA), 80
firewalls
routers, 268
viruses, 622
FireWire, 242
firmware hub (FH), 699
first series Pentiums, 98
fixboot command, 608
fixed disk drives. *See* hard drives
fixmbr command, 609
Flash BIOS, 53-55
flash memory, 186-188
Flash ROM, 55
flat architecture, 35
flat file databases, 544
flat panel displays. *See* FPDs
flat technologies, sockets, 34
flat technology monitor. *See* FTM
flickers, monitors, 203-204
Flipped Chip Pin-Grid Array. *See* FC-PGA
floating-point unit. See FPU, 39, 90
floppy disks, 160-161
floppy drives, 161-162
configuration, 164-165
controllers, 284

head actuators, 163
logic boards, 163
read-write heads, 162
spindle motor, 163
FM, 699
foam elements, 142
fonts, 224
bitmap, 224-225
raster, 224-225
TIF, 225-226
form factors (motherboards), 18, 27-28
ATX, 23-25
LPX (Low Profile Extensions), 25-26
Mini ATX, 25
NLX, 26-27
form feed printers, 218
FORMAT command, 341
FORMAT.COM, 346
formatting disks
boot sector, 381-382
logical drives, 341-347
FORTRAN, 699
forward slash (/), directory names, 331
FPBGA (Fine Pitch Ball Grid Array), 80
FPDs (flat panel displays), 201
FPM (Fast Page Mode), 66, 699
FPU (floating-point unit), 39, 90, 90, 699
fragments (memory), 52
frame relay services, 272
frames, buffers, 206
framework, A+ certification test, 634-635
Franklin, Benjamin, 121
Frankston, Bob, 314
frequencies, 123
friction feed paper, 221-223
Front Side Bus (FSB), 61-62
FTM (flat technology monitor), 211, 699
full pathnames, 330
full restores, 587
full-page monitors, 200
function keys, troubleshooting startups, 582-584
functions, calling, 524
fusing assemblies, 228
fusing process, IFS (Image Formation System), 233
fusing rollers, 233
Fylstra, Dan, 314

G

Gates, Bill, 312, 405
gateway leaks, 125
GB, 699
GDI.EXE, 412, 432
GIF, 699
global heep, Windows 3.x, 431-433
GMCH (graphics and memory controller hub), 699
GPU (graphics processing unit), 209
granted access, 535
graphics accelerator cards, 209-210
graphics and memory controller hub (GMCH), 699
graphics processing unit (GPU), 209
grids, address, 51
Group files, 417-418
groups, managing, 538-539
GRP files, 417-418
Guest account, 537
GUIs, 699

H

H command, 148
HAL, 699
HAL (Hardware Abstraction Layer), 526
HAL.DLL, 560
hard crashes, 379
hard disks, 166-167
controllers, 169, 284
IDE, 169-175
SCSI, 169-170
PCI specification, 176-177
random access, 168
sectors, 168-169
tracks, 168-169
hard drives, 166-167
clusters, 354
configuration, 178-179
controllers, 169
IDE, 169-175
SCSI, 169-170
PCI specification, 176-177
random access, 168
read/write heads, 354
sectors, 168-169, 354
tracks, 168-169, 354
hardware
compared to software, 139
detection, Windows 9x installation, 472
diagnostics, 501-502
troubleshooting, 613
circuitry failures, 614-615
Device Manager, 588-589
Device Resources, 589

jumpers, 613-614
System Information tool, 596-600
Hardware Abstraction Layer. *See* HAL
Hardware Compatibility List (HCL), 589
HAZMAT (Hazardous Material), 129, 699
HCL (Hardware Compatibility List), 589
HD (high density), 161, 699
HDTV (high definition television), 211, 699
head actuators, floppy drives, 163
heads (cylinders), 161
head actuators, 163
read-write, 162
Heinlein, Robert, 103
Help Desk, 508
hertz (Hz), 201
hexadecimal numbering, 132-134
hidden files, DEL command, 335
high definition television (HDTV), 211, 699
high density (HD), 161
high dielectric constant, 127
high memory, 435
high memory area (HMA), 431, 699
high performance file system (HPFS), 496, 699
high-voltage power supply, 228
HIMEM.SYS, 429-430, 482
global heep, 431-433
LIM 4, 433-434
system resources, 431
translation buffers, 430-431
UMBs (upper memory blocks), 430
HIMEM.SYS file, 387-388
History of motherboards, 18-19
HKeys, 529, 543, 462-464
HMA (high-memory area), 431, 699
home position (print heads), 220
hot swapping, 379
SCSI-3, 247-248
HPFS (high performance file system), 496, 699
HTML (HyperText Markup Language), 269, 700
HTTP (HyperText Transfer Protocol), 269-270
hubs, USB controller, 252, 255-256
human typist program, 221
HWDIAG.EXE, 502, 602
Hyper Terminal (Windows 98), 503
HyperText Markup Language (HTML), 269, 700
HyperText Transfer Protocol (HTTP), 269-270
Hz (hertz), 201, 700

I

I/O (input and output), 282, 700
addresses, 138
buses, 28
architecture, 28-30
data paths, 29
process speed, 29, 91-92
interfaces, 282-283
15-pin VGA connectors, 284-285
floppy and hard disk controllers, 284
scalability, 284
IBM (International Business Machines), 18, 700
8086 processors, 92-93
8088 processors, 92-93
80286 processors, 93-94
motherboards, 18
VGA, 204
8514/A, 204
XGA, 204
IC (integrated circuit), 36, 102, 700
IDE (Integrated Drive Electronics), 169-171, 700
ATA specification, 171
ATA-2 specification, 171-172
burst transfer rates, 173-174
fast ATA, 173
PIO modes, 172-173
disk, 242
Ultra ATA, 174-175
Ultra DMA, 174-175
IDs, user, 530-531
IEEE (Institute of Electrical and Electronic Engineers), 242, 700
IEEE 1394, 249, 257-259, 504
IEEE 802.3 (Ethernet), 262-263
IETF (Internet Engineering Task Force), 273
IFCP (Internet Fibre Channel Protocol), 248
IFS (Image Formation System), 229, 341, 495, 700
cleaning process, 229-232
end of cycle process, 233-234
fusing process, 233

Manager, 494-496
saving long file names, 499-500
TSRs, 496-497
VFAT, 497-499
IFSHLP.SYS, 482
image files, viruses, 623-624
Image Formation System. *See* IFS
images
resolution, 197-198
scanning, 200
size, monitor raster, 200
impact printers, 216
Imsai 8080, 313
indexing, 35
IneterNIC (Internet Network Information Center), 270
InfiniSAN RAID ATAboy2, 176
infrared (IR) wireless, 300
.INI files, Windows 3.x, 412-413, 458-459
file associations, 416
missing files, 415
PROGMAN.INI, 417-418
SYSEDIT.EXE, 413
SYSTEM.INI, 414-415
WIN.INI, 415
initialization events, 560
initialization files, Windows 3x, 412-413, 458-459
file associations, 416
missing files, 415
PROGMAN.INI, 417-418
SYSEDIT.EXE, 413
SYSTEM.INI, 414-415
WIN.INI, 415
ink jet printers, 216
ink pixels
ink bubble printers, 217-218
printers, 217
input and output. *See* I/O
input devices, 118, 147
Installable File System Manager. *See* IFS, Manager
Installable File System. *See* IFS
installations, Windows 9x, 468-470
copying files, 473
expanding files, 473
hardware detection, 472
log files, 475-476
restart, 474-475
startup, 470-472
system configuration phase, 474
Institute of Electrical and Electronic Engineers (IEEE), 242
insulators, 127
INT (Interrupts), 57
integrated circuit. *See* IC boards
Integrated Drive Electronics. *See* IDE
Integrated Services Digital Network. *See* ISDN
integration, processors, 97
Intel Pentiums, 97-98
Celeron, 104
clock multiplier, 100
first series, 98
over-clocking, 100-101
P6 family, 101-104
second series, 99
third series, 99
interactive partitioning (Windows 2000), 570
interfaces
ASPI, 694
ATAPI, 694
CGI, 695
Enhanced Small Device Interface. *See* ESDI
I/O, 282-283
15-pin VGA connectors, 284-285
scalability, 284
SCSI, 706
Small Computer Systems Interface. *See* SCSI
user, 318
interlaced mode, 202-204
intermittent failures, 125
internal commands (COMMAND.COM), 325
internal memory, 64-65
International Business Machines. *See* IBM
International Organization for Standardization (ISO), 701
Internet, 269-270
accessing, 271
broadband wireless, 272-273
cable, 271
DSL, 272
Internet2, 273-274
ISDN, 272
MMDS, 273
P2P networking, 275
email addresses, 270-271
Internet Engineering Task Force (IETF), 273
Internet Explorer 5.0, 504
Internet Fibre Channel Protocol (iFCP), 248

Internet Network Information Center (InterNIC), 270
Internet Protocol Next Generation (IPng) group, 273
Internet Protocol version 4 (IPv.4), 273
Internet Protocol version 6 (IPv.6), 273
Internet Service Provider. *See* ISP
Internet Small Computer Systems Interface (iSCSI), 248
Internet2, 273-274
InterNIC, 700
interpolation, 149
interrupt line controllers, 131
Interrupt Requests. *See* IRQs
interrupt vector table, 130
IO.SYS file, 383, 482-483
- 16-bit device drivers, 388
- CONFIG.SYS, 383-385
  - F5 key, 385-386
  - MSDOS.SYS, 386-387
- HIMEM.SYS, 387-388
- SYSINIT, 384

IOCH, 700
IP (Internet Protocol), 700
IPv.4 (Internet Protocol version 4), 273
IPv.6 (Internet Protocol version 6), 273
IR, 700
IRQs (interrupt requests), 39, 57, 130-131, 141, 700
- cascading, 132
- hexadecimal numbering, 132-134
- IRQ 14, 137
- IRQ 2, 131-132
- IRQ 9, 131-132
- MSD.EXE report of usage, 136-137
- PnP, 131
- ports, 138-139
  - COM, 139-140
  - LPT, 140-141
- Windows 98, 504

ISA, 700
- buses, 29-31

ISCSI (Internet Small Computer Systems Interface), 248
ISDN (Integrated Services Digital Networks), 271-272, 700
ISO (International Organization for Standardization), 701
ISPs (Internet service providers), 271, 701

J-K

jitter, 248
Jobs, Steve, 313
JPEGs, 701
jumpers, troubleshooting, 613-614

K-6 processor, 105
KB (kilobyte), 701
kernel mode
- Windows NT, 525-526
  - HAL (Hardware Abstraction Layer), 526
  - micro kernel, 526
  - system service, 527

keyboards, 141
- debouncing, 143
- PS/2 connector, 291-293
- switches, 142-144

keyed connectors, 24, 130
Kildall, Gary, 313
kilobytes, 290
KRNL286.EXE, 412
KRNL386.EXE, 412

L

L-2 cache processor buses, 30
LABEL command, 346
labels, volumes, 342
landscape, 200
landscape monitors, 200
LANs, 701
laptops
- LCDs (liquid crystal display), 96
- Personal Computer Memory Card Industry Association. *See* PCMCIA

laser printers, 216, 226-227
- components, 227-228
- IFS (Image Formation System), 229
  - cleaning process, 229-230
  - conditioning process, 230-231
  - developing process, 231-232
  - end of cycle, 233-234
  - erasing process, 230
  - fusing process, 233
  - transferring process, 232-233
  - writing process, 231

Last Known Good Configuration, 542, 593-594
LASTDRIVE= variable, 344-345
LastKnownGood subkey, 543

latent failures, 125
layers
HAL (Hardware Abstraction Layer), 526
OSI model, 267-268
LBA (Logical Block Addressing), 347, 701
LCDs (liquid crystal display), 96, 195, 210-211, 701
active matrix, 214
colors, 213
dual scans, 214
light, 213
liquid crystals, 211-212
panel construction, 212-213
passive matrix, 213-214
LD (low density), 161
LDAP, 701
LEDs, 701
legacy serial ports, 283
Level 1 (L-1) cache memory, 64-65
Level 2 (L-2) cache memory, 64-65
light
LCDs (liquid crystal displays), 213
monitors, 196
Lightweight Directory Access Protocol (LDAP), 701
LIM 4 (Lotus-Intel-Microsoft), 433-434, 701
linguistics, A+ certification tests, 10-11
liquid crystal display. *See* LCDs
listsvc command, 607
load events, 560
loading
device drivers, 482
programs, 323-324
Windows 9x, 480-481
loca heap, 432
local security authorization. *See* LSA
log files, Windows 9x, 475-476
Logged (Option 2) option, 491
logic boards, floppy drives, 163
logic gates, 187
Logical Block Addressing (LBA), 347, 701
logical devices, 139
logical drives, 340-341
extended partitions, 343-345
FORMAT.COM, 345-346
LABEL command, 346
LBA (Logical Block Addressing), 347
primary partitions, 343-345
SYS.COM, 346-347
terms, 341-342
volumes, 341-343
logical formatting, clusters, 354-355
CHKDSK, 357-358
FAT, 355-356
FAT32, 356
SCANDISK, 357-358
Logical Unit Number (LUN), 244, 701
LOGO.SYS, 488
logon command, 531, 609
logons, Windows NT networks, 531
LOGVIEW.EXE, 597
Longhorn, 461
Lotus-Intel-Microsoft (LIM), 4, 433-434, 701
low density (LD), 161
low memory, 421-425
Low Profile Extensions. *See* LPX
LPT (default printer ports), 140
ports, 140-141
LPX, 701
form factor, 25-26
LSA (local security authorization), 531-532, 701
SAT (Security Access Token), 532
session logs, 532
starting Windows NT, 543
LSASS.EXE (Local Security Authority), 543, 560
LUN (Logical Unit Number), 244, 701

M

macro viruses, 620
magnetic ink character recognition. *See* MICR
main logic assemblies, 228
main motor, 228
Maintenance Wizard, 510-511, 609-610
Make Directory (MD) command, 349
Make New Connections Wizard, 616
manufacturing masks, 64
manufacturing technology processors, 110
map command, 608
MAPI, 701
mapping, 422-423
masks, 533-534
Master Boot Record. *See* MBR
master boot sector viruses, 620
masters, 137
matrix (memory), 50
MB (megabytes), 701
MB/s (megabytes per second), 701
Mbps (megabits per second), 701

MBR (Master Boot Record), 378, 541, 702
  parition loader, 382-383
MCA (Micro Channel Architecture), 31, 702
  buses, 31-32
MD (Make Directory), 349
MDA (monochrome display adapter), 425, 702
MDRAM (multibank dynamic random access memory), 702
media
  networking, 261
  removable, 180
    DVDs, 184-186
    optical storage, 181-184
    tapes, 180-181
media sensor jumper, floppy drives, 164
megahertz (MHz), 201
membrane sheets, 142
MEMMAKER CONFIG.SYS file, 439-441
  DEVICE= directive, 441-443
  DEVICEHIGH= directive, 441-443
memory, 50-51, 70, 139, 419-421, 438-439
  640K barrier, 426
  addresses, 65
  aliasing, 422-423
  bus clocking, 59-60
  buses, 60-62
  cache, 60, 62, 64
    block, 65-69
    hierarchy, 63
    primary (L-1), 64-65
    secondary (L-2), 64-65
  chips, manufacturing masks, 64
  conventional, 421-422
  Direct Memory Access. *See* DMA
  DRAM, 56-57, 70
  evolution, 55-56
  extended, 429-430
    EMM386.EXE, 434-435
    global heep, 431-433
    LIM 4, 433-434
    page frame memory, 436-437
    page swapping, 436-437
    system resources, 431
    task switching, 435-436
    translation buffers, 430-431
    UMBs (upper memory blocks), 430
  external, 64-65
  flash, 186-188
  Flash ROM, 55
  fragments, 52
  high, 435
  HMA (high-memory), 431
  internal, 64-65
  Interrupts (INT), 57
  IRQs, 130
  low, 421, 423-425
  mapping, 422-423
  matrix, 50
  modules, 73, 76, 81
    continuity, 78
    DDR SDRAM, 79-80
    DDR-II, 80-81
    DIMMs, 74-75
    DIP, 73
    narrow channel bus, 77-78
    RIMMs, 75-76
    serial and parallel transfers, 76-77
    SIMMs, 74
  nonvolatile, 50
  page, 65
    Extended Data Out (EDO) memory, 66-67
    FPM, 66
    range, 65-66
    speed, 67-69
  page fault, 63
  parity, 81-82
    ECC, 83-84
    even and odd, 82-83
  RDRAM, 71-72
  Real Mode, 422
  ROM, 51-53
    BIOS, 53
    CMOS settings, 53-54
    Flash BIOS, 54-55
    programmable, 55
  SDRAM, 58, 71
  SIMMs (single inline memory modules), 98
  speeding up, 50
  SRAM, 57, 70-71
  types, 70
  upper, 425
  video RAM, 425-426
  virtual, 139, 426-427
    Control Panel, 428-429
    swap files, 427-428
  volatile, 50
  VRAM, 72
memory-resident viruses, 622

menus, Startup (Windows 9x), 490-491
- command prompt, 493-494
- F4, 494
- step-by-step confirmation, 492-493

metaphysical objects, 397
metastrings, 328
MHz (megahertz), 201
MICR, 702
Micro Channel Architecture. *See* MCA
micro kernel, Windows NT, 526
microcodes, 420
microkernels, 405
microprocessors
- bytes, 290
- microcodes, 420

Microsoft Anti-Virus (MSAV), 619
Microsoft System Information utility, 506
MIME, 702
Mini ATX form factor, 25
Mini-DIN (PS/2 connector), 290
MIPS, 702
MMDS (multichannel multipoint distribution services), 271, 273, 702
MMU, 702
MMX (MultiMedia extensions), 99, 702
modems, 145-146, 702
- commands, 147-148
- UARTs, 146-147

modules, SYSINIT, 384
monitors, 195, 214-215
- AGPs (Accelerated Graphics Port), 205-207
  - frame buffers, 206
  - modes, 208-209
  - pipelining, 207
  - queuing, 207
- contrast ratios, 200-201
- dot pitches, 199
- ELD (electro-luminescent display), 211
- flickers, 203-204
- FTM (flat technology monitor), 211
- full-page, 200
- graphics accelerator cards, 209-210
- interlaced mode, 202-204
- landscape, 200
- LCDs (liquid crystal displays), 210-211
  - active matrix, 214
  - colors, 213
  - dual scans, 214
  - light, 213
  - liquid crystals, 211-212
  - panel construction, 212-213
  - passive matrix, 213-214
- light, 196
- noninterlaced mode, 202-204
- pixels, 196, 198-199
- portrait, 200
- raster, 200
- refresh rates, 201
- resolution, 196, 198-199, 203
- scan cycles, 201
- screen size, 199-200, 215
- SVGA (Super VGA), 205
- triads, 196, 198-199
- UVGA (Ultimate VGA), 205
- VGA, 204
  - 8514/A, 204
  - XGA, 204

monochrome display adapter (MDA), 425
MOS Technologies, 313
motherboards, 17-18, 27-28
- AGPs (Accelerated Graphics Port), 205-207
  - frame buffers, 206
  - modes, 208-209
  - pipelining, 207
  - queuing, 207
- AT form factor, 19-21
- ATX form factor, 23-25
- Baby AT boards, 19
- bus structure, 18
- chipsets, 18, 38-41
  - AMD, 40
  - FC-PGA (Flipped Chip Pin-Grid Array), 40
  - North bridge, 60
  - South bridge, 60
- clock speed, 22-23
- CMOS (Complementary Metal Oxide Semiconductor), 21
- DMA controllers, 135
- expansion buses, 28-30, 42-43
  - AGP (accelerated graphics port), 30, 41-42
  - data paths, 29
  - EISA, 31-32
  - ISA, 29-31
  - MCA, 31-32
  - PCI, 29
  - processor speed, 29, 91-92
  - VESA, 32-33
- form factor, 18
- history, 18-19
- IBM, 18
- LPX (Low Profile Extensions) form factor, 25-26

NLX form factor, 26-27
PCMICIA, 43-44
power supplies, 20
processors, 90-91
8086, 92-93
8088, 92-93
80286, 93-94
80386, 95-96
80486, 97
AMD. *See* AMD
manufacturing technology, 110
mounting technologies, 33-37
names, 108-109
Pentiums. *See* Pentiums
performance, 108-109
protected mode, 94-95
real mode, 92-95
speed, 29, 91-92
resources, 48
slots. *See* slots
mounting processors
SEC, 35-37
SEP, 35-37
socket 7, 34
socket A, 34
socket indexing, 35
technologies, 33-34
mouse, 144-145
optical, 145
PS/2 connector, 291-293
trails, 214
wireless infrared, 145
mouse-overs, 505
MPEG formats, 702
DVDs, 185-186
MS Explorer, 486-487
MS-DOS, 315-317
MSAV (Microsoft Anti-Virus), 619
MSCDEX, 702
MSCONFIG.EXE, 509, 594-596
MSD Sheet, 702
MSD.EXE, 485, 502
IRQ usage, 136-137
MSDOD.SYS, 386-389, 478-479
multibank dynamic random access memory (MDRAM), 702
multichannel multipoint distribution services. *See* MMDS
MultiMedia extensions. *See* MMX
multimeters, 126-127
multimode fiber optic cable, 300
multipartite viruses, 623
multitasking, 398, 520
cooperative, 520
multithreaded, 521
NOSes, 396-398
preemptive, 400, 521
processes, 399
threads, 397, 399-400
time slices, 398-399
multithreaded multitasking, 521
My Computer (Windows 2000), 568-569
diagnostics, 603-604
My Network Places (Windows 2000), 570

N

name spaces, 452
names
files, 360
absolute, 360
characters, 360-361
extensions, 361-362
Windows 9x, 495, 498-500
processors, 108-109
narrow channel buses, 77-78
National Computer Security Council. *See* NCSC
National Television Standards Committee. *See* NTSC
NCSC (National Computer Security Council), 703
negative electrons, 121-122
Net Meeting 3.0 (Windows 98), 504
Net Watcher, troubleshooting Windows NT, 554
NETLOG.TXT, 475
network administrators, 529
network interface cards (NICs), 260
Network layer (OSI model), 268
Network Operating System (NOS), 260
networking, 259-261, 269
bandwidth, 263-264
bridges, 266-267
bus transfers, 259
cables, 294
coaxial, 294
fiber, 299-300
twisted-pair, 295-299
cables and connectors, twisted-pair configurations, 299
chaining devices, 242-243
client/server, 260-261
connectors, 294

Ethernet, 262-263
IEEE 1394, 257-259
Internet, 269-270
accessing, 271-275
email addresses, 270-271
media, 261
multitasking environments, 396-398
NICs, 261
OSI model, 267-268
peer-to-peer, 260
PnP, 256-257
redirectors, 261
routers, 266-267
SCSI, 243
LUN, 244
SCSI-1, 245
SCSI-2, 245-247
SCSI-3, 247-248
terminators, 263
throughput, 263-264
token-ring, 264-265
bus and star topology, 265
troubleshooting connections, 615-616
access, 617-618
NICs, 616-617
PROTOCOL.INI, 618-619
Services icon, 617
validation, 617
USB, 248-250, 254-255
hubs, 252, 255-256
NRZI encoding, 255
release 2.0, 253-254
releases 1.0 and 1.1, 250-252
wireless, 300
networking operating system redirectors (TSRs), 496-497
networks
accounts. *See* accounts
policies, compared to profiles, 539-540
profiles, 536, 542. *See also* profiles
compared to policies, 539-540
Windows NT, 529-530
logons, 531
LSA (local security authorization), 531-532
SAM (Security Account Manager), 530
SID (Security Identification), 532
user IDs, 530-531
user process, 532-533
New Technology File System. *See* NTFS
Nexsan Technologies, 176
NICs (network interface cards), 260-261, 616-617, 703
NLX form factor, 26-27, 703
Non-Return-to-Zero-Inverted encoding. *See* NRZI encoding
noninterlaced mode, 202-204
nonresident viruses, 623
nonvolatile memory, 50
Normal (Option 1) option, 491
North bridge (PCI), 37, 60
NOSes (Network Operating System), 260, 396-398, 703
NRZI encoding, 255, 703
/N switch (SETUP.EXE), 409
NT (New Technology), 404-405, 703
boot loader, 541-542, 611
NT File System. *See* NTFS
NTBTLOG.TXT, 598-599
NTDETECT.COM, 560
NTFS (New Technology File System), 496, 528, 543-545, 703
NTLDR (NT boot loader), 541-542, 611
NTLDR.COM, 560
NTOSKRNL.EXE, 560
NTSC (National Television Standards Committee), 703
numbers, volumes, 342-343
Nvidia chipsets, 41

O

O command, 148
Object Linking and Embedding. *See* OLE
objects, 452
metaphysical, 397
virtual, 397
Windows 95, 453
Windows 9x, 453
Windows Registry, 460
odd parity, memory, 82-83
OEM (original equipment manufacturer), 453, 703
ohms, 126
OLE (Object Linking and Embedding), 460-461
clients, 460
online resources. *See* Web sites
open standards, 23
operating systems, 310-312, 520-522
compared to shells, 363-366
file properties, 364
SHELL= variable, 366-367

DOS, 308, 312-313
- 86-DOS, 314-315
- Apple, 313-314
- ASCII text, 339
- ATTRIB command, 309-310, 333-335
- command interpreters, 318-319
- COMMAND.COM. *See* COMMAND.COM
- Control Program for Microcomputers (CP/M), 313, 316-317
- DEL command, 335
- DIR command, 335-336
- DOS COPY, 316
- environment, 325-332, 344-345
- error messages, 321-322
- file mask, 321
- file names, 310, 360-362
- MS-DOS, 315, 317
- parsing, 319
- PC-DOS, 315-317
- programs, 322-324
- saving searches, 338-339
- starting Windows, 310
- switches, 320-321
- syntax, 319-320
- VER command, 317
- wild card searches, 336-338
- Windows, 485-487
- Windows 9x, 317-318

Longhorn, 461
multitasking, 520
networks. *See* networks
OS/2 2.0, 406-407
OS/R-B, 453
troubleshooting
- Last Known Good Configuration, 593-594
- restores, 587
- Safe mode, 589-590, 592-593
- startups, 582-586
- strategies, 586-587
- System Configuration Utility, 594-596
- Windows XP Advanced Startup option, 596

Windows
- DOS, 485-487
- File Manager, 405-406
- NT, 404-405
- .PIF files, 402-403
- PROGMAN.INI file, 417-418
- Program Manager, 405-406
- resources, 403
- System VM, 402
- versions, 455-457
- Virtual Real Mode, 401
- WIN.COM, 409-412

Windows 2.x, 404
Windows 2000, 522-523, 558-559
- Active Directory, 562-564
- Administrative Tools, 602-603
- Computer Management tool, 462
- diagnostics, 565-574
- Disk Cleanup, 609-610
- Emergency Repair Disk (ERD), 591-592
- Last Known Good Configuration, 593-594
- Recovery Console, 309-310, 333-335, 450, 605-609
- Safe mode, 592-593
- starting, 559-562
- troubleshooting, 565-574, 584-586, 589
- WFP (Windows File Protection), 601

Windows 2000 Advanced Server, 559
Windows 2000 Datacenter Server, 559
Windows 2000 Professional, 558
Windows 2000 Server, 558
Windows 3.1, 406-407
Windows 3.11 Program Manager, 501
Windows 3.x, 418-421
- compared to Windows 9x, 502-503
- core files, 412
- global heep, 431-433
- INI files, 412-418
- LIM 4, 433-434
- memory, 419, 421-426, 434-439
- missing INI file, 415
- starting, 407-409
- virtual memory, 426-429

Windows 95, 451, 521
- Desktop, 452
- Emergency Recovery Utility (ERU.EXE), 591
- HwDiag.EXE, 602
- object properties, 453
- Safe mode, 590
- wizards, 451-452

Windows 98, 503-504, 521
- Active Desktop, 504
- Drive Converter, 454
- Explorer, 505

installation, 468-476
LOGO.SYS, 488
Registry Checker, 590-591
Safe mode, 590
Windows 9x, 489, 566
AUTOEXEC.BAT, 483-484
compared to Windows 3.x, 502-503
Control Panel, 489-490
Desktop, 452-453
file names, 495, 498-499
Help Desk, 508
IFS Manager, 494-500
loading, 480-481
loading device drivers, 482-483
Maintenance Wizard, 510-511
Microsoft System Information utility, 506
MSCONFIG.EXE, 509
object properties, 453
Registry, 463
Registry Checker, 507-508
Safe mode, 490-492, 589
saving long file names, 499-500
start sequence, 479-480, 484-485
starting, 476-479
Startup menu, 490-494
troubleshooting startups, 584
Windows Update Manager, 509-510
Windows Me, 511-512, 521
CPUs, 595
Registry Checker, 590-591
Safe mode, 590
SFP (System File Protection), 601
System Configuration Utility, 595-596
Windows NT, 521, 556-558
architecture, 524-528
boot partitions, 541
disk administration, 545-548
error messages, 554
missing BOOT.INI, 555
missing files, 556
missing kernel, 555
networking, 529-533
NT Detect, 554-555
NTFS, 543-545
NTLDR, 541-542
RAID, 549
Registry, 528-529
starting, 540-543
system partitions, 541
troubleshooting, 550-554
Windows NT 3.1, 522
Windows NT 4, 522
Windows NT 5.0, 522-523
Windows NT Server, 528
Windows NT Workstation, 528
Windows XP, 523-524, 574
Advanced Startup option, 596
Recovery Console, 450
startup time, 575
troubleshooting startups, 585-586
WFP (Windows File Protection), 601
WPA (Windows Product Activation), 575
operating systems technologies test, 3
Optical Carrier (OC)-1, 300
optical mouse, 145
optical resolution, scanners, 198
optical storage, 181
CD-Rs, 183
CDs, 181-183
transfer ratios, 183-184
optomechanical devices, 145
original equipment manufacturer. *See* OEM
OS/2, 703
development of, 404
microkernels, 405
Protected Mode, 397
OS/2 2.0, 406-407
OS/2 3.0, 405
OS/R-B, 453
OSI model, 267, 703
layers, 267-268
/O switch (SETUP.EXE), 409
Outlook Express 5.0 (Windows 98), 504
output
devices, 118
modems. *See* modems
printers. *See* printers
final, 194-195
transient, 194-195
over-clocking Pentiums, 100-101
overhead, 178-179

P

P command, 147
P2P networking (point-to-point networking), 275
P6 family
3DNow!, 103-104
Pentiums, 101-103
VID Pins, 102

page fault (memory), 63
page frames
  memory, 436-437
  switching, 398
page swapping, 436-437
PAL (Phase Alternating Line), 703
Palo Alto Research Center (PARC) labs, 226, 703
panels (LCDs), 212-213
paper
  feed process, 234
  jams in printers, 221
    continuous-form paper, 221
    friction feed paper, 221-223
  thermal, 219
paper control assemblies, 228
parallel cable connectors, 287
parallel ports, 283, 285
  36-pin Centronics connector, 288
  DB25, 286
  RS-232 and DB9, 287
  SCSI connectors, 288-289
  types, 289
parallel transfers, memory modules, 76-77
parallel wiring, 285
PARC (Palo Alto Research Center), 226, 703
parity
  error, 83
  memory, 81-82
    ECC, 83-84
    even and odd, 82-83
  striped sets with, 547-548
parsing, 319
partition loader, 382-383
partitions, 340-341
  extended, 342-345
  interactive (Windows 2000), 570
  FORMAT.COM, 345-346
  LABEL command, 346
  LBA (Logical Block Addressing), 347
  primary, 342-345
  status, 342
  SYS.COM, 346-347
  terms, 341-342
  volumes, 341-343
  Windows NT, 541
passive matrix, LCDs (liquid crystal displays), 213-214
passwords, 531
PAT, 703
pathnames, 329-332
paths, 329-332
Patterson, Tim, 314
PAUSE command, 322, 369
PB (petabyte), 704
PC cards, 28, 43-44, 704
PC-DOS, 315, 317
PCB, 704
PCI (Peripheral Component Interconnect), 33, 176-177, 704
  buses, 29
  North bridge, 37
  South bridge, 37
PCL, 704
PCMCIA (Personal Computer Memory Card Industry Association), 28, 43-44, 704
PDP (Plasma Display Panel), 211, 704
Peddle, Chuck, 313
peer-to-peer networking, 260
Pentiums, 97-98
  Celeron, 104
  clock multiplier, 100
  first series, 98
  over-clocking, 100-101
  P6 family, 101-102
    3DNow!, 103-104
    Pentium II, 102
    Pentium III, 102-103
    VID Pins, 102
  Pentium II, 102
  Pentium III, 102-103
  Pentium Pros, 101-102
  second series, 99
  third series, 99
performance, processors, 108-109
Performance Monitor, troubleshooting Windows NT, 553
Peripheral Component Interconnect. *See* PCI
peripheral devices, 118
  controllers. *See* controllers
  keyboards, 141
    debouncing, 143
    PS/2 connector, 291-293
    switches, 142-144
  mouse, 144-145
    optical, 145
    PS/2 connector, 291-293
    wireless infrared, 145
  scanners, 148-149
    bit rates, 151
    Charge-Coupled Devices (CCDs), 149-150

color, 151-152
connections, 150-151
resolution, 149-150
Personal Computer Memory Card Industry Association. *See* PCMCIA
PGA, 704
PGS (Pin Grid Array), 34
Phase Alternating Line. *See* PAL
photons, 197
physical devices, 139
Physical layer (OSI model), 267
piezoelectric crystal, 217-218
PIF Editor, 402
.PIF files (Program Information Files), 402-403, 704
Pin Grid Array. *See* PGA
PIO, 172-173, 704
pipelining, 207
Pixel Shader 1.4, 209
pixels
addressability, 196
colors, 198
monitors, 196, 198-199
printers, 216-218
triads, 196
plain text. *See* ASCII
planar boards. *See* motherboards
Plasma Display Panel (PDP), 211
platters, 167
plenum-type ceiling, 296
PnP (Plug and Play), 131, 256-257, 472, 704
point-to-point networking (P2P networking), 275
pointers, Windows Registry, 461-462
polarized sunglasses, 212
policies, 481, 539-540
polymorphic viruses, 623
portraits, 200
ports, 139, 293
IRQs, 138
COM, 139-140
LPT, 140-141
parallel, 285
36-pin Centronics connector, 288
DB25, 286
RS-232 and DB9, 287
SCSI connectors, 288-289
types, 289
serial, 290-293
positive electrons, 121-122
POSIX, 704
POST, 378, 704
routine, 477-478
potentiometers, 126
power supplies, 130
AC/DC, 228
high-voltage, 228
motherboards, 20
preemptive multitasking, 400, 521
PrepLogic, 682, 691
PrepLogic Exam Competency Score, 691
PrepLogic Practice Tests, 686
exam simulation interface, 686
Examination Score Report, 690
Flash Remove mode, 689
Flash Review mode, 688-689
installation, 687
Practice Test mode
Enable Item Review Button, 689
Enable Show Answer Button, 688
Randomize Choices, 689
starting, 688
studying in, 689
PrepLogic Exam Competency Score, 691
question quality, 686
removing from your computer, 687
reviewing exams, 691
software requirements, 687
study modes, 688
PrepLogic Practice Tests, Preview Edition, 682
Presentation layer (OSI model), 268
primary (L-1) cache memory, 64-65
Primary (PRI), 342
primary partitions, 342-345
PRINT command, 234
printed circuit card. *See* PC cards
printers, 215-216, 235-236
A/B box, 249
bubble jet, 216
commercial color-separation, 196
consumable components, 222
direct thermal, 216
dot matrix, 218-220, 223
dpi, 216
female connector, 287
form feed, 218
home position, 220
impact, 216
ink jet, 216
laser, 216, 226-234
paper feed process, 234

PCL, 704
piezoelectric crystal, 217-218
pixels, 216-218
resolution, 198, 217
thermal paper, 219
troubleshooting, 220
cleaning, 220-221
paper jams, 221-223
privileges, 525
probabilistic quiet times, 264
problems. *See* troubleshooting
processes, multitasking, 399
processors, 90-91, 106
32-bit processing, 107
64-bit processing, 107
8086, 92-93
8088, 92-93
80286, 93-94
80386, 95
coprocessors, 96
SX versions, 95-96
80486, 97
AMD, 104-105
Athlon, 105-106
Athlon XP, 108
Duron, 105-106
K-6, 105
Athlon, 41
Enhanced Mode, 96
integration, 97
manufacturing technology, 110
names, 108-109
Pentiums, 97-98
Celeron, 104
clock multiplier, 100
first series, 98
over-clocking, 100-101
P6 family, 101-104
second series, 99
third series, 99
performance, 108-109
protected mode
compared to real mode, 94
switching to real mode, 94-95
real mode, 92-94
compared to protected mode, 94
switching from protected mode to, 94-95
registers, 61
scalability, 97
slots, 33-34, 42-43
sockets, 33-34
7, 34
A, 34
indexing, 35
SEC, 35-37
SEP, 35-37
speed, 29, 91-92
upgrades, 97
profiles, 536
compared to policies, 539-540
Windows NT Last Known Good hardware, 542
PROGMAN.INI file, 417, 481
GRP files, 417-418
Program Information Files. *See* .PIF files
Program Manager (Windows 3.11), 405-406, 417-418, 501
programmable ROM (PROM), 55, 704
programming languages, 311
program commands, 322-323
loading, 323-324
running, 323-324
prompt, 319
PROMPT variable, 327-329
prompts, 493-494
properties
file, 364
Windows 95 objects, 453
Windows 9x objects, 453
proprietary standards, 23
Protected Mode, OS/2, 397
protected mode processors
compared to real mode, 94
switching to real mode, 94-95
PROTOCOL.INI, troubleshooting network connectivity, 618-619
protocols
LDAP, 701
TCP/IP, 708
PS/2 connectors (Mini-DIN), 93, 291-293
PSPs (segment prefixes), 316
pure mechanical switches, 142

Q-R

QDOS, 705
QIC, 705
quality gradation, twisted-pair cable, 296-297
questions
A+ certification test, 10-14, 632-634
sample A+ certification test, 636-656
queuing, 207

RADAR, 705
RAID (Redundant Array of Inexpensive Disks), 549, 705
RAID 1, 549
RAID 2, 549
RAID 3, 549
RAM (random access memory), 51-53, 705
  BIOS, 53
  CMOS settings, 53-54
  Flash BIOS, 54-55
  programmable ROM, 55
  video, 425-426
Rambus Inline Memory Modules (RIMMs), 75-76
RAMDAC (Random Access Memory Digital-to-Analog Converter), 705
random access, 168
random access memory. *See* RAM
ranges, memory, 65-66
raster fonts, 224-225
rasters, 200
RDRAM, 71-72, 705
read-only (R) memory, 51
read-write (RW) memory, 51, 162
read/write heads, 354
/R (Real Mode), 410, 422
real mode processors, 92-94
  compared to protected mode, 94
  switching from protected mode to, 94-95
Recovery Console (Windows 2000), 450, 573-574, 605-606
  commands, 606
    ATTRIB, 309-310, 333-335, 607
    CHKDSK, 607
    disable, 608
    diskpart, 608
    enable, 608
    EXIT, 609
    fixboot, 608
    fixmbr, 609
    listsvc, 607
    logon, 609
    map, 608
Recovery Disks, 450. *See also* disks
red, green, and blue (RGB), 196
redirectors, 260-261, 333
redraws, 201
Redundant Array of Inexpensive Disks. *See* RAID
reference points, clock tick, 255
refresh rates, monitors, 201
REGEDIT.EXE, 466-468
registers, CPU, 61
Registry, 450, 528-529
Registry Checker, 507, 590-591, 604-605
  Disk Cleanup, 508
  SFC (System File Checker), 507
  version conflict manager, 508
Registry Editor, 466-468
Registry, Windows, 457-458, 468
  backup files, 457
  backups, 465-466
  components, 462
    copies, 464-465
    HKeys, 462-464
  editing, 459-460
  .INI files, 458-459
  objects, 460
  pointers, 461-462
  shortcuts, 460
  SYSTEM.1ST, 464-465
relational databases, 544
relative locations, 350
REM file, 369
remark (REM), 369
removable media, 180
  DVDs, 184-186
  optical storage, 181
    CD-Rs, 183
    CDs, 181-183
    transfer ratios, 183-184
  tapes, 180-181
reports
  Windows, 500-502
  system, 603-604
resistors, 126
resolution, 196
  24-bit, 152
  colors, 198
  images, 197-198
  monitors, 196, 198-199, 203
  printers, 198, 217
  scanners, 198
resources, 403
  leaks, 433
  motherboards, 48
  online. *See* Web sites
  system, 431
restoring operating systems, 587
Rexx (Restructured Extended Executor), 705
RGB (red, green, and blue), 196, 705
ribbon cables, 284
right mouse button, 453

RIMMs (Rambus Inline Memory Modules), 75-76, 705
RISC, 705
RJ-45 modular connectors, 297
RLE, 705
ROM (read-only memory), 51-53, 705
  BIOS, 53
  boot sector, 381
    BASIC bootstrap loader, 381-384
    partition loader, 382-383
  CMOS settings, 53-54
  Flash, 55
  Flash BIOS, 54-55
  programmable, 55
root directory, 381
routers, 266-268
routines, 524
RPM, 705
RS-232 connectors, 287
RS-422 connectors, 287
RS-423 connectors, 287
rubber domes, 142
running programs, 323-324

S

S-Video (S-VHS), 210
SAA, 705
Safe mode
  Windows 95, 590
  Windows 98, 590
  Windows 9x, 490-491, 589
    F5, 491-492
    F6, 492
  Windows 2000, 562, 592-593
  Windows Me, 590
SAM (Security Account Manager), 530, 706
sample test, 632
  answers, 658-679
  questions, 636-656
SANs (Storage Area Networks), 248
SASI (Shugart Associates Systems Interface), 160, 706
SAT (Security Access Token), 532, 706
satellite wireless, Internet access, 272-273
saving
  file searches, 338-339
  Windows 9x file names, 499-500
scalability
  processors, 97
  upgrading, 284
Scalable Processor Architecture. *See* SPARC
ScanDisk, 358-359
SCANDISK, clusters, 357-358
scanners, 148-149
  bit rates, 151
  Charge-Coupled Devices (CCDs), 149-150
  color, 151-152
  connections, 150-151
  dual, LCDs, 214
  images, 197-198, 200
  motor, 228
  resolution, 149-150, 198
Scanregw.exe, 604-605
scheduling A+ certification tests, 4-5
scoring, 6
screen size, monitors, 199-200, 215
scripted viruses, 620-621
SCSI (Small Computer System Interface), 160, 169-170, 242-243, 706
  connectors, 288-289
  LUN, 244
  SCSI-1, 245
  SCSI-2, 245-247
  SCSI-3, 247-248
SCSI-1, 245
SCSI-2, 245-247
SCSI-3, 247-248
SDRAM (Synchronous DRAM), 58, 71, 706
searches (DOS), 338
  DIR command, 335-336
  paths, 331-332
  saving search results, 338-339
  wild cards, 336-338
Seattle Computer Products, 314
SEC (Single Edge Contact), 35-37, 706
SECAM, 706
second series Pentiums, 99
secondary (L-2) cache memory, 64-65, 71
sectors, 168-169, 353-354
security
  firewalls, 268, 622
  passwords, 531
  SAT, 706
Security Access Token. *See* SAT
Security Account Manager. *See* SAM
Security Identification. *See* SID
Security Reference Monitor, 533-535
segment prefixes. *See* PSPs
SEP (Single Edge Processor), 35-37, 706
serial devices, 290
serial ports, 283, 290-293
serial transfers, memory modules, 76-77

serial wiring, 285
Services icon, troubleshooting network connectivity, 617
Session layer (OSI model), 268
sessions, Windows NT networking logs, 532
Sessions Manager (SMSS), 542-543
SET command, 326, 328
SET TEMP= variable, 329
SET <variable>, 326-328
Settings command (Start menu), 249
SETUP.EXE, 407-409
SETUPLOG.TXT, 475-476
SETVER.EXE, 482
SFC (System File Checker), 507, 600-601
SFP (System File Protection), 601
SGRAM, 706
SHELL.DLL, 403
SHELL= variable, 366-367, 482
SHELLB, 409
SHELLC, 409
shells, compared to operating systems, 363-366
 file properties, 364
 SHELL= variable, 366-367
Shielded Twisted Pair. *See* STP
shielding, 296
SHIFT (Restart) key, 584
shortcuts, Windows Registry, 460
Shugart Associates Systems Interface (SASI), 160
Shugart Technology, Inc., 707
Shugart, Alan, 160
SID (Security Identification), 532, 706
signal skew, 248
signal traces, 29
signatures, 623
SIMMs (Single Inline Memory Modules), 74, 98, 706
Single Edge Contact. *See* SEC
Single Edge Processor. *See* SEP
single mode fiber optic cable, 299
single-sided single density, 161
SiS chipsets, 41
sites. *See* Web sites
sixth generation Pentiums, 101-102
 3DNow!, 103-104
 Pentium II, 102
 Pentium III, 102-103
 VID Pins, 102
size, images, 200
slaves, 137
slots, 42-43
Small Computer System Interface. *See* SCSI
SMARTDRV.EXE, 64
SMARTDRV.SYS, 64
SmartMedia, 187
SMI (Storage Management Initiative), 248
SMI (System Management Interrupts), 96, 706
SMSS (Session Manager), 542-543, 560
SNIA (Storage Networking Industry Association), 248
sockets, ZIF design, 90
software
 compared to hardware, 139
 drivers, 139
 requirements, PrepLogic Practive Tests, 687
SONAR, 706
SONET (Synchronous Optical Network), 272, 300, 706
Sony i.Link. *See* i.Link
Sony MemoryStick, 187-188
South bridge (PCI), 37, 60
spaghetti code, 525
spanning, 466
SPARC (Scalable Processor Architecture), 707
speed
 clocks, 22-23
 memory, 67-69
 processors, 91
SPGA (Staggered Pin Grid Array), 34, 707
SPI, 707
spindle motors, floppy drives, 163
SPP (standard parallel port), 289, 707
spyware, 624
SQL (Structured Query Language), 707
SRAM, 57, 70-71, 707
SSFDC (State Floppy Disk Card), 187
ST, 707
ST-506/412, 169
stacks, 435
STACKS=, 482
Staggered Pin Grid Array (SPGA), 34, 707
standard bi-directional parallel ports, 289
/S (Standard Mode), 410
Standard Mode (WIN/S), 410-411
standard parallel ports (SPP), 289
star topology, 265
Start menu, Settings command, 249

starting
- Windows DOS, 310
- Windows 2000, 559-561
  - boot options, 561-562
  - Emergency Repair Disk (ERD), 591-592
  - Last Known Good Configuration, 593-594
  - safe mode, 562, 592-593
- Windows 3.x, 407-409
- Windows 95
  - Emergency Recovery Utility (ERU.EXE), 591
  - Safe mode, 590
- Windows 98 Safe mode, 590
- Windows 9x, 476-477
  - after installation, 474-475
  - bootstrap, 477-478
  - DOS boot sequence, 478
  - MSDOS.SYS, 478-479
  - POST routine, 477-478
  - Safe mode, 589
  - start sequence, 479-480, 484-485
  - WIN.COM, 479
- Windows Me Safe mode, 590
- Windows NT, 540-541
  - boot partitions, 541
  - LSA, 543
  - NTLDR, 541-542
  - SMSS (Session Manager), 542-543
  - system partitions, 541
  - Win32, 543
- Windows XP startup time, 575

Startup menu (Windows 9x), 490-491
- command prompt, 493-494
- F4, 494
- step-by-step confirmation, 492-493

startups. *See also* bootups
- troubleshooting, 584-585
  - BOOTLOG.TXT, 597-599
  - crashes, 585-586
  - Emergency Recovery Utility (ERU.EXE), 591
  - Emergency Repair Disk (ERD), 591-592
  - Event Viewer, 599
  - function keys, 582-584
  - Last Known Good Configuration, 593-594
  - LOGVIEW.EXE, 597
  - NTBTLOG.TXT, 598-599
  - restores, 587
  - Safe mode, 589-593
  - strategies, 586-587
  - System Configuration Utility, 594-596
  - System Information tool, 596-597
  - Task Manager, 600
  - Windows 2000, 584-586
  - Windows 9x, 584
  - Windows XP, 585-586
  - Windows XP Advanced Startup option, 596
- Windows 95, 470-472

state voltage, 162

State Floppy Disk Card (SSFDC), 187

statements, routines, 524

static VxDs, 479

status, 342

stealth viruses, 621, 623
- firewalls, 622
- Trojan, 621-622

storage, capacitors, 128-130

Storage Area Networks (SANs), 248

storage devices
- controllers. *See* controllers
- flash memory, 186-188
- floppy disks. *See* floppy disks
- hard drives. *See* hard drives
- InfiniSAN RAID, 176
- removable media, 180
  - DVDs, 184-186
  - optical storage, 181-184
  - tapes, 180-181

Storage Management Initiative (SMI), 248

Storage Networking Industry Association (SNIA), 248

STPs (Shielded Twisted Pair), 296, 707

striped sets, Windows NT disk administration, 547-548

subdirectories, 352

sunglasses, polarized, 212

Super I/O chips, 283

Super VGA (SVGA), 205

superscalar technology, 97

SUWARN.BAT, 476

SVGA (Super Video Graphics Array). 205, 707

swap files, 194, 427-428, 435

switches (keyboards), 142-143
- capacitive, 143-144
- commands, 320-321
- foam elements, 142
- membrane sheets, 142

pure mechanical, 142
rubber domes, 142
SETUP.EXE, 409
switching
boxes, 249
page frames, 398
SX chips, 80386 processors, 95-96
Synchronous DRAM. *See* SDRAM
Synchronous Optical Network (SONET), 272, 300, 706
syntax commands, 319-320
SYS.COM, 346-347
SYSEDIT.EXE, 413
SYSINIT module, 384
System Agent
Windows 98, 504
Windows 2000, 571
system binders, 395
system boards. *See* motherboards
system clocks, 283
System Configuration Tool, 509
System Configuration Utility (Windows 2000), 565-567, 594-596
administrative tools, 567-568
System Diagnostics tool, 485
SYSTEM file, 560
System File Checker (SFC), 504, 507, 573, 600
System File Protection (SFP), 601
system files
CONFIG.SYS, 383-385
F5 key, 385-386
MSDOS.SYS, 386-387
HIMEM.SYS, 387-388, 429-430
system resources, 431
translation buffers, 430-431
UMBs (upper memory blocks), 430
IO.SYS, 383-384
16-bit device drivers, 388
CONFIG.SYS, 383
HIMEM.SYS, 387-388
MSDOD.SYS, 388-389
MSDOS.SYS, 386-387
System Information tool, troubleshooting hardware, 596-597
BOOTLOG.TXT, 597-599
Event Viewer, 599
LOGVIEW.EXE, 597
NTBTLOG.TXT, 598-599
Task Manager, 600
system maintenance, 609-610
System Management Interrupts. *See* SMI
systems
partitions, Windows NT, 541
reports, 603-604
resources, 431
service, Windows NT Executive Layer, 527
System VM (Virtual Machine), 402, 520
SYSTEM.1ST, 464-465
SYSTEM.DA0, 465
SYSTEM.DAT file, 457, 462, 481
SYSTEM.INI, 414-415, 480-481

T

T command, 147
T-connectors, 294
tagged image file format. *See* TIFF
Tandy, Charles, 314
tapes, 180-181
Task Manager, 552-553, 600
task switching, 396, 435-436
TB (terabytes), 707
TCP/IP (Transmission Control Protocol/Internet Protocol), 268, 708
Telecommunications Industry association (TIA), 287
television, HDTV (high definition television), 211, 699
terminate, stay resident. *See* TSR
terminators, 263
terms, 341-342
tests, 2-3
adaptive, 9-10
answers, 633
certification, 5
core hardware, 3
design, 10
exam requirements, 7
framework, 634-635
linguistics, 10-11
operating systems technologies, 3
preparation, 6-7, 13-14
qualifications, 2
questions, 10-14, 632-634
resources, 7
sample exam, 632
answers, 658-679
questions, 636-656
scheduling, 4-5
scoring, 6
signing up for, 4
site for taking exam, 5-9

text, ASCII, 339
thermal paper, 219
third series Pentiums, 99
Thomson Prometric Web site, 4
threads, 397-400
throughput, 263-264
TIA (Telecommunications Industry association), 287
tiered-star topology, 255
TIF (True Type Fonts), 225-226
TIFF (tagged image file format), 708
time slices, 398-399
token passing, 260
token-ring networks, 264-265
toner print process, 231-232
toner cartridges, 228
toolbar tips, 505
Top View, 396
topologies
  bus, 265
  star, 265
trackballs, 144
tracks, 168-169, 354
transfer corona wire, 233
transfer ratios, optical storage devices, 183-184
transferring process, IFS (Image Formation System), 232-233
transient output, 194-195
translation buffers, 430-431
Transmission Control Protocol/Internet Protocol (TCP/IP), 268
Transport layer (OSI model), 268
trapping errors, 322
triads, 196
  monitors, 196-199
  redraws, 201
Trojan virus, 621-622
troubleshooting, 582
  bootups, 610
    CMOS, 611-613
    hardware problems, 613-615
    NTLDR, 611
  hardware, System Information tool, 596-600
  printers, 220
    cleaning, 220-221
    paper jams, 221-223
  Registry Checker, 507
    Disk Cleanup, 508
    SFC (System File Checker), 507
    version conflict manager, 508
  SFC, 600
    SFP (System File Protection), 601
    WFP (Windows File Protection), 601
  startups, 584-585
    crashes, 585-586
    Emergency Recovery Utility (ERU.EXE), 591
    Emergency Repair Disk (ERD), 591-592
    function keys, 582-584
    Last Known Good Configuration, 593-594
    restores, 587
    Safe mode, 589-593
    strategies, 586-587
    System Configuration Utility, 594-596
    Windows 2000, 584-586
    Windows 9x, 584
    Windows XP, 585-586
    Windows XP Advanced Startup option, 596
  Windows 2000, 565
    Control Panel, 568-569
    Device Manager, 569
    interactive partitioning, 570
    My Computer, 568-569
    My Network Places, 570
    Recovery Console, 573-574
    System Agent, 571
    System Configuration Utility, 565-568
    System File Checker, 573
    Windows File Protection (WFP), 572
    Windows Update Manager, 571
  Windows NT, 550
    bootable disks, 551-552
    Emergency Repair Disk (ERD), 551-552
    Event Viewer, 550-551
    Net Watcher, 554
    Performance Monitor, 553
    Task Manager, 552-553
True Type Fonts (TIF), 225-226
truncating file names, Windows 9x, 498
TSRs (networking operating system redirectors), 496-497, 708
turnaround times, commands, 178-179
Tweak UI, 490

twisted-pair cable (10BaseT), 295-296
 configuration, 298-299
 quality gradation, 296-297
 RJ-45 modular connectors, 297
 STP, 296
 UTP, 296
 wiring problems, 297
typefaces, 224
 bitmap, 224-225
 raster, 224-225
 TIF, 225-226
types, 342

U

UARTs (Universal Asynchronous Receiver Transmitter), 146-147, 708
UDMA, 708
UDMA 2, 174-175
UDMA 3, 174-175
ULSI (ultra large-scale integration), 207, 708
Ultimate VGA (UVGA), 205
Ultra ATA, 174-175
Ultra ATA/66, 175
Ultra DMA, 174-175
ultra large-scale integration. *See* ULSI
Ultra SCSI, 246
Ultra Wide SCSI, 246
Ultra2 LVD SCSI, 247
Ultra2 SCSI, 246
Ultra2 Wide (U2W) SCSI, 247
Ultra3 SCSI, 247
ultraviolet light (UV), 219
UMBs (upper memory blocks), 430, 708
undirectional parallel ports, 289
Uninterruptible Power Supply. *See* USBs
Universal Asynchronous Receiver Transmitter. *See* UARTs
Universal Resource Locator. *See* URLs
Universal Serial Bus. *See* USB
Unix directory names, forward slash (/), 331
Unshielded Twisted Pair. *See* UTP
upgrades, processors, 97
upper memory, 425
upper memory blocks (UMBs), 430
UPS, 708
URLs (Universal Resource Locator), 269, 708
USBs (Universal Serial Bus), 242, 248-250, 254-255, 503, 708
 hubs, 252, 255-256
 NRZI encoding, 255
 ports, 283
 release 2.0, 253-254
 releases 1.0 and 1.1, 250-252
User accounts, 536
 groups, 538-539
 managing, 537-538
user IDs, 530-531
user interfaces, 318
User mode, Windows NT, 527-528
USER.DA0, 465
USER.DAT file, 457, 462
USER.EXE, 412, 432
utility files, bootable disks with, 394-395
UTPs (Unshielded Twisted Pair), 296, 708
UV (ultraviolet light), 219
UVGA (Ultimate VGA), 205
UVs, 708

V

validation, troubleshooting network connectivity, 617
variables, 325-326
 COMSPEC=, 327
 LASTDRIVE=, 344-345
 PROMPT=, 327-329
 SET TEMP=, 329
 SET <variable>, 326-328
 SHELL=, 366-367
VCRs, 708
VDTs (video display terminals), 195
VER command, 317
version conflict manager (Registry Checker), 508
versions, Windows, 455-457
vertical CPU slots, 36
very large-scale integration. *See* VLSI
VESA (Video Electronics Standard Association) buses, 32-33, 37, 211, 709
VFAT (Virtual Machine Manager), 453-454, 497, 709
 file name aliases, 498-499
 saving long file names, 499-500
 truncating file names, 498
VGA (Video Graphics Array), 204, 709
 8514/A, 204
 XGA, 204
VGALOGO.*, 409
VHD, 709
VIA, 41
VID, 709
VID Pins, 102

video displays. *See* monitors
Video Electronics Standard Association. *See* VESA
Video Graphics Array. *See* VGA
video monitors, 283
video RAM (VRAM), 206, 425-426
VIDs (voltage identification pins), 102
virtual device drivers (VxDs), 139, 401, 437-438, 479
Virtual File Allocation Table. *See* VFAT
Virtual Machine Manager. *See* VMM
Virtual Machines (VM), 93-94
virtual memory, 139, 426-427
  Control Panel, 428-429
  swap files, 427-428
virtual objects, 397
Virtual Real Mode, 401-402
viruses, 619
  adware, 624
  boot sector, 620
  image files, 623-624
  macro, 620
  master boot sector, 620
  memory-resident, 622
  multipartite, 623
  nonresident, 623
  polymorphic, 623
  scripted, 620-621
  spyware, 624
  stealth, 621-623
    firewalls, 622
    Trojan, 621-622
  Worm, 621
VisiCalc, 314
VL Buses, 709
VLSI (very large-scale integration), 207, 709
VM, 709
VMM (Virtual Machine Manager), 454, 479, 709
VMM32.VXD, 479-480
VMs (Virtual Machines), 93-94
volatile memory, 50
voltage, states, 162
voltage identification pins, 102
voltage regulator module (VRM), 102
voltages, AC, 693
volts, 122-123
volume sets, Windows NT disk administration, 546-547
volumes, 341-342
  FAT16, 349
  labels, 342
  number, 342-343
VRAM (video RAM), 72, 206, 709
VRM (voltage regulator module), 102, 709
VUE Testing Service Web site, 4
VxDs (virtual device drivers), 401, 437-438, 709

W

W command, 147
wait states, memory, 57
WAN, 709
watts, 122-123
Web browsers
  Explorer, 505
  Internet Explorer 5.0, 504
Web sites, 15
  CompTIA, 4
  Cruicial Technology, 56
  Thomson Prometric, 4
  VUE Testing Service, 4
WFP (Windows File Protection), 572, 601
wide channel buses, 77
wild cards, file searches, 336-338
WIN.COM, 409-410, 479-480
  386 Enhanced Mode (WIN/3), 411-412
  Real Mode (WIN/R), 410
  Standard Mode (WIN/S), 410-411
WIN.INI file, 385, 415
Win32, starting Windows NT, 543
Windows
  development of, 397
  DOS, 485-486
    booting to, 487-488
    MS Explorer, 486-487
  File Manager, 405-406
  NT, 404-405
  .PIF files, 402-403
  Program Manager, 405-406, 417-418
  reports, 500-502
  resources, 403
  starting, 310
  System VM, 402
  versions, 455-457, 521-522
  Virtual Real Mode, 401
  WIN.COM, 409-410
    386 Enhanced Mode (WIN/3), 411-412
    Real Mode (WIN/R), 410
    Standard Mode (WIN/S), 410-411

Windows 2.x, 404
Windows 2000, 522-523, 558-559
  Active Directory, 562-564
  Administrative Tools, 602-603
  Computer Management tool, 462
  diagnostics, 565
    Control Panel, 568-569
    Device Manager, 569
    interactive partitioning, 570
    My Computer, 568-569
    My Network Places, 570
    Recovery Console, 573-574
    System Agent, 571
    System Configuration Utility, 565-568
    System File Checker, 573
    Windows File Protection (WFP), 572
    Windows Update Manager, 571
  Disk Cleanup, 609-610
  Recovery Console, 309-310, 333-335, 450, 605-609
  starting, 559-561
    boot options, 561-562
    Emergency Repair Disk (ERD), 591-592
    Last Known Good Configuration, 593-594
    safe mode, 562, 592-593
  troubleshooting, 565
    bootups, NTLDR, 611
    Control Panel, 568-569
    crashes, 585-586
    Device Manager, 569
    hardware, 589
    interactive partitioning, 570
    My Computer, 568-569
    My Network Places, 570
    Recovery Console, 573-574
    startups, 584
    System Agent, 571
    System Configuration Utility, 565-568
    System File Checker, 573
    Windows File Protection (WFP), 572
    Windows Update Manager, 571
  WFP (Windows File Protection), 601
Windows 2000 Advanced Server, 559
Windows 2000 Datacenter Server, 559
Windows 2000 Professional, 558
Windows 2000 Server, 558
Windows 3.1, 406-407
Windows 3.11 Program Manager, 501
Windows 3.x, 418-419
  compared to Windows 9x, 502-503
  core files, 412
  global heap, 431-433
  INI files, 412-413
    file associations, 416
    missing, 415
    PROGMAN.INI, 417-418
    SYSEDIT.EXE, 413
    SYSTEM.INI, 414-415
    WIN.INI, 415
  LIM 4, 433-434
  memory, 419-421, 438-439
    640K memory barrier, 426
    aliasing, 422-423
    conventional, 421-422
    EMM386.EXE, 434-435
    low, 423-425
    mapping, 422-423
    page frame memory, 436-437
    page swapping, 436-437
    task switching, 435-436
    upper, 425
    video RAM, 425-426
  virtual memory, 426-427
    Control Panel, 428-429
    swap files, 427-428
Windows 3x, starting, 407-409
Windows 95, 451, 521. *See also* Windows 9x
  Desktop, 452
  HwDiag.EXE, 602
  installation, 470
    copying files, 473
    expanding files, 473
    hardware detection, 472
    restart, 474-475
    startups, 470-472
    system configuration phase, 474
  object properties, 453
  OS/R-B, 453
  starting
    Emergency Recovery Utility (ERU.EXE), 591
    Safe mode, 590
  wizards, 451-452
Windows 98, 503-504, 521. *See also* Windows 9x
  Active Desktop, 504
  Drive Converter, 454
  Explorer, 505

Registry Checker, 590-591
starting, Safe mode, 590
Windows 9x, 489, 566. *See also* Windows 95, Windows 98, Windows Me
AUTOEXEC.BAT, 483-484
compared to Windows 3.x, 502-503
Control Panel, 489-490
Desktop, 452-453
DOS, 317-318
file names, 495
aliases, 498-499
saving long names, 499-500
truncating, 498
Help Desk, 508
IFS Manager, 494-496
TSRs, 496-497
VFAT, 497-500
installation, 468-470
copying files, 473
expanding files, 473
hardware detection, 472
log files, 475-476
restart, 474-475
startup, 470-472
system configuration phase, 474
loading, 480-481
loading device drivers, 482
LOGO.SYS, 488
Maintenance Wizard, 510-511
Microsoft System Information utility, 506
MSCONFIG.EXE, 509
object properties, 453
Registry, 463
Registry Checker, 507
Disk Cleanup, 508
SFC (System File Checker), 507
version conflict manager, 508
Safe mode, 490-491
F5, 491-492
F6, 492
start sequence, 479-480, 484-485
starting, 476-477
after installation, 474-475
bootstrap, 477-478
DOS boot sequence, 478
MSDOS.SYS, 478-479
POST routine, 477-478
Safe mode, 589
WIN.COM, 479
Startup menu, 490-491
command prompt, 493-494
F4, 494
step-by-step confirmation, 492-493
troubleshooting startups, 584
Windows Update Manager, 509-510
Windows Explorer, creating bootable disks with, 393-394
Windows File Protection. *See* WFP
Windows Me, 511-512, 521. *See also* Windows 9x
CPUs, 595
Registry Checker, 590-591
SFP (System File Protection), 601
starting, Safe mode, 590
System Configuration Utility, 595-596
Windows Media (Windows 98), 504
Windows NT, 521, 556-558
architecture, 524-525
kernel mode, 525-527
User mode, 527-528
boot partitions, 541
disk administration, 545-546
Disk Administrator Tool, 546
disk mirroring, 548
duplexing, 548
RAID, 549
striped sets, 547-548
volume sets, 546-547
error messages, 554
missing BOOT.INI, 555
missing files, 556
missing kernel, 555
NT Detect, 554-555
networking, 529-530
logons, 531
LSA (local security authorization), 531-532
SAM (Security Account Manager), 530
user IDs, 530-531
user process, 532-533
NTFS, 543-545
NTLDR, 541-542
Registry, 528-529
starting, 540-541
boot partitions, 541
LSA, 543
NTLDR, 541-542
SMSS (Session Manager), 542-543
system partitions, 541
Win32, 543

system partitions, 541
troubleshooting, 550
bootable disks, 551-552
Emergency Repair Disk (ERD), 551-552
Event Viewer, 550-551
Net Watcher, 554
Performance Monitor, 553
Task Manager, 552-553
Windows NT 3.1, 522
Windows NT 4.0, 522
Windows NT 5.0, 522-523
Windows NT Server, 528
Windows NT Workstation, 528
Windows Open Services Architecture (WOSA), 562, 709
Windows Product Activation (WPA), 575
Windows Registry, 450, 457-458, 468
backup files, 457
backups, 465-466
components, 462
copies, 464-465
HKeys, 462-464
editing files, 459-460
.INI files, 458-459
objects, 460
pointers, 461-462
shortcuts, 460
SYSTEM.1ST, 464-465
Windows Update Manager (Windows 2000), 509-510, 571
Windows XP, 523-524, 574
Recovery Console, 450
startup time, 575
troubleshooting startups, crashes, 585-586
WFP (Windows File Protection), 601
WPA (Windows Product Activation), 575
WINFILE.EXE, 365
WinLogon, 531
WINLOGON.EXE, 560
wireless infrared mouse, 145
wireless networking, 300
wiring twisted-pair cable, 297
wizards
Maintenance, 510-511
Make New Connections, 616
Windows 95, 451-452
World Wide Web (WWW), 269, 710
Worm virus, 621
worms (write once, read many), 709
WOSA (Windows Open Services Architecture), 562, 709
Wozniak, Steve, 313
WPA (Windows Product Activation), 575
WRAM (windows RAM), 72, 710
write once, read many (worms), 709
write protection, floppy drives, 165
writing IFS (Image Formation System), 231
writing mechanism, 228
WWW (World Wide Web), 269, 710
WYSIWYG, 406, 710

X-Z

XCOPY.EXE, 485
XGA (eXtended Graphics Adapter), 204, 710
XML, 270
XMS, 710
XOF command, 148
XON command, 148
XT (eXtended Technology), 18, 710
XT connectors, 282

YB yottabyte, 710

ZB (zettabyte), 710
ZIF (zero-insertion force, 710
ZIF design (sockets), 90
Zn command, 148

How can we make this index more useful? Email us at indexes@quepublishing.com